Memoirs on the History, Folk-lore and Distribution of the Races of the North Western Provinces of India

Memoirs

on the History, Folk-lore and Distribution of the

Races of the

North Western Provinces of India

Being an Amplified Edition of the Original
Supplemental Glossary of Indian Terms

SIR HENRY M ELLIOT

EDITED, REVISED AND RE-ARRANGED BY
JOHN BEAMS

In 2 Vols. Bound in One.

Vol. 1

Low Price Publications

Delhi-110052

Distributed by
D.K. Publishers Distributors (P) Ltd.
4834/24, Ansari Road, Darya Ganj,
New Delhi-110002
Phones: 51562573, 51562575, 51562577
e-mail: dkpd@del3.vsnl.net.in
visit us at: www.dkpd.com

First Published 1859

Reprinted in LPP 2004

ISBN 81-7536-351-7

Published by
Low Price Publications
A-6, Nimri Commercial Centre,
Near Ashok Vihar Phase-IV,
Delhi-110052
Phones: 27401672, 27452453
e-mail: lpp@nde.vsnl.net.in
visit us at: www.lppindia.com

Printed at
D K Fine Art Press P Ltd.
Delhi-110052

PRINTED IN INDIA

MEMOIRS

ON THE

HISTORY, FOLK-LORE, AND DISTRIBUTION

OF THE

RACES

OF THE

NORTH WESTERN PROVINCES OF INDIA;

BEING AN AMPLIFIED EDITION OF THE ORIGINAL

SUPPLEMENTAL GLOSSARY OF INDIAN TERMS,

BY THE LATE

SIR HENRY M. ELLIOT, K.C.B.,

OF THE HON. EAST INDIA COMPANY'S BENGAL CIVIL SERVICE.

EDITED, REVISED, AND RE-ARRANGED

BY

JOHN BEAMES, M.R.A.S.,

BENGAL CIVIL SERVICE;

MEMBER OF THE GERMAN ORIENTAL SOCIETY, OF THE ASIATIC SOCIETIES OF PARIS AND BENGAL, AND OF THE PHILOLOGICAL SOCIETY OF LONDON.

IN TWO VOLUMES.

VOL. I.

LONDON:

TRÜBNER & CO., 8 AND 60, PATERNOSTER ROW.

MDCCCLXIX.

STEPHEN AUSTIN,

PRINTER, HERTFORD.

EDITOR'S PREFACE.

THIS work, the value of which has for more than twenty years been well-known and appreciated by all classes of Englishmen in India, as well as by Oriental scholars in Europe, is now given to the public in a form slightly different from that in which it first appeared. In previous editions the arrangement was strictly alphabetical, and the result was, in consequence, that it was difficult for the reader to find the subject of which he was in search. An article on some tribe or caste was followed by one on a totally different topic, and as some of the articles were extremely long, and there were no headings to the pages, such as are usually found in dictionaries, and no index, the task of finding any particular word was often a long and perplexing one. To remedy this defect in the form of the work, recourse has been had to the plan of dividing it into four parts, according to the subjects treated of. This four-fold division had, in fact, been already hinted at by the author in the Memorandum prefixed to the first edition. He modestly describes his book as "a few notices concerning the tribes, the customs, the fiscal and agricultural terms of this Presidency."

First in order has been placed the valuable and elaborate series of essays on the Castes, their septs and families. Copious additions have been made to this section of the work, some of which are derived from pencil notes in the author's own handwriting, made on an interleaved copy which he kept for that purpose. Recourse has also been had to the valuable Report on the Archæology of India, by General Cunningham, to a volume of the late Professor H. H. Wilson's Glossary of Indian Terms, in which that illustrious Orientalist had made in manuscript considerable additions with a view to the improvement of future editions of his work, and to the published records of the Government of the North Western Provinces, which contain many reports on the revenue settlements of various districts, and, as a matter of course, much information about the castes and families holding land therein. A residence of ten years in India, during which I have been employed in several Provinces as a Magistrate and Collector, has enabled me to add a considerable amount of information derived from my personal experiences. While, however, every effort has been made to bring the work up to the level of the present time, and to make it a fair exposition of our present state of knowledge on this confessedly extensive and difficult subject, it cannot be denied that there is very much still to be done before we can be said to have exhausted the subject. The people of the North Western Provinces are unfortunately not safe guides in questions relating to their own past history; the excessive pride of the higher castes, and the ignorance and apathy of the lower, added to the extravagantly legendary character of much that is recorded in early Indian Annals, especially of the pre-Muhammadan times, combine to puzzle, and often, it may be feared, to disgust the enquirer.

It may be assumed that the Aryan nation entered India from the North West many centuries ago, in the twilight dawn of human history; that they found it already occupied by men of another race, whose bitter and persistent hatred to the invaders armed them with strength to dispute their progress inch by inch; and that they were in consequence then, and for many centuries afterwards, compact and homogeneous. When, however, the country had been won, and the sentiment of union was weakened by the removal of opposition from without, the tendency to elaborate a complex social organization so characteristic of the Aryan race in all its branches, European as well as Asiatic, developed itself into that exaggerated state of social disunion known by the name of caste. The principle of disintegration thus introduced extended itself with amazing rapidity, so that each petty sub-division or family erected itself into a separate caste, and the process went on till the people themselves forgot their own origin, and invented grotesque and often disgusting fables to account for the state of things they saw around them. It is not wonderful that such a state of things should have presented insurmountable difficulties to successive generations of foreigners from a distant country, where such distinctions were unknown.

The discovery of the Sanskrit language, and the marvellous development given to the study of Indian literature thereby, are events which rank high in the history of the triumphs of the human mind; but the absence of anything like connected or reliable history in those wonderful, poetical, religious, and philosophical masterpieces of the Brahmins, has rendered them well-nigh useless to persons engaged in the class of investigations to which the present work is devoted.

A few gleams of light are thrown upon the darkness by the memorable incident of Alexander's invasion, and by the travels of the Chinese pilgrims, Fah-Hian (400 A.D.) and Hiouen-Thsang (648 A.D.); coins, rock and pillar-inscriptions, grants engraved on copper, and other waifs and strays spared by the waves of time, have been industriously and successfully attacked, and made to yield their scanty stores of information to an acuteness and energy which reflect honour upon many English names, both dead and living. But the darkness is still great, and we have still to confess that history, in the true sense of the word, does not begin for India till the advent of the Musulman on the scene. Then, however, it was too late, at least for our present purpose. Indian society was fixed, wars and migrations had taken place, legends had sprung up, the work of disintegration had wrought its full results of evil.

That it may yet be given to European skill and perseverance to lift the veil,—to build up the perfect statue from the scattered fragments lying hidden under the rubbish of time,—must be the hope of all those who have the good of India at heart; and to such Sir H. Elliot's researches supply a basis and a starting-point, the value of which, incomplete though they necessarily are, cannot be too highly rated.

With regard to the other three parts of the present edition, it remains only to add, that every available source of information has been used, both for correction and for the filling up of gaps in the original. Much has been supplied from Sir H. Elliot's own notes, much from Professor Wilson's, and somewhat from my own.*

* If every European official in India would keep a note-book, and put down from time to time such little points worthy of notice as come before him in the course of his daily work, he would end by possessing a vast mass of highly valuable information, which otherwise would be lost to himself and the world.

It must be observed that it was very difficult to decide where to draw the line between these three divisions of the book. Native life in India is somewhat monotonous and colourless, and there is none of that eager enjoyment on festive occasions which is shewn by the peasantry of Southern Europe. Superstitions and rites have a dull practical aspect to the Indian ryot; their due observance secures him a full crop, and this, again, enables him to pay his rent and his money-lender. Festival days are useful, because on them he and his family can go to the *mela*, or fair, and lay in a small stock of household requisites; bathing in the Ganges, or making some small offering to this or that shrine, are merely incidents, and not always very prominent incidents, in the process. It results from the above conditions that there are many words in the peasant's language—a language which is the faithful reflector of his thoughts and feelings—which might be entered with equal justice under any one of these three Parts. His superstitions, his tools, and his rent are all mixed up in the ryot's mind so closely, that it is difficult to separate them. To take an instance: in measuring land there are a dozen superstitious practises, such as the *dharm kotta*, or *biswa*, which is measured by a bamboo of six cubits length, and in order to get a good average measurement, a man measures the first cubit from his elbow to the tip of his thumb, the next cubit to the tip of the forefinger, and so on, changing a finger at each cubit, and a special virtue is supposed to reside in a bamboo thus measured. Such a custom as this might, it is evident, be noticed equally well either under Part II. or Part III.

Again, the distinction between various sorts of soils is a matter which in some parts of the country has an effect upon the revenue, while in others it has none. This requires explanation. In those districts where the "permanent settlement" is in force, the Government of Lord Cornwallis in 1793 assigned certain lands, as absolute personal property, to certain persons, on the condition that they should pay a certain quarterly rent. It is obvious that in making such an arrangement as this, the first thing to do was to ascertain who was the person with whom the land should be settled; next, how much land he was to have; and thirdly, what the land was worth, and how much he ought to pay for it. That none of these three important points received proper attention, and that the second and third points were in many instances entirely overlooked, is an extraordinary fact, only to be accounted for by the small number of Englishmen then in the country, and by their ignorance of the matters they were dealing with. Some of the largest estates in Bengal and Behar were settled in perpetuity with persons whose right to them was more than doubtful, the boundaries of the estate were left totally undefined, and the amount of revenue to be paid settled upon a report made by a native assessor, who only visited a small part of the estate, and was bribed handsomely to assess it at a low rate. The capabilities of the land never having been taken into consideration by the rulers of the country, it often happens that we find an estate containing the richest and most productive of soils paying a low rent, and a poor estate paying a high rent. The results of this system fall on the ryot: in a lightly assessed estate, provided the landlord is tolerably just, he can get his land cheap, whereas a few miles off, in a highly assessed estate, he may have to pay double for worse land. The distinction between the different sorts of soil is, under these circumstances, valuable merely as a guide to the treatment which it requires, and not for revenue purposes.*

It is far different, however, in the other provinces, where a more enlightened system prevails. There the capabilities of the soil, and all other circumstances which are likely to influence the outturn of crops, are carefully weighed and enquired into by experienced English officers,

* As shewing the condition of the wretched ryot of the old provinces of Bengal, Behar, and Orissa, which are under the "permanent settlement," I may quote a good Bengálí proverb which I heard from the Rev. J. Long:

Zamíndárer bhali bháshá
Musulmáner murghí poshá.

"A zamíndár's kind word is like the Musulmán's feeding his fowls;" *i.e.*, He feeds and cherishes them, in order to kill and eat them.

assisted by a large staff of trained native assistants; the ryots themselves are consulted, their grievances listened to; in short, every possible precaution is taken to secure a fair and equitable assessment, such as, while securing to the state its fair share of the profits, shall leave to the landlord and to the cultivator a fair return for their labour and outlay. In such a case the discrimination between the different sorts of soil becomes a revenue question, and may fairly be included in Part III.

It is necessary to mention these points, to explain the reason why some words are found in one Part, while others closely connected with them are placed in another; it is hoped, however, that, with the aid of the Index, the reader will be able to find at once any word he may require.

Those who are familiar with the earlier editions will observe that considerable alterations have been made in those parts of the work in which comparisons were made between Indian and European rites and superstitions. It has been thought better to omit all such allusions as foreign to the purely Indian character of the work, as well as many etymologies, which were probably hardly seriously believed in by the author himself, and could not be fairly reproduced after so long an interval of time, though when first penned they may have had a certain appropriateness as the lighter fancies of a refined and elegant scholar.

I am compelled also, in fairness to myself, to explain that the work was entrusted to me only in November, and being obliged to return to my duties in India in the middle of February, the time at my disposal has been hardly sufficient for the task. I have had to forego many inquiries which would have cleared up obscure passages and thrown light on uncertain points, because they would have taken more time than I could afford. Had I been able to devote six months to them, a better result might have been achieved.

In conclusion, my thanks are due, in the first place, to the distinguished Oriental savant and numismatist, Mr. Edward Thomas, under whose auspices the work has been executed, and by whose judgment I have been guided, as well as directed throughout: to my learned friend, Dr. Reinhold Rost, Secretary of the Royal Asiatic Society, for his ever-ready assistance and hearty co-operation at every stage; and to several other kind friends, whose names I need not here mention.

Mr. Stephen Austin's well-known printing establishment has also, under considerable difficulties, done its part well, and maintained its ancient reputation for beauty of type and excellence of workmanship.

JOHN BEAMES.

RICHMOND,
January, 1869.

PREFACES TO ORIGINAL EDITION.

MEMORANDUM.

As several months have elapsed since the receipt of the first Parts of the Glossary of Indian Terms, no further delay should occur in returning them to Government, under the Orders dated 14th December, 1842, No. 913.

The Board will regret to observe that the call for further information has not been responded to, except to a very limited extent, by any of the Officers under their control. Being therefore apprehensive that the Honorable Court of Directors, who have shown so much anxiety to prepare a comprehensive Glossary, may feel some disappointment at receiving no additions or suggestions from these Provinces, I have ventured to put together a few notices respecting the tribes, the customs, the fiscal and agricultural terms of this Presidency, in the hope that if they are found to convey any information not hitherto recorded, they may be deemed worthy of being incorporated with the work which is about to be compiled under the superintendence of Professor H. H. Wilson.

I have confined my attention chiefly to the words included under these four heads, though I observe from entries in the printed specimens, that if the scheme of the Glossary is fully carried out, it will include terms of Hindoo Mythology and Astronomy, an account of the principal Festivals, and much which will, perhaps, have to be excluded on a revision. I have not attempted to meddle with such subjects, on which there are several books which contain ample information; and even in such departments as I have undertaken, I have endeavoured for the most part to avoid words which may be found in the common Dictionaries. For a few terms I have been indebted to the Revenue Glossaries furnished to the Sudder Board in A.D. 1839; but I believe the extent of my obligations is confined to those of Saugor and Goruckpoor. It has been part of my plan to introduce articles on the old, and locally known territorial Divisions of the Country, as a subject not only highly interesting in itself, but as being intimately connected with the fiscal portion of the work. Indeed, such articles as Desh, Furingistan, Futtehpoor, etc. etc., in the Printed Glossary, show that the admission of such words is in conformity with the views of the Court.

The ethnological remarks I have tried to curtail as much as possible; but, with all my efforts, I fear that many notices will be considered very tedious. As some excuse, however, it may be mentioned that we are still almost as ignorant of the agricultural classes of these Provinces as we were on the first day of our occupation, and that even their names are entirely omitted from the Printed Glossary, though the tribes of the Deccan, Guzerat, and other Provinces are not only copiously noticed, but we are referred to an Appendix for fuller information respecting them. The Maps which have been added in illustration of this part of the subject will, I trust, be found of interest. Their preparation has been attended with considerable difficulty, but no pains have been spared to make them as correct as circumstances would admit.

I have not, except in very few instances, pointed out the mistakes in the Glossary itself; for the errors, both of orthography and statement, are so obvious, that they cannot escape the notice of the compiler. As for my own orthography, I do not profess to be satisfied with it, since most of the words have been taken from oral information; and as they have perhaps never yet been written, and their pronunciation is by no means fixed, the liability to error is very great. In writing them I have endeavored, as far as possible, to conform to the system of Gilchrist—or rather that modification of it in use in our Revenue Surveys—which certainly has the merit of enabling an Englishman to pronounce a word in such a manner as to make it easily comprehended by the natives of Hindoostan. Sir W. Jones' method is better suited to the learned; but since it is becoming of more general use, as our books and translations multiply, I have added a column for its admission; as far, at least, as respects the vowel system.

As my attempts to illustrate the barren themes which occupy these pages take up much time, and as they may, after all, be considered of no value, I shall for the present conclude with the letter J (to which the specimen last received extends); and shall be guided respecting the continuation of the work by the opinion which the compiler may be pleased to express of this first portion of my labours. If he judge of its merits by the extent of his own information on all the subjects discussed in it, he may be disposed to think that my time might have been more profitably employed. Even my own partiality cannot conceal from me that there is in this Supplement much worthless matter, which ought not to have been admitted; but as the revision would occupy nearly as much time as the original composition, I prefer allowing my notes to remain in their present shape, in the full persuasion that the Honorable Court will overlook all minor defects, in consideration of my earnest endeavours to fulfil their desires.

H. M. ELLIOT,
SECRETARY.

SUDDER BOARD OF REVENUE,
The 1st February, 1844.

From

THE SUDDER BOARD OF REVENUE, N.W.P.,

To

THE SECRETARY TO THE GOVERNMENT, N.W.P.

No. 75 A. OF 1844.

Dated 9*th Feb.*, 1844.

SIR,—With reference to the Order of the Government of India, No. 913 of 1842, dated 14th December, such portions of the Glossary of Indian Terms, then and subsequently received in this Department, as have undergone consideration and amendment, are herewith returned to be laid before the Honorable the Lieut.-Governor.

2.—The Sudder Board have great satisfaction in forwarding to the Government, for submission to the Honorable the Court of Directors, the accompanying Supplemental Glossary, prepared in accordance with the expressed wishes of the Honorable Court by Mr. H. M. Elliot, the Secretary to the Sudder Board, N. W. Provinces.

3.—The Board have perused this Supplemental Glossary with feelings of very great interest and satisfaction, and are persuaded it will be found to contain, so far as the limits allow, nearly all, if not all, the terms of known acceptation in the North Western Provinces, relating to the Revenue and Agricultural concerns of the country;—which, together with the very excellent commentary on the various tribes coming within the assigned limits, cannot but be regarded as a highly valuable addition to the original Glossary.

4.—Adverting to the great ability and research which have been displayed in the performance of so considerable a portion of the work, the Board beg to express an earnest request that Mr. Elliot may receive such notice from the Government and the Honorable the Court of Directors as will encourage him to bring the work to an early completion.

We have the honor to be, etc.,

(*Signed*) T. J. TURNER,
H. S. BOULDERSON.

SUDDER BOARD OF REVENUE, N.W.P.

Extract G. O., No. 450, *dated* 11*th May*, 1844, *in reply to a letter from the Sudder Board of Revenue, N.W.P., No.* 75A., *dated* 9*th February*, 1844.

The Lieut.-Governor [Mr. Thomason] has perused this interesting Volume with much gratification, and is very desirous that the curious matter it contains should not be exposed to the risk of loss from the existence of a single copy, or to perversion from the ignorance of transcribers. His Honor, therefore, requests the Board will take measures for having it printed at once under the immediate eye of their Secretary.

SUPPLEMENTAL GLOSSARY

OF TERMS USED IN THE

NORTH WESTERN PROVINCES.

PART I.

CASTES AND THEIR SUB-DIVISIONS.

[Under this head I have included all those articles of the original work which described any of the castes or sub-divisions of castes in the North Western Provinces, together with such additional notices of my own as seemed necessary to complete the subject. It will be understood that only those castes are mentioned which are found in these Provinces, and in the case of castes which live partly in and partly out of the North West, the original articles only refer to that portion which resides in the N. W. P. Those articles which I have added include some of the castes in Behar.—B.]

Agarwálá, اگروالا अगरवाला

A large sub-division of the merchant caste, comprising some of the wealthiest men in India. They derive their name from Agroha, on the borders of Hariána, which was the original seat of the tribe, and from which they emigrated to all parts of India, after the capture of that place by Shahábu'ddín Ghorí.—See Gogá Pír.

Agastwár, اگستوار अगस्तवार

Is the name of a small clan of Rajpúts in Havelí Benares.

Ahír,* اهیر अहीर

The origin of this tribe, as given in the printed Glossary, cannot be correct; for Kúp (properly Gop) signifies merely the occupation of a herdsman.—Wilson's Sanskrit Dict., p. 299, 2nd Ed. Manu (X. 15) says that they are descended from a Brahman by an Ambasthá woman, *i.e.* one of the Baid, or Physician tribe. In the Brahma Purána it is said that they are descended from a Kshatriya father and a woman of the Vaisya caste; but on the question of the descent of the different tribes, the sacred books, as in many other matters, differ very much from each other, and none are to be implicitly trusted.

This pastoral tribe of the Yadubansí stock was formerly of much greater consideration in India than it is at present. In the "Ramáyana" and "Mahábhárat" the Abhíras in the West are spoken of; and in the Puranic Geography the country on the Western coast of India, from the Tapti to Devagaṛh, is called Abhira, or the region of Cowherds. When the Káttís arrived in Guzerat, in the eighth century, they found the greater part of the country in possession of the Ahírs. The name of Asírgaṛh, which Ferishta and the "Khazána Amira" say is derived from Asa Ahír, shows that the tribe was of some importance in the Dekkan also, and there is no doubt that we have trace of the name in the Abiria of Ptolemy, which he places above

* References on this subject are: J.R.A.S. xiii. 141. J.A.S.B. ix. 478, 484, 756, 885. Bombay L. T. i. 287. Lassen, Alterthumsk. i. 539. J.R.A.S. i. 248. Tod's Western India, pp. 358, 421. E. *add.*

Patalene. Ahírs were also at one time Rajas of Nepal at the beginning of our era, and they are perhaps connected with the Pála, or shepherd, dynasty, which ruled in Bengal from the ninth to the latter part of the eleventh century, and which, if we may put trust in monumental inscriptions, were for some time the universal monarchs of India.—(As. Researches, Vol. ix., p. 438.)

In the North Western Provinces Ahírs are scattered over various Parganahs. We find them in great numbers in the southern parts of the Dehli territory, from Rewárí, on the borders of Mewát, to the Bikanír frontier, in a tract of country known under the name of Bíghoto, *q.v.* A dense population of Ahírs (Tíklewala) will also be found in a line extending from the Kála Nadí in the neighbourhood of Marehrah, to near Bíbameyú on the Jumna (see Atábú); and from Salempúr Majhaulí in Gorakhpúr to Singraulí in Mirzapúr. Indeed, the Parganah of Ahrorah in the latter district, though now without Ahír Zamíndárs, derives its name from them, being called Ahírwara in ancient records. The only districts which in the "Aín Akbarí" are said to have Ahír Zamíndárs are Nagína and Sirdhána.

The Ahírs of these Provinces all trace their origin to Mathurá, or places a little to the West of it. There appear to be three grand divisions amongst them:—the Nandbans, the Jadubans, and Gwálbans (see Gwál)—which acknowledge no connexion, except that of being all Ahírs. Those of the Central Doáb usually style themselves Nandbans; those to the West of the Jumna and the Upper Doáb, Jadubans; and those in the Lower Doáb and Benares, Gwálbans. The latter seem to have no subdivisions, or Gots. The principal Gots of the Nandbans are, Samarphallá, Kishnaut, Bhagtá, Bilehnia, Diswár, Nagowa, Kanaudha, Dúnr, Ráwat, Tengúrea, Kor,* Kamaria, Barausia,

* Kor or Kur are held to be inferior to the rest of the caste.—See Rec. N. W. P. iv. 137. E. *add.*

Mújwár, Dahima, Nirbán, Kharkarí, Dirhor, Sítolia, Jarwariã, Barothí, Gonda and Phátak; amounting in all to eighty-four. In Bíghoto, besides many of these, there are the Molak, Sántoria, Khosia, Khallia, Loníwal, Aphariya or Aphiriya, Mailá, Mhailá, Khoro, Sesotia, Gandwál, Gird, Bhámsará, Jánjaria, Kánkauriá, and Nigániá; amounting in all to sixty-four. Many of the two last-named clans have been converted to the Mahometan faith, and are known as Rángars.* The two villages whence they

* This term is more strictly confined to Rajpúts who have been converted to Mahometanism; but there are several tracts in Dehli, particularly in the district of Rohtak, where the term is indiscriminately applied to Rajpúts, whether Mahometan or Hindú.

The origin of the term is very doubtful, and those who have attempted its etymology are by no means agreed among themselves.

Tod ("Asiatic Journal," Feb. 1838, p. 107) says, that "Rangri, or Rangra, is an epithet applied to all Rajpút chieftains; from Ringa (in the dialects) signifying a field of battle."

The Enc. Metropol. (Art. "Dehli") says, "Rangars, *i.e.* turncoats, are Mahomedan renegadoes from the Hindu faith."

Mr. H. T. Prinsep, in a note to p. 443 of his "Life of Amír Khan," says, "Rangras are the lower classes bordering on the Western Desert. They are all thieves and robbers, and mostly Musulmans." He does not attempt the origin of the name.

Francklin, at p. 275 of his "Memoirs of G. Thomas," says, "Rangurs are Mahomedan Rajpúts," and suggests, like the Enc. Metr., that the word implies coloured, or stained, or of mixed blood.

Sir J. Malcolm ("Central India," ii. 123) says, "that all the Brahmans of Central India, except those who came from the Dekkan, are classed by the Mahratta conquerors as Rangrí, or barbarous." At vol. ii. p. 191, he says, "the language taught in Central India is a dialect of the Hindui, termed Rangrí, which prevails from Bundelkhand to the Indus." Again, at p. 304, he observes, "the Rajpúts say the word is derived from *Ran*, signifying battle, and *Garh*, a fort, an epithet asserted to have been given them by one of the Kings of Dehli expressive of their bravery, but the Mahrattas say, that the derivation is from *Ran*, a forest, and *Gurrí*, a barbarian.'

The probabilities are in favour of the Sanskrit रण, *ran*, battle—so that Rangur would mean "a warrior."—E. In the Marathi dictionary of Molesworth it is said "रांगडा is applied freely in abuse of persons or speech judged to be rude and uncouth."—B.

derive their name are celebrated in local legends for turbulence and contumacy.*

दिहली तें पैंतीस कोस कांहौर निगाना
अपनी बोई आप खाएं हाकिम ने† न दें दाना

"Thirty-five kos from Dehli is Kánhaur Nigáná;
What they sow, they themselves eat, they do not give the grain to the ruler."

Amongst these, the Khoro rank first; but their claim to superiority is denied by the Aphiriya, who have certainly in modern times attained the highest distinction. They all, including the Khoro, intermarry on terms of equality, avoiding, like all other Ahírs, only the four Gots nearest related. A man, for instance, cannot marry into his father's, mother's, paternal, or maternal grandmother's Got; and no intermarriages take place between distant clans. Thus, those of the Doáb and Bíghoto hold little or no personal intercourse, and each declares the other an inferior stock.

Ahírs conform to the customs of Gújars and Játs in respect to the marriage of elder brothers' widows, wherever they are much intermixed, as in the Dehli territory; but the Ahírs of the Central Doáb forswear all connexion with those tribes, which they consider of an inferior grade; but as each of these tribes, as well as the Ahar, *q.v.*, claims the superiority, it is not easy to settle their comparative rank, and the difficulty is increased, with regard to the latter, by the close similarity of

* This is the account they themselves give of their origin, but as Kánhaur and Nigáná are occupied by Powar Rangars, and *Kan*-k-*auria* can scarcely be derived from *Kan*-h-*aur*, I do not place much confidence in their assertion. Popular legends however, are not easily disproved.

† This ने is not the sign of the instrumental, but a local mark of the dative which is used in several other dialects, as, for instance, in Nepalese, under the form लाई or लै for the same case.—B.

name. In the Dehli territory, the Ahírs eat, drink, and smoke, in common, not only with Játs and Gújars, but also, under a few restrictions, with Rajpúts.* In other places, Rajpúts would indignantly repudiate all connection with Ahírs.

Besides the families above-mentioned, names are also given according to the place of residence. Thus we have the Dhúndarí of Mewar; the Hariániya of Hariána; the Púrbí, of the Eastward; the Birjia, of Brij; the Kohkohí of the Bindáchal Hills; and the Panjábí of Lahore.

Aheriyá, اهيريا अहेरिया

A fowler, a sportsman.—See Dhánúk.

Ahar, اهر अहर

Ahars are found on the banks of the Ramgangá, and in Sambhal, Rajpúra, Asadpúr, Ujhání, and Saheswán, and some other Parganahs in Rohilkhand, West of that river. These tracts, indeed, are known familiarly under the name Aharát. They are also found in great numbers in Faizpúr Badaria, and the country in the neighbourhood, between the Ganges and Búdh Gangá. They have *hukka pani* (smoke and drink) in common with Játs and Gújars, but disclaim all connexion with Ahírs, whom they consider an inferior stock; and the Ahírs repay the compliment. Ahars say they are descended from Jadonbansí (Yadu) Rajpúts; but Ahírs say that they themselves are the real Jadonbansí, being descended in a direct line from Krishna, and that Ahars are descended from the cowherds in the service of that illustrious Avatar, and that the inferiority

* In some of the eastern districts Brahmans will take milk, water, and even food from certain castes of Ahírs, such as the Baiswaria Gwálás. They explain this by saying that the Gwálás are purified by attending on that sacred animal, the cow, but it is possible that the alleged origin of the Ahírs from a Brahman father may have something to with it.—B.

cf Ahars is fully proved by their eating fish and milking cows. From the slight difference in the pronunciation of the two names, it is very difficult to ascertain what are the distinctive features in the two tribes. They are almost universally confounded by other classes, and very often disagree in the accounts of their own genealogies. Some of the most noted tribes of the Ahars in the N. West are Bhattí, Nagáwat, Naugorí, Rúkar, Básian, Ora, Bukiáin, Diswár, Bhúsiáín, and Birraria.—See Ahír.

Álíyá, آليا आलीया

A branch of the Turkia subdivision of Banjáras.—See Banjára.

Amethiyá, اميٹھيا अमेठिया

A tribe of Chauhán Rajpúts of the Bandhalgotí sub-division, of whom a few have settled in Salempúr Majhaulí, in the district of Gorakhpúr. They came from Amethí in Oudh.

Anṣárí, انصاري अनसारी

A tribe of Shaikhs who now are found chiefly in the Saháranpúr district, Kíratpúr in Bijnor, aud the Benares province. They are represented by Abú 'l Faẓl as being the proprietors of Sayyidpúr Bhitrí and Chanár in Akbar's time.

They profess themselves to be descendants of the citizens of Medina, who gave the prophet an asylum against his enemies when he fled from Mecca; hence called Ansárí انصاري auxiliaries. They appear to have come to this country from Herat in the time of Fíroz Shah.—See the "Mirát-i-Jahán," which was compiled from the papers of Mahomed Baḳa, an Ansárí.

Pocock ("Specimen Hist. Arab." p. 42) says, they are of the tribe of Azd and the family of Khazraj. "الخزرج Alkhazraj; Yathrebi (scil. Medinæ) incolæ qui الانصار al Ansar, Ansarii, scilicet Mahommediæ profugi adjutores, dicti"—deriving his information from Abulfeda.—See p. 473 of White's edition.

الخزرج اهل يثرب المسلمون منهم هم الانصار

It seems, however, more usual among Oriental writers of early Mahometan history to call the inhabitants of Medina generally, Ansárí.*

Áolániyá, آولانيا आओलानिया

A tribe of Játs holding about forty villages in Pánípat Bángar, so called from the name of their village in that neighbourhood. They are in reality Gatwáras. Though they are Hindús, they claim the title of Malik, which they say was bestowed upon them by some king as a token of their superiority to their brethren.

Aphariyá, اپهريا अफरिया

See Ahír, of which tribe they form a sub-division.

Áúdi, آودي or هودي आउदी or हदी

A tribe of Játs, proprietors of about twenty villages in Pánípat Bángar, and twenty in Sonípat Bángar. They are called indiscriminately Áúdí and Húdí, with perhaps a leaning in favor of the latter pronunciation.

Awasthí, اوستهي अवस्थी

One of the sub-divisions of Kanaujiyá Brahmans, *q.v.*

Báchhal, باچهل वाछल

A tribe of Rajpúts of the Sombansí stock. We find them in

* Dabistan, i. 20, iii. 27. The question is not an Indian one.

Jalálí of Aligaṛh; Kot Sálbáhan, Ujhání, and Nidhpúr of Badaon; Sahár and Aríng of Mathurá; and in Tilhar and Shahjahánpúr. They are recorded in the "Aín Akbarí" as being the Zamíndárs of Farída and of Kánt Gola, the old name of Shahjahánpúr; and the fact is interesting, as showing the changes of possession which have occurred in this tract within a short space of time. The Báchhal Rajpúts are said to have succeeded the Goelas or Gújars. They were in turn succeeded by Katherya Rajpúts, who themselves have been of late years succeeded by the Gaur Rajpúts, whom they called in as allies to aid them against the encroachments of the Rohillas.

Bágrí, باگری बागी

A tribe inhabiting the Bágar country, a tract between the South-western border of Hariána and the Ghára, who appear at one time to have been of great consideration, as we find a Bágrí Ráo mentioned by Chand Bardáí as accompanying Pirthí Rájá. They seem to have been originally Rajpúts, but are now held to be an inferior tribe, and are usually denominated Játs. Tod considers the Bágrís to be one of the aboriginal races of India, but he does not mention which Bágrís; and the term is so extensively applied, that any reference to them, without mentioning their locality, is very indefinite. There is an extensive clan of Bágrí Brahmans, and the name enters into the subdivisions of several other castes.—(See Jádon.)

Bágar is also the name of a large tract of country in Malwa,*

* "Among the tribes settled in Central India, who are professed robbers and thieves, the two principal are Baugries and Moghies, both Hindús of the lowest caste. They came originally from the Western parts of India, chiefly from the neighbourhood of Chittore. The Moghies can hardly be said to have passed the Chumbul, but the Baugries have settled in the Eastern parts of Malwa in considerable numbers."—Malcolm's "Central India," II. p. 182.

Probably Bágrís and Magahyas.—B. "A range of rocky hills intersects nearly the whole of Shekhawati in a N. E. direction and close upon its E. frontier. The country the inhabitants of which are called Bágrí; but in the North Western Provinces we rarely hear the word used except as applicable to the Bágrí Játs of Hissar and Bhattíána.

Bájpáí, باج پائي बाजपाई

See Kanaujia Brahman, of which tribe they are a sub-division. They are also called बाजपेई in Behar.—B.

Báláín, بالاين बालाइन

A large sub-division of the Játs, *q.v.*

Báland, بالند बालंद

A tribe which was formerly predominant in Agorí Barhar and the Southern parts of Mirzapúr, whence they were expelled by the Chandel Rajpúts. They retired to Manwás, where they retain a principality in subordination to the Raja of Rewa. They are said still to remember with fondness their former possessions in Agorí Barhar, and declare they will not bind on their turbans till their restoration to their ancestral rights is accomplished. It is not easy to say when this expulsion took place, but the immigration of Chandels to these parts appears to have occurred after the capture of Mahoba, some time previous to the defeat of Pirthí Rájá by Shahábu'ddín, towards the close of the 12th century.

It is sometimes said that Báland is merely the name of a Raja of the Kharwár tribe, but there seems more reason to suppose that it is the name of a distinct clan.

on the E. side of these hills is called Dhundar (a name which was formerly applied to a large portion of Rajputana), while that to the West is called Bágar, which includes nearly the whole of Shekhawati, and is generally applicable to the sandy country where water is only procurable at a great depth."—Boileau, MS. Journal. E. *add.*

Bándhalgotí, باندهلگوتي बांधलगोती

A tribe of Rajpúts of Chauhán descent, occupying part of Bundelkhand and Binaudha (which see). There are a few also in Havelí Ghazípúr. The name is frequently pronounced like Badhilgotí and Banjhilgotí.

Bárah sádát, باره سادات बारह सादात

A powerful tribe of Sayyids in the Eastern part of the Muzaffarnagar district. They hold a great portion of Parganahs Bhúkarherí, Bhúmá, Jánsath, Sambhalherí, Jaulí, and the Eastern parts of Parganahs Muzaffarnagar and Khataulí. A few colonies of them are occasionally found elsewhere, as in Amroha of Moradabad, and Sikandra of Allahabad; but their stronghold is the Muzaffarnagar district.

The origin of the name Bárah is ascribed to various sources; some say that, scandalized at the debaucheries of the Mína bazar of Dehli, which they considered unsuited to their sacred character, they obtained leave to reside outside (*bahir*) of the town—others that it was the chief town of twelve (*bárah*) which belonged to the clan: the spelling is opposed to the former derivation.*

There are four sub-divisions of the Bárah Sádát; the Tihanpúrí, whose chief town is Jánsath; the Chantraudí, whose chief town is Sambhalherí; the Kunḍalwál, whose chief town is Majhera; and the Jagnerí, who claim Bidaulí on the Jumna as their chief town. They assert that they have been located since the time of Mahmúd of Ghazni; but this is evidently false. There appears reason, however, to believe, from the col-

* I have always heard the derivation from باره twelve (which is sometimes written بارھ), but in E. *add.* it is mentioned that there is a place called Barhah. See article Budh Ganga in Part III. Sádát is the plural of Sayyid.—B. See Jehangir's Memoirs, p. 655, which is quoted by Barnes, Report on Bijnor, and confirms the derivation from *bára*, twelve.—E. *add.*

lateral evidence afforded by the interesting history of the Bilgrám Sayyids, called the "Júnaidiyá," that their occupation dates as far back as the time of Shamsu'ddín Altamsh. Besides these divisions, they have private marks of recognition, which they say have been very successful in excluding impostors from the tribe. Particular families have denominations, such as dog, ass, sweeper, etc., which are derived from the menial offices which it is said some of the Sayyids of this family performed for the Emperor Humayún, when reduced to extremities during his flight from Sher Shah.

The improbability of men assuming such humiliating designations without a good cause, gives some colour to the story; particularly when we learn the devotion of the Emperor's attendants, which is so amusingly detailed by his right reverential Aftábchí, Jauhar, in the "Tazkiratu 'l vikáyá."

The Bárah Sádát must have obtained their highest stage of prosperity in the time of Farrukhsír; but we read in the Memoirs of Jehángír and in the Táríkh-i-Badáoní that members of this family attained distinction not only in his court but in that of his father. Thus, the Sayyid Mahomed, mentioned in the article Bhadauriá, Sayyid Ahmed Khan, and Sayyid Hashim, were all men of distinction in Akber's court. Jehángír particularly mentions Sayyid Ali Asaf, as the son of the Sayyid Mahomed above-mentioned, "one of the great Amírs of his father's court." And in the Padshahnámah we find mentioned among the Mansabdars of Shahjahán's time, Sayyid Khán Jahán, Bárah, Mansabdar of 5000: and Shujá'at Khan and Debí Khan, each of 4000. In Aurangzeb's reign they were not less conspicuous.

Farrukhsír being indebted for his elevation to the assistance afforded by Husain Ali Khan, Governor of Behar, and Abdullah Khan, Governor of Allahabad, two brothers of the Bárah stock, their influence continued unabated during his reign, as well as for some time subsequent; and it is probable that to this period must be ascribed the handsome and expensive structures, of which the ruins are now scattered over so extensive a tract of country in the Upper Doáb, from Mawána to Jaulí.

The Sayyids having gained themselves honor by the constancy with which they adhered to the Minister's family during its decline, and the courage they displayed on the hard fought field of Hasanpúr, where Abdullah Khan was defeated and slain. This adherence, however, proved their destruction. Full particulars will be found in the "Sairu 'l Mutakharín" and the "Taríkh-i Múzaffarí."

Bíjheriya, بیجهریا बीझेरिया

There are a few of this clan of Rajpúts in the district of Gorakhpúr.

Bais, بیس बैस

One of the thirty-six royal races of Rajpúts, giving name to the province of Baiswára, in Oudh, and not in the Doáb, as Colonel Tod (Rajasthan, i. 118) supposes. Baiswara lies between Cawnpore on the west, and the Saí river on the east; and between the Chúáb rivulet on the south, and Dikhtan (the country of the Dikhit Rajpúts) on the north.

There are several Bais Rajpúts in these provinces, but they are not found to the westward of Dubhaí in Bulandshahr. To the east of that Parganah they are found in greater number than any other clan of Rajpúts; particularly in Koṭ Sálváhan, Nidhpúr and Saheswan of Budáon; in Barwar of Mynpúrí; in Atraulí of Aligarh; in Thattia, and Saurak of Farrukhabad; in Dehlí Jakhan of Etawah; in Jájmau, Ghátampúr, Akbarpúr and Sarh Salempúr of Cawnpore; in Fattihpúr Haswa (Musulman), Hatgáṅw, Ekdalla, Ayiah Sáh, Muttaur (Musulman and Hindú), and Gházípúr, of Fattihpúr; in Kurra, Kewaí, and Bara of Allahabad; in Banda, Jalálpúr, Chebú, Maudha,

Súmerapúr, and Hamírpúr, and many other Parganahs of Bundelkhand; in Sikandarpúr, Mahul, Bilhábans, Deogáṅw, and Chiryakot of Azimgarh; in Rattanpúr Bansí, Dhoriapár, Hasanpúr Magar, and Amorha of Gorakhpúr; in Khanpúr and Bahríabad of Ghàzípúr; and in Singrámau, Rárí, Zafarábád, and Karákaṭ of Jaunpúr. There are also several in the neighbourhood of Farrakhabad, especially in Paramnagar, whose turbulence has long been notorious; and who in A.D. 1391 and 1392 created such disturbances, in concert with the Rahtors, that it was thought necessary to send out large boḍies of imperial troops against them (Zíáu'ddín Barní).

All the Bais in our provinces state that they came from Dúndia Khera in Baiswara. Their accounts respecting the place, whence they emigrated to Dúndia Khera, do not coincide, but it is most usual for them to assert that they came from Múngí Paitun in the Dekkan. No other Rajpút tribe is represented to have come from that quarter. They state themselves to be of the same lineage as Sálivàhana, and he also is reported in ancient histories to have emigrated from Múngí Paitun to the banks of the Nerbudda, whence he expelled the famous Vikramáditya.*

The scale of the Bais in the rank of Rajpúts may be judged by their intermarriages, as is the case with all the Rajpút classes. The ordinary Bais of our provinces give their daughters in marriage, amongst others, to Sayngars, Bhadaurias, Chauháns, Kachwahas, Gautams, Parihárs, Dikhits, and Gaharwars; and receive daughters in marriage from Banáphars, Jinwars, Khíchars, Ragbansís, Raikwars, and the Karcholí Gahlotes. But the Tilokchandí Bais, who reside in Dúndia Khera, and their near relations, such as those of Barwar, Dehlí Jakhan,

* Colonel Tod in one place calls Saliváhana a Takshak, and in another a Yadu Prince. He is also of opinion that the Bais are a sub-division of the Suryavansi Rajpúts, and gives them a place in his list of the royal tribes. Múngı Paitun is on the Godavery, and is probably the Pithiana of the Periplus.

and Kot Salbáhan, consider themselves far superior to all other Bais, and profess to give their daughters to none but the very highest tribes. There is reason to suppose that they practise female infanticide, at least in the Oudh territory. Those Tilokchandís, who reside in our provinces cannot make away so freely with their offspring, and have consequently consented more readily to intermarriages. Thus the Tilokchandís of Dumráṅw, in Bhojpúr, give their daughters in marriage to the Harihobans of Ballía, in Gházípúr, and those of Deogáṅw give theirs to Rájkumárs. Besides the Tilokchandí, there are said to be no less than three hundred and sixty subdivisions of Bais Rajpúts, the descendants of as many wives of Salivahana. Amongst the progeny of these "queens of a day," the most noted in our provinces are the Tilsárí, Chak Bais, Nandwak, Bhanawag, Bach, Parsaria, Patsaria, Bijhonia, Khatbais, Bhatkaria, and Chanamia or Gargbans; but it may be doubted if all these are really Bais. (See these Articles, as well as Binaudha and Gautam.)

The Tilokchandí Bais of Dúndia Khera are subdivided into four clans of Ráo, Rája, Naihathá, and Sainbasí. These all profess to derive their rights from the Gautum Raja of Argal.

Baníwál, بنیوال बनीवाल

One of the subdivisions of the Bhangí caste, *q.v.*

Baresirí, بریسري बरेसिरी

A tribe of inferior Jadon Rajpúts in Fattihabad, and Shamsabad of Agra.

Barkalá, برکلا बरकला

An inferior clan of Rajpúts, found in some of the Western and Central Parganahs of Bulandshahr.

Barothí, بروتهي बरोथी

A tribe of Ahírs in the neighbourhood of Paindhat, in the Mainpúrí district.—See Ahír.

Básián, باسيان बासियान

See Gaur Tagá and Ahír.

Bilúch, بلوچ बिलूच

A few Bilúch Zamíndárs are to be found in the Parganahs of Hodál, Bághpat, and Jiwar. A large Bilúch Jágír in the Dehli territory has encouraged their resort to these parts.

Beldár, بيلدار बेलदार

A class of Hindús engaged in digging with a Bel, or mattock. They are said in the Puranas to be descended from a Tayúr boatman and a woman of the Ahír tribe ; but Beldárs are now rarely met with as a distinct caste, even if they ever were one, which may be doubted, as Beldár is a pure Persian word.

The Beldárs now met with are composed mostly of different inferior tribes—Káchhís, Kúrmís, Chamárs, and others, who follow the occupation of digging.*

Bhál, بهال भाल

A tribe of Rajpúts, proprietors of part of Sikandarabad in Bulandshahr, and Hatras and Tappal in Aligaṛh.

Bhálá sultán, بهالا سلطان भालासुलतान

A tribe of Rajpúts in Binaudhá, *q.v.* and Gorakhpúr. Both these tribes may be probably connected with the Balla, who are

* Kols and Santhals, calling themselves *ḍhangars* (which I believe is a Kol word meaning day-labourers), are now chiefly employed in road-making and the like.—B.

included in the Rajkula, and were the lords of Bhál in Saurashtra.

The Bhál and Bhála Sultán are the same tribe, but the Bhál by intermarriages with inferior stocks are not held in the same consideration as the Bhála Sultán.*

Bhánḍ, بھانڈ भांड

Bahrúpiya, بہروپیا बहरूपिया

The text of the Printed Glossary, under Bhánḍ, requires modification.

Bhánds are a separate clan from the Bahrúpiya, but are descended from them. Those also are called Bhánds who without reference to caste follow the occupation of singing, dancing, and assuming disguises. The Bhoí Sutr says that Bahrúpiyas spring from the intercourse of a Malláh, or boatman, with a widow of the Gangapútr tribe. Their name is derived from the Sanskrit बहु many, and रूप appearance—*i.e.*, multiform, assuming many disguises; a mimic.

It is an error to suppose that Bhánd is written by mistake for Bhát. The two are quite distinct, so much so that Bhánds are frequently known by the name of Bhandela, which shows the distinction more plainly. Bhánds are now all Musulmans. Bahrúpiyas are many of them Musulmans, but the greater portion have adhered to their ancient faith.

Bhát, بھاٹ भाट

Bhát is said in the Glossary to be one of the illegitimate tribes springing from the intercourse of a man of the Bais and a woman of the Kshatríya caste; so also says Wilson, *voce* मागध, as well as the Vocabulary to Johnson's "Selections from

* They have a tradition that their name means "spear-king," from *bhálá*, "a spear." See "People of India," *s.v.*—B.

the Mahábhárat," p. 207: but Bháts are usually considered to spring from the intercourse of a Kshatríya with a Brahman widow. Other authorities say that they were produced to amuse Párvati, from the drops of sweat on Siva's brow, but as they chose to sing his praises rather than her's, they were expelled from heaven, and condemned to live a wandering life, as terrestrial bards.—Sir John Malcolm, "Central India," Vol. II., p. 132, says: "According to the fable of their origin, Mahadeva first created Bháts to attend his lion and bull; but the former killing the latter, every day gave him infinite vexation and trouble in creating new ones. He therefore formed the Cháran equally devout as the Bhát, but of bolder spirit, and gave him in charge these favorite animals. From that period no bull was ever destroyed by the lion."

A Bhát is a genealogist, a family bard. By some tribes, the Bhát and Jága are considered synonymous; but those who pretend to greater accuracy, distinguish them by calling the former Birmbhát, or Badí, and the latter Jágabhát. The former recite the deeds of ancestors at weddings and other festive occasions: the latter keep the family record, particularly of Rajpúts, and are entitled by right of succession to retain the office; whereas the Birmbháts are hired and paid for the particular occasion. Jágabháts pay visits to their constituents every two or three years, and receive the perquisites to which they are entitled. After recording all the births which have taken place since their last tour, they are remunerated with rupees, cattle, or clothes, according to the ability of the registering party. Those of the North Western Rajpúts generally reside between the borders of Rajpútana and the Dehli territory. Many also live at Dáránagar on the Ganges, and travel to the remote East in order to collect their fees. Whereas the Birmbháts are residents in towns and Kasbas, and do not emigrate periodically.

Both of these classes are held in the same dread for their exactions; which are satisfied by their constituents for fear of being lampooned and paraded in effigy (Gudda) before the other members of the family.

Several communities of Bháts exist in the North of Oudh, and a few are scattered over our provinces. There are, for instance, several villages belonging to Bháts in Azimgaṛh, Gorakhpúr, and Gházípúr.

In Rohilkhand, the occupation of Bháts, as bards, is frequently usurped by Gaur Brahmans.

There are several sub-divisions among the Bháts of these Provinces, and an attempt is sometimes made, as with many other classes, to reduce them to the definite number of seven; viz., Atsela, Mahapátr, Kailea, Mainpúríwala, Jangira, Bhatara and Dasaundhí. But there are several which are not included under these heads, as Chaurásí, Gajbhim, Chúngele, Gújriwala, Síkatpúrea, Nagaurí, Baruá, etc., which shews that the classification into seven is not correct.

Steel, in his "Summary of Indian Classes," p. 108, divides Bháts into Bhát Rajpút, or Kaví, and Bhát Kúnbí; the former he says are in Hindústan, the latter in the Maraṭha country; but the difference, if any, between them, refers perhaps more to the tribes they serve, than to any family distinction amongst themselves.

Of Bháts, several have been converted to the Muhammadan religion; some are said to have become Musulmans as early as the time of Shahábu'ddín Ghorí, when they received the title of Raís.

Besides their employment as genealogists, it is, or rather was, considered their special duty to learn the Puránas, for which, it is needless to say, they are now no longer conspicuous. (Padma Purána. See "Journal of R. A. S.," No. V. 281.)

Bhíhar, بھیہر भीहर

This is the name of a tribe which, according to local tradition, appears to have been one of the aboriginal races of Rohilkhand and the Upper Doáb. They are said to have been expelled from Nirauli, Bahjoí, and the neighbouring districts by the Baḍgújar Rajpúts. In the Doáb they are more commonly called Bemhar, and in parts of Rohilkhand, Bíhar. There may have been some connection between them and the Bhars, *q.v.*

Bhuksá, بهكسا भुकसा

A tribe found inhabiting the forest under the hills from Púranpúr Sabna, on the Sarda, to Chandpúr, on the Ganges.

Bhuksas claim to be Powar Rajpúts, and assert that their chief, Udyájít, was driven from house and home in a quarrel he had with his brother Jagat Ráo, the Rája of Dháránagar, and came to dwell with a few dependants in Banbasá, a village in the Oudh territory. He had not been there long before his aid was solicited by the Raja of Kamáon, whose territories required defence against the invasion of some neighbouring potentate. Success attended the efforts of the Powar, and the gratitude of the Raja induced him to offer his defenders an asylum in his territories. Upon this they are represented to have left Banbasa, and to have taken up their residence in their present abodes under the hills, chiefly on the lower edge of the Bhábar, where the springs rise to the surface. A part of the tribe remained in attendance upon the Raja of Kamáon.*

* It may be proper to remark that there may possibly have been some connection between the Powars and Bhuksas; for Chand, the Bard, records that Ram, the Powar, or Pramar, bestowed Kattair upon Kehar; which shows that this province must once have been included within the dominions of the Chakwa lord of Ujjayin. It may also be added that an Udyájít, or Udyádit, Pramar, son of Bhoj, was Raja of Dhár in the first half of the eleventh century, as has been established by numerous inscriptions (Trans. R. A. S., Vol. I. 133), and that the Bhojpúr family of Sháhabad claim a similar descent. They differ, however, in saying that Jagat Deo was the *son*, not the *brother*, of Udyájít. Rana Deo, the brother of Jagat Deo, was the founder of the Bhojpúr family.

This close identity in the relation of the origin of two such distant tribes, which

Bhuksas are considered bad cultivators, and rarely remain in the same spot above two years, for by that time they generally contrive to exhaust the soil they have had under tillage.—See "Printed Reports on Rohilkhand Canals," p. 107.

Of Bhuksas there are fifteen different Gots, or Clans—twelve superior, and three inferior. The superior are Baḍgújar, Taábri, Barhanáí, Jalwar, Adhoí, Dugugia, Rathor, Negauria, Jalál, Upadhya, Chauhán and Dúnwaria. The three inferior are the Dímar Rathor descended from a Teli (oil-presser); Dhangra from a hill-woman; and Golí from a woman of the barber caste. The names of these tribes indicate considerable intermixture with other classes, both Rajpút and Brahman.

Bhuksas are prohibited marrying in their own Gots, but may select any other Got they choose. Those who reside in Kilpúrí and Sabna are said occasionally to intermarry with the Thárús.

The Bháts of the Bhuksas, who are descended from a follower of Udyájít, reside still at Banbasá, and pay occasional visits to their constituents.

The Parohits of the Bhuksas are Kanaujiyá Brahmans, who are also descended from one of the companions of Udyájít.*

Bhúínhár, بھوینہار भूंइंहार

A tribe of Hindús to be found in great numbers in Gorakhpúr, Azimgaṛh, and the province of Benares. The Maharaja

could have had no communication with each other for centuries, is rather favorable to the claims of the Bhuksas, and leads us to suspect that their name may possibly have originally had some connection with that of their great progenitor Raja Bhoj.

* A long and interesting article on the Bhuksas or Boksas will be found in the J. A. S. B. 1865, Part II. pp. 147-173, by Dr. J. L. Stewart. It is too long to quote here, but the whole description of the race tends to prove their aboriginal character. They are probably of the same class as the Thárús who occupy the Tarái to the eastward of them as far as the Bágmati River, and like them they are not affected by malaria.—B.

of Benares is of this caste. They call themselves sometimes Brahmans, sometimes Thakúrs. They were originally Brahmans of the Sarwaria stock; but from having, as they say, received the Parganah of Kaswár from Raja Banár, and become addicted to agricultural pursuits and cultivators of land (भूईं), they lost their rank as Brahmans, though they frequently receive marks of respect due only to that privileged class. Others say that when Parasuráma destroyed all the Kshatríyas, he introduced Brahmans to occupy their place, and hence they became proprietors of land.

We, perhaps, have some indications of the true origin of Bhúínhár in the names Gargabhumi and Vatsabhumi, who are mentioned in the Harivansa, as Kshatríya Brahmans, descendants of Kasya princes (p. 123). Their name of Bhumi, and residence at Kasí, are much in favour of this view; moreover, there are to this day Garga and Vaṭsa Gots, or Gotras, amongst the Sarwaria Brahmans; but Wilson seems disposed to give another meaning to the title ("Vishnu Purána," p. 410).

Bhúínhárs are congregated chiefly in Deogáṅw of Azimgaṛh; in Gorakhpúr; in Doabeh, and Saidpúr Bhitrí of Gházípúr; and in Majháwar, Mehwárí, Sheopúr, Narwan, Kol Asla, Dhús, and Kaswar of Benares; also in Majhowa, Simráṅw and Mehsí of Champáran, in Bahár.

Besides the Garga, and Vatsa Gots, there are several subdivisions of Bhúínhárs, such as Sandel, Gautam (of which family is the Benares Maharaja), Dichhit, Upadhya, Paṇḍe, Sankarwár, Kinwár. It will be observed that several of these are subdivisions of the Sarwaria Brahmans, and those whose origin is disguised by new names have all some title connecting them with the Sarwaria stock. Thus, the Sankarwar are Misr, the Donwar, Tewárí; and so on.

In their marriages they do not observe the same distinctions which are enforced among Sarwarias between the Gautam Garg, Sandel, and the inferior ranks; for all the Bhúínhárs intermarry on terms of equality. See Kanaujiya Brahmans and Sarwaria Brahmans.

** To the above remarks of Sir H. Elliot, I add the following notice, derived from personal reminiscences of my residence in Champáran. This caste is widely spread all over Northern Behar, Benares, and Gorakhpúr; and less frequent in Southern Behar. They call themselves Brahmans, but this statement is not admitted by other castes. The story mentioned in the text that they lost caste by taking to agriculture is incredible on the face of it, as there are many thousands of Brahmans in the same part of the country who are engaged in agricultural pursuits, but without losing caste; such as Tiwáris, Upadhyas, Ojhás or Jhás, and others. The popular account of their origin is that they are partly Rajpúts and partly of other castes, and that on some occasion a king—who some say was Janaka, others Ram, and others one or other of the old legendary heroes—being desirous of performing a sacrifice, part of which consisted in feeding a thousand Brahmans, was unable to find so many in all Mithili (Tirhút and Northern Behar). He therefore privately, the day before the feast, distributed Brahman's janeus, or sacrificial threads to all sorts of people of the inferior castes, and the next day had them assembled and fed together with the few Brahmans who were present. From that day they ranked as an inferior caste of Brahmans, and were called Bhúínhárs because they were the ordinary "people of the land" (भूईं, *i.e.* भूमि, land, and हार, *i.e.* वाला person). The Maharaja of Bettiah, in Champáran, is of this caste, as are also the Raja of Sheohar, the Rájkumár Bábú of Madhoban, and several minor zamíndárs in the same distict. They are connected by marriage with the Maharaja of Benares, and with many other influential landholders in Sáran and Gorakhpúr. They do not have "hukka pani" (drinking and smoking) with Brahmans, and only under some restrictions with Rajpúts. Thus, a Rajpút may eat rice with them only when it is without condiments; he may not eat bread; and he may drink water only from an earthen vessel, not from a brass lotah. Similarly, when he eats with them, his food must be placed on a dish made of leaves, and not on the usual brass tháli. The meaning of these apparently trifling distinctions is that the Rajpút, on an emergency, may eat hastily prepared food with them, but nothing that implies a long preparation or deliberate intention.

Bhúínhárs are also called Bábhan बाभन or बाह्मन, by which the people say is meant a *sham* Brahman; just as in some districts an inferior Rajpút is called a राउत Ráut, the corruption of the name betokening the corruption of the caste.

As to the *locale* of the sacrifice above-mentioned, there is some doubt. We have the same or a similar story told about the Sarwaria Brahmans,* whose habitat is Gorakhpúr, adjoining the Bhúínhár. It is well known that all Northern Gorakhpúr and Champáran were till recent times a dense forest, only broken by such sparse settlements of the Aryans as Simráṅw and Janakpúr. Two Bhúínhár brothers are reported to have immigrated into Champáran from across the Gandak, and to have founded the families of Bettiah and Sheohar, about two centuries ago. This would lead us to place the scene of the legend in the Doáb between the Gandak and Sarjú (Gogra) were it not for the presence of a Bhúínhár prince at Benares. It is useless, however, to speculate on the original seats and subsequent migrations of the more obscure castes in the present state of our knowledge. The heroes who have died *sine vate sacro* are so numerous in India, and the people are as a rule so careless of the past of their race, that it may be reasonably doubted whether we shall ever be able to pick up the lost and broken threads of Hindú history.

Bhúínhars do not marry with Brahmans, nor, I believe, with Rajpúts. They are a fine manly race, with the delicate Aryan

* See Kanaujiya.

type of feature in full perfection. Their character is bold and overbearing, and decidedly inclined to be turbulent.—B.

Bhrigubansí, بهرگبنسي भिगुबंसी

A tribe of Rajpúts.—See Barhauliá.

Bhadauriyá, بهدوريا भदौरिया

A branch of the Chauhán Rajpúts; but the Chauháns are disposed to deny this relationship, now that from motives of convenience the two tribes have begun to intermarry.

They are divided into the six Clans of Athbhaiyá, Kulhaiyá, Mainú, Tasselí, Chandarseniá, and Ráut.

We find Bhadauriás in Mehrabad of Sháhjahánpúr, Jánibrást of Etawah, in a few Parganahs of Cawnpore, and in the Saugor Territory, to which they were invited by Akbar after his partial conquest of that province. They are in chief force in Báh Panáhat of Agra, and the country to the south, which after them is called Bhadáwar. Some say their name is derived from Badara between the Chambal and the Jumna; others, more correctly, from Bhadaura in the neighbourhood of Atair.

The family of the Raja of Bhadáwar aspire to a high antiquity,* but the entire absence of any notice of them in Chand's description of the attack of Pirthí Raja on Kanauj, in which he takes occasion to mention all the tribes that joined either party, and in the annals of the early Musulman Empire, discredits their claim. Yet on the grounds of this antiquity of lineage, as well as of their fidelity to the British Government (which was otherwise most amply rewarded by a Sayer com-

* We are led to infer, from a passage in Tod's "Rajasthan" (ii. 44, 45), that the Bhadauriás were established on the Chambal by Manika Raí, Prince of Ajmír, or, at least, shortly after his reign. Now, as he flourished towards the close of the seventh century, the Bhadauriás must have preceded the Chauháns of the Doáb, if reliance is to be placed on his statement.

pensation of 24,000 Rupees per annum), a rent-free grant of thirty villages has been bestowed upon the adopted heir of the family. Amongst other pretensions advanced, it was stated that the Bhadauriá, Harchal Deo, joined Timúr's standard, and received Rápri and Chandwár as a reward for his allegiance. Now, it is evident from the accounts in the "Zafar-náma," "Habíbu's sair," "Rauzatu's safá," and "Matla'u's Sa'dín," which all treat in great detail of Timúr's invasion, that no Hindú chief united himself with that conqueror; and even if he had, the tyrant, during his rapid course in Upper India, could have bestowed no fief that was worth acceptance; and much less would his bigotry have suffered him to bestow it on an infidel. It also appears that he never advanced fifty miles to the south of Dehli,* and therefore could not have conquered the Raja of Rápri and Chandwár. Moreover, what serves entirely to disprove this alleged gift is, that it is expressly stated in the "Tawáríkh-i Mubárik Sháhi," that Timúr had scarcely turned his back on India, when Sayyid Khizr Khan sent his Wazír to levy the revenue of Chandwár, "which had been due for *some years*, and recovered Jalesar out of the hands of the Rajpúts of Chandwár;" so that the Chandwár family, instead of losing, must have increased their possessions during the troubles succeeding Timúr's invasion.

Again, it is said that in the reign of the Emperor Akbar, the holder of the Raj, Rajjú Ráut, distinguished himself by slaying Hetá, a Meo freebooter, who resided at Hatkánt,† a fastness in

* It may be as well to observe here, that the "Rauzatu-s safa," and "Tabakát-i Akbarí" state that Amír Jahán Shah was sent with other distinguished commanders to sweep the country on all sides (جانب) of Dehli; whereas Ferishta and the "Matla'u's sa'dín" say "the country south (جنوب) of Dehli." Whichever reading we assume to be correct, it is evident that if these foraging parties had reached even as far as Mathura, that important seat of idolatry would not have escaped the notice of these annalists.

† The first direct mention we have of their stronghold Hatkánt is in the "Makhzan

the ravines of the Chambal; but the contemporary author of the "Akbar-náma" confutes the assertion, as he states that, in the third year of the reign, the estate of Hatkánt was given in Jagír to Udham Khan, for the purpose of suppressing "the Bhadauriá Zamíndárs of that place, who had long been *famous for their turbulent opposition to the imperial authorities.*"

و از سوانح آنست که ادهم خان و جمعي را برسر هتکانت فرستادند شرح این اجمال آنکه هتکانت درنزدیکي دارالخلافت آگره است از و مستحکم ترجائي نیست و زمینداران آنجا از طایفهٔ بهدوریه و غیر آن بربسیاري مردانگي اشتهار دارند و همواره با سلاطین هند سرکشي کردند بیرامخان چون همیشه از ادهم خان متوهم بود اندیشید که آن محال بجاگیر او را مقرر شود تا باین وسیله از در خانه دور گردد وهم متمردان نواحي سزا یابند و بیک خیال دو کار نیکتر بتقدیم آید بنابر آن اندیشه آنرا بجاگیر مقرر کرده رخصت داد*

Afghání;" but in that they receive anything but honorable mention. It is said of Sikandar Lodi in 915 H.:

و درسن نهصد و پانزده از لهاور بنواحي هتکانت رسیده آن محال را از اهل شرک و طغیان مصفا ساخته و متمردان آنجا را بقتل رسانیده و جابجا تهانجات نشانده بدارالخلافت آگره نزول اجلال فرمود

"And in the year 915, having arrived from Lahore, in the neighbourhood of Hatkânt, having purged that estate of robbers and freebooters, and having slain the rebels of those parts, and having established police-stations in various places, he returned to his capital, Agra."

* The author has unfortunately omitted to mention the page or volume of the work. I have made a long search through the voluminous "Akbar-náma" in vain. A free translation of the passage is as follows:—"At this time Udham Khán was

This account is confirmed in the second volume of the "Jahángír-náma," a work of which the first parts have been too much neglected.

وهمدرين آيام ادهم خان كوكلتاش را به تسخير هتكانت كه درنواحي دارالخلافة اكبراباد ازان محكم تر جائي نيست و بهدوريه نام قومي درانجا توطن دارند و بشجاعت و مردانگي از اكثر زمينداران عام امتياز مي افرازند تعين فرمودند و گروهي از امراء نامدار مثل بهادر خان و حسين قليخان و سيد محمد بارهه و شاه قليخان محرم و صادق محمد خان و اسمعيل قليخان و خرم خان بكومك او مقرر شدند ادهم خان و ساير امراء بتائيد دولت ابد پيوند مفسدان بهدوريه را تاديب سزا داده آنولايت را كه بجاگير ادهم خان از ديوان اعلى مقرر گشته بود متصرف گرديدند*

It appears, therefore, that the Bhadaurias, so far from performing any service to the Imperial Government, were themselves the parties on whom punishment was inflicted. It is

sent with a force against Hatkánt, which is a very strong place near the capital, held by zemíndárs of the Bhadauria clan, who are renowned for valour, and have always been in rebellion against the kings of India. Berám Khán, who was always suspicious of Udham, in order both to get him away from court, and also to put down these rebels, gave him this estate and sent him off, thus killing two birds with one stone."—B.

* I have also been unable to identify this passage, which appears to be corrupt in some places:—"About this time he sent Udham Khán Kokiltásh to sudue Hatkánt, a very strong place near the capital, and the Bhadauria clan reside there, who are celebrated for valour above all other zemíndárs; and with him he sent a number of celebrated leaders, as Bahádúr Khán and others. Udham Khán, with his party, having chastised the Bhadaurias, the jagír of the estate was conferred on him."—B.

nevertheless said that for this service (that is of expelling the Bhadaurias), the Bhadauria Raja received not only an assignment of the conquered land, but also a Mansab of 7,000. Here again they are completely at fault, and disproved by the same author, who distinctly asserts, in the "Aín-Akbarí," that no dignity above 5,000 was ever bestowed upon any but the King's own sons. The higher and more extravagant Mansabs, which we read of in later periods, were not given during the reign of that monarch. They begun to be introduced by his son, who commenced the practice by bestowing a Mansab of 30,000 on his Queen, Núrjahán. Whether a member of the Bhadauria family ever attained in Akbar's time the dignity even of 500, which is claimed for him on the authority of the "Aín-Akbarí," may be doubted; for in several copies which have been consulted the name of the family is not given in the Register of the Mansabdárs of 500.

In the reign of Akbar's successor, the family does not appear to have been held in any higher consideration; for in the memoirs of Jahangir, translated by Major Price, it is said, "Among other objects which I accomplished about this period was the suppression of a tribe of robbers, called Fehndia, who had long infested the roads about Agra, and whom, getting into my power, I caused to be trampled to death by elephants." In all the Persian MS. copies which have been examined, this strange word Fehndia is written Bhadauria; and the fact tells much against the alleged respectability of the family. The words of the original are as follows:

بهدوریه جماعتي بودند که اکثر راهها میزدند و دردي میکردند

These instances have been adduced in order to shew that the high claims that have been put forward in favour of the family are somewhat unreasonable; and were, indeed, entirely needless, as its respectability for many years past has been unquestionable.

It was from the time of Jahangir's successor that they appear to have been held in consideration by the royal family of Dehli.

In Shahjahan's reign Kishn Singh Bhadauria is down as a Mansabdár of 1000.*

In Muhammad Shah's reign we find one of the family, Anirudh Singh, a Mansabdár of 6,000, and Faujdar of Laháwar; and although the patentee had to pay the handsome price of fifteen lacs of rupees, it must be confessed the dignity was high for a Rajpút of so small a principality. In the time of this Emperor, the personal virtues of Raja Gopal Singh, the father of Anirudh Singh, were also held in high consideration, as we may learn from the interesting correspondence of Naunidh Raí. The "Táríkh-i Muzaffarí" also says of Anirudh Singh, that Saadat Khán had such a regard for him that he used familiarly to call him his son; but it is evident, from the perusal of the many contemporary histories of that period, that the consequence of the Bhadaurias declined before the close of Muhammad Shah's reign. We find the Raja's Fort invested by the Maraṭhas, his country plundered, and afterwards subjected to heavy contributions, and one of his successors compelled to go into exile for several years to escape the ravages of the victorious Játs, who had subdued the Bhadaurias and confiscated the Raj: and when at last Raja Bakht Singh was restored, he succeeded to but little of his former possessions, for in the words of the accurate Murtaẓa Khán, "times are now changed, and weakness has fallen on the Bhadauria; much of his territory has been retained by the neighbouring Rajas, and he is obliged to be content with but a small principality." This was written about the year 1790 A.D.†

* "In the 22nd year of Shahjahan Raja Badan Singh Bhadauria is down for 1500, and his son, Raja Mahán Singh, for 1000. Kishn Singh is entered as Jauhar." E. *add.*

† From inquiries made in 1845 by the Commissioner of Agra it appeared that

To sum up all, it may be said that the immediate cause of their aggrandizement is obscure, but is as likely to have been a pair of large eyes, as the capture of a fort (see Bhatula); that their political importance lasted no longer than for a few years at the beginning of the last century; that their illustrious lineage even now invests them with consideration in the eyes of surrounding Rajas, who allow the Bhadauria to sit higher than themselves, who receive from him the investiture, or rather impress, of the Tilak, who confess that he alone can cover with grain the *lingam* at Batesar (the Rana of Gohad having tried twenty-one maunds in vain, while the Bhadauria accomplished it with seven)—and that though influential, they are not of that high importance which they would arrogate to themselves. It is to be feared, also, they are much addicted to infanticide; so that when we take all these circumstances into consideration, there seems reason to acknowledge that the indiscriminate bounty of the British Government might perhaps have been more worthily bestowed.

Bhadariyá, بهڈریا भडरिया

See Dakaut, of which tribe they are a sub-division.

Bhagtá, بهگتا भगता

A tribe of Ahírs.—See Ahír.

Bhangí, بهنگي भंगी

The name given to the low caste occupied in sweeping and other menial domestic services. The Puráns say they are descended from a Súdra and a Brahman's widow. They extend

Raja Bakht Singh's possession of Bah Panáhat was only interrupted by the Játs in 1768 A.D. (1176 F.S.), and recovered by the Raja from 1769 to 1784 (1177 to 1192 F.S.), when he lost it again.—E. *add.*

throughout the whole of Hindústan, and are called indifferently Bhangí, Lálbegí, Khákrob, Halálkhor, and Mihtar.* Those who have remained, like their ancestors, Hindús, chiefly worship Lál Guru, which is the familiar name of the Rákshasa Aroná-karat; and those who affect Musulman observances have converted this name into Lálbeg, and state that he was an immediate follower of the prophet. The names of some of their Gots are Baníwál, Bílparwár, Ták, Gahlot, Kholí, Gágrá, Sarohí, Chandáliá, Sirsáwal, and Siriyár. There are several besides these; but all the different Gots intermarry on terms of equality.

Low as this tribe is in the scale of social life, they consider others engaged in the same occupation far lower than themselves, such as the Dhánuks, Sekris, Ráwats, and Helas. Bhangis, however, eat the leavings of all classes. Helas pride themselves on eating only those of Hindús. The claims put forward by these lower classes show how much more caste is a privilege than a degradation.—See Chuhrá.

Bhangís cannot in general be said to be of any particular religion, but they are, perhaps, more Musulman than Hindú. They bury their dead; occasionally sacrifice, in the name of Lálbeg, a fowl which has its throat cut after the Musulman fashion; and perform Tíja after the death of relations, which is also a custom peculiar to Musulmans. They generally, nevertheless, profess to be Hindús, because their marriage, and a few other ceremonies conform chiefly to the Hindú modes.†

* Bhangí, probably, from their drunken habits, from *bhang;* Lálbegí, from their object of worship; Khákrob, from Persian خاک *khák*, earth, and روب *rob*, sweeping; Halálkhor, from Persian حلال *halál*, lawful; and خور *khor*, eating, because everything is lawful to them as food; Mihtar, from Persian مہتر *mihtar*, prince, said to have been applied to them in derision.—B.

† There is a Bhangía caste in Chota Nagpur. J.R.A.S., vol. viii., p. 411. E. *add.* Tod. Raj. ii. 624.

Bhangúriyá, بهنگوریا भगूरिया

A tribe of Tagás, which has a few villages in Siyána, a parganah of Bulandshahr.—See Gaur Tagá.

Bhansará, بهنسره भंसरा

A subdivision of the Ahír tribe, *q.v.*

Bhanwag, بهنوگ भनवग

A small class of Rajpúts, of which we find a few in Mariyáhú of Jaunpúr, and Sayyidpúr Bhitrí of Gházípúr.

Bhar, بهر भर

One of the aboriginal races of India, called also Rájbhar, Bharat, and Bharpatwa. Common tradition assigns to them the possession of the whole tract from Gorakhpúr to Bundelkhand and Saugor, and the large Parganah of Bhadoí, in Benares (formerly Bhardaí) is called after their name. Many old stone forts, embankments, and subterraneous caverns in Gorakhpúr, Azimgaṛh, Jaunpúr, Mirzapur, and Allahabad, which are ascribed to them, would seem to indicate no inconsiderable advance in civilization.

The wild Bhíls of Marwar are called Bhaunrís (Irvine on Ajmír, p. 17). See also A.S. No. 145 of 1844), but I know not whether there is any connexion between them and the Bhars. The Bhoyas and Bhuttias of Agorí and Singraulí, who are generally classed as Ahírs, may probably bear some relation to the Bhars, though no trace can now be had of their descent. The Cherús also, *q.v.*, are sometimes said to be a branch of the Bhars.

Bhars are now occasionally found in the original seats of their occupation, filling the meanest offices: swine are especially given over to their care; and they have credit with the common people for being well acquainted with the depositaries of hidden treasure.

On the hills to the eastward of Mirzapúr, they retain a few principalities. Korar, Karaich, and Húráha are each held by Bhar Rajas, and the country between Bijaygaṛh and Chainpúr is full of them. The famous fort of Bijaygaṛh, amongst many others, is attributed to them, being called a Bharávati fort.*

It is strange that no trace of Bhars is to be found in the Puranas, unless we may consider that there is an obscure indication of them in the "Brahma Purana," where it is said that among the descendants of Jayadhwaja are the Bharatas, who, it is added, "are not commonly specified *from their great number;*" † or they may, perhaps, be the Bhargas, of the "Mahabharata," subdued by Bhim Sen on his Eastern expedition.

The Bhars consider themselves superior to Rájbhars, notwithstanding the prenomen of Ráj; but this claim to superiority is not conceded by the Rájbhars. They do not eat or drink with one another.—E.

The whole of Azimgaṛh was formerly occupied by Bhars or Rájbhars, who were dispossessed by Rajpúts of the Gautam clan, and are now swineherds, and possess no estates.—Records N.W.P. iii. 133. They also held the Parganah of Bára in Allahabad, but were there also dispossessed by Rajpúts of the Banáphar, Baghel, and other clans. They have left behind them several architectural works of great merit, as the ruins of a fort at Bhiṭa, and a palace at Sheorájpúr. They are said also to have held Khairagaṛh down to the dismemberment of the Kanauj kingdom.—Rec. N.W.P. iv. 401, 413.—B.

* Bharwá is a parganah of Chota Nagpúr. See J.R.A.S., vol. viii. p. 409. There are also some Bhars near Simla, whose features have a Kol type.—E. *add.*

† So also the "Harivansa" says of the Bharatas, I. p. 157. "They form an immense family whose numbers it is impossible to mention."

Bharbhúnjá, بهربهونجا भड़भुंजा

In the Glossary Bhadbhújá, and again Barbhúnja; in which place they are said to be the same as Halwaí, which is not quite correct. The literal meaning of the word is Grain-parcher, and denotes the general occupation of the tribe. They are traditionally said to spring from the intercourse of a Kahár with a Súdra woman. They are generally considered to be divided into seven Kúrís or clans, of which the most famous appear to be the Kanaujia, Sukhsena, and Utarráhá. They do not intermarry.

A class of Káyaths, particularly those of the Máthúr tribe, who follow this occupation, are distinguished by the same name. but have no other connection with the original Bharbhúnjas. They can never be got to enumerate the names of the seven clans with any uniformity; and it may therefore be doubted if that definite number of them exists.

Bharpatwá, بهرپتوا भरपत्वा

A subdivision of the Bhar tribe, *q.v.*—See also Gaharwár.

Bhartkúl, بهرت کول भर्तकुल

One of the subdivisions of Gaur Brahmans, *q.v.*

Bhaṭ, بهٹ भट

The name of a Brahmanical tribe in Ḳariát Síkhar, and other parts of the Benares province. They derive their origin from a Maraṭhi Brahman of the name of Mor Bhaṭ, and a Sarwaria mother.

Bhaṭ Gaur, بهٹ گور भटगौर

A subdivision of the Gaur Rajpúts, *q.v.* Also of Káyaths; see next Article.

Bhatnágar, بهتناگر भटनागर

A large tribe of Káyaths, who derive their name from Bhatner. They are found in great numbers, almost conterminous with the Gaur Brahmans, from Sambhal and Moradabad to Agroha and Ajmír: but are also scattered over some of the Eastern provinces, in which their establishment dates from the time of Ghyásu'd-dín, in the middle of the 13th century. When the King's son, Náṣiru'd-dín Karrá Khán, was appointed to the Government of Bengal, he was accompanied by several Bhatnágar Káyaths, who were high in his favor. These men soon became much intermixed with the Gaur Káyaths, the old residents of that country, at which the old Bhatnágars were scandalized; insomuch, that when Náṣiru'd-dín returned, some years after, to Dehli, to dispute the succession with Kaikobad, and was for some time encamped at Kásna, the old Bhatnágars refused to associate with them, and the heretics consequently became distinguished by the name of Gaura Bhatnágar or Bhatgaur.

The Bhatnágars are not considered very pure Hindús, and are more addicted to drinking than other Káyaths, but their official position has enabled them in some places to acquire considerable influence. They are the Kanúngoes of Gwalior and of Mahában in Mathurá.

The Gaura Bhatnágars are Kanúngoes of Mariyáhú in Jaunpúr, of Chapra and Múngír (Monghyr). To these Eastern divisions they appear to have been appointed by Náṣiru'd-dín. The females of these families are taken in marriage by the Western Bhatnágars, but a reciprocal privilege is denied to the Gaur Bhatnágars, as they are considered to have forfeited their claims to an equal rank by their amalgamation with the Gaurs.—See Gaur Káyaths.

The Káyaths in the N. W. P. are entered in the census 351,463, diffused all over the province.—B.

Bhaṭṭáchárj, بهٹاچارج भट्टाचारज

See Kanaujiyá Brahman.

Bhaṭṭí, بهٹي भट्टी

A Rajpút tribe of Yadúbansí descent, the rulers of Jaysalmer, giving name to the Bhaṭṭí territory between Hissar and the Garra. (See Bhattíana.) The once formidable Fort of Bhatner, perhaps, also derives its name from them, though a different origin is ascribed to it. The Bhaṭṭís of those parts were, it is said in the "Survey Report," converted to Mahomedanism in the time of Akbar, but the fact is not probable, as few conversions took place in his reign. It is stated in the "Annals of Rajasthan" (ii. 213, 260) that they were converted shortly after Timúr's invasion, and that on this occasion they changed their name from Bhátti to Bhatti. It does not appear, however, that there is any authority for this latter statement.*

It was shortly after Timúr left India, that a colony of Bhaṭṭís migrated from the neighbourhood of Bahawalpúr, under their leader Bersi, and captured Bhaṭner from a Mahomedan chief, who had himself lately conquered it from the Játs. It is not improbable, however, that there were Bhaṭṭís even at that time already in the neighbourhood, though the annalists of Timúr's invasion mention the Játs only. The son of Bersi was, after his father's death, compelled to sustain three several attacks of the Mahomedans, and on the third occasion was reduced to such straits as to be obliged to consent to conversion as the condition of retaining his conquest. The circumstantiality of the account invests it with some probability.

A large clan of Bhaṭṭí Rajpúts are said to have come to

* In Bikaner they are called Bháṭí. The conversion of their Raja to Islam was effected by Firoz Shah. Prinsep's Tr. ii. 368. Tod, i. 85, 534; ii. 186, 211. The Hindú traders of Shikárpúr, in Sindh, are Bháttias. E. *add.*

Bulandshahr under a Raja Kánsal in the time of Pirthí Rajá. A few of the descendants of the original stock are now in Tilbegampúr, Dádrí, etc., but the greater part of them have by intermarriages become Gújars. The Bhaṭṭís are held to have had 360 villages, and the tract from Loni to Kasna was called after them Bhatner. There are a few also in Tigrí and Ujhárí of Rohilkhand.

Bijhoniyá, بجهونيا बिझोनिया

A tribe of Rajpúts in the Parganah of Ghisua, Zilla Jaunpúr.

Bilkhariya, بلكهريه बिलखरिया

A tribe of Rajpúts of the Bachgotí Chauhán stock. There are many of them in Dhuriapár, a Parganah of Gorakhpúr. They derive their name from Bilkhar, in Oudh.

Badgújar, بڈگوجر बड़गूजर

One of the thirty-six royal races of Rajpúts, descended, like their opponents the Kachhwáhas, from Ráma, but through Lava, the second* son. We find them in great numbers from Sambhal, Seondara, and Salempúr in Rohilkhand to Atraulí and Koel, and even Jalesar in Mathurá. They are also in Shamsabad of Farrakhabad, Ayta of Mainpúrí, and in Gorakhpúr. Another clan, now entirely Musulman, is found to the Westward of Muzaffarnagar.

Colonel Tod says that it was in Anúpshahr that the Badgújars, on their expulsion by the Kachhwáhas from Rajor, found refuge; and that is still the chief town of the Badgújar family. But, as this expulsion occurred only in the time of the illustrious Siwaí Jay Singh, in the beginning of the last century, the chief of Rajor must have chosen for his residence a part of

* The *elder* son (*vide* Tod, Rajasthán, i. 46, 117; ii. 364).—B.

the country which was already in occupation of his brethren; for Baḍgújars are mentioned, even in Akbar's time, as the Zamíndars of Khúrja, Dhabáí, and Pahássú.

Their own assertion is that they came from Rajor, the capital of Deoti, in the Mácheri country, under Raja Partab Singh, and first resided in Kheria, near Pítampúr, and that the Raja, after marrying at Koel into a Rajpút family of the Dor tribe, which at that time occupied the whole country between Koel and Bulandshahr, obtained favor in the sight of the Dors, and got authority to establish himself as far Eastward as he chose. Having, in consequence, exterminated the Mewátís and Bhíhars, who are represented to have been in previous occupation, he was so successful as to acquire the possession of sixteen hundred villages, eight hundred on the East, and eight hundred on the West of the Ganges. At the time of his death, Chaundera, near Pahássú, was reckoned the chief possession of the Baḍgújars, and one of the descendants of Partáb Singh, Raja Salibahan, whose residence was at Chaundera, gave his own name to a Parganah which comprised the present divisions of Pítampúr, Pahású, and Birauli.

Raja Partáb Singh left two sons, Játú and Ránú. Játú took up his abode in Katehr, or Rohilkhand, and Ránú remained as chieftain of Chaundera.

The antiquity of the Katehr Baḍgújars may be surmised from a passage in the Rathor Genealogies, "Bharat, the eleventh grandson of Nayan Pál, the Rathor, at the age of sixty-one, conquered Keneksir, *under the Northern Hills*, from Rudrasen of the Baḍgújar tribe." Nayan Pál is supposed to have lived in the fifth century. Though there appears no occasion for ascribing to his reign so early a date, he must, at any rate, have long preceded the final Mahomedan conquest of Kanauj.

While the Katehr Baḍgújars and the Anúpshahr family have preserved their ancient faith, nearly all the Doáb tribes, which preceded the expulsion of their chief from Rajor, have turned

Mahomedans; and the early opponents of the British in Famonah and Pandráwal were Baḍgújars of that persuasion. They still, however, appear proud of their Rajpút lineage, for they assume the appellation of Ṭhákúr. Thus we hear the strange combinations of Ṭhakúr Akbar Ali Khán, and Ṭhákúr Mardán Ali Khán.*

At their marriage they paint on their doors, and worship the image of a Kahárí or female bearer, under whose instructions they executed a stratagem by which they exterminated the Mewátas who had been engaged in a drunken revel during the Holí. Some of the Musulman families have of late discontinued this custom.

The Baḍgújars to the west of Muzaffarnagar were all converted to the Mahomedan faith in the time of Alá-ud dín Khiljí, but they still retain most of their old Hindú customs. A stricter conformity to the Musulman tenets was endeavoured to be introduced by some reformers, and all Hindú observances were sedulously proscribed by them; but when it was found, as they themselves assert, that all their children became blind and maimed, in consequence of their apostacy, they were induced to revert to their ancestral customs, and still adhere to them with so much pertinacity, that it is almost doubtful which faith prevails most.

The Muzaffarnagar Baḍgújars state that they came from

* The converted Rajpúts of Northern Behár are similarly called Ṭhakuráí, which title they *affix* to their name, as 'Ináyat 'Ali Ṭhakuráí. In Eastern Behár we find a still more singular combination of names, the converts to Muhammadanism retaining Hindú names with the prefix of Shaikh; as Shaikh Ram Chand, Shaikh Kishn Singh, and other eccentricities. In the parganahs of Dhaphar and Náthpúr, of Puráníyá (Purneah), is a tribe of Brahmans who use the Pathán title Khán, which was given them by Sher Shah, I believe, or some other of the emperors of Delhi. The females of this tribe do not, however, take the title of Khánum (which would be the proper feminine of Khán), but call themselves, oddly enough, Kháṅyáiṅ (खांयाईं), an almost unpronounceable title, which is evidently formed on the Hindí principle, as *kunjrin*, a huckster, *baṛhaiṅ*, a carpenter's wife, *chamáin*, a midwife, etc.—B.

Debandesár near Dhaín Dawása, south of the Alwar country, under one Kurásen, whose ancestor, Bába Megha, is still invoked when they make their offerings at the time of naming their children. They intermarry with the converted Puṇḍír Rajpúts of Sakraudá in Sahéranpúr, and the Ráo Baḍgújars in Farídabad of Ballabhgaṛh, to the south of Dehli. They seem to know but little of their brethren who reside in the neighbourhood of Anúpshahr.

The place whence they emigrated may be easily traced, for Dawása, or Deosah, lies on the Bangangá river, about thirty miles east of Jaypur, and Dháín is about eight miles to the south of Deosah. Deosah is famous as being the first place belonging to the Baḍgújars, which was occupied by the Kachhwáhas after their emigration from Narwar in the middle of the tenth century. It is not improbable that the Kachhwáhas may at this period have compelled the Baḍgújars to emigrate in search of other seats, and they in their turn may have wreaked their vengeance on the Kachhwáhas of the Upper Doáb, and established their Chaurasí among the brethren of their distant foe. Certain it is, that tradition assigns a large tract of country in these parts to the Kachhwáhas, before the Baḍgújars, Játs, and Pathans obtained possession.—See Kachhwáha.

The Sikarwál Rajpúts state that they are a branch of the Baḍgújars; but they are separately entered among the thirty-six Royal Races in Tod's list. It is to be observed, however, that in some of the other lists which he has given ("Annals of Rajasthan," vol. i. p. 81), neither Baḍgújars nor Sikarwáls are entered.

Barmbháṭ, برم بهاٹ बर्मभाट

See an account of this tribe under the article Bhát.

Bisen. بسین बिसेन

A powerful tribe of Rajpúts in the eastern parts of these

provinces. To the westward they do not extend beyond Rasúlábád of Cawnpore. We find them in Kewaí, Karárí, Karra, Chail, Bára, Khayrágaṛh, and Aṭharban, in the Allahabad district; Chibúmau in Banda; Badlapúr and Mariáhú in Jaunpúr; Bhadoí, Pandra, and Aṭhgáwán in Benares; Shádiábád, Pachhotar, Bahriábad, and Haveli in Gházípúr; Muhammadabad Gohna, Nizámabad, Mahul, and Bhadáṇw of Azimgaṛh; and Chillopar, and Salempúr Majhaulí of Gorakhpúr. In Oudh they have three hundred and sixty villages.

The Bisen families to the north of the Gogra intermarry with the Sarneṭ, Súrajbans and Kalhans Rajpúts, and receive the daughters of Chandel, Bais, and inferior Chauhans.

The acknowledged chief of the Bisen stock is the Raja of Salempúr Majhaulí. The founder of the political influence of the family was Mewar Bhat, whose ancestors had for many generations resided as devotees in the neighbourhood of Nawápúr, now known as Salempúr Majhaulí. Mewar Bhat, though himself a religious man, was not able to withstand the solicitations of ambition, and taking up arms after returning from a pilgrimage to Benares, acquired possession of the greater part of the country between the Ganges and the great Gandak.

Mewar Bhat had four wives. By one, a Rajpútní, he had issue Bisú Sen, the founder of the name of Bisen, and the ancestor of the Raja's family. By a Bhúinhar he had Bagmar Sahí, the ancestor of the Kawarí and Tamakhoí Rajas. By a Brahminí he had Nages, whose descendants hold a few villages in Salempúr Majhaulí. By a Kurmí he had the ancestor of those now resident in Ghosí of Azimgaṛh.

The present incumbent of the Raj is said to be in the hundred and fifteenth generation from Mewar Bhat.

Bishṇaví, بشنوي बिश्नवी

A tribe of growing importance in Rehar, Sherkoṭ, and some of the neighbouring parganahs of Rohilkhand. They are found also in great numbers in Bikanír, Nagor, and Hissar; and small communities of them are also found in the Upper Doab. They are not to be confounded with the ordinary Vishnavas, of whom Wilson has given us an account in the "Asiatic Researches," yet they do not appear a sect of modern origin, as they are mentioned in the "Aín Akbarí" as the Zamíndars of Islampur in Sirkar Badanw. The "Tambíhu'l jahilín" says that they derive their name from Bishnu, a Tagá Brahman, a pupil of a Musulman Fakír, who appears to have been a freethinker; and that hence arises their regard of Musulman observances. They worship according to the Hindu ceremonial three times a day, and pray after the Musulman fashion five times a day. They keep twenty-eight holidays during the year, and observe the fast of Ramzan. They read both the Ḳuran and Hindu Pothís. They refrain from meat and intoxicating drinks, and intermarry. They generally call themselves Shaikhs, adding that title to a Hindu name, or adding sometimes a Hindú title to a Musulman name. Sometimes they bury, and sometimes burn their dead. They consider themselves more Hindús than Musulmans; which gives the author of the above-mentioned work the opportunity of remarking how strange it is that, notwithstanding most of the teachers of the dissenting sects have been Musulmans, as is the case with the Kabírpanthí, Parnamí, Daudpanthí, Sádh, Kalalpanthí, and Bishnaví sects; yet they all call themselves Hindús.

In Coleman's "Mythology of the Hindús," p. 310, there is a description of a sect of Bishnavís, called Dhamian, inhabiting Bundelkhand, but it is evident from the description given of their tenets that they are followers of the famous Prán Náth, who established a notorious influence over the mind of Raja Chattar Sál.

Bohra, بوهرا बोहरा

A class of money-lenders frequently met with in the North

West Provinces, more especially in the Upper Doáb. A description of those who have been converted to the Mahomedan faith is given in Vol. VII. of the "Asiatic Researches," and Malcolm's "Central India," II. 212. The printed glossary would seem to imply that there are in India none except those on the Western coast.

The Bohrás of these Provinces, either come from the neighbourhood of Jaypúr, or are descendants of the original settlers from that quarter, and preserve some peculiarities of speech and dress by which they are readily known. An inferior class of Bohrás is known under the name of Kaiyáns and Rahṭís. They lend money to agriculturists and others in a small way, generally by tens, and for every ten rupees take a bond for twelve rupees, payable by instalments of one rupee per mensem, by which means they realize a large interest upon their money. The continually revolving nature of their dealings, and monthly visits to each of their debtors, have, with reference to the constant revolutions of the Rahaṭ, or Persian wheel and buckets, procured them the designation of Rahtís. The derivation of the term Kaiyán is not so certain.

The Bohrás, who probably derive their designation from the word Beohar or trade, are monied men, and possessing credit elsewhere, have larger dealings, and with higher classes than the Rahtís have, but, like the latter, are generally eager to acquire possession of profitable estates; there is, however, this difference between the two, that the Rahtís lend, and will take in return, only money; whereas the Bohrás are ready to receive every marketable article, including the produce of the soil as well as cattle, among which may be enumerated horses, camels, sheep, and goats, in payment of their debts.*

* The "Borah" in Bombay is a travelling pedlar, or, as we say in Bengal, "box-wallah." The Kaiyáns are generally Jains, or rather the Jains are called in Behar by the name of Kaiyán.—B.

Búhar, بوهر बूहर

A predatory tribe on the frontier, between Bikanír and Bháwalpúr (See Report of Boundary Commission, dated 10th June, 1849, p. 26).—E. *add.*

Búndelá, بونديلا बूंदेला

A spurious tribe of Rajpúts, who give name to the province of Bundelkhand. They are descended from Gaharwárs of Kantit and Khayrágaṛh, Various accounts are given of the origin of the name. They themselves state that they are so called from the devotion to Binda (Vindhya) Basní, for which their ancestors were conspicuous. The "Kshatr Prakásh" says, that Raja Pancham, one of their ancestors, determine to sacrifice his life in honor of Binda Basní Bhawání, but that she kindly interposed just after he had begun to inflict a wound on himself, and that the drop of blood (बूंद *búnd*) which fell from the wound on the earth became a Kuṅwar, or Prince, and hence his descendants are called Búndelás.

The whole genealogy, however, of this work, which is the foundation of Colonel Pogson's "History of Bundelkhand," is completely wrong, and this story has been made up to cover the disgrace of a humble origin.

The intelligent author of the "Hadiḳatu'l-aḳálím" gives a much more probable origin of the name. He says that Hardeo, one of the Gaharwár family, came with a slave girl from Khayrá-gaṛh, and took up his abode at Gaṛh Karár, in the neighbourhood of Urcha. He was there invited to give his daughter in marriage to the Raja of Urcha, which he refused to do, as the Raja was a Khangar. After much importunity he consented, on the condition that the Raja and his family should come to the marriage feast, partake of the viands, and thus lose all distinction of caste. The Raja consented, was poisoned with all his family, and the Gaharwár obtained possession of the country.

His son was called Búndela, because he was the son of a slave girl (Bandí), some say the daughter of the Khangar Raja; and this name has been given to his descendants.

The establishment of the Búndelas, to whatever it owes its origin, probably occurred about the beginning of the thirteenth century, after the Chandels had been humiliated by the Chauhans, and they in their turn had been compelled to yield to the supremacy of the Musulmans. The country around Kalinjar and Mahoba must then have been in so distracted a state, as to have invited the attack of the first chieftain who could muster a band of followers sufficiently strong to maintain their occupation.*

Narsingh† Deo, one of the descendants of Hardeo, obtained the appellation of Dáng, equivalent to a dacoit, and hence arose the name of Dángaya applied to Eastern Bundelkhand, particularly the part East of the Dassan, which was held by the descendants of Chattarsal; so that neither from the name of Bundela, nor that of Dangaya, does this stock derive any honor. The estimation in which it is held for fraud and chicanery may be learnt from the familiar proverb:

न सौ डंडी न एक बूंदेलखंडी

That is, one native of Bundelkhand commits as much fraud as one hundred weighmen.

* Franklin (Trans. R. A. S. Vol. I.) gives a later origin to the Búndelas. He says that from the time of Mahmúd to Timúr anarchy prevailed in the country of Bundelkhand; and that about the time of Timur's invasion Dewadri Bir from Goharbhani (evidently the country of the Gaharwárs) established himself with his followers at Mao Mahoni (Máu on the Jumna), and thence by degrees the dominions of the Gaharwárs extended to the Westward, till they included the whole of what is now called Bundelkhand.

† More correctly Bírsingh, according to E. *add.*, but he seems in some doubt as to which is the correct name. Tod Rajasth. i. 117, mentions Bír Singh, but it is doubtful if this be the same man. The original name of Gahawár, or, as Tod writes it, Gherwal, is still retained in the original seat of the family. Urcha and Dhattiá are their chief places.—B.

In British Bundelkhand there are few Bundelas, except in the Parganah of Panwarí.

Bauriya, باوریا बौरिया

A tribe of robbers in the district of Muzaffarnagar, said to number two thousand and upwards. These men were possessed of a perfect organization for thieving purposes, and carried on their trade all along the Grand Trunk road, and into the Panjab. They are also known as Bagrís (*q.v.*) and Magahyas, and though attention has been chiefly drawn to them from their assembling in the Muzaffarnagar district, yet they are known to be spread all over the country from the Jhelum river to the Narbadda. They claim to be Rajputs from Chittor, and are mentioned, under the name of Báwari, by Tod (Raj ii 318) among the degraded or apostate tribes, and as professional thieves. In the N.W.P., however, they seem to be neither Hindu nor Musulmans. This name is said to be derived from "Báwar," a snare; but I doubt this. They, like all other doubtful and low castes, say they have seven clans, to which they give grand names, as follows:—Powar, Soharki,* Dobas, Chauhan, Tuar, Dhandhara, and Gordhí. They add sometimes an eighth, called Chami. They admit a connection with the well-known bold, inveterately thievish, and dacoity-practising Badhaks of Bhojpur and Ghazípur, also with the Magurs and Bagoras of Gwalior. (See, for a full account of these men, Sel. from Rec. N.W.P. Vol. IV. pp. 109, 253.)—B.

Bach, بچ बच

An inferior tribe of Rajputs in Mongra of Jaunpúr.

Bachgotí, بچگوتي बचगोती

A Rajput tribe, said to be descended from the Mainpurí

* It is so written in the report from which I take the information, but is probably a misprint for the well-known Rajpút name of Solankhi.

Chauhans. The names of their progenitors were four brothers Guge, Gage, Gautam, and Raní.

There are several Bachgotís on the borders of Jaunpur and Gorakhpur, and in the South Eastern part of Oudh, where the two most conspicuous chiefs of the tribe are the Raja of Kurwar and the Dewan of Hasanpur Bandhwa. The last, notwithstanding his being a Musulman, and hence called Khanzada, invests all the Rajas of Binaudha with the Tilak. The Sombansí chief of Araur, the Bisen of Rampur, the Kanpurya of Tiloí and Bandhalgotí of Amethí would not be considered entitled to the privileges exercised by their ancestors without receiving it from his hands. The consequence of this family has, however, somewhat declined since the Dewan Roshan Ali Khan Khanzada was killed in action by Muhammad Kulí Khan, the nephew of Nawwab Safdar Jang.

It may be proper to add, that most people deny the right of the Hasanpur Bandhwa family to the title of Dewan, which they say belongs only to the Bilkharia family; and in practice it is certainly usual to give the title to the latter.

The Bachgotí are of old notorious for their turbulence. We read of it as early as the time of Sikandar Lodi and Sher Shah, in the "Tawaríkh-i-Afághana;" and again in Muhammad Kazim's history of the reign of Alamgír From these histories, and from the "Tabakát-i-Akbarí" and "Táríkh-i-Badaoní,"*

* There are two works called the "Ṭabakát-i-Akbarí," and two works called the "Táríkh-i-Badáoní." Of the former, only that by Názimu'd-dín Ahmad Bakhshí has been quoted throughout these notes: and of the latter, that by Abdu'l Ḳádir bin Maluk Shah. He himself calls the work "Muntakhabu't-Tawaríkh;" but this is the title of so very many works, that I have preferred "Táríkh-i-Badáoní," by which title the work is now more generally known in Hindustan. The other "Táríkh-i-Badaoní," contains "a valuable history of Hindústan by Abdu'l Razzak Malúk Shah, of Samarkhand," which I have never had an opportunity of seeing. This description of the work rests on the highly respectable authority of Dr. Lee (Preface to Ibn Batuta, p. xiii.): yet I cannot help thinking he may possibly have been mistaken; and what somewhat encourages the suspicion is, that the next work he quotes is the "Matlau's-Sa'dín,"

we learn also that the Khánzádas must have been converted to Mahometanism before the Mogul dynasty commenced, as we read of Bachgotís with Musulman names before that period.

The Bilkharias (*q.v.*), Rajwárs, and Rájkumárs are offshoots of the Bachgotís.

Bárí, باري बारी

A class of men who occupy themselves in making and lighting torches, and occasionally as barbers. They are said in Brahma and Padma Purános to be descended from a barber and female tobacconist.

In the Oudh service they have acquired the reputation of being very excellent soldiers, and some of them have attained to the dignity of Rájá.

Bhaṭkariyá, بهٹکریا भटकरिया

The name of a class of inferior Bais Rajpúts resident in the district of Jaunpúr.—See Bais.

Baghel, بگهيل बघेल

Literally, tigers' whelps, from باگه a tiger.*

Abdu'l Razzák ibn Isḥák, of Samarkand, which title is perfectly correct. As the names so closely resemble each other, and follow so closely, may we not suppose that Razzák and Samarkand have been given to Dr. Lee's "Táríkh-i-Badáoní" by some oversight, and that it may really be the same work which has been occasionally cited in this supplement.—E.

For further information about these works the reader should consult the valuable and learned article entitled "Materials for the History of India," by Major Nassau Lees, which has recently appeared in the J. R. A. S., Vol. III., p. 414. The "Muntakhabu't-Tawaríkh" of Abdu'l ·Ḳádir has been published in the Bibliotheca Indica of the Asiatic Society of Bengal, but I do not find anywhere any notice of the other "Táríkh-i-Badáoní" mentioned by the author. The "Ṭabakáṭ-i-Akbarí" of Nizám (not Názim) u'd-dín is also noticed in Major Lees' article, but has not yet been published.—B.

* Tod (Raj. i. 99) spells the word Bhagel, and says they are so called from their founder, Bhág Ro, which is, I think, the most probable story. See also Records N.W.P., iv. 413.—B.

A branch of the Solankhí tribe of Rajputs. They give name to the large principality of Baghelkhand, or Rewa, to the South of Allahabad, and were formerly rulers of Guzerat, where some chieftains of this family are still to be found. They acquired considerable influence during the time of Akbar, who in his youth was for a long time a companion of Raja Ram Baghel, and whose mother was indebted to him for protection during the troubles of Humayun.

In our own provinces we find Baghels in Bundelkhand; Chibramau, Tirua and Thattia of Farakhabad; (the Raja of Thattia is a Baghel) in Sarh Salempur of Cawnpore; Barah and Arail of Allahabad; Bhadoí of the Benares Raja's Domains; Salempur Majhaulí of Gorakhpur; and Sohagpur.

The Baghel chief of Rewa, or Bhagel (for it appears to be written in both ways), is the descendant of the famous Sid Raí Jay Singh, the ruler of Anhalwara Pattan from A.D. 1094 to 1145. His Court was visited by the Nubian Geographer, Edrisi, who distinctly states that at the time of his visit the chief adhered to the tenets of Buddha.

Bagsariyá, بگسریا बगसरिया

A small clan of Rajputs chiefly found in Kundurkí and Sirsí of Moradabad. It is also the appellation of a clan of Kanaujia Brahmans, of which there are a few families in Gorakhpúr.

Baheriya, بہیریا बहेरिया

A clan of Rajpúts in Ghiswa of Jaunpur and in Chanar.

Bahlím, بہلیم बहलीम

This tribe has a few villages in Dasna and Mírat. They are Shaikhs, but do not rank high in the scale of respectability. Some of the sub-divisions of Rohilkhand Banjáras are called Bahlím, and evidently derive their name from this tribe.

Balesar, بليسر बलेसर

A sub-division of the Gújar tribe, *q.v.*

Bamhaniyá, بمهنيا बम्हनिया

A sub-division of the Káchhí tribe, *q.v.*

Bamhangaur, بمهن گور बम्हनगौर

See Gaur Rajpút.

Bamtelí, بمتيلي बमतेली

The name of a Rajpút tribe which preceded the present Zamíndárs of the Eastern portion of parts of the Central Doáb. They still remain in the original seats of their occupation, but are not held in high consideration.—E.

They appear to be found now only in Farakhabad and Cawnpore, where their name is also pronounced Bhúíntelá, which is probably more correct than the other.—B.

Banafar, بنافر बनाफर

A tribe of Yadúbansí Rajpúts which is found in considerable numbers in the Southern parts of Oudh. There are some also in Kárra of Allahabad; in Narwan, Havelí, and Katehar of Benares; in Garra Mandla; and in Bundelkhand.* Their original seat is Mahoba, and they have acquired much celebrity from their clansmen, Ala and U'dal, whose desperate bravery in their contests with Pirthí Raja forms the subject of several well-known ballads, and gives title to one of the sections of Chand's voluminous poem.†—See Chandel.

* There is a tract in Parganah Chandla called after them, Banapharí.

† It is the twentieth prastáv of the Prithi Raja Rásá, and is entitled आल्हा ऊदल महोवा जुद्ध "The fight with Ala and Udal at Mahobá." It contains 308 kavitts, about 3000 lines in all, and is consequently rather too long to quote.—B.

Banjára, بنجاره बनजारा

In addition to what is stated in the printed Glossary, it may be as well to mention that the word appears to be derived from the Sanskrit Banij वणिज a merchant, and not, as Shakspeare's Dictionary tells us, from the Persian Biranjár برنجار rice carrier; the word being of higher antiquity than the Indian connection with Persia.* Thus we find mention of a cock fight in a Banjara camp in the story of Ramati in the "Dasa Kamára Charitra," written by Dandi, a predecessor of Kálidása, according to Colebrooke ("Introd. to Hitopadesa"). It is to be confessed, however, that Wilson does not assign an earlier origin to this compilation than the ninth century ("Journ. R. A. S." No. IX. p. 135). Nevertheless, independent of this testimony, Banjáras seem to be clearly indicated, even by Arrian, as constituting one of the classes of Indian society (Indic. xi.). We may therefore rest assured that we are not to look to Persia for the origin of the name.

The Banjáras of these provinces are not always wandering merchants, but many are denizens of the long tract of country under the Northern hills from Gorakhpúr to Hardwár. Most of those who are Musulmans ascribe, like the Lodanahs of Central India, their origin to Multan, or its neighbourhood, and state that they were converted to Mahometanism by Shaháb'ud-dín Ghorí; but it is probable that, like the Multanis of the Deccan and the Lodanahs, they did not leave their native country till about the time of Nádir Shah's invasion. The Hindú genealogical records usually consider Banjáras to be Chárans, or bards, who have chosen a wandering life, and disregarded the literary accomplishments which are considered to be their birthright. Their origin, however, as the text says, is involved in great obscurity.

* They are, however, frequently called Brinjaras in India: which gives some colour to the derivation from the Persian.—B.

Those of Central and Western India are doubtless usually Chárans. The sacred character of their office inspires respect among the lawless, but superstitious, people with whom they have to deal, and grain and merchandize under their charge are allowed to pass without question.

The original stock of Banjáras mentioned above as living in the Northern forests have become much intermixed with other classes, and men of all tribes are constantly deserting their homes, and joining the Banjára fraternity.

The mere names of their tribes are sufficient to show this. The Turkia Banjáras are divided into thirty-six tribes: Tumar, Chauhán, Gahlot, Dilwárí, Alwí, Kanothí, Búrkí, Dúrkí, Shaikh, Nathámír, Aghwán, Badan, Chakíráha, Bahrárí, Padar, Kaník, Gharí, Chandaul, Telí, Charkhí, Dhangaia, Dhanhíkaia, Gaddí, Gotahní, Títar, Hindia, Ráha, Marauthia, Khákhará, Kareya, Bahlím, Bhattí, Bandwarí, Bargadda, Alía, and Khiljí. These assert that they came originally from Multan, and left their newly chosen country of the Dekkan under a leader called Rustam Khan,* and first of all took up their abode at Badlí Tánda,† near Moradabad, from which they have gradually spread to Bilaspúr, Richha, and the neighbouring tracts. They are for the most part occupied as carriers.

* They probably mean the famous Rustam Khan, who held the Government of Sambhal for some time during the reign of Shahjahán. He was the founder of Moradabad, which he originally called Rustamnagar; but as that name gave offence to the Emperor, he called it after Prince Murad; to whom, however, he was subsequently opposed in the famous action in the Chambal, in A.D. 1668, in which he lost his life.

† Táṇḍa is a settlement or camp of Banjáras. There are many towns called Taṇḍa in various parts of India, from their having once been depôts or encampments of some Banjára patriarch. The large village called Taṇḍa in Gujrát district in the Panjab, a few miles from the place where the Chenab river issues from the hills, is entirely inhabited by Labánas, which is the Panjabi name for this tribe. The assertion in the text that Labanas are employed entirely in agriculture is very erroneous. I know many large gangs of them who spend their time entirely in carrying grain from mart to mart on bullocks.—B.

The Bayd Banjaras came from Bhatnír under a leader called Doalha. Of them there are eleven Gots: Jhaloí, Tandar, Hatar, Kapahí, Danderí, Kachní, Tarín, Dhorpahí, Kírí, and Bahlím. Their occupations are more various than those of the Turkias, as they are occasionally employed as doctors and weavers. They are found in Pilibhít, Kant, and in the neighbourhood of those places.

The Labána Banjaras have also eleven Gots. They state that they are descended from Gaur Brahmins, and came in Aurangzeb's time from Ranthambor. They engage almost entirely in agricultural pursuits.

The Múkerí Banjáras of the Northern Parganahs of Bareilly assert that they derive their name from Mecca, which one of their Naiks, who had his tanda in the neighbourhood, assisted Father Abraham in building! Leaving Mecca, they came and resided at Jhajjar, where their illustrious name became corrupted from Meccaí into Múkerí. Their fabulous history is not worth recording, but their names also betray a strange compound of tribes, Musulman and Hindu: Aghwan, Moghal, Khokhara, Chauhan, Simlí-Chauhan, Chothya-Chauhan, Panjtakya-Chauhán, Tauhar, Katherya, Pathan, Tarín-Pathan, Ghorí, Ghoríwál, Bangaroa, Kanthya, and Bahlím.

The Bahrup Banjaras are for the most part Hindús, and lead a more wandering life than the Musulmans. They are divided into the tribes of Rathore, Chauhán or Kurrí, Powar, Tumar, and Bartia. The origin of the first four is sufficiently apparent from their names. The fifth is said to be derived from a Gaur Brahman. Of these tribes again there are several ramifications. Of the Rathore there are four: Muchharí, Bahúkí, Murhawat, and Panot. Of the Múchharí there are fifty-two divisions; of the Bahukí there are twenty-seven; of the Murhawat there are fifty-six; and of the Panot there are twenty-three. The Chauhán, who have forty-two Gots, are unanimous in stating that they came from Mainpurí. The Powars have twenty Gots, and sta*e that they came from Dháranagar. The Tumar, Tuar, and Torí have forty-two Gots, and state that they came from Dehli. The Bartia have fifty-two Gots. They claim Chittor as their original seat. Bahrup Banjaras, like all the other clans, intermarry, but do allow of any connexion between members of the same Got. They receive the daughters of Nats in marriage, but do not allow their own daughters to marry into Nat families; and they have some curious customs at their marriages, which need not be detailed here.

It is evident that the Bahrúp Banjáras have a close connection with those of the Dekkan. In a paper in the "Bombay Literary Transactions" (Vol. I.), General Briggs divides them into Chauhán, Rathore, Powar and Bartia. In a paper published in the "Journal Asiatic Society" (No. 145, for the year 1844), the last is omitted. It seems strange, where the subdivisions are in the four cases mentioned in the "Bombay Transactions" identical, we should miss the fifth (Tumar), who form so large a clan of our Bahrúp Banjaras.

Before the predominance of the Rohilla Afghans, the jurisdiction of the Rohilkhand Banjáras was of great extent, and in the middle of the last century they held a great portion of the forest, as well as of the country to the South of it. But after the defeat of Raja Harnand by Ali Mahomed Khan, the parganah of Pilibhít was wrested from Daispat Banjara by Payinda Khan, and added to the Jagír of Hafiz Rahmat.

The Banjáras of Gorakhpur used to commit extensive depredations in that district, and were not put down till a short time previous to the British accession, when they were severely punished by Raja Sarbajít of Bansi.

The turbulence of the Banjaras has now been entirely suppressed, both in Gorakhpur and elsewhere, and they have become, under our pacific rule, a quiet and well-conducted people. They now confine themselves principally to the occupations of cattle graziers and carriers, especially the latter.

During the early part of the cold weather, many parties of them visit the Northern and Eastern forests to graze their cattle, and dispose of their cargoes of salt; and on their departure in the hot season load them with rice, tumeric, and other produce of those regions; and as they are distinguished for the honesty of their mercantile transactions, their credit is considerable. They usually take advances from a native merchant to purchase the goods they require, and repay him by a bill from the market where they are disposed of. Each community has a chief or Náik, whom all implicitly obey, and trust in all matters connected with their traffic and conduct. Through him the city merchants make their bargains, for the punctual execution of which he is security. Any Banjára committing an offence against the tribe, or its head, in his public capacity, is tried by Panchayat, and punished by fine or expulsion, as may be thought proper. Their decisions, indeed, are said sometimes to extend to the length of inflicting capital punishment, and such may possibly have, till within the last few years, been the case, for the regions they visit are so remote, that they are pretty secure of escaping detection.

Barhaí, بڑهئی बढ़ई

A carpenter.—There are usually said to be, as in many other inferior tribes, seven sub-divisions. Their names are never given accurately; but it is easy to ascertain that there are many more than seven; even the list of the most conspicuous exceeds that number, for among them are enumerated those of Kúka, Mahúr, Tánk, Khátí, Uprautiya, Baman-Barhaí or Mathuria, Ojha Gaur, and Chamár Barhaí.

Barhaiyá, بڑهیا बढ़ैया

A small clan of Rajpúts, of which we find a few in Sikandarpúr and Bhadaon and Azimgarh, and Sayyidpúr Bhitrí of Gházípúr.

Birheriya, بڑھیریا बिढ़ेरिया

One of the sub-divisions of the Chamár tribe, *q.v.*

Barhauliya, بڑھولیا बढौलिया

A branch of the Bhrigubansí* stock of Rajputs, and the chief proprietors of Barhaul in Benares, from the principal town of which Parganah they derive their name. They are said to have come from Raingarh in Marwar, and were on their way to the celebrated shrine of Jagannath, in Orissa, when their chief, Narotam Rae, accepted service with the Seorí, or Cheru, Raja. —See Cheru.

The Raja rewarded him with several villages, in consequence of being relieved from some dangerous illness by his skill. Rae Narotam was also authorised to raise troops for the expulsion of the Ragbansí Rajputs, who ravaged the borders of the Raja's territory. When the Raja died, Narotam usurped the chieftainship, and from that period the Barhauliyas have increased their possessions, and still hold several villages in Majhwar, Havelí, Dhus, Mawí, and Mehwarí. Raja Balwand Singh's favourite wife was a Barhaulia girl, whom he seized in one of his forages, and her influence was much exercised in advancing the interests of her own tribe.

Birjiyá, برجیه बिर्जिया

One of the sub-divisions of the Ahír tribe, *q.v.*

Barwáik, بروایک बरवाईक

A class of hereditary Chokídars, introduced into the South Eastern extremity of the Bhábar, *q.v.*, for the purpose of guarding and patrolling that inhospitable region. Nearer the hills,

* And therefore of the same illustrious lineage as Parasuráma, who was descended from Bhrigu, one of the first Prajápatis or sons of Brahma. The Bisen Rajpúts also claim the same descent.

in the same direction, we have the Jutiyal, who have been introduced into that tract for the same purpose.—E.

Barwáík is also the name of a tribe of Thárús, a race of Tibetan origin, living in the lower hills, and occupying villages in the plains in Northern Gorakhpúr and Champáran. They now chiefly speak Hindi, but state that those of their tribe who still remain in the submontane districts of Nepal continue to use their own original speech, which, like Magar and Gurung, is Tibetan at base.—B.

Barwar, بروار बरवार

The name given to a class of people engaged in cleaning and selling rice —See Dhanwaiya.

It is also the name of a tribe of Rajputs in Mansurnagar and Chiluapar of Gorakhpur; Sagrí, Ghosí, Sikandarpur and Muhammadabad of Azimgaṛh; Kharíd and Kopachít of Ghazípur; and Havelí, Benares.

Batar, بٹار बटार

A tribe of Gújars, who are considered to hold a Báwan (*i.e.* fifty-two villages) in Gangoh and Lakhnautí in Zillah Seháranpur. There are many also in Bijnor, on the opposite side of the Ganges.—See Gujar.

Baigar, بیگار बैगार

One of the names by which the Kharwar tribe are known. Affecting also a Rajput lineage, they frequently call themselves Benbans.

Bainsí, بینسی बैंसी

A sub-division of the Gújar tribe, *q.v.*

Cháhil, چاهل चाहिल

Cháhil, or Cháhira, is the name of a tribe of Rajpúts, of

which the greater part is now converted to Mahometanism. There are a few in the Hissar district and on the borders of Bikanír. A peculiar interest attaches to them from their connexion with Goga Chauhán, whose wife, Siriyál, was the daughter of Sinja, the Cháhil, Raja of Sirsa Patan. The memory of this relationship is still preserved by the Cháhil tribe being the exclusive managers of the Saint's tomb.

According to some authorities the Cháhil ranks as one of the thirty-six royal races; but the distinction is not usually conceded to them.—See Goga Pír.*

Chándam, چاندم चान्दम

Rajpúts of this clan are found in Allahadad and Jaunpúr.—E.

The census does not mention any class of Rajpúts with this name; but in Allahabad there are Chandans 393; none in Jaunpúr. They are probably classed under Chandel, as local variations of the pronunciation of names of clans are frequently met with.—B.

Chíhe, چیہي चीहे

See Gújar, of which tribe they form a sub-division.

Cherú, چیرو चेरू

Cherús appear to be the aborigines of Gházípúr, a part of Gorakhpúr, the Southern portion of Benares and Mirzapúr, and of Behar. They are sometimes said to be a branch of the Bhars.

There seems great reason to suppose that Cherús are called also Siviri, or Seorí; though Buchanan is of opinion that the two are distinct, and that the Seorís subdued and expelled the Cherús. At the same time, he considers the Kols and the Cherús to be the same, and even to be the ancestors of the Bais Rajpúts ("Eastern India," Vol. I. pp. 24, 406, 407, 457, 465,

* See J.A.S.B. for 1836, p. 635.—E. *add.*

466, 494, and Vol. II. pp. 345, 348, 372, 460); but his statements can rarely be relied on, and are especially confused when he has to deal with the abstruse subject of Indian Ethnography.

It is, however, confessedly very difficult to trace the connexion or difference between the aboriginal tribes of Bhars, Cherús, Seorís, and Kols, and to learn whether their occupation of the above-mentioned tracts was successive or synchronous. As the Cherús declare themselves to be descended from the great Serpent, we may possibly have in them the remnant of the Nágbansí dynasty of Magadha.—(See Gaur Tagá.)

Remains of buildings attributed to them are found near Buddh Gya, Sahasrám (Sasseram), and Ramgaṛh, and the images of Siva and Hanumán, which are found in them, indicate the prevalence of the Hindú religion.

They appear to have been expelled from their ancient abodes by the Pramars of Bhojpúr, the Hayobans of Hardí, and the Bhúinhárs, not long, perhaps, before the first Mahometan invasion, about which time there appears to have been a general convulsion throughout India, during which several tribes acquired their present possessions. The features of the Cherús are said ("Eastern India," I. 495) to mark them as belonging to the aboriginal tribes of the Vindhya mountains. They live chiefly by cutting timber, collecting drugs, and killing game, and though their numbers are reduced very low, they continue to create a Raja for every five or six houses, and invest him with the Tilak in due form.

We do not read of Cherús anywhere in history, except in the life of the Emperor Sher Shah, who is said to have ordered out Khawas Khan against Maharta, the Cherú, Zamíndar of the districts of Behar. Thus far had the progress of the Rajpúts compelled the aboriginal clan to emigrate; and the extravagant joy shewn by the Emperor at the conquest of Maharta shews that the last efforts of the Cherús to maintain their independence was sustained with considerable vigour. The present chief of

Singraulí in Mirzapúr is said to be a Cherú, but he attempts to disguise his origin by the assumption of the title of Benbans. (See Baigar and Kharwar.) Cherús are still found in the Southern parts of the Province of Benares, and in the fastnesses of Ramgaṛh.

It is probable that the limits assigned in the first paragraph to the Cherús are too narrow, for in the Central Doáb a tradition is still preserved that the Rajpúts of that quarter expelled Cherús. The Kayaths also of Bhúigáṅw state that their predecessors were Chirars; and the Chírahs, who are alluded to in the Glossary as slaves in Etawah, are perhaps of the same race; unless, which is not improbable, this word has been written by mistake for Chela. It would be highly interesting to obtain any authentic memorials of this race, but it does not at present appear that there is any likelihood of adding to our information respecting this or any other aboriginal tribe.

It may not be out of place to hint the bare possibility that in the Siviras, Seorís, and Cherús we may have the descendants of the ancient Suraseni. There is a passage in the "Harivansa" worth transcribing: "From this race came the Sauras, Saurávíras, and Saurasenís. The great king Saurasena has given his name to the country over which he reigned" (p. 158); and the following passage from a note by the translator is also worthy of record, as shewing the connection between the countries of the Suviras and the Saurasenas: "Le Târâ-tantra appelle le Souvira le pire des pays, et le place á l'est du Soûraséna" ("Harivansa," p. 141). But how does this Eastern position of Suvari coincide with that which is assigned to it on the better authority of Wilson?—See "Vishnu Purana," p. 177, and notes to "Johnson's Selections from the Mahábhárata," p. 65.

May it not be possible also that there may be some allusion to the Seorí, where the Chauhán Raja describes the Súrji as being to the Eastward of Chandelkhand?—See the "Transactions of the Royal Asiatic Society," Vol. I., p. 260.

Chúhṛá, چوهڑا चूहड़ा

The lowest caste of village servants. They are known also by the names Bhangí, Halálkhor, and Khákrob (see Bhangí); but Chúhṛá is the most usual term in villages. The head of this tribe, as well as that of Chumars, is known by the title of Mihtar, and receives perquisites under the name of Mihtaraí; so that the word Mihtar, far from being contemptuous, as is usually supposed, is one of honour and dignity. In Persian Mihtar مهتر signifies a prince; literally, greater, being the comparative of مه great. In Sanskrit, also, महत्तर signifies greater, more—a man of the fourth or servile tribe; from महत great, with the affix of comparison: "perhaps," according to Wilson (Sanskrit Dict., p. 648) "given in derision, or in comparison with the mixed tribes." The latter is more probable than the former, but it appears more likely that the title was derived from the fourth being more in number than the other three tribes. Either way, both the Persian and Sanskrit terms convey no dishonourable distinction.*

Chúla, چوله चूला

Chúla, or Chúlat, is a tribe of Tagas in Baghpat; so called from their having come from Chúlú in Bikanír; which is more commonly known as the mart of Chúrú on the Eastern border of that territory.

Chaube, چوبي चौबे

A class of Brahmans who originally received their names from reading the four (*chau*) Veds, as Dube was derived from reading two, and Tribedí from reading three, of the Veds.—See Kanaujiyá.

* This is a mistake. The word مهتر is used of all members of this caste, and is generally supposed to have been conferred in derision by the Mughal invaders India.—B.

Chauhán,* چوهان चौहान

This highly interesting tribe of Rajpúts traces its origin from the neighbourhood of Sambhar and Ajmer. They have many sub-divisions, such as the Khíchí, Nárbán, Nikumb, Thún, Bhadauria, Bachgotí,† Rajkumár, Hára, Bilkhariya, Chiráiya, Bándhalgotí, etc. These are not all honored with mention in the "Annals of Rajasthan," where, however, twenty-four Sachæ are enumerated, most of which are not at all known in our N. W. Provinces.

Chauháns are very generally distributed throughout the districts of these Provinces, but we find them in great numbers chiefly to the North and East of Saharanpúr, in Jahangírabad, Faizábad, Sirsáwa, Behat, Jáwálápúr, and Sakraudah (these are now many of them converted to Mahomedanism); in Khair, Chandaus, Sikandra Rao, Mahrera, and Múrthal of Aligarh. In Rohilkhand we find them in Ajaon, Aṅwla, Saneya, Satásí, Mandáwar, Chándpúr, Nagína, Nithaur, Haldaur, and the Eastern Parganahs of Bijnor. In Hamírpúr; Rattanpúr, Bansí, Salempúr Majhaulí, and Tilpúr in Gorakhpúr; in Sagrí and Bhadáon of Azimgarh; and in the environs of Dehli and Mirat. But the most important clans of the Chauhán branch

* This name is spelt in a variety of ways. In two MSS. of Chand's great poem, in the Library of the R.A.S., and in one in the Bódleian the following variations occur: चाहुमान the oldest and original form; चाहुवान, चाह्रवान, चाउहान. The first syllable is also sometimes written short—चहुवान *metri gratiâ*. Much of these variations is due to the unsettled state of Hindi orthography. In a pencil note on his private copy of this work, the author proposes to re-write this article, which is, it must be confessed, rather a scanty notice of this valourous old royal and patriotic race; *sangre azul* of Aryan chivalry. It is, however unnecessary to do more than note their present geographical distribution in the N.W.P., as Colonel Tod, in his "Annals of Rajasthan," devotes much space to an ample and enthusiastic account of the noble Chauhans. The reader who wishes to know more about the pluckiest race that Indian history has to show, cannot do better than go to the Colonel's glowing pages for information.—B.

† All Chauháns are, in fact, Bachgotí, inasmuch as they are of the Gotra of Bach.

in these Provinces are those of the Central Doáb, in Khandaulí of Agra; Lakhnau, Jánib Rást, Deolí Jakhan, and the Hazúr Tahsíl of Etawah; in Akbarpúr of Cawnpúr; and in Mústafabad, Gihror, Sonj, Etah, Kishní Nabíganj, and Bhúngańw in the district of Mainpúrí. Of these the most conspicuous are the families of Rajor, Pratápnír, Chakarnagar, and Manchana, the head of which latter is usually known as the Raja of Mainpúrí.* These four families, as well as their relatives, do not allow other Chauháns to associate with them on terms of equality, being descended from the illustrious Pirthí Rájá, and and therefore connected with the regal stem of Nímrana.†

Raja Sangat, the great grandson of Chahir Deo, the brother of Pirthí Rájá, had twenty-one sons.‡ Of these twenty-one,

* The Pratápnír man says the Chakarnagar family is inferior to his own; and that four princes founded Rajor, Pratápnír, Mainpúrí, and Chandwár, which latter afterwards became Bhadauríyá; that four princes more went to Bardwán. That the Pratápnír family went from Rintambhor to Nímrána, and thence to Chibramau; thence successively to Kudarkoṭ, Asáí, Etawah, and, finally, to Pratápnír, in Shujau'd daulat's time. Of these eight princes Sumer Singh was the eldest, who founded Sumer Mau, near Chibrámau, and the fortress of Etawah. The Pratápnír family claim Sumer Singh as their ancestor, thus elevating themselves above Mainpúrí.—E. *add.*

† These four houses have the title of Raja. The house of Sakraulí in Etawa has the title of Rana; and the houses of Jasohan and Kishní have the title of Rao, Thus, also, amongst the Bhadaurias, besides the title of Raja, we have that of Dewan, which is held by the house of Parna in Bah Panahat; that of Chávaṇd Rai, held by the house of Chitauli in Atair; and that of Rao held by six different houses. The Mainú and Tasselí are altogether excluded from these dignities, being of inferior quality, and contaminated, it is said, with a little Mewatí blood in their veins.

‡ In Tod's Genealogical Table ("Annals," vol. ii. p. 451), this number is ascribed to Raja Lakhansi, the father of Sangat. He mentions also Nanad Singh as the present chief Nimrana. But this is a mistake. Nanad Singh, who is still alive, was never chief; being the illegitimate child of Chandarbhán, the grandfather of the present Raja, Bijay Singh, who is in the twenty-ninth generation from Pirthí Rájá, the last Hindú king of Dehli, who died in prison at Ghazni.

The Musulman historians say that Pirthí Rájá was killed at the battle of the Gaggar, or shortly afterwards; but Chand represents him as dying in captivity at Ghazni; and the Bard would gladly have concealed so humiliating a fact if he could.

the youngest (as in the case of the sons of Dasaratha, and of Raja Sankar in the "Mahábhárata") succeeded to the throne, in consequence of an agreement to that effect made by Sangat in his old age, when he married a bride of the Tauhar clan, and of the house of Jíla Patan: the issue of this marriage were Láh and Laure. Láh became Rao of Mandáwar, and is now reckoned the head of the clan. Laure became Raja of Nímrána, and receives investiture from the Rao, who marks his superiority by fixing on the Tilak with his great toe, instead of with his hand.

लाह मंडावर बैठियो आठों मंगलवार
जो जो बैरी संचरे सो सो गिरे मार

"Láh, dwell at Mandáwar, prosperous for ever;
Whatever foe attacks thee, let him be smitten dead."

is a common saying indicative of the superiority of Láh.

The other sons sought their fate and fortunes in different parts. Two are said to have established principalities in the Hills, one of which is now represented by the influential lords of Jamú; two went to Sonkra Sonkrí; one to Khayr; five to Pachwára; from one, the Sheorám Játs are descended; from another, the Khoro Ahírs; and from another, it is said, the vagabond Baunrís, *q.v.*

Sahesh Mal and Harsarú remained in the neighbourhood of Nímrána. Bíghá Raja, the grandson of the former, established the name of Bíghoto बीघोतो *q.v.*; the latter that of Dhúndhoṭí धुंधोटी *q.v.* The country of the descendants of Láh is known by the name of Ráth राठ *q.v.* All the Chauháns of this neighbourhood, and of similar descent, are known by the name of Alanot.

The Mainpúrí family are represented to be the descendants

Several of our Chauhán sepoys, after the capture of that fortress, sought out, and professed to find, the Chhatrí (or monument) of their ancestor, where they shewed their devotion to his memory by presenting their humble offerings in honour of the champion of their faith.

in the direct line of Pratáp Rudr, another son of Raja Sangat. He, and some others of the same family, left their original seat at Nímrána, and, invited by the distractions of the Doáb not long after the Mahomedan ascendancy, founded the several principalities of Pratápnír, Rajor, Sakíth, Chandwár, Mainpúrí, etc. etc., of which the last named is considered to rank the highest.

These Chauháns of the Central Doáb formed a sufficiently strong confederacy to oppose frequently a successful resistance to the imperial troops; and the principalities of Rápari and Chandwár on the Jumna, and Mainpúrí Bhúngáṅw, are always spoken of with respect, even by Musulman historians.

In the reign of Bahlol Lodi we find Raí Pratáp, Hákim Zamíndár,* sufficiently strong to obtain the Government of Mainpúrí Bhúngáṅw; † and his descendants appear to have maintained for some time subsequent a show of independence, which says much for the credit of their adroit management; for, during that period, this part of the Doáb was constantly

* At that period most native princes were called zamíndárs; consequently, the value of this expression, as applied to Pratáp Raí, is considerably different from what it would be in our days. The author contemplated discussing it under the word Talúkdár, had he progressed so far, as is evident from the note to the first edition.—B.

† و از آنجا بپرگنهٔ کول آمده تمام محال عیسی خان را بدستور سابق مقرر داشت و ازانجا بپرگنه سکیته آمد مبارك خان حاکم سکیته ملازمت نمود محال جاگیر اورا نیز مسلم داشته و راي پرتاپ حاکم و زمیندار نواحي بهون گانون را نیز برو مقرر داشت و ازانجا به راپری و چنداور آمد

(Makhzan Afghaní.)

"And thence he came to Pargana Kol, and confirmed Isa' Khan in it as heretofore, and thence to Pargana Sakíth, where Mubarik Khan, hákim of Sakíth, did homage, and received the mehál as a jagir. He also confirmed in his possessions Rai Pratáp, ruler and zamíndár of the region round about Bhúngáṅw; and then went on to Rápari and Chandwár."—B.

exposed to hostile incursions, and was the seat of war for more than half a century, being on the borders of the rival kingdoms of Dehli and Jaunpúr.

To the East of the Rewah territory, and to the South of the Kaimúr range, between Sirgúja and Sohagpúr, there is a district called Chauhánkhand, of which the occupants trace their descent from the Mainpúrí Chauháns, and the same origin is asserted by the Chauháns of Benaudha.—See Bachgotí.

Chauhánkhand is better known to the people themselves* as Chandarkona, so called from their leader Chandarsen,† from whom also Chandwár takes its name; and did not the Chauháns of Chandwár and Chandarkona concur in the same story, it might have been supposed that the latter were descended from the original Chauháns who peopled Gwálkhand and Gara Mandlá.

The Chauháns of Upper Rohilkhand, as those of Nihtor, Haldaur, Sherkot, Afzalgarh, Nagíná, Chandpúr, and Mandawar, are considered a very inferior stock, and are frqeuently not ranked with Rajputs.

The Chauháns of the Gorakhpúr district, branches of which have extended into Behar, are said by Buchanan ("Eastern India," Vol. II. 426) to be descended from Raj Sen, son of Ratna Sen, the last Raja of Chittor. But the whole account was evidently furnished to him by some ignorant scribe, who has mingled the histories of Chauháns and Sísodiás. Nevertheless, the Doctor has accepted and recorded the statement

* The Chauháns of the Upper Provinces say Chandarkona is near Calcutta, or, more accurately, forty miles from Calcutta on the road to Jaggannath, which would bring it very close to Midnapore. Others, again, say it is near Burdwan; and there is a place of that name near Burdwan, according to As. Res. vii., 459. This is a more probable site for a Rajput colony than the wilds of Sirgúja, which are inhabited almost entirely by non-Aryans, such as Kols, Uráons, and the like.—B.

† With respect to Chandersen, he is claimed not only as the leader of these Southern Chauháns, but as the ancestor of the Bhadauriás, *q.v.*, of which one subdivision bears his name to this day.

without question; like too many others of a more injurious tendency which have been industriously circulated from his works to the prejudice of the natives of India.*

In the history and traditions of the Chauháns of our provinces, there is little to confirm, or disprove, the alleged modern origin of the race. Many arguments may be adduced against that view of the case, notwithstanding some respectable authorities maintain it. But there is no space for the controversy in this place. (See "Transactions R.A.S.," Vol. I. p. 133.—"Oriental Quaterly Magazine," No. XV.—"Bird's Guzerat," p. 79.—Tod's "Annals of Rajputana," I. 94; II. 439, and "Journal Asiatique," May, 1827.)

*** The following notice is chiefly taken from General Cunningham's report :—

The Chauháns are one of the Agnikula or "Fire races" of Rajputs. These are four in number—the Parihár, Pramár, Solankhi, and Chauhán, and are fabled to have sprung into existence from the sacred fire-fountain or Analkuṇḍ on the summit of Mount Abú. "But this claim must be of comparatively modern date, as the common gotráchárya of all the Chauhán tribes declares him to be of the race of Vatsa through five famous ancestors (*Bach gotra pánch pravara*). Now, in Fell's inscription of Jaya Chandra of Kanauj, we have a record of a grant of land made in A.D. 1177 to a Kshatriya named Rao Ráshtradhara Varmma, who is said to be of the Vatsa Gotra with the five pravaras (or ancestors) of Bhárgava, Chyavana, Apnavana, Aurva, Jamadagnya. From this document, therefore, we learn that the Chauháns, so late as the reign of Prithí Raja, laid no claim to be sprung from fire, but were content to

* In justice to Dr. Buchanan it must be explained that his account of the districts he visited, when derived from personal observation, is strikingly correct; and his laborious and lengthy enumeration of the castes has been so ruthlessly massacred by Mr. Montgomery Martin, that it is not fair to pass an opinion on it in its present state.—B.

be considered as descendants of the holy sage Bhrigu through Jamadagnya Vatsa." (Report, Part iv., p. 7.) The fable of the fire-fountain appears according to the same authority to have risen from the name of a Chauhán cowherd, Anala, which means fire, who is traditionally said to have pointed out to the Solankhi Vana Raja, the site of the city called Analwára Patan, long the capital of the Solankhi race; but it may be doubted whether the legend of the cowherd is a bit more authentic, though less violently improbable, than that of the fire-fountain. It is, however, in favour of the legend that Mukji, the bard of the Khichi Chauháns, makes only the Chauháns to be fire-sprung. As regards the name, it means literally "the Desired," as is shown by the original spelling *cháhumána*, from *cháhná* "to desire," and the modern spelling *chaturman* had its origin in the later amplification of the legend to include the *four* tribes *(chatur)*, "*chau*" in Hindi being the usual form of *chatur* in composition. The earliest prince of the race is Ajaypál, whose date is uncertain, and who is said to have founded Ajaymera, or Ajmer. Manik Rai, whom Cunningham fixes in A.D. 800, is considered to be the real founder of the race, and in his time they acquired possession of the country as far as the Sakambhari or Sámbhar Lake, and retained it as long as the Muhammadan conquest.

The Chauháns ruled at Ajmer till the sack of that place by Muhammad Ghori in 1193 A.D. It was again attacked and finally annexed by Kutbu'ddin in 1195 A.D.—(See Khichi, Kachhwaha, and Tomar.)—B.

Chakwáin, چکواین चकवाईन

A small class of Rajputs in Kopachít, Zillah Ghazipur.

Chamár, چمار चमार

A tribe employed in the curing of leather. They are said, on the authority of the Padma, Varaha, and Brahmavaivartta

Puranas, to be descended from a Mallah, or Boatman, and a Chandál woman. The Chamárs are generally said to be subdivided into seven classes—Jatúá, Kaiyán, Kuril, Jaiswára, Jhusía, Azimgaṛhia, or Birheria, and Korí, or Korchamra.* These seven do not eat together or intermarry. The Jatúás are chiefly in the North-West. The Dehli Territory, Rohilkhand, and the Upper, and part of Central, Doáb are their seats. The Kaiyáns are in Bundelkhand, and Saugor. The Kurils occupy the greater part of the Central and Lower Doáb. The Jaiswárás meet them in the neighbourhood of Allahabad, and extend through Jaunpúr, Mirzápúr, and Benares, to the neighbourhood of Sayyidpúr Bhitrí, where they are to be met by the Jhusias, who occupy Ghazipur and Behar. The Azimgaṛhias have their seats in Azimgaṛh, and Gorakhpúr; and the Korís, or Korchamras, in Oudh. The last are generally engaged in the occupation of weaving.

Other names are mentioned besides these seven, as the Jatlot of Rohilkhand; the Aharwar, Ṣakarwar, and Dohar† of Central Doáb: but as these latter avow some connection with the Kurils, they may perhaps be included in that tribe. In Behar we meet also with subdivisions of Garaiyas, Magahyas,‡

* All the lower castes attempt to establish a sevenfold division into Gots; but few, if any of them, can enumerate the seven correctly, and no two agree about it. The division is, probably, purely fanciful in most cases. In the list of Chamárs subdivisions given in the text, Kaiyán is a name of the Marwárí merchants, who are generally Jains; Jhusía and Azimgaṛhia are merely local names, from Jhusí, near Allahabad, and Azimgaṛh; Korí should probably be written कोढ़ी koṛhí, or leprous, as the Chamárs, from their filthy habits, are peculiarly liable to this disease.—B.

† The Dohars are mentioned in "Steele's Summary," p. 128, as existing in the Dekkan along with Katnís (cobblers) and Daphgars (Dabgar, maker of oil bottles): but he does not include them amongst Chamárs, of whom he enumerates the following classes—Saltangar, Marathe, Paradosh, Pardesí, Haralbhakt, Dabalí, Woje, Chaur.

‡ The Magahyas are not Chamárs, but wandering Doms, who live in *sirkas*, or portable reed-huts, like the Naṭs, Khâna-ba-dosh, Bázigars, and others; and, like them, are incorrigible thieves.—B.

Dakshinias, Kanaujias, as well as the Jhusía and Jaiswára above mentioned: all tending to show that the division into seven clans is imaginary.

Chamárs are reputed to be a dark race, and a fair Chamár is said to be as rare an object as a black Brahman.

करिआ ब्रह्मन गोर चमार
इन के साथ न उतरिये पार

That is, do not cross a river in the same boat with a black Brahman or a fair Chamár; both objects being considered of evil omen.

Chamáín, چمایں चमाइन

A clan of Gújars, proprietors of about twelve villages in Panipat Bángar.

Also a woman of the Chamár caste, who usually acts as midwife in Hindu villages. (Probably contracted from Chamárin.)—B.

Chamargaur, چمرگور चमरगौर

See Gaur Rajput.

Chandáliyá, چنداليا चनडालिया

See Bhangí.

Chandel, چنديل चंदेल

A tribe of Rajputs scattered in various parts of these Provinces, who for the most part derive their origin from Mahobá in Bundelkhand, which before the Musulman conquest, appears to have been the capital of a principality which extended to the Nerbudda, and included the province of Chanderí, or Chandelí, which is called after their name. Though they are styled Sombansi, they are not considered to be of pure descent, and their sons are carefully excluded from marriages with the higher clans.

The Chandels are found in Osahat, Míhrabad, Púranpúr Sabna, Baragáṅw, Jalálabad, and Imratpúr, Parganahs in the South-East of Rohilkhand; Havelí, Sidhúa Jobna and Rattanpúr Bansi, of Gorakhpúr; in Bara, Karra, and Chail, of Allahabad; in Máhul, Sikandarpúr, Muhammadabad Gahná, Nathúpúr, and Nizámabad, of Azimgáṛh; in Mariyáhú, of Jaunpúr; in Narwan and Havelí, of Benares; in Bhagwat, Bijaygaṛh, and Agorí Barhar, of Mirzapúr; in Sheorajpúr, Jajmáu, Akbarpúr, Sheolí, and Bithúr, Parganahs of Cawnpúr; and in Bundelkhand. There is also a large clan of them South of Bardí, giving name to a Province called Chandelkhand. They are divided, at least in the Lower Doáb, into the four families of Raja, Rao, Rana, and Ráwat, like the Gautams of the same neighbourhood. Thus the chiefs of the Sheorajpúr Chandels are known as, the Raja of Sheorajpúr, the Rao of Sánpai, the Rana of Sakrej, and the Ráwat of Ráwatpúr, the respective residences of the parties. We learn the turbulence of this Doáb tribe at the early part of last century from the letters of Ranchhor Dás.*

The Chandels of Mirzapúr came from Mahobá after the defeat of Brimaditya, the son of their chief Parimál, by Pirthí Raja. For this was not a mere victory: it led to the temporary occupation of the country; since we learn from Chand (Books 60 and 61), that after the Chauháns had taken Kálinjar, it was occupied by a garrison from Dehli under the Amber prince, Pajjún. These Mirzapúr Chandels are said to have expelled the Bálands, and they themselves in their turn had to flee from the victorious arms of the Gautam Raja of Benares. The chiefs of Agorí Barhar and Bijaygaṛh, after seeking refuge in Bhoj-

* The chiefs of Nálagaṛh, Kahlúr, and Biláspúr are Chandels, and the first named acknowledges a connection with the Raja of Kamáon.—E. *add.*

púr, returned to their old seats on the occasion of the British ascendancy.

Those of Azimgaṛh migrated also from Mahobá, but appear to have lingered for some time about Jaunpúr, before proceeding in their onward course to Sikandarpúr.

The period of Chandel emigration eastward is very doubtful. Though no date is so probable as the one above mentioned for their departure, yet we have some incidental testimony respecting those of Rohilkhand and the Doáb, which appears to point to an earlier period.

We find one of the Banaphar heroes boasting in the "Ala Udal Prastáv." (Chand Bk. 20.) "Our heads were the pillars of Mahoba; by us were the Gonds expelled, and their strongholds Deogaṛh and Chanbari added to his sway. We maintained the field against the Jadǒn, sacked Hindaun, and planted his standard on the plains of Katter." This refers to a period long previous to Pirthí Raja's defeat of Brimaditya. We may also be allowed to conjecture that the Chhindú race, which Mr. Prinsep (J. A. S. B., Vol. vi., p. 780) declares to be utterly unknown, and which we find recorded in a very interesting inscription, dated A.D. 992, discovered by Mr. H. S. Boulderson in the neighbourhood of Bisalpúr, is no other than the Chandel, and that they might then have been inhabiting that part of Rohilkhand, on the way to their more distant principality of Champáwat,* and Almorah, of which the representative is the present titular Raja of Kamáon, or, more strictly speaking, his cousin, who is a British pensioner at Almorah. Chand is the title of the holder of the Raj: his Rajput brethren are generally known as Rautela.

* Som Chand, Chandarbansí, established the Raj of Champáwat, A.D. 1178. This period would be in accordance with the Bísalpúr inscription. It is a vulgar, but almost universal error to trace the origin of the Chandels from Jhúsí opposite Allahabad; but the proper reading is Jhansí, in Bundelkhand, a position which connects them immediately with the Chandels.

The Chandels of Rohilkhand themselves state that they derive their origin from Sheorajpúr; and here, again, we have a gleam of evidence that the Sheorajpúr Chandels are older than Pirthí Raj's conquest.

In the famous Arabic work, the "Kitab-al-Yamini," we find that the victorious Mahmúd, after conquering Kanauj, in A.D. 1017, and proceeding lower down into the Doáb, before passing over to Bundelkhand, encounters what appears to be a Chandel chief, and subsequent mention is made of another chief, called Chand Rai, who might also have had some connexion with the same clan.*

*** General Cunningham writes this name Chándel (though in all the copies of Chand it is written Chandel), and as his researches into the history of the race are more minute and explanatory than those of any former investigator, a summary of them is here given.

The Chandels claim to be descended from Chandramá, or the moon, and Hemávatí, daughter of Hem Raj, a Brahman, who was the parohit or family priest of Indrajit, the Gaharwár monarch of Benares. The founder of the race was named Chandra Varmmá, and his immortal father promised that his race should reign as long as they bore the name of Varmmá. The result of this promise will be seen hereafter. At the age of sixteen he performed a sacrifice to obliterate the shame of his mother's illicit intercourse with the god. The place where this sacrifice occurred was named Mahotsava Nagara, or the

* In the first edition there was an extract in Arabic, but it was far from being correct or intelligible; and as no reference was given beyond the name of the work, I have been unable to verify it, and have therefore omitted it. It appears to mean that Mahmúd took the fort of Ásí, whose chief was called "Chandál púr!" and further on we come to a word جَنَّدَ بَال "Channadabála," the vowel points of which, at any rate, are wrong. The author admits that his extracts were taken "from a very incorrect copy, and there is no saying how much the names are disguised."—B.

city of the great sacrifice, since corrupted to Mahobá.* The date of this sacrifice is variously given by different annalists: General Cunningham, after an examination of the subject, fixes A.D. 800 approximately as the date of the rise of the Chandel dynasty, irrespective of the legend, which is only another of those frequent instances of the introduction of a divine father to cover the indiscretions of frail princesses, so common in Greek and Roman, as well as Indian story. If the lady were a Brahmaní, it is difficult to see how her descendants can be ranked as Rajputs. The matter, however, is scarcely worth discussing, save for the purpose of shewing how entirely the legendary lore of the people disproves the Brahmanical or priestly view of the rigid separation of caste from caste in early times. The General goes on to analyze the conflicting accounts as to the history of the Chandel race. It would not be in accordance with the plan of this work to go into this question at full length. The result of the inquiry is, that a dynasty of eighteen kings sat on the throne of Mahobá, among whom Raja Gandá (or Nandá as he is called by Ferishta) conquered Kanauj, but was in consequence attacked by, and in his turn obliged to yield to, Mahmúd of Ghazní. This Raja was possessor of the celebrated fort of Kálinjar, which appears to have been his residence. The date of Mahmúd's raid against him is A.D. 1023. Gandá's great-grandson, Kirti Varmmá, was subdued by Karna Kulachuri, Raja of Chedi, between 1065 and 1075 A.D.; but Kirti Varmmá's son appears to have thrown off the yoke, and to have made conquests in the Antarbed or Doáb.

Passing over several monarchs, we arrive at Madana Varmmá (A.D. 1130–1163), whose kingdom stretched from the Jumna to the Nerbudda. His son and successor (omitting a doubtful Kirti II.) was the famous Parimál Deva (or Paramárddhi), the

* Mahobá is fifty-four miles South of Hamirpúr, and thirty-four North of Khajuráho, the other capital of this clan.

first of the race who did not bear the charmed name of Varmmá, whose reign "has been rendered famous by his long-sustained contest with Prithi Raj Chauhán, which forms one of the most interesting portions of Chand's poem. The warlike deeds of his two champions, Ala and Udal, are also celebrated by Chand, and they still form the theme of many of the most favorite songs of the people of Northern India." In this battle the Chandel was defeated, and the western portion of his dominions wrung from him. He retired to Kálinjar after the loss of Mahobá, retaining only those districts of his former kingdom which lay east of the Kayán (or Cane) river. Kuṭbu'ddín Aibak. however, subsequently beseiged and sacked Kálinjar in 1196, after which we hear no more of the unhappy prince, whose misfortunes are said to have arisen from his being the first who did not bear the name of Varmmá, a name which, apparently warned by Parimál's reverses, his successors revived. Nothing worthy of note is recorded of them; save that their fortress Kálinjar sustained sieges, in A.D. 1247 from Ghiásu'ddin Balban, and in A.D. 1530 from Humáyún, from Shir Shah in A.D. 1545, and was finally taken and annexed by Akbar in 1569. Kirti Rai, who held the fort in the sieges of 1530 and 1545, was probably "the father of the celebrated Chandel princess Durgávati, the dowager queen of Garra Mandala, who so gallantly died defending her country against Akbar's general, in 1564."

As usual with the ancient Rajput kingdoms, when finally annexed to the Mughal Empire, the Chandel monarchy expired, the princes of the race subsided into feudatories, and no further notices are given of them in the historians.—(See Banáphar.)—B.

Chandela, چندیلا चंदेला

A clan of Gujars in Mairwara (Dixon's Mairwara, p. 6).—B.

Chanamiyá, چنميا चनमिया

The name of a tribe of Chandarbansí Rajputs in Parganah Rárí of Jaunpúr; Sagrí and Mahul of Azimgaṛh; and in Amorha of Gorakhpúr. They are generally included among the Bais of inferior descent, and are known also by the name of Gargbans; but the Chanamia and Gargbans are separately entered in the Jatimala in the "Hindí Selections."

Dángí, دانگي दांगी

Is the name given to Búndelas in the Saugor Territory, and parts of Bundelkhand.—See Búndela.

Díchhit, ديچهت दीक्षित

(See Kanaujiyá Brahman.) There are Rajputs also of this name in Ghazipur, Azimgaṛh, and Benares.

Díkhit, ديكهت दीखित

See Dikhit.

Demráut, ڈيمراوت डेम्रावट

One of the twelve Pals of Mewátís.

Deswál, ديسوال देसवाल

A tribe of Tagás who hold about twelve villages in Bághpat.

Dháhimá, دهاهما धाहिमा

A tribe of Rajputs recorded amongst the thirty-six royal races. They were the lords of Biana, and bore a high name for deeds of chivalry. Colonel Tod considers the tribe to be extinct ("Annals of Rajasthan," Vol. i. p. 119), but they have three or four villages in Baghpat. There are also Dháhimá Ahírs and Dháhimá Játs in the same neighbourhood.

Dhákará, دهاکرا धाकरा

A tribe of Rajputs who hold a few villages in Khandaulí in the Agra district, Jalesar in Mathurá, and Dehli Jákhan in Etawa; and are scattered over other parts of the Central Doáb and Rohilkhand. We learn from the letters of Izad Bakhsh that this tribe gave the imperial officers in the neighbourhood of Agra much trouble in the beginning of last century. The following extract is otherwise interesting, as showing the defenceless and dilapidated condition of Agra, even at that early period.* (See Janghárá.)

Dhámiyán, دهامیان धामियान

See Bishṇaví.

Dhangal, دهنگل धंगल

One of the twelve Pals of Mewatís.†

Dhánuk, دهانک धानुक

This tribe is employed as archers, fowlers, and house guards, and is engaged in several menial occupations both of the house and field, wherever they reside. The females are especially in request as midwives.

* I give a translation of the important part of this passage :—"And the reason is this that Akberabad (Agra) has no fortifications, and most of its buildings are in ruins and lurking places of thieves, and in its neighbourhood live rebels and marauders. At present one of them, Iraní Dhákara, zamíndár of Mauza Bálimpúr, Parg. Janwár, a Jagír of the Vakíls of the Goverment, lying seven kos from the city—having no fear of the officers of justice in his heart,—from Etawah to the capital commits violence and robbery, and stops the roads. Your servants, from respect, have hitherto done and said nothing, in spite of the continual robberies; and I also have been guilty of some little neglect, as I saw that in the absence of fortifications there is no chance of safety for the city and the roads. I cannot venture to act without orders, but request permission to extirpate this rebel."—B.

† More correctly दहंगल *dahangal.*—E. *add.*

Dhánuks are descended, according to the Padma Purana, from a Chamár and a female Chandál. From Dhánuks have proceeded the Aheryas, who are also occupied as fowlers. Aheryas are said not to consume dead carcases, as the Dhánuks do. Of Dhánuks there are reported to be seven subdivisions—Longbasta, Mathuriá, Katharia, Jaiswar, Magahya, Dojwar, and Chhilatya.* These do not intermarry, or even eat or smoke together. They mix, indeed, so little with one another, that an individual Dhánuk is seldom able to mention more than two, or at most three, of these names as belonging to his fraternity.

There are several Dhánuks in Dehli, and they are scattered over the north-western provinces, but Behar is the country in which they most abound.†

Dhanwaiyá, دهنویا धनवईया

A thrasher, or seller, of rice.—See Barwar.

Dhandel, دهندیل धंदेल

A tribe of Hara Rajputs giving a name to Dhandelkhand in Bundelkhand. They intermarry with Powar and Bundelas. Also apparently written दंदेल as in the following extract: "The Powars are a shade higher than the Dandeles, and the Dandeles a shade higher than the Boondeylas, the reigning chiefs of Bundelkhand, with the exception of Jhúsí and Chattarpúr. These chiefs in consequence almost all take their wives from the Powars, who in return make them pay dearly in land and money grants on service tenures. . . . They are by far the

* The usual statement, but not to be believed implicitly. Magahyas are generally classed under Doms, and the author gives them both under Dhánuks and Chamárs, showing how uncertain these classifications are.—B.

† Dhánuks are usually employed as domestic servants in the houses of Rajas, and form in Behar the bulk of the Khawás, as this class is generally called.—B. They are said to fill the office of village watchmen all over Farrukhabad.—E. *add.*

most troublesome people in Bundelkhand in time of disorder, as they are bold, brave, poor, ambitious, and unscrupulous.—Sleeman."—E. *add.* He does not give the name of the work nor reference to volume or page.

Dhe, ڈھي ढे

See Ját.

Dhímar,* دهيمر धीमर

A caste of Hindus, chiefly employed in fishing. They are, properly speaking, a branch of the Bearer, or Kahar, caste; though they are sometimes said to be offshoots of Mallahs, or Boatmen.†

Ḍherh, ڈھيڑه ढेढ

Name of a caste found in these provinces, chiefly in the Saugor territory. The name is also applied to Bhangís and Chamárs.‡ They eat dead animals, clean the skins, and sell them to Chamárs. In the Nagpúr territory they have acquired some consideration from their employment as Delals.

In the Deccan they are said to be the same as the Mahrs of

* Sanskr. धीवर a fisherman.

† They are also called धीश्वर and तीश्वर and मकूआ, and are very abundant in Behar and Benares. Two years ago a prophet arose among them, who said that the goddess Bhawáni had appeared to him out of a pillar in his house and commanded them to leave off eating fish; he collected an immense crowd at Kadba, in Púraniya (Purneah), who came to see the miraculous pillar and offer goats to it, and the prophet in consequence fleeced them considerably. In connection with this revival, the Tíars of Benares nearly killed a man as a sacrifice to Bhawáni; the police fortunately arrived in time to prevent the consummation of the offering.—B.

‡ This word is spelled धेड in Molesworth's Maraṭhi Dictionary; and I think this is more correct than in the text. But so much uncertainty exists as to the spelling of Hindi that, in the absence of a conclave of paṇḍits, I cannot venture to decide. Wilson, both in Glossary and "Sel. Works," i. 186, spells it ढेढ.—B.

the Mahrattas (Journ. R. A. S. p. 224).—See also the Printed Glossary under Dheda and Dheyr.

In the Western provinces, though they are now not often found in any numbers, they appear to have left the remembrance of their name, for it is a common term of abuse to call a man a "bará Dherh," or a low-caste fellow.

In Rajputana, Dherhs will not eat hogs, either tame or wild: the latter they hold in great abomination, notwithstanding their Rajput masters look upon them as a luxury.

Ḍhiṛhor, ڈڑھور ढिढोर

A tribe of inferior Ahírs in Benares and Gorakhpúr. They are reckoned in the Tashriḥu'l aḳwám amongst the Doáb Ahírs.*

Dhobí, دھوبي धोबी

A Washerman. This is considered one of the lowest castes of Hindus. Of Dhobís, as of several other of the inferior tribes, there are generally reckoned to be seven subdivisions. Kanaujia, Magahya, Pagahya, Belwar, Bátham, Srí Bátham, and Bharká. The Kanaujia are to be found chiefly from Kanauj to the borders of Behar, and extend into Gorakhpúr. The Magahya and Belwar throughout Behar. The Pagahya in Rohilkhand and Farrukhabad. The Bátham, and Srí Bátham in Baiswara; and the Bharká from Mainpúrí and Etawah to the far west. About three-fourths of this latter clan have been converted to the Mahomedan faith. None of these tribes eat, or drink, or marry together. They are as much strangers to each other as the members of any other caste.

The seven subdivisions are not retained under the same names

* There is a subdivision of Kirars, whose name is either ḍhiṛhor or ḍaṛhor; but the native informant himself was uncertain as to the spelling.—E. *add.*

in other provinces. In Behar, for instance, we meet with Ajodhyas and Gosaṛs, which are not in the above list.

Dhundhoṭí, دهندهوٿي धुंधोटी

Is the name given to a tract of country in the Gurgánw district, in possession of the descendants of Chaudharí Harsarú, one of the twenty-one sons of Raja Sangat.—See Chauhán.

The Alanot Chauháns are found in Bighoto, Dhundoti, Chandain, and Ráth. All these names are of mere local application. In the public registers they are not known, nor are they known much beyond the boundaries of the tracts themselves. Bighoto includes the whole of Rewárí, and much more, both to the west and east. Chandain is generally reckoned to be a part of Bighoto, but has been considered for some time past separate. It includes the greater part of Taúrú, and derives its name from the twelve villages of Chand Chauháns, who are descendants of Sahes Mal, another son of Raja Sangat. Ráth is the largest of these districts, and is for the most part included in Alwar. The principal places within this tract are Mandáwar (the chief of which has the title of Rao), Nímrana (the chief of which has the title of Raja), Biroda (the chief of which has the title of Rana), Lahpotí, Bíjwar, Kot Putlí, Harsuran, and Narnaul.

Dharmgaur, دهرم‌گور धर्मगौर

See Gaur Brahman.

Dharwáí, دهروائي धरवाई

The Patwarí who weighs grain.—Dehli. The word is derived from Dharí, a measure or weight of five seers, which is generally considered his perquisite at the harvest.*

* Or from धरना "to hold," from his holding the scales; the word is also pronounced धरवाहा, which is equivalent to dharnewálá, in Behar.—B.

Digwár, دگوار दिगवार

A Watchman; literally, a protector of the different quarters, or points, of the compass. See under Dig; and Dígwan and Degwar in the Printed Glossary.

Dikhit, دکهت दिखित

A tribe of Rajputs inhabiting the Parganahs of Kutia, Fattihpúr, Ekdalla, Mutaur, and Ghazipur, in the Fattihpúr districts. They have also sixty or seventy villages to the north of Baiswara, in the Oudh territory, in a tract called after them Dikhtan, and several in Bundelkhand and Benares. The Dikhits of Pachhotar in Ghazipur are called Pachhtariya. They give their daughters in marriage to Sombansí, Raghbansí, Gaharwár, and Bais, and take from Sayngur, Donwár, and Kausik.

The correct denomination of this clan is Díkhit, but Dikhit accords better with the ordinary pronunciation.

Dogar, دوگر दोगर

A tribe scattered over various tracts of the North-West of Hindústan. There are a few in Hansi, Sonam, and Ferozpúr, which latter place, together with a considerable tract along the bank of the Satlaj, they held for a long time during the last century in almost undisputed sovereignty. Their occupation is divided between pasture and plunder. They are Mahomedans, and state that they were originally Chauháns; but the Ḳáim Kháni, and other converted Chauháns of those parts, will not acknowledge the fraternity, asserting that Dogars were nothing but Játs and Gújars. This appears to be the case, notwithstanding all their emphatic negations. Dogars are held in no consideration by their neighbours, but in former times they were much dreaded on account of their predatory habits, which a civilized neighbourhood and a strong Government compel them now unwillingly to relinquish.

Their personal appearance is in their favor. They are a tall and muscular race, and are generally remarkable for having large aquiline noses.

*** Dogar or Dugar is also the name of a family of Kaiyáns, or Marwari Jain merchants, to which belong Rai Lachmipat Singh Bahádur and Rai Dhanpat Singh Bahádur, the wealthy and public-spirited bankers and landed proprietors of Murshidabad. These are not the same as the Doghras of Jammú, in the hills between Kashmir and the Panjab; the latter are considered a mixed race, and are despised accordingly by their neighbours. They, however, call themselves Rajputs, and, apparently, with justice. There is not much in their appearance to indicate a mixture of race. They eat and smoke with the Bhojpúrí Rajputs. Guláb Singh, the ruler of Kashmir, was of this race.—B.

Dom, ڈوم or ڈومرا डोम or डोम्रा

Said, in the Printed Glossary, to be a race of out-castes: slaves in Kaṭṭak and Kamáon. Their history is worth enquiring into, as they seem to be one of the aboriginal tribes of India. Tradition fixes their residence to the North of the Gogra, touching the Bhars on the East, in the vicinity of Rohini. Several old forts testify to their former importance, and still retain the names of their founders; as, for instance, Domdiha and Domangaṛh. Ramgaṛh and Sahankot, on the Rohini, are also Dom forts. Buchanan considers that the Doms are the same as the Dom Katar (Domtikar). ("Eastern India," Vol. II. p. 453.) He also conceives that the Doms expelled the Thárús, and were afterwards expelled by the Bhars: but this order of precedence cannot be admitted.

There are several Doms, or Domras, scattered over the Western districts of these Provinces, and in Bundelkhand and

Saugor, who are engaged in the menial occupations of making ropes, fans, mats, and such like articles. In Oudh the term Dom is applied to sweepers, as Bhangí and Chúhra are elsewhere.

Dom is also the name of a tribe of Musulmans descended from Bhats. They are, perhaps, more generally known by the name of Mírásí and Pakhawají. The name of Mírásí is abbreviated into Mír: and thus the Mírs of the Kala Naddí, after whom Mírapúr is called, having assumed this distinguished title, are frequently able to conceal the truth of their being really descended from the Mírási Surkh.*

*** The Magahya Doms of Champáran are a race of professional thieves. They extend their operations into the contiguous districts of Nepal. They are rather dainty in their operations, and object to commit burglary by digging through the walls of houses; they always enter a house by the door, and if it is dark, they carry a light. Of course all this is merely done by way of bravado. Magahyas never live long in one place. They move about, constantly pitching their ragged little reed tents or *sirkas* outside a village, or on a grassy patch by the road-side, like our gipsies, till they have done all the plundering that offers itself in the neighbourhood, when they move off again. They are small and dark, with long tresses of unkempt hair, and the peculiar *glassy* eye of the non-Aryan autochthon.—B.

Domṭikár, دومٹکار डोमटिकार

One of the sub-divisions of Sarwaria Brahmans, *q.v.*

Ḍonwár, ڈونوار डोनवार

We find Zamíndárs of this mixed Rajput-Brahman tribe in the Parganah of Sidhúa Jabna in Gorakhpúr; in the Parganahs

* See for a short notice of the religion of the Doms "Select Works of H. H. Wilson," i. 60, 181.—B.

of Havelí, Karenda, and Sayyidpúr Bhitrí, of Ghazipur; and in Kariát Mithú, Mahomedabad-Gohna, Sikandarpúr, Bhadáon, and Maunáth-Bhanjan, of Azimgaṛh. They call themselves Thákúrs, but they are generally considered Bhúínhárs, or Military Brahmans.* Even those who claim Brahmanical descent marry into Rajput families, so it becomes doubtful in what class they ought to be included. They were strong enough at one time to establish a principality on the Kosi in Western Tirhút, and there are several monuments still existing in that neighbourhood which attest the power of the Donwár Raja, Karná Deo. The word appears to be pronounced indifferently, Donwár, Danwár, and Dunwár.†

Dúbe, دوبي दूबे

See Kanaujia Brahman.

Dugdhá,‡ دگدها दुग्धा

A tribe of inferior Brahmans on the borders of Fattihpúr and Allahabad. They date their origin from the time of Jay Chand, who figures in so many fabulous legends of those parts. A certain Paṇḍe Brahman, by name Barú, set up his abode as a recluse in Parsakhí, between Shahzádpúr and the Ganges, and withdrew himself entirely from worldly concerns. His credit as a holy man was so great, that Jay Chand became anxious to see him, and promised to reward any person who would bring him into the presence. After several unsuccessful attempts by all the chief officers of his Court, a woman of the Rajput tribe, and of great personal charms, ventured on the difficult undertaking. Her wiles and blandishments could not be withstood, and before long the holy hermit confessed himself father of

* But see the article on Bhúínhárs.—B.

† The Parganah of Danwár, in Shahabad, is probably named from them, or they from it.—B.

‡ Sansk. दुग्धा doubt.

several children; and as the lady succeeded in the object of introducing him to an audience with Jay Chand, a grant of several villages was bestowed upon her. On the death of the hermit she is said to have married a Ḳází, but it is not probable that such a connexion took place at that early period of the Mahomedan conquest. However, she divided the inheritance, it is asserted, amongst her children. Those by the Paṇḍe, who were Dugdhá Brahmans (*i.e.* of mixed blood), received forty-eight villages, of the greater part of which they are in possession to this day. The Musulman descendants also retain some of the villages said to have been granted at the same time.

The Dugdhás are reckoned in no repute as Brahmans; indeed, they are properly Bhúínhárs, and are very indifferent about the rank of the families with which they intermarry, not unfrequently receiving the daughters of Rajputs as wives.

Durgbansí, درگ‌بنسي दुर्गबन्सी

Name of a clan of Rajputs who hold villages in Garwára, Ghisua, and Rárí, in the district of Jaunpúr, and Máhul, in Azimgaṛh. The Raja of Garwára is a Durgbansí. They are descended from Díkhits, and came to the neighbourhood of Jaunpúr from Simauní in Bundelkhand, about fourteen generations ago. Their relative position in the rank of Rajputs is shown by their giving daughters in marriage to Chamargaur, Bandhalgotí, Tilokchandí, Bais, Sombansí, Súrajbansí, Sarnayt, Baghel, and the Gaharwár of Kantit. Their sons marry into the families of Chandel, Powar, Gautam, Raghubansí, Ujayin, and the inferior grades of Bais.

Ḍor, ڈوڙ डोड़

A tribe of Rajputs, said by Tod to be extinct. Before the immigration of the Baḍgújars, they were the chief proprietors of Aligaṛh; and a remnant of them now exists in Dabhaí, Atraulí, Koel, Shikarpúr, and Baran. They are now nearly all Mahomedans. The whole of Kundarkhí and Seondara,* in Moradabad, were also held by the Ḍoṛs, where they have now been almost entirely supplanted by the Powars. They hold also several villages in Seondha, in the district of Banda, as well as in the Saugor territory, so that they are far from being extinct, though most of them have abandoned the faith of their forefathers. They are included among the thirty-six royal races of Rajputs, and Pirthí Raja honored them by raising a tablet in commemoration of a victory gained over them.—(See Trans. R.A.S., Vol. I., p. 133.)

Dahiyá, دهيا दहिया

A tribe of Játs met with in the Parganahs of Rohtak, Kharkhauda, Mandauthí, Panípat, and Sonípat-Bangar.

Dahlán, دهلان दहलान

A tribe of Tagás on the banks of the Hindan, in the Upper Doáb.

Dakaut,† ڈکوت डकौत

A tribe of mendicants of Brahman descent. They are considered to be proficients in astrology. The Bhadauriás are a branch of the same tribe. Both are considered troublesome vagabonds.

Dalál, دلال दलाल

A tribe of Játs, who hold some villages in the Parganah of Mandauthí, Zillah Rohtak.

Dalímá, دليما दलीमा

A clan of Tagás in Sirsa, a Parganah of Moradabad.—(See Gaur Tagá.)

* The old name of Seondara was Deora, so called after this clan.

† Hindi डाकना to bawl, because they beg aloud in the streets.—B.

Damwast, دموست दमवस्त

A inferior tribe of Rajputs in Tappah Guzára, Zillah Benares.

Dangast, دنگست दंगस्त

A clan of Rajputs in Parganahs Shádíabad and Pachhotar of Ghazipur.

Gáín, گاین गाईं

The name of a small clan of Rajputs in Kopá Chít, Zillah Ghazipur, and in Benares.

Gágrá, گاگرا गाग्रा

See Bhangí.

Gáṛa or Gaṛhá, گاڑا or گاڑھا गाड़ा or गाढ़ा *

A tribe of industrious cultivators in Saharanpúr. We find them chiefly in Rúrkí, Rampúr, Súltanpúr, and Malhaipúr. They are Musulmans, and are frequently considered to be, like the Jhojhas, converted slaves. They themselves assert that they were formerly Sombans Rajputs, that they came from Nagra Bambera (to the west of Dehli), and that Akbar located them in desert tracts, which have now been cleared by their industry. There seems reason to believe that they are the progeny of Rajput clans, because amongst themselves they have the subdivisions of Baḍgújar, Chauhán, etc., but there are also perhaps amongst them descendants of several inferior castes. All these, on being converted to Mahomedanism, were called (perhaps contemptuously) by their neighbours, Gáras, from the new practice they had adopted of burying (Gárna), instead of burning, their dead. They now apply the term to themselves, but endeavour to disguise its origin by pretending to high

* Hindi गाड़ना or गाढ़ना to bury.

birth. The Gáras generally intermarry in their own clan, but there is a set of villages in Saharanpúr, called Sayyid Gára, from the fact of the daughters of Gáras marrying into Sayyid families.

Gahlot, گہلوت गहलोत

A tribe of Rajputs from which have branched the two illustrious stems of the Sisodia and Aharya. They are spread over different parts of these provinces, but though they sometimes style themselves Sisodia, they are rarely known by any other name than that of Gahlot. We find them as proprietors in Bhoelí, a Parganah of Mirzapúr; in Khanpúr of Ghazipur; in Nizamabad of Azimgaṛh; Bilhaur, Bithúr, and Rasúlabad of Cawnpore; in Sadabad, Sahpú, and Jalaisar of Muttra; in Thattia, Tirúa of Farrakhabad; in Ránia of the Bhattí Territory; in Hatras of Aligaṛh; and in great numbers in the N.W. parts of Bulandshahr. We find them also as cultivators in Khotar of Shahjahanpúr. Those of Bulandshahr say they emigrated to Dehra and Dholana, near Dasna, under Raja Khoman, after the capture of Chittor by Akbar; but it was evidently prior to that period, as they are recorded as Zamíndárs of Dasna in the "Ayín Akbarí." The more probable period is, after the capture of Chittor by Aláu'd dín Khilji. Others say that one of their ancestors, Govind Rao, married Raí Pithaura's (*i.e.* Prithí Raja) sister, and obtained these villages as a marriage gift. What gives an air of probability to this story is that Govind Rao is mentioned by Chand Bardai as one of Raí Pithaura's auxiliaries. Their neighbours, who, for some unexplained reason, are fond of imputing cowardice to them, say their name of Gahlot is derived from Gahla, a slave girl; but the real origin is the following, which is universally believed in Mewar. When the ancestors of the Rana of Mewar were expelled from Guzerat, one of the queens, by name Pushpávatí, found refuge among the Brahmans of the Mallia Mountains. She was shortly afterwards delivered of a son, whom she called, from the cave (Goha) in which he was born, by the name of Gahlot, and from him are descended the present Ranas of Udaypúr.

** Dr. Fitzedward Hall, the well-known erudite scholar, has favoured me with the following notice :—

"It seems probable that the term Gahlot is connected with Guhila, the name of the second king of the Udaypur dynasty. See the "Asiatic Researches," Vol. xvi., pp. 292, etc. The apparent eponymist of the Gahlots is called Gobhila in an inscription from Chedi, which I have published and translated in the "Journal of the American Oriental Society," Vol. vi. Guhila may have been corrupted from Gobhila, a name occurring in ancient Sanskrit literature; or, which is rather more likely, Gobhila may have been Sanskritized out of Guhila. In popular pronunciation, Guhila must have become Guhil; and we know that *gotra* was broken down into *got*. The coalescence of these shortened forms, after both had become still further depraved, may have given rise to Gahlot; a result which would in no wise transgress the lawless licence of Hindí analogies."

In support of this opinion, I may add, that throughout the Prithvi Raja Rasa, Chand always uses the form Gohil, गोहिल The following passage from the "Ala udal prastav" of that poem is interesting, as shewing the Gohil in good and valiant company at an early date, in spite of the later imputation of cowardice. It will be seen that they are decidedly on the side of Parimál, the Chandel king of Mahoba, and opposed to Prithí Raja, though the author above says their chief, Govind Rao, was an ally of the Chauhán :—

किये परिमाल सु ऊकम गाजि।
चले सब रावत जंग पै साजि॥
चन्देल बनाफर मुष सु सूर।
बघेल अरु गोहिल लोह करूर॥

"The monarch shouted his commands,
To battle marched the Ráwat bands;
Chandel, Banáphar, heroes leal,
Baghel and Gohil, fierce as steel."

I venture to differ from Dr. Hall about the origin of the last syllable. Having devoted much time to the consideration of the changes which compound consonants undergo in Hindí, I am in a position to affirm that had the word *gotra* been the origin of the last syllable, the initial *g* must have held its place, and the final *l* of Gohil would have been assimilated to it, thus resulting in a form Gohiggot or Gohgot. My theory is, that like so many names of places, clans, and persons, the final syllable is the Sanskrit adjectival termination वन्त् (वान, वती, वत) which coalesces with a long *á* in the termination of the preceding word into *ávat*, *aut*, and *ot*. Compare Dakaut from ḍakávant (*i. e.*, "shouters" or "criers"), Chandraut from chandrávant, Mahaut from mahávant, etc.; so that the word Gahlot arose from a form Guhilávant, or "Guhila's people." Colonel Tod gives in his lists Grahilot (Sisodia) as a separate clan from Gohil, and says the *former* are the Gahlot of modern times; but Tod's lists are very incorrect in many respects, and his etymologies are not worthy of the slightest notice.—B.

Gentú جنتو जेंतू

An Indian, a Hindu. The Printed Glossary says that at Madras the term appears to be used to designate the language and people of Telingana.

This word is a corruption of the Portuguese "Gentio," a "Gentile." Dr. Fryer (Travels, 1672 to 1681) says "the Gentues, the Portugal idiom for Gentiles, are the aborigines." He appears to be the first English writer by whom the term is used, but before his time Pietro della Valle speaks of the Hindus as Gentili, following the example of the Portuguese; yet, notwithstanding these unquestionable authorities, Halhed

(Gentú Code, xxi. xxii.) supposes that the Portuguese borrowed the term Gentú from the Sanskrit word Jant, a sentient being. —(See Ency. Metrop. *voc.* Gentú.)—E. Further notices from the early travellers on the origin of this singular word (now long since passed out of use) are as follows :—

Nieuhoff, in 1662, calls the natives "Jentyves or Pagans" (Churchill's Collection of Travels, II. 198). Gemelli Carreri (Works, Part III. Book ii. c. 8) in 1695 says, "As for courage, neither the Mahometans or Gentiles have much of it ; the best of them are the Baluccis (Bílúchís), borderers on Persia ; the Patans of the kingdom of Bengala, and the Rasbootis (Rajputs), very great thieves." Ralph Fitch, in his travels in 1583 (Hakluyt, II. 385), speaks of "Moores and Gentiles." Gaspar Balbi, in 1579, has "Gentiles" (Purchas, II. 1723). In the title page of Baldœus, printed in Churchill's collection, they are styled "Malabars, Benjias, Gentives." In the body of the work occurs "Moors and Pagans ;" again, "the Gentives are sorely oppressed by the Persians and Moors," p. 591. "As well Gentiles as Mahometists," says Antony Jenkinson, in 1558 (Hakluyt, I. 372). In all these cases the term Gentile means Hindu as distinguished from Musulman.—E. *add.*

Ghorcharhá, گهورچڑها घोरचढ़ा

A sub-division of the Kurmís. The literal meaning of the word, if rightly spelt, is a horseman. I am not sure that there may not be some connexion between them and the Kurcharra, whom Tod puts down in Chand Bardái's list of the royal races.

Ghosí, گهوسي घोसी

Herdsmen. They are said to be descended from Ahírs. Most of them have now been converted to Mahomedanism ; indeed, the name is generally considered, according to the Dictionaries, to be exclusively applied to Musulman milkmen. The name is derived from a Sanskrit word signifying a cattle pen. The Eastern Ghosís who have been converted are called Bandí Ghosís.

In many parts of the country, as in Dehli, Ghosís are those who trade in milk, without any reference to their caste or religion.

Ghand, گهند घंद

A subdivision of the Játs, *q. v.*

Ghanghas, گهنگهس घंघस

See Ját.

Gobrí, گوبري गोब्री

This is the name of a tribe in Rohilkhand, of which there are a few traditions preserved in the Taraí. From that they have been expelled, and now live on, or just under, the Hills.*

Godárá, گودارا गोदारा

See Ját.

Golá, گولا गोला

An inferior caste, employed in the manufacture of salt. The following contemptuous distich of popular poetry perhaps exalts them above their deserts :—

जाट गडरिया गूजर गोला
इन चारों का हेला मेला

"Ját, Gadarya, Gújar, Golá,
These four are all the same sort of people."

Golá púrab, گولا پورب गोला पूरब

An inferior tribe of Sanadh Brahmans, but very spirited

* They were formerly Ahírs. Their great hero was Raja Parsun, who was bitten by a snake, and of whom Rohilkhandís still sing.—E. *add.*

cultivators, in Parganah Irádatnagar of Agra. Their origin is decidedly Brahmanical, but carpenters often include them in their own class.

Gonḍ, گونڈ गोंड

The aboriginal inhabitants of the Saugor Territory, a simple primitive race, now chiefly confined to the hilly tracts, though some have been tempted to settle in the plains. Their great characteristics are a love of truth, drunkenness, and superstition. A writer in "Rushton's Gazetteer," (Vol. iv., Part 1), says :—

"To the north of Saugor, the representative of a royal household, styling themselves Raj Gonds, still exists in Bundelkhand, and is regarded with great deference by the scanty Gond population now to be found in that quarter. On the west, in the Bhopal Territory, similar traces of a formerly powerful dynasty are to be found, and acknowledged as such by the still considerable Gond Zamíndars, Thakurs, and Rajas, who abound in the south of Saugor, and in Hoshangabad and Narsingpur: while as regards the whole of the eastern portion, the royal houses of Deogarh, Balaghat (or Chandwara), and Garha-Mandla retained more or less sway until a very recent period, the representative of the former being at present a pensioner of the Nagpur Government, and that of the latter, of the British.

"In the western portion, or Saugor, it would appear that the Gonds were subjected by a tribe named Dangi, to which the present chief of Shahgarh belongs, and of the ruling house of which the representative still exists at Bilehra of Saugor. These were, in their turn, subdued by the Bundelas, from whom the territory passed to the Peshwa.

"The Gonds included amongst them several different sections: the Baiyas, who are very generally regarded as sorcerers, living apart from all, in solitary habitations, in the most dense forests, where they clear spaces with their axes, and sow their grain, without further labour, in the ashes left after the felled timber has been burned; but subsisting, for the most part, on the roots and fruits of the forests (with which they are especially familiar), the wild honey, or the beasts of game, which, in some parts, they occasionally destroy with bows and poisoned arrows:—the Bhumias, a nearly similar and almost equally wild race, without whose consecration a village is not considered habitable or safe from tigers, and who are universally the referees in all disputes regarding boundaries and established usages amongst these tribes:—the Purdhans, who preside at their orgies, are their beggars and bards, and unquestionably the most roguish and worthless part of their community:—the Patharis, who greatly assimilate to the latter; with some other divisions."

*** I here subjoin some information about these tribes, abridged from the late Rev. Mr. Hislop's recently published papers, containing much that was not known in the days when Sir H. Elliot wrote:—

"The Gonds and Konds are closely connected, and the name is probably derived from the Telugu *kondá*, 'a mountain.' They live in the mountain ranges lying between 18° 40′ and 23° 40′ N. latitude, and between 78° and 82° 30′ E. longitude. This corresponds with the old Muhammadan division of Gondwáṇa; but the Mughal geographers appear to have confounded them with the Kols, and not to have been aware of their connection with the Khonds of Bastár and Kalahandi.

"In the North they are met with about Saugor and near the source of the Hasdo; on the East they cross that river into Sargujá, where they border on the Kols, and are found with Konds and Uriyas in Navagaddá, Kariál, and Kalahandi; in the South they form the mass of the population of Bastár, and a portion of the inhabitants of Jaypúr (in the Madras Presidency), while they occupy the hills about the left bank of the Godávarí about Nirmal; and on the West they are intermingled with the

Hindus of Berar for thirty miles from the right bank of the Warda and along the Kúrrs, extend along the hills, both North and South of the Narbaddá, to the meridian of Hindia, where they give place to the Bhils and Nahals."

They are divided into twelve and a half classes—Ráj Gond, Raghuwál, Dandave, Katulyá, Pádál, Dholi, Ojhyál, Thotyál, Koilabhutál, Koikopál, Kolám, Mádyál, and a low Pádál as a half-caste. The first four, with the addition, by some, of the Kolám, are the highest and purest Gonds, and are called Koitor.

The Ráj Gonds have supplied the chief royal families, and live in Nagpúr, Berár, and the jungles South of the Wardá, as well as those North of the Narbaddá. The Raghuwál and Dadave are near Chindwara. These three are agricultural, eat together, but do not intermarry. The Katulyá are few, and scattered. They ape Hinduism, and are often received into that faith, and marry the daughters of needy Rajputs. Like all proselytes, they are over-zealous. The Raja of Khazradad is now a Hindu. They all go in for being Rajputs when converted.

The Pádál is also called Páthádi,Pardhán, and Desi; they live near and among the Ráj Gonds, to whom they act as spiritual guides (प्रधान). They are also bháts, or bards. The Ḍholís, so called from the ढोला ḍholá, or drum which they beat, are musicians, and attend at feasts: there is a sub-caste of them called Nagárchis (from the kettledrum), also known as Chherkya in the jungle districts, where they are employed as goatherds. Their wives act as midwives. The Ojhyáls are wandering bards, who play on castanets and bells, which they make themselves.

The Thotyál or maimed, also called Penda bariá, or minstrels of God, are wandering singers, who play a tambourine; they also make baskets; their women are great at simples, and practise physic. This caste knows charms against small-pox (mátá), whence it is sometimes called Matyál. They like to be called Thákur.

Koilábhutáls are wandering dancers, the men pimps and the women prostitutes. The Koikopáls are settled cowkeepers: the word is derived from Koi, *i.e.* Gond, and Kopál, *i.e.* Gopal.

The Madya Gonds are wilder than the others, and in some parts, as in the Beiládilá Hills, they are perfectly savage. The men wear very little clothing, and always carry battle-axes. The women in the more remote districts wear no clothing at all, only a bunch of leafy twigs before and behind hung from a string round the waists. (J.A.S.B., xxv., p. 295.) Bachelors live in a common house in the villages. They fly at the approach of strangers, even of their own race if not of the same tribe. Their tribute to the Raja of Bastar is paid in kind, and is collected by an official "who beats a tomtom outside the village, and forthwith hides himself, whereupon the inhabitants bring out whatever they have to give." Their ceremonies are very peculiar and curious, and have nothing in common with Aryan popular customs. They are too long to detail here.

The Koláms extend all along the Pindi Hills to the South of the Wardá river, and along the table land extending East and North of Manikgad, and thence South to Dántanpalli, running parallel to the Western bank of the Pranhita. They do not intermarry with the common Gonds, but eat together and dress alike. The Koláms worship Bhimsen, and have the custom, common in other nations, of pretending to carry off their brides by force.

The Gonds in general wear the dhoti, or waist-cloth, and a small kerchief on ther heads. The better classes also wear a scarf (angwastra) on their shoulders. The women wear a lower garment tucked up so as to expose the thighs and legs, and a sari, or cloth like a sash, over the breast and back, and are loaded with jewels and tattooed. Their religion is to a great extent un-Aryan.—B.

Gonda, گونڈا गोंडा

See Ahír.

Gwál or Gwálá, گوال or گوالا ग्वाल or ग्वाला *

A Cowherd.—See Ahír. They do not appear to acknowledge any subdivisions in these parts, but in Behar there are several, as Bihota, Banarasya, Kanaujia, and Chautaha.†

Gújar, گوجر गूजर

A very numerous clan in the N. Western Provinces, formerly notorious for their thieving propensities, but gradually becoming more addicted to habits of peaceful industry. Their importance may be rated by their having given names to the provinces of Guzerat on the western coast of India, and to Gujrát and Gujranwala in the Panjab. They are sometimes considered to be among the aborigines of India, and have been so reckoned by Tod, who somewhat inconsistently declares them also to be a tribe of Rajputs. Sir R. Jenkins says that in the Nagpur Territory they consider themselves to be Rajputs, and that, as they are descendants from Lava, Rama's second son, they have an undoubted right to be so considered. In these provinces, however, they do not aspire to so high an origin, contenting themselves generally by saying their ancestors on the male side were Rajputs, who had united themselves with women of inferior lineage. Thus the Rawal Gujars of Panípat say that they are descended from a Khokhar Rajput (a clan which has been considered to be the same as the notorious Ghakkar); the Chhokar from a Jadon; the Chamáyin from a Tuar; the Kalsian of Kaírana, and the Maví, from a Chauhan; the Pílwan from a

* Sanskr. गोपाल cowherd.

† In parts of Behar Gwála and Ahír are convertible terms; and all the remarks under Ahír will therefore apply to them.—B.

Púndír; the Ádhaná from a Badgujar; and the Bhattí from Raja Kansal, a Bhattí Rajput from Jaisalmír.

The Gújars are spread all over the Dehli Territory, the Upper Doáb, and Upper Rohilkhand, and enumerate eighty-four different tribes.* In Dehli, the chief tribes are the Chamáyin, Khatána, Kháre, Barsoí, Chhokar, and Rawál. In the Doáb,—Sukal, Baisalí, Máví, Ráthí, Bhattí, Kasauní, Balesar, Dede, Jindhar, Pílwan, Batar, Adhaná, Cheche, Kalsían, Rámáyan, Nagrí, Chhotkaná, Badkána, Kasaná, Rausá, Khúbar, Múndan, Kadáhan, Tauhar, Gorsí, and Kanáná. In Rohilkhand,—Batár, Khúbar, Khare, Jatlí, Motlá, Surádná, Púrbar, Jindhar, Mahainsí, and Kasane. All these tribes intermarry on terms of equality, the prohibited Gots being only those of the father, mother, and paternal and maternal grandmother.

A great part of the district of Saháranpúr was called Gujrát during the last century. By the Gújars themselves it was said to consist of three parts, and the division is not only known amongst them to this day, but is usually adopted in ordinary converse. The Khádar, or tract which extends from the upland as far as the Ganges, was called Ghar. From the upland to the Jumna, running along the skirts of the town of Saháranpúr, and maintaining a high name for productiveness, was called Rutolá. Almost all the rest of the district, from the Ganges to the Jumna, was called Gujrát proper; the small parganah of Kata only excepted. Gujrát extended down to Kairanah and Jhinjanah, and included Gahgoh, Lakhnautí, Nanauta, and Títron. A part of this tract, tenanted by Khubars, was known also as Badanon, a name affixed by themselves, in order to feed their vanity of being reputed men either of lofty

* In a pencil note the author quotes a Lt. Robinson as stating that Musulman Gújars are found in Chach Hazara, on the Indus, in Swat, Yusufzai, and on Mahában; also in Bonair. They are all zamíndárs, and state that they came from the Province of Gúzerat, by way of Vazirabad, in the Panjáb. They do not intermarry much with other tribes.—E. *add.*

stature, or eminent in war or council. Their common estimate of 125,000 subordinate villages within Gujrat must vanish when it comes to be examined. Three thousand is the utmost they could have possessed. They might perhaps have doubled that, had they included the tract they called Taliayin, which extended from Hastinapur and Baisuma, in a semicircle to the south of Mírut, up to Bagput. The Gujars of this tract were rather despised, chiefly because they shaved, and did not live in such a lordly fashion. The tract opposite to Dehli, from Loni to Kasnah, was called Bhatner, from the prevalence of the Bhattí Gújars.

Gujars are rarely found to the eastward of Aligaṛh in any numbers; but crossing the Jumna, we find them in Kunch and the northern parts of Bundelkhand, and the independent state of Sampter is ruled by a Gujar chief. There are many also near the Chambal and the Narbaddá. The Gujars, like the Játs, all state that they came from the west country into these parts. Many have been converted to the Mahomedan religion. Upon conversion they are generally styled Thatthar by their brethren of the ancient faith.*—E.

*** Gújars are also found in large quantities as far west as the Indus. Those in the Panjab are all Musulmans. As to their origin, the most probable story is that which makes them a cross between Rajputs and Ahírs.† Their habits are more pastoral than agricultural; and I have heard their name derived from *gau*, a cow, and *char* (of *charná*), to graze. I do not

* This is probably only a local term in Panipat.—E. *add.*

† General Cunningham considers that the Gújars are the same as the Tochari, *alias* Yuchi, *alias* Kushán, *alias* Kaspiræi, *alias* Thogarii, *alias* Kuei-Shwang, *alias* Korson, Korsea, Khoransu, or Korano. This remarkable tribe were, it would seem, originally Tartars, but by a series of events, related apparently by Chinese, Muhammadan, and Greek historians, they were led to give their name to Khorasan: also to Gurjjara-ráshtra, the modern Guzerat. It is sufficient merely to mention these speculations: those who care to read them will find them at pp. 25-29 of Part IV. of the General's report.—B.

accord much credit to this derivation, but it is remarkable that the province of Guzerat, which seems to have been their first abode, lies between the Rajput province of Malwa, etc., and Sindh, where the Abhiri, who are supposed to be the Ahírs, formerly lived. That they are aborigines is clearly disproved by their fine manly Aryan type, in which they closely resemble the Jats, who are constantly found as their neighbours. Gujarat in the Chaj Doab, Gujaranwala in the Rechna, and Gujar Khan in the Sindh Sagar, are named after them; the former is an ancient city which gives name to a district, and was re-built in A.D. 1588 by the Gújars.—B.

Gujar-gaur, گوجرگور गुजरगौर

See Gaur Brahman.

Gaura, گورا गौरा

A tribe of Ahírs, *q.v.*

Gaur brahman, گوڑ برهمن गौड ब्रह्मन

These form one of the ten tribes of Brahmans. They all state that they came from Gaur in Bengal, but there is much improbability in the story. There can be little doubt of Kanaujias emigrating on the invitation of Adiswara from Kanauj to Bengal; how then can we account for the whole tribe of Gaurs not only leaving their native seats, but crossing through the country of the Kanaujias, and dwelling on the other side of them? If they emigrated in or about the time of the Pándavas, as universal local tradition would induce us to suppose, it would lead to the inference that Kanaujias are a more modern race. Gaur, moreover, was only made the Bengal capital shortly before the Mahomedan conquest, and that is too late to admit of its giving a name to one of the ten tribes. Mr. Colebrooke seems to help us out of this difficulty by saying that

Gaur is not the Mahomedan capital, but a Des, or country below Patna; but admitting this, the difficulty would still occur, how they came to overleap the Kanaujias? and how happens it that all the Gaur Brahmans now in Bengal are very recent importations from the West? There is ample room for speculation, and it may, perhaps, amongst other things, be conjectured, that the Ta-Gauria, mentioned by Polybius, which Wilson, in his excellent work on "Ariana Antiqua," says affords some indications of Gaur, may be found to have something to do with their "incunabula," at any rate, if their connexion with it could be proved, it would solve the chief difficulty respecting their present Western position. A fuller examination of the point might result in important discoveries respecting the origin of the Brahmanical tribes.—See Gaur Taga.

We find Gaur Brahmans throughout the Súbah of Dehli, extending from Rampur to Hariana, and from Aligarh to the Hills. They appear in general a more ignorant race than the Kanaujias, and can seldom be got to give an intelligible account of their own subdivisions; but it may be gathered that they amount to the number of forty-two. The most noted tribes of Gaur Brahmans are the Adh, Júgad, Kaithal, Gújar, Dharam, and Sidh Gaur.*

Gaur káyath, گوڑ کایتھ गौड़ कायथ

One of the twelve sub-divisions of Káyaths. As their name implies, they are chiefly to be found in Bengal, though Násir-u'ddin, the son of Balban, introduced several of them into the Western Districts about 600 years ago, when he appointed them Kanúngoes of Nizamabad, Bhadoí, Kolí, Ghosí, and Chiriakot, in the Súbah of Allahabad.

There are two chief divisions of Gaur Kayaths—Kharrí and

* The Jatimala gives six divisions: Gaur, Parík, Bahínú, Khandelwál, Sarsut, Sundbel; but these are not all admitted by some Gaurs.—E. *add.*

Nizamabadí. The latter are subdivided into Nizamabadí proper, Brahman Gaur, Utarea or Shumálí. To these perhaps may be added Bhat-gaur or Gaura-Bhatnágar; but on this subject authorities are not very clear.

The Nizamabadís are now for the most part Sikhs, or followers of Nanak Shah.—See Bhatnágar.

Gaur rajput, گوڑراجپوت गौड़ राजपूत

One of the Chattís Kula, or thirty-six tribes of Rajputs. According to Colonel Tod* (Vol. I. p. 115), the ancient kings of Bengal were of this race, and gave their name to the capital Lakhnauti There are several of this clan in these provinces. We find many of them as Zamíndárs in Majhaulí of Gorakhpúr; in Bundelkhand; in Bisauli, Nidhpúr, Badánw, Satásí, Usahat, Ujhaní, and Saheswan in Zillah Badaon; in Powayin,

* It is difficult to say on what authority he makes this assertion. Gaur is generally supposed to have been founded by one of the Physician Dynasty of Bengal, not long before the Mahomedan invasion; though it must be confessed that Dow and Rennel state that it was the capital of Bengal 730 years before Christ. As another illustration of the unsubstantial theories entertained by this enthusiastic annalist, it may be mentioned that he considers the Gaur to be descendants of Bahrám Gaur, who is said, in some apocryphal histories, to have visited India in the fifth century, and to have left progeny there by a princess of Kanauj. In a subsequent passage, he has no doubt that the Gaur appanage was West of the Indus, and that this tribe, on conversion, became the Ghor, and returned to India as the Ghorí Kings of Dehli (Annals, Vol. I., p. 233; Vol. II., p. 449).

While, however, we cannot but dissent from several of the author's extravagant surmises and assertions, it would be ungracious not to acknowledge how deeply we we are indebted to him for his interesting "Annals of Rajasthan," a work which contains much novel information, and is a repertory of important facts and traditions, which are invaluable to an enquirer into the history of India previous to the Mahomedan invasion. He would have conferred a still deeper obligation on us had he published his promised translation of the poem of Chand Bardai. A perfect copy of the original is now rarely procurable, even in the best native libraries.—E.

I have procured two copies, and am about to publish an edition and translation of this interesting poem.—B.

Zillah Shahjehanpur; in Sambhal and Sirsí, Zillah Moradabad; in Aonla, Zillah Bareilly; and in Chibramau, Shamsabad, Alipur Patti, Phaphund, Dehli, Bilhour, Akberpur, Rasulabad, Ghatampur, and Dera Mangalpur, in Central Doab. In Khairabad of Oudh, they are found in considerable numbers. They gave great trouble in the time of Burhanu'l-mulk, Saadat Khan, and at last met with severe retribution.—(Imadu's Saádat.)

Tod gives the names of five "Sachæ" of Gaurs, which do not at all correspond with those known in these provinces. Here they are divided into three classes, called Bhat Gaur, Báman Gaur, and Chamár Gaur,—names derived from some intercourse with Bhats, Brahmans, and Chamars. To these are sometimes added Katherya Gaurs, descended from a Katheri, or carpenter; but it may be doubted if the Katherya are really Gaurs. No argument, however, can be derived from the fact that the daughters of Gaurs marry into Katherya families, because the Chamar Gaur and Baman Gaur also intermarry.

The Chamar Gaur, who are subdivided into Rajas and Raís, rank the highest, which is accounted for in this way. When troubles fell upon the Gaur family, one of their ladies, far advanced in pregnancy, took refuge in a Chamar's house, and was so grateful to him for his protection, that she promised to call her child by his name. The Bhats and Brahmans, to whom the others fled, do not appear to have had similar forbearance, and hence, strange as it may appear, the subdivisions called after their name rank below the Chamar Gaur.

The Chamár Gaur themselves say their name is properly Chaunhar Gaur, from a Raja who was called Chaunhar. Sometimes they say their real name is Chiman Gaur, and that they are called after a Muni, whose name was Chiman. The fact is, they are ashamed of their name, as it presumes a connexion with Chamars, which they are anxious to disclaim.

The strongest clan of Gaur is in the Central Doab. They say

that they came from Narnaul, from which place Nar in Rasulabad, the residence of a Gaur Raja, derives its name.*

Gaur taga, گوڑ تگا गौड़ तगा

An important tribe, of Brahmanical descent, in the northwest of India, extending over a great part of Upper Rohilkhand, the Upper Doáb, and the Dehli Territory. They are a tribe of peculiar interest, from the traditions which attach to their occupation of their present seats. They state that they were invited from Bengal to these parts by Raja Janamejaya,† for the purpose of exterminating snakes; which fable, though sufficiently ridiculous in itself, no doubt veils under an allegorical type a most important historical fact. The circumstances attending the sacrifice of the snakes by Janamejaya are preserved in local tradition in almost precisely the same form as they are given in the "Adi Parva" of the Mahábhárata. A garrulous old Taga, who has perhaps never read a line of that sacred poem, will tell you how that Raja Paríchit (Parikshita) was bitten to death by a snake, notwithstanding all the precautions he took to avoid it, by seating himself on a platform in the centre of the Ganges; how that Atang (Atanka), a Muni, persuaded Janamejaya, who had lately returned victorious from Takshasila, to avenge his father's death; how that Janamejaya determined on having a Hom, or sacrifice, of the entire race of snakes; how that they were all exterminated except Takchak (Takshaka, brother of the Adityas) and Basuk (Vasuki, sove-

* The Rajas of Suket, Kishtawar, Mandí and Keonthal, in the Himalayas, between Simla and Kashmir, are all Gaur Rajputs. He of Suket is a Chamár Gaur. They all state that their families came originally from Bengal.—E. *add.* He also refers to Tod, I., 115, 233; II., 449. Buchanan. II., 613, 728; and III., 42, 68, 154. Burnouf, Bud. Ind. I., 632. Raja Tarangini, I., 488, 508. J.A.S.B., Jan. 1847, p. 18.

† The same tradition is preserved in Bengal also.—See "Buchanan's Eastern India," Vol. III., pp. 42 and 154.

reign of the Nagas of Patala); when, towards the close of the sacrifice, Astik, a holy man (of whose birth some marvellous particulars are given), came forward, and obtained the promise of Janamejaya to spare their lives, which promise he dare not break, as it was exacted by a Brahman; and how that he was thus foiled in his object of sacrificing the chief offenders, whom he had reserved for the close of the ceremony, in order that none of their followers might come to their assistance.

The extent to which this tradition of the serpent-sacrifice (Sarpa Satra) has spread is very surprising. Here we not only have it preserved by the common people of the north-west, the very scene of the operation, but in inscriptions and legends from distant parts of India. Thus, in the "Asiatic Researches" (Vol. IX.) we have an inscription from a copper-plate found at Bednor, which purports that Janamejaya made a progress to the south and to other quarters, for the purpose of reducing all countries under his dominion, and performed a *sacrifice for the destruction of serpents* at the confluence of the rivers Tangabhadra and Haridra, at the time of a partial eclipse of the sun. Having completed the sacrifice, the king bestowed gold and lands on certain Brahmans of Gautama Gráma,—a name evidently of Buddhist origin. Though the genuineness of this monument is distrusted by Colebrooke and Colonel Mackenzie, they both concur in thinking it no recent fabrication. If it is forged, it must of course have been drawn up in conformity with notions and traditions generally current on the spot. Again, Stirling ("Report on Orissa," p. 25) says that the Brahmans of Agrahat, eight miles north of Kaṭak (Cuttack), state that the spot was visited by Janamejaya during his progress over India with all the feudatory princes of the country in his train; and they "point out the spot where he performed the *sacrifice for the destruction of the serpents*."—See also "J.A.S.B.," September, 1837.

It can scarcely be doubted that these serpents, for whose

annihilation so much trouble was taken, were Takshak Scythians of the Buddhist persuasion, and the chief supporters of that religion. From the time of the Great War, when we find them already in the north-west, to about 500 B.C., they extended their conquests in India; and, as they had a serpent for their national emblem, they were known as the Takshak, or serpent race. There can be no question also that the early legends of Persia are to be interpreted with this key, and that the voracious snakes of Zahhak were hordes of barbarous Scythians from the north.

The period of their chief, though perhaps not their first, invasion of India, under their leader Sahesnag, occurred about 600 B.C. Many memorials of the bloody wars in which the Hindus were engaged with these invaders exist in the records of Indian history. They extended their usurpations to the Magadha Empire of Behar, the throne of which was held by the Nag, or Serpent dynasty for ten generations, and a branch of them, the Nagbansí chieftains of Ramgaṛh Sirgúja, have ("Trans. R. A. Society," Vol. ii. p. 563), the *lunettes* of their Serpent ancestor engraved on their signets in proof of their lineage,—while the capital and district of Nagpúr are called after their name. The Vayu and Matsya Paranas call the Saisanagas, Kshatra Bandhís, which may designate, says Wilson ("Vishnu Pur.," p. 467), an inferior order of Kshatriyas. The use of the title serves to show that they had already begun to be included in the military class, and is confirmatory of the view that they are included in the Agnikula. The invasion above-mentioned was, according to Colonel Tod's supposition, nearly contemporaneous with the appearance of the 23rd Buddha, Parisnath, whose symbol is that of the race he accompanied, and hence he is called Sahasphann, "the thousand-hooded." It is supposed that the Brahmans made converts of some powerful branches of these new sectaries, and that it is to them the term Agnikula (fire-race) is applied, as signifying their spiritual regeneration by the element of fire. If so, the Takshaks must be the progenitors of the most distinguished tribe of Rajputs; and yet it is strange that no vestiges are now to be found of the original name Tak,* or Takshaks, though it is recorded amongst the thirty-six royal races. I am aware that Elphinstone ("History of India," Vol. i., App. ii.) opposes the doctrine of a Scythian admixture with the Rajputs; but there is much in Indian history which could not well be explained without it, at least without the admission of an incorporation of some northern family, and even he is disposed to concede the point with regard to the Játs.—See also "J.A.S.B.," Vol. vi. p. 677.

* It may be remarked that Tak is one of the sub-divisions of the Bhangís, but they are not likely to be in any way connected with our Rajput Taks.

There is also a community of Tank Rajputs in Gihror of Mainpúrí, and in the South of Rohilkhand. They trace their origin from Tank Tora in Karaolí, and receive the daughters of Baman Gaur, Chamar Gaur, Gahlot, and Dhákara in marriage, which would argue them to be of respectable lineage. The probability of their connexion with the Tak race will be further discussed under the article Tank.

It is also to be observed that Takshak is still one of the Gram Deotas, or village gods, of the Bhagalpúr district.

The "Mirát-i Sikandarí" says the tribe was called Tak, because it became Tyágí, or separated from its brethren: ascribing, therefore, the same origin to the name as is given to our Tagas.·

سدهارن از قوم تاک است در تاریخ هنود مسطور است که تاک و
کهتري برادران یکدیگراند يکي از ایشان بشرب شراب رغبت نمود
اورا کهتریان از قوم خویش اخراج نمودند و چنین مخرجي را بزبان
هندي تیاگي گویند یعني از قوم برآورده شده از آن باز رسم و آئین
و دین کهتري از تاک امتیاز یافت

The translation of the passage is as follows:—"Sidháran is of the Tak tribe. In the Histories of India it is written that Tak and Khattri are brothers; one of them took to drinking, and the Khattris expelled him from their tribe, and an expelled person is, in the Indian language, 'tyágí.' From that time the customs and laws and religion of the Khattris differed from those of the Tak."—B.

This spiritual regeneration must have occurred three or four centuries subsequent to the allegorical tradition mentioned above, which evidently implies that the edict of extermination was not entirely fulfilled, and that Janamejaya was induced to forego his purpose at the instigation of Astik, who, according to the "Mahábhárata," was the son of Takshak's own sister; so that intermarriages with the Takshaks could not have been altogether uncommon even in the Court of King Janamejaya.

It is evident that we are to construe in a similar way those frequent allusions in the "Mahábhárata" and the "Puranas" to the intercourse between mortal heroes and the Nága Kanyas, or Serpent nymphs. For instance, when it is mentioned that an Apsara from Naglok was married to Chatrgupt, and that more than half the Kayaths of the country are the offspring of this union, and when it is mentioned that the seventeen daughters of Basuk, the king of the Nágas, were married to the seventeen sons of Raja Agarsen, we are to understand that a nuptial alliance united a Scythian family with that of Chatrgupt and Raja Agarsen. Those who, like the Agarwala Banias, are descended from the Raja, would not willingly acknowledge this interpretation, as they would rather adhere to the fable; but it need not alarm them, for a little examination would show that, even as it is, they cannot be pure Vaisyas, since the Raja was himself a Kshatriya. In a similar manner, almost all the mercantile tribes of Hindustan are of Rajput descent. But these anomalies do not appear to strike the credulous Hindu, and he is content to leave the subject without enquiry.

It was for the purpose of officiating at the serpent sacrifice above-mentioned, that Janamejaya is said to have invited Brahmans from Gaur. After they had performed all that he requested of them, he offered them remuneration, which some rejected, and others received in the shape of land; on which account they are called Tagas, from having consented to a Tyág (relinquishment) of their creed as Brahmans, by pursuing agriculture, which they are forbidden by the Shasters to practice.

Those who continued to retain their titles and privileges as Brahmans—(See Gaur Brahman)—took up their abode chiefly in Hariana, while the Tagas remained in the immediate neighbourhood of Hastinapúr, within a circle of about one hundred miles round the ancient capital, where they are found to this day. This is the usual account. It is remarkable, however, that almost all the clans of Tagas state that they came from Hariana, not from Gaur, and even derive their names from places in that country, as, for instance, the Chulat, who say that their name is derived from Chúlú in Bikanír, and the Bikwans of Púr Chapár, who came from Bikanír. It is therefore far more probable that the Brahmans were already tenants of Hariana, that they must have settled there before Janamejaya's reign, and that the Tagas only, not the Brahmans, owe their residence to that powerful Raja; otherwise it is difficult to reconcile the apparent contradiction that he called Gaur Brahmans from Bengal, and Gaur Tagas from Hariana; or it may be, that the Brahmans were invited from Gaur by Janamejaya, and afterwards settled in Hariana; and that the Tagas were invited by some succeeding prince or princes, after the Brahmans had fully established themselves in Hariana; so that the occupation of the country round Hastinapúr by the Tagas may be later than the occupation of Hariana by the Brahmans. But what militates against this, and confirms the other hypothesis is, that it is expressly stated in the concluding section of the "Mahábhárata" that Janamejaya, "having concluded the ceremonies of the sacrifice on which he had been engaged, *dismissed the multitude of Brahmans*, and other pious mendicants who had thronged to the place, loaded with presents, to their *several abodes*."

There are some Tagas in the Upper Doáb, who state that they do not proceed from the Gaur stock. For instance, on the banks of the Doáb Canal, near Dehli, there are a few villages held by Tagas of Sirsútí Brahman descent. With this exception, it is generally acknowledged that all the Tagas were originally Gaur Brahmans.

They are divided into several separate clans, amongst which some of the most important are Mungal, Títwal, Mahesara, Basian, Dattian, Karáwal, Makta, Dikhit, Aimlí, and Dabhe.

There are several Mahomedan converts among them, particularly in the line of country between Mírat and Moradabad.

In the Dehli Territory the Gaur Brahmans and Tagas frequently intermarry, but the practice is not observed by the Gaurs of the Doáb and Rohilkhand.—E.

*** There is, doubtless, in the legends of the early Aryans much that is obscure on the subject of their connection with the Nágas, or serpent race. Any speculations here would be out of place, as Mr. Fergusson has just published a magnificent work on this subject, which will be found to contain valuable information. As, however, Gen. Cunningham has many notices about a tribe which may, or may not, be allied to the above, I give an abstract of them, without in the least committing myself to approval of the General's opinions (which appear to me to be in many cases ill-founded), because in the dearth of information on the subject of castes, it is useful to collect all that has been written, with a view to the ultimate sifting of the mass when the proper time shall come.*

* What a pity it is that our Indian savants so habitually neglect the proper division of all philosophical enquiry into its two great branches: first, the collection of facts; next, the induction from a sufficient quantity of collected and ascertained facts! We are really, at present, as regards the pre-Muhammadan history of India, only in the first of these stages, and we have not yet collected half our facts. It is much to be desired that our learned workers in this school would abstain for the present entirely from making deductions, which only our grandsons will be in a position to make, and devote themselves solely to collecting facts, for which they have still ample scope. We are not yet ripe for Indian Niebuhrs: we are still in the age of Scaliger and Reuchlin.—B.

The Takkas are denominated by the above-named writer "early Turanians," and he ascribes to them a connection with "the famous city of Takkasila or Taxila." They were formerly, he thinks, in possession of the Sindh Ságar Doáb, or the country between the Indus and Jhelum rivers in the Panjáb, but must have been expelled thence by the Gakkars (who are also said to be Turanians) during the reign of Darius Hystaspis, or thereabouts. The reason for this supposition would seem to be that "in the first century of our era, the district of Taxila was already called Amanda or Amandra, a name which at once recalls the Awáns of the present day and their country Awánkári." In another place (p. 8) the Awáns are said to have been in possession of Taxila at the time of Alexander's invasion, and to have been expelled by the Indo-Scythians two centuries later. These speculations, however, are confessedly rather uncertain, and some confusion exists in this part of the report. The curious custom mentioned by Q. Curtius, and by Fa-Hian, the Chinese traveller (A.D. 400), as prevalent among the people of Taxila, of entertaining guests for three days, and obliging them to depart on the fourth, is adduced to show that the same people occupied that site from the time of Alexander to that of Fa-Hian, a period of seven hundred years.

Attok is also supposed to recall the name of the Takkas. Rashídu'd dín calls it the fort of Tankur, which with the Arabic article (التنكور at-tankúr) is said to have suggested to Akbar the name Attok (Aṭak) meaning obstacle. Though I strongly doubt this supposition, it is certain that the name was given by Akbar. The Játs in the Gujrát district of the Panjáb have a legend that they were Rajputs, and lost caste by crossing the Indus, which the others refused to do. They were taunted, says the story, by Akbar, in the following verse:—

सारा भूं गोपाल का है।
ता में चटक कहां॥

जा के मन में अटक है ॥
ता में अटक रहा ॥

"All the earth is God's: In it where is there any hindrance?
He in whose mind there is a barrier, in that (alone) is the hindrance."*

"In A.D. 900 we find the district of Takkadesa forming part of the kingdom" of Gujrát "when Raja Sankara Varmma of Kashmír, who reigned from A.D. 883 to 901, annexed it to his own dominions. At that time Takkadesa must have been situated to the north or north-east of Gujrát, towards Kashmír. Now this is the very position where we find the Takkas of the present day, namely, in the hilly country on both banks of the Chenab, within the Jammu territory" (p. 4). This would seem to me to be conclusive against the identity of Takkadesa with Taxila, as the General himself fixes the latter in the north-western part of the Sindh Ságar Doáb, at Shahdheri, near Kála Saráí.

There are also Táks in Sindh who are connected with the Panjábí Takkas, a chief of whom held the fortress of Aser in Rájwára, and is stated to be mentioned by Chand under the name of Chátá Ták, and to have been wounded at Kanauj. "Two centuries later one Sárang Ták became the first Muhammadan king of Gujrát under the name of Muzaffar Shah" (ib.)

These Takkas and Taks are said to have been descended from Takshaka, the founder of the Nágas, or serpent race; and the legend of Paríkshita's death by the bite of a snake may be interpreted as showing a conflict between the Pándavas and the Takkas of the Panjáb, in which the latter were victorious. "This event may be dated about 1400 B.C."

These Takkas are considered to have originally peopled Kash-

* I quote this verse from memory, from the valuable manuscript Settlement Report of the district, by Captain Hector Mackenzie, which is a perfect storehouse of curious legendary and other information. I do not know if it has yet been published.—B.

mír, where serpent-worship prevailed till the time of Kanishka, about the beginning of the Christian era, who introduced Buddhism; but shortly after his death the Nága sacrifices and ritual were re-established by Gonarda II. There was a Nága king named Durlabha in Kashmír in the seventh century, who established a dynasty.

On the whole there appears to be no valid reason, in the present state of our knowledge, for supposing the Takkas to be anything but low Aryans. The arguments adduced at p. 5 of the Report prove nothing at all.—B.

Gauráhar, گوراهر गौराहर

An obscure tribe of Rajputs in Saheswan, and in Gangerí, Pachlánah, Badarea, and Bilram, on the borders of Badaon and Aligaṛh. They are said to be descended from the Chamár Gaur, and it is sometimes added, by way of reproach, that there is a little Ahír blood in their veins.

Gauruá, گوروا गौरुआ

An inferior clan of Rajputs in Rehar, and Nagína of Bijnor; Irádatnagar of Agra; and Sahár, Shergaṛh, and Hazúr Tahsíl of Mathura. Those to the west of the Jumna are said to have emigrated from Jaypúr about nine hundred years ago. They are frequently confounded with the Gauráhars, but are, in fact, quite distinct.

Gautam rájpút, گوتم راجپوت गौतम राजपूत

This tribe is now usually rated among the Chandarbans; but they are not considered as holding a place among the thirty-six royal races. There are a few of them in Bundelkhand and Benares, but they are found in large numbers in Ghazipur, Ayia Sah, Mutaur, Kora, Kútia Gunír, and Bindkí, Parganahs of Fattihpúr; Jajmau and Sarh-Salimpúr of Cawnpore; in Islámnagar of Badaun; Deogáńw, Chiryakot, Kariat Mittú, and Nizamabad of Azimgaṛh: and in Máhul, Atraulia Tilhení, and Aurungabad Nagar of Gorakhpúr.

The Gautams were once a very powerful clan in the Lower Doáb. Their chief village was Argal on the Rinde in Parganah Kora, and their representative, now shorn of all his power, still resides there, and is honored with the title of Raja. They themselves state that they were originally Brahmans, that Siringí Rikh, their ancestor (so called from a prominent horn on his forehead), was invited to court by the Gaharwár Raja of Kanauj, who bestowed his daughter in marriage on Ingí Rikh, the son of Siringí, and accompanied the gift with the splendid dowry of all the villages from Kanauj to Karrá.

The tradition is good for nothing. It is, in the first place, impossible that Siringí Rikh could have been a contemporary of any Gaharwár Raja, and, in the second place, it is highly improbable that the Gaharwárs should have preceded the occupation of the Gautams. Nevertheless, the story is most devoutly believed by many Gautams. They are divided into the tribes Raja, Rao, Rana, and Rawat. The representative of the Rajas lives at Argal; of the Raos at Biṛáhanpúr, in Bindki; of the Ranas at Chillí, in Parganah Majháwan, now included in Sarh-Salímpúr; and of the Rawats at Bháúpúr, in Bindkí.

Besides the possessions which they themselves retained, they are said—and here probability is in favour of the tradition—to have bestowed upon their allies several large tracts which are to this day tenanted by the grantees. Thus the Chandels of Sheorájpúr in Cawnpore are represented to have received from them sixty-two villages in that Parganah, having been induced to leave their original seat of Mahoba, after the defeat of their chief Brimaditya by Pirthí Ráj. The Jaganbansí Kanaujía Brahmans of Kora are said to have received the Chaudrahat of that Parganah from Birsingh Deo, a Gautam chieftain. The Thatbarár Kanaujía Brahmans are said to have been Bakhshís of the Argal family. The Athya Gautams, who are reckoned inferior to the general stock, and considered to have been originally Jinwar Rajpúts, are said to have received twenty-eight villages in Bindkí from the Argal Raja, with whom they had contrived to ingratiate themselves by teaching him the game of chess.

But the largest assignment of land which was attributed to their bounty is that of Baiswara, in Oudh. The reason of this gift is thus given by the traditions of the country. The Argal Raja, having given offence to some king of Dehli, the king directed his myrmidons to seize the Raja's wife, who was then on a pilgrimage at Allahabad. They were nearly succeeding in their attempt, when a large party of the Bais Rajputs from Múngí Paitan, who had come under their leaders Bhao and Bebhao to the sacred confluence, came forward to the rescue, and kept the royal army at bay till they reached Karra, when there was no longer any fear of danger. To mark the Rani's gratitude, the Bais were invited to Argal, and there, after a short time, a marriage was celebrated between Bhao and Gúrdandí, a Rajpútní of the Rao Gautam tribe. The Raja, though he considered it a humiliation to unite one of his own stock to the stranger, was nevertheless pleased to authorize a marriage with the Rao, and to bestow upon the Bais, as a dowry, 1,440 villages on the eastern side of the Ganges, which now constitute the country of Baiswara. The story goes that the Gautam Raja offered the bride all the villages of which she could pronounce the names without drawing breath. She accordingly commenced, and after reciting five lines of names, had proceeded so far as Panchgáṅw, when the Raja's son, fearing that his possessions would be lost to him, seized hold of the bride's throat, and prevented further utterance.

If we are to put faith in the essentials of this tradition, it would shew that the Gautam country must really have been an important tract, extending from Kalpí to the neighbourhood of

Gorakhpúr, since we find a Gautam Raja still residing, as head of his tribe, in Nagar in that district, and that the Azimgarh family, now Musulmans, were, before their conversion, Rajputs of the Gautam stock. We find it also stated in Buchanan ("Eastern India," Vol. II. p. 458), that the Gautams of Gorakhpúr considered that their ancestors were once in possession of Bundelkhand. Though his statements are never to be taken without reservation, yet we may fairly receive them for the evidence of a tradition respecting the Gautams, which concur with that of their Western brethren in assigning to their ancestors the possession of a very large principality in and around the Lower Doáb.

It must be remembered that both the Gautam and Bais Rajputs concur in this story, and such a concurrence is almost equivalent to authentic history. Now, as the Bais are descendants of Salivahana, and a Salivahana was sovereign of Pratisthana, the modern Jhúsí ("Asiatic Researches," Vol. X. p. 32), it gives at once an established antiquity to the Gautams, which makes it possible that we may have in them the descendants of the illustrious Shakyas. There are of course difficulties* attending this hypothesis, but the bare mention of it raises questions of considerable interest, which invite a longer discussion than can be bestowed upon them here.

For some generations the Gautams of Argal seem by their own accounts to have continued in great prosperity, dating their decline from the period of Hamáyún's return to India, who avenged himself upon them for their zealous adherence to the cause of his victorious rival, Sher Shah. Musulman history,

* Il résulte de là qu'il n'est pas aisé de comprendre comment Shakya à pu porter à la fois ce nom, qui rappelle la tribu guerrière à laquelle il appartient, et celui de *Gautama*, qui rappelle une famille brahmanique. La seule manière de résoudre cette dernière difficulté, c'est d'admettre que le nom de *Gautama* a dû appartenir, non pas seulement à Shakya *mouni* seul, mais à toute la famille guerrière des Shakyas, comme le pensent les Chinois.—M. Burnouf, *Foe Koue Ki*, p. 309.

however, is silent on this subject, both of this warfare of extermination, and of the presumed importance of Argal and the Gautams, and it is therefore difficult to say what portions of truth are mixed up with the fictions of these relations.

The Gautams of Jaunpúr and the Eastward give their daughters in marriage to Sombansí, Bachgotí, Bajhalgotí, or Bandhalgotí, Rajwar, and Rajkúmar. Those of the Doáb give their daughters to other tribes, the Bhadauria, Kachhwáha, Rathor, Gahlot, Chauhán, and Túar, and they vary as much with respect to the tribes whose daughters they receive.

Gautamiyán, گوتمیان गौतमियां

A clan of Rajputs in Azimgaṛh and Gorakhpúr. They are offshoots of the Gautams, but of a spurious breed.

Gabr, گبر गबर

An infidel, in general; but the word is more specially applied to a fire-worshipper. Meninski says, "Ignicola, magus, infidelis, quivis paganus." The word is more familiar to us in Europe under the aspect of Guebre—the Parsee of Western India. There seems reason to suppose that there were colonies of refugee fire-worshippers established in Upper India also till a very late period. One of the governors of Mírat, even as late as the time of the capture of that town by Timúr in A.D. 1399, was of that persuasion; and though the "Rauzatu's Safá," the "Timúrnama," and "Zafarnama" mention him merely under the term of Gabr, which is also applied by them to Hindus in general, yet the "Mutlau's Sayyidín" distinctly says that his son worshipped fire; and the language of Khondemir in the third volume of the "Habíbu's Sair" is too plain to be mistaken on that point:—

و آخر ماه ربیع الاخر صاحب قران عالي ماثر بدآنجا رسیده عساکر

منصور آغازِ جنگ کردند و قهرًا میرت را گرفته صفي گبر را در حين قتال بزخم تيغ آبدار بدارالبوار فرستادند و پسرش را بآتشي که مي پرستيد سوزانيدند * اگر صد سال گبر آتش فروزد * چو يکدم اندر و افتد بسوزد * غره ماه جمادي الاولی اکثر گبران انحصار بر دست اهل اسلام کشته گشته بروجِ قلعه مانند خاکِ راه هموار شد*

Gaddí, گدي गद्दी

A tribe resembling the Ghosís. They are now mostly Musulmans, and have a few scattered communities in several Parganahs, such as in Gaṛhmuktesar and Sarawa of Mírat, and the Rampúr territory. It is not unusual to call any converted Hindú a Gaddí, which is looked on by a true Musulman as a term of reproach.

Gadariyá, گڈریا गडरिया

A shepherd. There are several sub-divisions of Gaḍariyás in these Provinces—Níkhar, Tasselha or Pachhade, Chak, Dhengár, Bareiya, Paihwar, and Bhaiyatar. Of each of these there are also many divisions, which are not worth recounting.

These hold no intimate communication with one another, being as much strangers as any two distinct castes. The most liberal relaxation of this social bondage being that the Níkhar and Dhengár smoke each others hukḳas.

* "And at the end of the month Rabíu's-saní His Majesty arrived, and the army commenced the attack, and having taken Mírat, they sent to hell Safí, the Gabr, who had been wounded by a sword at the time of the slaughter, and burnt his son in the fire which he worshipped.

Though a Gabr kindle fire for a hundred years,
If he once fall into it he will burn.

On the first of Jamadi-ul-úla' most of the Gabrs of that fort fell into the hands of the Musulmans and were killed, and the fortress was levelled."—B.

As with the Játs and Gújars, so with the Gaḍariyás, the younger brother marries the elder brother's widow, but the elder brother is prohibited from forming a similar connection with the younger brother's widow.—See Karao in Part II.

Gaharwár, گہروار गहरवार

A tribe of Rajputs found in Dera Mangalpúr, Bithúr, Jájmau, Kanauj, and Bilhaur in the Central Doáb; in Islámganj on the left bank of the Ganges; in Bundelkhand; in Gorakhpúr; in Katehar and the Hazúr Taḥsíl of Benares; in Pachhotar and Mahaich of Ghazipur; in Khairagaṛh of Allahabad; and Kantit of Mirzapúr.

The Gaharwárs* of Khera Mungrore in Mirzapúr are converted to Mahomedanism, and those of Mahaich in Ghazipur are reckoned an inferior branch. The chief of the Gaharwárs resides at Bijaypúr, a few miles to the west of Mirzapúr, where the liberality of the British Government enables him still to keep up some show of respectability. At the time of our first occupation of Benares, he was a fugitive from the tyranny and oppression of the Gautam Bhúínhárs, who had expelled the Gaharwár family in 1758 A.D.

The Gaharwárs may be considered one of the most interesting races of the Upper Provinces, yet much obscurity hangs over their origin and lineage. They are recorded among the thirty-six royal tribes of Rajputs, and are said to be of the same family as the Rathors, with whom they deem themselves on an equality, and with whom it is said they never intermarry. But this is a mistake, for those of the Central Doáb and Gorakhpúr intermarry with Rathors, and the observation can only apply to the *soi-disant* regal family of Kantit. They are mentioned, moreover, in the "Prithiraja rásá,"

* The Jatimala in the "Hindí Selections" spells the name गहड़वाड़, but it seems more usual to spell it as in the text.

under the distinct appellation of Gaharwár. Thus, in the "Alhá-prastáv"* we read,

सज्जि गहवीर गोहिल अनेक
"Many Gaharwárs and Gohils were arrayed."

So that they were acknowledged to be a separate tribe at the time of the final subjugation of Kanauj by the Mahomedans.

They assert that they were originally masters of Kanauj, local tradition confirms their claims, and the Gautam Rajputs attribute their own residence and possessions in the Lower Doáb to the bounty of a Gaharwár Raja of Kanauj. The "Ḥadikatu'l-Akálím" states that they come from Benares, and settled at

* There is also very curious mention of them at the end of another Khand. Bír bhadr is made to deliver the following prophecy respecting the future greatness of this family:—

ता पाछे पूरब देसीयं उपजै कोऊ नरेसीयं
विंदासु चल मधिवासीयं वेद भेद उपासीयं
कुल गहरवार सुमझियं नर्पमहों हिंदूसहीयं
हरिचंद निजुध की जातीयं प्रिथिराज तेज समातीयं
धर्म राज विक्रम सूरियं सकवंध अवतर पूरियं
फिरि जसो हिंदू अवतरें मिलि गहरवार सगोतरं
धरिजीति सकति चलाई है हिंदूवान सर्व मिलाई है
उन सिर तिलकु सी से दियौ दीसो पति साहदिल्ली को कियौ
जौं छषन पंडव थापीयं त्यौं गहरवार सुथापीयं

After saying that the Empire of India will be swayed by the Pathans, a Banya (?), the Moguls, and a hero from the Deccan (?), he states that the Gaharwárs will finally attain the sovereignty. But both the style and sentiment betray marks of modern interpolation; and the passage was no doubt written by some courtly poet of the holy city, when it was under the dominion or influence of the Gaharwár family.—E.

I leave this passage as it stands, because it is one of the few bits of Chand that have yet got into print. Every one talks about Chand, but few have really read his poem, which is very scarce. As to this extract, though it is manifestly incorrect, yet no correction of it can be attempted till a collation has been made of the original, which I hope to do shortly, as also to publish an edition and translation of the whole poem.—B.

Kantit, in A.D. 1155. Other authorities say that Gadan Deo (by some reckoned the son of Manik Chand, brother of Jay Chand, the Rathore) came from Kashmír, about the end of the same century, and after expelling the Bharpatwas, at that time the occupants of the southern bank of the Ganges, settled at Kantit, and assumed for himself and brethren the name of Gaharwár. Kashmír is most likely a mistake for Kási (Benares), which is generally considered to be their original country; and if so, the two reports would be nearly identical with respect to the place and time of emigration.* The probability, however, appears to be that the Gaharwárs preceded the five Rathore princes of Kanáuj, and fled to their present seats, on the occupation of the country by the Rathores; or, it may be that, after living in subordination to, or becoming incorporated with, the Rathores, they were dispersed at the final conquest of Kanauj by Muhammad Ghorí.

What has chiefly puzzled the English historians of this eventful period is the name of Korah, which was borne by the Raja of Kanauj at the time of the invasion by Mahmúd of Ghazní. The Rauzatu's-safá calls him Jaipal, but the Habíbu's-sair, the Táju'l-maasir, the Tabakát-i-Akbarí, and Ferishta call him Korah or Gorah.† Now it is not at all improbable that

* Colonel Tod, in the "Annals of Rajasthan" (Vol. I., 116), says, "The Gherwal Rajput is scarcely known to his brethren in Rajasthan, who will not admit his contaminated blood to mix with theirs. The original country of the Gherwal is in the ancient kingdom of Cassi. Their great ancestor was Khortaj Deva, from whom Jeponda, the seventh in descent, in consequence of some grand sacrificial rites performed at Bindabassi, gave the title of Búndela to his issue. Búndela has now usurped the name of Gherwal."—This is not correct. The Gherwals (Gaharwárs) have allowed no usurpation of their name by the Búndelas, and would consider the assumption very impertinent. The author, who admits the Gherwals into his own list of the thirty-six tribes, does not state what ground he has for considering their blood contaminated.

† Briggs, nevertheless, by some inadvertence, calls him, in his translation, Kúwar Raí.—Dow, more correctly, gives it Kora.

It may be here proper to mention the origin of the name Korah assigned in the this was the designation of a tribe, and that tribe was Gaharwár, converted by a misapprehension of the Musulman historians into Korah or Gorah, which, with an entirely new language, character, and pronunciation, is not at all an unlikely transfiguration. If this supposition is correct, it would afford a very simple explanation of one of the chief historical difficulties of this period, and serve at the same time to confirm a local tradition which is adhered to with surprising pertinacity. It is not to be concealed that there would still be much requiring explanation; amongst other matters, the connection between the Rathores and the Gaharwárs is not easy to be accounted for, because inscriptions of the period show that Srí Chandra Deva, the Rathore, "*conquered* by his own arm the unequalled kingdom of Kanauj;" and it could therefore scarcely have been held by a kindred tribe before him, unless, indeed, he may have reconquered it, as a member of the Gaharwár family, from those who had usurped the dominion after the death of Jaipal, the Gorah, who was slain by the Raja of Kálinjar, in revenge for his too easy submission to the demands of Mahmúd. If this is allowed, and there is nothing to militate against it, it would sufficiently account for the Gaharwárs not fleeing to their new seats till the end of the eleventh century, and there would then be little to demand further explanation.*

Rathore genealogies. "The fourth grandson of Nayn Pal was Umrabhíjai, who married the daughter of the Pramara prince of Koragarh on the Ganges, slew 16,000 Pramaras, and took possession of Korah, whence the Korah Camdhas." Korah, however, is not on the Ganges, and is evidently mistaken for Karra, which has still the remains of a large Rathore fort, known by the name of "Little Kanauj," and haunted by the undying Álá, one of the chief heroes of the popular songs and tales of Upper India.

* To show what difficulty attends the prosecution of this enquiry, it may be as well to add the Gorakhpúr traditions, as given in "Martin's Eastern India" (Vol. II., 458). One is, that the Gaharwárs are descended from the famous Raja Nala, and came to Kasi from Narwar, near Gwalior. Another is, that Baldeo, Raja of Kasi, was expelled from that town by a King of Maghada, and entered into the service of Tripura, King of Kashmír, from whom he contrived to seize the government of that

Gandhílá, گندھیلا गंधीला

A vagrant tribe, a few degrees more respectable than the Baorí, *q.v.*

Gandhú, گنڈھو गंढू

See Jat.

Gangáputr, گنگاپتر गंगापुतत्र

A tribe of inferior Brahmans (literally, sons of the Ganges), found chiefly in Benares, Bithúr, and Sheorájpúr in Cawnpore. In the two latter Parganahs they hold several villages in proprietary right. They declare their descent from Kanaujias, and preserve the same sub-divisions, asserting that they assumed a distinctive name, merely because they receive gifts and assist at ablutions on the banks of the Ganges.

Gardezí, گردیزي गर्देजी

The name of a class of Sayyids in Jaula of Muzaffarnagar. They wish to claim connection with the Barah Sadat (*q.v.*), but they do not really belong to any of the four branches of that stock. The family has been somewhat ennobled of late by a member of it having been raised by adoption to the Masnad of Purneah.* In our own provinces there are few Gardezís, but

country. His descendants enjoyed it for 121 generations, when they were expelled by the Kings of Ram, Turkestan, and Iran, and retired to Kanauj, which they held for fifty more generations till the time of Jai Chand. His third son, Banar, Raja of Kasi, was ancestor of the Gaharwár chiefs." It is not worth while to attempt to disprove this improbable legend.

See also "Bird's Guzerat," p. 34.; and pp. 351–354, 358, 455, and 478 of Col. Sykes' admirable Essay on Ancient India, in the Journal of the R.A.S." No. xii.

* This is incorrect. Sayyid Reza Ali, a Gardezí, came to Puraniya (Purneah) in Eastern Behar, and married the daughter of Momin Ali, zamíndár of Parganahs Badaur and others in that district, and, on Momin Ali's death, succeeded to the estates in right of his wife, and still holds them, or rather did when I was at Purneah last year. There is, however, no title of Raja or Nawab attached to the estates, nor is there any Masnad in any sense, and the estates are twenty miles from Purneah.—B.

in Multan and the Westward there are several. According to the Manba'u-s Sádat, the ancestor of the Gardezís of India is Mír Sayyid Shahábu-d dín, whose tomb is at Manikpúr.

Garg, گرگ गर्ग

See Kanaujiya Brahman.

Gargbansí, گرگ‌بنسي गर्गबंसी

Rajputs of this clan are found in Sagrí and Máhul of Azimgaṛh; and in Amorha, Rattanpúr Bansí, and Rasúlpúr Ghaur, of Gorakhpúr.—See Chanamia.

Gaṭwárá, گتوارا गटवारा

Gaṭwárá, or more correctly Ganthwárá, is the name of a tribe of Játs who hold villages in Gohana (where they are called Aolanía, after their chief town), in Sonípat Bangar, and in the Doáb, on the opposite side of the Jumna. They trace their origin from Ghazní, from which place they were accompanied by the Bhat Búrdia, the Dom Sámp, the Brahman Shawál, the Barber Bajwáin, and the Blacksmith Badia,—all of whose descendants are now living, and engaged in the occupation of their fathers in the villages of the Ganthwárá fraternity.

Háṛá, هاڑا हाड़ा

A branch of the Chauhan Rajputs. There are a few of this distinguished tribe in Rattanpúr Bansí of Gorakhpúr, but they are very rarely met with elsewhere in the North-Western Provinces. The chief of the Hárás is the Raja of Kotah Búndí or Harautí.

Helá, هيلا हेला

See Bhangi.

Hele, هيلي हेले

Is the name given to the tribe of Játs which was in occupation of the country previous to the arrival of the Dhe.—See Ját.

Herí, هيري हेरी

A tribe of Musulman Rajputs chiefly found in Jaspúr, a Parganah of Moradabad. They were introduced for the same purpose as the Barwaík, *q.v.*

Húriyá, هوريا हुरिया

A small clan of Sombansí Rajputs in Athgáṅwan and Mariyáhú, in the Province of Benares.

Ḥalálkhor, حلال خور हलालखोर

See Bhangí.

Ḥalwáí, حلوائي हलवाई

A Confectioner. In the Lower Doáb it has become an appellation of a caste or tribe. In most other places it is applied to the trader only. The caste is sub-divided into Chailha, Bakarra, Dúbe, Kanaujia, Tilbhúnja, etc., etc.

Hardehá, هرديها हरदेहा

Is the name of one of the tribes of Káchhí.—See Káchhí.

Hardwás, هردواس हर्दास

There are a few of this clan of Rajputs in Deogáṅw of Azimgaṛh, and Salempúr Majhaulí of Gorakhpúr.

Harihobans, هَرهوبنس हरिहोबंस

A clan of this name exists in Ballia, a Parganah of Ghazipur. —See Hayobans.

Haratkul, هرتکل हरतकुल

One of the sub-divisions of Gaur Brahmans, *q.v.*

Hayobans, هیوبنس हयोबंस

See Benaudha and Harihobans. The Raja of Haldí in Ghazipur is of this conspicuous clan, which once held large dominions on the banks of the Narbadda ("Journal A. S. Bengal," August, 1837*); and has the credit of having been instrumental in expelling the Cherus from the southern bank of the Ganges. The Hayobans are Sombansí; and Mahesvati, or Maheswar, on the Narbadda, the first capital of the Lunar race, was founded by Sahasra Arjuna of the Hihya (Hayobans) race. A small remnant of them yet exists in Sohagpúr, and they are recorded as Zamíndárs of several villages in Ballia of Ghazipur.

Jádo, جادو जादो

One of the low castes in a village,—the same as Kamín. In some places the term is equivalent to Súdra.

Jádon, جادون जादौ

Classically, Yadu, or Yádava, a tribe of Rajputs of the Chandarbans division, who profess to trace their origin in a direct line from Krishna.

Yadu is the patronymic of all the descendants of Buddha, the ancestor of the Lunar race, of which the most conspicuous are now the Bhattí and the Jareja; but the title of Jádon is now exclusively applied to the tribe which appears never to have strayed far from the limits of the ancient Suraseni, and we consequently find them still in considerable numbers in that neighbourhood. The large tract south of the Chambal, called

* The reference is to J.A.S.B., Vol. VI., Part II., p. 623, where there is a long and interesting article on the Garha Mundala Rajas by Sleeman.—B.

after them Yaduvati, is in the possession of the Gwalior Mahrattas, and the state of Kiraulí on the Chambal is now their chief independent possession.

Some of the tribe, or at least professedly of the tribe, are Zamíndárs in our provinces,—as the proprietors of the Talukas of Awa Mísa in Mathura, Somna in Aligaṛh, and Kotila in Agra. There are many of them also in Fattihabad and Shamsabad of Agra; Mustafabad and Gihror in Mainpúrí; Sahar and Aríng in Mathura; Sohnah in Gúrgaon; and in Koel, Hasangaṛh, Goreyí, Marẹhra, Jalálí, Akbarabad, Sekandra Ṛao, and Khair in Aligaṛh. They are considered spirited farmers. All these have adopted the practice of second marriages, and are now considered of an inferior rank to their brethren in Kiraulí, and in Jewar of Bulandshahr, which was the first spot they occupied on their emigration to the Doáb. The Jádons of Jewar are distinguished by the title of Chaukarzáda; but, by way of reproach, the inferior Jádons are called Bágrí by their neighbours. They are regarded as of servile descent; and they are certainly not admitted generally to intermarriages with the higher Rajputs of the neighbourhood. It is very probable that their increasing wealth and importance will soon soften these prejudices; indeed, some marriages lately made by the family of Awa Mísa have raised its respectability to a high standard, insomuch that the Talukdár now lays claim to a direct descent from Anand Pál, the son of the Kiraulí Raja, Kumár Pál, and asserts that the Baresirí, Jaiswar, and other self-styled Jádons are altogether of an inferior stock.

Jádons are also found in Hoshangabad, whither they emigrated after Akbar's conquests on the Narbadda.

Jáis, جایس जाईस

A tribe of Surjbansí Rajputs resident in the parganahs of Nohjhíl, and Máat in Mathura, in which they were originally much larger proprietors than they are at present.

The Jáis themselves assert that they had thirty-six villages, and not twenty-four, as is mentioned in the article Chaubísa, in compliance with the prevalent opinion. They trace their origin from Ajudhya, like true Súrjbansí Rajputs. Their rank may be judged by their receiving in marriage the daughters of Kachhwáha, Jaiswar, and Bachhul Rajputs.

Jágláín, جاگلاین जागलाइन

A clan of Játs, proprietors of a few villages in Panípat Bangar.

Jákhar, جاکھر जाखर

A subdivision of the Ját tribe, *q.v.*

Ját, جاٹ जाट

This is the Jaut and Jhut of the printed Glossary. There are several clans of this interesting tribe in the North-West Provinces, particularly in Dehli and the Upper Doáb. They are rarer in Rohilkhand, and in the Doáb do not extend below Mainpúrí.

The chief clans of the Dehli Territory are Sangwán, Sheoram, Bágrí, Dahia, Ganthwárá, and Dalál. The Sangwán extend West from Dádrí till they meet the Sheoram. To the West and North-West of them extend the Bágrí. From Bowána to beyond Kharkhauda, are the Dahia, whence that tract is called Dahian. The Ganthwaras surround Gohána, and from Mandhautí to Dadrí are the Dalál. There are many others of less importance, as the Katíra, Lohaín, Rongí, Antal, Sayil, Bora, Jatární, Jákhar, Ahláwat, Kadíain, Sakel, Sataungí, etc., etc.; and on the borders of Hariána we meet with the large tribes of Púnya, Bhangíwal, Godára, Kasua, etc., etc. In the Doáb we have the Salaklaín, Balaín, Ganthwára, Ráthí, Ghanghas or Gangas, Múndian, Gand, Lákri, Nohwal, Thukarel, Thenwan, Khúthel, etc., etc. In Rohilkhand there are the Cháhal, Dhanok, Dhalíwal, Berhwal, Untwal, Bangi, Alúma, Khobra, Dhanoí, Láthar, Dighelya, Machhar, Sangwán, Jatrání, Chhílur, Sekráwat, Harrí, Sheko, Gillu, Dharíwal, Siddhú, Gandhú, and sundry more equally euphonious.

The Játs of the North-Western Provinces are separated into two grand divisions—the Dhe and the Hele of the Doáb, or Pachhade and Deswale of Rohilkhand and Dehli. The former (the Dhe and Pachhade*) are a later swarm from that teeming hive of nations which has been winging its way from the North-West from time immemorial. They are in consequence frequently called Panjábís, and scarcely date their residence beyond a century before the present time, when the troubles of the empire enabled them quietly to extend their usurpations. The Dhes frequently have no Jaga, or family genealogist, as the Heles have, and are accused by the latter of adopting some Muhammedan practices in their marriages, particularly in discarding the Mor, or nuptial coronet, and adopting the Sehra, or veil. They have hitherto, in short, been entirely separate, and never intermarried till very lately, when the Balamgarh Raja consented to an union with the Kaithal family, from which time the connexion has increased, and all differences of habits or origin will perhaps before long be obliterated.

The Játs, who were always considered as one of the thirty-six royal races, are now never admitted to intermarriages with the Rajputs. Colonel Tod † assigns as the reason of this, that their

* The term may be derived either from Pachchhim, "the west," or from Píchhe, "afterwards." The Pachhadas are contemptuously spoken of by their elder brethren, and a common proverb couples them with a black snake and worn-out cattle :

बूढो भैंस पुराणा गाडा
काला सांप और सगा पछादा
कुछ लाभ हुआ तो हुआ न खादर खादा

† On the subject of their descent he is contradictory. He asserts in one part that

immigration was so long subsequent to that of the Solar and Lunar Races, that their alliance has been rejected. But, notwithstanding this repugnance to a complete amalgamation, it is evident that connexions have frequently been formed between Játs and Rajputs, though they may not be dignified with the name of marriages.

We find them, as in the case of the Gújars, frequently attributing their origin to a Rajput. Many of their tribes indeed bear Rajput names, such as Dahima, Kachhwaha, Powar, Johya, Bágrí, Dahia, etc. The Balaíns, Nohwal, and Thukarel say they are descended from Chauhán, the Sarawats and Salaklaíns from Tuar Rajputs, and so forth.*

It is strange that almost all the Játs, as well as the Gujars so descended, concur in the same ridiculous story respecting their connexion with the Rajputs—namely, that a female Ját or Gújar was going along with water pots on her head, and that

they are not of pure blood, yet includes them in his own corrected list of the Chattís Kala. From an inscription at p. 796 of the first volume of the "Annals of Rajasthan," it is evident that, in the fifth century, the Játs intermarried with the Rajputs.

* This is to be observed also of the Rye, or Re, and other tribes of similar descent, who have *húkka pani* in common with Játs and Gújars. Among them we have Birgújar, Kachhwaha, Tuar, Chauhán, Johiyá, Katherya, etc. etc.

Sir J. Malcolm, in his "Essay on the Bhills" (Trans. R.A.S., Vol. I., p. 80), says: "The answer from a chief, skilled in the legends, was the following short fable: . . . . . In former times, when Parasu Ráma (Avatára) declared a war of extirpation upon the Rajputs (in revenge for an offence against his father), numbers of that tribe were obliged to save themselves by denying that they belonged to it, professing to be members of other classes of the community. To punish this evasion, Parasu Ráma insisted that every individual should eat the food of the tribe to which he declared himself to belong. Those Rajputs who did so lost their caste, and were obliged to adhere to the tribes of their adoption, but retained their former name, . . . and this (said the old man) accounts for your finding men who call themselves Rhatores, Solankis, etc., amongst the Bhills, and many other low castes, with whom their ancestors, when in dread of extirpation, associated. Some of these degraded Rajputs are found among the Telis, or oilmen, and the Baláyas, or guides; and even, I am informed, among the Chamárs, or shoemakers, who are deemed the vilest and most unclean of the Hindu community."

she stopped a runaway buffalo by pressing her foot on the rope tied to its neck, and did so without spilling the water. This feat of strength and agility so pleased some Rajput chieftain who was looking on, that he took her to his home, and thus a new family, or Got, sprang from the connexion. Others are fond of arrogating to themselves a still superior lineage, asserting their procreation from the matted hair (Jatá) of Mahadeo; and some will have it that their name is corrupted from the illustrious Yádavas, or Jádos, to which latter opinion Tod and Wilson (Select. from Mahabh. p. 46) both seem to incline.

Almost all the Játs of our Provinces, who do not acknowledge any descent from Rajputs, trace their origin from the far North-West, and some of them, as the Ganthwárás, say that they have heard from their ancestors that Gajni or Gaṛh-Gajni, was their original seat, by which names the town was known to the Hindus, before it became famous under the Muhammedans, as Ghazní or Ghaznín.* Here, without any knowledge of the learned discussions about the identity of the Játs and the ancient Getæ, we find the traditionary legends of these ignorant tribes pointing to the remote Ghazní as their original seat, the very spot we know to have been occupied by the Yuechi, or, as Klaproth (Tabl. Hist. de l' Asie, p. 288) says, more correctly, Yu-ti,† in the first centuries of our era, after the Sakas

* There are also other Gajnis known to the Hindus; one was the ancient name of Cambay (the port of Balabhipúra); the ruins of it are still to be seen about three miles from the modern city. There is another on the estuary of the Maihi. These, however, are quite out of the line of the Ját migration.

† Professor Lassen says that the substitution of Yuti for Yuechi, or Yuetschi, is quite unauthorized, and accuses Klaproth of monomania in his endeavours to trace the identity of the Getæ, Goths, and Játs. Dr. Prichard, who is much of the same opinion, adds, "the supposition that the Játs, or Juts, upon the Indus are the descendants of the Yuetschi does not appear altogether so preposterous; but is supported by no proof, except the very trifling one of a slight resemblance of names."—"Researches into the Physical History of Mankind," Vol. IV., p. 132.—E.

It is much to be regretted that this opinion of one of the highest and soundest were repelled back from the frontiers of India, and left the country between India and Persia open for their occupation. The Ját tribes no doubt emigrated, not all at once, but at different times, and it is probable that those in the North-West are among the latest importations. Elphinstone, in his "History of India" (Vol. I. p. 445), draws a distinction between the Jăts of the Indus and the Játs of Bhartpúr (Sinsinwar); to which it may be sufficient to answer that in the Parganahs where Játs are now, they are recorded as Játs in the Ayín-i-Akbarí. So that the difference of the long and short *a* is a mere fashion of spelling,* and shows no difference of origin, family, or habit. The priority of occupation is perhaps to be conceded to the Játs of Scinde and Rajputana.

The last arrival is the Dhe, and as this tribe had been hitherto excluded from complete union with the older Játs, they may probably be descendants of the Dahæ, whom we know (Strabo, xi.) to have been on the shores of the Caspian, the conterminous neighbours of the Massagetæ (the great,† or as Larcher supposes, the Eastern Játs) in the South-West, and on terms of amity with them during the latter period of their residence in that quarter, and may therefore have advanced with them on their onward progress towards India, after the destruction of the Bactrian empire. This would sufficiently account for their not

authorities should not have had the effect of restraining those speculations about Indo-Scythians, and the like, which some English writers so largely indulge in; mere verbal resemblance is, especially in Indian philology, the most unsafe of all arguments.—B.

* In the N.W.P. they are called Játs; in the Panjáb, Jăts. This is a mere dialectic difference. Panjábi always shortens the long *á* of Hindi: witness काम, P. कम्म, etc. General Cunningham tells me that in Rajputana, where there are found both Hindu and Musulman Játs, the latter are known as Jăts, in distinction to the former; but this remark does not hold good for the Panjáb.—B.

† Massa means "great" in Pehlevi. Vans Kennedy ("Ancient and Hindu Mythology," p. 94) is not disposed to agree with Dr. Jamieson and others, that the Getæ and Massagetæ were originally the same people.

being entirely incorporated with the great Játs. At all events it must be confessed that the resemblance between Dhe and Dahæ or Daæ, gives some colour to the hypothesis. Dahas are also mentioned among the Western tribes in the Pauranic Geography.—(See Vishnu Purana, ed. Wilson, p. 192).

Few of the North-Western Játs have been converted, like those of Sindh, to Muhammedanism, and yet they can scarcely be called pure Hindus, for they have many observances, both domestic and religious, not consonant with Hindu precepts. Second marriages are common, and they are still accused by their neighbours of having a community of wives.*—(Clio. 216.) There is a disposition also to reject the fables of the Puranic Mythology, and to acknowledge the unity of the Godhead. Hence probably one of the chief causes of their becoming such ready and devoted disciples of Nanak Shah (*i.e.* Sikhs).

⁂ Much ingenuity has been wasted in guesses as to the origin of the Játs or Jats. The hypothesis which is gaining ground among *sound* philologists, and which, moreover, rests on universal native tradition, makes them either Rajputs who have lost caste, or the offspring of Rajputs and some lower caste. In some parts of the Panjáb, where they are exceedingly numerous, they say they lost caste by crossing the Indus.† They all say they came *originally* from the N. W. P., though they have some traditionary reminiscences of a sojourn in Persia. I have been obliged to let some of the author's remarks about Getæ, etc., stand, as they are mixed up with valuable matter, but it should be understood that the line of inquiry he adopts is purely tentative, and cannot now be supported.

The Játs of the Panjáb amount to nearly one-half of the entire population of that province, and are found in every part of it; west of the Rávi they are nearly all Musulmáns. Two

* But the accusation is quite unfounded.—B.

† See the remarks about Attok, *s.v.* Gaur Tagá. The Játs crossed the river when the Rajputs refused to do so.—B.

of their most numerous and important septs are the Vahráich and Gondal; the latter, who are numerous about Soháva of Gujrát and in Shahpúr, are massively built, stalwart, and bold, with large beards, which they generally dye blue with indigo. They were not long ago notorious cattle-thieves, nearly as bad as their neighbours the Gújars. The practice of *chádar dálná*, or marriage of a widow with the younger brother of her deceased husband (v. "Karáo," Pt. II.) is prevalent among them, and arises, I fancy, from the fact that women are rather scarce, and have to be bought by the father of the bridegroom, who naturally desires to economise; and if his eldest son dies, utilises the piece of female property he has bought (*mál* is the common term in use) by handing her over to the next son, who marries her by the simple process of throwing his scarf *(chádar)* over her head, whence the name. The Jăts of Gujrát call the low fertile tract of country along the Chenab, where they dwell, Herát, from some traditionary reminiscence of their having once dwelt at Herát; but this can scarcely have been before the arrival of the Aryan race in India. Those who wish to see how much can be made of the Indo-Scythian theory are referred to Gen. Cunningham's Report, Pt. iv., p. 19, where they will not fail to notice that whereas in India at the present day the Dhe is a subdivision of the Ját, in the time of Strabo the Xanthii are a subdivision of the Dahæ, so that if we are to identify Xanthii with Játs, and Dahæ with Dhe, an interchange of names, or inversion of some sort must have taken place.

It would seem that at that undefined date, and in those undetermined regions alluded to by the above-named writer, the various tribes and races enjoyed a multiplicity of names which must have been *tant soit peu* bewildering to themselves and their neighbours; for we are taught that the Játs were once called Abars, which is connected with Abiria in India, generally supposed to be the land of the Abhiri or Ahírs. They also had the name of Sus, and many others. All this may be true, but the application of it to the Játs rests on the single link afforded by the similarity of Xanthii to Játs. On the other hand we have the whole of Sindh peopled with Jăts. Dr. Trumpp says* "The original race in Sindh are the Jăts (जतु or जट्ट) cultivators of the soil, and camel-drivers. It is no argument against this that they are Mahomedans, and looked down on by Hindus. There is no doubt that these Jăts, who appear to be the original race in the country, belong to the real Aryan Stock, which stretches from the mouths of the Indus as far as the valley of Peshawar, and through the whole length of the Indus has retained its own speech, though with some modifications. I have long ago convinced myself, from my journeys from Karachi to Peshawar that the Jăt-folk is not more separated from the rest of the community than can be accounted for by various circumstances." The argument derived from language is strongly in favour of the pure Aryan origin of the Játs. If they were Scythian conquerors, where has their Scythian language gone to, and how comes it that they now speak and have for centuries spoken an Aryan language, a dialect of Hindi? In Peshawar, the Derajat, and across the Sulaymaní range in Kach Gondava this language is known by the name of Hindki, or Jăt's speech (जत की गाली). The theory of the Aryan origin of the Játs, if it is to be overthrown at all, must have stronger arguments directed against it than any that have yet been adduced. Physical type and language are considerations which are not to be set aside by mere verbal resemblance, especially when the words on which reliance is placed come to us mangled beyond recognition by Greeks or Chinese.—B.

Jáṭlí, جاٹلي जाटली

See Gújar, of which tribe they are a sub-division.

* Zeitsch. d. Deutsch. Morg. Gesellsch., xv., p. 690, "Das Sindhi in Vergleich zum Prakrit, *u.s.w.*—B.

Jáṭú, جاٹو जाटू

The name of a Rajput tribe in the neighbourhood of Karnál, and in Hariana, in which tract of country they are considered at one time to have held 1440 villages. They are one of the four divisions of the Tuars,—viz., Jatú, Jaraita, Raghú, Satraura. The Játús are now chiefly Musulman, or Rangar, but there are a few Hindus in Hissar, and in Bidaulí in Muzaffarnagar.

Jáṭuá, جاٹوا जाटुआ

A branch of the Chamár tribe, *q.v.*

The word is also frequently pronounced Jatua.

Jewár, جیوار जेवार

A clan of Rajputs of this name is found in Saugor and Bundelkhand. As they receive in marriage the daughters of Saraswár and Rathore Rajpats, they may be considered to hold a respectable rank.

Jhinjar, جھنجر झिंजर

See Gújar, of which tribe they form a sub-division.

Jhojhá, جھوجھا झोझा

The word literally means the stomach, and is the designation of an inferior class of Musulmans. The Jhojhás, in Parganah Baran of Bulandshahr, represent themselves as converted Rathores, Chauháns, and Tuars; but by others they are considered to be converted slaves of these tribes. In like manner, those of Anúpshahr are said to be slaves of Moghals, converted to Mahomedanism. They are despised by the Baḍgújars and other converted Rajputs of the neighbourhood, with whom they are not suffered to intermarry; from which their servile origin may be fairly presumed. They are scattered over different parts of the Doáb and Rohilkhand, and are reported to be good cultivators. Hence the saying :—

झोझा हाली लाकर घर बैठो चौपड खेल

"employ a Jhojhá as a ploughman, and you may sit at home and play at backgammon."

One of the chief causes of the value attached to their services is, that being Musulmans, they are not restrained by Hindu observances of certain festivals. Thus, while Hindus are waiting for the Dithwan (*q.v.*) before they cut their sugar-cane, the Jhojhás have already begun to press their cane and manufacture their sugar.

Jhonaiyá, جھونیا झोनैया

One of the classes into which the Kurmís are divided.—See Kurmí.

Jhaṭiyáná, جھٹیانا झटियाना

The Jhatiyáná, or Jhutiyáná, is a small clan of Rajputs found in Parganahs Sirdhana, Baghpat, Soron, Shikarpúr, Budhana, and Khúrja in the Upper Doáb.

Jijhoṭiyá, ججھوٹیا जिझोटिया

This is a branch of the Kanaujia Brahmans (*q.v.*), which ranks low in public estimation. Their more correct name is Yajurhota, derived originally, it is said, from their having made burnt-offerings according to the form of the Yajurveda. Their sub-divisions are much of the same character as those of the Kanaujias, but it is needless to enumerate them. Amongst their chief families are reckoned the Chaubes of Rúpraund, the Dubes of Dauria, and the Misrs of Hamírpúr and Karíá.

Jinhar, جنہر जिनहर

Is the name of one of the numerous Gots of Gújars, *q.v.*

Johiyá, جوهيا जोहिया

Johiyás are by some authorities included among the thirty-six royal races of India; by others they are considered a mere ramification of the Yadu Bhattí. In the gathering of the Rajpúts to defend the Mori prince of Chittor, they are styled Lords of Jangaldes, which included Hariána, Bhatner, and Nagor. There are, I believe, no Rajputs of this clan, except a very few in Khairagarh of Allahabad, and those in the Doáb, who form a Chaurásí in the neighbourhood of Allahabad and Chail, and who are all converted to Mahomedanism. Colonel Tod considers the Johiyás to be entirely extinct. The Johiyás, who held 1,100 villages in Jangaldes were completely subdued, and perhaps in part expelled from their ancient abodes, by the Godaras, with the aid of Bíka, the Rathore, the founder of Bíkanír. This occurred at the close of the fifteenth century, but the occupation of the Lower Doáb was perhaps of an earlier date. That there was not a complete expulsion at the period above-mentioned we know, from Johiyás being recorded as late as the time of Akbar, as still holding Zamíndárís in Sirsa. The Johiyá are considered the same as the Jinjúta of Bábar, but the position thus assigned appears too far to the westward.

Jugád gauṛ, جگاد گوڑ जुगाद गौड

See Gaur Brahman.—The name would be more correctly Jugádí.

Júṭiyál, جوٹیال जूटियाल

See Barwáik. The word is also pronounced Jutiyal.

Joshí, جوشي जोषी

An inferior tribe of Brahmans employed in casting nativities and fostering other superstitious practices of the natives. Their name is corrupted from ज्योतिषी, an astrologer, and they are known also by the names of Bhadaria and Dakaut. A very different meaning, however, is conveyed by calling a Brahman a Baṛá Jotishí, which is a title of great consideration, and implies that he is learned in the Jyotish Shastras, without engaging in the actual occupations of Joṣhís. It is with reference to this original meaning that the Joṣhís of Kamaon maintain a high character for respectability.*

Jagá, جگا जगा

The word is more properly Jágá جاگا ; but the common pro-pronunciation is Jagá.—See Bhat.

Jaganbansí, جگنبنسي जगनवंसी

A tribe of Brahmans who hold Zamíndárí possessions in Parganah Kora, Zillah Fattihpúr.—See Gautam.

Jandauliyá, جندوليا जंदौलिया

A small clan of Rajputs in Chíbúmau, Zillah Banda.

Janghárá, جنگھارا जंघारा

A large and somewhat turbulent tribe of Rajputs of the Tuar clan, in the south-east of Rohilkhand, whence they appear to have expelled the Katheryas. They are large proprietors in Usahat, Farídpúr, Mehrahbad, Bísulpúr, Salempúr, Tilhur, Jalalpúr, and Khera Bajhera, and are found as asamís in Khotar, and Bísulpúr. They are sub-divided into the Bhúr and Taraín Jangharás, and these again have their sub-divisions, which it is needless here to detail; but it may be mentioned that the Bhúr rank first, on account of the Turaín clan having adopted the practice of Karao, *q.v.* They profess to have come

* This distinction of meaning is not preserved in the Eastern districts.—B.

to these parts under a leader called Dhappú Dhám, whose name is immortalized in popular poetry for his gallant opposition to some chief of Badaon.

नीचे धरती ऊपर राम
बीच में लडे ढप्पू धाम

"Below is earth, above is Rám,
Between the two fights Dhappú Dhám."

The Janghárás were once a powerful clan in the neighbourhood of Koel, where, though they are now but small proprietors, they once held four separate Chaurásís—that of Mandrak, held by the descendants of Ladhar; of Chandpúrí, held by the descendants of Chand; of Barain, held by the descendants of Megh Raja; of Aglás, held by the descendants of Ajay Raj. One of his descendants, Madhukar, is also famous in local ballads.

मधुकर मधुकर हूं कहूं हूं आयो मधुकर पास
जो मधुकर घर नहिं हैं तो कौन काम अगलास
जहां मधुकर तहां केतकी तहां भवर करें गुंजार
एक मधुकर को कमल देहि खडग दान संभार
पांसै छप्पन दीजिये पीठ न एकौ लगिया
पांसै छप्पन मांगिया धकरा गांव से भगिया

"Madhukar, Madhukar I call, I have come to Madhukar;
If Madhukar be not at home, what good is Aglás?
Where Madhukar is there is the ketaki: there the bee hums.*
Give (but) a blanket to Madhukar, and (you will) receive a sword as a gift.
'Give 556;' not a back was touched;
He asked 556; the Dhakará fled from his village."

These lines are often quoted in allusion to his splendid donation of 556 horses to his Bhat, for which the Dhakara of

* A sort of pun on the name of Madhukar, which means "a bee." The ketaki is a fragrant tree (*Pandanus odoratissima*, Roxb.) much affected by bees.—B.

Goreyí, as he was unable to present the saddles, was compelled for shame to leave his ancestral home, and take up his abode in Kherí Barhan of Jalesar. The whole story exemplifies the power of the bards, as well as the generosity of Madhukar, whose lineal descendant is still Raí of Aglás, and chief of the clan.

These Jangháras intermarry with Púndírs, give their daughters to Chauháns and Badgújars, and receive daughters from Bhals, Jáis, and Gahlots.

Janútúrwá, جنوتوروا जनूतूर्वा

A small clan of Rajputs in Gangapúr, Zillah Benares.

Janwár, جنوار जनवार

There are a few of this tribe of Rajputs in Sihonda and Simauní of Bundelkhand; Rasúlabad and Bithúr of Cawnpore; and Kútiya Gunír of Fattihpúr.

Janwariyá جنوریا जंवरिया

A tribe of Ahírs.—See Ahír.

Jaráitá, جرایتا जराइता

One of the divisions of the Tomar, or Tuar, clan.—See Jatú and Tomar.

Jariyá, جریا जरिया

One of the seven divisions of the Lodh tribe, a widely spread caste, chiefly fishermen, whose numbers amounted to 585,932 in the census of 1865 throughout the provinces.—B.

Jarethá, جریتھا जरेथा

The name of one of the clans of Kachhís.—See Kachhí.

Jasáwar, جساور जसावर

Jasáwar, or Jasáwat, is the name of a tribe of Rajputs in Aríng of Mathura. They are held in no great consideration.

Jatrání, جتراني जतरानी

A tribe of Játs in Rohilkhand and Dehli.—See Ját.

Jawanpúriyá, جونپوريا जवनपूरिया

A sub-division of the Kachhí tribe, *q.v.*, which takes its name from the town of Jaunpúr.

Jaiswár, جيسوار जैसवार

See Jasawur and Juswar in the printed Glossary.

A tribe of inferior Jadonbansí Rajputs in the Parganahs of Alípúr Pattí, Kishní Nabíganj, and Azimnagar in Central Doáb. Jaiswár, or rather Jaeswára, is also the name of a sub-division of Chamárs, Dhanuks, Kalals, Moraos, Kurmis, Telís, Banias, and many other inferior tribes; and implies perhaps that they came originally from Jaís, a large manufacturing town in Oudh. It must have been a place of much greater importance than it is at present, to have given name, like Sankasya, Sringavera, Kanauj, and Sravasti,* to so many

* In the article Chaurasí the position of Sankasya has been indicated. Sringavera is mentioned in the "Rámáyana" as a village which was in the midst of a forest extending on both sides of the Ganges, inhabited by Nishadas, or wild tribes, who assisted in ferrying Rama, Lakshman, and Sita over the river. Sringravera is the modern Singraur, of which the consequence has declined only lately, for it is mentioned as the chief town of a Parganah in the "Ayín-i-Akbarí," and by the Jesuit Tieffenthaler in the middle of last century. It lies on the left bank of the Ganges, about twenty-five miles above Allahabad, and is now included in the Parganah of Nawabganj (V., p. 274). The Singrauria Kachhís and Kurmís derive their name from this town.

distinct families. Kasba Jaís is also mentioned with distinction by the early Mahomedan authors, particularly in the Lataif'i-Ashrafí, or record of the acts and opinions of Ashraf Jahangír. On one occasion when this sainted personage visited Jaís, it is stated (in the fifty-seventh Latífa) that nearly three thousand pupils came out to pay their respects. In the Imperial Register also it is mentioned as the chief town of a large Parganah.

Káchhí, کاچهی काछी

A tribe of industrious cultivators extending throughout the greater part of Hindústan. They are much employed in market and flower gardens. Those of the North-Western Provinces assert that they have, like the Kurmís and Chamárs, seven sub-divisions, which are generally enumerated as the Kanaujia, Hardíha, Singrauria, Jawanpúria, Bamhania or Magahya, Jaretha, and Kachhwaha. These tribes do not eat together or intermarry. The Kanaujia are considered to rank the highest of the seven; the Kachhwaha the lowest. By the Kachhwahas themselves this relative rank is reversed.

The Kanaujia extend from about Kanauj to Benares. The Hardíha are chiefly in Eastern Oudh and Baiswara, the Singrauria in the South-West corner of Oudh, the Jawanpúria in Benaudha, the Bamhania and Jaretha in Behar, and the Kachhwaha are chiefly found to the Westward, as in Birj and Jaypúr.

There are, however, other Káchís besides these, such as the Dhakolia, Sukhsena, and Sachan; in short, like the Kurmís, Káchis seldom coincide in the names of their seven sub-

The Kanaujia familes have been frequently mentioned throughout this work, and of course derive their name and origin from Kanauj.

From Sravasti we appear to have the Sríbastam Káyaths and Naís, and the Sirí Batham Dhobís; if so, they would lead us, like the Suksena Káyaths with respect to Sankasya, to an identification of the old town of Sravasti, for they trace their origin to a place which still bears nearly the same name, about eight miles to the West of Faizabad, near the ancient Ajodhya.

divisions; and it is evident that that definite number does not exist.—See Kachhwara, Koerí, Morao.

Kanaujiyá, كنوجيا कनौजिया

This is the name of a sub-division of several tribes in the North-West, who trace their origin from the ancient city of Kanauj (see Kurmí and Káchí); but, taken by itself, it is more especially applied to a large and influential clan of the Brahmanical order.*

Of Brahmans there are ten well-known sub-divisions, of which five are Gaur, and five Dravira. Of the five Gaur, Kanaujia is one, and may also be considered the most numerous; as it extends from the Siwalik Hills to the Narbadda, and the Bay of Bengal. The sub-divisions of the Kanaujias are five. Kanaujia proper, Sarwaria, Sanadh or Sanaudha, Jijhotia, and Bhúínhár. These Kanaujias again, according to the statement in the "Tambíhu'l-Jáhilín," are sub-divided into sixteen denominations, of which most, as in the other Brahman classes, are derived from the occupations and abilities which each was supposed to possess. The sixteen names are here repeated from the same work:—Garg, Gautam, Sandel, Pande, Díchhat, Patakh, Súkul, Dube, Tewarí, Chaube, Awasthí, Tirbedí, Bhattacharj, Upadhya, Bajpaí, and Misr, of which the first three are said to be far superior to the rest. There seems reason to believe that the author is quite wrong in this classification, and that his error partly arises from his confusing the accounts of the Sarwarias and Kanaujias. The first three are the chief amongst the Sarwarias, but amongst the Kanaujias are either of no importance, or not extant.

* It should be observed that whenever the lower castes begin to talk about their sub-divisions, they always give them the grandest possible names, such as Chauhán, Kanaujia, and so on. This shews how little reliance can be placed on their accounts.—B.

Amongst the Kanaujias the chief families are called the Khatkul, or six houses. There are, however, really six and a-half chief houses, and their names and Gots (Gotra) are as follows :—

1	2	3
Sandel Got.	*Upaman Got.*	*Bharadwaj Got.*
Parsú ka Mísr, etc.	Lakhnau ka Bajpaí, Garhwas ka Dube, Parbhakar ka Awasthí, etc.	Bala ka Sukul, etc.

4	5	6
*Bhuradwaj Got.**	*Katiáyan or Viswamitra Got.*	*Kasyap Got.*
Khor ka Pande, Gargásan ka Pande, etc.	Manjgáṅw ka Misr, Súthian ka Misr, etc.	Jahangírabad ka Tewarí, etc.

6½

Sakrint Got.

Nabhele ka Sukul, Fattíhabadí, etc.

* Professor Wilson, in a note to the "Uttara Rama Charitra," observes that the accounts of Bharadwaja are rather obscure. "In some places he is called the son of Vrihaspati, and in the 'Harivans' is said to have been adopted by Bharata, as King of Pratisthana. In the 'Rámáyana,' Bharadwaja appears as a sage residing at Prayága or Allahabad, where a temple dedicated to him still exists on the high bank of the Ganges. In the 'Mahábhárat' he is described as residing at Haridwar, and the father of Drona, the military preceptor of the Pandava and Kaurava princes. He is also the parent of Arundhati, the wife of Vasishtha." May not this obscurity be cleared up by supposing, as the above genealogy purports, that there are two saints of nearly the same name, Bhàradwaja and Bharadwaja? The Kanaujias certainly acknowledge the distinction, and this kind of evidence being founded on immemorial tradition and usage in respect to intermarriages, is not to be slighted.

In Sanskrit the long *á* indicates descent: as Ságara from Sagara; Bhágirathí from Bhagiratha. In the same way Drona, the son of Bharadwaj, is called Bháradwaj in the "Mahábhárata" (see p. 3 of "Johnson's Selections," "Wilkins' Sanskrit Grammar," p. 494, and Langlois' "Harivansa," pp. 70, 71, 145). But this cannot be the relationship existing between these two persons; because, if they had been father and son, the son could not have established a separate Got, being already of the Got of his father—himself the child of two fathers (see "Vishnu Purana," p. 449). The "Prabar Manjarí" appears to explain the difficulty. Bharadwaj, the father, established no Got, but his son Bháradwaj did—and the Bharadwaj, whose Got we now

The divisions below these are almost endless, and few Kanaujias can ever be got to enumerate them. It may be sufficient to remark that these six and a-half houses, or the Khatkul, are of much greater consequence than the rest, and receive from them daughters in marriage; but do not allow their own daughters to marry, except in one of the Khatkul tribes. The honor of an alliance with these privileged classes is so great, that like the Kulíns of Bengal, some of them have as many as twenty or twenty-five wives.

The equally intricate divisions of the Sarwarias will be noticed in their proper place, but it may be as well to mention here that amongst them are included the Sawalákhí, who are said to have been made Brahmans by Raja Ram Baghel, when he was in a hurry to make a sacrifice, but as he could not perform it without assembling a lakh and a quarter of Brahmans, he collected people from all classes and parts, and invested them with the janeu, or sacred thread. Others say that Manik Chand, the brother of the famous Jay Chand Rathore, others, that one of the Surneyt Rajas, others that the redoubtable Ram Chandar himself was the manufacturer.* However this may be, they rank very low in the scale of Brahmans.

have was the son of Angiras (see also the "Nirnai Sindh," Chap. III., in which the "Prabar Manjari" is quoted).

Again, in Vol. II., p. 12, of the "Hindu Theatre," Professor Wilson says, "It is asserted that thirteen Gotras or families of Brahmans owe their origin to as many divine sages called after their names. Kasyapa (Kasip) is one of their number. The Aswalayana Sutra of the "Rig Veda" contains the enumeration of the Gotras, and their sub-divisions, but in a very involved and unintelligible style. The popular enumeration of them, however, is not uncommon; but it is *nearly, if not wholly*, confined to the South of India, where several of the reputed representatives of these tribes yet exist."

He again says, at p. 3 of his Notes to "Johnson's Extracts from the Mahábhárata," that in the *South* of India Brahmans are still found pretending to be sprung from some of the patriarchal families. Do not these statements require qualification with reference to the Gotras of the Kanaujias given above?

* A precisely similar story is told of the Bhúinhárs, *q.v.*—B.

The Kanaujias are found chiefly in the Central Doáb, where many, particularly in Etawa, are possessed of Zamíndárís. They extend also into Kúnch and the Western portion of British Bundelkhand, and into Baiswara in the Oudh territory.

The Sanaudhas, or Sanadhs, as they are more familiarly called, touch the Kanaujias on the North-West, extending over Central Rohilkhand, and part of the Upper and Central Doáb, from Pilibhít to Gwalior.

The boundary line (which has been delineated on a small map) runs from the North-West angle of Rampúr, through Richa, Jahanabad, Nawabganj, Bareilly, Farrídpúr, to the Ramganga; thence through Salempúr and the borders of Mihrabad; thence down the Ganges to the borders of Kanauj; thence up the Kalínaddí to the Western border of Alipúr Pattí, through Bhoígaon, Soj, Etawa, Bíbamau, and down the Jumna to the junction of the Chambal. Instances of course occur of occupation by either party on the other line, but they are very rare.

On the North-West, the Sanadh are met by the Gaur Brahmans, whose boundary line is also sufficiently definite to admit of description. It runs through the Rampúr territory as far as the Ramganga, thence through Seraulí, Seondara, Neraulí, Bahjoí, Rajpúra, Dubhaí, and the Western borders of Koel, Chandaus, Noh Jhíl, and Kosí.

The whole of the British territory to the Westward of this line is in their occupation. It might have been expected that a great portion of this would have been occupied by Sirsútí Brahmans, but they are not to be found in any numbers, except in a small tract on the borders of Rampúr.

The Jijhotias commence only in the South-West portion of Badausa, and thence extend Southward and Westward.

The Sarwarias, including the Bhúínhárs, touch the Kanaujias on the East, extending from Bahraich in Oudh, through the Parganahs of Kotila, Hatgaon, Ekdalla, U'gasí, Darsenda, and Badausa, to the hills of Bundelkhand.

The name of Sarwaria is an abbreviation of Sarjúparia,* or people living in Sarwar, *i.e.*, the other side of the Sarjú, or Gogra. Sarwar is pretty nearly comprised within the limits of the present district of Gorakhpúr. They say that they offended the great Ram Chandar, because they would not officiate at a sacrifice which he wished to perform without divesting himself of his arms. They refused, as this was contrary to the Shástras. The Sanaudhas, however, were not so scrupulous, and satisfied his desires. He subsequently respected the independence of the Sarwarias, and promised to give them as much land for their residence as the flight of his arrow would cover. The hero drew his bow on the banks of the Sarju, and the arrow, as is devoutly believed, sped as far as the Tarái. Hence that country was assigned to them, and from it they derive their name.

It is strange that a somewhat similar legend is told respecting the location of Brahmans and other colonists in Malabar. The traditions of the Peninsula relate that Parasurama stood on the promontory of Dilli, compelled the ocean to retire, and shot his arrow over the site of Kerala or Malabar, and presented the new territory to the colonists whom he invited from the North, and thus, to the present day, the Brahmans of Malabar and Kanara are most of the five Northern nations. ("Catal. of the Mackenzie Collection").—See Jijhotia, Bhúínhár, and Gaur Brahman.

*** In the census of the N. W. P. in 1865 the Brahmans of the province are thus classified and enumerated :—

Drávir̤ (Tamil)	75	in Fattihpúr
Tailang (Telugu)	231	Benares and Muttra
Maharáshtrí (Marat̤hi).....	3,749	Cawnpore chiefly

* In the Jatimala, given in Price's "Hindí Selections," Kanaujia Brahmans are divided into four clans; namely, Sarwaria, Sarjúparia, Jijhotia, and Sanaudha. But it is surely a mistake to divide the Sarwaria from the Sarjúparia. Perhaps by the former is meant the Kanaujia proper, for of this, the most important sub-division, no mention is made; but the Kanaujias would be very loth to acknowledge such a title.

Kanaujiyá	566,888	Kanauj in Cawnpore	
Sáraswat	14,073	diffused	
Gaur	170,182	do.	
Ojha or Maithil (N. Behar)	8,479	Gorakhpúr and Jaunpúr	
Utkal (Orissa)	43	Mirzapúr	
Málwí	7,380	do.	
Trivedi	2,538	Banda and Etawah	
Gautam	10,895	Muttra and Allahabad	
Jijhotia	22,731	Lallatpúr	
Bharadwaji	34,808	Banda	
Párikh	699	Murádabád	
Sákhaldípí	2,258	Azimgaṛh	
Pushkarná	121	Mirzapúr	
Mathuriyá	1,583	Agra	
Tiwárí	213,565	diffused	More numerous in the Eastern district than in the Western or Central. (Tiwárí to Upadhyá)
Sukul	64,371	do.	
Misr	150,231	do.	
Chaubé	59,993	do.	
Dubé	132,612	do.	
Pandé	167,735	do.	
Upadhyá	75,007	do.	
Sarwariá	102	Allahabad	
Awasthí	5,155	Banda	
Gujaratí	6,427	Benares chiefly	
Sanádh	163,993	diffused	
Bhatt	610	Gorakhpúr and Benares	
Banowa	935	do.	
Kashmírí	719	Agra chiefly	
Bargháiyán	20	Allahabad	
Rikhepúrí	11	Allahabad	
Nágar	1,180	Benares and Farrakhabad	
Belhán	41	Allahabad	
Páṭak	53,532	diffused	
Bajpai	4,925	do.	

Piásí	20	Allahabad
Garrai	961	do. and Banda
Dikshit	51,085	Jhansi chiefly
Dhatúrá	9	Allahabad
Gangáputr	6,161	do. and Farrakhabad
Demái	150	Muradábád
Shorduj	12	do.
Jhwásí	9,894	Muttra
Trephallá	13	Jaunpúr
Kauli	1,082	Mirzapúr
Golápúrb	9,732	Agra
Paháriá	525	do.
Athwariá	59	do.
Katárá	117	do.
Pandá	678	diffused
Aginhotri	933	do.
Tirgunáit	969	Farrakhabad, Etawa, and Jaunpúr
Ráwat	82	do.
Rájauriá	2,810	Etawa
Marwárí	556	Jhánsí
Bhúínhár	52,199	Gorakhpúr, Benares
Naik	1,990	do.
Palná	13	Benares
Gandharb	677	do.
Kaṭak	78	do.
Bhát	78,351	diffused
Tagá	105,035	do.
Badowá	19	Allahabad
Dakauṭ	31,848	diffused
Mahabrahman	7,773	do.
Dosadh Brahman	159	Allahabad.
Total	2,311,887	

It will be seen that this classification is made according to the familiar local designations in use among the people, and takes no notice of their genealogical divisions into Gots. It is, however, all the more useful for that reason, as it shows the English reader what is the real practice among the people.

There is also a column in the returns headed Brahmans (without distinction), which is explained to mean those Brahmans whose special Got was not mentioned by the reporting officer. They number 1,198,216. The total number of Brahmans in these provinces thus amounts to 3,510,103.—See Census of N. W. P., 1865, published by authority, Vol. II., Table III..—B.

Kol, کول कोल

A few of this primitive tribe are found in the province of Benares, particularly in the Southern part, and in Bundelkhand, near the hills. Their occupations are of a most servile kind.

Saktísgaṛh was formerly called after them Kolana, and the Parganah of Kol Asla in Benares still bears their name, and testifies to their former importance, before the Rajput immigrations.

From a consideration of the condition, habits, and position of the Kols of Benares and Behar, they may probably be found to have some connection with the Kolís of Guzerat, and the Kolaris of the South of India. I know not whether their languages have been ever compared; but there is no *primâ facie* improbability that they should be found to resemble each other; for the Moravian Missionaries of Amarkantak declared that they could converse with the Gonds of that neighbourhood in the Kanarese language, the origin of which is entirely distinct from the Sanskrit.* It is to be regretted that the sudden death of these ex-

* It is now an established fact that the languages of the Kols and Gonds form a distinct non-Aryan family closely allied to the languages of the Dravidian family, Telugu, Tamil, and the rest.—B.

cellent men, in the year 1842, prevented their giving public testimony to this interesting fact. If two countries so remote as Karnata and Amarkantak, between which there is no communion or commerce whatever, are found to have essentially the same languages, the Kols, Kolís, and Kolaris, between whom at least there is a resemblance of name, may be found to be similarly connected.

From the "Harivansa," Vol. I., p. 68, one might conclude the Kols to be of Rajput descent.

⁂ The best modern account of the Kols is in an article by Colonel Dalton, published at p. 153 of the "Ethnology of India," of which it forms by far the most valuable portion. ("J. A. S. B.," Vol. XXXV., Pt. ii. for 1866.)

The Kols live in Chota (or properly Chuttia) Nagpúr, the eastern portion of the extensive plateau of Central India, which is connected with the Vindhya range to the west, with an average height of over 2000 feet, and a climate less oppressive than that of the plains. Its area is about 7000 square miles, and its population about a million, more than half of whom are Kols. Col. Dalton asserts that this name was given to them as a term of reproach by the Brahmanical tribes. They fall into two great classes—Mundas and Uráons; of whom the former are traditionally said to have occupied the country first. Connected with the Mundas are the Sonthal, Bhumij, Khorewahs, Kheriahs, and Juangas or Pattuns (leaf-clad). A few of them have turned Hindus, but the mass preserve their old "mad" religion—devil-worship or whatever it be. The Uráons have a tradition that they were once settled in Guzerat, and there are reasons for believing this to be true. They call themselves "Khunkir." Their physical characteristics are different from those of the Mundas. They are very small in stature, but well-proportioned and dark-complexioned. It would be beyond the scope of this work, which is devoted to the N. W. Provinces only, to go into greater details, as the

Kols scarcely touch at all on those provinces. The reader who is interested in the question is referred to the article abovementioned.—B.

Ḳulí (Cooly), قلي कुली

A carrier, a porter. This word is in all probability derived from the Turkish Kulli قلي a slave, though that word is also known in Hindustan as the designation of several influential families who may have been originally slaves, but whose servile origin is now forgotten; or it may have been derived from the Kolis of Western India, as they were found to be frequently engaged in menial occupations.—E.

*** It is an error to say that kulí is the designation of any families in India. Mahomedans often give their sons names which, in respect of the final word, are the same as their own, and thus a semblance of a family name is established. Thus, Ali Razá will name his son Hasan Razá, and his son will be Muhammad Razá, and so on. It is in this way that we find the word kulí employed; as, *e.g.*, Allah Kulí, son of Muhammad Kulí, son of Hasan Kulí, which only means that these gentlemen called themselves respectively slaves of God, of Muhammad, of Hasan, etc. The assumed connection of the word Cooly with the Kols is, I am convinced, quite imaginary. The ignorant munshis of the Lower Provinces, it is true, often spell the word كولي *kúli,* but they confess that they write it merely by ear; it always written قلي in the districts of the Panjáb and Western Provinces.—B.

Kurmí, كرمي कुरमी

A large class of cultivators in the Eastern and Central portion of this presidency, but there are few in Dehli and the Upper Doáb. Under the different names of Kurmí, Kumbhi, Kunabi, or Kúmbhí, they extend throughout the greater part of Hindustan, Berar, and the Dekkan.* They are famous as agriculturists, but frequently engage in other occupations. The Kurmí women, like the Játnís, assist the men in husbandry, and have passed into a proverb for industry,—

भली जात कुंबिन की खुरपी हाथ
खेत निरावे अपने पी के साथ

"A good caste is the Kunbin; with hoe in hand,
They weed the fields together with their husbands."

The Kurmís of these provinces are said to have seven subdivisions, which are usually enumerated as Kharíbínd, Patarya, Ghorcharha, Jaiswar, Kanaujia, Kewat, and Jhúnaiya. These do not eat together or intermarry. The two first are chiefly in the Lower and Central Doáb, Benares, and Oudh. The Ghorcharha far to the Westward, the Jaiswar in Saugor and Bundelkhand, the Kanaujia in the lower parts of Central Doáb, the Kewat to the East of Benares, the Jhúnaiya to the West of the Upper Jumna. There are, however, other divisions which appear to be independent of these, as the Singraur and Chaparya of the Lower Doáb; the Jharí of Nagpore; the Ghameta, Samsawar, Kachisa, and Chandani of Behar; the Saithawar, Putanawar, Atharya, Chunanaun, and Akharwar of Gorakhpúr and Benares; the Rawat, Jadon, Bhartí, Kattiar, and Gangwarí of Rohilkhand. These also have no communion of food or marriage. In short, Kurmís are never agreed as to the seven tribes of which they are composed, and it is evident that they were never confined to that number.

There are several Kurmís, or Kumbis, among the Marattas,

* Those of the Dekkan are divided by Steele (p. 107) into Marathí, Kúnbi Waní, Kanárí Kamatí, Tailang Kamatí, and Hindústaní, amongst whom he includes Lodhí Pardesí and Chapparband. But Lodhís are not Kurmís, nor can we receive them as such on this authority: for it must be confessed that, however excellent the "Summary of Indian Classes" may be with respect to law, the second book, on the subdivisions of Castes, appears not to be executed with that care which the interesting nature of the subject required.

and the Gwalior, as well as the Satara families are of that stock. In our own provinces, we find Kurmís chiefly in the following Parganahs, Rudarpúr, Bísalpúr, Nawabganj, Pilibhít, Negohí, Ajaon, and Shahjehanpúr in Rohilkhand; Nidhpúr, Kanaujia, Bilhaur, Akberpúr, Shamsabad, Sikandra, Bhognípúr, Sheorajpúr, Sarh Salempúr, Dhata, Chaile, Ekdalla, and Ghatampúr in the Doáb; Aurangabadnagar, Sidhoa Jobna, Dhúreapara and Shahjehanpúr in Gorakhpúr; Seondha, Darsenda, Jalálpúr, and Kúnch in Bundelkhand; Khairagaṛh and Bari in Allahabad; Bhagwat, Bhoelí, Agorí Barhar and Singraulí in Mirzapúr; and Nathúpúr, Nizamabad, Sugrí, and Mahomedabad Gohna in Azimgaṛh.

In Oudh also there are several, and the notorious Darsan Singh has ennobled his tribe by the designation of Raja.

Kausik, کوسک कौसिक

A tribe of Sombansí Rajputs; but their name would seem to imply Brahmanical descent or connexion. Considerable numbers of them are in Deogaṅw, Mahul, and Gopalpúr in Azimgaṛh; Dhúriapar in Gorakhpúr; and in Chít Ferozpúr and Sayyidpúr Bhittrí in Ghazipur. In the Áín Akbarí they are recorded as the Zamíndárs of Jaunpúr, Kharíd, and Mariyahú. They pretend to derive their origin from Kusika, whose son, Gadhi, built Gadhipúr, or Kanauj. (See "Harivansa," p. 148, and "Vishnu Purana," p. 405.)

Kachhaurá, کچھورا कछोरा

A small clan of Rajputs, of which there are a few in Gorakhpúr.

Kachhwáha, کچھواها कछवाहा

Properly Kashwaha, being descended from Kasha, the eldest son of Rama. This tribe of Rajputs is now predominant in the territory of Amber, or Jaypúr, from which they expelled the Mínas and Baḍgujars. They also give name to Kachhwahagaṛh, a tract between the Sindh and Pahauj rivers, ceded by Gwalior in January, 1844, for the payment of the new British Contingent. There are a few in Muzaffarnagar, Belah, and Phaphúnd in Etawa; Sahár and Aríng in Muttra; Mahul in Azimgaṛh; Sakatpúr in Farrukhabad; and Anglí in Jaunpúr. They assert that they once held 360 villages in the neighbourhood of Muzaffarnagar. This may have been the case, for amongst those who went to aid the Chauhán Prince Bísal Deo, in his invasion of Guzerat, we find the Kachhwáhas of Anterbed enumerated, and as they are not found in any numbers elsewhere in the Doáb, except in Etawa, those of Muzaffarnagar are perhaps indicated; but they must have been in much greater strength than they are now, whether we consider them as occupants of Muzaffarnagar or Etawa, to have been honoured with any notice in such a gathering of Rajputs. (See Antarbed). The mention of the Kachhwáhas of Antarbed in the middle of the eleventh century is interesting, as showing that those of Amber had not yet risen into notice; and that those of Narwar, who are recorded by Chand as proceeding to the defence of Chittor in the beginning of the ninth century, must have been on the decline.

⁂ The story of the descent of the Kachhwáhas from Kusa, the son of Ráma, is evidently an idle fabrication of later days, concocted with a view to the aggrandizement of the tribe.

The word is, in all probability, a corruption of the Sanskrit Kachhapagháta, or "tortoise-killer," as the race is mentioned by this name in old inscriptions. Kachhapa becomes in Hindu Kachhúá, and *há* is derived from *han*, or killer, the nominative of which in Sanskrit is *há* (*han* and *gháta* are only different forms from the same root). This derivation, which is as nearly certain as any such etymologies can be, shows that this race is very ancient. Their original seat was Kuntipura, or Kutwár. One of their kings, Suraj Sen, is alleged to have founded the city of Gwalior, forty miles South-East of Kutwár, and they became independent under Vajra Dáma, one of whose inscriptions is dated A.D. 977. They retained the sovereignty of Gwalior, together with that of Narwar, till 1129, when Tejkaran, "the bridegroom prince," as he is called, eighty-fourth in descent from Suraj Sen, left his capital of Gwalior, and went to Deora, to marry the king's daughter of that place, and was so charmed with her society that he never returned. His nephew Parimál, a Parihára, supplanted him in Gwalior and Narwar. The Kachhwáhas then migrated to Dundár (or Jaipúr, as it was subsequently called), where they established themselves a new principality (Cunningham, Report, Part IV., pp. 27, 51, etc.)—B.

Kachhwár, کچھوار कछवार

See Kurmí, of which tribe they are a sub-division.

Kasbhará, کسبھرا कसभरा

Is the designation of the class which works in bell-metal; from کانسا kánsa, bell-metal, and بھرنا bharná, to fill. They are also employed in fusing precious metals, and making ornaments which require to be formed in moulds. They comprise one of the sub-divisions of Sonars, or goldsmiths, of which the others are Mathuriá, Mair, Khattrí, Kamethika, Lahauria, Púrbiyá, Kanaujia, Máhaur, Mahamania, Agaria, Birpúria, Chhainiwán, and Mangoria. Of these the Mathuriá ranks the highest. Kasbhará is below them all.

It is not generally known that amongst these tribes there is a secret language which is adopted for the purpose of concealing their fraudulent acquisition of property. Many, even of those deemed most respectable, are accessories to thefts and robberies; for nearly all the precious metals, obtained by the craft and dishonesty of others, fall ultimately into their hands, for the purpose of being melted down and formed into some other shape.

As their slang vocabulary is very difficult to obtain, and its existence even is commonly denied by the parties who use it, a few words are subjoined in a note,* but it is of much

* SLANG VOCABULARY OF INDIAN METALLURGISTS.

Damisahu,	Speak.
Neet,he hohu,	Be quiet.
Mat,h,	A house.
T,hag,hatu,	Sit down.
**Cheeta lawahu,*	Fix a little wax at the bottom of the scale.
**Chimaree jin lawahu,*	Do not make crooked the pin of the balance.
Lao karau,	See.
Pat,hau,	Beat.
**Sagawahu,*	Return it.
**Jhas karahu,*	To do a thing so that some benefit may accrue from it.
**Poot,h toongeo,*	Weigh it correctly.
**Bag,hat toongeo,*	Weigh it so as it may be less.
**Bearas toongeo,*	Weigh it so as it may be more.
**Kit kira jin karahu,*	Do not change the weight.
Boolaee,	An *Ushurfee.*
Gandhanu,	Gold.
Kooloo,	Brass.
Bhasooa,	*Justa.*
Kyanu,	*Ranga.*
Gariyara,	Lead.
Karasooa,	Iron.
Parikaha,	A Rupee.

Bajna,	A Rupee.
Talee,	Eight Annas.
Badilla,	Four Annas.
Cheeta,	Two Pice.
Sariya,	One Pice.
Poochhariha,	Half a Pice.
Sowhan,	Quarter Pice.
Soobaree,	A Dumree.
Hoorookee,	A Cowrie.
Tora,	One Tolah.
Mala,	One Masha.
G,hooree,	A *G,hoonchee.*
Indra,	Camphire.
Bhoos,	Mouth.
Nadik,	Belly.
Sat,ha,	Cloth.
Gowna,	Legs.
Hut,hna,	Hands.
Lanjhee,	Fish.
Tiratiya,	Meat.
Soong,hnee,	Nose; also the nose jewel.
Manu,	One.
Sownan,	Two.
Ekwaee,	Three.
Ahirin,	Four.
Palo,	Five.
Poochhuree,	Six.
Pynt,	Seven.
Karha,	Eight.

* **These expressions are used by them when weighing stolen property brought them by thieves, and enable them to rob the robbers successfully.—B.**

larger extent than this limited extract might lead one to suppose.

Korag,	Nine.	*Nat,h,*	A Village.
Agoor,	Ten.	*Soong,hna,*	A Dog.
Soot,	Twenty.	*Najoora,*	A large Well.
Bheedu,	An Hundred.	*Najoharee,*	A small Well.
Tik,hariha,	{ *Sah* (a respectable person).	*K,hajoora,*	Wheat.
		Sekooree,	Paddy.
Kotu,	A thief.	*Larihaddra,*	Arhur.
Hariyara,	One *Beera* of Pân.	*Phalehra,*	Gram.
Bhasuka,	} Tobacco.	*Bhasee,*	Mud or Earth.
Phanphee,		*Raresika,*	Salt.
Lodhikaru,	*Goor.*	*K,hoosan,*	A Brahman.
Karsoodhee,	A Sword.	*Liharu,*	A Rajpût.
Karsingee,	A Buffalo.	*Makar,*	A Villager.
Bakrasu,	Milk, and Buttermilk.	*Kong,*	A Musulman.
Sondkaha,	Ghee.	*Selu,*	A Buniya.
Nanwikaha,	Oil.	*Phitkara,*	A Washerman.
Tapooce,	Bread.	*Maska,*	A *Kayeth.*
Nik,harahu,	Eat.	*Chooskar,*	A *Kulwar.*
Loree,	Fire.	*Tachar,*	A *Lodh.*
Laree,	Wood.	*Lariteona,*	A Carpenter.
Bersiya,	Meat.	*Memanaha,*	A Shepherd.
Memna,	A Goat.	*Baraph,*	A Brahman.
Bakahoonwa,	Bullocks.	*Jholahra,*	A *Bhoonjwa.*
Gowk,ha,	Paper.	*Piskaru,*	A *Bhat.*
Kiaree,	A Bed.	*Rhabaja,*	A Weaver.
Loree jin ootareo,	{ Do not put it in the fire.	*Pariparu,*	A Barber.
		Sabhar,	An Assembly.
Loorhow,	Sleep.	*Oolgar,*	Disgrace.
Biarho,	Sing.	*Teonee,*	Hire.
Najooa,	Water.	*Toogna,*	Scales (for weighing).
Hariyan,	A *Tumbolee.*	*Rasoora,*	A Horse.
Lodhikaha,	A *Hulwaee.*	*Dobhikaru,*	A Tailor.
G,hoorkan,	A *Pasee.*	*Dhatoorahu,*	Go.
Kajaree ka teona,	A Singer.	*T,hawana,*	An old man.
Karasoobar,	A Blacksmith.	*T,hyat,ha,*	Father.
Niknarchhata,	A *Baree* (a link boy).	*T,hent,hee,*	Mother.
Totwokar,	A Leper.	*Badhooka,*	Brother.
Lajihanu,	A brass pot.	*Choonwa,*	Son.
Masbeta,	A *Koomhar* (Potter).	*Kootee,*	Wife.

Tomar, تومر तोमर*

This ancient royal race of Rajputs is now but scantily represented in these provinces. There are about 3,000 of them in Agra, and a mere handful in each of the districts of Banda, Jhansi, and Farrukhabad.

We first hear of them in anything like authentic history in A.D. 736, when Bilan De, or Deo, also called Anang Pál, the Tomar, rebuilt Dehli, and established there his capital. He was succeeded by eighteen sovereigns of his race, who sat on the throne successively till 1153, when Visala Deva, better known by the popular corruption of his name into Bisal Deo, the Chauhán, conquered Dehli. Anang Pál II., however, the then king, appears to have been retained in power as a subordinate to the conquering Chauhán, who proceeded to subdue the rest of Northern India. Bisal Deo's son, or grandson, Samesar, married Anang Pál's daughter, and from this union sprang the chivalrous Príthí Raja, the hero of Chand Bardai's celebrated epic poem, who sat on the throne of Dehli till con-

Kansee,	Bad.	*Byjanat hai*	He knows the language of the Goldsmiths.
Katamb,	Labourers.		
Sedhahu,	To dress.	*Tarooa,*	A Goldsmith's bag.
Kasaree,	(*Dhar*) Large Ear-rings.	*Tachu,*	Belonging to the legs (such as shoes, etc.)
Gark,ha,	Silver Necklace (*Huslee*).	*Oochhmioa,*	An Elephant.
		Beroee,	A Woman.
Hat,hna,	Bangles and arm ornaments.	*Lowkarat hai,*	He is seeing.
		Ak,hilat hai,	He is joking.
Gawanee,	Feet ornaments.	*Kodee,*	Theft.

These words are not given by the author in the original character, and are apparently written according to the Gilchrist system. I have not ventured to alter the spelling, except in a few instances where the words are such as I have heard used. A few of the words in the above list are merely reversed from Hindi; as *náth*, a village, which is simply *thán* said backwards; *gaukha* paper for *gazkha*, from *kághaz*, etc.; but the principal part of them are pure inventions. Many Indian tribes use such vocabularies, as the Naṭs, the Ramúsis, and others.—B,

* Also often written तूमर and तुअर.

quered by the Musulman invader, Shahábu'ddín, when the dynasty came to an end.

The Tomars make no mark in history after this till the reign of Aláu'ddín Khilji, or shortly after the death of that sovereign,* when Bir Singh Deo, an obscure Tomar, became possessed of Gwalior, which had been previously held successively by the Kachhwáhas, the Parihárs, and the Muhammadans.

After him a long line of illustrious princes ruled, subject more or less to Musulman influence, among whom Dungar Singh (1425-1454) is noteworthy, inasmuch as in his reign the celebrated rock-sculptures of Gwalior were executed. They appear to have been sometimes at feud with, and sometimes faithful allies of the Musulman rulers of Dehli. The princes of the house of Lodi, Bahlol, Sikandar, and Ibrahím, attacked and defeated them, or were defeated by them several times in those troublous and unsettled ages. The strong fortress of Gwalior, however, more often defied the Mughal forces. Raja Mán Singh (1486-1576) was a prince of great power and ability, and in his reign the power of the Tomars was at its height. He was a wise ruler, a patron of the arts, and himself a skilful musician, and a beneficent administrator. Under his successor, Bikramajit (Vikramaditya) the fortress of Gwalior succumbed to the Musulmans under Azim Humayun, and the Raja was captured and sent to Agra, where, though treated with honour, he sank into an ordinary Jagírdar (A.D. 1518). Vikramaditya fell at the battle of Panipat, fighting by the side of Ibrahím Lodi, his suzerain, in 1576. His troops held the fort of Agra, but yielded to Bábar, to whom they presented some valuable jewels, including a famous diamond, once the

* The date, according to General Cunningham, is 1357, which, as Alá died in 1316, would be after his death There is still some uncertainty as to the actual date, as all the chroniclers, according to the above-mentioned authority, agree in placing Bir Singh's rise in the reign of Alá.—B.

property of Aláu'ddín, which is supposed to be the same as the since famous Koh-i-núr. From this time forth, though the Tomar chiefs are still regarded by the people as the Rajas of Gwalior, they appear to have sunk into mere Zamíndárs, and finally emigrated to Udaypúr, where their descendants are still living.

From the ease with which these Rajput families rose into power, and sank again into insignificance, often without any sensible diminution of their numbers, it will be seen that many of the proud family names of the caste, such as Chauhán, Chandel, Tomar, Solankhi, and others, do not indicate for the bearers of them any real distinctiveness from the other septs or tribes of Rajputs, but that so far from being separate castes they are merely families, who probably all had a common Kshatriya origin, though legends of all degrees of extravagance were invented for them when in power, by adulatory bards, with the view of proving that in their veins ran some special "sangre azul," not possessed by their caste-fellows. (See Dahal in Part IV).—B.*

* The whole of this account, with some trifling exceptions, is compiled from various parts of General Cunningham's Report on the Archæological Survey of India.—B.

APPENDIX A.

NUMERICAL STRENGTH AND DISTRIBUTION OF THE CASTES OF THE HINDUS IN THE NORTH-WESTERN PROVINCES, AS SHOWN BY THE CENSUS OF 1865.

[*By the Editor.*]

TWICE since the original publication of this work, a census of the North-Western Provinces has been taken, in 1853 and again in 1865. The latter census has been carried out on a very comprehensive system, and a special section is devoted to the various castes.

As Sir H. Elliot did not continue his work beyond the letter K,* many castes were necessarily omitted whose names began with letters from M to Z. It is not in my power to complete the work for the reasons mentioned in the preface; but as the census papers include every district in these provinces and every caste in each district, I hope by giving an analysis of them to supply much of the deficiency, as well as to bring the work down to the present time.

It will be observed that the classification of the different castes adopted in the census differs very much from Sir H. Elliot's. In the first place, Manu's old fourfold division of the people into Brahmans, Kshatriyas, Vaisyas, and Sudras

* It was really only done as far as J, but under an improved system of spelling, the words which he put under C now come under K.

has been introduced. This is a most inopportune piece of pedantry or ignorance, I know not which, and has had the effect of very much diminishing the value of an otherwise admirable report.

As regards the Brahmans, they are still as they have ever been, Brahmans, and very little harm results from the use of Manu's division in their case. As to Kshatriyas, the Rajputs claim, and with justice apparently, this title, but no other class has any shadow of a claim. The Játs and Gujars, indeed, were probably of Rajput origin, but not of pure blood, and so could not rank as Kshatriyas. The Vaisyas, I have always been told by well-informed natives, are extinct, with the exception of a small body of Bais Baniahs in Oudh, whose claim, however, is doubted by some. Sudras, as such, no longer exist by name in Northern India. The so-called Sudras of Madras owe their name to their Brahman converters, who place their Dravidian converts in the lowest rank of their social system, as it then stood.

The attempt made by the early Indian lawgivers to divide society into classes, which should hold no communication with each other, was one which broke down at a very early period. Even in India "love will still be lord of all," and intercourse between men and women of different castes very soon occurred, to puzzle and disgust the sages who were (or would be) superior to human passions. They adopted the plan of placing the issue of such intercourse below the four original castes, and thus in time a great number of so-called mixed or impure castes arose, mention of whom occurs even in Manu himself. The result of this, at first sight, cruel arrangement, has been highly beneficial. It is like the process in nature by which granite rocks are disintegrated by the slow and constant action of the elements till they form fertile soil. It was all very well for priest and sages to say that the offspring of a man and woman of different castes was impure, and to rank him below the Sudra, but, in practice, a man who had a Brahman or a Rajput for his father was not likely to be ashamed of it, or to be looked down upon by his fellow men. Hence it came to pass that no man was ashamed of his caste. The Sudra, starting from a position of degradation, found himself above the sons of Rajputs and Vaisyas, and the mixed classes were proud of their connection, left-handed though it were, with the highest castes. Thus one of the great evils of caste, the elaborate system of social degradation prepared for the lower ranks, became impossible, and the barriers between caste and caste once overstepped, that mixture and fusion of the people began which has gone on to our own day, and promises to continue till there shall, in some happy and perhaps not far distant future, be no remnant of caste left.*

In the present time, then, there are no Sudras and no Vaisyas; no Kshatriyas except the Rajput. Only the Brahman is recognizable. The lower castes fused more readily than the higher, and the Sudras probably were soon absorbed in the mixed classes, and ceased to have any distinct existence *as Sudras.*†

* A laconic modern proverb in North Behar says, "Jât bhât," that is, "caste is rice," *i.e.*, merely an affair of eating or not eating with others. This proverb is, I take it, one of the hopeful signs presaging, like the Brahma Samáj, a new and better order of things in India.

† I do not pretend to have said anything new in the above remarks, but it was necessary to say so much to prove my argument against the revival of the old fourfold division. Moreover, I by no means wish to be understood as believing that the Brahmanical theory was ever an established fact. Modern researches are upsetting so much of what the Sanskrit writers tell us, that one would not be surprised to find that the Sudra, as a caste, never existed at all, save in the minds of recluses and Paṇdits. May not the Cheru and Bhar and others be the Sudras after all? Non-Aryans, too powerful to be at once cast out and subdued, and therefore consigned to an infinite depth of social ignominy, *if they should ever catch them*, by scolding Brahmans. But did they ever catch them? My argument above is founded upon the old received belief that the four original classes did really exist, simply because all I want to prove is, that even if they ever did exist, they do so no longer, and that it is impolitic and pedantic to resuscitate the memory of them. If they did not exist, it is still worse to introduce them, and so to revive a pestilent Brahmanical dream, which for many centuries has wrought untold evils on Indian society.

This being the case, why at the present day revive in an official publication an obsolete system, which while it existed was baneful, and which has long ceased to have any practical meaning? The only result of so doing is that the compilers have had to ignore the existence of the mixed classes altogether, and to place among Sudras those who on their own system would rank below them. In the following analysis I shall as far as possible ignore this Sudra and Vaisya system altogether.

A second point which it is necessary to notice, is the nomenclature of the divisions of the different castes. Sir H. Elliot, in publishing the results of his own enquiries, was able to group the clans of Rajputs and others without reference to local names, but in the census each collector of a district sends in his own return, and being as a rule very busy, and probably rather indifferent, besides knowing little of any district save his own, he enters or allows to be entered in his return, all sorts of local names, without reference to the real or universal name of the family. This makes the analysis difficult to execute, and still more difficult to reconcile with the text. Explanatory notes will, however, be added, with a view to simplify the matter as far as possible. In defence of the district officers it may be said that as a rule local names for the divisions of castes are very prevalent, and in many instances, among the lower orders especially, supersede the real names, so that though Sir H. Elliot, with the means at his disposal, could comprise the whole province in one view, and place the various tribes and clans in their proper connection, a district official would find it very difficult to do this.

I must also notice that there is considerable want of uniformity in these returns. In some districts the census is divided according to Parganahs, in others only one figure for the whole district is given; the divisions of castes also differ very much.

I mention all this to account for any irregularities that may be apparent in the following analysis, to which I now proceed.

1. Brahmans. A full list of these will be found under the head of Kanaujia.

2. Rajput. The name Rajput only occurs once in the general tables of the census, though in the district returns it is of frequent occurrence, in many varieties of erroneous application.

Under the general head Kshatriya, 175 different clans are given. This arises from the fact that the table is compiled from all the district returns, and the same clan is known by one name in one district, and by a different one in another. Moreover, in one district the generic name will be given, in another the specific, but in the table they appear as two different classes. Thus one column gives us Súrajbansi, another Jais, though the latter are only a sub-clan of the Súrajbansis, known locally by this name in Muttra. To give in detail the whole 175 columns of the table would merely be to weary and puzzle the reader. I will therefore take this caste geographically, noting its divisions as they occur in each district. For a regular genealogical classification, the reader should refer to Tod's Rájasthán, which gives the best, though not a perfect summary of the ramifications of this royal race.

I. I begin with the Mírat division, which comprises the districts between the Ganges and Jumna, as far down as Aligaṛh, also the submontane dún or valley, of Dehra, in the Himalayas.

In Dehra dún there are—

Chandarbansís	29,324
Chauháns	67
Khattrí	281
Total	29,672

No attempt is made to give the various clans of the great Chandarbans or Lunar race.

In Sahâranpúr, the next district going southwards, we have—

Rajput	230,108
Khattrí	2,849
Chauhán	6,439
Total	239,396

Here the Rajput is treated as distinct from the Chauhán!

Muzaffarnagar, the next district, has—

Khattrí	767
Shuniál (a local term)	18,114
Chauhán	2,245
Súrajbansí	2,819
Chandarbansí	2,233
Total	26,178

Shuniál, also written Shumál, occurs in no other district.

Mírat gives only Rajput 60,887

A note tells us that these Rajputs are principally Nirbhán, Gahlot, Tuar and Chauhán, but gives no details; oddly enough it adds, "there are no Súrajbansís, Rajbansís, etc."

Bulandshahr, south of Mírat, has—

Rajput	79,099
Khattrí	2,942
Total	82,041

with no specification of details.

Aligaṛh, south of Bulandshahr, gives—

Ṭhákur or Rajput*	69,691
Khattrí	588
Total	70,279

II. The division of Kamáon in the Himalayas contains the districts of Kamáon and Gaṛhwal.

* All Rajputs all over India prefer to call themselves Ṭhákur, or lord.

Kamáon has	204,285
Gaṛhwál	30,963
Total	235,248

No details are given.

III. Rohilkhand is the province to the East of the Ganges, bounded on the North by the Himalayas, on the West and South by the Ganges, and on the East by Oudh.

Bijnor occupies the North-Western angle of this division.

Rajput	2,433
Chauhán	71,685
Khattrí	921
Total	25,039

The Chauháns of this district are stated to be "a collection of the lower branches of almost all the Kshatriya tribes," and not the same as the royal Chauháns of Nimrána, Mainpúrí, etc. This is very likely true, as natives are fond of dubbing themselves by grand names, to which they could not establish a right.

This Bijnor return is very carefully executed, and gives many useful explanations.

Moradabad lies to the east of Bijnor, and gives a list of twenty Rajput clans, amounting to 33,632, and including among others

Baḍgujar	10,406
Kathairia	13,108

The other clans are—Pasnín 29, Janwár 106, Chandela 18, Powar 1,686, Sengar 29, Chauhán 495, Dikhat 55, Gaur 465, Gautam 1,284, Raghwar 28, Gahlot 16, Tumar 10, Parihar 11, Mehror (Maḍawar) 13, Gadhwár 10, Bais 125, Bhadauriá 25, Súrajbansí 203, Kachhwáha 17, Jadobansí 741, Rathaur 8, Báchhal 5, Dor 1,005, Pariwál 10, Kirár 1,371, and Khattrí 2,448.

Badáon, to the south and east of Moradabad, gives us briefly

Thákur	72,073
Khattrí	287
Total	72,360

Bareli (Bareilly), the chief district of the division, lies north of Badáon, and exhibits

Thákur	42,320
Khattrí	2,300
Total	44,620

Shahjahánpúr, the most eastern district of Rohilkhand, has also

Thákur	69,588
Khattrí	1,384
Total	70,972

In the Rohilkhand tarai, or district under the Hills, are

Rájbansí	3,365

III.—The Agra division includes the districts of the Central Doáb, and a considerable tract of country west of the Jumna, extending southwards to the Chambal.

Muttra (Mathurá), partly on the west of the Jumna and partly in the Doáb, is the most northerly district.

Rajput (unspecified)	40,439
Khattrí	1,918
Chauhán	1,651
Jadon	23,433
Jais	7,306
Gauruah	22,460
Gahlot	9,894
Total	107,101

Agra, south of Muttra, and on both sides of the Jumna

(though chiefly west of it), contains forty-two clans of Rajputs. besides Thákurs lumped together *en masse*. The classification is avowedly imperfect, and not the same for the different Tahsils. It gives a total of 187,065, including about 23,000 Súrajbans, among whom are Sikarwar, Chauhán, Tuar, and Powar; also a curious item, "Rajputs 11,205," as though the others were not Rajputs. This comes of the fourfold division.

On the eastern side of the Doáb is Farrakhabad, with a total of 70,650 Rajputs in twenty-three classes, most of whom bear local names—but Chauhán 551, Bhadauria 138, Rahtor 31, Tuar 58, and Kachhwáha 72, occur among others.

Mainpúrí (Mynpoory) is in the centre of the Doáb, next to Farrakhabad, and gives

Thákur	49,458
Kirár	6,527
Total	55,985

The meagreness of detail in this district is disappointing, because there are here several important seats of the Chauhán and other principal Gots.

Etawa, south of Mainpúrí, and on both sides of the Jumna, gives more detail. The Rajput is there divided into

Súrajbansí—	
Gahelwar Gahlot	1,012
Gaur	2,766
Rahtor	314
Raghbansí	571
Kachhwáha	5,692
Chandarbansí—	
Chandel	145
Sonbansí	78
Jadon	111

Agnibansí—	
Parihár	3,743
Powar	16*
Chauhán	15,300
Byás	651
Baghel	98
Sengar	6,368
Miscellaneous—	
Thákurs	15,898
Total	52,763

Without expressing any opinion as to the correctness of this classification, it is clear that we have here a more intelligent grouping than elsewhere. We do not find Rajputs treated as separate from Chauháns, and such like eccentricities.

Etah is a small district north of Mainpúrí, and gives

Thákur	53,132
Khattrí	127
Total	53,259

IV. The Allahabad division† includes the Lower Doáb, and some large tracts south and west of the Jumna, bordering on the independent states of Bundelkhand.

Kánhpúr (Cawnpore) is entirely in the Doáb, which here narrows considerably. The return is very elaborate. It exhibits fifty-seven descriptions of Kshatriyas, but many of the names are purely local, as "Cawnpoorea;" others are apparently imaginary, as the Nekhats and Jerkas, of whom there are only 8 each, and who occur nowhere else. We also find "Chandarbansis" 6 only, though there are several thousands of sub-

* Only in Parganah Phappúnd.

† I have omitted the Jhansi division, as it is, strictly speaking, only a sort of outrider to the N.W.P., and is not under the general regulations.

sidiary gots of the Lunar race enumerated. The total number of Rajputs is 130,347.

Fattihpúr, the next district going down the Doáb, gives—

Súrajbansí	9,125
Chandarbansí	14,434
Dikhit	7,303
Gautam	13,538
Bais	8,302
Sirkí (only in Haswa Parg.)	11
Gaur	1,727
Khetri	491
Total	54,931

Banda lies west of the Jumná, and south of Fattihpúr, and has twenty-nine clans of Kshatriyas, including "Rajput or Chattrí" 9,389, different from whom apparently in the writer's mind are Bais, Baghel, and others. The total is 64,635, and the list includes—

Baghel	1,123
Bais	15,480
Kachhwáha	756
Dikhit	9,429
Gautam	3,140
Chandel	583
Gaur	4,333
Powar	2,712

with other minor and doubtful clans.

Allahabad, the chief place of the division, and capital of the North-West Provinces, is the principal town of a district lying at the apex of the Doáb, and on both sides of the Ganges and Jumna, both above and below their junction. The same absurd system of nomenclature exists; we have Rajputs side by side with Súrajbansí, Chandarbansí, Powar, Chauhán, etc., all distinct, besides three persons called Mungaráhas, who exist nowhere else. The total is 57,647. It is not surprising to find mention of castes which we hear of nowhere else, at such places as Allahabad, Benares, Muttra, and even Cawnpore,—because, these being places of great sanctity, many devout Hindus, from all parts of India, go there on pilgrimage, and many, when they feel themselves getting old, leave their homes and take up their abode permanently in Muttra or Benares, in order to secure the spiritual advantages which they believe will result from dying in those sacred spots. As some of these men come from the Mahratta country, others from the South of India and such-like distant places, they do not belong to any of the clans known in the N. W. P., and hence we get isolated names represented by two or three individuals only.

Hamírpúr, which lies above Banda, west of the Jumna, has 44,202 Rajputs, in twelve classes:—Súrajbansí, Raghubansí, Chandarbansí, Bais, Baghel, Parihár, Powar, Chauhán, Sikh Rajput, Solanki, Gaur, and Khattrí.

V. Gorakhpúr is an extensive district lying between Oudh on the west and the Gandak on the east, the Himalayas on the north, and Gogra and Behar to the south. It contains 123,328 Rajputs in twenty-nine classes, but badly arranged. Chandarbansís are put down as "nil," though several Lunar Gots are given immediately afterwards.

VI. Benares gives its name to a division occupying the south-eastern part of the North-West Provinces, having Oudh and Gorakhpúr on the north, Behar on the east, and the independent states of Bundelkhand on the south.

Azimgarh, the most northern of the districts of this division, exhibits sixty-six classes of Kshatriyas, many of whom contain only a few families, and seem peculiar to this district, such are—

Bhrigubans	24
Bargaiyan	451

Sangjál	236
Sawahya................................	30
Láhút................................	35
Pachotaría	8

These most probably are really offshoots from some more celebrated clans. The total of Rajputs in this district is given at 171,480, but we must deduct from this 46,642 Bhúínhárs, who are not Rajputs at all, leaving 124,838 as the real total.

Jaunpúr is a small district west of Azimgaṛh, and shews fifty-seven Gots of Rajputs, one of which, called Turkmán, consists of two persons! another, the Khajái, of three! The most numerous are—

Bais................................	35,536
Raghubansí	30,493
Bachgotí................................	23,988
Nauwak	22,806
Chaupatkhamb (not in Elliot)	15,158

Total of all clans, 223,938, which is a very large amount for so small a district.

Mirzapúr lies south of the Ganges, and extends a long way into the independent states, and embraces much wild country along the Kaimúr range.

Twenty-four clans occur here. The Giharwár number 26,892, the Gautam 18,178; the total, deducting 4,241 Bhúínhárs, amounts only to 95,383, which is a small number for the size of the district, and considering its proximity to Rewa and Bundelkhand, with their large Rajput populations.

Benares is a small district on both sides of the Ganges round the sacred city. Twenty-seven clans amount to 54,445. The most numerous is the Raghubansí, 43,131, the least so the Bhanwag, which consists of *one* solitary specimen!

Ghazipur lies along the north bank of the Ganges as far as its junction with the Gogra (Deohá or Sarja) river, and contains 206,262 Rajputs.

Ajmer, a province in the centre of Rajputana, has 17,539 Rajputs.

I could have wished to exhibit a perfectly homogeneous table of this important caste, showing the ramifications of its numerous Gots, but the irregular, heterogeneous, and unsettled nature of the returns, and the want of any uniform system of nomenclature, has rendered this impossible. I can therefore only add that the grand total of Rajputs for the province is as follows:—

Mírat division	507,686
Rohilkhand do.	249,528
Agra do.	526,853
Kamáon do.	235,248
Allahabad do.	351,762
Benares do.	804,871
Gorakhpúr	123,328
Ajmer	17,539
Total Rajputs in N. W. Prov.	2,816,815

In other words, a little short of three millions—or very nearly one-tenth of the whole population. The Dehli division is not included in this enumeration, as it has since 1857 formed part of the Lieutenant-Governorship of the Panjáb. The same remark holds good for the three districts of Hissar, Sirsa, and Rohtak, composing the division of Hissar. The population of these two divisions at the last Panjáb census amounted to 2,265,770, and the Rajputs probably numbered two hundred thousand out of the whole.

3. Bhúínhár.—This caste, which I have explained to be in reality bastard Brahmans, is sometimes classed with them and sometimes separate. In the N. W. P. they are found in the eastern districts only.

Gorakhpúr	30,739
Benares	21,460

Azimgarh	47,926
Jaunpúr	3,333
Mirzápúr	4,241
Total	107,699

4. Játs.—This important and wide-spread caste, which is in the census absurdly enough classed among Sudras, is stated to amount to only 682,712. This, I cannot but think, must be a mistake. There are many sub-divisions of Játs, and some of them may have been treated as independent tribes. The census returns, however, support Elliot's assertion that their region is chiefly the Upper Doáb, and it must be remembered that when he wrote, the Dehli division formed part of the N. W. P.

The districts in which Játs are most numerous are

Mírat	118,216
Muttra	120,494
Alígaṛh	76,689
Muzaffarnagar	75,694
Agra	66,538

They are extremely numerous under the name of Jăt in the Panjáb, where General Cunningham estimates them at four-tenths of the population, or about five millions.

5. Gújar.—These also come, according to our census compilers, under the head of Sudras. They number 264,496, and, like the Játs, side by side with whom they are always found, are settled chiefly in the Upper or North-western portion of the Provinces. They have in

Sahâranpúr	51,855
Mírat	54,035
Bulandshahr	44,112

They have a very bad name in this district, where they were particularly troublesome and riotous during the Mutiny, plundering the town of Sikandarabad, and doing a deal of mischief. They and the Rángars of Dehli are unenviably notorious as being among the few rural populations who rose against us at that trying time.

Muzaffarnagar	17,315
Ajmer	32,270

The constant occurrence of Játs and Gújars in the neighbourhood of Rajputs, and the way in which, so to speak, they fill up the gaps between various settlements of the Rajputs, together with their fine *physique* and manly bearing, lends great support to the only really probable theory as to their origin, which supposes them to be offshoots of the great Rajput caste.

6. Ahír.—Number, 2,196,786—over two millions. These are also, somewhat oddly, classed as Sudras. They rank high however as regards purity, and are probably partly of Brahman origin. They are especially numerous in the eastern part of these provinces, though well diffused over the whole,—there being five or ten thousand of them in nearly every district. Their profession of herdsmen secures them a certain respect wherever the sacred cow is worshipped, and the legendary connection of their caste with the popular god or demigod Krishna is still held in remembrance.

They are most numerous in

Gorakhpúr	408,903
Azimgaṛh	210,868
Ghazipúr	168,308

In those parts of Behar which are under the Government of the Lower Provinces of Bengal they are extremely numerous. Avoiding to some extent the agricultural and well-cultivated parts of the country, they are to be found in immense numbers wherever there are vast grassy plains for their herds, as in the wide jungles of Gorakhpúr, and the equally wild plains of Northern Behar, and as far east as Purneah.

7. Káyath.—This class is known as the "writer" caste. They are the clerks and men of the pen all over India. Their tradition is that when Parasu Rama destroyed the Kshatriyas,

the pregnant women of that caste fled, and the children to whom they subsequently gave birth having been concealed during the massacre in the wombs of their mothers, were called Káyasths (Sansk. काय: body स्थ remaining). They are a fine handsome race, with delicate intellectual features, and some of the cleverest natives of India have sprung from their number. In Lower Bengal, especially, they are distinguished by the rapidity with which they acquire a wonderfully perfect knowledge of the English language, and of European literature. They are the "Greeks of the lower empire," subtle, clever, intellectual, but wily and treacherous. Perhaps no race in India has so eagerly responded to the attempts which have been made to civilize, in the European fashion, the natives of this country.

They are, however, also found as cultivators in many parts of the country, and in that capacity are, perhaps, not superior to their neighbours. Their numbers in the N.W.P. are 351,463. They are very equally diffused, though perhaps rather more numerous "down country," or in the eastern part of the provinces.

In Gorakhpúr they number	39,689
Ghazipur	23,597
Bareilly.............................	23,012
Allahabad	21,869

8. Kurmí or Kunbí, amount to 971,285. They are more numerous in the lower or eastern districts than in the Central or Upper Doáb. They are, however, returned as amounting in Bareilly to 162,232, but

In Gorakhpúr	242,388
Allahabad	121,140

9. Kachhí, better known in the eastern districts as Koerí, also called Muráo, or Moráí. The market gardeners of India, wonderfully industrious and neat, and skilful cultivators of all the finer kinds of produce. There are 1,348,316 of these useful

people. They are tolerably equally diffused all over the provinces except in the Upper Doáb, where they seem scarce. In North and South Behar they are very frequent, and wherever the poppy is grown between Benares and Patna, they are found engaged in its cultivation and the production of opium from it.

To sum up these remarks, I exhibit in a brief tabular form the totals of the various castes. I do not attempt to give the whole of them, more especially since they are drawn out with elaborate and somewhat fanciful detail in the census. I include the castes treated of above, with several of the servile castes who are extremely numerous.

1.	Brahman	3,510,103
2.	Rajput	2,816,815
3.	Bhúínhár	107,699
4.	Ját	682,712
5.	Gújar	264,496
6.	Ahír	2,196,786
7.	Káyath	351,463
8.	Kurmí	971,285
9.	Káchhí	1,348,316
10.	Kewat	388,258
11.	Teli* (oilman)	427,857
12.	Sonár (goldsmith)	176,615
13.	Lohár (blacksmith)	314,552
14.	Baṛhái (carpenter)	301,471
15.	Kumhár (potter)	453,614
16.	Mali (gardener)	167,597
17.	Hajjám or Náí (barber)	430,564
18.	Dhimar or Kahár (bearer, also fisherman)	693,519
19.	Gaḍariyá (shepherd)	566,981

* I have drawn a line above these names, to shew that they are not, strictly speaking, castes, but professions or trades.

20.	Bharbhúnjá	163,882
21.	Lodhá	585,932
22.	Kalwâr (distiller)	262,884
23.	Dhobí (washerman)	270,568
24.	Chamár (leather-worker and general drudge)	3,580,385
25.	Mihtar (sweeper)	310,795
26.	Nuniá * (saltpetre worker)	199,936
27.	Banias in general	383,202

* Chiefly in the Eastern districts, and in Oudh and Behar.

APPENDIX B.

NUMERICAL STRENGTH AND DISTRIBUTION OF THE MUHAMMADANS IN THE NORTH-WESTERN PROVINCES, ACCORDING TO THE CENSUS OF 1865.

[*By the Editor.*]

THE arrangement of the Musulman populations is a simpler affair than that of the Hindus. They fall into two great classes, of which the first consists of the descendants of foreign invaders, and the second of converts from Hinduism. This division is of course ignored to a great extent by themselves. Throughout Hindustan they recognize a fourfold classification, into Sayyid, Mughal, Pathán, and Shaikh.

The Sayyid, as claiming descent from the Prophet, is of course the most honoured of the four, he takes either the word Sayyid before his name, or in some places the title Sháh; the latter custom prevails more in the Panjáb and western parts of the Provinces, where the respectful form of address, "Sháh Sáhib" is used to all Sayyids of rank, and "Sháh jí" to others.

The Mughals are, as their name implies, descendants of the companions or followers of the Tartar conquerors of India. They are less numerous than the other classes, and in many cases still preserve a markedly Turanian type of countenance. They are generally known by the title of Beg affixed to their name, and often use the prefix Mir or Mirzá (shortened from Amírzáda, *i.e.*, "son of a noble").

The Patháns are of Affghan origin, and are always known by the affixed title Khán.

The class of Shaikhs is a mixed one. Any ordinary Musulman who belongs to none of the three above-named classes, is called Shaikh. A vast number of the converts from Hinduism give themselves this title, which from being so promiscuously used has long ceased to have any special meaning or value as a title of honor.

The large populations in all parts of the North-Western Provinces who were originally Hindus, but are now Musulman, take great liberties with these titles; many affect the title Khán, and some go so far as to call themselves Sayyid, especially if they have attained high social position. In the Panjáb, where the process of conversion has been carried out on a very large scale, there used to be a proverbial couplet to this effect, supposed to be spoken by a convert—

"Last year I was a weaver, this year I am a Shaikh,
Next year, if grain is dear, I shall be a Sayyid."

meaning that if he sold his crops well, he should be wealthy enough to assume this latter title.*

The census classes the Muhammadans of these provinces under the four general heads given above, and gives besides a column of "miscellaneous Muhammadans," including converts of all sorts. The analysis is as follows:—

1. SAYYID.—There are 170,248 of this class in these Provinces. They are most numerous in Muzaffarnagar, where there are counted 21,837 of them. It is in this district that the Gardezís are located. Bijnor and Moradabad contain

* Much amusement was caused, I remember, in 1860, at Gujrát, in the Panjáb, by the Sarrishtadar, or principal clerk of the judicial department, describing himself in an official return as "Sayyid Háshimí Ḳuraishí," that is, of the family and lineage of the prophet. His father, who was living in obscurity in his native town, was discovered to be a *lohár*, or blacksmith.

respectively 10,285 and 16,439. Lower down, Allahabad has 11,558, Jaunpúr 12,771, and Gorakhpúr 10,078. In one or two districts the Musulman population has not been classified, so that something would have to be added to the above total to obtain the full number, say 10,000, so that we may fairly assume the Sayyid population to be 180,000 throughout the Provinces.

2. Mughal.—There are stated to be 41,748 of this class, who are most numerous in Sahâranpúr, where they amount to 8,370. There are more of them in the Upper Doáb and Rohilkhand than in other parts, but in no district except Sahâranpúr are there more than four thousand of them. With regard to the Mughals it must be noted that they seem, as a class, to have amalgamated less with the native population than any others. They were of the clan of the conquerors, and fierce truculent Tartars to boot. From passages in the Institutes of Timúr, and other writings of the early Mahommadan invaders, we get an impression that the Mughals were rather unwilling participators in the plans of their sovereign. They had no objection to a raid on India, with a prospect of a speedy return to their steppes, but a lengthened sojourn in the plains of the Ganges seems to have been viewed by them with great aversion. Comparatively few, therefore, and they merely hangers on of the court, appear to have stayed on permanently in the country. The Mughals are often found holding very respectable positions, but are almost entirely, as far as I know, townspeople, not having any taste for rural pursuits.

3. Pathán.—This class is very much more numerous than either of the two preceding ones. But there is a possibility that many persons who do not properly belong to this head may have been entered under it. The favourite Pathán title of Khán is often adopted as a stepping-stone to that of Sayyid by ambitious plebeians, and in this way many have probably crept into this column of the returns who have no right to be there.

The Patháns, true or false, are set down at 515,526, or nearly three times the number of Sayyids.

They are very numerous in the Mírat and Rohilkhand divisions, as the following list shows:—

Sahâranpúr	92,226
Muzaffarnagar	13,995
Mírat	13,634
Bulandshahr	39,171
Moradabad	18,926
Badáon	13,150
Bareilly	44,468
Shahjahanpúr	42,356

In Agra and Farrakhabad also they are found in considerable quantities, and are tolerably equally diffused over the whole province, though there is a marked diminution of their numbers in the Benares division.

4. SHAIKH.—I am in doubt about the way this class has been treated in the census. So many that are really not Shaikhs call themselves so, that I apprehend there has been much diversity of practice on this head. The Shaikhs are put down at 1,140,108. By this title we ought strictly to imply those Musulmans who, on the one hand, are neither Sayyids, Mughals, nor Patháns, and on the other are not Hindus converted to Islam. The Shaikh, properly so called, is the lowest class of the descendants of the invaders. He is often of Affghan descent, though his forefathers were not of sufficient social standing to acquire the title of Khán. There is also much Persian, Bokhariot, and Turki blood in his veins. Judging from the appearance of this class on the whole, one would say that the non-Aryan element preponderated considerably. I notice, however, in many districts, converted Gújars and others are entered under this head. Saháranpúr gives eleven classes of Shaikhs. Mírat gives Shaikhs "sprung from Patháns," which is only true of some of them. Most districts draw a distinction between the

four classes of true or original Musulmans and the long list of inferior or miscellaneous.

Sahāranpúr contains the largest number of Shaikhs, 164,819. But there are few districts which have less than twenty or twenty-five thousand of them.

Below the four great classes, there is a large population described as miscellaneous Mahommedans. These are the converts from Hinduism, or more strictly speaking, the descendants in the ninth or tenth generation of such converts, together with those who follow certain petty trades in towns, and who are a very mixed multitude, not connected in any particular way with one another, save by the accident of following a similar trade. As the general tables of the census give no details of this motley rabble, whose numbers, however, amount to 2,207,576, or nearly two millions and a-quarter, it will be probably useful to give an analysis of them, as far as it can be extracted from the district returns.

1. Julláha.—This well-known class is that of weavers; they are as a rule poor and of little consideration. In some districts there are Hindu Julláhas also, but in most cases the term is applied to Musulmans only,—Hindu weavers being known by the names Tánṭí and Tatthiá.

They are located as follows:—

Mírat Division—

Dehra Dún	1,361
Muzaffarnagar	18,922
Mírat	29,457
Bulandshahr	9,558
Aligaṛh	1,844

Rohilkhand Division—

Bijnore	57,000
Moradabad	44,190
Bareilly	61,401

Shahjahánpúr	16,969
Tarai	3,520
Agra Division—	
Agra	607
Etah	2,827
Allahabad Division—	
Fattihpúr	3,282
Banda	182
Allahabad	33,875
Hamírpúr	915
Benares Division—	
Azimgaṛh	51,973
Jaunpúr	21,125
Mirzápúr	19,774
Benares	23,711
Ghazipur	46,268
Total	449,661

Those districts whose names are not found in this list are those in which the Julláhas are not specified by name.

2.—Nái or Hajjám (barber).—This caste, like the Julláhas, is both Musulman and Hindu, and is found in every village in the country. The barber is an important person at betrothals and weddings, though of more consequence among the close-shaven Hindus than the bearded Musulmans. They are often found employing themselves in agriculture.

They are settled as follows :—

Dehra Dún	86
Muzaffarnagar	7,239
Mírat	10,263
Bijnore (about)	10,000
Moradabad	11,308
Baṛeilly	20,188

Tarai	570
Agra	21,574*
Etah	396
Cawnpore	18,950*
Fattihpúr	1,243
Banda	13,849
Hamírpúr	123
Azimgarh	3,950
Jaunpúr	2,243
Mirzapúr	1,426

3. Bihishtí (*vulgo* Bhisti), water-carrier.—These are the men who carry water in goat-skins for the supply of the upper classes. They are chiefly found in towns, and are also called Máshkís, from the Mashak, or water-skin, and Sakká.

Dehra Dún	70
Muzaffarnagar	3,689
Mírat	7,569
Aligarh	10,512
Bijnore	2,603
Moradabad	4,061
Bareilly	3,041
Tarai	299
Agra	14,308
Fattihpúr	331
Allahabad	591
Hamírpúr	29

The Bihishtí is generally found in the service of Europeans, but his trade is not in much request, as most people draw their own water. The word Bihishtí means literally an inhabitant of "Bihisht," or paradise, and the name is said to have been

* In the return it is stated that some of these are Hindus and some Musulmans, but it is not known how many belong to each religion.

applied to them by the Mahomedan invaders, either in derision, or from the relief they gave to the thirsty soldiery.

3. Kassáí, or Kassáb, butcher.

These are thus given:—

Dehra Dún	132
Muzaffarnagar	10,420
Mírat	15,376
Aligaṛh	4,154
Bijnore	6,442
Moradabad	9,179
Bareilly	5,933
Tarai	442
Agra	3,376
Etah	2,251
Fattihpúr	1,191
Allahabad	4,157*
Hamírpúr	7*
Azimgaṛh	1,740
Jaunpúr	883
Mirzapúr	661
Benares	1,089*
Ghazipur	1,652

6. Rangrez, or dyer.—This is like the Julláha, a very useful and wide-spread class. They are found in all the large towns. There are in—

Mírat	4,127
Bijnore	2,063
Moradabad	2,270
Bareilly	2,488
Agra	515†

* Locally known as Bakar kassáb, *i.e.*, ox-butcher.

† The Agra return is careless in these points. I suspect this figure is too low by half.

Etah	579
Allahabad	979
Azimgaṛh	1,281
Mirzapúr	3,227
Benares	609
Ghazipur	1,099

In addition to this there are several large classes of Musulman Dhobis (washermen), Darzís (tailors), and others, who are mentioned in some returns but not in others. I give their names only; an approximation to their total numbers is all that it is possible to offer.

Halwáí, confectioner	15,000
Dhuniá, cotton-carder	70,000
Mi'amár (معمار), builder	12,000
Bhaṭṭiyárá, serai-keeper	8,000
Tawáif (طوايف), prostitute	15,000
Kiltibán, pimp and cinædus (also called Kaláwat or Bharúá)	1,500
Kunjrá, vegetable seller	18,000
Dhobi, washerman	30,000
Telí, oil-seller	55,000

The total of Musulmans is 4,075,206 against 25,971,420 Hindus, or nearly in the proportion of one to six and a-half.

PART II.

CUSTOMS, RITES, AND SUPERSTITIONS.

[This Part has been constituted in accordance with the fourfold division of the work mentioned by the author. The number of articles it contains is, however, small; and I have experienced some difficulty in deciding what articles should find a place in this Part, as being illustrative of customs, rites, and superstitions. It has not been found possible in practice to draw the line accurately, and the reader is therefore requested to refer to Part IV. for any words he may not find in this Part.—B.]

Ajaulí, اجولي अजौली

Perquisite of the lower castes, from the threshing-floor.—Benares. The word may perhaps be derived from Anjalá or Anjalí, *i.e.*, as much as one can carry in two hands joined.

Akhtíj, اکهتيج अखतीज

The 18th day of the month Baisakh, upon which frequently the obligations incurred by the agriculturists to enable them to provide for the cultivation of the Rabí season are adjusted, on the principle explained in the article Bara-bhao.

The Bara-bhao system prevails most to the East, and Akhtíj ka Bhao to the West. The Akhtíj is to the Rabí what the Dewalí is to the Kharíf—the day appointed for settling the accounts of the past harvest. It is proper to commence the manufacture of agricultural implements, and to feed Brahmans on the Akhtíj, as well as to eat new grain, which scrupulous men generally forbear doing till the return of this auspicious festival. A plough is also slightly passed over the fields, as the ceremony is supposed to secure good luck; but to sow seed on that day, except on certain conditions, is expressly forbidden in the points and precepts of some Oriental Tusser.

पोई माउस मूल बिन बिन रोहिनी खेतीज
स्रवण सलोनो बारि क्यूं बखेरे बीज

The name of this festival is derived from अ not, क्षय decay, and तीज (तृतीय) third; the undying 3rd of the lunar half of Baisakh; or 18th, according to the usual computation: "The consequences of meritorious actions performed on this day being permanent, as it is the first day of the Satya Yuga, or the anniversary of creation."—Sanskrit Dict. p. 4.

Angaungá, انگونگا अंगौंला

Perquisites from the threshing-ground to the Brahman, Purohit, Guru, Grazier, and Village God.—Benares.

In the North-West, the corresponding term is Siyáudí or Thapa; and Anjalí in Bundelkhand.

From the time of distributing the Angaungá to that of weighing, a deep silence is observed, and strangers are carefully excluded. A short time since, a party of peasants engaged in this operation were brought before the magistrate for conniving at a criminal's escape; whereas, they had merely made a sign to him to keep off, and not profane the ceremony with his unhallowed presence.

In Dehli, and the North-West, as well as in some parts of Benares, this deep and mysterious silence is observed at an earlier stage of the proceedings. When the corn is ready to be formed into a heap, a man seats himself down with a ploughshare in his hand, which he digs into the ground, and which is supported on each side by some kús grass and cowdung. Another person from behind then throws some corn over the head of the man sitting on the ground, who employs himself in carefully adjusting it around the ploughshare, taking care all the time to keep it as much as possible concealed from the gaze of inquisitive persons. When it is well covered, he gets up, and every one present assists in forming the heap. This is the Dehli custom.

In Rohilkhand a somewhat different ceremony is observed. After burning a hom, or a little sacrificial fire, a ploughshare and a pot full of water are placed to the north of the pole round which the bullocks are driven when treading out the corn. The heap of corn is then raised to the south of the ploughshare, and not over it, as in Dehli. The subsequent proceedings will find a more appropriate place under Chánk.

But in whatever way the ceremony is observed, during the whole time the strictest silence is observed, and is not to be broken within the threshing-ground until the corn is measured out and distributed.

It would be deemed unlucky were any talking to take place; even if an articulation or ejaculation of any kind were made, mischievous sprites would come, and extract much of the strength and substance of the corn.

It is from the apprehension of a visit from these malignant goblins that the agriculturists of these provinces commence forming their heaps of winnowed corn either exactly at twelve in the day time, or shortly after twelve at night, at which times sprites are said not to wander.

If the work is begun in the day time, and not over by sunset, the party retire from the threshing-ground, and do not recommence operations till starlight; the intermediate period being very inauspicious.

Angauriyá, انگوریا अंगौरिया

A ploughman. Allowing the use of a plough, instead of paying wages in money or kind.—Benares.

This practice is called Jítrá in Bundelkhand and Rohilkhand.

Anjalá, انجلا अंजला

As much as can be held in the cavity formed by joining the two hands together in the shape of a bowl.

Anjalí, انجلي अंजली

This has the same meaning as Anjalá, but is current chiefly in Bundelkhand. It is also applied to a mode of salutation by carrying the hands in this form to the forehead.—See also Angaungá.

Anúá, انوا अनूआ

The place where men stand who throw the Daurí (which see). —See also Berí and Boka (Part IV.).

Annaprásan, انپراسن अन्नप्रासन

The first feeding of children with grain; from the Sanskrit अन्न *anna*, corn, and प्रासन *prásan*, feeding; also called in some places पसनी *pasní*, which appears to be merely a corruption of the above words.

The Pasní takes place (see "Menu," II. 34) usually six months after birth. It is an important ceremony with a Hindi child, who is then considered to enter on a new stage of life.

अन्नमूल प्राण । प्राणमूल पुरुष । पुरुषमूल हरमजदगी

"Corn is the staple of life, life is the origin of man, and man is the essence of viciousness (حرامزادگي)."

Argh, ارگهه अर्घ

The ceremony of making a libation of water between the threshold and the spot where the first bundle of corn is deposited after being brought home from the threshing-ground. This particular ceremony is supposed to be propitious, as it unites the two chief elements of man's sustenance.

Another kind of agricultural Argh consists in placing on the threshold, at seed-time, a cake of cowdung formed into a cup, filling it with corn, and then pouring water upon it. The practice is supposed to propitiate the deities, and secure a good harvest.

The word Argh means in Sanskrit any libation of water to a deity.

Arwan, اروں अर्वन

The first cuttings of corn, not taken to the threshing-floor, but brought home to be eaten by the family, and presented to the family gods and Brahmans. It is not cut without previously ascertaining the fortunate moment for commencing the harvest. In the Kharíf, Shamakh,—in the Rabi, barley,—is the grain used in the Arwan. When the Arwan is brought home, the grain is taken out of the ear, mixed up with milk and sugar, and every member of the family tastes it seven times. The season is of course one of festivity.

फुला फुला क्यूं फिरे घर अर्वन आया
झुका झुका क्यूं फिरे पिआदा आया

"Why do you go about swelling (with joy)? Because the Arwan has been brought home.

"Why do you go about bent (with grief)? The peon has come (to collect the revenue)."

Arwan is chiefly used in Rohilkhand and the Upper Doáb. The more general and the proper term is नवान्न from नव new, and अन्न corn.—See Dithwan and Júrí.

Asárh, اسارّه असाढ

The name of the third Hindu Solar month (June-July). The first month of the rainy season, and consequently of cultivation. It is therefore a busy period in the country, and cultivators are on the alert. There is an old proverb—

असाढ नांधे हाथी बांधे
सावन नांधे घोरा बांधे
भादों नांधे कुंभि बांधे

That is, "begin in Asáṛh, and you will become a proprietor of elephants; wait a month till Sáwan, and instead of elephants you will have horses; wait two months till Bhadon, and your family will become slaves."

In the printed Glossary, Assam (evidently a mistake for Asáṛh), is called the sixth month, but it can only be considered so according to the European calendar.

The same error occurs under Asin, also called Kúár, and under Augun, usually Aghan.

Asáṛhí, اسارّهي असाढी

This word does not preserve an identical meaning throughout these provinces. In the North-West it is used only for the Rabí, or spring harvest, and is frequently corrupted into साढ़ी Sáḍhí. Sáwaní is used in the same parts for the Kharíf, or autumnal harvest. This latter word is not known to the eastward. In Benares, Eastern Oudh, and Saugor, Asarhí signifies the Kharíf, and not the Rabí harvest. The people in the North-West say their meaning is derived from the *ploughing* in Asarh; those of Benares say theirs is derived from the *sowing* in Asarh. The latter have the more reason on their side, for the land is ploughed in Asarh for either harvest.—See Asarh.

⁂ The following extract from a recently-published work, "Handbook of the Economic Products of the Panjáb," by Baden

H. Powell, Roorkee, 1868, gives so good a general view of agricultural operations in the upper or western portion of the country under notice, that although it is specially written for the Panjáb, I feel no apology is necessary for introducing it here:—

METHOD OF SOWING, WEEDING, AND GENERAL TREATMENT OF CROPS.

The great harvests are called universally Rabí and Kharíf, or by the villagers "Hárí" and "Sáwaní," from the names of the months in which the crops are ripe.

Rabí is the spring harvest; Kharíf the autumn; but it is not all land that bears two harvests. Land that will, is called "dofaslí," and land that bears only once, "ekfaslí;" but there are certain tracts of country where two or even three harvests will be taken off the soil.

The spring crops are the important ones, for they are sown just at the great rain-fall of the year—the "barsát," or rainy season—about the month of September, and the crop, which has been sustained during its growth by the winter or latter rains, is cut at the end of the spring of the year following in the month of Baisákh, and the months following. In the bángar lands of the Cis-Satlaj States, Mr. Winyard writes that the rabí crops are not sown where artificial irrigation is not procurable, and that the autumn crops are the staple. The kharíf or autumn crops are sown before the rains, and reaped after their close in October and November.

Mr. Melville, writing from Hushyárpúr, says:—"The rabí crop is reared after great labour; the kharíf with but little trouble; the latter invariably follows the former, and the ploughings of the rabí are almost sufficient for the kharíf also. When the spring crop is cut, the husbandman will wait for a shower in June, plough over his land once or twice, and sow his kharíf crop."

Fallow lands are never turned up for the first crop at kharíf;

but always begin with a ploughing and sowing for the rabí harvest. The principal crops of the rabí are wheat, barley, gram, "mattar" (*Vicia*), lentils, tobacco, linseed ("sarshaf" or "sarsoṅ," "rai," etc.) The kharíf sowings are "jawar," bájrá (millet), maize, rice, "moth," "múng,". "másh," and other pulses, sugar-cane, and cotton. These are produced by the efficacy of the rains, which occur when they are in full growth. These crops require much moisture, and most of them, except the pulses, get artificial irrigation beside the rain. The land is subjected to repeated ploughings, the number of them depending on the industry and the means of the farmer; but their number seems much to influence the success of the crop. The fields to be sown with the (zabti) best crops are often ploughed over and over again, ten and twelve times; six times is about the average. The plough seldom goes deeper than six inches, while in England nine inches depth is considered to give the best crops.*

Land intended for sugar-cane receives the greatest number. The land intended for this crop is ploughed up as if the land were to be sown for a rabí crop, and then left till *Har*, when the planting is effected.

Annexed is a Table showing the number of ploughings given to each kind of crop.

Crop.	No. of Ploughings in *rohi* land.	Do. *dushahi* land.	Do. *maira* land.	Remarks.
	Rabí.			
Wheat	12	11	10	The number of ploughings will vary much with the skill, industry, and means of the cultivator.
Gújí (wheat and barley together)	7	7	5	
Barley	5	5	4	
Gram	2	2	2	
Poppy	10	9	9	
Tobacco	9	9	9	
Linseed	12	12	11	

* Sealkote Report, p. 116.

Crop.	No. of Ploughings in *rohi* land.	Do. *dushahi* land.	Do. *maira* land.	Remarks.
	Kharíf.			
Makai (maize)	7	6	6	The number of ploughings will vary much with the skill, industry, and means of the cultivator.
Cotton	5	5	5	
Mustard	7	7	7	
Sugar-cane	11 to 27	11	11 to 27	
Charí (jowâr grown as a fodder)	2	2	2	
Dhán (rice)	4	...	...	
Munjí (rice)	5	...	...	
Moth } pulses	...	...	1	
Múng and Másh } pulses	...	...	2	

It will be observed how much fewer are the kharíf ploughings than the rabí, with the single exception of sugar-cane land, which, however, is no real exception, for this land, as before remarked, is prepared at the same time as the rabí lands, but left to lie to the kharíf sowing time.

A pair of good bullocks will plough half an acre daily, but weak ones less. Cattle are never kept at work continuously for more than five hours in a day, or two-and-a-half at a sugar-mill. Generally speaking, there is in "bángar" lands about one pair of bullocks to seven or eight acres. "Bár" lands, where the wells are deep, take one pair to five acres, and buffaloes are there much in use on account of their strength. In the well lands it is said that the animals die off quickly because of the constantly rotatory motion which they undergo at the well. "Khádir" land requires less, and weaker animals will do.* In submontane and hill villages a pair can be purchased for Rs. 16, sufficient for ordinary ploughing purposes.

Land after being ploughed is levelled with a "sohága," called "dáh" in the submontane districts; a flat, straight, heavy piece of wood dragged over the surface of the field by cattle. Some-

* Major Clarke's "Agriculture of the Rechna Doáb."

times they are made with teeth, and called "much." Some crops are then sown broad-cast, and after the seed is down the land is twice ploughed over, and the field marked out into beds or divisions for irrigation purposes, the divisions being little banks of earth dividing the field into squares. The exact time for sowing is dependent on considerations of weather, rains, etc., and varies for different crops; the people are also superstitious, and often consult Múllahs and Bráhmans, according as they are Hindús or Musulmáns, to ascertain favorable omens and times for sowing. Sowing is generally done broad-cast, but in khádir lowland along the banks of rivers, it is effected by the drill: a hollow piece of bamboo is attached to the plough, through which seed is dropped, and the ploughing and sowing are thus done at one operation; but this practice is not followed in lands irrigated by wells (*cháhi*). Sowing, when broad-cast, is performed by the farmer with the aid of the "Kamínán,"—the Tirkhán, Lohár, and Chamár, etc., who receive certain dues for their work.

Reaping is done by laborers, who are paid either so much per "kanál" of wheat cut, or else so much per diem.

Manuring is done by Chúras (low caste of sweepers) who receive a small due, and the gleanings of the gathered grain.

Cotton is usually sown broad-cast like wheat. Poppy, tobacco, rice, and some other crops, are sown in nursery beds, called "lab," and when the seedlings appear are planted out. Sugar-cane grows from pieces of the cane containing some joints. They are put into furrows made in the soil.

In sowing, the quantity of seed required to one acre is proximately given in the following Table.

Each kind of crop has generally some peculiarity as to its management, or the method of sowing and rearing it. Such details will be noticed in the catalogue along with the name of the particular product to which they refer.

Biswansí. The twentieth part of a Kachwánsí is an Unwánsí, or Nanwánsí. The word Kachwánsí is rarely used in account books; the more usual denomination is Pitwansí. But it must be confessed that great difference of opinion prevails respecting these fractions. It is even sometimes stated that a Kachwánsí is the twentieth part of a Biswansí, but as these denominations were, even under native governments, rarely used in practice, and are now less used than ever, it is a matter of little consequence what precise value is attached to them.

Sirkár, سرکار सरकार

This word is more correctly spelt Sirkár, but is more familiar to Europeans as Circar, in consequence, perhaps, of the geographical division of the Northern Sirkárs being so written. In other parts of this Supplement it will appear as Sirkár.

A Sirkár is a sub-division of a Súbah. The North Western Provinces, excluding the Saugor and Nerbudda territories, comprise no complete Súbah, but only portions of the four Súbahs of Agra, Allahabad, Dehli and Oudh. Each Súbah is divided into a certain number of Sirkárs, and each Sirkár into Parganahs or Mehals (which are used as equivalent expressions), and the Parganahs again are aggregated into Dastúrs or districts; and as the Parganahs of the same Dastúr are of course always contiguous, the Dastúr statement in old registers, if copied with any regard to correctness, frequently forms a very important means of the verification of doubtful names.

Súbah is an Arabic word, signifying a heap of money, or a granary. Sirkár is literally a chief, a supervisor. Dastúr besides signifying a rule is also a minister, a munshi; Parganah means tax-paying land:

پرگنه زميني را گويند كه ازان مال و خراج بگيرند

It is strange that the "Burhán-i Ḳáti'," while giving this Hindustani meaning, does not speak of it also as a sub-division of a province, for it is so given in the older lexicons, as for instance in the "Farhang-i Jahangiri;" and though it is omitte in the "Farhang-i Ibrahímí," the word was undoubtedly in use ir the time of that compilation, being not only found in the almost contemporary memoirs of Baber, but in the "Tabakát-i Násirí," and the "Fatuhát-i Fírozshahí" (in which we find that about A.D. 1350, there were fifty-two imperial Parganahs in the Doáb) and even on an inscription dated A.D. 1210, discovered at Piplianagar in Bhopal ("Jour. A.S. Bengal," Vol. V. p. 377).

The other words do not appear to have been in use till introduced by the Moghuls, nor do any of them appear to be used in similar senses in foreign countries, except Sirkár, which is stated in the "Chiragh-i Hidayat" to be used in Western Asia also, in the sense of a territorial sub-division, the authority quoted being the translation of the "Mujalis-ul Nufais."

The words used before Akbar's time to represent tracts of country larger than a Parganah, were Shaḳḳ شق, Khitta خطه, 'Arsa عرصه, Diár دیار, Viláyat ولایت, and Iktá' اقطاع, but the latter was generally, though not always, applied when the land was assigned for the support of the nobility, or their contingents, and the presiding officer was called Mukta or Iktadar. Thus, in the early historical writers before the close of the fourteenth century, we find Shaḳḳ-i Sámánah, Khitta-i Oudh, Arsa-i Gorakhpúr (this term is rarely used for any other tract), Diar-i Lakhnautí, Viláyat-i Mián Doáb, and Iḳta -i Karrá.

Between Sirkár and Dustúr there app rs a connexion; one meaning chief, and the other minister; between Súbah and Parganah a connexion may also be tr ; one being a large, the other a small collection; but whether the words were chosen with reference to this connexion may be doubted.

The title of Súbahdar, or lord of the Súbah, is long subsequent to Akbar's time. Sipáhsálár was then the only designation of the Emperor's Viceroy in each Súbah.

I have endeavoured to restore the Sirkárs, Dastúrs, and

STATEMENT OF THE AVERAGE QUANTITY OF SEED REQUIRED FOR ONE ACRE OF LAND.

Crop.	Maunds.	Seers.	Chittaks.	Remarks.
Wheat	1	10	...	*Sailábi* land requires less seed than *chahi* land.
Goji	1	10	...	
Barley	1	10	...	
Gram	...	20	...	
Poppy	...	...	7	
Linseed	...	14	...	
Tára míra	...	15	...	
Moth, múng, and másh	...	2	8	
Munji (rice)	...	12	...	
Chari	...	20	...	
Makai (Indian corn)	...	9	...	
Cotton	...	8	...	
Mustard	...	3	...	
Turnip	...	2	8	

When the crop is sown, the number of waterings that it receives greatly depends on the district, the fall of rain, and other natural and local circumstances.

Hand-hoeing and weeding are often given to crops. The operation is called "godí," and is effected by a flat kind of shovel or hand-hoe, "rambha," very like the "khurpá" of Hindústán; but much depends on the class of cultivators, and these operations are little attended to by the lazier castes of agriculturists before-mentioned. In the Cis-Satlaj districts, weeding appears to be much more attended to than in the others. In Thanesar it is stated that sugar-cane is weeded ten times; the poppy seven; tobacco five; cotton four; and maize three. Sugar-cane, cotton, Indian corn and tobacco, and even rice, require manuring.

The following statement, indicating the ploughings, waterings, sowing time and reaping time of the various crops, has been compiled from the valuable tables given by Major Clarke, in his account of the Rechna Doáb Agriculture; the list applies directly to the Gujranwalla district, but gives a good general idea of the practice and results of the various operations of agriculture in other similarly situated districts of the Panjáb proper.

RABÍ.

Kind of Crop.	No. of Ploughings.	No. of Waterings.	No. of Handhoeings.	When Sown.	When Reaped.
Wheat	4 to 8	4 to 8	None	Rabí, Kartik, and Maghar	Bysákh
Barley	4 to 8	4 to 8	Ditto	Ditto	Chet
Gojí	4 to 8	4 to 8	Ditto	Ditto	Bysákh
Gram	2	None	Ditto	Bhádon	Bysákh
Flax or linseed......	2	Sown in Sailábí	Ditto	Assuh	Bysákh
Mustard ...	8	3 or 4	1	Assuh	Chet
China	6 Rabí 4 Kharíf	10 to 16	None	Phágan and Sáwan	Bysákh, Kirtik, or Maghar
Kangní ...	5, 6, or 7	5 or 6	1	Chet, Sáwan, and Bhádon.	Bhádon, Assuh
Tobacco ...	4 or 5	15	3 to 5	Kartik, transplanted in Magh or Phagan	Jeth and Hár
Onion......	4 to 8	16	3	Planted out in Magh	Ditto
Carrot	4 to 6	3 or 4	None	Assuh	Chet
Turnip.....	5	3 to 5	Ditto	20th Bhádon to 10th of Assuh	Maghar to Magh
Methi and sinji	...	2 or 3	Ditto	Kartik	Phagan and Chet
Poppy	10 to 12	Every 4th or 5th day	10 to 12	Assuh	Chet

It must be borne in mind that the real number of ploughings for some of the above crops is more than appears in the statement, because no account is taken of the primary ploughings on wheat lands afterwards appropriated to the other crops, which land lies fallow till it is determined what shall be sown.

KHARÍF.

Kind of Crop.	No. of Ploughings.	No. of Waterings.	No. of Hand-hoeings.	When Sown.	When Reaped.
Sugar-cane	14 to 15	16 to 25	4 to 6	Phágan	Maghar
Cotton	4 to 6	Uncertain	4	15th Hár to 15th Sáwan	Assuh to end of Maghar
Maize	3 or 4	6 or 7 in chahi lands	2	Hár	Assuh or Kartik
Jawár	3 or 4	3 or 4	For corn, once	Hár	Kartik
Bájra	2	2 or 3	1	Sáwan	Assuh or Kartik
Moth	1	None	None	Sáwan and Bhádon	Maghar
Múng	2	Ditto	Ditto	Hár	Maghar
Til	2	Ditto	Ditto	Sáwan	Maghar
Másh	3	Ditto	Ditto	Sáwan	Kartik and Maghar
Ráwan.....	3	Ditto	Ditto	Hár and later	Kartik
Rice	*Vide* details of cultivation in the sequel under "rice."				
Sawánk ...	2	3 or 4	None	Hár and later	Bhádon, Assuh, and Kartik
Mustard ...	5 or 6	5 or 6	1 or 2	Bhádon	Kartik

Lands are generally manured at about 250 maunds per acre, or nearly nine tons. Twelve tons is rather a low rate in England.

PRODUCE.

I now come to the last head, namely, the productiveness of the land and the costs and profits of cultivation.

The produce per acre in the various districts may be best gathered from a tabular statement from all districts,—such a one now follows:—It was compiled from returns supplied to the Lahore Museum in 1860. The rates vary much; but we must bear in mind that the estimate is only a proximate one; and that the differences of local situation, the facilities of irrigation, the absence of presence of "kalr" in the soil, the character and caste of the agriculturists, the prosperity of the district generally, the moderation and justness of the Government assessment (amounting on an average to a third or a fourth of the essential produce),* the definition and security of proprietary rights, have all of them great power to modify the agricultural prosperity of a district, and consequently to affect the area of land brought under cultivation, as well as the style of cultivation, and amount of produce.

Division.	District.	Name of Grain, etc.	Produce in grain per acre.	Produce in straw.	Average height of crops.
LAHORE.	Lahore.	The particulars are given in a separate and detailed Table.			
			mds.	mds.	ft. in.
	Gujranwalla.	Wheat, Khádir lands	8	...	...
		Wheat, Near the bar	10	...	...
		Wheat, On the bar	14	...	...
		Barley, Khádir	7½	...	...
		Barley, Bar	9 to 12	...	...
		Barley, Sailábi	6	...	...
AMRITSAR.	Amritsar.	Wheat, white (on rohi land)	16	12	3 6
		Barley (on dosháhi land)	12	9½	2 0
		Red Wheat (on rohi land)	16	10	2 6
		Chola (gram) ditto	14	2	1 3
		Saron ditto	9½	...	3 0

* Or to one-sixth in fairly lightly assessed tracts.

Division.	District.	Name of Grain, etc.		Produce in grain.	Produce in straw.	Average height of crops.
				mds.	mds.	ft. in.
AMRITSAR.	Sealkote.	Vadának Wheat (1st quality)		15	12	4 6
		Red Wheat, "lál kanak,"		12	10	4 0
		Barley		0	9	4 0
		White Wheat, from Adálatgarh		10½	...	...
		Ditto, from Syjoké		18	...	...
		Rice, from Chukrandás		?12	...	...
		Ditto, from Síráṅwalla		8¼	...	...
		Ditto, from Bakupúr of Pasroor		8¼	...	...
	Gurdaspúr.	Mustard Seed		2¾	...	...
		Sugar		3½	...	...
		Rice		10½	...	...
		Wheat		7	...	..
		Linseed		2⅝	...	...
		Taramíra		3½	...	...
RAWALPINDI.	Gujrát.	Wheat, kanak dágar (of 1st quality)	Rohi	22	8¾	...
			Doshábi	18¾	8¼	...
			Maira	15	8	...
		Ditto (of 2nd quality)	Rohi	17½	8	...
			Doshábi	16½	7¾	...
			Maira	15	7¾	...
		Red Wheat, "lál kanak" (of first quality)	Rohi	18	8¼	...
			Doshábi	16¼	8	...
			Maira	15	8¼	...
		Ditto (of 2nd quality)	Rohi	17	8	...
			Doshábi	16	8	...
			Maira	15	7¾	...
		"Ghoni kanak" (of 1st quality)	Rohi	13¼	6	...
			Doshábi	12	6	...
			Maira	11	6	...
		Ditto (of 2nd quality)	Rohi	12	6	...
			Doshábi	11	6	...
			Maira	10	5¾	...
		Barley, "jau" (of 2nd quality)	Rohi	14	3¼	...
			Doshábi	13	3	...
		Gram		8¾	...	...
		Rice (cháwal)		14	...	...
		Maize (makkai)		10½	...	...
		"Jawár" (*Holcus sorghum*)		7	...	...
		Bajra (*Penicillaria spicata*)		8¾	...	...
		Dálmúng (*Ph. mungo*)		7	...	...
		Ditto, massúr (lentil)		7	...	...
		Dal másh, or úrad (*Ph. radiatus*)		7	...	...
		Mót kála (*Ph. aconitifolius*)		4	...	...
		Mót safaid (*Cyamopsis psoraloides*)		4	...	...
		Chalodra or mandal (*Eleusine coracana*)		5¼	...	...
		Kaiyúṅ (black pulse)		3½	...	...
		Cheena (*Panicum miliaceum*)		7	...	...
		Dángrí (pulse), (*Cajanus*)		5¼	...	...
		Karain (pulse), (*Cajanus*)		5¼	...	...
		Kodra (*Paspalum scrobiculatum*)		5¼	...	...

Division.	District.	Name of Grain, etc.	Produce in grain.	Produce in straw.	Average height of crops.
			mds.	mds.	ft. in.
RAWALPINDI.	Shahpúr.	Millet (china)	12	...	...
		Ditto (kangni), (*P. italicum*)	11	...	...
		Ditto (sawánk), (*Oplismenum frumentaceum*)	5 or 6	...	...
		Ditto (bajra)	8	...	...
		Ditto (jawár)	9	...	...
		Pulse (másh)	7	...	...
		Múng	6	...	...
		Massúr	7	...	...
		Moth	8	...	...
		Lobiya	2	...	...
		Gram (chana)	10	...	...
PESHAWUR.	Kúhat.*	Wheat (kanak) (of 1st quality)	34	32	5
		Ditto (of 2nd quality)	34	32	5
		Barley (jau)	48	60	3½
	Peshawur.	Barley (jau)	40	5	2½
	Hazara.†	Wheat (kanak)	5-8	...	...
		Barley (jau)	6-12	...	...
		Rice (cháwul)	8-12	...	...
		Oil Seeds—sarshuf	4	...	...
DERAJAT.	Dera Ghází Khán.	Wheat (kanak)	10½	...	...
		Ditto (makkewalla)	5¼	...	...
		Ditto (pamban)	7	...	...
		Barley (jau)	8¾	...	...

* Kúhat—I believe this and the Peshawur rate to be a mistake, unless the maunds are "kucha," from 13 to 20 seers instead of 40.

† The list given by Major Abbot to the Agri-Horticultural Society of produce in Hazara (where the soil is classed according to the number of harvests it yields), is as follows:—

Name of grain.	Tín-fasli soil.	Do-fasli soil.		Ek-fasli soil.	
		mds.	srs.	mds.	srs.
Maize	12 maunds	8	0	6	0
Cotton	2¼ maunds	3	0	2	0
Rice	,,	...	...	12	0
Jawár	,,	4	0	...	...
Kungni	,,	...	...	2	20
Bajra	,,	...	...	2	0
Másh	,,	...	...	1	8
Múng	,,	...	...	2	0
Moth	,,	...	...	2	0
Rawan	Sown always with other grain	...	...	2	0
Wheat	4 maunds, 34 seers	3	20	8	32
Barley	9 maunds	6	0	4	20

Division.	District.	Name of Grain, etc.	Produce in grain.	Produce in straw.	Average height of crops.
			mds.	mds.	ft. in.
Derajat.	Dera Ghází Khán.	Black Barley	8¾	...	...
		Rice	12½	...	...
		Ditto	12¼	...	...
		Bajra	10½	...	...
		Jawár	10½	...	...
		Gram	8¾	...	...
		Peas	8¾	...	...
		Moth	3½	...	...
		Dal (múng)	5¼	...	...
		Mohrí	8¾	...	...
		Simuka	3½	...	...
		Sawánk	5¼	...	...
		Gram	5¼	...	...
	Bunnoo.	Kangni	6-10	7-16	3-4
		Barley	8-16	6-14	2-3
		Chína	9	8	12
Múltán.	Múltán.	Wheat	9	16	3
		Barley	10	12	2
	Jhang.	Wheat (called rodi kanak)	12-19	10-17	2¾-½
		Ditto (inferior land)	9-12	7½-10	2-2¼
		Wheat (canal land)	13-20	15-21	½-33
		Ditto (inferior land)	10-13	8-15	2-2¼
		Barley (canal land)	12-24	8-16	2½-3
		Ditto (inferior land)	6-10	4-6	2-2¼
Jálandhar.	Jálandhar.	Wheat, Cháhi	10	...	...
		Wheat, Baráni	4	...	...
		Barley, Cháhi	11	...	...
		Barley, Baráni	4	...	...
		Gram	20	...	...
		Bajra	4	...	...
		Maize, Cháhi	16	...	...
		Maize, Inferior	8	...	...
		Charí (jawár)	5	...	...
		Mash	8	...	...
	Hushyarpúr.	Wheat of 2nd quality, Cháhi	8	15	...
		Wheat of 2nd quality, Baráni	6½	10	...
		Wheat of 2nd quality, Best rohi	12	22	...
		Ditto of 1st quality, Cháhi	24	25	...
		Ditto of 1st quality, Baráni	12	20	...
Cis-Satlaj States.	Amballa.	Wheat (rausli)	18	54	3
		Gram (khádir)	15	30	1½
		Linseed (khádir)	3	...	1½
		Lentils	5	5	1½

Division.	District.	Name of Grain, etc.	Produce in grain.	Produce in straw.	Average height of crops.
			mds.	mds.	ft. in.
Cis-Satlaj States.	Ludhiana.	Wheat	16	...	...
		Rice	14	...	...
		Barley	14	...	...
		Maize	19	...	...
		Jawár	19	...	...
		Bajra	13	...	...
		Gram	19	...	...
		Moth	66	...	...
		Másh	...	...	...
		Múng	10	...	...
		Sesamum (*til*)	6	...	...
		Sarsóṅ	11	...	...
Dehli.	Dehli.	Wheat	6½-16	...	...
		Barley	6-16	...	...
		Barley, on unirrigated land	2-4	...	...
		Jowar	5-10	...	...
		Rice	9-15	...	...
		Gram	6-14	...	...
		Gawár (*Cyamopsis*)	15-20	...	...
	Karnál.	Wheat... Irrigated best land	13	15	3
		Wheat... Bángar	7	7	2¾
		Wheat... Rausli	9½	9½	2¼
		Barley... Irrigated best land	12	12	2¾
		Barley... Bángar	7	7	1½
		Barley... Khádir	9½	9½	2
		Gram ... Irrigated best land	9½	6½	2
		Gram ... Bángar	10	8	1½
		Gram ... Khádir	9½	9½	1
		Sarsoṅ	5	5	4
Hissar.	Hissar.	Rice, the kind called básmátí	12	...	...
		Ditto (shakar chiní)	10	...	...
		Ditto (múnjí)	10	...	...
		Jawi or javi (oats)	15	...	...
		Jowar	9	...	...
		Gram	18	...	...
		Moth, gawár, múng	9	...	...
	Rohtak.*	Daúdi wheat	6-14	...	...
		Rice	7-12	...	...
		Barley	8-14	...	...
		Maize	6-18	...	...
		Kangní	6-12	...	...
		Gram	6-24	...	...
		Múng	3-6	...	...
		Urd	3-6	...	...
		Moth	3	...	...

*** More recently I have received from the Deputy Commissioner of Rohtak, under his letter**

One or two districts, from the peculiarities of the situation, or means of irrigation, could not conveniently be included in the above table; they are given separately.

Such are the Sirsa and Kangra districts; the former remarkable for the irrigation effected by the overflow of the river Ghagár, the latter by its mountain streams and peculiar rice crops.

PRODUCE OF SIRSA.—I. PRODUCE OF TRACT ON THE BANK OF THE SATLAJ.

Local name of the grain, or quality of the grain.	Whether grown with irrigation or not.	Average height of stem.	Soil in which grown.	Average yield per acre. Grain.		Average yield per acre. Straw.		Remarks as to outward appearance.
		Feet.		md.	sr.	md.	sr.	
Kanak "paman" (wheat of large size, long grain, and translucent appearance).	By irrigation.	4½	Rausli and dakur ...	10	0	15	0	Long and dark colour beard.
Kanak "dáúd-khání" (wheat of very white colour).	"	3	"	7	20	11	10	No beard at all; consumed chiefly by wealthy people.
Kanak "lál" (wheat of smaller size, and reddish appearance).	"	3	"	9	0	13	20	Short and white beard.
Jau (barley)	By irrigation and rain ...	4	Rausli and bhúr	12	0	12	0	Short beard and ear.

No. 592, dated 18th August, 1864, the following table, showing the produce in canal and rain irrigated villages;—

	Average produce per pucka beegah of canal villages.	Average produce per pucka beegah of barani villages.
Wheat	10 maunds.	7 maunds.
Paddy	12 "	... ...
Barley	12 "	5 maunds.
Imphee	6 "	7½ "
Indian Corn	7 "	8 "
Bajra	6 "	10 "
Kangní...	7 "	2½ "
Gram	12 "	10 "
Múng	8 "	7 "
Urd	8 "	7 "
Moth	... ...	11 "
Gawár'...	... ...	12 "
Mustard or Rape Seed	7 maunds.	4 "
Til	... ...	6 "
Goor, (molasses from sugar-cane) ...	18 maunds.	... ...

II. Produce of the Tract on the Bank of the Stream Ghagár.

Local name of the grain, or quality of the grain.	Whether grown with irrigation or not.	Average height of stem.	Soil in which grown.	Average yield per acre. Grain.	Straw.	Remarks as to outward appearance.
		Feet.		md. sr.	md. sr.	
Kanak "lál" (wheat of small size and reddish colour).	By irrigation	3	Rausli and dakur ...	12 0	24 0	Long and white beard.
Jau (barley)	By irrigation and rain ...	3	Rausli, dakur, and bhúr ...	12 0	12 0	Long beard and short ear.
Chola (gram).........	By ditto	1½	Dakur and rausli ...	15 0	30 0	
III. By Rain.						
Jau (barley)	By rain	2½	Rausli......	4 26	9 12	Long beard and ear.

Kangra District.

Crop.	Produce per acre.	Quantity of seed required for sowing.	Remarks.
Wheat	7½ maunds	26½ seers..	Principally in Kangra valley.
Barley	6½ "	35 "	Grows also higher up on the mountains.
Maize..............	8½ "	8 "	One return gives about 16 maunds an acre, or 10 maunds a beegah; perhaps this includes the cobs.
Rice	14½ "	44 "	Mr. Barnes mentions that he has counted 1100 seeds on one head of rice. One return gives only 3½ maunds of husked rice, but that was a fine quality.
Amaranth (*Chaulai*).	4 "	....	
Mandal (*Eleusine*)...	6 "	....	
Másh	2 "	5½ seers..	Usually sown mixed with *kúlth*.
Gram	9½ "	2 "	
Chínán	4 "	....	Both Kúlú and Kangra.
Ginger	4 "	....	

STATEMENT SHEWING THE QUANTITY OF THE SEVERAL SORTS OF GRAIN PRODUCED AT LAHORE.

Name of Grain.	Time of Sowing.	Number of times of Ploughing.	Quantity of Seed per Acre.	Cost per Acre.	Quantity of Grain produced.	Remarks.
Wheat	October ...	7 or 8 times	1 to 1⅓ maunds	It does not need hoeing	25 to 30 maunds	Abundantly produced in mahjah and kalr lands (high lands from the river), but very little near the Rávi banks; if sown there, the crop produces more grain.
Barley	October ...	4 or 5 times	35 to 40 seers	Ditto	35 to 40 maunds	Kalr land produces more grain and less straw than the others. Barley is mostly used as a food for horses, and very little by men of the lower classes. It is made into sattu, or flour, made after parching the grain. The crop does not need hoeing. Barley parched is called *khat*, and with gram, *channa-chabina*.
Gram	September and Oct.	2 or 3 times	12 to 15 seers	Ditto	20 to 25 maunds	It is eatable when parched, and is used as dál (split gram); when ground into "besan" it is used for making sweet-meats. In its raw state it is food for horses.
Mustard	October ...	4 or 5 times	10 to 12 chs.	It needs hoe-ing	3 to 4 maunds	From its seeds oil is extracted, which is used for many purposes; the stalk is useless.
Masúr or lentils	Ditto	2 or 3 times	25 to 28 seers	It does not need hoeing	15 to 20 maunds	It is used as dál, and is made into bread; the *bhúsa* answers well for the food of animals, and the grain is given to the bullocks.
Churál	Ditto	2 or 3 times	Ditto	Ditto	Ditto	Cooked as dál, its flour is baked into chapaties, and its stalk for cattle.
Linseed	September and Oct.	5 or 6 times	10 to 28 seers	It needs hoe-ing twice	Ditto	If it is cultivated for its fibre, it is sown with 28 seers of seed to an acre, otherwise 10 seers is sufficient. If grown for oil its stalk is useless: the land is manured before sowing: the crop is watched.

Name of Grain.	Time of Sowing.	Number of times of Ploughing.	Quantity of Seed per Acre.	Cost per Acre.	Quantity of Grain produced.	Remarks.
Rice, of all descriptions.	May and June	4 or 5 times	12 to 15 seers	Rs. 3-8	35 to 40 maunds	Kalr land produces very good rice, but not so the mahjah land. It is a very wholesome food; from it are made sweetmeats, the flour is baked into chapaties. The straw is not so useful for fodder as the other straw, therefore its chief use is as a litter: the land in which it grows is manured: the crop is watched when standing green in the field.
Sesamum ...	July	3 or 4 times	10 to 12 chs.	...	$2\frac{1}{2}$ to 3 maunds	It yields an oil, and is used in making sweetmeats. Hindús on one of their fasts use it for food.
Jawár (*Holcus sorghum*)	Ditto	Ditto	20 to 25 seers	No need of hoeing	...	When green answers well as fodder for cattle, and called "charrí," The parched grain is eaten by the country people. Its flour is baked into chapaties.
Másh	July and August	2 or 3 times	5 to 8 seers	No need of hoeing	5 to 7 maunds	It is used as dál, and mixed with rice makes "kichri." In famine its flour is made into chapaties by the country people; also "baris" are made of it by soaking the grain in water for a night; next morning the soft grain is gently rubbed to remove the skin; it is next ground on a flat stone and mixed with spices. This paste is made into balls, which are put for a time in the sun till they dry.
Moth	June and July	2 or 3 times	5 to 7 seers	Ditto	4 to 5 maunds	Dál and kichri is made of this, and very seldom chapaties of its flour.
Múngi	July	2 or 3 times	3 to 4 srs.	Ditto	7 to 8 mds.	Ditto, ditto, ditto.
Bajra	June or July	3 or 4 times	3 to 4 seers	Ditto	8 to 9 maunds	The people when in need make bread of it, and also kichri: it is food for birds. It is much eaten, however, in the tract of country called Phattowar, between the Jhilam and Indus.

Kangní	Ditto	twice	1½ to 2 srs.	Ditto	10 to 12 ms.	Ditto, ditto, ditto.
Chína	Ditto	twice	2 to 2½ srs.	Ditto	8 to 10 mds.	Ditto, ditto, ditto.
Sawánk	Ditto	4 times	2 to 2½ seers	Ditto	8 to 10 maunds	It is made into "khir" (grain and milk boiled together), khushkah, gram boiled in water, kichri, etc.
Maize	Ditto	6 or 7 times	28 to 30 seers	Ditto	40 maunds	It is made into bread; the boiled grain is used for eating. It is generally parched and sold in bazar by people for eating, called "challi" and "sitta;" also it is used as dalya.
Mandal	July	2 or 3 times	10 to 12 srs.	Ditto	10 to 12 ms.	Useful for making bread, and is a sort of food for animals.
Kodra	Ditto	2 or 3 times	10 to 12 seers	Ditto	10 to 12 maunds	Bread is made of it; also kichri,—grain and rice boiled in water.
Arve or gú-yáṅ	Feb. and March	8 or 10 times	6 to 7 seers	Rs. 18	100 to 105 maunds	The root is used by natives and Europeans as an article of food. It is procurable in every season of the year.
Potato	October	15 times	6 to 7 seers	Rs. 25	140 maunds	Ditto, ditto, ditto.
Sugar-cane...	Feb. and March	15 or 16 times	Rs. 19	Rs. 20	150 maunds	It is much esteemed by all classes, who chew it as a sweet-meat; the process of sugar-making is described later in the book.
Musk-melon, water-melon, etc.	Ditto	12 or 14 times.	Rs. 3 to 4	Rs. 15 or 16	Rs. 37 to 63	Esteemed as a fruit.
Cotton	April & May	5 or 6 times	9 to 10 srs.	Rs. 12	5 to 6 mds.	A fibre.
Red pepper...	Ditto	5 or 6 times	Rs. 2½	Rs. 12	Rs. 20	When dry, the produce is about five maunds per acre.

It is now time to close this somewhat protracted agricultural sketch, with some tables illustrating the costs of cultivation and the profits of agriculture. I need hardly remind the reader that the Government assessment on lands is intended to be at the rate of about a fourth, and should not be more than one-sixth of the gross produce, ascertained at the time of settlement by careful enquiry, both as to existing assets and future capabilities. There can be little doubt that the majority of settlements are now on equitable terms, although it must be admitted that there is much inequality on the pressure of the assessments. The revision of settlement, at present in progress in many districts, cannot fail to remedy this defect to a great extent; and the security of a just and moderate assessment for a long period cannot fail to encourage agriculturists.* It has been said that, in some of the fertile districts of the Panjáb, a portion of the kharíf harvest alone is sufficient to pay the Government share, leaving almost the entire rabí as clear profit to the farmer, that is as his own assets, from which he pays his costs and expenses, and draws his profit. There can be little doubt that this is the case, and in a state of profound peace, when the agriculturist knows that the sum once assessed cannot be augmented during the continuance of the term specified in his settlement contract, he has every inducement to enlarge his efforts, and thus surely increase his profits. It only remains for us to overcome the great drawbacks to improvement that exist in the slothfulness of the people, and where they are not slothful (as many agricultural tribes are not), to overcome that aversion to change which leads them to be perfectly satisfied to plod on at the same rate now as they did 2000 years ago.

* The question of a permanent settlement is also under discussion; the subject is one of the greatest importance, but cannot be entered on here, because if any remarks were offered either on one side or the other, it would be impossible to avoid going into the whole subject.

Suggestions on these points will be found on the report of the jury on this class. I will only add here that one of the most powerful checks on cultivation that is in existence consists in the taxation of capital in assessing lands. It requires the nicest discrimination on the part of the assessing officer, and ought to receive his earnest attention, to see that capital is not taxed, otherwise the people will cease bringing land under cultivation, and cease sinking wells from the mere dread of an enhanced rental, which, if carelessly assessed according to mere *apparent assets*, will surely result in the crushing of agricultural enterprise.

I now give some lists showing the costs of cultivation in different parts. The first is a transcript of Major Clarke's estimate, which gives the costs and profits on 34 acres of land attached to a first-rate well, in the parganah of Shekopúra in the Rechna Doáb, which will give a fair representation of the majority of good lands in the Panjáb (excluding of course bar lands, and sandy, "tibba," tracts,) where the produce is assumed to be first-rate in quantity.

The 34 acres sown for the year are supposed to be sown thus: 12 acres for kharíf, 22 for rabí :—

12 Acres for Kharíf.
- 2 ghumaos of land for sugar-cane, or nearly 2 acres.
- 2 acres of cotton.
- 1 acre of rice.
- 1 acre of sarson (rape or mustard seed).
- 4 acres of jawár (*Holcus sorghum*).
- 2 acres of maize.

22 Acres for Rabí.
- 18 acres of wheat.
- 2 acres of barley.
- 2 acres of gújí (wheat and barley mixed).

Then the cost and profit will be as follows:—

KHARÍF.

Quantity of land under crop.	Crop.	Produce in kind.	Produce in money.			Expenses, including revenue, and all cesses at ¼th of produce.			Expenses of ditto at ⅓rd of produce.			Profit to cultivator or farmer paying ¼th of produce.			Ditto paying of ⅓rd of produce.		
			RS.	A.	P.	RS.	A.	P.	RS.	A.	P.	RS.	A.	P.	RS.	A.	P.
2 Acres.	Sugar-cane	80 mds. (goor)	200	0	0	149	9	0	163	3	6	50	7	0	36	12	0
2 „	Cotton	24 „	48	0	0	34	9	6	39	2	6	13	6	6	8	13	6
2 „	Maize	40 „	26	10	0	17	11	9	20	6	9	8	14	3	6	3	6
1 „	Rice	24 „	24	0	0	13	9	9	15	14	6	10	6	3	8	1	6
1 „	Mustard ...	8 „	8	0	0	4	8	0	5	3	9	3	8	0	2	12	3
4 „	Jawár	32 „	21	5	0	22	3	0	Is used as fodder, and the cost becomes almost nothing.								
12 „	....	....	327	15	0	242	3	0	243	14	9	86	10	0	62	10	9
			RABÍ.														
18 Acres.	Wheat	304 mds......	304	0	0	198	0	9	226	14	6	105	15	3	77	1	6
2 „	Barley	32 „	21	5	3	11	14	6	14	1	3	9	6	9	7	4	0
2 „	Gújí	32 „	25	10	0	14	8	0	16	14	6	11	2	0	8	11	6
22 Total.	....	....	350	15	3	224	7	3	257	14	3	126	8	0	93	1	0
	Grand Total		678	14	3	466	10	3	501	13	0	213	2	0	155	11	9

I have added one more table of the costs and profits of land, extracted from that very able and interesting volume, the Report on the Revised Settlement of the Sealkot District in 1865, by Mr. E. A. Prinsep. These tables are interesting from their great accuracy, as well as from their showing the state of things in a richly cultivated district like Sealkot. From the appendix to these tables a very good idea will be obtained of the proportion in which the Government revenue tax falls on the produce, and how equitable rates can be ascertained: the tables as here given are somewhat reduced in form from the originals, which, together with the illustrative matter of para. 241, *et seq.*, should be studied in the original report; the whole work will repay perusal.

The land taken as a standard is 30 ghumaos, attached to one first-class well in the Charkari Mahál, or well-abounding tract of the district.

The total expenditure for a year from pucka well, irrigating 30 ghumaos, in the Charkari Mahál of Sealkot is:—

		R.	A.	P.
Wages of labour.	Ploughman, @ 2 maunds kucha per mensem and 1 rupee cash	22	0	0
	Coolie, per annum	4	0	0
	Cowherd	26	0	0
		52	0	0
Farm service.	Potter, @ 1 máni per harvest	10	0	0
	Carpenter, @ ½ máni	5	0	0
	Carpenter, @ ½ máni	5	0	0
		20	0	0
Cost of fodder and keep of stock.	5 yoke of oxen's feed, besides grass and clover, @ ½ a máni per head per annum, or cash charge for salt, Rs. 2	27	0	0
Repair of ploughs and tools.	5 Ploughs @ Rs. 0–8 per plough per annum	2	8	0
	Iron for trowels (*rambha*), scythes (*dátri*), etc.	1	0	0
	Ditto for spades	1	0	0
	Well-rope required every two months, @ Rs. 1 per "mál"	3	0	0
		7	8	0
Value or cost of seed.	1 Ghumao sugar-cane, @ 1 pai per 4 marlahs	2	0	0
	2 Ditto cotton, @ 16 ditto	0	4	0
	4 Ditto maize, @ 1 topa per kanal	2	0	0
	4 Ditto, "charri," @ 3 ditto	2	8	0
	Total (*Autumn Crop*), 12 *ghumaos*	8	12	0

Value or cost of seed.		R.	A.	P.
	10 Ghumaos wheat, @ 1 pai per kanal	8	0	0
	4 Ditto, "guji," ditto	4	0	0
	2 Ditto barley, @ 3 pai ditto	2	0	0
	3 Ditto turnips, @ 1 pai per ghumao	1	0	0
	½ Ditto flax, @ 1 pai per kanal	0	3	0
	½ Poppy, @ Rs. 2 per ghumao	0	1	0
	Total (*Spring Crop*), 18 *ghumaos*	15	4	0
	Grand Total Rs.	130	8	0

NOTE.—One mání is equal to 12½ maunds kucha. A maund kucha is variable, from 13 to 20 seers, being usually counted 2½ kucha = 1 pucka; the standard maund is 40 seers of 80 tolahs each.

The standard maund is sometimes called *pakka* or *Angrezi*, but more often the term *pakka* is applied to the "Lahori maund," the old weight which is rather heavier, viz., 3 kucha maunds = 1 Lahori.

Annual gross income for one pucka well, irrigating 30 ghumaos of land, in the Charkari Mahál, Sealkot district.

Harvest.	Area under crop, in ghumaos.	Usual distribution of crops.	Average yield per ghumao, in kucha maunds.	Average market price for 30 years (per rupee).	Yield in the deduced money equivalent.	Total value in money for whole crop.	Grand total value.
Autumn (kharíf) 12 ghumaos, at an average gross rate of Rs. 12-10	2	Sugar-cane ..	45	1½ maunds	32	64	
	2	Cotton	20	1¼ "	16	32	
	4	Maize	24	2 "	12	48	
	4	"Charri" ...	...	per ghumao	2	8	152
Spring (rabí), 18 ghumaos, at an average gross rate of Rs. 17-2	10	Wheat	30	2¼ maunds	13-4	140	
	4	Guji	35	3½ "	10	40	
	2	Barley	40	4 "	10	20	
	1	Turnips (not counted, as consumed by cattle).					
	½	Flax	10	2 "	5	5	
	½	Poppy.........	...	per ghumao	6	3	208
Grand total of the 30 ghumaos, for both harvests...							360

Space forbids me to extract from the Sealkot Report the remaining table, which fills up the page in the original, and which shows how an equitable revenue rate per well can be deduced from the above data. To summarize the results in the form of a per centage, it will be found that calculating the gross proceeds of 30 acres, at a money value of Rs. 360, this gives Rs. 12 an acre; and the following scheme will show the costs and profits according as the Government revenue is assessed at Rs. 2-8 or at 2 per acre.

	At Rs. 2-8.			At Rs. 2-0.		
	RS.	A.	P.	RS.	A.	P.
Expenses	130	8	0	130	8	0
Subsistence	100	0	0	100	0	0
Interest, etc.	17	10	0	15	8	0
Revenue and cesses	85	8	0	68	6	0
Profits	26	6	0	45	10	0
Profit at 7 per cent.				Profit at 13 per cent.		

Where the Government revenue demand is at the rate of Rs. 2-8 per ghumao, the farm expenses and subsistence of two families are 64 per cent.; interest on revenue and cash payments of farm, 5 per cent.; Government revenue, 23·5 per cent.; leaving nett profit, 7·4 per cent: or if the Government rate be Rs. 2 per ghumao, then these figures will become 64 per cent., 4·2 per cent., 18·6 per cent.; and profits, 13·0, respectively.

Under the various headings of the collection will be found an occasional list of costs in detail of the cultivation of the various crops.

When the owner does not cultivate, but receives his malikana, the profit to him is nearly the same.

The last point I shall notice is the native classification of diseases and blights incident to crops, and again quote Major Clarke* and Mr. E. A. Prinsep.

* Agriculture of the Réchna Doab.

Corn is lodged (hawá-zad) by strong wind, and is injured by want of rain, by frost, hail, rats, jackals. The following are the names of insects, animals, and diseases which injure crops:—

Sugar-cane.—Tela, huda, kírí, soka, pála, nisarna, músh, kuchra, and kangíárí.

Cotton.—Phirtí, tela, soka, pála (frost) and rats.

Makai.—Kírí, toka, siyank, tupkí.

Charí.—Kírí, toka, and tela.

Rice.—Jholur and rats.

Moth, mung, and *mash.*—Tela, toka, and bhutoth, or poachur.

Wheat, barley, and *gúji.* — Kúngí, lakha, jholur, patáka, toka, kangíárí, and trel.

A few of the above may be specifically mentioned.

Kúngí.—A red rust. The "kúngí," as far as I can discover, is a blight that comes upon young wheat (which is sown late) in the months of January and February, after much rain. If there has been several days of rain, and followed by a cessation for three or four days, and during this time the sun does not appear, but heavy lowering clouds hanging about, bringing sultry weather, then this red "rust" appears on the ears of wheat. The damp is said to bring it on, but it goes away if the sun shines after rain, or the cold wind ceases. It attacks wheat and nothing else, barley is quite free from it, because it is believed that barley is not a grain that is heating. Gram and masúr, which are sown at the same time as wheat, are free from it. This "kúngí" is the chief disease wheat is liable to. It appears always first at the junction of the large leaf, with the blade, and thus spreads to the young ear; if it should disappear in three days, then there is hope for the crop. If it lasts and spreads beyond that time, then the crop is ruined,—generally it reduces the yield by about one-third; sometimes by half; the disease lasts altogether about ten days, and when in its height so extensive is the "red rust" that is accumulated, that, if a man walks through the field, his feet and legs will be quite covered over with a coating of red.

If the clouds break, after rain has ceased, and the sun comes out, then the blight is driven away. If a breeze blows from east at the time, it is intensified, but if the wind shifts round to west, it is blown off on the ground. The chief cause is assigned to the pressure of lowering clouds. If they are disturbed by the sun breaking out, or by a breeze removing the sultriness in the air, then there is hope of the blight disappearing in such cases; all that will remain will be mere discoloration. If, however, the sultry state of the atmosphere continue for three or four days continuously, then the disease is looked upon as certain to affect the whole crop. If timely rain, or west wind intervenes, *within the first three days* of its first appearance, then it is washed or blown off, and no real harm is done, for the disease has had time only to get on the leaf, and not to spread to the ear of wheat in the leaf. The wheat leaf will gather its strength and greenness as it grows, and all trace of the discoloration, even, will in such cases disappear.

The actual loss sustained by the crop is not known till the wheat ripens. The ear is found to have no grains, and where most of the blades turn out grainless, they turn yellow, and show what loss has been done about one month and a half after, *i.e.*, in the first fifteen days of April.

Tela.—Is a dark-coloured powder, saltish to the taste, which lies between the outer and inner coating of sugar-cane and stops its growth; the only remedy for it is to wash it off with water. In wheat it causes the plant to turn black. (The "smut" on wheat, etc. is called *kali atta;* it is a fungoid growth).

Huda.—The drying up of leaves, and their becoming yellow in Sáwun and Bhadoṅ, without any apparent cause.

Nisarna.—This is not a disease, but it is esteemed very bad for sugar-cane to blossom (nisarna), and such canes as blossom, being evil-omened, are taken up and given to whomsoever will have them.

Pála.—Frost, when the north wind blows piercingly, and the cold discolour the cane, the taste of which becomes saltish, and the produce is inferior; the cane has also a disagreeable smell, and the top dries up.

Kuchra.—In Jeth and Har, when the young cane is about 20 inches high, this insect eats the heart, and does very great injury to the crop, destroying as much as half, perhaps.

Kangiári.—These are barren branches, growing out of the cane, which do not give juice,neither will cattle eat them; if kangíárí prevail much in a crop, it injures it to the extent of one-twentieth.

Kirí.—An insect so called, which eats the germ of young plants, particularly sugar-cane. In Jeth and Baisákh, sometimes the crop is destroyed by it; rain or water is the best remedy; sometimes the "madár" plant (*Calotropis Hamiltonii*) is cut, and laid in the water which is to irrigate the field; the bitterness thus given destroys the kírí.

Soka.—Is occasioned by want of water, the cane dries inside, becomes hollow, and throws out great quantities of "choee," or outer leaf.

Phirti.—In Jeth and Har, young cotton plants, in maira soil, are liable to be injured by sand storms, which wound them and they dry up. The remedy for this is to water the crop, by which means the sand holds together. Phirtí also injures sugar-cane.

Toka.—Is a moth, which injures young shoots by nipping them off, as if with a pair of scissors.

Dhimak or *white ants.*—If rains do not fall in Sáwun and Bhadoṅ white ants do great damage; rain kills them.

Trel or *dew.*—If heavy dews fall in Assuh and Kartak, the jowar crop is much injured, the grain cracks and becomes dark, and almost friable.

Bhutoth.—This disease arises from the east wind blowing, which causes moth, mash and múng to shrivel up, and the pods do not fill.

Lishk or *Lightning.*—Should it lighten much when gram is about to form its flowers, it injures them, and the pods do not fill well, and an insect is also produced thereby.

Tupki.—When the rains are very heavy, the stalks of Indian corn shoot up, and spindle, and yield no grain.

Another drawback to good crops, particularly in districts below the hills, such as Gujrát, Sealkot, and Gurdáspur, is the frequency of hail-storms, which are prevalent in the months Phaggan and Chet, sometimes they come in October. At the former season they always cause much injury to wheat when it begins to ripen. In Tila in the Jhilam district, the "jogis" are propitiated by presents, to come and forewarn the people of storms. They plunge into a field with a drawn sword, or a knife is stuck into a mound with offerings placed round it; goats are often sacrificed, and people are stupid enough to pay for this deception. Lightning does damage to such crops as gram, masúr, flax, and tíl, which are called "phoilsah," or lishk-már, lightning-struck, in consequence. The flowers fall off and the seed is lost.

Crops are preserved from birds by scare-crows, or "daránas." A blackened earthpot stuck on a stick being a favourite method. In the case of tall crops, such as sugar-cane, etc., light platforms, called "manas," are erected, on which a person is stationed day and night to frighten birds, by shouting and discharging clay pellets, etc., etc.

Notwithstanding that the Panjáb is a great grain-producing country, some grain is imported from Malwa and the fertile districts, in its neighhourhood, the mart for whose produce is the city of Jhánsi, whence the grain is exported northwards. The internal traffic in grain is considerable, from the fertile districts. Large quanties of grain comes down the Satlaj to Fírozpúr. Rice is largely exported from Kangra to other districts. Hushyarpúr and the Jálandhar districts supply much grain also to other districts. Sugar is exported largely from parts of the Panjáb, both in a finished state and as "goor," or molasses. Latterly there has arisen a large export trade of wheat and sugar, cotton and oil seeds, towards England, *viâ* Múltán and Bombay.

Ast, است अस्त

A Sanskrit word signifying the setting of the sun. Astáchal अस्ताचल is the name of the Western mountain, behind which the sun is said to set. Uday उदय is the word used in opposition to Ast, to signify the rising of the sun. It is the name also of the mountain over which it rises. As Ugmana is used with Athmana,* *q.v.* so is Uday used with Ast. Thus, it is a common benediction in the North-West to say to an English

* I have put this word in Part IV., because of a note attached to it containing a long string of miscellaneous words, which do not come under this head.—B.

functionary, أدي است تک تمهارا راج هو "May your dominion extend from East to West.

Bíjkhád, بيج كهاد बीजखाद

A term used in Rohilkhand to signify advance of seed and food to agriculturalists: Taḳḳávi being understood to apply solely to advances for cattle, and for sinking wells.

The word is derived from بيج seed, and كهاد manure.

Bísar, بيسر बीसर

Gleanings left in the field for the lower orders.—E. Oudh.

Silá or Salla are the words used in the Doáb, Rohilkhand, Dehli, Bundelkhand, and Benares.

Bíjwár, بيجوار बीज्वार

Perquisite of the lower classes, consisting of a portion of seed-corn, which is brought away each day from the field.—Rohilkhand.

It is called Bijáí in Dehli. Both words are derived from بيج seed.

Bengat, بينگت बेंगत

Seed.—Seed given to an indigent ryot for sowing, who is to repay the same at the time of harvest, with such additional quantity as may be agreed upon.—Benares. See Bísar.

Berí, بيڑي बेडी

Fetters.—Irons fastened to the legs of either men or animals; also the basket used for raising water for the purpose of irrigation. It is generally made of bamboo in the East, and of leather in the West. It is suspended from four ropes, and swung by two men. The word is used in the Doáb and Rohilkhand, as are also Lihṛí, Chhapa, and Boka. In Benares the word Daurí is used, and sometimes Boka. In Dehli Dal, and in Bundelkhand, Dalea and Dúgla.—See these articles.*

A drawing of the *beri* will be found in the plate at the commencement of Part IV.

Bháolí, بهاولي भावली

Distribution of the produce of a harvest between Zamíndár and cultivator. Rent paid in kind instead of money.—See Glossary under Behavilly and Bhaweley.†

Bhogbandak, بهوگبندهك भोगबंधक

Mortgage.—A debt in which lands, trees, or animals, are pledged to the lender; the produce in corn, fruits, milk, labour, etc., being considered an equivalent for interest.

"The rent, or use, or occupation of a pledged house, or the produce of a pledged field, is called bhoga labdha, interest by enjoyment."—"Vrihaspati, Digest," B. I., c. i. s. 35.

The word is derived from भोग enjoyment, and बंधक pledge.

Patbandhak is a pledge, the usufruct of which pays principal and interest within a certain period, and therefore ensures its own redemption. A debt is thus said pat jana, from the Sanskrit Root pat, to fall.

Dishtbandhak, *q. v.* is equivalent to hypothecation. These expressions, though in general acceptation as law-terms, are not much used in the transactions of the common people, except in the Lower Doáb and Benares.

Bhúíndagdhá, بهوئيندگدها भूइंदग्धा

Gifts at marriages and funerals. The word is derived from

* Káli Rái spells these words त्रिहडी, बेंडी and डाल.—E. *add.* This Káli Rái appears to have been a Tahsildar, or, perhaps, a native settlement officer. He is often quoted in E. *add.*—B.

† This kind of tenure is very common in Southern Behar, and is similar to Batai, *q.v.*—B.

the ceremony of burning earth, which is performed previous to their presentation: from भूईं earth, and दगधना to burn.—E. Oudh.*

Bhúínbhái or Bhúnbhái, بهوئنبهائي or بهونبهائي
भूईंभाई or भूंभाई

A term used in the Dehli Territory to signify a man invited by a proprietor to reside in a village, and invested by him with a portion of land, which he is not at liberty to dispose of to others. From भूईं or भू earth, and भाई brother.

Bhúnḍarí,† بهونڈري भूंडरी

A small patch of cultivation. Lands let without rent by Zamíndárs, either to village servants, such as barbers, bearers, watchmen, and the like; or to indigent relations, fakírs, and friends who come to sojourn in a village for a season.

Baunda is the term used generally in Rohilkhand and the Doáb; but it is variously pronounced Bhaundarí, Bhúnda, Bhundarí, and perhaps most correctly Bohndarí.

Bhadáhar, بهداهر भदाहर

The cutting of grain when it is only half ripe. It is a common saying—

चना भदाहर श्रौर जौ कुरा
काटो गेहूं ढेंका ढारा

"Cut your gram half ripe, your barley ripe, your wheat when the ear bends down."

The word is confined to Rohilkhand. Bhadbhadána and Hureha are used in a similar sense in the Doáb; and Dhesar

* Buchanan II. 496.—E. *add.* He probably refers to Montgomery Martin's Edition of the Buchanan Papers, called "Eastern India."—B.

† I think this should be spelt भूईंधरी from धरना to hold.—B.

and Gadra in other places. These last terms are applied generally to any half-ripe fruit.

Bhanṭá, بھنٹا भंटा

Ploughman's wages in kind.—Rohilkhand.

Bhaṭṭa is used in this sense in Dehli and the Doáb.

Bharpáí, بھرپائي भरपाई

A release in full in Ságar and Benares; the corresponding word is Bharautí भरौती.

It is derived from two words which are entered in the receipt, as in the endorsement, मैं ने कौडी कौडी भर पाई "I have received every Kauṛí in full."

The equivalent term in Persian is رسيد rasíd, a receipt, from رسيدن rasídan, to arrive.

Bhaṭṭá, بھٹا भट्टा

Ploughman's wages in kind.—See Bhanṭa.

Bijhgáh, بجھگاه बिझगाह

A scare-crow. The word is in general use, and is derived from बिझकाना Bijhkáná, to frighten. Ḍaráwá ڈراوا is more frequently used in Dehli, and Dháí دھائي if it is moved by a string, as when a bambú or a stick is pulled against a bough of a tree, to produce a noise and frighten away the birds. Other words in common use are Dhokhá دھوکھا, Dharakká دھرکا, Dharallá دھرلا and Dhúhá دھوھا *q.v.*

Binahar, بنہر बिनहर

A gatherer of cotton; from Binná بنا to pick.—Benares.

The corresponding word in the Doáb and Rohilkhand is Paikar; in Bundelkhand, Paihara; and in Dehli, Púí. He generally receives one-tenth of the gross produce, as well as a share, sometimes amounting to a fourth, of the cleaned cotton.

Bisár, بسار बिसार

Loan of seed, upon stipulation of ample refund after harvest.—E.

⁂ In some parts of Gorakhpúr and Champáran, and for aught I know to the contrary, in other parts of the country as well, a simple and ingenious system called the देवढ़िया deoṛhiyá or "one-and-a-half," is followed. At sowing time the cultivator borrows, say one maund of seed, value two rupees, and engages to repay it at harvest with interest at fifty per cent., or in simpler words to repay one-and-a-half for every one he receives, whence the system takes its name. He generally applies, not to grain dealers or banias, but to one of the wealthier peasants, or to his zamíndár, many of whom have large accumulations of grain stored up on purpose to trade with. The zamíndár, nothing loth, advances the necessary grain, and when the harvest comes round demands instant repayment. The ryot tenders him a maund and a-half of grain; but the price of grain has fallen, as it always does at harvest-time, to, say, one rupee a maund, a maund and a-half would only be worth at that time 1 rupee 8 anas, which would not repay the lender, who therefore refuses to take it, and demands three rupees, two as the cost of the seed and one as interest, and he insists on immediate payment of either three rupees in cash, or the equivalent in grain at the market rate of the day, in other words three maunds. The ryot of course has no cash, and therefore pays in kind three maunds of grain, as an equivalent for three rupees. This grain the lender keeps for months, till the price of grain rises to two or two and a-half rupees a maund, when he sells, and by this process pockets seven and a-half rupees in return for his outlay of one maund! But this iniquitous system is sometimes pursued a step further. Suppose that the harvest is a bad one, as often happens. The ryot comes to the lender and says, "I cannot pay you till next harvest." "Very good," says the lender, "I shall charge you deoṛhiyá on the whole amount, principal and interest," compound interest in fact. The account then stands over till next harvest when it assumes this shape—

Lent originally one maund of grain, value ...	2 rupees.
Interest at 50 per cent.	1
	3

Market rate of grain at harvest time, 1 rupee = 1 maund.
Therefore due 3 maunds.

Market rate of grain at sowing time (after a bad harvest), 3 rupees.

Therefore 3 maunds	= 9 rupees.
Interest at 50 per cent.	= $4\frac{1}{2}$
Total................	$13\frac{1}{2}$

Market rate of grain at harvest time, 1 rupee = 1 maund.
Therefore due $13\frac{1}{2}$ maunds

which will be sold three months later at $2\frac{1}{2}$ rupees a maund = 33 rupees 8 anas. And all this for one maund originally lent! The trick consists in shifting the terms of the account from kind to cash and back again as often as the state of the market requires it. I have given above a very simple and moderate example, but by raising the interest, as is sometimes done at each renewal of the loan, it may be imagined what immense profit to the lender, and what hopeless ruin to the borrower, results. I have heard of cases where grain was lent at siwáiyá, or 25 per cent. the first harvest, at deoṛhiyá, or 50 per cent. the second, at tínpáwiyá, or 75 per cent., the third, and so on; so that out of an original amount of one maund lent, a debt of 100 maunds had (owing to bad harvests, and various additional extortions) arisen in two years! The lenders are generally Zamíndárs, and there is a class of Rajputs converted to Islam, and called ठकुराई Thakuráis, who have earned a specially bad name by this practice. During the famine of 1867, the houses of these men were naturally frequently pillaged. In some cases bands of starving ryots, headed by their paṭwárí, surrounded the bursting granaries of these men, and helped themselves to the contents, the paṭwárí writing down each person's name, and the amount taken by him, and handing the list to the owner, when they all departed quietly and orderly to their homes, after promising to repay when times improved. Perhaps the most serious, though not the most striking results of famines in India, are the long train of indebtedness which they leave behind, entanglements such as it takes the ryot years, and sometimes generations, to wipe off. The native Zamíndárs seem to have no pity on such occasions, and it is impossible to interfere without making matters worse. The detestable system I have described above was never in fuller force than during the dreadful summer of 1867, when the agricultural population was decimated by famine.—B.

Bohní, بوهني बोहनी

The first money received during the day by shopkeepers and hucksters. No credit is allowed, nothing but ready money being received on such occasions. The practice is universal in India, and is precisely like the Handsel of England.

Bau, بو बौ

Is the name of the fee or perquisite of the Zamíndár, whenever the daughter of any cultivator in his village is married. The word is probably a corruption of Bahú बहू, a bride.

Múṛásá and Manḍwach are also used in this sense.

Badní, بدني बदनी

A contract by which the borrower gives a bond at high interest, and in satisfaction of which he assigns his crops valued far below the market price. It is called Buddunní in the Glossary. The word is derived from بدنا to wager, to agree.

Bahoro, بہورو बहोरो

The name given to the sloping pathway for bullocks drawing a well; especially that by which the bullocks return towards the well. The more general word is Pairí.

Bahoro is chiefly used in the Central Doáb; but the origin of the word can be traced, where Bahoro is unknown, in the verb بہورنا *bahúrná,* to return, to come back. Thus, a man standing at the well-head, amongst other ditties which he chants, as well to soothe his toil as mark the time, will frequently say—

बहुरके ले आव भाई मेरा राम *

That is "bring back the bullocks," as the water bag is raised. Hence Bahoro comes to signify the road by which the bullocks are brought back. We trace it again in the common Hindí word بہورن "again."

Banotsarg, بنوتسرگ बनोत्सर्ग

Is the name given to the marriage ceremony performed in honour of a newly-planted orchard, without which preliminary observance it is not proper to partake of its fruit.

A man holding the Salagram personates the bridegroom, and another holding the sacred Tulsí (Ocymum sanctum) personates the bride. After burning a hom, or sacrificial fire, the officiating Brahman puts the usual questions to the couple about to be united. The bride then perambulates a small spot marked out in the centre of the orchard. Proceeding from the south towards the west, she makes the circuit three times, followed at a short distance by the bridegroom, holding in his hand a

* Ram is a mode of salutation and friendly address almost always used during well irrigation. Hence the common proverb—

गांडी की मसकरी कुआ राम राम

In which a driver's rudeness and incivility are contrasted with the courtesy of the well-man.

strip of her chádar or garment. After this the bridegroom takes precedence, making his three circuits, and followed in like manner by his bride. The ceremony concludes with the usual offerings.

The word is derived from the Sanskrit बन a forest, a grove, and उत्सर्ग abandoning, resigning, a donation, a presentation of anything promised to a god or Brahman with suitable ceremonies. (Wilson's Sanskrit Dictionary, p. 144.) Thus also वृषोत्सर्ग is applied to the ceremony of marriage performed in the name of the bullock which is abandoned to the wide world on the eleventh day of mourning for a near relative, and which infests our streets and high roads under the name of Bijar, Sáṇr, and Brahmaní Bull.—See Jalotsarg.

Barábháo, بڑابہاو बडाभाव

A kind of appraisement. Literally, a high price, from बड़ा large, and भाव rate. The term is used in distinction to the Akhtíj ka bhao, in which, when money is borrowed by a cultivator, he agrees to re-pay it in corn, with the úp or interest, at the price prevailing on the day of Akhtíj. (See Akhtíj.) The grain merchant can scarcely ever lose under this engagement, as in consequence of the season of the year, the average necessarily ranges high.

In borrowing money on Barábháo, the cultivator agrees to re-pay it with interest at the highest rate of the whole season. Suppose a man, at the beginning of the season, when wheat is selling at 20 seers per rupee, borrows 10 rupees on Barábháo, at the rate of 5 seers úp; and supposing corn subsequently at any time during the season to range up to 25 seers, he will have to pay $1\frac{1}{4}$ maund as interest, added to $6\frac{1}{4}$ maunds principal, in all $7\frac{1}{2}$ maunds, having borrowed only a few months previously what was equal to 5 maunds.

⁂ It will be seen that this system, where the grain merchant is the lender, though somewhat exorbitant, coming to as much as 50 per cent., is still tolerably fair when contrasted with that pursued by the petty zamíndárs of Champáran, described under Bisár, *q.v.*—B.

Barháwan, بڑھاون बढावन

A round cake of cowdung placed on the top of a heap of corn, to prevent the effects of an evil eye, and for good luck's sake, in order that the corn may increase. There is a well-known satirical couplet in ridicule of the practice.

जग बौराहा त्रिष्णा बिबस भूत पूज भावलेवें
बढे र बढे बढावना जन किसान रचदेवें

"The world is mad, and for the sake of avarice will worship devils, and will still put on the Barháwan, whether increase result from it or not."

The word is used chiefly to the East of Allahabad. To the Westwand Chank and Chhattúr, *q.v.* are applied in the same sense.

Barrá, بَرّا बर्रा

A rope; especially that which is pulled on the fourteenth of the light half of the month Kuár, which day is known as the Bantá Chaudas, **बांटा चौदस**. The rope, which is made of the grass called Makra, is thicker than a man's arm! and that village party in whose quarter the rope is broken, or by whom the rope is pulled out of the hands of their antagonists, remain the champions during the ensuing year, and retain possession of the rope. If, during the next year, no other party succeed in breaking the new rope, that also remains as their spoil, and so continues till more successful competitors are found. The practice is observed chiefly in the East of these Provinces, being unknown, even by name, in the West.

Barsodiyá, برسوديا बरसोदिया
Barsáliyá, برساليا बरसालिया

A servant engaged in cultivation, who contracts for one year's service; from बरस a year.

Bayá, بيا बया

A person appointed in bazars to measure grain. The word is principally used in the Lower Doáb and Bundelkhand; in other parts the word *kayál* is more usual.

Bayáí, بيائي बयाई

Weighman's perquisite; from the preceding word.

Chánk, چانك चांक

Chánk, or Chanka, is a stamp fixed on a stack or heap of grain, called also chhapa, from छापना *chhápná*, to print.

The Chánk is cut on wood, and is impressed on a cake of moist earth, called the Barkat kí mittí. The legend engraved upon it generally consists of such words as عاقبت بخيرباد "may the result be happy," or ايمان كي سلامت "the safety of good faith," to imply that the honour of the parties to whose care the corn is entrusted is appealed to against any dishonest alienation of it. The seal is then placed on the sides of the heap, never as in the Chhattúr, *q.v.*, on the top, lest the increase of corn may be thereby prevented. The Chánk is only impressed where Baṭáí tenures prevail, and only on heaps which are to be divided, or, having been divided, are left under charge of only one of the parties.

Another meaning of Chánk is given under the articles Chhattur and Barháwan, *q.v.*

Chánk is also the name of the ceremony which is observed in the threshing-ground at the time of forming the winnowed corn into a heap.

After the foundation has been laid as described in the article Angaunga, or according to any other mode in local use, and after the heap has been raised about a foot, a man, standing with his face to the North, takes the winnowing basket in his right hand, his left hand being full of grain, and commencing from the South goes round from West to East, and again to the South, pressing the basket against the bottom of the heap. When the heap is raised to about three feet, each hand changes its occupation, his left hand holds the basket, and his right the grain, and he circumambulates the heap the contrary way, from East to West, pressing the basket against it. When the heap is raised about five feet, he changes hands again, and goes through the same form as he did on the first occasion, pressing the basket against the top of the heap. It is seldom that more than three circuits are made, but if the heap is very high, as many as five, or even six are made.

Sometimes the Chánk is not performed till the entire heap is made, when it is perambulated three times successively in the order above-mentioned.

When the performer again reaches the South at the conclusion of his last circuit, he places the basket before him on the ground, and joining the palms of his hands together, makes a low bow to the corn, exclaiming :

स्यावढ परमेश्वर जी
से बर्कत दीजिये

"Lord God of the corn-heap,
Give a hundred blessings."

or,

अन्न देवता जो
सहेस गुना हजिये

"Corn, God and Lord,
Mayest thou multiply a thousand-fold."

or,

सहदेवन गोशाईन हम को तुम राज ब्योहर उर्गिन करो

"God give us prosperity in our affairs."

or some other ejaculation, by which he hopes to obtain a blessing on his corn.

This is the mode as it is practised in the Upper Doáb and Dehli. In Rohilkhand it is different. In the northern parts of that province, a man, holding nothing in the left hand, goes from the South towards the West, then towards the North till he reaches the Merh or limit, or pole: he then returns the same way, and goes towards the East till he reaches the pole, and back again to the South—he then places the basket on the ground, and makes the same obeisance, concluding with some pious ejaculation. In the Southern portion of Rohilkhand they generally press their hands from bottom to top in six different parts of the heap, and repeat each time the name of one of the Chakravartti Rajas, such as Mandhata, Ben, Dalíp, etc.

In the Lower and Central Doáb and Saugor, the ceremony generally consists in making a circle with cow-dung or ashes round the Ras and Thapa at the same time, commencing from the East, and going from South to West till the East point is again reached; the operator taking care all the while to hold his breath. Sometimes the South is again reached by going back again from the East, and thus a complete circle is not formed. The part from the East to the South being left, because from that part the presentations to the Brahmans and gods are taken and put aside. The same happens at the Pakarma in worship, for a more obvious reason, that the foot may not overstep the running water.

In most other places the ceremony of going round the Thápa, or heap formed for the village servants, is somewhat different. The man goes from the South to the North, and back again, not placing his foot anywhere on the Eastern side, because that is the aman or kand, which contains the refuse corn belonging to the Chamars, which having fallen behind the winnower, is of a very inferior quality.

The entire ceremony of Chánk is gone through with the utmost silence, which is to be observed till the grain is measured and distributed. The reason is said to be that evil sprites who "bootless make the breathless housewife churn," injure the corn if any talking takes place.

All these rites, ridiculous as they are, are devoutly supposed to be efficacious for obtaining the advantages which it is their aim and object to secure, and though from the influence of the opinions of their utilitarian masters the common people are getting gradually weaned from their credulity and superstition, and these trifling observances begin to be less thought of than they were a century ago, a long time yet will elapse before they cease to be practised.

Chhaur, چھور छौर

Walking a boundary with a raw cowskin on the head, under a solemn oath to decide correctly. Five sticks are also held in the hand, to imply that the arbitrator is the representative of the Pancháyat.

The word is in use in the North-West. Muṅhchhandarí (मुंहछन्दरी) is used in Saugor and Rajputana, and Dill in Benares, in which latter province the Harbans Purána is laid on the head.—See Gola.

Chhattur, چھتر छत्तुर

Is the name given to the covering placed on a heap of winnowed corn, from the Hindi छत्तर Chhattar, an umbrella. It is known also by the names of Barháwan and Chánk, *q.v.* In Benares it is generally a mere cake of cow-dung; elsewhere, it is a shoot of grass, or a dry stick of Arhar, with several (generally five) projecting twigs, on each of which a small piece of cow-dung is placed, or a flower of the Ak or Madar (Asclepias gigantea). Sometimes a spear is stuck in the ground, not on, but at the side of the heap, and sometimes an artificial flower is placed at a short distance from the bottom of the heap.

The object in fixing the Chhattur upon or near the corn, is to prevent the effect of an evil eye, or the injury which is sure to be sustained from the praises of any casual visitor. It is for this reason that natives, when their children are sent out on a visit, always place upon their cheek or forehead some black spot, as it is considered to have the virtue of preventing the effects which would be occasioned by any expression of admiration. By the superstitious natives of this country, the Chhattur is devoutly believed to offer a sure remedy against the disastrous effects of fascination. If his Rás or heap be but surmounted with this fanciful emblem, the husbandman may sleep secure; but as sure as he neglects it, should an evil eye fall upon the grain, it is infallibly gone, and he will have to weep over the lost hopes of a year's labours.

Chamráwat, جمراوٹ चमरावट

The perquisites of Chamars.

Dáen, داین दाएं

Dáen, or Dáona, is the tying of a number of bullocks together for the purpose of treading out the grain from the ear. As in this action they are invariably driven from the right to left, these words may perhaps have some connection with Dahina, the right hand.

Dánt tinká, دانت تنکا दांत तिनका

The taking a straw, or piece of grass, in the mouth, to deprecate anger, or to express complete submission. The action is generally accompanied by standing on one leg, which puts the supplicant in a ludicrous position. The custom shews the reverence of the Hindús for the cow, the action implying, "I am your cow, and therefore entitled to your protection." The custom is very old, and is alluded to in the inscription on the

Lat of Fíroz-Shah, at Dehli. "Tears are evident in the eyes of the enemy's consort; blades of grass are perceived between thy adversaries' teeth ("As. Researches, Vol. VII. p. 180). The image also is not rejected by the poets. Muhammad Aman Nisar says—

رنگ دکھایا جو زرد عاشق رنجور نے

خوف سے تنکا لیا دانتوں میں کافور نے

"When the afflicted lover shewed his sallow face,
Káfúr, through fear, seized the grass with his teeth."

Dáridr khedná, داردر کھیدنا दारिद्र खेदना

Literally, to drive out poverty; a custom observed on the morning of the Dewalí, of taking a sieve, or winnowing basket, and beating it in every corner of the house, exclaiming at the same time—

ईश्वर पैठो दरिद्र निकलो

that is, God enter, and poverty depart; or some equivalent prayer. The basket is then carried outside the village, generally towards the East or North-East, and being there thrown away, is supposed, like the scape-goat with respect to the sins of the Israelites, to bear with it the poverty and distress of the people. In some places this ceremony is called Serua, and, instead of beating a sieve, the people brush the house, and carry out the dirt in a basket.

The night preceding this observance is passed in watchfulness, and is hence called Kojagara; as Lakshmi descended on this night, and promised wealth to those who were awake. It is enjoined that men should play on this night some game of chance with their wives, which requisition is in practice construed to mean a general indulgence in gambling.

People do not now, as a rule, play cards with their wives, but parties of merchants collect for the purpose and play all night. Large sums of money change hands over the cards on this night.

Dáwan, داون दावन

The process of thrashing by means of bullocks, in the mode adopted by almost all Eastern nations.—See Dáen.

Dípdán, دیپدان दीपदान

Land assigned to Brahmans on the banks of rivers, to deprecate river encroachments.—E. Oudh and Benares. The word is derived from द्वीप, an island, and दान, a gift.

The same word, but derived from dípa, a lamp, is applied to a ceremony observed for ten days after the decease of a relative. It consists in suspending from a Pípal, or some other tree, a lamp, for the purpose of lighting the departed spirit on the dark road to Jampúrí (Yamapuri). This place is declared in the sacred books to be the general rendezvous of the departed from all parts of the world, from which they proceed in a body with a proper guard, composed of the servants of Yama (Pluto), to Dharmapuri.—As. Res., Vol. X., p. 145.

Díwár, دیوار दीवार

Perhaps more correctly Dihwar, is the god under whose special care a village is placed; the Genius loci for whom a portion of grain is always set apart at each harvest.—Benares.

The corresponding term in the North-West is Thanapati (the lord of the place). In Bundelkhand, Gram Deota. In Saugor he is styled Miroyá मिड़ोया, from the fact of his being the guardian of boundaries (see note to Damcha). The Díwár is very commonly, and even where these local names prevail, styled Bhúmia, from Bhúm, land.

The Díwárs have various names, such as Katesarí, Barnaichu, Hanwat, Bhúm Sen, Chanwar, Kashínath, Mansa Ram, Hardaur, Ratnú, Harí Ram, Jharkhand Iswar, Kall Sen,

Bisharí; oft times they are the spirits* of good men, Brahmans, or village heroes, who manage, when they become objects of worship, to be generally considered very malicious devils; and oft times they are nothing but mere epithets of the Dii Majores. In some places their images are of male, in others of female, figures. In many places the villagers, for fear of misrepresenting their Gram Deota, erect a stone without form or feature; like the "si Deo si Deæ" of the Romans, which ambiguous expression was addressed to their tutelary gods, to obviate all chance of mistake.

The worship of these village gods is fixed to no stated day. In some places it occurs on the 14th of every month; in others, on the full moon of Chait; at others, on the full moon of Katik, and so on.

It has been supposed by Dr. Stephenson, of Bombay, that these Díwárs, or Grama Deotas, are the remnants of the ante-Brahmanical religion; but the supposition cannot be received as correct concerning our provinces, though it may be conceded with respect to the Gods of the South of India that there are many circumstances of their worship which are not of Hindú origin.—(See "Bombay Literary Transactions;" "Journal R. A. S." Nos. IX. and X.; Buchanan's "Eastern India," Vol. II. pp. 138, 352, 478; and Wilson's "Hindú Theatre," Vol. I. p. 21, and Vol. I. p. 64.)

Deoṭhán, دیوٹھان देओठान

See Dithwan.

Ḍhák, ڈھاک ढाक

Ḍháka, ڈھاکہ ढाका

Dhákhá, دھاکھا धाखा

Name of a tree (Butea frondosa). The bark furnishes an

* An instance is mentioned by Lieutenant Colonel Sleeman, in his "Rambles and Recollections," of a village settlement having been made with the ghost of a former, instead of with the living, incumbent.

important exudation called the Palas gond, or Bengal Kino; and a strong kind of rope is also made from the root, called Bukel. It has also many other uses. Its wood is valued for coating wells, and it is also much sought after for the purpose of making a hom, or sacrificial fire. The flowers are in clusters and bright red. When pounded, they produce an excellent yellow dye, which is frequently, amongst other purposes, applied to form the Holi powder. The "Tálíf-i-Sharíf" says, that "when the white flowers are found, and any one shall eat the seeds, his heart will be cleansed, his understanding increased, and he shall be endowed with supernatural knowledge." The common Dhak which is found all over the uncultivated plains of Northern India is a stunted tree, and never attains the height that it does in and under the hills.—See Chhíúl.

Dhokhá, دهوكها धोखा

A scarecrow; from a word signifying deception. In Rohilkhand the term Ujká is sometimes used; in Central Doáb, Ojhak and Ojpo, from उजकना *ujakná*, to start, to be alarmed; and for the same reason a scarecrow is called Daráwar in Dehli, from डराना, to frighten.—See Bijhgah and Dhúha.

Ḍhúhá, ڈهوها ढूहा

A scarecrow. Dhúhá, or more correctly Dhúá· ढूआ, also signifies a clod or mound of earth raised as a boundary mark. These mounds are about four feet high, and fixed round the limits of each township, at the distance of about two hundred yards from one another. As the Dhúhá is merely made of earth, it requires constant renewal and repair.—See Damcha, Daula, and Hadbandí.

Dhajá, دهجا धजा

A standard, a strip of cloth. Dhajá, or rather Dhojá, which

is more in accordance with the Sanskrit ध्वज, is also the name given to the pole, with a strip of cloth attached, which is erected in fulfilment of a vow near some place of worship, by a person who has succeeded in any important object. It is also the name given to the standard tied to a tree, or raised in some elevated position on the Pavan Paríchha, the last day of the month Asáṛh. From the direction of the wind at sunset on that day, the people draw their auguries of the coming season. On this occasion the banias, or grain-dealers, are observed to be more anxious consulters than the agriculturists, and their anxiety gives rise to the saying of "Bania ka paní." This is the response if the pendant shows a westerly wind, and indicates the probability of a dry season. If a little more favorable, it is "Kumhár ka paní," or suitable to potters, as they also delight in dry weather. If from the north, moderate rains may be expected, and the answer is "Málí ka paní," or suitable to gardeners. If from the east, copious rains are to be looked for, and the season is said to enjoy "Dhobí ka paní," or a deluge sufficient to satisfy a washerman. These sayings, though not general, have currency in many parts of the country, especially in Brij.*

Diṭhwan, دٿهون दिठवन

The Ekadasí, or 11th of the bright half of the month Katik, which day is also known by the name of Bodini.† On this day a ceremony is observed in celebration of Vishnu's return from

* Kâli Râi says, "On that day the villagers weigh out carefully one or two tolas of each kind of grain, and leave them in little earthen dishes in a clear place in the jungle all night. In the morning they go and weigh them again. If the weight is greater than it was overnight they anticipate a good season, and *vice versâ*.—E. *add*.

† J.R.A.S., XIII., 6, Kâli Râi says, "This is the first day of reaping the sugar-cane: after lighting a lamp and doing pûjâ, they tie a red thread round five canes, and breaking a little off, they distribute it among their neighbours."—E. *add*.

his slumber of four months, during which he is represented to have been with Raja Bal in Pátál, or the infernal regions.

> May Vishnu's shrinking glance
> Yield peace and joy—as waking from his trance
> His opening eyes are dazzled by the rays
> From lamps divine that blaze:
> Those eyes that with long slumber red
> Ambrosial tear-drops shed,
> As pillowed on his snake-couch mid the deep
> He breaks reluctant from his fated sleep.
>
> —*Mudra Rakshasha.*

No marriages and but few festive ceremonies have taken place in the meantime, and the Dithwan is the signal for their commencement. Houses are cleaned, and smeared afresh with cowdung, and the fruit of the Singhara and Ber and Chanaka-ság, and other dainties of the season may be lawfully enjoyed.

But amongst agriculturists it is more especially celebrated for its connexion with the cutting of the sugar-cane. All Hindus of correct habits will carefully abstain till this day from touching the crop; but on the Dithwan, a little is taken from the corner of the field, brought home, and spread out for the reception of the Saligrám, which in due form is lifted up several times, an action significant of Vishnu's rising from his slumber. He is waked, according to the "Matsya Purana," by this incantation—"The clouds are dispersed, the full moon will appear in perfect brightness, and I come in hope of acquiring purity to offer the fresh flowers of the season: awake from thy slumber, awake, O Lord of all worlds."

When this worship is duly performed, and the officiating Brahman declares the fortunate moment for beginning operations, the cutting is commenced. The whole village is a scene of hilarity, and dancing and singing are the order of the day.

Dithwan is variously called Dataund, Daiten, Dashtun, Dutaon, according to the degree of ignorance of the speaker

The proper name of the ceremony is Deothan, or "the standing up of the God." In Shakespear's and Smyth's Dictionaries this is said to occur on the second day of the light half of the month of Kátik; but that festival is usually called Bhaiaduj Jamdutya, or in Sanskrit Bhrátṛidwitíya, on which day sisters feed and pay some kind of ceremonial worship to their brothers.

What the ceremony of Dithwan is to the sugar-cane, that of Arwan is to the shamakh and barley grain.—See Arwan and Júrí.

Ḍaliyájhár, ڈلیاجھار डलियाझार

The conclusion of the sowing season; literally, the brushing out of the sowing basket. It is called by various other names as Kuṅr mundlá, Hariar, Bai-bharí, and Kuṅr-Bojí. Amongst the agricultural population of the Upper Provinces, as in most other parts of the world, it is a season of joy and relaxation.

Dam madár, دم مدار दम मदार

The ceremony of performing the Dhammal, or Dam Madar, is very popular with the agricultural and lower classes in Upper Hindústan. It consists in jumping into a fire, and treading it out, with the exclamation of "Dam Madar! Dam Madar!" that is, "by the breath of Madar, by the breath of Madar." It is devoutly believed that not a hair of these devotees gets singed, and that those who have practised the ceremony are secure against the venom of snakes and scorpions.

Badíu'ddin Shah Madar, in honor of whom this ceremony annually takes place, was, according to the Mirat-i-Madarea, a converted Jew. He is said to have been born at Aleppo in 1050 A.D. and to have come to India in the reign of Sultan Ibrahím Sharkí; and having taken up his abode between Cawnpore and Farrakhabad, and expelled therefrom an evil genius, called Makan Deo, who infested the place, he gave the name of Makanpúr to his residence, and was buried there in 1433 A.D. at the good old age of nearly four hundred years! The tomb, which is a handsome structure, was raised over him by Sultan Ibrahím. He is believed still to be alive, and hence is frequently styled Zinda Shah Madar. The prophet Mahomet gave him the power of habs-i-dam, or retention of breath, and hence arose his longevity, as the number of his respirations was diminished at pleasure.

There is a large concourse of people at his tomb during the first seventeen days of Jamadiu'l awwal, and the fair, or festival, is known by the names of Chharí, Mední, Charaghan, and Badi. The two ceremonies of Dhammal Khelna and Gaí lútana, which take place on the seventeenth of the month, are fully described in the Kanún-i-Islam. Mrs. Mír Hasan Ali tells us that women can never with safety to themselves enter the mausoleum containing the saint's ashes, for they are immediately seized with violent pains, as if their whole body was immersed in flames of fire.

There is a class of Fakírs called Madarea, after his name. They generally wear black clothes, and are much addicted to the use of intoxicating drugs.*

Dandázaní, ڈنڈازنی डण्डाजनी

A mode of torture said in Mr. W. W. Bird's Report, dated 25th May, 1827, to have been practised by the subordinate officers in the private domains of the Raja of Benares. It consists in fastening a man's arms behind his back with a cord, which is twisted round by means of a stick, so as to increase the tension until the pain inflicted by it becomes intolerable. The other modes were Áwangilli and Sundrízaní.

* References are: As. J., 1831, Vol. IV., p. 76: Ṭabaḳat-i Shahjahâni, p. 15; Yâdgâr-i Bahâdurí, p. 281; Daulat Râi Chaman, I.; Dabistan, II., 244; III., 307.—B.

Áwangilli is compelling a man to stand astride with each foot on an inverted earthern vessel, placed so far apart as to endanger his dropping between them; while a Chaprassí stands by to flog him, unless he exerts himself as much as possible to keep erect.

Sundrízaní is striking with a double flapper made of thick leather; although the particular instrument made use of at the Raja's Kutcherry was the leathern case of a Gadka, or single stick, stuffed with bran. It was used instead of a slipper to coerce the better sort of defaulters, as being less disgraceful.

Daijá, دیجا दैजा

A dowry, or portion which the wife brings a husband in marriage.

Wilson, in a note to Mill's India (Vol. I., p. 447), says that "amongst the Hindus the practice of purchasing a bride by a dower is apparently of modern growth, and a violation of the law." There are passages in Manu on the subject which appear contradictory.

"Let no father who knows the law receive a gratuity, however small, for giving his daughter in marriage; since the man who through avarice takes a gratuity for that purpose, is a seller of his offspring."—Institutes III. 51.

"He who takes to wife a damsel of full age shall not give a nuptial present to her father" (IX. 93); which implies that under ordinary circumstances a present *was* given.

Again, "If after one damsel has been shown, another be offered to the bridegroom who had purchased leave to marry her from her next kinsman, he may become the husband of both for the same price. This law Manu ordained."—VIII. 204.

These passages would imply the observance of both practices; and the same may perhaps have continued till the time of the Greek invasion, for Arrian (Indica, CXVII.) says the Indians neither took nor gave money in marriage; while Megasthenes

(Strabo, Lib. XV.) says their wives were purchased for a yoke of oxen.

Amongst the agricultural tribes in the North-West Provinces. the present practice is most usual for the bride's father to purchase the bridegroom, so that the man receives the dowry,* or Daijá, which consists for the most part of money and household utensils. Thus, even when the daughter of Jai Chand was forcibly abducted by Pirthí raja, the father sends to him "the richest gems, the fruits of the victory of Bijay Pal, inestimable wealth, pearls, elephants, and dyes." Thus also, the same hero, when he marries the daughter of the Dahima of Biana, receives from his father-in-law "eight beauteous damsels, sixty-three female slaves, one hundred chosen Irak horses, two elephants, ten shields, a pallet of silver for the bride, one hundred wooden images, one hundred chariots, and one thousand pieces of gold."

This system, the fruitful source of female infanticide, arises from the almost universal desire to obtain for the daughter the privilege of marrying into a higher family, which is only to be acquired by purchase. Thus among Rajputs and Brahmans, the relative position of the several clans can be easily ascertained by learning with what families sons and daughters respectively intermarry. The sons marry those of an inferior stock, and receive money for the condescension; the daughters marry those of a superior stock, and their parents have to pay for the privilege. Where perfect equality reigns (and mutual convenience, as well as the gradual extinction of ancient prejudices, are slowly tending to this result), sons and daughters of three or four different stocks intermarry; and as alliances are thus not sought for mere honor and distinction, the payment of exorbitant prices is obviated. Sometimes, indeed, an imaginary purchase is made, as a type of a custom of which the breach is thought preferable to the observance.

It may be as well to subjoin, in further illustration of this

* Dower the wife is of course entitled to by the laws of inheritance.

subject, the following passages from Steele's "Summary of the Law and Custom of Hindoo Castes":—

"Usoor is the 5th variety of marriage, where the girl is taken in exchange for wealth, and married. This species is peculiar to the Byse and Soodra castes." "The sale of a girl in marriage is forbidden, and the money, if unpaid, is an unlawful debt."

"The lower castes often receive money on the marriage of their females, called Hoonda, which is the characteristic of the 5th (Usoor) variety, and it is suspected that Brahmins occasionally, in the present avaricious generation, incur sin on this account."

"A poor family, to avoid the disgrace of receiving Hoonda, will sometimes marry their daughter into a family of similar circumstances; or an intermarriage may be agreed on both sides."—Pp. 31, 161, 166.

See also Macnaghten's "Principles and Precedents of Hindu Law," Vol. I., chap. 5.*

Ghází míyán,† غازي ميان गाज़ीमीयां

This saint is in high repute with the agricultural and lower classes of these provinces, except in Dehli, and is included among the Panchpírí. (See Hathíle.) Notwithstanding he did his best to exterminate the Kafirs, he is as much worshipped by the Hindus as the Musulmans. An annual fair‡ takes place

* On the subject of female infanticide among the Rajputs there is an interesting chapter in Mr. C. Raikes's "Notes on the N. W. Provinces," 1852, which details the steps taken to put a stop to this crime. A much older work by E. Moor, published in 1811, on the same subject, is also worth looking at, as it contains curious notices of the habits of the people in several parts of India. See also "Selections from Rec. N.W.P.," III., pp. 1-10, and pp. 167-210, as regards Agra.—B.

† Dabistan, III., 213; Firoz Shah, p. i., 272, 320; Yádgár-i Bahádurí, p. 262; Beale's Miftah, 56.—E. *add.*

‡ Sikandar Lodi endeavoured to suppress this fair, as partaking too much of Pagan idolatry, but without success.

in his honour in the month of Jeṭh. On these occasions, a long pole is paraded about, crowned at the top with bushy hair, which is said to represent the head of the martyr, which kept rolling on long after it was separated from the trunk.* The fair takes place at most large towns, but the greatest concourse of pilgrims is at Bahraich, where he lies buried. This fair is commonly styled the "Nuptials of Ghazí Miyan," because it is said he had on his bridal clothes, and was about to be married, when he was martyred. The "Mirát-i Masa'udi," however, says only that he had a dream the night before his death, in which his mother came and placed a bridal chaplet on his brow, as being indicative of the crown of martyrdom with which he was to be honoured on the following day. It is said in the "Araish-i Mahfil" that an oilman of Radaulí first established the custom, by carrying a bed and other nuptial paraphernalia every year to Bahraich, being persuaded that the saint annually renews the ceremony. He is, partly on this account, called Gajna Dúlha, and Salar Chinala. M. Garcin de Tassy, in his "Memoire" on the Musulman religion in India, page 81, states that Mr. H. H. Wilson entertains doubts about the representation of the marriage, and conceives that Shadí, "Marriage," has been written by mistake for Shahadat, "Martyrdom," but there is no occasion to dispute the correctness of the word or the fact of the ceremony.

Who this Ghází Míyán was is a question on which even Musulman authorities are not agreed. In the "Ḳanun-i Islam" he is said to be the same as Rajab Sálár. In the "Akhbár-ul Akhyár," he is said to be the same as Pír Bahlím. Some say he was a Sayyid, others a Pathan. Ferishta and the author of the "Súbah-i Sadiḳ" say he was a descendant of Mahmúd of Ghaznı, and was killed at Bahraich in A.D. 1162. Abu-l Fazl says he was a relation of that king. The most detailed, and apparently the most authentic, account of him is given in the

* There is no authority for this statement.—E. *add.*

"Mirátu-l Asrar" and the "Mirát-i Masa'udí.* In them he is stated to have been the son of Mír Sahu, who married Satr-i Mu'alla, the sister of Mahmúd of Ghazní. He was born at Ajmír in A.H. 405, and by his feats of arms in Guzerat, and advice at Somnath, obtained so much notice from Mahmud, as even to have excited the envy of the Emperor's favourite slave Ayaz.† These histories then enter into an account of his proceedings at Ghazní, Kashmír, Multan, Dehli, Mírat, and Kanauj, the Raja of which place, Jaypal, is said to have been restored through the saint's intercession with the angry Emperor. His subsequent conquests, and those of his followers, on the other side of the Ganges and Gogra, are then given, and if they could be thoroughly relied on, would be of much interest. It is then related how the news of the death of Sultan Mahmúd inspired the Indian princes with the hope of retrieving their independence, and how an army of infidels assembled at Bahraich, under Raja Sháhar Deo, for the purpose of exterminating the faithful, and how, after three severe contests he gloriously fell a martyr on the field of battle in A.H. 424, at the early age of nineteen. The memorial verse which gives the dates of his birth and death runs thus:—

"In four hundred and five he came into existence; in four hundred and twenty-four he took his departure!

The cause of his being frequently called, both in Khurasan and India, Rajab Sálar, is that there is a tomb of that personage also at Bahraich, and the name of Sálár, meaning prince,

* These works were written in Jehangir's time, by 'Abdu'r raḥmán, who states that his details are founded on the account given by Mulla Muhammad of Ghazní, a companion of our Saint and his father. As this work is said to give a full account of the Emperor Mahmúd, it would be worth examination.

† This person frequently figures among the anecdotes of the East, and there are some which tell greatly in favor of his humble deportment in the midst of prosperity. He is the subject of a famous Masnaví by Jalálí.—See Stewart's "Catalogue of Tippoo Sultan's Library," p. 57.

which is common to both, has created confusion in the minds of those who have not sufficiently examined the question.

Who this Rajab Sálár was is also a doubtful point, but it is certain that he has no claims to saintship, like our Sálár Masa'ud, or Ghází Míyán. Abú'l Fazl, in his account of the Suba of Oudh says he was the father of the illustrious Fíroz Shah; and we learn from the "Shams-i Siráji" that Rajab Sálár was the name of Fíroz Shah's father, but from this account it does not appear that he died in the neighbourhood of, or was buried at, Bahraich. Now, the "Mirát-i Masa'udí" expressly says that Rajab Sálár was one of the followers of Ghází Míyán, that he was induced to seek his fortunes in India because some rent-free land of his was unjustly resumed, that he was made the Kotwal of Ghází Míyán's camp, and that he was buried at Bahraich. This latter, therefore, would appear to be the Rajab Sálár, who is frequently taken for Ghází Míyán.

Ghegará, گهیگرا घेगरा

Ghegará, or Gheghará, is the unripe pod of Gram. Also, the unripe bole of cotton, which is known also by the names of Gúlar, Ghentí, and Bhitná. When it bursts it assumes another name.

When this change begins to occur in a cotton field, some kind of superstitious ceremony is observed in most parts of the country, which is generally known by the name of Phurakna. To the Eastward of the Jumna it is most usual to select the largest plant in the field, and having sprinkled it with butter-milk and rice water, it is bound all over with pieces of cotton, taken from the other plants of the field. This selected plant is called Sirdar, or Bhogaldaí, *i.e.*, mother-cotton, from bhogla, a name sometimes given to a large cotton-pod, and daí (for daiya) a mother, and after salutations are made to it, prayers are offered that the other plants may resemble it in the richness of their produce. To the West of the Jumna there is rarely a

Bhogaldaí, but when the pods begin to burst, women go round the field, and, as a kind of lustration, throw salt into it, with similar supplications that the produce may be abundant.—(J. R. A. S., XIII. 29.)

Ghelauní, گهيلوني घेलौनी

Ghelauní, which is more generally known by the name of Rúk رونك, is much the same in kind as dastúrí is in money—something taken by the purchaser in addition to the nominal selling price. A familiar illustration is given of this in the article Harbong ka Raj. Another instance of Ghelauní is found in the common practice of adding so many Panjas or fives, to the hundred, without which it is not considered a complete hundred. Thus 110 bamboos, 120 mangoes, 130 melons, 115 carrots, and so on, will only be considered in the light of perfect hundreds of each respectively, according to the practice prevailing in the several bazars.

Goga pír, گوگا پير गोगा पीर

The agriculturists of the Dehli territory and the Upper Doáb regard this saint with superstitious reverence, and crowd to his shine with their offerings in the month of Bhadon. The Kánun-i Islam, and M. Garcin de Tassy, quoting the Barah Masa, say his tomb is somewhere in the Doáb ; but in this they are mistaken, as it lies nearly two hundred miles to the South-West of Hissar, and twenty miles beyond a place called Dadrera. As these authors confess their entire ignorance* respecting Goga, it may be as well to subjoin a few particulars respecting him. He is called by the Mahrattas Zahir Pír, and is with them a favourite saint. The local tradition respecting him is

* Cet ouvrage (Barah Masa) est le seul, de ceux que j'ai pu consulter, où il soit question de Goga.—Mémoire sur des part. de la Rel. Musulmane, p. 89.

that he was the son of a Chauhán Rajput, called Vachá, according to some; according to others, Jewar, whose wife Bachal, a Túar, produced him, after being long barren, at the kind intercession of Gorakhnath. There is a clan of Musulman Chauháns even now resident in the neighbourhood of his tomb (see Chahil); the Gogáwats of the desert are descended from him, and the Gogadeo ka thal is called after his name. His territory extended from Hansi to the Garra (Ghara), and his capital was Mehera on that river. In a quarrel about land he killed his two brothers, on which account he drew down upon himself the anger of his mother. To escape her imprecations he fled to the jungles, and there wished that the earth might open and swallow him up, but a voice from heaven declared that he could not have the satisfaction of being buried alive, horse * and all, unless he uttered the Kaláma and became a Musulman. He appears to have had no difficulty in doing this, upon which the earth opened before him, and he leaped into its bosom.

His claims to saintship are not very distinct. He is said to have been a contemporary of Pirthí Rájá, and to have fought with desparate valour against the Mahomedans; but there is more reason to suppose that he must have contended with the earlier Ghaznivide monarchs, for several favorite ballads relate how he fell with his forty-five sons and sixty nephews, opposing the great Mahmud on the banks of the Garra. The above is an abridged account of the tradition, with the omission of all the detailed particulars, some of which are interesting.

In the Eastern portion of these Provinces, where distance overcomes the zeal for pilgrimage, it is usual for the Bhangís

* His horse has been immortalised under the name of Javadia. The chroniclers relate that Goga was childless, until his guardian deity bestowed upon him two barley-corns (*jao* or *java*), one of which he gave to his wife, the other to his favorite mare, which produced in consequence the famous steed Javadia. Some accounts assert that these two barley corns, or cocoa-nuts, were given to Goga's mother. The story, however, is too long and trifling to be inserted here.

to carry round the sacred symbols of the Pír in the month of Bhadon, and to raise contributions. The Agarwala Banyas are particularly sought after on this occasion. Their original emigration from Agroha, beyond Hariana, was no doubt once considered a sufficient reason why the symbols of their illustrious countryman, Gogá, should be paraded before their eyes. But perhaps few in these times have ever thought why the Agarwalas are supposed to be, more than any other class, especially favorable to Gogá, and the present continuance of this ceremony on the return of the proper season, after all knowledge of its origin has utterly faded from remembrance, shews the marvellous permanence which usages, in themselves puerile, will sometimes attain, when they are commemorative of an historical fact. The one we are now alluding to has been preserved through a succession of ages, and under the most unfavorable circumstances. At Ujayyin there is a temple of Gogá Sháhid, and his day is the ninth of the dark half of Bhadon. His votaries carry a black flag.—See "As. Res." VI., 41; Cunningham's "Sikhs," p. 13.

Gohar, گوهر गोहर

A broad pathway for cattle, of which the preservation is considered as obligatory as that of a boundary. The rural denunciation, attributed, like so many others, to Sahdeo, one of the five Pandu heroes, runs—

जो कोई तोडेगा डौल वा गोहर वा करे
कि बोएंगे और कि रहेंगे परे

That is, "may the man who destroys a boundary, a cowpath, or a ditch, have his lands sown by others, or may they lie waste." It is also called Dagar, and Dahar.

Golá, گولا गोला

A mode of ordeal formerly much practised in fixing boundaries. It consisted in taking a red-hot ball in the palms of the hand, which were only protected by Pípal leaves. If the arbitrator, in walking the boundary with the Golá, escaped unscathed, his testimony was considered true, and the boundary adjusted accordingly.—See Chhaur.

Guptdán, گپت‌دان गुप्तदान

Literally, a hidden donation; an ostentatious mode of giving alms in secret to Brahmans, especially at Kurchhettar (the ancient Kurukshetra, about thirty miles south of the British station of Amballa), during the sun's eclipse, at which times this sacred place is as much resorted to as Benares is on the occasion of an eclipse of the moon. The devotee immerses himself in the sacred pool, and leaves his donation at the bottom, which occasions the Brahmans no small trouble to recover.

Guptdán also consists in leaving horses or clothes in the pretended care of a Brahman, and not returning to claim them; also, in giving a closed bag of coin, so that the receiver does not know, till the donor's back is turned, whether gold or copper has been bestowed upon him.

Gopashṭamí, گوپشتمي गोपष्टमी

Is the name given to the eighth day of the bright half of the month of Kátik. On this day, as well as on the Godhan (Govardhan), the day after the Dewálí, garlands are suspended from the necks of cows, their horns, hoofs, and bodies are painted, and salutations are made to them.

Gadhe ká hál, گدهي کا هل गधे का हल

Literally, a donkey's plough. Before the British accession, it was not uncommon to yoke donkeys in a plough, and drive them over the ruins of a captured fort, as a mode of shewing supreme contempt for the vanquished enemy. The furrows thus raised were levelled by the Lohe kí maí, or iron harrow.

This mode of wreaking vengeance has been in especial favour with Eastern nations, and was practised by Jenghiz Khan and Timúr with unrelenting severity. Hence the common expression "I shall sow barley where you now stand." See the vaunt of the Bandit-Minstrel Kurroglou, at p. 138 of "Popular Poetry of Persia."

Gadhe par charhána, گدھے پر چڑھانا गधे पर चढ़ाना

Literally, to seat upon a jackass. This is a punishment more commonly known by the Arabic تشہیر publication, celebration; which is rendered by Golius, "Per urbem duci jussit sontem in exemplum: fere asino aut camelo impositum." In India, when this punishment was ordained, the criminal was seated with his face to the tail of a donkey, and old shoes, rags, and the like were suspended from his neck in derision.

A tashhír, or public exposure with the face blackened, is expressly declared to be the punishment inflicted by Umr upon a false witness, in addition to forty stripes: though Abu Hanífa and his two disciples differ as to whether the punishment should be considered a sentence of Tázír or Síasat.—See "Hedaya," Vol. II., pp. 715, 716; and "Harington's Analysis," Vol. I., p. 287.

The first intimation we have of a Tashhír in the Mahomedan history of India is when Saifu'd dín Ghorí was captured in Ghazni. He had his forehead blackened, and was seated astride on a bullock with his face towards the tail; and after enduring the shouts and insults of the mob, he was tortured and finally beheaded.—Tawáríkh-i Guzída.

It is generally supposed that this punishment was introduced into India by the Mahomedans; but this is a mistake, for in the Institutes of Manu (Cap. VIII. 370) it is ordained, "If a woman shall be guilty of the offence mentioned, she shall have her head instantly shaved, and two of her fingers chopped, and she shall ride mounted on an ass through the public street."

The punishment has for many years been discontinued in British territories in India.

In Europe there was formerly a superstition that sitting on, or speaking to an ass was a cure for scorpion-bites. In India it is also believed that, if a person is bitten by a scorpion, he may be cured by the following ceremony:—A young male buffalo-calf is selected, in preference to a donkey, as being a purer animal, and into its ear is whispered the following incantation (which probably has no meaning at all; at least, only faint glimmerings of sense can be detected in it):—

बीछी बीछी तोरे कै जाती वारह वरन अठारह जाती
अठारहौ चली समुद्र अन्हाय छाकारी छापेरी छारवाररवाई
समुद्र के तीर एक वर का विरवा तेहिमा रहै बीछि का किरवा
झारीं बीछि उतारीं किरवा उतरो बीछि डांसे आउ

When this jargon has been duly uttered by the messenger, he returns to the bitten patient, and is sure to find him fully recovered.

Whether, as in the case of the Fables of Syntipas and the Arabian Nights, the origin is to be ascribed to India, is doubtful. It is more probable that the superstition is derived from some of the translations of the Greek medical writers, which were made in the time of the Khalífa Mamun; and this is somewhat confirmed by observing that it is not so much the common people who entertain this persuasion, as those who profess to have made some acquaintance with Oriental literature.

Híráná, هیرانا हीराना

Manuring a field by penning a herd of cattle or flock of sheep in it for several hours.—E. Oudh. Khatáná is used in a similar sense in Rohilkhand.

Halbarár, هلبرار हलबरार

Assessment according to the number of ploughs. Collections at a certain sum per plough.

Haláitá هلایتا हलाइता

The first ploughing of the season, which is generally preceded by the taking of omens, and other superstitious ceremonies. The note of the Koil bird, amongst other auguries, is considered very favorable, and its utterance is of such authority as to enable the cultivator to dispense with a formal application to a Brahman.—See Haríta. This bird directs other operations besides agriculture. Thus, **कोइल बोली सिबन्दी डोली**, *i.e.* the disbanding of the armed men for collection of revenue depended on the Koil's note, "Sibandy" being a corruption of Sipah Hindí, in distinction to Mughal or foreign troops, who were always kept up.

The Koil, indeed, occupies much the same place in India that the cuckoo does in Europe.

It also resembles the European species is being "the nursling of a stranger nest;" and, according to popular belief, selects a crow's nest for the place of deposit. A Hindi verse says, "Whose property has the crow taken, to whom has the Koil given it? Her sweet notes have captivated the whole world."

Harbong ká ráj, هربونگ کا راج हरबोंग का राज

This expression, which literally means Harbong's Government, is applied to signify civil disorder and mal-administration. Roebuck ("Oriental Proverbs," Part II., p. 187) says that "Hurbhoom is the name of a village near Ilahabad, infamous for injustice." But the name of Harbhúm, which is more usually pronounced Harbong, and sometimes Harbhong, is given to the Raja, and the scene of his injustice is called Harbongpúr.

Harbongpúr is now known by the name of Jhúnsí, or Jhúsí, on the left bank of the Ganges, opposite to Allahabad,* and opposite to Arail,† on the right bank of the Jumna. It will be seen from the notes below that the names of these places were changed by Akbar, and Jhúsí itself shared the same fate,

* Immediately before Akbar's time this place was known as Píág, or Prág, both corruptions of the Sanskrit Prayága; by him it was denominated Allahabas, which subsequently became Allahabad. The name is more correctly Ilhabad, or Ilahabad, as given by Captain Roebuck, but I adopt the usual practise of writing it Allahabad. Whether, when Sháhjahán changed the terminal *bas* into *bad*, which had been adopted by his grandfather in deference to the Hindús (see Dastúr), he also changed the Ilah into Allah, does not appear from any author who treats of the subject; but the alteration would not have been unreasonable, for there is a marked distinction between the two terms. [Ilah اله means a god in general; Allah الله is the same word having incorporated with it the article ال. It therefore means "the God," *i.e.* the only God. Ilah thus means an idol, a false god, and Prayág was so called by the Mahomedans as being the shrine of the false gods of the Indians. Allahabad is a mere English corruption of this name. The correct pronunciation of Ilahabad is still retained and used by all educated natives. There is no reason for supposing that Sháhjahán or any one else ever thought of changing the first syllable of the name. —B.] From some passages in the early Indian historians it would appear that they confounded the famous Somnath with the Arabian Ilah or Ilat; and though it certainly would be no uninteresting enquiry to trace the real circumstances of the counexion, a mere reference only can be made to it here. See in the Rauzatu's Safá, Habíbu's Sair, and Ferishta, the passage quoted from Faríd-u'd-dín Attar. Sale's Koran, I. 23, II. 390. Hyde de Rel. Vet. Pers. p. 130. Pococke, Spec. Hist. Arab. 4, 92, 110. Bird's Guzerat, p. 39. D'Herbelot, voce Lat. Al-Makkari's Mahomedan Dynasties in Spain I. 346, and Herod. III. 6. The same fanciful and nice distinction respecting the value of single letters in these devout exclamations is also observable in the Bismillah, on which Zamakhshari in his commentary on the Koran observes, Rahmán denotes a more extensive idea than Rahím; for this reason people say in speaking of God, "the merciful (Ar-Rahmán) in this world and the next," and "the clement (Ar-Rahím) in this world."

† The name of this place was also changed by Akbar. He called it Jalalabad, after his own name of Jalálu'ddín. That he was not above this common and venial weakness we know from his public edict abolishing the salutation of Salam 'alaykum, and substituting the Allahu Akbar, and the reply of Jalla jalálahu, in both of which we have parts of his name Jalálu'ddín Muhammad Akbar. The Sipah Salar was ordered to see that the same exclamations were made at meals; and the Aftábí, the rupee, and several other coins of his reign, as well as his seal, bore the

being called Hadíábas, yet it is strange why it was not called Jhúsí in the Imperial Registers, for that town was in existence long before Akbar's time. It has frequent and honorable mention in the Treatise Fí Hálat-i-Murshid, containing an account of Sayyid Ali Murtazá's Miracles. The Sayyid died A.D. 1369, so that as the place was called Jhúsí in his days, there appears no good reason why the Parganah was not so denominated in the records of Akbar's reign.

Harbongpúr, which preceded the name of Jhúsí, is itself a comparatively modern name, for the site of Jhúsí is by common consent allowed to be the Pratishṭhan, or Kesi, of the Puranic Histories, the residence of the first prince of the lunar dynasty, Pururavas, the son of Budha, the son of the Moon.*—(Wilson's Introd. to Univ. Hist., p. 8; As. Res., Vol. X. p. 44; Vishnu Purana, p. 350.)

But it may be enquired, if Pratishṭhan is considered to have occupied the present site of Jhúsí, how could Kalidasa thus describe the position of the palace of Pururavas.

> "We are there, behold it
> White gleaming in the moonlight, whilst below
> The Yamuna's blue waters wash its feet."
> —"Hindu Theatre," Vol. I., p. 231.

Might not Pururavas, as the second Act of the "Hero and the Nymph" opens with a "scene in the palace at Prayaga," have had his palace on the neck of the Doáb, and actually on the Jumna? or even on the point overlooking the confluence of the

inscription أللّٰه اكبر جلّ جلاله. We have several instances of Arail's being mentioned prior to Akbar's time. In the Tárikh-i-Badauní it is stated, that the Parganah of Arail was in A.H. 977 (before the composition of the Ayín-i-Akbarí) given in Jagír to Raja Ram Chand, and even before this time, we have frequent mention of it in the history of the Afghan reigns; when the place appears to have been sometimes visited by troops marching in the neighbourhood. In the last century it was celebrated as the residence of several Persian nobles, of whom there is now no trace or record, except in the ruins of the houses which they occupied.

* This is very doubtful.

Ganges and Jumna (Ibid. p. 214) ? or are we suppose that in the poet's time the Jumna joined the Ganges in an earlier part of its course, and ran under the high bank on which was the hermitage of Bharadwaj, still known by his name, and the scene of the feast given by him to Bharata, the brother of Rama, together with his large army; which feast, though given by a Brahman (so little do the habits of those times consort with present Hindu notions) consisted among other luxuries, of peacocks! venison!! and pork!!! eagerly washed down with foaming bowls of spirituous liquor!!!!—(Ramayana, Book II. section 77, p. 301.)

If we are to allow that the Jumna took that course in ancient times, it becomes another question for consideration, was the ancient Prayag on the site of the modern Allahabad, and what was there which occupied the position of the present fort?

On this subject the only materials we have are calculated to make us form different conclusions; but as even the faintest light * thrown on the origin of ancient cities is precious, they may, contradictory as they are, be not unworthy of record and observation.

When Mahmúd of Ghazní captured Asní, on the banks of the Ganges, near Fattihpúr (see extract at p. 74 of this supplement), he would not have crossed over into Bundelkhand without visiting Prayag, had there been a city there worth plundering. Again, when Muhammad Ghorí captured Benares,†

* L' oscurissima e ben sovente imperscrutabile origine delle più antiche città, prezioso rende e singolare ogni piccol lume, che negli accrediti scrittori interno a così remoti notizie ci ramaso.—(Scipione Maffei.)

† Abu'l Fazl tells us that Benares was twice visited by Sultan Mahmúd, once in A.H. 410, and again in A.H. 413; but the truth of this statement is open to considerable doubt, for not only do other historians omit all notice of these expeditions, but had not Muhammad Ghorí been the first to capture this stronghold of idolatry, he could scarcely have had a thousand temples left him to destroy, and loaded four thousand camels with the spoils.—Wilford also stated that Mahmúd captured Benares (As. Res., Vol. IX., p. 203); but Wilford's assertions are not always to be depended on.

we should have heard of his taking Prayág on his way; but it is not even noticed by any of his historians.

And yet that there was something like a town at Prayag, before Allahabad was founded, we are authorized to believe, not only on the ground of the extreme improbability of there being no permanent residents at so important a place of pilgrimage, but because there are evidences of the present fort having been built on, and partly composed of, the ruins of some former building. This may be seen by examining the face towards the confluence, and became further evident by the discovery of Hindu sculptures and architectural remains, when a few years ago the foundation of the Jumna face was undergoing repairs. The Patalpúrí also, enclosed within the fort, is manifestly of great antiquity, even allowing that the Akhaibar is, as is most probable, a modern fixture.* Wilson, however ("Hindu Theatre," I. 207), considers that Allahabad, or Prayaga, was not a city till Akbar made it one. That Vaisali was not the ancient Allahabad (as asserted in the "Jour. R. A. S.," No. XII. pp. 302, 325; and "Jour. A. S. Beng.," Vol. I. p. 4), is evident from the position assigned to it in the Chinese Travels; and the question so warmly espoused at one time of the confluence having been the site of the famous Palibothra, may now be considered fairly set at rest, to the exclusion of Allahabad from that high honour.

After this digression on the subject of the cities which may

* "The tree should be the imperishable Ber tree, which has long been famed at Allahabad, and which is still represented by a withered stem in the cave of Pátála puri underground; but it should appear from the text that it grew in daylight, and the play probably preceded the construction of the cavern. There was, no doubt, a very ancient and venerable fig-tree at Allahabad, perhaps for some centuries, for it is alluded to in various vocabularies, as Medini, etc.; it is also described in the 'Kási-khanda' and 'Kurma Purana.' The first notice, however, is in the 'Rámáyana' (Bk. II., Sect. 41 and 42); Rama with his wife and brother resting under the shade of it after crossing the Jumna; so that not only was the tree in the open air, but it was on the opposite side of the river to that on which it is now traditionally venerated."—"Uttara Rama Charitra," note, p. 302.

be supposed to have been the principal scenes of his vagaries, we may now revert to Raja Harbong, and the expression which forms the subject of this article. In the traditional stories recorded of him, there appears, as in the parallel instance of Shaikh Chillí, examples both of folly and shrewdness; sometimes reminding us of the wise men of Gotham or the Tamil stories of the Guru Paramartan, at others of the ingenuity of some of the actors in the Pancha Tantra and the Greek fables of Syntipas. Many remind us of stories still current in Europe; adding another link to the chain which connects the fictitious histories, as well as languages, of Europe with those of India. But it is for injustice that the Raja is most celebrated at the present day, though it must be confessed that this appears to arise less from intentional violence than from his ignorance of jurisprudence and of the dictates of common sense.

One of the most familiar couplets expressive of the evils of his administration is—

अनधेर नगरी बेबूझ राजा
टका सेर भाजी टका सेर खाजा

"The city is in darkness, the Raja is without understanding, greens and sweetmeats are both sold at a pice a seer;" in allusion to the orders to that effect issued by the Raja of Harbongpúr, where everything, moreover, was in such disorder and confusion that the people are said to have worked by night and slept by day.

A common story of his discrimination on the judgment seat has given rise to a proverb. A man having purchased a buffalo, was leading it home, when a stranger, meeting him on the road, declared the animal was his. After much altercation they went before the Raja. The proprietor explained the circumstances of his purchase, when his accuser exclaimed, "Has your worship ever seen a man driving horned cattle without a cudgel? He has not got one, I have; it is therefore evident that the buffalo must be mine." "True," said the Raja, "now I reflect upon it, I have certainly observed that graziers always have a cudgel in their hand. Let it be decided, then, that the buffalo belongs to him who has the cudgel." Hence the proverb, जिस की लाठी उस की भैंस which is now used to express the supremacy of club law.

On another occasion, a man who had purchased a buffalo-calf, demanded, after he had paid the money, something as Ghelauní, *q.v.* that is, something extra in kind. The seller refused, and they went before the Raja. "Assuredly," said the Raja, "I never heard of anything being sold in the bazar without some allowance as Ghelauní. Something therefore must be given. Have you no other cattle?" "Nothing whatever," replied the seller, "but the mother of this very calf." "Let the mother then be given as Ghelauní," said the Raja, "for we must not infringe old customs." Hence the proverb, पर्या लेनी भैंस घेलौनी "Buy the calf, and take the mother into the bargain, as a perquisite:"—something equivalent to "Give an inch and take an ell."

These tales will serve to show the nature of Harbong ka ráj, without drawing further on the stock of similar examples of the Raja's mal-administration. But the account of his death is too characteristic to be omitted. The great Gorakhnath and his teacher Machhander were on their travels, when they came to the kingdom of Harbong. Gorakhnath, hearing that everything, whether rare or common, was sold at the same price, determined to take up his abode in Harbongpúr, contrary to the persuasions of Machhander, who counselled retreat. They had not been there many days before a murder was committed, and gallows (?) were erected for the punishment of the culprit. But on the day appointed for the execution no criminal was forthcoming, and as the rope was very thick and strong, the Raja ordered that two of the largest men should be selected from the assembled crowd and punished on the following day. The two largest men happened to be Gorakhnath and Machhander, who after taking counsel together about their proceedings, were brought out for execution. No sooner had they reached the gallows, than they began to quarrel about precedence, each loudly pretending to desire to be strung up before the other. The Raja enquired the meaning of this singular quarrel, when Machhander stepped forward, and said he had ascertained from his books and learned Pandits, that whoever should obtain the honor of being hanged first on that day, would go immediately to Paradise. "If that is the case," said the Raja, "the fate is too good for either of you; I will swing first, if you please," and so was hanged at his own desire. These pious devotees were so shocked at his atrocities that, immediately after the execution, they made a complete *bouleversement* of Harbongpúr, and it remains a shapeless ruin to this day.

This is the Hindu account. The Mahomedans ascribe its destruction to a miracle effected by the Sayyid Ali Murtaẓá mentioned above, who died as late as A.D. 1359, and who changed the name of the place from Harbongpúr to Jhúsí.

بعد ازان دوم بار نعرہ یا مریخ نمودہ نگاہ بطرف قلعه او کردند قلعه
مذکور ازبیخ براوردہ غلطید چنانچه عمارت ان قلعه تحت برفت و
زمین بالا گردید و ان کافر مع فوج خود بجهنم شتافت و رسم اسلام
جاري گردید باقي همه هنودان از ترس این زلزله مسلمان شدند مخدوم
صاحب سید شعبان الملت استقامت کردند آخرش چند مدت آنجا
ماندند بعدہ پارگنگ درحویلي پیاک در موضع جرئي استقامت کردند
وچند فقرا در جهونسی گذاشتند * (Manba'u's Sádát.)

* "After this having a second time cried out, 'Yá mirríkh,' he looked towards the fort which suddenly fell down and sank beneath the earth, and that infidel with his army went to hell; and the religion of Islam was introduced and all the rest of the

He is represented to have visited Jhúnsí for the purpose of introducing the Mahomedan religion amongst the infidels; but that surely must have been effected before this period, and though the story is devoutly believed by the Mahomedans, and more especially by his descendants, some of whom now hold high judicial offices under our Government, we can scarcely believe Ali Murtazá to be a contemporary of Raja Harbong, who, if he had any existence at all beyond the imaginations of the people, must have preceded that saint by several centuries.

Hardaur, هردور हरदौर

Is the name given to the oblong mounds raised in villages, and studded with flags, for the purpose of averting epidemic diseases, and especially the cholera morbus. It is called after Hardaul Lálá, the son of Bír Singh Deo, from whom are descended the Rajas of Dattea. The natives have a firm persuasion that the cholera broke out in Lord Hastings' camp, in consequence of beef having been killed for the European soldiers within the grove where repose the ashes of this Bundelkhand chief. So rapid has been the extension of this worship, that it now prevails throughout the Upper and Central Doáb, a great part of Rohilkhand, and to the banks of the Sutlej. To the Eastward, the worship of Hulká Deví (the goddess of vomiting) has been prevalent since the same period.

Harí, هري हरी

Contributions of assistance by Ryots in ploughing the fields of Zamíndárs. The service is compulsory, and occurs in Asarh and Kátik.—Lower Doáb, Benares, and E. Oudh.

It is occasionally applied as Angwara, *q.v.*

Hindus embraced it through fear of that earthquake, and the saint lived there for some time, but subsequently crossed the Ganges to Jarai, and lived there; a few poor people remained in Jhúnsí."—B.

Harítá, هريته हरीता

The first commencement of ploughing in the rainy season.—Rohilkhand. In Dehli the word Halsotea is used, and elsewhere Haláitá, Harainí, Haráit, Harautá, Harwat, and Harái, *q.v.*

Hariyar, هرير हरियर

This bears the same meaning in Oudh, and its immediate neighbourhood, as Kuṇr muṇdha and Daliájhár do elsewhere, viz., the closing of the sowing season.—See these articles, and Harpúji.

Harpúji, هرپوجي हरपूजी

The worship of the plough. This takes place on the day which closes the season of ploughing and sowing. It generally occurs in the month of Kátik, but in some places it occurs both after the Kharíf and Rabi' sowings, *i.e.*, in Sawan and Kátik. The plough is washed and decorated with garlands, and to use it or lend it after this day is deemed unlucky.

Though the plough is in some places decorated at the opening of the season (Haláitá), yet it is the more general practice to do so when its labours are closed.—See Kunr, Mundlú, and Duliájhar. Kálí Rái says, "After sowing the Kharíf and the Rabi', when they leave off ploughing, they feast the blacksmith, carpenter, potter, barber, and shoemaker, and that day they call 'nibauní.'"—E. add.

Harwal, هرول हरवल

Advances without interest made to ploughmen.—Eastern Oudh and Benares.

Haṭhíle, هتهيلي हठीले

One of the Pachpírí, or five noted saints of the lower orders of these provinces. He is said to be the sister's son of Ghází Míyán (*q.v.*), and lies buried at Bahraich, near the tomb of that celebrated martyr. Monuments are erected to the memory of Hathíle (who derives his name from Hathi, an elephant, on account of his elephantine stature), and fairs are held at several villages in honor of his name.

Ikhráj, ایکهراج ईखराज

Ikhráj, or Ukhraj, is the name given in some places to the day on which sugar-cane is planted, which is generally attended with some festive ceremonies. In the Eastward it is usual for the women of the villages to take out to the field a mixture of rice and turmeric, called Aipan, into which they dip their hands, and impress them on the heap of sugar-cane which is to be planted. They then proceed towards the ploughmen and planters, and leave the same impression on their backs. The man who drives the first plough is decorated with necklaces and other ornaments, lamp-black is rubbed on his eyelids, and on him the first hatha, or impression, is made. The women then begin to dance and sing, and after a short time has elapsed, the proprietor of the field throws a bundle of sugar-cane amongst them as the signal of dismissal, and after much scrambling they depart. The labourers also are well fed by the proprietor on their return home.

In the Eastward the Ikhráj seldom occurs on a Sunday, but to the Westward that day is considered propitious for the planting. The customs which are observed are also different. In Dehli, for instance, the wife of the man at the plough, who turns up the ground for the reception of the sugar cuttings, follows a little behind with a ball of cotton in her hand. At some unexpected moment he turns on her, and after a sham contest bears her to the ground. The cotton being forced out of her hand spreads upon the ground, and the parties present exclaim, "may our sugar-cane grow and spread like this cotton."

The sugar-cane is called ईख íkh in the West, and ऊख úkh in the East, of these Provinces. Kálí Rái says the day on which they sow the seed they worship the plough with rice and turmeric, and call that day उखरहज "ukharhaj." He says there are three kinds of sugar-cane: 1. The parvi or púrbí. 2. dusáhí (also called bastwá and karakh), sown after the kharíf is cut. 3. That which grows from the root of last year's cane, and is called munḍha. The sugar-cane grown from cuttings is called भटमई bhaṭmaí.

Istikbál, استقبال इस्तिक़बाल

A ceremonious meeting in the open air, by advancing to receive a visitor.

Jákar, جاکڑ जाकड़

A pledge in deposit, until goods, which are taken away, are finally approved of. This is the usual pronunciation; but the correct word is Jankar.

It is also used in Behar to signify money deposited in a Government treasury as security, being equivalent to the more usual word ضمانت ẓamánat.—B.

Jíterá, جیترا जीतेरा

Mutual assistance in tillage; also allowing the use of a plough and bullocks, instead of paying wages in money or kind.—Rohilkhand and Bundelkhand. The word is pronounced also Jitta, and the custom is known by various other names.—See Angwara, Dangwara, and Harsot.

Jehaṛ, جیہڑ जेहड़

A pile of waterpots placed one on the other. The word is pronounced also Jeghar. To take the waterpots off the head of a divorced woman, is to imply consent to marry her. The custom prevails amongst the Játs, Ahírs, and Gújars, but principally amongst the former, and more commonly in Rajputana than in these provinces.

Jeoṛá, جیوڑا जेओड़ा

Perquisites of Blacksmiths, Washermen, Carpenters, and other village servants.

Júṛí, جوڑي जूड़ी

From joṛna, to join: a small bundle of sugar-cane. The tops of the Júrí, brought home on the festival of the eleventh of Katik (see Dithwan), are kept suspended from the roof of the house till the Holí, and burnt during that festival.

Jalotsarg, جلوتسرگ जलोत्सर्ग

The ceremony which is gone through when a pond, baolí, or well is married. It has been already described under Banotsarg, *q.v.* The only difference is that the bride is personated by an image, instead of the Tulsí. The word is derived from the Sanskrit जल water, and उत्सर्ग donation. The advantages to be derived from the ceremony are shown in the 3rd chapter of the Nirṇaya Sindhu. It is the general impression amongst Europeans that this marriage ceremony takes place only between a well and a garden, but this union is exceedingly rare; the most usual practice being, as mentioned before, to perform the marriage ceremony of each separately.

Kuṇṛ mundlá, کنڑمنڈلا कुंड मुंडला

Is the name given to the day on which the sowing is concluded.—Benares. It is in the Lower Doáb and Baiswara generally called Kunr bojí and Hariar. In the North-West it is well known by the name of Dalea-jhar, or Palea-jhar, that is, the cleaning out of the sowing bag or basket. The real meaning of Kunr mundlá is the closing of furrows, from कुंड *kunr*, a furrow, and मुंदना *mundná*, to be closed or shut. The meaning of Kunr bojí is the filling of furrows. Bojí is from बोझना to be full. This word should be written, I think, बोझी.

It is usual to devote this day to festivity, and, amongst other ceremonies, to decorate the ploughs; and to make the residue of the seed-corn into a cake, which is partaken of in the open field, and in part distributed to Brahmans and beggars.—See Daleajhar, Hariar, and Harpújí.

Karáo, کراو कराओ

The name given among Játs, Gújars, Ahírs, and other inferior tribes in the Western part of these Provinces to concubinage generally; but more especially to marriages of widows with the brother of a deceased husband. The practice (which is also known to the Eastward by the name of Urbarí, in the Deccan of Bathí, and, in other Provinces, by the name of Dharícha) is common among these classes, but is not very openly confessed even among them, as some degree of discredit is supposed to attach to it. It is only younger brothers who form these connections, elder brothers being prohibited from marrying their younger brothers' widows; but among the Dehli Játs even this is not prohibited. The practice has been common among several nations of the East.

When the laws of Menu were enacted Karáo appears not to have been confined to the lower classes; but, as is not unusual with the Institutes, there is much contradiction between the enactments relating to it. From a consideration of all the passages on the subject, it appears that failure of issue was the point on which the legality turned.

"On failure of issue by the husband, the desired offspring may be procreated by his brother, or by some other Sapinda, on the wife who has been duly authorized."—(Ch. IX., v. 59).

The Commentator confines this licence to the servile class,

and he is borne out by the passages immediately succeeding (60, 64); but the following section appears to recognize generally the lawfulness of such marriages.

"He who was begotten according to law on the wife of a man deceased, or impotent, or disordered, after due authority given to her, is called the lawful son of the wife."—(Ch. IX., v. 176).

All the modern schools of Hindu Law prohibit the practice entirely;* and the later commentators and abridgers of the Mahábhárata show the utmost anxiety to slur over or explain away a most conspicuous case of Karáo, or worse than Karáo, recorded in that sacred poem. From the fact of Draupadí marrying the five Pándav brothers, we learn that polyandry must have prevailed amongst the heroes of that period; and if polyandry, the more venial offence of Karáo was, no doubt, not uncommon; indeed, the compiler of the Mahábhárata, Vyása, was himself appointed to raise up offspring to his deceased brother! Most of our English historians of India † take us to the Panjáb for the scene of this incestuous marriage of the Páṇḍavs, and invite us to search for a Kampilanagar in that country, where it is not improbable that a remnant of Scythic manners might be found. But we surely need not go beyond our own Kampil on the Ganges. It seems strange that it should have been overlooked, that when the five brothers in the "Mahábhárata" proceed to all parts of Hindústan in search of allies, the first place visited by Raja Bhím, going East from Indraprasthá (Dehli), was Kampil, the capital of Raja Drupada ("Sabhá Parva," Vol. I., p. 354, Cal. Ed.). Kampil is certainly

* It has nevertheless been admitted by the Sudder Dewany Adawlut as the *lex loci* of Orissa. See "Reports," Vol. II., p. 175, the "Digest," Vol. III., p. 276, and "MacNaghten's Hindu Law," Vol. I., p. 102.

† Even Marshman has fallen into this error, at p. 26 of his excellent "History of India for Schools," under which unpretending title, he has written by far the most clear and intelligible account which we possess of the ante-Mahomedan period.

of sufficient antiquity for mention in the "Mahábhárata." It is a place, moreover, of sacred resort among the Jains, where they annually bury an image of one of their Tirthankaras, and has been immemorially established among them as a holy city. The origin of the mistake appears to be that Kampila is in Panchála, which has been considered to be the Panjáb; whereas it is the name of an old country on the banks of the Ganges, including Farrakhabad and Southern Rohilkhand.

This practice must have prevailed even before the time of the Páṇḍavs, for Yudhishthira replies to the expostulations of King Drupada, "We pretend not to determine what is proper: we follow the path successively trodden by those who have gone before." There is, perhaps, no circumstance which so strongly shews the Northern descent of the deified heroes as this marriage. Herodotus tells us that the practice prevailed among the nomadic Scythians, as it does at present among the Bhotias. The practice is adopted also by the Nairs of Malabar, between whom and the people of the Himalaya Wilson traces the obscure vestiges of a connection (See "Selections from the Mahábhárata," pp. 8 and 66).

Amongst Játs, Gújars, and Ahírs, children born in Karáo are considered legitimate, and are entitled to inheritance accordingly. Children brought forth by the woman previous to Karáo, except in the case of fraternal Karáo, are known by the name of Kadhelara कधेलड़ा, and do not inherit the property of the father-in-law.

Khoj, کھوج खोज

_ Literally, tracking. This term is applied to an elaborate system prevalent in the Panjáb, and in certain parts of these provinces where the crime of cattle-lifting is very frequent. The foot-prints of thieves, and the hoof-prints of cattle, are tracked by a class of men called khojis, whose skill is very extraordinary. Such men are met with in nearly every village, and having once struck the track, will carry it on for miles, over all sorts of country, and nearly always succeed in finding the cattle. The chief difficulty which a khoji has to encounter in the course of his tracking is when he comes to the entrance of a village. In the Panjáb, and the Upper or Western parts of these Provinces, the villages consist usually of clusters of houses huddled close together on a mound, and having only very narrow lanes between them. In many districts, especially in the Cis-Satlaj provinces, or the country between the Jumna and the Satlaj, where the incessant broils carried on by the petty chieftains of that district among themselves have long rendered life and property insecure, the villages are surrounded by a wall, and have only one large and strongly defended gateway, in whose deep recesses the patriarchs of the community meet to smoke their evening hukka, and watch the cattle coming home. It is obvious that the mass of cattle all entering at one gate, or even at two or more, must leave a multiplicity of footprints, amongst which the track of one particular animal is indistinguishable. The cattle-thief is well aware of this, and leads his booty home through as many villages as he can on purpose to baffle his pursuers; by doing so, however, he exposes himself to the danger of being seen and recognized by many people, questioned about his cattle and himself, and if the village chokidár, or watchman, be on the alert, of being seized and detained. This danger, however, is less in reality than it sounds, because the thief can in a great many, perhaps the majority of cases, count upon the sympathy and silence of the villagers. Inasmuch, however, as without connivance on the part of the people through whose villages he passes, the thief could not well escape detection and detention, a system sprung up under native rule, which was for some time, and I believe still is, allowed to remain in operation under the British administration. It is this:—if on following up a track the khoji and his witnesses can bring it into the mass of hoof-prints immediately surrounding a village, he carefully covers the last mark over with a potsherd, or leaves some one to watch it, and going into the village summons the lumberdars, or headmen, and calls on them to "pahuncháo," or carry on the track beyond the limits of the lands belonging to their village. If they, with the assistance of their own khoji, are unable to do so, they are considered responsible for the stolen property, and have either to produce it or pay the price of it in money.

In the Barr, or desert, through which the five rivers of the Panjáb flow for many miles of their lower course, the soil is often a hard caked sand, which does not retain the impress of the foot, and in those parts it is only by making the most of such foot-prints as he can find in the patches of soft sand which occur here and there that the khoji can follow his game. The patience and ingenuity, and the marvellous keenness of sight, which a good tracker displays, are equal to anything that has been recorded of the red men of North, or the gauchos of South America. Out of many anecdotes current on this interesting subject I select two, one of which fell within my own observation. A camel was stolen from the market-place of Multan, a locality where thousands of these animals, coming from all the neighbouring countries, are assembled. This particular camel, like many others, had been branded on the soft spongy soles of his feet with his owner's private mark. The brand was shown to a khoji, who, after making a careful circuit of some miles round the city, found foot-prints with this mark leading northwards. Mounted on another camel he took up the track, and followed it for more than two hundred miles, till he reached Gujrát, a town only thirty miles from the foot of the Kashmír hills. Here the country becomes fertile, and is extensively cultivated, and for a time he lost the track, and applied to me in consequence for assistance. Another khoji was associated with him, and the two together found the track again, and, accompanied by the owner of the camel, found the beast at last in the market-place of a little town in the Kashmír territory, close under the hills, whence they brought it back in triumph to Gujrát.

In another case a buffalo was stolen from the neighbourhood of Ferozpúr. The thief took it to the Satlaj, which he crossed, swimming and holding on by the animal's tail. The khoji followed the track to the banks of the river, which at that place is nearly two miles broad; on the other side was the vast sandy plain of the Barr, where hundreds and thousands of buffaloes graze. The khoji calculated so accurately the force of the current and its effect in carrying a swimmer along with it, that without any hesitation he crossed and landed on the other side exactly at the spot where the thief had come out, and after carrying the track a little further, found both man and animal.

In tracking human foot-prints the khoji is sometimes aided by three little straws, with which he measures the length of the foot, its breadth at the ball and at the heel; but many of the best khojis disdain any such mechanical aid, and trust solely to their eye.—B.

Panch, پنچ पंच

Pancháyat, پنچایت पंचायत

*** The rustic tribunal known by these names is one the origin of which is lost in antiquity, and whose popularity has remained unimpaired through the ages. पंच में परमेश्वर "In the panch is God," is a common saying in India. In its strictest acceptation the panch consists, as its name implies, of *five* persons, who ought to be residents of the same village, or of the same caste and rank in life as the parties concerned; but this number in modern times is seldom adhered to: three is the smallest number of which it can be constituted, and it may consist of as many as fifty or a hundred. This irregularity arises from the fact that the panch has, and probably has always had, two distinct characters, according to the functions it is called on to discharge. First and most important is the judicial panch. This generally consists of five only, and not less or more. In the Panjáb, and, I believe, in the non-regulation districts generally, previous to the introduction of the Indian Penal Code (Act XLV. of 1861), the institution of the panch was utilized to a great extent by the district officers in the trial of civil, criminal, and revenue suits, and its decisions were always acquiesced in cheerfully, and, except in cases where unfairness had been practised, never appealed from. The procedure was for the plaintiff to name two men, and the defendant two, either party having, as in the case of a jury in England, the right of challenging the other's nominees. The magistrate or other presiding officer then chose a head, or *sar panch*; the point in dispute was clearly stated to the panch, all the necessary papers were handed over to them, and they were sworn to decide fairly and honestly, and to return a judgment in a certain number of days. The particular value of this mode of trial was that in intricate points of native customs, often depending upon a state of feeling which it was difficult for the English officer, as being a foreigner, to enter into, the members of the panch were thoroughly at home in their subject, and were able to give due weight to a variety of minor considerations which none but a native could perfectly understand. Even in the older provinces, where the regulations are in force, it is found at times convenient to have recourse to this time-honoured method of decision, and the result is always so satisfactory, that one is tempted to wish it were more largely resorted to.

There are some cases, such, for instance, as those relating to the peculiar customs of the Kashmiri shawl-weavers in the Panjáb, which can only be settled by a pancháyat composed of members of the fraternity. Such also are questions connected with partitions of estates, or the assessment of lands for revenue purposes; or those, again, in which damages have to be awarded for breaches of contract; or settlements of accounts between a peasant and his money-lender, where the panch, from being residents of the same village as the parties, can bring their local knowledge to bear on points which could not well be decided by a judicial officer, from the total want of reliable evidence as to minute credits and debits running on through a long series of years. Moreover, the influence of the elders of the village is often strong enough to induce one or both of the contending parties to yield certain points in order to obtain a settlement, or even to forgive the injury which has been the origin of the case.

Different from this judicial panch, is that self-constituted court whose edicts owe their validity to the force of public opinion; and these are often very terrible tribunals indeed. The questions they are most often called upon to decide are matters connected with the great institution of caste. As a rule a man can only be put out of caste, or received back into it, by a pancháyat of his caste-brethren, and, especially in Behar and Bengal, such pancháyats consist often of very large numbers of persons. A case which I remember in Purneah illustrates the operation of this caste-panch fully. A man of a low caste, as far as I recollect, a dhobi, or washerman, was suspected of living in illicit intercourse with his aunt. He denied it, but refused to remove the woman from his house, and some time afterwards went and was openly married to her. None of his caste-fellows attended the marriage feast, as the woman was with child, as was supposed, by this man. Public opinion ran strong against the pair, and at last the whole of his caste in the parganah, amounting to some hundreds, met and elected a numerous pancháyat, who, after carefully taking and recording a mass of evidence, solemnly found both parties guilty, and put them out of caste. A singular letter was then written in a rude Hindi scrawl, to which the members of the pancháyat affixed their marks or names, and this was sent round from hand-to-hand through a large circle of country, comprising three or four districts, informing all whom it might concern, that so-and-so, having been judged guilty of conduct immoral in itself and opposed to the practices of the caste, had been deprived of his rights, and that no one was thenceforth to eat, drink, or smoke with him on pain of sharing his fate. The wretched man, after bearing his sentence for some weeks, finding his life intolerable, and all the neighbouring country closed to him, at first contemplated turning Musulman, but eventually gave in, was separated from his wife, and made submission; he was then directed to give a feast, at which all the fraternity attended and ate with him, whereupon he was re-installed in his caste.

But the pancháyat, though a singularly just tribunal, and displaying generally a sound common sense, is of course not infallible, and it sometimes occurs that bribery or other corrupt practices are resorted to. From the general uncertainty prevailing as to the way such tribunals, when not summoned or charged by a magistrate, proceed to arrive at their decision, it has been in practice found unadvisible to endorse or uphold their judgments, and taking into consideration the immense increase of material wealth in the Lower Provinces, and the important interests at stake, it must be admitted that the system is not so applicable to that part of the country as it is to the rude and simple peasantry of the Panjáb. It is probably destined to be swept away, or at least to be retained only among the people themselves in such cases as are not susceptible of rigorous legal investigation before the constituted tribunals.—B.

APPENDIX C.

PREVALENT CASTES IN THE NORTH-WESTERN PROVINCES, AS DESCRIBED IN THE CENSUS REPORT (1865), VOL. I.

The subsequent pages (283–92) have been taken from Mr. W. C. Plowden's Digest of the Census, §§ 230–310. For the statements contained in the extracts that follow (marked in the original as Appendix B.) the several District Officers must be held responsible whose names are appended :—

The classification of castes in the general statement is a singular table. There are no less than 560 castes shown among the Hindus, and there are fourteen other columns, raising the total number to 574, embracing Bengalís, Madrasís, Thibetans, Chinese, Parsís, Mahomedans, and Christians.

The four great primary castes of Hindus are thus sub-divided :—Brahmans into 70 sub-divisions, Kshatriyas into 175, Vaisyas into 65, Súdras into 230. Then come five columns—one comprising Sikhs, four comprising different sects of the Jain religion; then fourteen columns relating to religious sects—Gosains, Jogís, Sannyásís, and the like. Finally, three columns relate to travellers, and one to Hindus whose caste is not known.

The Brahmans are 3,451,692 in number; the Kshatriyas amount to 2,827,768; the Vaisyas are much less in number, namely, 1,091,250. The Súdras form the great bulk of the population, counting 18,304,309 individuals. Then come 12,336 persons whose caste was unknown. Only 1,425 Sikhs are shown; but it must be remembered that the Statement of Castes does not embrace military or persons employed on the railway. According to the present composition of the native army, we should expect to find a large number of Sikhs classed among military; and there is no doubt that Sikhs form a considerable portion of the native troops stationed in these Provinces; but the information received from the several Brigade Majors and Cantonment Magistrates is not complete on this head—the troops merely being shown in several cases according as they are Hindus or Mahomedans, without any reference to the castes of the former.

Going on with the statement, we find 49,983 of the Jain sect, and 195,977 of other religious sects—Gosains, Fakírs, Sannyásís, etc.; 1,348 persons are returned as Bengalís, 26 as Madrassís, 67 as Thibetans, 37 as Chinese (of whom 36 are to be found in the districts where tea-planting is going on, and one is at Allahabad); 76 Parsís are entered as residing at Ajmír, but no specimens of this enterprising race are to be found in any other part of the North-West.

Of the Mahomedans, 2,207,576 have not been classified at all; of the remainder, 1,140,108 are Shaikhs, 515,526 are Patháns, 170,248 are Sayyids, and 41,748 are described as Mughals.

Of the sub-divisions of the four great castes, we find the following prevalent:—

Among the Brahmans, excluding 1,198,216 who have returned themselves merely as Brahmans, without reference to sub-divisions of castes, the sub-divisions mentioned below are most numerous, and prevail most largely in the districts named:—

Names of Sub-divisions.	Total Number.	District where most prevalent.	Number.
1. Kanaujia	506,888	Cawnpore	235,805
2. Tewarí	213,565	Gorakhpúr	62,250
3. Gaur	170,182	Sahâranpúr	46,948
4. Pandey	167,735		67,513
5. Sanauria	163,993	Muttra	90,287
6. Missir	150,231	Gorakhpúr	41,835
7. Dúbey	132,612	Ditto	34,826
8. Taggah	105,035	Mírat	46,603
Total..............	1,610,241		626,067

The Kanaujias are not found in any number above Etawah; in fact, in the Mírat Division they are not known, and in Rohilkhand they number little more than 1,000—a small colony of 998 existing in

Moradabad, and 16 persons of the same sub-division being recorded as residents of Bijnore.

Almost half the Gaur Brahmans belong to Muzaffarnagar and Saháranpúr. There are large numbers also of this sub-division in Moradabad and Muttra.

The Tewarís belong almost entirely to the Gorakhpúr and Benares Divisions. Allahabad and Banda, however, contain 68,000.

The Chaubeys are met with in greatest numbers at Mirzapúr, Benares, Gorakhpúr, and are not to be found above Muttra.

The Dúbeys also belong to the south of the Province; and the Pandeys (a name not unfamiliar to English ears, for, owing to the first of the Sepoy mutineers belonging to this caste, the name was not uncommonly applied to designate all sepoy mutineers) are likewise found almost exclusively below the Mírat and Rohilkhand Divisions.

Seven-eighths of the Sanauria Brahmans belong to the Muttra and Agra districts; while the Taggahs, on the other hand, are found exclusively in Saháranpúr, Muzaffarnagar, Bijnore, Mírat, and Moradabad—a cluster of adjoining districts forming the extreme north-west of this Province. The smallest class among the Brahmans is the Dhatúrah sub-sect, which consists of nine individuals living in the Allahabad district.

Turning now to the great military family of the Kshatriyas, with their 175 divisions, we find twelve-fourteenths (1,282,454) classified as Chhattrí Thákurs, Kúer or Rajputs. Saháranpúr contains 230,118, and Ghazipur 206,262, of their total number; but they are found in large numbers throughout the Province.

The sub-divisions, comprising the largest numbers, and the districts in which they are prevalent, will be seen in the accompanying abstract:—

Names of Sub-divisions.	Total Number.	District where most prevalent.	Number.
1. Khassia	204,190	Kamaon..........................	204,190
2. Bais	146,953	Jaunpúr..........................	35,536
3. Chauhán	118,714	Bijnore	71,685
4. Gautam	66,633	Mirzapúr	18,178
5. Bhoimhar..................	55,500	Azimgaṛh	47,926
6. Gaur......	53,937	Muttra	22,460
7. Khattrí....................	46,332	Widely scattered throughout the Province.	

The Khassias are peculiar to the Kamáon hills. The sequel contains a brief account of them, *vide* the Memorandum of Castes for the district of Kamáon.

With the exception of 5,912 in Farrakhabad, the Bais clan is confined entirely to the Allahabad, Benares, and Gorakhpúr Divisions, that of Allahabad containing the greatest number.

The Chauháns are found in nineteen districts, but in large numbers only in Bijnore and Etawah. Three-fifths almost of the whole are found in the former district, and 15,000 in Etawah.

The Gautams belong to the Allahabad, Gorakhpúr, and Benares Divisions.

The Bhoimhar caste is met with only in Azimgaṛh, Jaunpúr, and Mirzapúr, the bulk of the tribe belonging to Azimgaṛh.

The Gaur tribe is found mostly in Muttra and Cawnpore.

Khattrís are to be met with in all but five districts, but are not found in large numbers in any one district. The greatest number, 8,457, is found in Cawnpore.

Of the Mansal and Mallú Kshatriyas severally, only one representative appears, and in both cases in Agra.

Of the Vaisyas, or mercantile class, 383,202 are recorded as Banniahs. 232,862 are classed as Agarwals, of whom the largest number (68,661) are entered in the Mírat return.

Of the remainder, the following classes are most largely represented :—

Names of Sub-divisions.	Total Number.	District where most prevalent.	Number.
1. Kandú	72,149	Ghazipur	38,005
2. Umar	55,827	Mirzapúr	16,693
3. Kasserwani	49,528	Allahabad	31,763
4. Kassondhan	31,782	Gorakhpúr	21,832
5. Mahajan	31,691	Etawah	13,529
6. Agrehrí	29,874	Jaunpúr	6,514
7. Baranwal	20,328	Azimgaṛh	6,293
8. Dúsar	15,429	Cawnpore	15,254

With the exception of 175 in Hamírpúr, the Dúsars are recorded only in Cawnpore; the Kandús in Ghazipur and Gorakhpúr; the Baranwals, with the exception of 2,428 in the Moradabad District, are found only in Gorakhpúr, Azimgaṛh, Jaunpúr, and Ghazipur; the Mahajans principally in Etawah and Etah; the Kassondhans in Gorakhpúr; the Kasserwanís in Allahabad; the Agrehrís in the districts below Cawnpore, and the Umars in Mirzapúr, Cawnpore, Farrakhabad, and Jaunpúr.

The Agarwals and the Banniahs, who have been recorded without subordinate distinctions of tribe, are found in all districts throughout the Province.

Proceeding now to the lowest of the four great castes, we find among the Súdras, exclusive of those whose castes are designated by their profession, that the following sub-divisions are conspicuous by their numbers: the districts in which they are most numerous are also shown:—

Names of Sub-divisions.	Total Number.	District where most prevalent.	Number.
Ahír	2,196,786	Gorakhpúr	483,903
Kayasth	351,463	Ditto	39,689
Málí	167,597	Bijnore	42,736
Náí	430,564	Gorakhpúr	55,508
Kumhár	453,614	Ditto	61,646
Dhímar or Kahár	693,519	Ditto	67,426
Kúrmí	971,285	Bareilly	163,232
		Gorakhpúr	242,388
Gadariyá	566,981	Cawnpore	40,200
Lodhá	585,932	Hamírpúr	59,864
Kalál	262,884	Gorakhpúr	46,739
Káchhí	1,348,316	Ditto	163,839
Kolí	444,992	Agra	36,457
Pasí	272,151	Allahabad	82,345
Chamár	3,580,385	Gorakhpúr	412,600
Gújar	264,496	Mírat	54,035
Ját	682,712	Muttra	120,494
Mallah	388,258	Gorakhpúr	134,652
Kisan	335,305	Bareilly	105,506

Among the remaining Súdras the following are noticeable:—

Mhair	50,570	Khassiah	107,648
Kol	62,463	Nat	25,095
Gond	48,430	Kanjar	15,236
Thag	2	Sansia	116
Dom	51,199	Bhar	233,373
Chauhán Chaudrí	37,313	Bind	63,501

The Kayeths, or Kayaths, are found throughout the Province, with the single exception of the Gaṛhwal District. In Kamáon, however, they are very few in number, only 25 being found there; and these it may be considered are emigrants from the pláins who have settled at Naini Tál, or in some of the Government offices in the hills.

The Ahírs, too, are numerous throughout the plain districts, and Muzaffarnagar is the only one in which they do not appear in force. The Kachhís, who are admirable cultivators, are found throughout all the divisions of the North-West proper, *i.e.*, excluding the mountains and the Ajmír Division. In Mírat, however, they are few, and are found only in one district of that division in anything like numbers. In the Mírat District they amount to 27,418, and in Bulandshahr to 2,421. They do not appear in the other districts of the division. The Kolís and Jaláhas are found in all the plain divisions except Gorakhpúr; but in the Benares Division, where little cotton is produced, they dwindle down to less than 1,200.

The Bhars, supposed by some to be aborigines, are found in the extreme east of the Province. With the exception of 2,377 in the Allahabad District, they are confined to Gorakhpúr and the districts of the Benares Division.

The Pásís, too, belong to the south-east: a few are found in Mírat, and nearly an eighth of their whole number in Shahjehanpúr, Bareilly, and Moradabad.

Chamárs are to be met with in all the districts of the Province, hill or otherwise.

The Gújars belong principally to the north and north-western districts; three-fifths of them reside in the Mírat Division, and 32,270 are entered against Ajmír. Játs are found in all but four districts, but not in large numbers south or east of Agra. More than a quarter of their number are residents of Muttra and Agra, and nearly a half of the whole is found in the Mírat Division, where they amount in round numbers to 330,000.

The wandering tribes, Nats and Kanjars, are, as might be predicted, to be met with in most districts; they appear in thirty out of thirty-five cases.

The Mallahs have evidently been incorrectly distinguished, as none are found in many districts bordering the Ganges and the Jumna, where they notoriously exist.

The Khassiah Súdras are, like their Rajput brethren, peculiar to the hills. In Gaṛhwál they number 107,627, and 21 are found in the Tarai immediately below the hills.

The greater number of the Doms appear to reside in Gaṛhwál. It is probable they are included in other cases with Methars and Khakrobs.

Bijnore has the distinction of giving a home to the two Thags recorded as residents of the North-West.

The Chauhán Chaudrís, entered as a Súdra caste, belong exclusively to Moradabad.

The four districts of Bareilly, Shahjahanpúr, Farrakhabad, and Mainpúrí contain ten-elevenths of the whole Kisan class: 344 of this class are found in Moradabad, 1,693 in the Tarai, and the remaining 11,966 in Etah.

The Gonds, an indigenous tribe, are found almost exclusively in Gorakhpúr, Benares, and Mirzapúr. There are also a few in Allahabad, and a few scattered throughout the Jhansi Division.

The Kols, a somewhat similar race, are found principally in Allahabad and Mirzapúr, which two districts contain 52,275. The remaining 10,188 are residents of Banda.

The Mhairs belong exclusively to Mhairwara, in the Ajmír Division.

Of the Jain religionists, numbering 49,983, by far the larger number belong to Ajmír, where they amount to 23,795; but Muzaffarnagar contains 9,354 Saráogís, and Lallatpúr 11,264 Jains. The remainder are scattered in small bodies, principally in Agra, Farrakhabad, Etawah, Allahabad, and Mirzapúr.

The Gosains muster strongest in Mírat, Muttra, and Bulandshahr; the Jogís in Moradabad, Aligaṛh, Agra, and Cawnpore. The Sannyásís are peculiar to Gaṛhwál, and the same may be said of the Dúm Jogís. The Jangan and Nanakshahí sects are peculiar to Benares; the Atíth to Azimgaṛh. Nearly half of the Fakírs enumerated are found in Allahabad and Gorakhpúr, while the Ladhú, Bhartí, and Bankhatta classes are to be met with only in Benares.

The accompanying statement shews the percentage of each of the four great castes on the total Hindu population of each district:—

STATEMENT OF DISTRICTS, SHEWING THE COMPOSITION OF THE HINDU POPULATION IN REGARD TO THE FOUR GREAT CASTES.

Names of Districts.	Percentage of Brahmans on total Hindus.	Percentage of Kshatriyas on total Hindus.	Percentage of Vaisyas on total Hindus.	Percentage of Súdras on total Hindus.
Dehra Dún	10·05	32·58	2·84	54·53
Sahâranpúr	11·55	41·03	7·19	40·23
Muzaffarnagar	12·88	5·42	8·03	73·67
Mírat	17·47	7·16	7·57	67·80
Bulandshahr	14·30	11·99	4·97	68·74
Aligaṛh	16·44	8·45	6·81	68·30
Kamáon	17·22	76·73	1·12	4·93
Gaṛhwál	22·67	11·78	0·47	65·08
Bijnore	8·34	15·45	3·74	72·47
Moradabad	8·25	4·60	4·59	82·56
Badáon	8·09	9·29	3·42	79·20
Bareilly	6·79	4·12	2·83	86·26
Shahjahanpúr	7·89	8·01	1·85	82·25
Tarai Parganahs	7·15	5·81	·97	86·07
Muttra	20·12	14·60	7·11	58·17
Agra	15·44	10·64	6·96	66·96
Farrakhabad	11·27	8·77	1·63	78·33
Mainpúrí	10·29	8·45	5·22	76·04
Etawah	16·22	9·	5·62	69·16
Etah	10·24	9·66	5·25	74·85
Jhansi	14·78	5·70	4·30	75·22
Jalaun	16·85	12·03	5·46	65·66
Lallatpúr	9·59	6·46	5·16	78·79
Cawnpore	22·27	11·45	3·90	62·38
Fattihpúr	13·98	8·99	3·96	73·07
Banda	16·79	9·50	3·99	69·72
Allahabad	15·10	4·71	4·13	76·06
Hamírpúr	13·19	9·06	3·95	73·80
Gorakhpúr	12·79	4·11	4·06	79·04
Azimgarh	8·43	14·27	1·19	76·11
Jaunpúr	19·34	24·50	3·11	53·05
Mirzapúr	13·87	10·10	4·50	71·53
Benares	15·25	8·07	2·67	74·01
Ghazipur	10·13	16·90	3·97	69·0
Ajmír	6·47	4·90	9·31	79·32

The Statement of Castes may be accepted as correct in so far as it classifies the primary castes; but the details of the sub-castes are only approximately correct, as it is evident from the tables that in some cases no distinction of subordinate caste has been observed.

There is but one other portion of the papers included in the Census Report which still requires remark. I refer to Appendix B., containing the replies of the several District Officers in regard to the castes prevailing in their respective districts, and the mode in which the subsidiary castes have taken their origin. This is a subject on which I am not in a position to add any information. Babú Siva Prasad, Joint Inspector of Schools in the Benares Circle, who is well acquainted with the subject, has, however, been good enough to furnish the following comments on this Appendix :—

"Appendix B. contains much valuable and interesting information, though mixed up with much that is worthless, badly arranged, and sometimes contradictory. The reader will often find the statement that Aheer (Ahír) is derived from *ahi*, a snake, and *heer*, love. He will meet with such glaring errors as the following :—

"'Doms came from Arabia.'—(Page 4, line last.)

"'Suraogees take their names from Jeynee, a woman who married one Rigdeojee, a Chuttree. This man became a hermit. Zeenuth was his first disciple.'—(Page 26, line 29.)

"'The Cashmeree Pundits, who attempt to pass themselves off as an offshoot of the Brahmin class, are in reality Kaeths.'—(Page 51, line 3.)

"'Mahajuns.—These are the illegitimate children of a man called Jin, hence called Mahajin, which in course of time became corrupted into Mahajun.'—(Page 52, line 19.)

"'They are said to have descended from Maicasur, a demon.'—(Page 95, line 28.)

"'Gharwars.—This race call themselves descendants of Bindar, of the Lunar race. They originated in Rewah. Akbar of Dehli was born at the house of some Rewah Chuttree; he therefore called Rewah his *ghur* (house), and hence the derivation of the name Ghurwar.'—(Page 115, line 5.)

"To anybody with a slight acquaintance with Sanskrit it will be evident that Ahír is a corruption of *abhira* (cow-herd), as mentioned in page 70, line 38.

"It is not probable that Doms, who are generally considered to belong to the aborigines of India, could have come from Arabia.

"'Suraogee is a corruption of *srávak*, meaning the lay votary of a Buddha or Jina.'—(Wilson.)

"'Jeynee (Jaini) is derived from *Jina*, the generic name of the personage peculiar to the Jaina sect, who is ranked by them as superior to the gods of the other sects.'—(Wilson.)

"'Rigdeojee (Rishabha Deva) is the first of the twenty-four principal *jinas* or Jaina saints.'—(Wilson.) His first disciple was Pandarik, and not Zeenath. The latter (really Zinat) can only be the name of a Mahomedan, and is commonly met with among the occupants of the Mahomedan *zenanas*—*e.g.*, Zinat-ool-Nissa. These few remarks show how absurd is the derivation which has been assigned for the term Suraogee."

The Babú adds: "There is no reason to suppose the Cashmeree Pundits are in reality Kaeths; that Mahajun (*Maha-jun*) simply means 'great man,' and is applied to bankers of all castes, like its synonym, Seth, which is a corruption of *shrishti*, meaning pre-eminent and president. It is a great mistake to connect the word Mahajun with Jina (the god) or Maicasur (*Mayasur*, a demon).

"If by 'Akbar of Dehli' is meant Akbar the Great, of Agra, everybody conversant with history knows that he was born in Amarkot (Sindh), and not in Rewah; while Binár (not Bindar) was the famous Rajah of Benares said to be a Goharvor. Whatever may be the origin of the term, it has nothing to do with *ghur*."

The Babú pronounces the Memorandum by Kaur Lachman Singh, of Bijnore, to be by far the best; and he remarks that the note from Moradabad contains much interesting matter, as also does that for Etawah.

The names "Chamachhe and Ujeg Chand" in the Memorandum from Mírat and Bulandshahr (page 12, line 18; and page 15, line 23) are errors: they should be Rajahs Janmejay and Jaichand.

DEHRA DÚN.

In very early ages Rajputs and Brahmans from the plains settled in Gaṛhwál. The Rajputs intermarried with a race known as Kassies (a hill race of very low caste), and thus themselves lost caste, but continued to call themselves Rajputs. When the Rajah of Gaṛhwál wished to people the Dún, he brought these men down from Gaṛhwál. Though they called themselves Rajputs, they were not acknowledged by their brethren of the plains, and could not (and cannot now) intermarry with them. The better class of these gradually took the titles of Ráwat, Bisht Negí, and Karaulí, and the inferior classes (the dependants who came with them) were called Rauleor. The families of Rajputs who from time to time have come from the plains and intermarried with the Dún Rajputs have lost caste, and there are only ten or twelve houses of Rajputs who intermarry with families in the plains.*

The Brahmans who settled in Gaṛhwál soon lost sight of the obligations of caste, and intermarried with the Rajputs and with the hill tribes, and they adopted to a great extent the customs of the Rajputs. They separated into smaller castes, such as Notal, Matana, Dabál, Dangwal, Bhangána, Otal, Kukraití. The two chief sub-divisions of castes were the Seraulí and Gangrárí. The Gangrárí will eat bread from the hand of a Seraulí; but the Seraulís will only eat from the hands of one of their own caste, and not from one of their own caste who has married a Gangrárí. These Brahmans came from Gaṛhwal to the Dún with the Hill Rajputs. The Gaur Brahmans came direct from the plains, and still keep their purity of caste, and marry only with Brahmans from the plains. Of this class is Jowála, Brahman of Raepúr, and his family.

These latter (the Gaur Brahmans) are recent immigrants. But the Seraulí and Gangrárí Brahmans are old inhabitants.

The Baniahs and Mahájans, who originally came from the plains, have in many cases intermarried with the Hill Rajputs, and have thus lost caste. Their descendants are called Ghatta Baniahs.

The lower castes, such as Carpenters, Chamárs, etc., are supposed to have been imported by the Maharaja of Gaṛhwál from the plains.†

* In the Dún at the present time there are families of Rajputs who have comparatively recently come from the plains, and who still keep up their connection by marriage, etc., with the parent stock. These families will not eat or intermarry with the original Dún and Hill Rajputs.

† The mass of all the lower castes, such as Chamárs, Káhárs, etc., have probably come to the Dún as cultivation has been extended, and also in consequence of the great influx of Europeans to the Dún. These have brought in their train domestic servants and farm labourers, who have gradually settled in the Dún. But, besides these, there

Besides the above-mentioned castes, there are a few Udásí Fakírs, who came to the Dún from the Panjáb with Guru Rám Ráe.

The origin of the Mehras in the Eastern Dún is not well known. They are supposed to correspond to the Bokhsars of Rohilkhand, and are believed to be the degenerate offspring of Káhárs and Banjáras.

Soba Ram, *Kánúngi.*

SAHÁRANPÚR.

The following table gives some information regarding the different castes inhabiting the district:—

"The district seems to have been first generally inhabited about the year 1300 A.D., and, with the exception of this universally acknowledged date amongst the natives, all seems to be enveloped in mist and uncertainty."

HISTORY OF CASTES IN ZILLAH SAHÁRANPÚR.

Numbers.	Caste.	Remarks.
1	Brahman	The Gaur Brahmans came from Bengal, the Gujratí Brahmans from Gujrát, and other Brahmans from the vicinity of Kanauj, from 1300 to 1400 A.D.
2	Baniah	The Aggarwal, etc., came from Agroah, beyond Hisár, about 1400 A.D.
3	Dhúsar	The Dhúsar Baniahs came from Rewarí, in Gúrgáon, about 1840 A.D.
4	Rajput, Hindú	The Hindú Rajputs came from Oudh about 1400 A.D.
5	Khatrí	This caste came from Peshawar and Múltán, in the Panjáb, about 1500 A.D.
6	Kaith..............	Came from Bhatnair, Zillah Sirsah, and other parts of the North-Western Provinces, from 1300 to 1500 A.D.
7	Sayyid	Came from Arabia originally, and have been in Saháranpúr since it was inhabited, about 1300 A.D.
8	Shaikh	Ditto ditto ditto.
9	Patháu	Ditto ditto ditto.
10	Kamloh..............	Came from Kamudnagar, and have located themselves in Sahâranpúr for the past 300 years.
11	Raen, Hindú...........	Came to Sahâranpúr from the Gur Gazní and Sirsawal, in Afghanistan, about 1650 A.D.

is a large floating population of the lower classes, who depend for their livelihood on domestic service, or come as Bildárs to the tea plantation, and who, when it suits their purpose, go away and are replaced by others.

Numbers.	Caste.	Remarks.
12	Bilúch	Came from Bilúchisthan about 1400 A.D.
13	Ját	Ditto Sirsapathan, in the Dekkan, about 1600 A.D.
14	Ahír	Ditto Muttra and Riwarí, and have been in Sahá-ranpúr since first inhabited, about 1300 A.D.
15	Thattra, { Hindú / Musulman }	Ditto Múltán, in the Panjáb, 250 years since.
16	Kalal, Hindú	Ditto Panjáb, about 1400 A.D.
17	Ditto, Musulman	Ditto Dehli, about 1750 A.D.
18	Khojah	Ditto Hírat, 200 years since.
19	Kamangar	Ditto Arabia, 300 ditto.
20	Tírgar	Ditto Persia, 500 ditto.
21	Múchie	Ditto Arabia, 500 ditto.
22	Mihmar	Ditto Ditto, 400 ditto.
23	Mamárí	Ditto Ditto, 550 ditto.
24	Juláha	Ditto Ditto, 550 ditto.
25	Lohar, Musulman	Not known where they came from, but have been in Sahâranpúr 400 years.
26	Badhie, Musulman	Came from Múltán, in the Panjáb, 200 years since.
27	Pherai	Ditto Khelat, 550 ditto.
28	Bissatí	Ditto Kirana, in Zillah Muzaffarnagar, 200 ditto.
29	Banjára	Ditto the Lower Provinces, 400 ditto.
30	Sabúngar	Ditto Dehli, 400 ditto.
31	Kágazí	Ditto Arabia, 500 ditto.
32	Kangígar	Ditto Múltán, in the Panjáb, 550 ditto.
33	Garah	Ditto all parts of the country, ditto.
34	Darzie	Ditto ditto ditto.
35	Kassie	Ditto Arabia, 500 years since.
36	Khúmra	Ditto the Lower Provinces, 100 ditto.
37	Hajjam	Ditto the Panjáb, 550 ditto.
38	Bhistí	Ditto the Lower Provinces, ditto.
39	Dhobí	Ditto Jodhpúr, ditto
40	Tehlie	Ditto Múltán, 400 ditto.
41	Khairaddí	Ditto Bengal, 500 ditto.
42	Atasbaz	Ditto Arabia, 550 ditto.
43	Tabbak	Ditto Dehli, ditto.
44	Bhattíara	Ditto Turkey, 500 ditto.
45	Sekalgarh	Not known where they came from.
46	Mallie (Musulman)	Came from Dehli, 200 years since.
47	Gagra	Ditto Jíndh, etc., 550 ditto.
48	Rangrez	Ditto Múltán, in the Panjáb, 550 ditto.
49	Ghosí	Ditto Khelat, 550 ditto.
50	Bildar	Ditto Panjáb, 80 ditto.
51	Fakír	Ditto all parts of the country.
52	Mirdah	Ditto Oudh, 550 years since.
53	Súnar	Ditto Dehli, 500 ditto.
54	Bansphor	Natives of Sahâranpúr, etc., took this appellation 150 do.
55	Chauhán	Came from Oudh, 500 ditto.
56	Kúnjra	Ditto the Lower Provinces, 125 ditto.
57	Meu	Ditto Riwarí, 550 ditto.
58	Bandúkchí	Ditto Híra Hirí, Zillah Bijnore, 300 ditto.
59	Dom	Ditto Arabia, 400 years since.
60	Kanchan	Ditto the Panjáb, 550 ditto.
61	Pazzawagar	Ditto ditto, 300 ditto.

Numbers.	Caste.	Remarks.	
62	Zahúrí	Came from Arabia, 400 years since.	
63	Jhojah	Natives of Sahâranpúr, etc., took this appellation 500 years since.	
64	Jhoghí	Came from Gujrât, 550 years since.	
65	Gújar, Hindú, and Musulmans	Ditto	Karnaul, 550 ditto.
66	Bharbúnja	Ditto	Bhatnair, in Sirsa, 400 ditto.
67	Barwa	Ditto	Srínagar, in Gaṛhwál, 300 ditto.
68	Patwa	Ditto	Agra, 300 ditto.
69	Lore	Ditto	Dehli, 400 ditto.
70	Chepí	Ditto	the Panjâb, 300 ditto.
71	Kaprí	Ditto	Rohilkhand, 300 ditto.
72	Bewra	Ditto	Marwar, 90 ditto.
73	Kuzágar	Ditto	Rohilkhand, 400 ditto.
74	Kumhár	Ditto	the Lower Provinces, 400 ditto.
75	Saini	Ditto	Dehli and ditto, 200 ditto.
76	Kahar	Ditto	Dehli, 550 ditto.
77	Dakauth	Ditto	Bengal, 550 ditto.
78	Bairagí	Ditto	Ujjain, in Dekkan, 500 ditto.
79	Bhat	Ditto	Gujrât, 500 ditto.
80	Kolí	Ditto	the Lower Provinces, 500 ditto.
81	Sainsí and Banwaria...	Ditto	all parts of the country, 300 or 400 ditto.
82	Lodah	Ditto	Gúrgaon, 550 ditto.
83	Rone	Ditto	Hansí, 500 ditto.
84	Bengalí	Ditto	Bengal, 100 ditto.
85	Bhíl	Ditto	Bundelkhand, 150 ditto.
86	Mairah	Ditto	Hills of Central India, 100 ditto.
87	Herí	Ditto	the Lower Provinces, 200 ditto.
88	Pasí	Ditto	Oudh, 100 ditto.
89	Kúrmí	Ditto	ditto, 200 ditto.
90	Gadaria	Ditto	the Panjâb, 550 ditto.
91	Khattiks	Ditto	Ditto, 550 ditto.
92	Chamár	Ditto	Riwarí and Muttra, 550 ditto.
93	Mihtar	Ditto	Natives of Sahâranpúr, 550 ditto.
94	Gosain	Ditto	Ujjain, in Dekkan, 500 ditto.
95	Mughal	Ditto	Turkey, 500 ditto.

H. D. Robertson, *Collector*.

MUZAFFARNAGAR.

Sayyids.—The Sayyid families, forming what is known as the Bárhá Sádát, may be regarded as the characteristic element in the population of this district. This influential tribe, although shorn of much of the power and splendour it appears to have possessed under the empire of the Mughals, is still in the enjoyment of extensive zamíndárí rights in the east, south-east, and north-western portions of the district.

The Bárhá Sádát claim to be descended from Fátima, the daughter of Mahomed, and assert that their ancestor, Abu'l Fera, accompanied Mahomed of Ghazní on his first entry into India in the year 1001 A.D. From an early period of the Mahomedan rule they would seem to have obtained grants of land in the Muzaffarnagar District, and finally succeeded in acquiring the zamíndárí possession of a very large share of the finest parganahs.

The Bárhá Sádát are divided into four branches:—

1. Tainpuri, whose chief town is Jansath.
2. Chatbanúri, whose chief town is Sambalhera.
3. Kandlival, whose chief town is Majhera.
4. Jagveri, whose chief town is Bidoli.

A detailed account of the history of this family, with a narrative of the fortunes of each of the four branches, was submitted in English with the Settlement Report at the close of 1864.

There are, moreover, a few families of Sayyids who are not included in the Bárhá Sádát, but they are unimportant in either numbers or influence.

SHAIKHS.—This tribe of Musulmans is located in considerable numbers in the towns of Púr, Khandla, and Thanah Bhowan.

They claim to be descended from the four Khalifs, Abu Bekr, Omar, Usman, and Murtazá 'Alí, and are known respectively as the Shaikh Sadíki, Shaikh Farakhí, Shaikh Usmání, and Shaikh Abbasi, or Ulví Shaikhs. They assert themselves to have come into India with Mahomed of Ghazní, and to have been located in this district since that time.

PATHÁNS.—Several influential families of this tribe are to be found in the western portion of the district, and others in a lower condition of life are scattered over the whole of it.

They, too, assert that they have been settled in the Muzaffarnagar District since the time of Mahomed of Ghazní; but Mansúr 'Alí Khan, of Jallalabad, the present head of the family, states that the Patháns of that part to have come into the country in the time of Shahábu'd-dín Ghorí, and that the town of Jallalabad was founded by Jallal Khan in the reign of the Emperor Alamgir. The Patháns appear to have taken a leading part in the contests with the growing Sikh power established by Nanak.

Mughals.—This tribe, although not very numerous, is yet sufficiently so to claim a brief notice. They, like the other tribes of Musulmans, claim to have settled in the district on the first conquest of the country. They came originally from Turkistan.

Gárhás are an industrious race, originally Hindu Rajputs it is supposed, though some say they were only slaves of Rajputs, and others say the name is a general one given to Hindus who have been converted to Mahomedanism; but such, at all events, does not appear to be the case in this district, where the classes enumerated above are as distinct to all appearance as so many castes of Hindus. Gáṛhás are so called from their having adopted with their new faith the Mahomedan practice of burying their dead. Little can be learnt of their history, but they state roughly that they were converted to the Mahomedan faith between 200 or 300 years ago.

Jojhás.—This tribe is in all probability composed of converted Rajputs; but why they have taken the distinctive name of Jojhás is not clear. They are said by some to have been converted slaves, and the name Jojhá, signifying stomach, may have been given to them in derision by the Hindus, as typical of the inferiority of their position.

Játs.—These are simply Játs converted to the Mahomedan religion, and are known as Musulman Játs. They are numerous throughout the district.

Gújars.—Like the Játs, they are known by their own name with the affix of Musulman.

Rajputs.—The Musulman Rajputs are generally, but by no means invariably, distinguished from the Hindu Rajputs by the name of Rangwár. It is uncertain at what period the four last-mentioned classes seceded from their ancient faith. Other converts, following various trades, have retained their old names and many of their caste distinctions.

Brahmans.—The chief tribes are the Gaur, the Gujrátí, and the Paliwal Brahmans.

Another tribe of Brahmans are known by the name of Bohrás: they follow the profession of money-lending and banking, and came into this district from Marwar in the time of Shah Alam.

Ṭhagas.—A fine race, mostly employed in agriculture, and claiming to be descended from a Brahman father and a Chatrani. They are said to have come from Bikanír, but the date is uncertain.

KÁYATHS.—The Káyaths in this district are of the Monahar family, and mostly belong to one of its *gots* known by the name of Batnagar. The Káyaths of Kyrana state that they came from Barh in the time of the Rajput sovereigns of Dehli, about 1,000 years ago. There are numerous sub-divisions of each *got*, that of Batnagar alone having, it is stated, no less than eighty-four. The Káyaths in other parts of the district are of more recent date, having settled about 200 years ago, in the reign of the Emperor Shahjahan.

KSHATRIYAS, CHATRÍS, OR RAJPUTS.—This caste is divided into two great families, the Chandarbansí and the Súrajbansí, and sub-divided into innumerable *gots* and *áls*; besides which it has thrown off a large number of what now rank as independent castes. The Súrajbansí Rajputs originally came from Ajúdhia, and the Chandarbansí from Hastinapur and Badrakanshí.

Members of either family are to be found in the district in considerable numbers, and many of them, as before-mentioned, have been converted to Mahomedanism. The castes which have sprung from Rajput fathers by women of other tribes, and which are to be met with in Muzaffarnagar, are as follows:—Khatrís, Játs, Gújars, Rowas, Sanís, Banjaras, Bhats, Mahesrís, Bedhaks, Bewarís, Barhís, Lohars, Zargars, Champís.

Khatrís are descended from a Rajput father by a woman of the Vaishya caste. They are not numerous.

JÁTS.—The origin of this race is obscure, and the accounts given by the members of the caste differ greatly. Many of them had come within the last hundred years from the Panjáb, but others have been settled in the district for a very much longer period. The common story is that they are descended from Rajput fathers by women of the Vaishya or Súdra tribes. They were formerly ranked among the thirty-six royal families of Rajputs. The Játs of Bhainsí, a large and flourishing community, assert that they have been settled in that spot for 1,600 years, and that they are called Jáls or Játs from Játra, the matted hair of Mahadeo, from which they sprang. I have not heard any mention of the story to which Elliot alludes of their having come originally from Ghazní, but their customs certainly point to an origin different from that of other Hindus. This industrious race of agriculturists is very numerous in this district, and has a great many sub-divisions.

R. J. LEEDS, *Assistant Collector.*

MI'RAT.

JÁTS.—They are the most numerous of all the land-owning castes in Mírat, and are supposed to have seceded or been excommunicated from the Rajputs on account of some irregular ideas they held on the subject of marriage.

As in the case of Tagas, it is more probable that they are the descendants of a marriage of a Rajput into a lower caste; and one legend distinctly points to Rajah Jaswant Singh as their original ancestor, and he, as the story goes, married beneath his rank.

They all point to Hariana and Rajputana as the country whence they originally came, and it is probable that they emigrated thence in large bodies, occupying and settling down in the country from Dehli westward along the Jumna and lower rivers of the Panjáb—first appearing in the peaceful characters of agriculturists, but afterwards showing the natural instincts of their race by now and again following the pursuit of arms.

They gained their first footing in the Chapraulí, Kútanah, and Barote Parganahs of the Mírat District, pushing out before them the Taga occupants of the soil; and thence they spread themselves, though in less compact colonies, over the whole districts.

The Játs, as a caste, are again sub-divided amongst themselves into distinct families or tribes, which in many respects, particularly as regards marriage, hold aloof from each other.

There are the "Hela" Játs, the "Dehta," the "Salkhan," and the "Des", or "Desí" Játs, all distinct from each other, and recognizing some distinguishing customs.

The latter, or Desí, tribe are found in the greatest numbers.

W. FORBES, C.B., *Collector.*

GARHWÁL.

The manner in which Gaṛhwál became peopled is enveloped in obscurity. The most recent immigration on a great scale is assigned to a period as remote as 745 Samvat, or 688 A.D., when a number of Brahmans and Rajputs from the plains are said to have come in with Kanakpal, a Guzeratí adventurer, who established himself in Chandpúr, and thence extended his conquests until he or his descendants reduced to one sceptre the petty chiefs who had ruled each, from his hill fort, a small portion of the country.

The descendants of these immigrants, whether as a conquering race or because they have better preserved their distinctions of Hinduism, still pride themselves on superiority to the older inhabitants. The Brahmans belonged to the Dravida, Adigarh, and Kanaujia branches of the great Brahman caste. The Rajputs included Chauháns from Dehli and Rantimbor, Powars from Guzerat, Tawars from Dehli, and others. Most of these families now take their names from the villages in which they are first settled, lying for the most part in Parganah Chandpúr; but have since extended themselves over the district, and are often not to be found at all in their original seats.

Next to these in consideration come a mass of Brahmans and Rajputs, who, though undoubted members of these two families, and immigrants from the plains of India, can give no account of themselves. They derive their names from villages in which they reside, or resided, and believe themselves to be indigenous to the hills.

A third class is that of the Khassias, who generally call themselves Rajputs; they are, however, pronounced to be Súdras by discerning Hindus: they do not wear the mystical thread of the two great castes. Another external custom which at once distinguishes them from the true Rajputs is their not disdaining to handle the plough—an act which the poorest Rajput in the hills delegates to a man of lower caste. They are generally believed by the natives to be the oldest inhabitants of Gaṛhwál, and they doubtless are the oldest of the Hindu inhabitants, properly so called. They form nearly one-half of the entire population of Gaṛhwál.

Closely connected with them in social bonds, and probably in history, are a large class of Brahmans sometimes called by their prouder brethren Khassia Brahmans, who do not disdain to act as *purohits* to the Khassias, and to officiate at temples of petty local deities; they are probably the old Brahmans of Khasdes, the ancient name of Kamáon and Gaṛhwál.

Lower yet in the social scale we find the remarkable race, the Doms. Their huts may be seen in every village subordinate to, and separate from, the Bithana, or patrician quarter of the Rajputs and Brahmans. Though totally opposed to all Hindu notions and traditions, which would rather represent them as the dregs of Hinduism, the inference is irresistible to a European mind that these are the aborigines of the hills, who have been reduced to their present state, or rather to the state of slavery and degradation in which they were found at the beginning of British rule, by successive waves of Hindu conquerors from the plains. They are distinguished from Hindus by their high cheek-bones, smaller but well-set frames, and greater vivacity of feature and gesture; and high authorities have discovered in them a resemblance to the Gonds, and other undoubted aboriginal tribes of India.

Distinct from all the above-named classes, though they love to confound themselves with Rajputs, are the Bhotias, who inhabit the villages at the entrance of the passes into Thibet, and engage in the Thibetan trade, spending half their time in Thibet and half under British rule, and worshipping alternately at Hindu and Buddhist shrines. The eyes obliquely set to the nose, the high cheek-bones, thin beard, and large projecting ears, proclaim undoubtedly an admixture of Mongolian blood; but there can be as little doubt that they are right in claiming a Hindu origin.

There are besides a few families of genuine Mongolians, some of whom during the last few years have taken up their homes permanently in this district. They are confounded together under the name of Khampas, and occupy one or two villages in the Niti Pass.

A connecting link between the Hindus and Mahomedans is formed by the Bisnoís, an eclectic sect, some of whom have come up from the Bijnore District and settled in Srínagar. They are said to be a turbulent class, and disliked by the rest of the community.

D. M. Gardner, *Assistant Commissioner.*

BIJNORE.

Brahmans, 27,519.—Of the 27,519 Brahmans (exclusive of their degraded branches), the largest number belong to the Gaur class. There seem to be no Maithil, Utkal, Driaur, Tailang, Karnátak, or Mahárasht Brahmans in the district; but there are about fifty families of Gujrátís, the same number of Saraswats, and two or three of Kanaujias. According to their own tradition, the Gaur Brahmans were invited from their native land in Bengal to this part of the country by Rajah Janmejay, son of Paríkshit, to assist him in the great sacrifice performed by him for the destruction of serpents, in retaliation of his father's death by the bite of the celebrated *takshak*. Having received largesses and assignments from the Rajah, they never returned to their homes. The reason why the Gaurs were invited from so long a distance, when other Brahmans of the Saraswat and Kankúbj classes were to be got in the neighbourhood, is said to be this,—that the latter classes were either reluctant to assist at so cruel a sacrifice, or they were not so well acquainted with the requirements of this particular kind of ceremony as the Brahmans of Bengal, who were always ahead of the inhabitants of any other part of India in the art of charming and controlling serpents.

Tagás, 10,572.—The Tagás are a class of Upa Brahmans (extra Brahmans), similar to, or perhaps synonymous with, the Bhúínhárs of Benares.

Having been *tyagdia* (abandoned) by their relations, they were originally styled Tyágá, and that word has been corrupted into Tagá.

The above is their own story, unsupported by written evidence; but by other people generally the Tagás are supposed to be the offspring of a Brahman by some low-caste woman. They are divided into two clans—the Bíssa, or uncorrupted; and the Dussa, or corrupted. Widow marriage is allowed among the Dussas, and not among the Bíssahs.

Ocharaj Mahabrahman or Kattya Brahman, 179.—These Brahmans receive gifts offered for the benefit of the dead *within* thirteen *days* from the death, and are for that reason considered the most impure and degraded.

Dakaut, or Pudia, or Joshí, or Bharára, 1,234 persons.—They are a degraded class of Brahmans. Their profession is to interpret the influence of the stars on persons of different names and at different times, and to receive gifts offered for averting the consequences of the influence of evil stars.

BHÁTS, 998.—The Bháts are said to be the progeny of a Brahman by a Súdra mother. One branch are called Brahma Bhát, their profession being the recitation or composition of poetry in praise (and sometimes in disparagement) of individuals. The second branch are called Jágas, and they are the pedigree-keepers of the Rajputs in particular, and other castes in general. Third class, Chárans, are the bards and heralds of the Rajput tribes. They are not to be found in these Provinces, but in Rajputana.

RAJPUTS, 2,319: THÁKURS, 87.—Rajput (king's descendant), and Thakur (lord of land) are terms of respect for a Kshatriya. The Rajputs and Thakurs enumerated in this district are mostly of the Bais and Gond tribes.

CHAUHÁNS, 71,685.—These Chauháns do not claim their descent from Prithíráj, the last Hindu King of Dehli, or his ancestors, like the real Chauháns of Mainpúrí, Pratápnír, and Nímrána.

KHATTRÍS, 921.—It is a subject of dispute whether the Khattrís are the old Kshatriyas, or a mixed class.

KAMBOH, 433.—According to their own account, the Kambohs are the old inhabitants of the trans-Indus country, and most of them were converted to Islam by Mahmúd of Ghazni. The Sanskrit name of Cabúl is Kamboj, and this is so similar to Kamboh, that, on the authority of the above tradition, these people may be safely conjectured to have been the ancient inhabitants of Cabúl. Their Mahomedan brethren state that they are the descendants of the ancient Kai dynasty of the Kings of Persia. On the last king of the dynasty having been dethroned and expelled from the country, he wandered about for some time with his family and dependants in the neighbouring countries. The company, wherever they went, was termed Kai Amboh (assembly of the Kais), and that appellation is corrupted into Kamboh.

Another tradition is that their ancestors were of the same descent as the Khattrís, and lived in the Panjáb.

The Musulman portion of the Kambohs are held in the same contempt by the other Mahomedans as the Afghans and Kashmírís are. The Persian proverb is :—

Yeke Afghan, doyam Kamboh, Sium badzat Kashmirí.

The Afghan, the Kamboh, and the Kashmírí are rogues.

Banniahs, 18,151.—All sorts of traders of the Vaisya class are included in this head. The greater portion of them are of the Agarwala branch, inclusive of the Dassas, Bísas, Jamís, and Vaishnos.

Bishnoís, 4,308.—They are Banniahs who, without regard to their caste, follow the religion of Jhamájí. This man propagated his precepts in the country of Marwar about the year 1460 A.D. With the exception of Vishnu, they worship no Hindu deity, and are therefore held in contempt by the Hindus.

Ahírs, 4,748.—This caste is usually put down among Súdras, but according to the "Bhágwat Púran"—which distinctly says that Nand Ahír, the adoptive father of Krishna, was a Vaisya,—they claim to be of the Vaisya class. Abhír, of which Ahír seems to be a corruption, is a mixed class according to Manu. A Gopa, which is another name for an Ahír, is a true Súdra according to the "Jatimala;" but tradition makes them the progeny of a Vaisya slave girl and a Rajput slave. They seem to be very old inhabitants of the district, for the "Ayín Akbarí" shows that there were many Ahír zamíndárs in Parganah Naggína in Akbar's time.

According to one tradition, the word Ahír is derived from the word *ahi*, a snake, and *her*, to love (or lover of snakes), because when the children of the slave and slave girl lived in the jungle they used to feed snakes with milk.

Kaisth, 3,516.—According to the "Jatimala" Kaisths seem to be the true Súdras. They are there mentioned immediately after the Gopas, and before the mixed classes. Their origin is said to be thus :—That a Súdra of the name of Bhútidatta was so clever in household affairs, that the prince, his master, styled him Kaisth (*kai*, a house, and *stittei*, to settle) as his future designation. The following are the twelve branches of the Kaisths :—

1.—Mathar.	5.—Súrajdhaj.	9.—Balmak.
2.—Bhatnagar.	6.—Amisht.	10.—Aithana.
3.—Sríbastab.	7.—Gaur.	11.—Kalserisht.
4.—Saksena.	8.—Karan.	12.—Nigam.

Ját, 54,989.—This caste is nowhere mentioned in the ancient Hindu books. They everywhere call themselves degraded Rajputs, and there is no doubt that this assertion is correct to some extent; but the conjecture that they are emigrants from the trans-Indus regions is also well founded. According to their tradition, the original Ját tribe, called Ponea, sprung from the locks (*juta*) of Mahadeo, or one of his chief attendants at Mount Kylas. It must be observed that Mount Kylas is not very far from the Hindu Kush, which, according to the Greek historians of antiquity, was the abode of the Getes, of whom the Játs are conjectured to be a colony. From Kylas the Játs are said to have descended into the plains of the Panjáb, and thence to have spread themselves in all Upper and Western India, increasing their numbers by admitting degraded and excommunicated Rajputs to the tribe, and marrying women of almost every class. During the decline of the Mughal dynasty, they became independent princes and sovereigns of parts of Western India.

In this district there are three sorts of Játs—Chaudrís, Deswalas, and Pachandas.

Gújars, 6,851.—Originally Gochar, or cattle-graziers. They sometimes pretend to be degraded Rajputs, and sometimes Ahírs.

Sanís, 42,736.—This caste is the same as Malís.

Rowas, 9,093.—Very good cultivators. They call themselves low Rajputs, and are said to have settled in this district in the reign of Shahjahan. The mode in which women of this caste procure their divorce is peculiar in itself—all they have to do is to throw an *upla*, or dried cake of cowdung, from outside into the house; seeing this done, the husband separates himself from his wife without further formalities, and for ever.

Sayyids, 10,285.—Descendants of Fatima, the favorite daughter of Mahomed.

Mughals, 1,564.—Originally inhabitants of Central Asia. Their tribes are Barlash, Choghatta, Kazalbash, Uzhí, Tark, Kye, Chak, and Tajak.

Jolahas, 60,333.—Very few of these are Hindus, called for the sake of distinction Bhainbar.

Kaur Lachman Singh, *Deputy Collector*.

BAREILLY.

Before entering upon the points noticed in the orders of the Board, I think it would not be uninteresting and out of place if I attempt to give a brief and rapid sketch of the antecedents of this district, so far as I have been able to ascertain. I do not and cannot vouch for the accuracy of the narrative, for, as it is well known that there are no authentic works to assist me in the matter, I merely give the facts as I have been able to gather from conversation with the intelligent native gentlemen of this city, and from certain extant manuscripts in possession of some of them.

The country was previously covered with dense jungle, and sparsely inhabited by Ahírs in charge of herds of cattle, sent here to graze by rajahs and other large cattle-owners. A little cultivation was also here and there attempted for providing their own simplest necessaries. The country was then called Tuppa Ahíran. Matters continued in this primitive state till the subjugation of Hindustan by Timúr, and his ascension to the throne of Dehli, when, the Ahírs becoming turbulent, Rajah Kharack Singh and Rao Harrí Singh, feudal lords of Tirhut, were deputed by the Emperor to bring them to their senses. They came to the place, easily routed the ill-formed and undisciplined Ahír hordes who opposed their progress, and finally took possession of the country. Timúr's lieutenants being of the Kather caste, the country was named Mulki-Kather.

Some of the relatives, attendants, and retainers of the two brothers went to Powayen, Kharral, and other places in the Shahjahánpúr District, where, forcibly or otherwise taking possession of a large number of villages, they became talúkdars. A second party went to and settled in Chaupalla, now called Moradabad, after the name of Moradbaksh, son of Shahjahan, in whose reign the district was subjugated from the Katherias.

The now ruined feudal family of Shísgarh is descended from Kharack Singh, and the Rajah of Khatar and Talúkdar of Mahal from Rao Harrí Singh.

At or about this time one Basdeb and his brother, Barreldeb, of the Katheria caste, built a small town, now called the old town, erected a fort, the ruins of which can still be seen, and called the settlement after their joint names Bas Barell, which in course of time became corrupted into Bans Bareilly, the present name of this city and the district.

In Akbar's time the management of the country was withdrawn from the Katherias.

I now proceed to the question of sub-divisions of caste. The question, I confess, is a very difficult one, and rendered more intricate in the absence of all authentic and faithful work on the subject. In the books which are available for reference the facts are so commingled with ridiculous traditions and ludicrous stories of mythology, that it is very difficult to separate the one from the other. Almost all the sub-sects claim their descent from one or other of the heavenly bodies, or of the several millions of Hindu mythological deities. However, I have made an attempt to separate the chaff from valuable historical facts, and the result is embodied in the following paragraphs.

Originally there were only four castes amongst the Hindus—1st, Brahman, *i.e.*, priests, lawyers, and professional mendicants; 2nd, Kshatriyas, *i.e.*, the governing class; 3rd, Baishyas, traders and cultivators; and 4th, Súdras, who had menial services assigned to them. From these four primary classes have sprung up the present scores of sub-sects we find in the country.

First, as regards the Brahmans. Originally there was only one class of Brahmans, called Sanadh. Subsequently they emigrated towards the Vindhya chain, and those who settled on the south of it took the name of Panch (*i.e.*, five) Dravir, and those on its north, Panch Gaur—those who did not so emigrate retaining their original name of Sanadh. Under the first there are again five sub-classes, *i.e.* :—

1.—Guzeratí, from the men having settled in Guzerat.

2.—Drávir, from Dravar, near the River Narbadda.

3.—Maharast, from Maharatta.

4.—Tilang, from Tilang.

5.—Karnatack, from Karnatic.

Under Panch Gaur have sprung up a like number of sub-classes, each being called after the name of the country where they settled, *i.e.* :—

1.—Gor, from Gor, in Bengal.

2.—Sarsúth, from the name of the stream Sarosottí, on the banks of which they settled.

3.—Kankubj, from Kanauj, in the district of Farrakhabad.

4.—Maithal, from Mithila, near Tirhut, in Bengal.

5.—Utkal, *pandahs* or priests of Jaggarnath, of Kattack.

Besides the above, there are nine additional classes of this sect, but they do not appear to be of pure blood, though they would, if questioned, vehemently assert their claim to it.

1.—Mathúr.—Chaubeys of Muttra. Rumour has it that the men were previously Játs.

2.—Magat.—Priests of Gya, in Behar.

3.—Paukarn.—Priests of Pushkar, in Ajmír.

4.—Gautam.—Alleges to be descended from a saint named Gautam.

5.—Ekbassy.—Priests of Baldeo, near Muttra.

6.—Mohaverry.

7.—Golab Púrab.

8.—Pandey.

9.—Taggah.

There is another sub-sect which I omitted to mention before,—I allude to the Pahárí Brahmans. Some eight centuries ago the then Rajah of Nepaul, with the view of inducing the different sects of Brahmans to have intermarriage between them, sent for them. Brahmans of seven out of the ten sects went to Nepaul, acquiesced in the proposal of the Rajah, and settled in the country.

KASHMERES.—The Kashmere pandits, who attempt to pass themselves off as an offshoot of the Brahman class, are in reality Kaeths, and, like them, are the descendants of the illegitimate children of Chittar Gupta, of the Byás caste. They emigrated to Kashmere, took the name of pandits, and formed themselves into a separate caste. They therefore have no intermarriage between their brother Kaeths of the plains, nor do they mess together.

BÁBÚ RAJKISSEN MÚKERJÍ,
Head Clerk, Collector's Office.

SHAHJAHANPUR.

The tribe of Hindus found in the greatest numbers in this district are as follows:—The Chandela and Kátheya tribes, who in the parganah of Jallalabad hold, the former 197, and the latter 49, villages.

Different families of the Kanaujia stock, such as Sanadh, Misr, Súkal, and others, also hold 23 villages in the same part of the district. The Kayeth tribe, chiefly of the Saksena, Bhatnagar, and Siri Wásthab families, hold 18 villages, and were at one time more opulent than now.

In Khera Bajhera the prevailing clan is the Jangahara, and in Tilhar and Jallalpúr the same tribe in smaller numbers—the Bachhal and Katharya being more numerous. Tomar and Gor are also met with. The Pathak Brahmans also hold some villages. The Bachhal tribe appear to be the earliest recorded occupants of that part of the district lying to the north of Shahjahanpúr, where there are also found Katharyas in considerable numbers. The tract thus occupied includes the parganahs of Negohí, Powayan, and Khotar. In the latter parganah and its immediate neighbourhood the Katharyas hold 147 villages. The Gor Rajputs also have several villages in the same tract. There is also a tribe which is said to have descended from the Nepal Hills, now settled in Pullía, called Parbattí. The Bachhal clan is again found in the Shahjahanpúr Parganah, where there are also Gor and Pomar families. The Bachhal Thakurs hold 71 villages in this parganah; the Gor Thakurs hold some 50 villages near Powayan, Seramau, and Khotar; and the Pomars, 36 in the same parganah, in the same neighbourhood. The limits of this note do not permit me to particularize the sub-divisions of each of these clans which are to be found in the district, or to enter in detail into an account of other inferior or servile castes, which form a large part of its population.

As regards the origin of the tribes inhabiting the district, I gather from local traditions that Gújars, Ahírs, Banjarahs, and Játs are the earliest known inhabitants, and that those tribes which have established themselves here in more recent times drove out or conquered them, to be themselves in turn in a great measure supplanted by Musulmans from beyond the Indus. In the south of the district the Chandela tribe is the most powerful and numerous, and many years ago gave much trouble to Government from their intractable and quarrelsome habits, by whom they were known as the Kanddhar Thakurs, from the chief village in an iláḳa of that name, held by a numerous family comprising nearly 300 proprietors, of whom Rajah Dalel Sing is the head.

This tribe originally came from the Chandelí Des, in Southern Bundelkhand, where they are found in great numbers, under one Rajah Sirpal. His descendant in the fifth generation, Rajah Pirmal, moved from Sheorajpúr (in Cawnpore) and occupied Mohamdabad (in Farrakhabad), from whence the sons of his relation, Petamber Singh, by name Dhir Sah and Bhir Sah, crossed the Ganges and occupied Chachnapúr, a village belonging to the Chachúa Kúrmís, in Jallalabad, and spread themselves over the neighbouring villages, seizing those they found deserted, and expelling the possessors of others when able to do so.

The Kanaujia Brahmans appear to have followed the Thakúrs both of the Chandela and Bachhal clans, and to have received in gift, as religious offerings for their maintenance, the villages they possess.

The Rathores, who are not numerous in this district, though found very frequently on its southern border, hold one village, which they acquired through one of their tribe, Kasib, marrying the daughter of Sahdal, the Katheya Thakur of Barah Kallan, who bestowed on him Mauzah Kajarí, Parganah Jallalabad, which they still possess. This occurred some 400 years ago. The Katheya Thakurs state that they came originally from Jallander,—a tradition similar to that of many tribes, *e.g.*, Banjaras and Játs, etc., who describe their ancestors as being immigrants from the west.

Their settlement in this district is said to have taken place 300 years ago, when Rajah Mokat Sing came from Patialí (in Etah) and occupied Usain (in Badáon), which was then included in the dominions of Rajah Jaychand Rathore, of Kanauj. The name of the hero has been better preserved than the date of his conquest, as we find that the Emperor Humayún bestowed the government of Sambhal on Askarry Mirza in the year 1532 A.D. The incursion of this tribe probably occurred much earlier, at a time when the Musulmans had not established themselves in this part of the country, as the Katheyas speak of their ancestors clearing the jungle and planting villages, and peopling the land with their tribe. The death of Jaychand, the famous Rajah of Kanauj, is, moreover, placed in the era of Kutbu'd-dín at the end of the twelfth century A.D.

The Pomar Thakurs, who hold between 70 and 80 villages in the parganahs of Jallalabad and Shahjahanpúr, describe themselves as coming originally from Ujjain, in Central India, under the leadership of Rawat Singh, who seized on Kúría Bans Kiria, in Parganah Shahjahanpúr, and, clearing the jungle and expelling the inhabitants of neighbouring villages, established themselves in this part of the country.

The Gotam Thakurs, like all their tribe, describe themselves as coming from Arghal in Parganah Kora (in Fattihpúr) where a family claiming to be the head of the race is still to be met with. They hold 37 villages in the south of the district. The Badúría Thakurs have only three villages, and the Chauhán Thakurs only two, in the south of the district. They are to be found scattered about in other parts. Some of the latter have also a zamíndárí acquired by marriage in Pallea, a parganah under the Tarai in the north of the district. These tribes are respectively offshoots of the Badúrías of Bah Pinahat (in Agra), and the Chauháns of Mainpúrí and Baugaon (in Mainpúrí).

The Gor Thakurs ascribe their possessions in this district to permission having been given them by the Emperor of Dehli to dispossess the Gújars of their lands in this neighbourhood, and that their incursion took place some 900 years ago, under the leadership of Khag Rae and Bagh Rae, who came from Oudh and took possession of 62 villages, of which they still hold 50.

They are allied to the Katharyas, and, as these two tribes are found generally dwelling together, and the Gor Rajputs claim to be Katharyas, their immigration into this part of Rohilkhand may be placed at a very early date, for in ancient times the province was called Kathair, as is said, from its being chiefly occupied by that tribe, whose warlike habits secured them from conquest by the Musulmans until the era of Shahjahan.

Kathair, however, appears to have been often invaded by Musulman armies; and many villages now inhabited by these tribes were included in the Sirkar of Badaon as belonging to the district of Gola; but they claim to have been independent of the Emperor of Dehli for three generations after Akbar's fiscal divisions of sirkars and parganahs were framed.

The Rajah of Powayan is the head of the Gor tribe, and the Rajah of Khotar of the Katharyas. The country inhabited by the Gor and

Katharya Thakurs is nearly coterminous with the parganah of Gola, as described in the zillahbandí of Akbar's reign: but they spread themselves into parts of the modern divisions of Pillibhít and Lackímpúr (in Bareilly and Oudh), which were not altogether included in Gola. Whether the ancient town of Gora in Powayan, or Gola in Lackímpúr, gave its name to this division, I am unable to say.

The same district was to a great extent peopled by the Bachhal clan, and the Katharyas state that their occupation of Eastern Rohilkhand dates from the defeat of the Bachhal Thakurs in one of the incursions of the royal army, when the Emperor gave the Katharyas their villages.

The tribe appears, under all circumstances, to have been established here from very ancient times. They are said to have occupied the chief part of the district of Gola, before mentioned, and are now to be found in parts of the Shahjahanpúr parganah, in Negohí and Tilhar. Their first appearance in this part of the country is said to have been in the year 1000 A.D., under the leadership of Daro Pad, who occupied some territory near the modern Farrakhabad. They spread through the country in a northerly direction, and count among their famous men Raja Ben, who founded Matí, which afterwards gave its name to one of the tappahs of the fiscal division of Gola. Elliot records their occupation in Eastern Rohilkhand as antecedent to that of the Katharyas, and local traditions confirm his view. From this tribe arose the family of Rajah Deo and his twelve sons, whose descendants, or rather those who claim to be so, are to be found scattered throughout the Shahjahanpúr, Tilhar, and Farrídpúr parganahs. The parganah of Negohí was occupied by this man's family. As late as the middle of the sixteenth century, Chabbi Singh, one of the tribe, obtained, partly by a grant of the Emperor and partly by violence, a territory extending over parts of the Kant, Powayan, Tilhar, and Shahjahanpúr parganahs; and at a later date one of his descendants obtained possession of Semaría, which, along with seventy other villages in these parts, is still in the possession of this tribe. One Rajah Tilokchand Bachhal is said to have occupied Tilhar, and to have settled his tribe in Pattah Chirkola, now called Jallalpúr, driving out the Gújars and Banjaras. The Katharyas again appear on the scene, and local tradition survives of their coming from the neighbourhood of Benares, which confirms Elliot's view that they took their name from Katehar, in the neighbourhood of Benares, and not from their connection with the Katharia Gor Rajputs, who assert their designation to be derived from *kathiri*, a carpenter. Their leader is said to have been one Nagdeo.

There are also found Tomar and Gor families. These are no doubt the descendants of the aboriginal inhabitants, the Banjaras, who number among the numerous *gots* of their claim both Tomars and a family who call themselves Gor, from their descent through a Gor Brahman, with whom one of their tribe intermarried.

The tradition that the Bachhal tribe cleared land and settled themselves in Tilhar and Negohí indicates their origin as being more ancient than the Katharyas, who only ousted the Gújars in Jallalpúr.

The Bachhal tribe brought into the country the Páthak Brahmans, who still hold villages in Tilhar, which they received as a religious offering for their maintenance.

The tribe of Jangahara Rajputs are chiefly found in the Khera Bajhera parganah. This clan has always had a name for fighting, and they state their designation to be derived from the words *jang*, war, and *áhára*, a Baka word for *bhank* (hunger),—the men who hunger for war. It is a common joke against a Jangahara to say that their name means beaten in war, *jang hara*, an interpretation which they will not admit to be correct. The tribe are found in other parts of the district, but their chief seat is in the neighbourhood of Khera Bajhera parganah.

The Kayaths own 18 villages in Jallalabad, and have zamíndárís in other parts of the district as well.

There is a tradition that 50 villages in Jallalabad were in very ancient times held by Sayyids, who maintained themselves on the north bank of the Ganges by the assistance of their brethren in Shamsabad, but that they were driven out by an incursion of Rajputs, and have now only four villages in their possession. The town called Jallalabad is said to have been first known by the name of Karankolapúr Patheyn, in the era of Rajah Prithí Raj, of Hastinapúra (Dehli); and it next was occupied by some Jogís, from whom it derived the name of Jogípúr, and retained it until Jallalu'd-dín Akbar, obtaining possession of it, called it after his own name; that Hafiz Rehmat Khan, the Nawab of Bareilly, built a fort on the khera in the village. The village is partly owned by Kayaths as above-mentioned, and partly by Kanaujia Brahmans, who were brought into the country by the Chandela and Bachhal Thakurs.

The Musulman proprietors in the neighbourhood are chiefly Yuzofzaie, Warakzaie, and Mahmand Afghans.

The site of Shahjahanpúr was formerly called Noner Khera, and its neighbourhood was inhabited by Gújars, defended by a fort at the junction of the Garra and Kanhaut rivers, built by Maghi and Bhola, two of their leaders.

C. J. DANIELL, *Officiating Collector.*

TARAI PARGANAHS.

There are only two tribes in the Tarai which call for remark. The others have moved in from neighbouring districts at various periods; and information regarding them will be forwarded in the report of the district in which they preponderate; as, for instance, the Rains in Pilibhít.

The two castes and tribes above referred to—namely, the Bhuksas and Thárús—are unable to afford any information regarding the period or the reason of their settling in the Tarai, beyond that the former state that they came from Dharanagar, and the latter from Chittor.

The Bhuksas still claim to be addressed as Thakur, and a few wear the thread, or *janeo.* Sir H. Elliot, in page 258, under the article "Des," alludes, among others, to a district entered in the ancient registers in Sirkar Kamaon as "Bhuksar, now Kilpúrí and Rúderpúr." Bhuksar is the name still used for localities inhabited by Bhuksas, without reference to any particular boundaries, as Thárúat signifies tracts inhabited by Thárús.

The Thárú traditions state that they come from Chittor, and refer to Jaimal and Pattah. They state that they were driven from their home and settled here. The reference would appear to indicate the third sack of Chittore—*i.e.*, that by Akbar, about 1560 A.D. They claim to have been originally Rajputs, and state that their ancestors lost their caste by taking to intoxicating liquors and rearing fowls. I have never heard from them any allusion to a Gúrkha or hill origin, an idea which their type of feature itself suggests. The Thárús, as the Bhuksas, are sub-divided into *gots*; and interspersed with them are other tribes, who are generally called Thárús, but who are quite distinct, such as Gaharwár, who claim to be Rajputs, and are probably some of the Gaharwárs whom Sir H. Elliot describes as a most interesting race, over whose origin and lineage much obscurity hangs. These never intermarry or eat with the Thárús, abstain from liquor, and never rear fowls; others, again, as Dangras, are looked down on as a lower caste by the Thárús.

Sir H. Elliot says, referring to the Bhuksas, that "those who reside in Kilpúrí and Tabna are said occasionally to intermarry with the Thárús;" and states them to be "a tribe found inhabiting the forest under the hills from Púranpúr Tabna, on the Sardah, to Chandpúr, on the Ganges." At present no village of Bhuksas is situated to the east of the Kitcha or Gola river, which is about thirty miles west of the Sardah river, and which is the existing boundary between the two tribes. The Bhuksas range from its west bank to the Ganges, and the Thárús to the east, as far, I believe, as Gorakhpúr. I have never heard of the two tribes intermarrying; indeed, the Bhuksas marry on attaining puberty, while the Thárús are married as young as their means will permit. Cases occur of men of one tribe eloping with women of the other, and a small village exists chiefly inhabited by the progeny of such left-handed marriages. It is situated exactly between where the Bhuksa villages end and the Thárú villages commence.

Either tribe claims superiority in caste, and repudiates any attempt at tracing them to a common origin, or of any connection between them; nor is there, in my opinion, any evidence on which such an attempt could be based. Their claims to respective superiority, however, rest on very small grounds,—the Bhuksas charging the Thárús with rearing fowls, which they do; while the Thárús say Bhuksas sell flesh and fish, which they deny indignantly.

It is a circumstance worth remarking that two tribes, under such similar circumstances, should have kept so distinct while living in such close proximity. They are both superstitious, and, as a rule, truthful, much given to intoxicating drink, and not very chaste; both more or less migratory, only continuing to cultivate the land until it is exhausted, and then moving off to fresh grounds; both utterly reckless with water, with which they inundate their fields, if allowed to, and utterly careless of the swamps they may be forming: indeed, most of the worst swamps could be easily proved to owe their origin to the rude irrigating means used by these people. Both tribes are supposed to be adepts in magical arts. A few Bhuksas in conversation with me have claimed such powers for persons of their caste; but generally they laugh at the idea, though they attribute their comparative immunity from marauders during the disturbances caused by the Mutiny to the general belief in their superhuman powers, which the Desís, or plains-people, entertained. At the same time they have the greatest confidences in their *bararars,* or medicine-men, who are consulted on every occasion, and who mulct them heavily for their services.

As a general rule the Thárú is more intelligent than the Bhuksa.

It is uncommon to find a Bhuksa village with the same name as a Thárú village. If the Bhuksas had gradually retired before the Thárús from the Sardah to the Golah, names still common among them might be expected in the three parganahs inhabited by Thárús east of the Golah, *alias* Kitcha, river; but I do not know of any instance, except such common names as Biria or Mahola, which offer no clue; and where Bhuksas are found living in villages called Khanpúr, Hussainpúr, Fattihgang, and Dímarkhera, any attempt at tracing them through their village names is hopeless.

Neither of the tribes have any acknowledged leaders, through whom, or through whose title, a clue might be obtained. The office *barwaick* or *barbaik* of the Thárús, being hereditary, continues in certain families; but they now exercise no function. It appears to have been given to certain Thárú head-men by Kamaon Rajahs for the reasons assigned by Sir H. Elliot in his "Supplementary Glossary." The Bhuksas in the Tarai still recognize the authority of a man who is, I believe, a resident of a village in Kashípúr; but this authority appears also to have been conferred by Kamaon Rajahs, and is chiefly exercised in settling private disputes relating to family matters, and is generally exercised by administering a whipping with a cloth.

Thárús in this district declare themselves distinct from those who live to the east of the Kanaita river, in Oudh, whom they declare to be a very inferior caste,—a compliment invariably returned by the few Thárús I have met from that locality. They do not intermarry.

Neither of these tribes claim for their ancestors the credit of excavating the tanks, erecting the buildings, or sinking the masonry wells, ruins of which still exist in the Tarai; nor do they connect them in any way with their own history. To this day neither the Thárús or Bhuksas build even earthen walls for their houses, which are made of posts driven into the ground, with beams resting on them. The walls are made of reeds, locally termed *tant,* tied with grass, and generally smeared over with mud and cow-dung, with a thatched roof. The Thárús keep their residences scrupulously clean. For wells, which they only use for drinking purposes, and never for irrigation, a hollowed tree is sunk into the ground. They employ hill or plains men as *lohars,* etc., which all tends to prove that they never possessed knowledge sufficient to admit of their erecting the places and wells above referred to.

Generally, all that can be considered as tolerably certain is that the Bhuksas came about the 11th century from Dharanagar, and the Thárús in the 16th from Chittor, into the Tarai, which they sought as a refuge, and which tract was never practically under Mahomedan rule, and indeed was looked on as wild and dreadful by the troops of that power till the time of the Rohilla Pathans; that these tribes assisted the Kamaon Rajah, by whom they were protected, and from whom they received *sannads,* etc.; that they were ever, as now, distinct; and that they were probably different branches of Rajputs.

E. Colvin, *Superintendent.*

MUTTRA.

The population of the Muttra District consists almost entirely of Hindus, nearly half of whom are Játs. Next to the Játs, in point of number, are the Brahmans, Chamárs, Rajputs, Kolís, and Gaḍariyas.

The history of the Játs is a most curious one. It seems that about fifty years ago they consisted of two distinct and separate tribes, comprising many subordinate *gots* or clans. These tribes were,—the Deswala, that is, the old inhabitants of the country; and the Pacháda, who were, as their name imparts, settlers from the west or north-west. Tradition varies as to the origin of the Deswala, but the commonest story is that they are descended from Rajputs who married slave girls; and it is certain that they have been in the country from time immemorial. The Pachada, on the other hand, are, comparatively speaking, a modern race. In all probability they did not appear in Hindustan till the 5th century of our era. Most of them speak of the Panjáb and neighbouring countries, and all agree in pointing to the north-west of India as their original seat. There is historical evidence that they were settled in large numbers on the lower Indus about 200 A.D., and they seem from time to time to have been making their way into these provinces. I am told that not more than 150 years ago, numbers of these Pachada Játs came and settled in and around the Muttra District.

It is not known whence the Játs derive their name; it is, however, supposed that they were once identical with the Gauta of classic history. Be this as it may, we know from the "Zafarnama" of Sharfu'd-dín that Timúr, when he invaded India, believed the Játs of the Panjáb to be of the same race as the Tartars whom he met in Central Asia.

There is little to be said regarding the Brahmans of Muttra. They are principally of the Sanadh tribe. Two classes, however—the Chaubeys and Ahvásís,—are deserving of notice. The Chaubeys are so named from their supposed knowledge of the four Vedas, and are found in many parts of India; but there is a distinct clan peculiar to the city of Muttra. It is said that Muttra is their original seat, though they were compelled by persecution to leave it for a time, and seek the protection of King Sarsein, the grandfather of Krishna, at his capital on the Jamna, near Batesar.

I have not been able to ascertain when and how the Muttra Chaubeys seceded from their brethren. They have probably been separate from time immemorial, yet their separation is marked by no great distinction of manners and customs. There is one strange practice peculiar to the Muttra Chaubeys, due, I believe, to their limited numbers.

C. Twigg, *Assistant Magistrate and Collector.*

AGRA.

Of the Brahmans there are ten sub-divisions, as given in the margin—sub-divisions purely local. With respect to the five Drávira clans, I may note that, whereas Colebrooke gives "Kashmírí" as the fifth, all accounts in this district give "Karnatik." The latter would seem to be the more

5 *Gor.*—Gor (proper), Kankúbj, Sarsút, Mithila, Utkal.
5 *Drávira.*—Tailang, Mahárásht, Gúzeratí, Drávira, Karnatik.

correct. None of these are found here; and of the five Gor clans, the Gor proper, the Kankúbj, and the Sarsút are the only three with which we have to deal, and of these, the Kankúbj alone hold any prominent place. Gors are found in the parganahs of Pharrah, Fírozabad, and Khandaulí, as *purohits* to Ahír and other zamíndárs, while members of the Sarsút clan are found in these three parganahs, also in that of Fattihabad; but they are only in small numbers, and possess no landed property. Members of both clans are found in the city of Agra. There are five divisions of the Kankúbj Brahmans, given in the margin. The first two appear in great force in this district, but of the others I have discovered no traces, and their true country lies to the east of the Ganges. The country of the Sanadhs and Kanaujias proper may be roughly represented as a triangle, having for its western side a line drawn from Pilibhít, in Rohilkhand, to the south-west of Muttra; and for its eastern, a line from Pilibhít to the junction of the Jumna and Ganges at Allahabad; and for its base, the country bordering upon the Jumna and Chambal rivers. Of this triangle the western half forms the country of the Sanadhs, and the eastern of the Kanaujias.

1.—Gors.

2.—Sarsút.

3.—Kankúbj.
1.—Kanaujia proper.
2. Sanadh.
3. Sarwarra.
4. Jijhoti.
5. Bhurhar.

Sanadhs.—Tradition assigns the separation of this clan from the parent stock to their founder having condescended to officiate at a *jág* performed by Rám Chander after the defeat and death of Ráwan—an act which alienated them from their stricter brethren, who, from the murdered Ráwan having been himself a Brahman, had refused to take part in it. This district forming part of the original country of the Sanadhs, they prevail in great force, and apparently outnumber the representatives of any of the other clans. In Parganah Pináhat especially, there is scarcely a village in which they are not found as zamíndárs, cultivators, or *purohits*.

Kanaujias proper.—Of these there are in all sixteen sub-divisions, but only the following appear to be represented in any force:—

Díchhit.—Why this appellation of "the initiated," properly common to all Brahmans, should have become applied specially to this clan, is scarcely apparent, nor have I been able to trace the origin of the tribe. They are scantily represented here, and appear chiefly in Parganah Pharrah, where they have been residents for some 500 years.

CHAUBES.—So called from their reading the four Veds.

GOHAN.—Of this clan there are very few representatives.

CHAURASÍAS.—These are noticed in the Report from Khandaulí only. They appear to have followed the migration of the Sikarwar Thakurs in the capacity of *purohits,* and beyond a doubt received their name from the "Chaurasí" of the Thakurs. Most probably they came from Gwalior, as Elliot mentions having discovered traces of a Chaurasí of Sikarwars there at Pahargaṛh.

RITORIAS.—The countries of Jessalmír, Bikanír, Udeypúr, and Rajputana generally form the head-quarters of this family, members of which have from time to time journeyed eastwards. Within the Agra District they are found mainly in the Parganahs of Fattihabad and Fírozabad, and in one or two villages of Parganah Kheragaṛh.

LAHARIAS.—Said to be a degenerate branch of the Sanadh tribe.

GOLAPÚRABS.—Said by some also to have originally belonged to the Sanadh family, and to have sprung from Galib Rishi—some say by a low-caste widow, others by Saksení, daughter of the Chanderbans Rajah Chandersen.

BHÁTS AND JOSHÍS.—From their wearing the Brahmanical thread, the classes of Bhát and Joshí, bards and astrologers, may here be noticed. But they are not true Brahmans, and accept as offerings iron vessels, cloths, etc., which none but the most degenerate of the priestly class would take.

CHATTRÍS.—These claim next attention, and in historical interest might even claim precedence of the Brahmanical tribes. The following are the prominent clans in this district:—

CHAUHÁNS—Who belong to the Súrajbansí branch. A fabulous origin is assigned to them. It is said that they were "created" at a *jág* performed by a great *rishi,* Basisthmuni. They are found in all parts of the district, but their chief residence is in the Khandaulí parganah, where they boast descent from the great but ill-fated Pirthí Raj. Tradition states that Sangat Rai, the grandson of Chahie Deo, Pirthí's brother, had twenty-two sons, of whom seven settled at Balrám, in the Etah District, whence their descendants, the Chauháns, subsequently migrated to parts of Muttra and Agra. The time of this movement it is impossible to ascertain, but they would seem to have occupied their present positions for upwards of 500 years. Their dispersion in all probability took place very soon after the downfall of the Hindu monarchy.

Bhadaurias.—These are a branch of the Chauháns, gaining their distinctive name from Bhadáwar, near Atah, south of the Chambal. This place appears to have formed the centre of their territory, which included the parganah of Pinnáhat in this district. Only in Pinnáhat do they appear in any force.

Sikarwár.—Also belonging to the Súrajbansí family. They appear to be so styled from their residence about Sikarwári, in the Gwalior territory. Thence they have at times, from 400 to 600 years ago, moved northwards, and sent their representatives into this district.

Morís.—Also Súrajbansís. The true origin of this name is unknown. One account derives it from an alleged ancestor, Moraddúj. Their true country is Dholpúr, and the tract round Chitorgaṛh.

Parihárs.—This term also appears underived, nor have I been able to trace out the original locality of this clan.

Pomárs.—Originally seated in Oujein. Their appearance in these parts is thus explained:—Raja Bijípál, of Baiana, wished to bring about an alliance between his daughter and the son of Tindpal, of Oujein, and with this view sent an embassy with presents. Tindpal, however, objecting to the proposed marriage, ordered the ambassador to return; but his son Lakansí, meeting them on his own account, accepted the proposal, and, in spite of Tindpal's objections, brought back the party to Baiana, and there the marriage took place.

Jadons.—These are the descendants of the Chanderbansí Raja Yadu, and were first seated in the parts round Keraulí, on the Chambal, and Baiana.

Baresirís.—These are a branch of the Jadons, and descendants of Raja Tindpal, originally settled round Baiana. Their distinctive appellation is ascribed to Akbar, to whom they afforded great assistance in the capture of Chitorgaṛh. The term *baresir* appears to be equivalent to Bahadur. They are principally resident in the Fattihabad and Pharrah parganahs, and appear to have come across from Bhartpúr some 200 years ago.

Tomars.—To this family belonged Anangpal and Pirthí Raj. Upon the dissolution of the Hindu monarchy, the Tomars migrated southwards and settled in various parts of Gwalior.

Kachhwáhas.—These claim descent from Kash, the eldest son of Rám. They are traced back to Jaipúr, which now forms their chief seat, and whence they expelled the Mínas and Bargújars.

Tarkans.—The origin of this clan is Brahmanical. It is said that four brothers, Brahmans, who in the time of Raja Tindpal were notorious dacoits, were offered pardon if they would abandon their evil courses. They did so, and, to show their complete severance from their old caste, threw aside (*tark kiyá*) the Brahmanical thread, and hence their name. They are found chiefly in parganahs Pharrah and Pinahat, and appear to have come from Muttra.

Bargújars.—They claim to belong to the thirty-six royal races, descendants of Lava, Ram's younger son. Their true country is Rajore and Jaipúr. Expelled thence by Kachhwáhas, they sought refuge in Anúpshahar, Rohilkhand, Muttra, Etah, and Aligaṛh.

Rahtors.—Originally residents of Jaipúr and Jodpúr, and allied to the Rajas of Kanauj. Relationship to the old Pomar and Sikarwar settlers seems to have drawn them here. In Parganah Khandaulí they have resided some 100 years, while in Kharegaṛh they scarcely date back beyond the last decade.

Dhakrahs.—The illegitimate descendants of Súrajbansí Rajputs, the offspring of slave girls. They are said to have come originally from the banks of the Narbadda river, and to have journeyed northwards in search of a livelihood.

Índolias.—This clan, originally from Indore, is but scantily represented here; they mainly appear as zamíndárs and cultivators in the parganah of Khandaulí, but the time of their coming is unknown.

Bachal.—The original country of this small clan is unknown, but their main residence is in Muttra, Aligaṛh, Badáon, and Shahjahanpúr.

Gehlots.—These are noted as residing chiefly in the parganahs of Fírozabad and Khandaulí, and are said to have been settled here for several hundred years. Members of this clan, from which have proceeded the two great families of Sísodya and Aharya, Rajas of Udaipúr, are dispersed as landholders over almost all parts of these provinces.

Jassáwats.—A branch of Jadons, originally residents in Jessalmír and Jaipúr. They are noted as settlers in the parganah of Khandaulí.

Bais.—This is one of the twenty-six royal races, and from them Baiswara, in Oudh, takes its name. They are scattered in considerable numbers over the whole of the North-Western Provinces, and in this district appear chiefly in the parganah of Khandaulí; but their residence here scarcely dates back beyond the last 100 years.

Chandels.—This clan is also now dispersed over the greater part of the north-west. They were originally seated in the province of Chandelí, by the Narbadda, and held a principality there. They have been for several hundred years residents in a few villages in the Khandaulí parganah.

The next three tribes to be noticed are the Khattrís, Kachís, and Játs,—all originally connected with the Chattrí class.

Khattrís are scattered about the district without any special locality, and are said to have immigrated here from Dehli.

Káchís.—Descended from the Kachwaha Thakurs by slave girls. They abound throughout the district, and are very old residents; but they seem to have settled especially in Parganahs Khandaulí, Kheragaṛh, and Pinahat. Those of the latter parganah state that they came from Dholpúr,—and this seems to have been their most recent movement.

Játs.—These are said to be the illegitimate descendants of Thakurs and low-caste concubines. Their sub-divisions are numerous, the names of which, equally with those of the Kachí clans, bear testimony to their origin. The fabulous origin assigned to them as sprung from Mahadeo's *jattá* scarcely merits notice. Most of the clans are represented in this district, and appear to be most conspicuous in the parganahs of Pharrah, Khandaulí, and Fírozabad. They date back many centuries, and appear to have settled here from Aligaṛh, Muttra, and Bhartpúr.

Banniahs.—Representing the third or Vaisya *baran*. Their subdivisions are numerous, more or less true in blood. The following are the most prominent here:—

Agarwálas.—Respecting the original seat of this tribe, accounts differ greatly: the most reliable seems to be that which ascribes their name to their residence in Agroha, on the borders of Hariana. In the parganahs of Khandaulí, Pharrah, Hasúr Tehsíl, and Kharegaṛh they appear in great force: in Pharrah some 300, in Kheragaṛh some 500; in the other parganahs there are not many.

Pallíwals.—So called from Palle, in Marwar. These are not thorough Vaisyas, having Birbújar blood in them. In the time of

Aláu'd-dín Ghorí (1150 A.D.), they migrated eastwards, and settled in the parganahs of Pharrah, Khandaulí, Fattihabad, and Pinnahat. From Pharrah there has recently—some twenty-five years ago—been a movement to Kharegaṛh.

KANDELWALS.—Mentioned as resident in Parganahs Kharegaṛh and Pharrah, whither they came several centuries ago from Bhartpúr.

MAHORS.—Muttra is said to have been the original seat of this clan. They are old residents of the district, and are found in large numbers in all parts except the Kharegaṛh parganah, where they have only one village. Their settlement appears to have extended over several centuries, and various periods are stated—from 100 to 400 years. They are not true Vaisyas, being descended from a Vaisya by a Chaubey woman.

DILWARÍAS.—This clan is mentioned only in the Pharrah parganah, where it has settled some 300 years, having migrated from Dehli.

KÁYATHS.—The Kayath class occupies an intermediate place, and is variously reckoned as the only representative of the true Súdra caste, and as one of the mixed classes: Mathor, Bhatnagar, Saksena, Siríbast, and Súragdúj, Nigam, Gor, Amisht, Karran, Aitana, Kalsirisht, and Bálmík, severally giving their names to the twelve Kayath clans. Of these, the Bhatnagar, Saksena, Siríbast, and Kalsirisht clans are represented throughout the district, and in large numbers. A few members of the Aitana clan are found in the Pharrah parganah; as also some Pentálísas, a sub-division of the Mathor Kayaths.

It now remains to notice the most prominent of the mixed classes.

AHÍRS.—Said to have sprung from a Chattrí father and Vaisya mother. Tradition here gives Hariana as their original seat, but this most probably refers to a sub-division only. Their antiquity is great, "Abhírs" finding mention in the "Rámáyan" and "Mahábhárat." They are found in all parts of the district, and seem to have come mainly from Muttra. Their migration dates back from 200 to 500 years.

KÁHÁRS are numerous throughout the district, and have settled at various times.

MALLAHS.—These seem to belong to the old Nishád, or fisher class.

NAHÍS.—Accounts vary as to the origin of this tribe. They are abundant throughout the district.

BURJÍS.—Their origin is also variously stated.

KÚRMÍS.—Described as the descendants of a slave girl and the illegitimate son of a Chattrí.

GADARIYÁ.—The descendants of an outcast Kúrmí by a concubine. Alienated from the brotherhood, they lived apart in the jungle, gaining a livelihood by grazing herds. Such is one account. Another makes them to be the offspring of a Karan (Kayath?) mother and a Vaisya father; while a third account asserts them to be Gújars, and a fourth Ahírs. The latter explanations have this plausibility, that amongst Gaderiyás, equally with Gújars and Ahírs (and also Játs), there prevails the custom of the younger brother taking to wife the widow of the elder. The time of their settlement here cannot be definitely ascertained, but they are beyond a doubt old residents. Their sub-divisions are manifold, and keep as aloof from one another as if they were distinct castes.

LOHÁRS.—Explained as the descendants of a Kúrmí by a concubine, caste unknown; and again, as merely a sub-division of the Chattrí caste, probably separated from the original stock by the speciality of trade.

KÚMHÁRS.—The offspring of a Brahman's Kahárí concubine by a Súdra. Another account, however, quoted by Colebrooke, makes them descendants of a Brahman and a Chattrí girl. There are three classes, arranged according to their manner of working,—(1) Mathúriya, working by hand; (2) Gola, working by the wheel; and (3) Parodia, toy-makers.

LODAHS.—Of the origin of this tribe also various accounts are given; one making them the descendants of an Ahír by a Chattrí woman, another, of a Chattrí father and low-caste mother. They appear to have come here from Muttra and Bhartpúr some 400 years ago, and are found in the northern parganahs chiefly, being very rare in those of Irádatnagar and Pináhat.

CHAMÁRS.—The most reliable accounts state this tribe to be descended from a Mallah by a Chandál woman; others from a Súdra father and Nishád mother; while another, stated by Colebrooke, makes them the offspring of a Bhangí woman and a Brahman.

KOLÍS.—Descended from a Bais father and a slave girl.

DHÁNUKS.—Descendants of an outcast Ahír and a Chamárí, or, as given by Sir H. Elliot, of a Chamár and a Chandál woman.

A. SELLS, *Officiating Deputy Collector.*

MAINPURI.

Agarwálas.—Agarwálas are found in the town of Mainpúrí, and also Shekoabad and its immediate neighbourhood. They profess the Jain religion, but are by descent Hindus, and state that they came from Agra or Agroha (supposed to be so called from Agrasen), near Dehli, about 116 years ago.

Ahírs.—The Ahírs are very numerous throughout the whole district, and are also considerable landholders, more especially in the parganahs of Shekoabad and Mustafabad. Their principal sub-divisions here existing are as follows:—Phatak, Nigana, Jiwariya or Jarwariya, Dhamar, Dunr, Kamariya, Karaiya, Sondele, Rant, Lehngaya, Angere, Bhragade, Badosiya, Malgoraya, Gaindua or Gadua, and Ghosí. All these claim to be Nandbansí except the Phataks, who are really by descent Thakurs, and, like them, have a bad character for female infanticide.

Bais.—Some Bais Thakurs settled at Bhewar about 250 years ago, in consequence of an intermarriage between a member of their family and the Raja of Mainpúrí, who gave them sixty villages, which they still hold. They are sub-divided into two *gots*—the Bharadwaja and the Garg, the former being the more numerous.

Bhadoris.—A Brahman caste, found scattered in small numbers here and there. They accept alms from all classes indiscriminately, and are therefore held in very low esteem.

Bháts.—The Bháts are Brahmans by descent, though now scarcely reckoned amongst the Brahmanical families.

Brahmans.—The principal sub-divisions of Brahmans found in the district are the Sanadh, Gor, Saraswat, Kanaujia, Mathuríya, and Byohra.

Byohras.—All Brahmans of this class are dealers and money-lenders, and so derive their distinctive name. They profess to have come from Marwar and Charn, in Rajputána, about the middle of the last century, and now hold several zamíndárís here.

Chauháns.—The Chauhán Thakurs are the most numerous and influential class in the district.

Chirars (local name, Chobdars).—It is said that the Chirars were in occupation of the country when the Chauháns invaded it and dispossessed them.

Kamariyas.—The Kamariya Ahírs hold eleven villages in the Mainpúrí, and forty-six in the Mustafabad, parganah.

Kachhwáhas.—There is a small settlement of Kachhwáha Thakurs at Devapúra, close to the town of Mainpúrí. They say that their original home was beyond the Chambal.

Kayaths.—There are twelve families of Kayaths, all of whom claim descent from a certain Chitra Gúpt.

Kirárs.—The Kirars hold thirty-five villages in the Shekoabad parganah, and claim to be a branch of the Jadava Thákurs. They say their great ancestor, Kanwar Pal, invaded the west country and took a strong city called Kirárwar, from which they derive their distinctive name. They settled in the district which they now occupy about 500 years ago. Sada Sakh, Kirár, Zamíndár of Karera, puts in a pedigree beginning with Varadeva, in which Kanwar Pal, *alias* Karoli Pal, figures as a direct descendant of Krishna; and two of his near descendants, Chattar Pal and Puran Pal, are stated to have settled, the first at Akhrend, the second at Chattarauli, about 1445 Sambat. This is the only date introduced throughout. Wilson, in his Glossary, describes the Kirárs, though with a query at the end of the sentence, as a low tribe, whose occupation is to sell grass and exercise horses, and identifies them with the *kiráts* (barbarians), the *cirrhadæ* of the ancients. There can be little doubt that Kirár and *kirát* are really the same word, but the description above given is much too unfavorable a one for the people answering to the name in this district; and Wilson appears to have overlooked for the moment a passage in "Manu," x., 43, 44, where the Kiráts are included in a list of Kshatriya castes (so far confirming the local tradition) which have become degraded in consequence of neglecting their proper religious duties.

शनकैस्तु क्रियालोपादिमाः क्षत्रियजातयः
वृषलत्वं गता लोके ब्राह्मणादर्शनेन च किराताः

The Kiráts of whom Wilson was thinking are no doubt those mentioned in the "Padma Purana," with the Nishads, Bhils, Pulindas, etc., as descendants of the dwarf who was supernaturally born of King Vena, and was the embodiment of his sins.

Mathuriyas.—The Mathuriyas are a class of Chaubey Brahmans who, as their name indicates, have come from Muttra. They say that they first settled in Mainpúrí about 300 years ago, and that Chittor was their original home before they moved to Muttra.

RAGHUBANSIS.—Some Raghubansí Thakurs hold three villages in the neighbourhood of Ghiror. They state that they came from Ajudhia in the time of Raja Jaichand of Kanauj.

RATHORS.—The Rathor Thakurs are Surajbansí, and came from Ajudhia in the time of Raja Jaichand. They have a *chaurasí* in Karraulie which now comprises eighty-eight villages, though some of these have been recently acquired.

PHATAKS.—The Phatak Ahírs hold twenty-one villages in the Shekoabad Tehsílí, and give the following account of their origin:—There was a Raja of Chittor of the Sissodhia line of Rajputs, commonly designated the Kateri Rana. His capital was attacked by the King of Dehli, and, of the twelve gates of the city, one only held out. Therefore, when the invading army had retired, the Raja decreed that the guard of the twelfth gate and their descendants should ever thereafter be distinguished by the name of Phatak. They profess to be actually descended from this Rana by a *dola* marriage with the daughter of Digpal, Raja of Mahaban, an Ahír, and they are accordingly reckoned among the Ahírs. From this marriage two sons were born, Bijay Singh and Hansraj: the former abandoned his native district, and, with a disorderly band of followers, roamed the country till he came to Samohar, then in the hands of the Mewatís, whom he dispossessed and there established himself about the year 1106 Sambat. The lands in the occupation of their descendants are still called the Samohar *chaurasí*. The family of Hansraj, the second son, settled at Khat Khera, in the vicinity of Dehli.

SANADHS.—The Sanadhs form one of the largest and most influential Brahman classes in the district, being most numerous in Bhangaon. They are divided into two main lines. The first contains sixteen *gots*, of which the Sandil, the Gautama, the Vasisht, and the Bharadwaja are the principal here found: they say that they came as the *purohits* of the Rathors, first to Rampore, and thence to Bhangaon. The second line comprises three-and-a-half *gots*. They say they came from Sambhal 400 years ago.

SONARS.—The Sonars of Bhangaon claim to be Thakurs from Kanauj, which locality they profess to have left 1500 or 1600 years ago.

Saraugies.—The Saraugies (Jains) are numerous in the town of Mainpúrí. There are two divisions, which have no intercourse with each other, the Saraugie proper, and the Lohiya Saraugie. The latter, so called from the trade which they follow, are considered the inferior. The former have a temple of some antiquity by the Ganesh Darwaza, and the Lohiyas have recently erected a new temple for themselves at very considerable expense. The separation between the two classes would appear to be of recent date.

Tanks.—The Tank Thakurs hold eight villages in the Mainpúrí Tehsílí. They claim to be Jadubansi, and say that they came from Karraulie and Tank, and settled in the village of Kosma, dispossessing the former occupants, who were Brahmans.

Thákurs.—The Thakur classes found in the district are as follows, of which several have already received special mention:—Chauhán, Bargujar, from Gujrát, Kachhwáha, Tank, Raghubansí, Rathor, Jadava, Gor, Bais, Gahlot, Tomar, Dhakara, Bhadauriya, and Baghela.

F. S. Growse, *Assistant Collector*.

ETAWAH.

The early history of Etawah, and that tract of country now included in the district of that name, is involved in the same doubt and obscurity which rests upon everything Indian prior to the commencement of the eleventh century.

The pandits produce *slokes*, said to be derived from the "Mahábhárat," in which the name of Etawah occurs, but these appear to be forgeries; indeed, though there are reasons to believe that the place is of considerable antiquity, and though the current tradition is that Mahmúd of Ghazní* took Etawah after a three days' fight in 1022–23 A.D., after his unsuccessful attempt to protect his ally, the Raja of Kanauj, no-

* Though it is not, I believe, the commonly received identification, I have no doubt myself that the famous place of Munj, which Mahmúd destroyed in 1017–18, is no other than the Munj situated in the district, fifteen miles north of Etawah, the size and height of whose khera is almost, if not quite, unequalled in the Doab. The account of Mahmúd's marches is confused to a degree in all the Persian histories; but I think that, taken as a whole, the present situation of Munj will suit their narratives as well, if not better, than any other.

thing authentic is known of its history until towards the close of the twelfth century.

Etawah formed part of the *antarbed* according to later historians, and it seems probable that it was at one time an integral part of the kingdom of Kanauj; but long before our authentic history commences the country (over which the Kings of Dehli then seem to have claimed sovereignty) had ceased, I think, to own even a nominal allegiance to the Rathor Dynasty, and the whole tract seems to have been overrun with Meos, whose turbulent lawlessness had reduced it almost to a wilderness. A time came, however, when two powerful Rajput races —the one from the south and the other from the west—swept over it, and, having exterminated the Meos, founded a number of princely houses, many of which to this day retain the titles, and (notwithstanding our anti-talúkdarí policy, so pertinaciously clung to for more than half a century) something of the possessions, of their great ancestors.

Of these two races, the earliest to appear on the scene were the Senghars.

Claiming, like the Gautam Rajputs (well known in Azimgaṛh, Jaunpúr, Ghazipur, Fattihpúr, etc.), to be descended from Singhí or Siringhí Rish and a daughter of the then monarch of Kanauj, they pretend that their own immediate ancestor, Púrandeo (or Sorandeo, as some have it), son of Padam Rish and grandson of the horned sage, Singhí Rish, having received the *tilak* from Raja Dulíp of Antar, migrated southwards and established an important kingdom in the Dekkan, or, as most will have it, in Ceylon.

For seventy-two generations the Senghars ruled in the far south, whence, moving to Dhara (Dhar ?), for fifty-one more generations their sovereignty remained intact. Thence they appear to have been forced to migrate to Bandhu, whence again, six generations later, they moved to Kanar, a place near Jaggammanpúr. Here it was that, in the 137th generation from Singhí Rish, Raja Bisúkdeo—or Súkdeo, as he is indifferently called,—the founder of the modern fortunes of the Senghar Raj, first saw the light.

I entertain no doubt that he is a real historical personage. His birth in all the *kursi-namehs* is assigned to the year Sambat 1122, or 1065 A.D.; but I am myself inclined to believe that his birth has been thrown 100 years too far back, and that the correct date would be 1165 A.D.

He married Deokúlah, the daughter of Jay Chand, apparently the Rathor Raja of Kanauj, who in 1194 A.D. was defeated somewhere in the Etawah District by Shahabu'd-dín Ghorí, who, it is said, plundered Etawah itself about the same time.

This victory destroyed for ever the great kingdom of Kanauj, and paved the way for the Senghar and Chauhán principalities. Bisúkdeo took possession of the whole of the eastern parts of the present district. His descendants allege that he received it in dower on his marriage with the daughter of the Kanauj Raja, on condition of exterminating the Meos, who were then ravaging the whole country. But this seems scarcely likely, since at the time of his marriage the kings of Dehli claimed sovereignty over this tract, and had made, about the time of the famous battle of Tiraurí, a grant of a portion of it to their own employés.

In 582 H., or 1186 A.D., one Udaikarn, of Ajúdhia (a Sríbastam Kayath of the Dúsera division), presented himself at the Court of Pirthí Raj as an aspirant to the royal favor. Proving himself both brave and clever, he was sent with a force to Phapund to reduce the Meos to order; and in A.D. 1191 received a formal *sannad* conferring on him a *jaghir* of Rs. 50,000, with the title of Chaudhrí.

Then came the destruction of the Dehli Raj in 1193 A.D., and of that of Kanauj in 1194 A.D., after which both the Kayath and the Senghar appear to have obtained the favor of the conqueror. Poker Dass, Udaikarn's son, was confirmed in his father's *jaghir* and title, with the addition of being nominated hereditary Kanúngo of the shag of Phapund, with further emoluments; while Bisukdeo and his sons obtained firm hold of the whole of the rest of the eastern half of the district.

Of the Kayaths, Chaudhrí Ganga Persbád, of Búrhedanna and Umrí, Talúkdar and Honorary Magistrate, still (with branches of his family) hold nearly the same villages they obtained in grant some 650 years ago; while the Rajas of Bharrai, Jaggammanpúr, Ruru, Sakkat, and all the multitudinous "Ruá," "Rawat," and "Kúnr" kinsmen, holding some 300 to 400 villages between them, sufficiently maintain the name and position of their great ancestor.

It was somewhat later than the advent of the Senghars that the

Chauhán Raja, Sumersa (grandson of Hamír Shah, killed at the taking of Rattambúr in 1230 A.D., by Altamsh), with his two brothers, the founders of the Rajore and Mainpúri Dynasties—all being sons of Raja Uram Rao, and great-great-grandsons of Pirthí Raj,—made their way from Nímrana to this part of the country; when Samer Shah with his Chauhán followers and friends took possession of the whole of the western portion, as the Senghars already had of the eastern portion, of the district. This I take to have occurred somewhere about 1266 A.D., and I gather that the Chauháns obtained a certain amount of countenance from Ghyasu'd-dín, in consideration of their having aided to exterminate the Meos, who were then, as ever, the very *bête noirs* of all regular administration.

From this stem the Rajahs of Pertabnír and Chakkernagar, the Rana of Sikrorí, the Raos of Jassohan and Kisní, and other princely houses, sprang, and though they probably no longer hold more than a fifth at most of the 1,122 villages over which Sumersa once exercised regal authority, the Chauháns are still the dominant race of the west, as the Senghars are of the east, of the Etawah District.

But though the Chauháns and Senghars are, and have been for fully 600 years, the ruling races here, it must not be supposed that these are the only castes, or even the only Rajputs, who deserve our notice. Before the Senghars, the Gaur Thakurs in the north-east, and, after the advent of the Chauháns, the Bhadauriás in the west, were in their turns powerful, and have left till this day representatives in many village communities.

The Gaurs belong to those dim middle ages in which nothing can be distinguished with certainty. According to their own traditions, they migrated from Sopar in the west as early as 650 A.D., and took up their head-quarters at Parsú, reclaiming much of the surrounding country from the everlasting Meos, whom everybody was always conquering, without, it must be confessed, their appearing much the worse for it.

In about 1000 A.D. the Gaur Thakurs were, they assert, in great force in that tract of country now known as Phapund, Akbarpúr, Oreyah, Rassúlabad, and Dera Mangalpúr parganahs, having their head-quarters at Malhausie, and founding fifty-two (*bawan*) gharís, amongst which Phapund, Umrí, Búrhedana, and many others later granted to the Kayath Chaudhrís, are enumerated. Who exactly Allah and Udal (the worthy Rajas of Mahoba whose prowess is sung to this day at the commencement of the rains by all the minstrels and peasants of the Central Doáb) may chance to have been, and whether they were men or myths, the works of reference at my command do not enable me to decide; but it is to those doughty warriors—but specially the matchless archer, Udal—that the Gaur Thakurs ascribe their defeat and ruin at the very commencement of the twelfth* century. Elsewhere they again, on various occasions, rose into importance, but here they never regained their lost supremacy, though their descendants to this day continue to hold Sahail, Karchalla, Jaura, and other villages in this and the Cawnpore Districts.

The Bhadauriás on the west, whose head-quarters are in the Bah Pinahat parganah of the Agra District, claim, as is well known, great antiquity, and are (owing to the favour in which they stood in the later times of the Mahomedan Emperors, which are least forgotten) allowed precedence by the Chauháns of Manchhana (or Mainpúrí) and Pertabnír; but in reality these Bhadauriás were of *no* importance when the great Chauhán houses were founded hereabouts, and only rose into notice when the Chauháns of Etawah had been for nearly 400 years the rulers of the whole country round about. It was during the time of Shahjahan and his successors that the Bhadauriás (always a troublesome and disreputable set) obtained a permanent hold, which they still retain on much of the Chauhán territory.

Mingled with the Bhadauriás are a few communities of Dhakera Rajputs, who appear to have migrated hither from the direction of

* How they reconcile this early date with the alleged fact that Údal married a daughter or sister of Jaichand of Kanauj, I cannot pretend to say. Everyone knows Udal's story,—how as a boy he broke the Kahari's *ghara*; and how, taunted by her, he went and recovered his father's skull; his loves, his conquests, and his sad fate—are they not told in all our chronicles? *One* such contains nearly 1,000 pages of close manuscript, solely devoted to Udal and his family. But for all that, I am by no means convinced that he and his exploits are not pure myths, and that his whole story, as *originally* told, was not a semi-religious fable. If he was a *man*, and not a myth, the story of his marrying Jaichand's daughter need give no trouble. Every family who ever married in old days into any Rathore family of Kanauj *now* give out that their ancestor married Jaichand's daughter. Probably it may have been one of his great-grandfather's *chobdar's* daughters; but this is all the same to them.

Ajmír early in the sixteenth century, and to have early joined themselves with the Bhadauriás. For nearly two centuries they bore a reputation as robbers and cut-throats second only to that of their prototypes, the Meos, and to this day they are, I think, the least respectable of our village communities.

In the east, again, where this district marches with that of Cawnpore, a good many of the Gahlor—or, as it is sometimes written, Gahlot—Thakurs are to be found. The head-quarters of this clan, hereabouts at least, is Parganahs Rassúlabad and Tirúa Thattia, Zillah Farrakhabad. They profess to have made their way, about 1400 A.D., from Muttra and Dehli, to assist Sultan Mahmúd Taghlak in maintaining order in and about Kanauj, and to have received the 600 villages they still profess to hold in reward for their services. That they obtained their present holdings about the time that that most blood-thirsty ruffian, Tamerlane, had reduced the whole of Upper India to a state of anarchy is, I deem, probable enough; but although Mahmúd Taghlak was residing for a short time at Kanauj, it was as a mere refugee, and I doubt whether he ever *attempted* to keep order *anywhere*, or possessed any power to reward allies. I suspect by "their own good swords they won those lands," as certainly later "by those same swords they kept them."

A considerable number of Parihar Thakurs are to be found in that portion of the district south of the rivers Kúarí and Chambal, known as the Talúka Sandús. Inhabiting, as these people have done, that intricate and inaccessible net-work of ravines that abuts on the Panchnaddí (as the confluence of the Jamna, Chambal, Sinde, Koarí, and Pahúj is here termed), they have ever been a peculiarly lawless and desperate community.

The great ancestor of these Parihars was Belan Deo. From him, in the seventh generation, descended Nahir Deo, one of whose fourteen sons, Paup Singh, founded this particular clan, who were then located in Biana, Zillah Amritpúr. Very early in the eleventh century, and consequent on (though why consequent, none can explain) the defeat of Anang Pal by Mahmúd of Ghazní, Samit Rai, the then surviving head of the house, fled to Sandús and colonized the country thereabouts, which his clan still continue to occupy.

The Kachhwáhas are also represented in this district. The Kaurs of Bailah were once rather important landholders, and, with their numerous kinsmen, still hold Bailah itself and a few other villages.

The Kachhwáhas appear to have emigrated at an early period from Gwalior or its neighbourhood to that tract of country now known as Kachhwáhí Ghar. Thence in 1656 A.D. came one Ajab Singh, who took service with the then Raja of Ruru, and later, through his master's influence, obtained possession of Bailah and other villages. Besides this family, there are a good number of this caste (all emigrants from Kachhwáhí Ghar) sprinkled here and there about the eastern parganahs of this district.

To return, the Rajput races were the pioneers, but with them and after them came tribes of Brahmans, as *pandits*, *purohits*, and *pújarís*, who soon obtained villages or portions of villages as *maáfís*, or as subsistence provisions, from their warlike patrons.

Throughout this district, if we except the Oreyah parganah, the Kanaujias are in majority. A very considerable proportion of these belong to the Dúbai division (or *got*); and one celebrated Dúbai, Shivnath, is recorded as having accompanied Raja Sumersa when he first established himself in Etawah. Throughout the north-east of the district Kanaujias abound, but all admit that they only came by degrees, finding their way one by one to the courts of the Senghar chieftains, from whom they obtained grants of lands, and whose rights they in many cases usurped in the course of time.

In the centre of the district, for some reason, there always remained a broad belt of debateable land between the Senghars and the Chauháns, and in this neutral ground, about 1500 A.D., appeared two Kanaujia Brahmans, Dhun and Mun (*query*, should these be Dhan and Man?), born, it was said, at Nandhaha, near Bithúr. These soon possessed themselves peacefully of a very considerable tract of country.

In the Oreyah parganah (which is not generally known), the Sanaurias or Sanadhs predominate, and are represented chiefly by Singías and Merhas, two well-known *gots* of that sub-family. There are a considerable number of Singía* Brahman zamíndárs, and these

* The Singías are also called Gargia Chaubeys. They say that Garga Cháraj, Sri Krishen's *guru*, belonged to their family. Their name is derived, they allege, from that of their native country—a tract near Dehli, which was once known as Singhí.

all date their origin from one Basdeo. According to them their ancestor first settled at Sabhda under the protection of the Senghars, and then one of his sons went to Dehli, where he obtained service late in Shahabu'd-dín Ghorí's reign.

They are probably in error in dating their advent so far back as 1200 A.D., but they are unquestionably one of the first of the Brahman septs now existing that settled in the district.

The Merhas profess to have been from early times the family priests or the Senghar Raj of Bharrai.

In the Etawah parganah, besides the gradual influx of Kanaujias, two distinct immigrations of other Brahmans are noticeable as having to this day left numerous representatives.

Very early in the fourteenth century, when Alau'd-dín took Rantampúr, Chitorgaṛh, and other places, one Harrípant, a famous pandit, made his way to Etawah. With him came Ugarsen, Mathúria, and others of that sub-division of the Sanaurias. Ugarsen's two sons, Radho and Madho, rose to more or less importance, and at this present moment their descendants of the twelfth, thirteenth, and fourteenth generation, as well as the descendants of their father's companions, are to be found almost throughout the Etawah parganah.

Another and far more important sept of Sanaurias are the "Sabarn" Chaudhrís of Manikpúr. Their ancestors, it is generally allowed, accompanied Raja Sumersa on his first settlement in the district, and from him obtained the title of Chaudhrí and a grant of several villages.

In later times they possessed, it is said, a *chaurasi* of villages.

Of the Kayat or writer class, besides the important Phapund family already noticed, a considerable number are to be found in the Etawah parganah. Of these the most noticeable are the Ayara family (Suksenai Kayats of the Pardhan *ál*), whose ancestor, an inhabitant of Kanauj, migrated to Etawah after Raja Jaichand's death, and when Sumersa took possession of Etawah, entered his service.

Besides these, there are the Chakwa and Parasna Kayats, to whose family belonged the famous Raja Nawal Rai, whom the Nawab Bangash killed. These are Suksenai Kharrai. Again, there are the Ekdill Kayats, Suksenai, Dúsera, and others, whose ancestors were one and all followers or servants of the Chauhán Rajas.

For traders the Etawah District has never been famous. Inaccessible ravines, dense jungles, and the unchecked rule of virtually independent petty Thakur chieftains were not elements conducive to the rapid development of commerce.

About 400 years ago one Mota Mal, a Khattrí of Jalaun, settled in the old city, and there, with a number of relatives and kinsmen, grew to importance. He built a magnificent residence—one might almost call it a palace—which still, though ruined (and all its best marble and stonework long since sold away by his numerous pauper descendants), attest the builder's wealth and taste.

Of the humbler traders or Banniahs scattered everywhere about the district, a large proportion are Aggarwallas. These Aggarwallas are said by Elliot to derive their name from Agroha, on the borders of Hariana; but I believe that this statement is incorrect, as by all tradition, written and oral, they are descended from a person named Augar, or Ugar. According to some accounts he was a Brahman saint, Augar Rikhisúr; while others call him a Kshatriya Raja, Ugar Sen. Be this as it may, he had seventeen sons, whom he married to the seventeen daughters of Basuk Deota, King of the Nagas.

The descendants of these Nág-kannies, or snake-daughters, were called Aggarwallas, and these comprise to this day seventeen *gots*,* named after Augar's seventeen sons. Those snake-ladies brought with them a number of slaves, and the descendants of these were called *Dassa*, to this day a well-known though inferior race of Banniahs. How these Aggarwallas, descendants of saints or monarchs, came to sink into the position they have ever occupied within the historical period, is, I think, easy of explanation. Admitting, as is now unquestionable, that these serpent-kings, of whom we hear so much, were nothing more than the chieftains of tribes of invaders whose birthplace was beyond the Himalayas, Scythians, as Elliot calls them, and concurring with Elphinstone that any considerable admixture of the blood of these barbarians in the pure Rajput stocks is highly improbable,—I believe that many of the inferior castes, and amongst others the Aggar-

* *Viz.*, Garag, Gotal, Basal, Nayal, Tandal, Metal, Sangal, Mangal, Gon, Chaudan, Abarn, Dhabaran, Kusal, Gangal, and three others which I have never been able to find out.

walla Banniahs, the Kayats, the Gújars, and the Játs, originated in marriages between males of the pure Brahman and Rajput stocks and females of the later hordes of invaders. The subject, however, is one which I cannot here discuss further.

Then we have the Jameya Banniahs, of whom there are a good many in Oreyah, and who are remarkable as having until quite recently always buried their dead, whom they now place on a mat and fling into a river. They claim descent from Pahlad, son of Hiranya Kasyap, but they take their name from Jameya, their more immediate progenitor, who, abandoning the "panth" or sect of Hiranya Kasyap, became initiated in the worship of Bishen (or Vishnu), and prescribed the same to his descendants. Like others of the trading and laboring classes, their advent to this part of the country seems to have been subsequent to the comparative restoration of order under the Rajput chieftains. Besides these Jameya Banniahs, there are the Gaharwár, Gahore, Didhomra, and Púrwar, or Ajúdiahbasís, and others, whose traditions, though useful in discussing the general question of the origin of the inferior castes, would be too tedious to dwell on here. And lastly, before concluding this passing notice of our traders, we are bound to name the Marwarís—commercial adventurers—of many castes, who, second to none in enterprise and industry, periodically seek in these provinces the fortunes they generally return to spend in their distant homes in Marwar.

Hitherto we have considered only the Hindu races, and the truth is that ours is an essentially Hindu population, amongst which here and there a few Mahomedans only have been permitted to find homes. Not as conquerors or rulers, for the most part came the Mahomedans to Etawah: nature had so fortified the Rajput principalities here that neither Shah nor Nawab ever ventured to interfere much with them, though in course of Akbar's time the whole was duly included in the subah of Agra, under the dastúrs of Etawah, Bhaugáon, and Kalpí.

In early times the whole northern half of the district was traversed from west to east by a portion of that broad ten-*kos* belt of *dhák* jungle, which—though now in many localities replaced by cultivation, and everywhere greatly diminished in breadth, is still to be traced through the Mírat, Bulandshahr, Aligaṛh, Etah, Mainpúrí, Etawah, and Cawnpore Districts—was once a dense continuous and jungle forest.

The whole of the south of the district was, and indeed still is, a net-work of terrible ravines (then everywhere densely wooded), fringing throughout their whole course the Jamna, Chambal, and Kúarí rivers. Lastly, right through the centre of the district runs the Senghar, which for the last thirty miles of its course here is bordered on either side by a belt of ravines, in many places several miles in breadth. These latter ravines, even up to a recent date, were so densely clothed with khair,* rewaj,† chenkar,‡ babul,§ and others of this thorny race, that it was difficult in many places for even a single footman to thread his way amongst them; and all tradition leads us to believe that in past times the Jamno-Chambal ravines were no less densely clad.

It is therefore no matter of surprise that, close as Etawah was to the capital of the great Mahomedan Emperors, the Hindus always contrived to hold their own, so that we have but few, and these but little important, Mahomedan families to chronicle here.

Phapund and Etawah alone have any Mahomedans. To Phapund, early in the sixteenth century, from Jaunpúr, came Sayyid Yusuf, a native of Bokhara, known to us now as Shah Jaffer Bokharí. With this good man came his brother, Sayyid Tayab, and his family; and this latter's descendants are now the leading Mahomedans of Phapund. About the same time appeared also at Phapund one Baba Sejhanand, who is said to have been born in Totadarí, near Ajmír; and with this Baba the Bokharí contracted the strongest friendship. Both Sejhanand and Shah Jaffer, who died in 956 Hijrí,‖ left a name for goodness and sanctity, revered alike by Hindu and Musulman,—and flowers are sprinkled, lamps are lit, and snow-white sheets are still spread upon the Mahomedan's tomb at festivals by the pious of *both* creeds; while the great fair of Shah Bokharí, held yearly at it to this day, shows how long and brightly "good deeds shine out upon this naughty world," and how, even in the darkest ages and amongst the most ignorant people, a career of pure unselfish piety and good works will conquer sectarian prejudices, and live to distant generations in the hearts of multitudes, who, though they will not imitate, can at least admire, its virtues.

In Etawah we have two families or clans of Mahomedans. The first

* Acacia Catechu. † Acacia Lencophlæa. ‡ Acacia Trispinosa.
§ Acacia Arabica. ‖ The date is on his tomb.

are Shaikhs, who, emigrating from Bagdad, settled in Dehli in Chengiz Khan's time, early in the thirteenth century, and thence in the time of the Emperor Akbar (whose sannads they retain to this day) moved to Etawah, of which they became the hereditary kazís, although they never appear to have become landholders. The other clan are Sayyids, whose progenitor, Sayyid Jabba, of the Barah Sadat, obtained in Faruksír's time a small grant of land in Etawah from the Vizier Abdulla, who, as is well known, belonged to the same famous Sayyid stock.

There still remain the inferior castes, of whom in this district the Ahírs, Chamárs, Kachís, and Lodhís are perhaps the most noticeable and most important. Of the origin* of these, or the times at which they first occupied the district in considerable numbers, nothing can be said with certainty.

Looking back through the dim vista of receding ages, we seem to discern traces of a time when the Etawah District was widely different from anything it has ever been within the historic period: a time when population was very dense, and when arts long since forgotten, and a religion now unknown, grew and flourished everywhere about the district. Even in the midst of barren plains, ancient sites † of considerable magnitude, and in some instances extraordinary height, attest the importance and antiquity of the towns under which they once slowly grew. Fragments of a highly glazed and ornamental pottery, such as in Asia is now scarcely produced anywhere out of China, and portions of sculpture, which even now, weather-beaten by unnumbered seasons, are almost Grecian in the purity of their design, from time to time crop up—mute records of arts and civilization, such as in the last thousand years have found no parallels here. Even the principal mosque in Etawah itself is nothing ‡ but a modified Buddhist temple, to which it is impossible to assign a later date than the fifth century of our era.

* From such scraps of tradition as I have at various times collected from the people and from native books, modern and ancient, I hope some day to be able to show good grounds for believing that most of the more important of the lower castes spring from unions between the *males* of the higher castes and females of the aboriginal inhabitants of the country, or in some cases (and these are the most respected of the lower castes) the females of the so-called Scythian races.

† Known as *kheras*.

‡ I was the first to point this out, and even now it is not generally known.

Some great calamity then devastated the country. War and pestilence may have contributed; but there are nowhere the faintest traces of irrigating channels—water is very far from the surface, and it is to one of those terrible famines to which this part of the Doáb is peculiarly liable that I myself am inclined to attribute the change.

The next glimpse we catch of the country—it is almost tenantless, a straggling wilderness, overrun with scattered hordes of robber savages; then came that widely-extended *reflex* movement of the southern Rajput tribes towards the north and north-east, which, commencing long before the earliest important Mahomedan invasion, has never, I think, been adequately explained. Other tribes doubtless preceded them, of whom even such faint traces as we have of the Gor occupation no longer remain to us; but the first to obtain a lasting footing here were the Senghars' and Chauháns' bold hearts and strong arms, before whom the plunderers soon melted away. Once more something like protection to life and property is afforded: the Brahmans come with science, such as it is, and all that still remains to them of a declining civilization; agriculture becomes possible; herds multiply in something like security; commerce and banking spring up to aid the distribution of growing wealth, and the Tatars, Mughals, and Mahrattas have successively held nominal sway, and exercised a more or less real authority over them.

Brahmans.—I note, though it is probably so perfectly well known as to require no repetition, that Brahmans are divided into two great classes—the Panch Gor, who reside north, and the Panch Dravira, who reside south, of the Vindyachal mountains.

The Gor contains five great families:—1, Sarasút; 2, Kankubj; 3, Gor; 4, Maithal; 5, Utkal.

The Dravira contains five other great families:—1, Tailang; 2, Drawar; 3, Maharasht; 4, Karnatic; 5, Gújar. These do not intermarry, I believe.

The Kankubj, with whom chiefly we are concerned in these provinces, contains five sub-families:—1, Sanauria, or Sanadh; 2, Kanaujia; 3, Jijhotia; 4, Bhúínhár; 5, Sarwaria. These do intermarry.

The Kanaujias, again, comprise sixteen divisions and 104 *gots*; and similarly each of the sub-families include a vast number of divisions and *gots*. No two authorities agree as to these, and some years ago, after recording some hundreds, I came to the conclusion that these distinctions were of no value. Doubtless, however, Brahmans of the same *gots* cannot intermarry. The distinction of *gots* had their origin in the *jágs* and *oms* performed by their ancestors and founders.

Kayaths.—These, as is well known, claim descent from Chandar, or Chittor Gupt, who had two wives and twelve sons, each of whom was founder of a separate clan. There ought, therefore, now to be only twelve such clans, but a thirteenth has been somehow introduced, and the Kayaths are always said to contain twelve and a half families. These are—1, Mathur; 2, Bhatnagar; 3, Sríbast or Sríbastam; 4, Suksena; 5, Kalserisht; 6, Negam; 7, Gor; 8, Súraj-thúg; 9, Amisht; 10, Aithana; 11, Balmek; 12, Karan; 12½, Unais.

These cannot intermarry, but each of these are divided, first, in great sub-divisions, as the Sríbast into (*a*) Kharai, (*b*) Dúsera; and all these sub-divisions into innumerable *áls*, the members of each *ál* being unable to marry in their own *ál*, or out of their own great family.

O. A. Hume, C.B., *Collector.*

ETAH.

Out of a population of 614,351 souls, there are 71,662 Chamárs and 10,900 Kolís.

It is not known from what part of the country the Chamárs came, but it is possible that they have settled here on account of the leather trade. They are sub-divided into seven classes—viz., Jatúa, Kaien, Kúrah, Jaiswar, Jhosia, Azimgaṛhía and Kúrís.

Ahírs and Ahirs.—Of these there are 63,193.

Lodhas—Of whom there are 58,758 souls in this district. They are chiefly to be found in the parganahs of Etah and Marehra; they hold zamíndárí in this district, and are old inhabitants. There are six sub-divisions of caste amongst them, viz., Pataria, Mathuria, Sankallajaria, Lakhia, Kharia, and Pania. The Pataria caste abounds in Etah, and came from the west—the districts of Aligaṛh and Dehli. Atranjí-kherah is an ancient seat of the Lodhas. Lodhas are said to have come from the hills.

Thakurs.—Of these there are 53,132. The principal tribe of Thakurs, inhabitants of this country, are Chauhán, Rathors, Solankhí,

Tomars, Kattíar, Bais, Dhakre, Powar, Jadon, Bhatalai (or Bamtalai), Bargújars, Pondair, Goraher, Jaiswar, Kattia, Gor, Kachhwáha, Raghbansí, and Jais.

CHAUHÁN.—These Rajputs or Thakurs trace their origin from the neighbourhood of Sambhar and Ajmír; they came into this district from that quarter and Dehli.

RATHORS.—This is a very old tribe of the Thakurs.

SOLANKHÍS.—They first came into this district from Gujrát, some say Tonk.

SONKHÍS.—A branch of the Solankhís, and are to be found in Eklehra and Garhía.

TOMARS.—The famous Pandús are said to have been of the Tomar caste. Their original country was Hastnapúr, Indar Prast, or Dehli.

KATTÍARS.—They are only to be found in Parganah Azimnagar, and they came into this part of the country from Jallandhar.

KATTIAS.—They are only to be found in Parganah Azimnagar. They came likewise from Jallandhar.

BAIS.—They are to be found only in Parganah Nidhpúr. They say that they came from Daondía Khera, in Baiswara (Oudh), and belong to the royal race.

DHAKRAIS.—A tribe of Rajputs who are now to be found in Mauzahs Súndrain and Meholí, Parganah Nidhpúr.

PANARIRS.—They are to be found in Parganah Azimnagar.

JADÚNS.—The Raja of Awa and the Zamíndár of Rústamgaṛh are of this tribe. The Raja of Awa holds zamíndárí in Parganahs Marehra, Etah, Sonhar, Azimnagar, Patialí, and Soron.

BHATAILIAS.—They are to be found in Mauzah Mogarra Tatyí, Parganah Nidhpúr. They came from across the Ganges.

BARGÚJARS.—They are to be found in Ujhaipúr and Nandgáon, in Parganah Sakkít.

PUNDÍRS.—They are said to have come from Hardwar some 1100 years ago, and hold zamíndárí in the Balgram Parganah, Tehsíl Kassganj, Ulayí Khass, Indrayí, and Jaitpúra.

GARHAHERS, OR GAURAHERS.—An obscure tribe of the Rajputs found in the Parganahs of Pachlana, Badria, and Bilram. They are said to have come from Ajmír some 225 years ago.

JAISWAR, or JAIS are to be found only in Parganah Azimnagar, and they are stated to have come from Jaisalmír or Jagnair, while Sir H. Elliot mentions they came from Kasba Jais, in Oudh.

GAURS.—A royal race of Rajputs—the ancient Kings of Bengal were of the Gaur caste. They came from the east of Kashí (Benares). Barhola and Sanorí are their zamíndárí villages. They are sub-divided into Bhat Gaur, Brahman Gaur, and Chamár Gaur. Barhola zamíndárs are Brahman Gaurs, while the Barona zamíndárs are Chamár Gaurs.

KACHHWÁHAS.—Akbarpúr, Tamraura, and Sikandarpúr are the abode of Kachhwáha Thakurs.

RAJBANSÍS.—To be found in Nidhpúr Parganah.

BRAHMANS.—There are 53,132 souls, principally Sanadhs.

KACHÍS.—They are sub-divided into Kanaujia, Hardía, and Suksena.

GADARÍAS.—Of these there are 21,479.

BANNIAHS.—Of these, 15,412 are in this district.

MAHAJANS.—There are 12,907.

KISAUNS.—There are 11,966.

BARHYÍS.—They are probably aborigines.

KAISTHS OR KAITHS.—The Suksenas are original inhabitants of Sankesah, near Serai Agath, in this district, and this district may be said to be their native country. Other sub-divisions are—

KULSHIRISTS.—From Oudh, thence to Jallaisar and Shekoabad, and in this district.

SRÍBASTAMS.—Came from Oudh, Khairabad, and Gonda. Sríbastam Suksena, and Kulshirist hold zamíndárí.

C. H. T. CROSTHWAITE, *Deputy Collector.*

JALAUN.

The principal castes of this district are:—1, Kachhwáha Rajputs; 2, Senghar Rajputs; 3, Gújars; 4, Kúrmís; 5, Brahmans; 6, Mahratta Pandits.

The Kúrmís hold 107 villages.

Next in this district come the Brahmans: they hold 198 villages; the Gújar caste have 105 villages; the Kachhwáha Thakurs hold 84 villages; and the Senghars 62 villages.

It will be remarked that, though this district is considered in Bundelkhand, yet the Búndelá clan only have three villages.

KACHHWÁHA THAKURS.—The Kachhwáha Thakurs, who inhabit the north-western part of the district, situated on the banks of the Pahuj and Jumna, are represented by the Raja Mansingh, of Rámpúr. A branch of the same clan is the Raja of Gopalpúr, another *jaghírdar*. The Raja of Sikrí is also of the same clan.

SENGHAR RAJPUTS.—The Senghar clan holds many villages in the north-eastern part of the district, near the banks of the Jumna. Their representative is the Raja of Jaggammanpúr.

GÚJARS.—The Gújars state they came from the west of India. The principal Gújar families are Dhantolí, Hardoí, and Babye; but none are of any note, or hold large estates.

MAHRATTA PANDITS.—The first appearance in these parts of the Mahratta Pandits was on cession to the Peshwah in A.D. 1726, by Chattersal, of a large tract of land containing 3,481 villages, given in payment of assistance rendered against the Nawab of Farrakhabad, who had invaded this part of the country.

KÚRMÍS.—The Kúrmís, although playing a most important part as agriculturists, hold no influential position. The same remark as to position applies to Ahírs, and all the inferior castes. A native tradition exists that this district, anterior to the conquest by Chattersal Búndelá, was entirely held by the Meo caste, an inferior clan of Rajputs.

A. H. TERNAN, LT.-COL., *Deputy Commissioner.*

JHANSI.

Very little can be said in this district on the subject regarding which the Board have called for information. There are no records or *sannads* extant, and, as a rule, the people have no traditions of their own histories. There are no large colonies of Rajputs or other well-known castes, and no tract or portion of the district is occupied by any one particular tribe. Here and there may be found the scattered members of the same family, but with very few exceptions there is no one family holding more than two or three villages.

There have never been any inducements to settle in this part of the country. There are, indeed, signs of its having been a prosperous and well-populated country in the time of the Chandels; but since their expulsion (probably about 850 years ago) the country has been overrun and held by different conquerors, and the people have been badly governed, and were, when the English took possession of the district, very much reduced in numbers, and generally wretchedly poor.

The castes which exist in the greatest numbers in this district stand, as regards numbers, in the following order:—

1.	Brahmans	46,818
2.	Chamars	36,566
3.	Kachhís	31,772
4.	Koerís and Khushtahs	24,202
5.	Ahírs	23,274
6.	Rajputs	15,847
7.	Garereahs	15,232
8.	Kurmís	13,150
9.	Bundelas	10,507
10.	Lodhís	10,420
11.	Kangars	8,592
12.	Kayaths	7,889

SAHEREAHS.—These people are said to be Gonds; they live in the jungles in the southern part of the district: they are no doubt the aborigines of this part of the country. They are very wild in their habits, and look more like monkeys than men. They have no traditions, and can give no information about themselves.

CHANDELS (Rajputs).—These number only ninety-four in this district.

KANGARS.—These people are said to be one of the many castes who owe their origin to Bishwa Karma, a Brahman, and Ganashí, a woman of low caste. They say that they settled here about 650 years ago, but this is not at all certain. It is most probable that, taking advantage of the misrule and disorder which prevailed after the great victory gained by Pirthí Raj over the Chandels, they invaded and took possession of a large portion of this district; for when the Bundelas came they found the Kangars rulers of nearly all the tract of country which lies between the Dassan Naddí and the River Pahuj. They had in those days their capital at a place called Kurar, about seventeen miles from Jhansi. They are like the Bhars in the Jaunpur, Benares, and Mirzapur Districts, who also were rulers once of that part of the country—the thieves and chaukídars of the district.

BUNDELAS.—These men, as well as those of the Dhandelas and Ponwar castes, are spurious Rajputs. They are sprung from the Gaharwars, one of the thirty-six Rajput tribes. They came from Kantit and Khairaghar in the Mirzapúr District. They were probably forced to emigrate and come westwards by the pressure caused by the Mahomedan invasion of the Doáb and Oudh, and the colonization of Oudh and the Jaunpur, Azimgarh, and Benares Districts by the Rajputs, who were driven eastwards by the Mahomedans. They conquered Bundelkhand at the commencement, I believe, of the thirteenth century, but it is impossible to fix the exact date.

Dhandelás (spurious Rajputs) —I have not been able to find out how or when they lost caste. They intermarry with the Búndelás and Ponwars. They say that they settled here 700 years ago, and that they are descended from Dhandhú, one of the officers in the army of Pirthí Raj. There are only 353 of them in this district.

Ponwars (spurious Rajputs: see above).—They settled here after the conquest of the country by the Búndelás, about 400 years ago.

Parihárs (Rajputs).—The head of this family lives at Jigní—an independent State on the right bank of the Dassan river—and the clan hold twenty-seven villages in this and the Hamírpur District, and in adjoining Native States. Those in this district are descended from Gobindeo and Sarangdeo, the grandsons of the head of the family, Raja Júǰhar Singh. They were here long before the Búndelá conquest, probably in the time of the Chandels. They came no doubt from Marwar, of which country the Parihárs were in possession up to the commencement of the twelfth century.

Khattís (Rajputs).—There are now only sixty-five of this tribe in this district.

Saingar (Rajput).—These number 409. They came from Jagmohanpúr, on the Jumna, about 300 years ago.

Bais (Rajputs).—These number 710. They came from Dúndea Khera in Oudh. Like all other Bais, they state they are true Tilok Chandí Bais, and are descended from the great Raja Salbahan, the conqueror of Raja Bikramajít, of Ujjain. They settled here probably at the close of the fifteenth, or at the commencement of the sixteenth, century.

Gaur (Rajputs).—Say they came from Indurkhí, Scindiah's territory (formerly in the Jalaun District), 300 years ago.

Dhangís.—These men assert they are descended from Lav, one of the sons of Raja Ramchand, and that they came here from Narwar, in Scindiah's territory, 900 years ago.

Marwarís.—These are the money-lenders in this district.

Gújars.—This tribe numbers in this district 3,860.

Koerís and Khushtahs.—These are the weavers in this part of the country. They are in great numbers in the towns of Mau, Erick, Gúrserai, and Bhandere. They number 24,202. The Koerís came, so they say, from Benares some 700 years ago, and the Khushtahs from Chandairí (a place renowned for its silk manufactures) 600 years ago; but I do not think it likely that they have been here so long. The Koerís make *Kharúa* and other cotton goods, while the Khushtahs make silk articles only. The Koerís assert that they are descended from Bishwa Karma, a Brahman, and Ganashí, a woman of inferior caste.

Játs.—The number of this tribe in this district is 350. They say that their ancestor was born from the matted hair *(jaṭá)* of Mahadeo —hence their name. They settled in this district about 700 years ago, and came from Gohad, a place in Scindiah's territory, about twenty-five miles north-east of Gwalior.

Kurmís.—These people state that they emigrated from the south 1200 years ago.

Lodhís say they came from Narwar, in Scindiah's territory, 1000 years ago. They have a tradition that they originally came from Lúdianá, in the Panjáb.

Kachhís.—These people also assert that they came from Narwar 1000 years ago. They claim descent from the Kachhwáha Rajputs.

It is a matter of great difficulty—indeed, it is next to impossible—to trace out the origin of the numerous castes and sub-divisions of castes; but it will be found that there were two great causes which led to these sub-divisions,—the one, the marriages of men of higher with women of inferior caste; and the second, the adoption by some member of the family of a particular profession. Originally there were very few castes; but caste in India became a social usage, and anyone becoming an outcast, or withdrawing himself from his own caste, found himself compelled to institute a new caste or sub-division of caste. Thus the Kachhís ascribe their origin to the union of a Rajput and a woman of a lower caste. The Koerís and the Khangars claim descent from Bishwa Karma, a Brahman, and Ganashí, a woman of low caste.

The Garereahs take their name from their occupation—*gádar* (गडार) being the Hindí for sheep. So also do the Lohars, Sonars, Chípás, Mochís, Baraies, Chamars, and Rangrez. The Ahírs are divided into two castes (there are, I believe, no Yadbansís here)—the Nand Bans and the Guala. The Nand Bans, again, have several sub-divisions. The Guálás are named after their ancestor, Guál, who some say was a Bakal; at any rate the Nand Bans Ahírs look down upon the Guálás. The Ahírs came from Muthra, and derive their names from *ahi* (अहि), the Sanskrit for serpent. They say they had an ancestor called Hír, who used to be on good terms with serpents and snakes, and used to give them milk to drink. The origin of this tribe is not, I believe, known.

E. G. JENKINSON, *Deputy Commissioner*.

LALLATPUR.

BRAHMANS.—It is not known when the Brahmans first settled in this district, but it is supposed that a sect called Jagjotia came from the eastern regions of Kanauj; they are said to have been descended from the family of Kanauj Brahmans. Raja Jújanat, of Bundelkhand, sent for thirteen Brahmans from Kanauj and settled them in his country, whence this sect had its origin, and took the appellation Jagjotia. These Jagjotias are also known under several names, such as Panday, Dúbai, Súkal, Tewary, Pathak, Chaube, Díabat, Misser, etc. When Rama (the god incarnate among the Hindus) returned to Oudh (Ajodhia), his country, having killed his inveterate foe, Rávana, King of Ceylon (Lanká), his countrymen refused to take gifts from his hands on account of his having slain the said Rávana, a Brahman. Rama in consequence brought some boys from the Muthra School and gave them gifts of lands, and from their descendants the Sonadh sect took its origin. The tribe Bhagaur is descended from the family of Bhirgu Muni (monk) and Gaur. They are scarce in this part of the country. Came from a place of the same name, formerly the capital of Bengal.

BÚNDELÁ.—This tribe has its origin from the Chattrí family, commonly known as Kashesar Gairwara Rajputs. As an endowment from Daibí they, under the name of Búndelá, took possession of this country, and hence from their time this province is termed "Bundelkhand."

Their customs differing from others, they messed apart and formed a separate sect. They first emigrated from Benares and came and settled at Urcha, and thence their head subdued Barr (a village in Lallatpúr District), and resided there.

Ahírs.—The exact time of the Ahírs settling in this country is uncertain: it was about 400 or 500 years ago. They are known under several names at different places, such as Kamaria, Nagal, Bhalia, Boyla, Pachlara, Bangnah, Tar, Thanga, Salkhya, Gairwa, Rewrah, Thanik, Khaisar, Nata, Tilwar, Khandelah, Gotaylah, Pattaylah, and others; and all these different sects take their food together.

Lodhí.—About 300 or 400 years ago this tribe came from the northern climes and settled themselves in these parts. They are said to be the original race.

Kachhís.—The original advent of this tribe cannot be traced. This caste consists of four principal sects—viz., Kachhwáha, Salloria, Hardia, and Amwar,—named from the places whence they came.

Banniah.—This tribe came to this district from Marwar about 400 or 500 years ago. They are of two sects, viz., Parwar and Banikawal. The former is the more numerous. The Banikawal sect sprung from the Parwars, from whom they separated themselves. The Banikawal race seem to be the illegitimate descendants of the Parwars.

BANDA.

As far as I have been able to discover, it appears tolerably certain that the original inhabitants of the district were the tribes now generally known as Kols, Bhíls, Khonds, and Gonds. By the incursions of other tribes these have been by degrees relegated to the hilly parts of the country, and now are to be found, in this district at least, only in the hills of Parganahs Tirohan, Chibú, and Badausa.

They differ, of course, in almost every respect from the inhabitants of the plains, but are somewhat civilized and engaged in agricultural pursuits. Their way of living is of necessity in general wild in the extreme: from poverty, they go about almost naked, and, though nominally Hindus, yet have not the smallest hesitation in eating any animal or bird they may catch. They very little differ from the other wild tribes of India.

They would seem to have been driven from their homes many centuries ago by the incursions of the warrior tribes of Rujputs, who eventually took full possession of the country, and who now, under various names, form the majority of the proprietors of the soil of this district. Here they are known by the generic name of Rajput Búndelás, or, in common parlance, as simply Thakurs.

Their principal tribes here are the Súrkí, Rathor, Tekan, Bilkait, Kachhwáha, Ḍikhit, with a few Bais Thakurs, etc.

The Rajput Búndelás differ in many important respects from their fellow tribes—men of the Doáb and other parts of northern India. They do not intermarry with them, dress differently, have a different way of shaving their heads, and also do not disdain personally to engage in agricultural pursuits.

In the train of the Rajputs, the tribes now known as Bundelkhandí Brahmans entered and settled in the district.

Like the Rajputs, the Bundela Brahmans differ considerably from the Brahmans of the Doab in habits and costumes, as well as in language.

In the parganah of Tirohan there is a considerable number of Mahrattas, settled there by Omrit Rao, of Púna. They form a community by themselves.

W. R. Burkitt, *Officiating Collector.*

MIRZAPUR.

TEHSÍLDAR OF HAZÚR TEHSÍL.

Brahmans, Chattrís, Gautams, and Kaseras are the prevalent castes who have settled in this district. Mirzapúr is in the midst of Benares and Allahabad, and is close to Bindachal. As these are places for Hindu worship, the Brahmans, Chattrís, and Gautams have settled in great numbers. The reason of the Kaseras settling in great numbers is that the trade of brass and copper pots, etc., is actively carried on in this district. All the Kaseras here manufacture brass pots, etc., and despatch their articles of commodity to distant stations for sale.

Gautams have sprung up from Misr Brahmans, and Bhurtias from Gújars.

In this tehsíldarí there are no other castes except Gautams residing in Talúḳa Majhwa, and Bhurtias in Tappeh Opraudh, who took their origin from the chief castes. The Gautams were originally Sarwaria Misrs, the most of whom, with a view to show their pomp and splendor on being *iláḳadars*, commenced smoking *húkah*, and consequently the rest of their brethren discontinued eating and drinking with them. These Gautams being thus excommunicated, commenced intermarriages with Bhúínhárs, who settled in the eastern districts, and since then this tribe is increasing.

As these Gautams sprung up from Misrs, who had their *gotra*, or family title, Gautam, they became known by that appellation.

The Bhurtias who inhabited Tappeh Opraudh originally sprung up from Gújars, who were residents of Guzerat. Owing to Guzerat being thickly populated, they abandoned their native place and emigrated to Tappeh Opraudh, of this district, and here they assumed the title of Bhurtias, by which name they are now known, and forsook their primary title, Gújars.

TEHSÍLDAR OF CHUNAR.

Kúnbís have settled within the jurisdiction of this tehsíl in great numbers. It appears they first came from Jainagar and other places in the east, and entered in the service of the Bijaipúr Raja; but when their numbers increased, most of them emigrated here, and became zamíndárs. Among them one Ujaib Singh was a man of great influence, who invited others of his tribe from his native land to settle with him. The Kúnbís are more numerous here; most of them are kashtkars and few as zamíndárs.

Most of the Brahmans who are residing here emigrated from Sarwar; the rest from other localities. Some settled here to earn their livelihood by their own profession, *panditai* (priesthood), and others to obtain *Krishnarpan*, and a few others came along with their relations and settled here. Now Brahmans have become very numerous here: most of them hold zamíndárí and kashtkarí tenures.

Of the Bhuínhárs, Gautams, etc., who reside here, some came in search of employment, others settled as zamíndárs and kashtkars, and some came along with their relations from the Benares and Azimgaṛh Districts.

Chattrís are said to have emigrated from the various localities of the east—some from Garh Chittor, and some from Sausopur, close to Naddí Poshkar, and other places. They came in search of employment, and settled here. Now most of them are kashtkars and zamíndars.

There are no tribes within the jurisdiction of this tehsíldarí who have in course of time formed themselves into various sub-divisions, and eventually lost their primary castes. Among the Kunbís there are ramifications, but they are not very numerous. These sub-divisions are quite distinct from the beginning, and have undergone no change except this,—that those who came from Jainagar have commenced ploughing the land with their own hands, and making re-marriages (*sagai*), which they never did before. The Kúnbís who reside in Jainagar do not eat and drink with those that have settled here. Nothing can be known regarding the origin and position of this tribe; hence it has been concluded that they belong to very low caste. They received promotion in the service of the Setara Rajah, where, having accumulated wealth and possessed *iláḳas*, they reckoned themselves among the high castes.

There are various classes among the Brahmans from the beginning. The real fact regarding them is this,—that the Brahmans are the earliest inhabitants of Kanauj, three of whom at first emigrated into Sarwar; since that time the Sarwars became famous and highly esteemed. From these three sprung up thirteen, which made the total sixteen; and from the latter started up three and a half more, making the aggregate number nineteen and a half, which, by gradually increasing, reached to 125,000 in number—each of which was reckoned a separate clan. The reason of their being divided into numerous sects is this, that each of them assumed his family title from the name of the village he at first settled in, and is consequently known by that name. Most of the Brahmans who emigrated from Sarwar having commenced taking *dan* (charity), and acting as priests, are permitted to eat and drink and to have inter-marriages with those Brahmans only who follow the same profession here. The Brahmans who are residing in Sarwar abstain from eating and drinking with those settled here.

There are several sub-divisions among the Bhuínhars. They are the descendants of Ujach Brahmans. In this country the Ujach Brahmans are called Chitpawon. In other countries the Ujach Brahmans are known by different denominations. The Brahmans have *gotras*, which they have assumed from the Rishis from whom they have sprung up; for instance, Gautambans, who are said to be offsprings of Kithu Misr, who descended from Gautam Ujach Brahman, Kripa Charje family. There is no distinction between them and the other Brahmans besides this,—that the former carry arms and lead a military life, and consequently they have assumed the title of "Singh," and have forsaken eating with other Brahmans. Owing to their title of "Singh" being celebrated, their original titles of Misr, Gond, Opadhia, etc., have fallen into disuetude. Still up to this day in some places they are known by their old titles.

Chattrís also from the beginning have various sub-divisions. Like the Brahmans, they were enumerated into 125,000 sects, which still exist, only their original titles are now changed in some respects.

In Parganah Karíat Síkhar there are numerous Chattrís whose ancestors are said to have emigrated from Sausonpur, close to Naddí Poshkar, in the east, in search of employment. They were originally known in their native country by the appellation of Chamargaur. Since they arrived here, owing to their being the former inhabitants of Sausonpur, they are known as Sonepurwar, which has now been abbreviated into Sarwar.

Within the jurisdiction of this tehsíldarí, Brahmans, Chattrís, Bhúínhárs, and Kúnbís are more renowned.

TEHSÍLDAR OF ROBERTSGANGE.

In times of yore, when Balind was reigning over these parts, Kols, Kharwars, Majhwars, and Chamars were the prevalent tribes who settled there, and Brahmans and Kúnbís were very few. Since the Chandels obtained possession of the kingdom, the Sarwaria Brahmans came from Gorakhpúr and Hussainpúr, in the district of Shahabad; and Kúnbís from the latter place and Parganah Bhoelí, of this district, and, being well received by the Chandels, settled here. These classes of men are still found here in great numbers.

In Parganah Singraulí, the Rajas of Singraulí, including their relations, were known as "Kharwars" formerly; but since they ruled over that part of the country they assumed the title of Benbans Chattrí. Those Chandels, Baghails, and Kharwars who emigrated there from other places, owing to their having intermarriages with the Raja of Singraulí, were excommunicated from the castes they originally belonged to, and consequently they have now no connection with them.

TEHSÍLDAR OF KERA MANGRORE.

Ahírs are reckoned among Sudras. They subsist upon milk and curds; they prefer settling close to mountains and valleys, on account of their having ample pasturage there for their large herds of cattle. There are various ramifications in this caste, but here we have only Dhandúr and Gowals.

Kharwars appear to have settled in these mountain tracts from a considerable time. There are various sub-divisions among this caste, which are known as Rajwars, Kharwars, Chero, Manjhís, etc. Some of these sub-divisions think themselves equal, some superior, and some inferior, to the others. Almost all these tribes are found to be upright and honest men. They seem to have sprung up from Níkhad, a primitive race. They are generally of dark complexion; their voice and features are unlike those of other tribes who inhabit these parts.

Chamárs include themselves among the Hindus. There was once among them a man known by the appellation of Raidoss Bhagat, a pious devotee and well-behaved man, and, as he was remarkable for his principles, all the Chamárs take a pride in calling themselves Raidoss, and pretend to be the descendants of that personage, in order to share in the celebrity he had attained. They generally live upon carcasses of animals, and as they deal in leather and skins, which in Hindí are called *chamra*, they have derived their title of Chamár from their profession.

The Brahmans are said to be the aborigines of Kanauj, from whence a portion of them emigrated to Sirwar and several other places. Among them there are two sects, Ghatkarma and Paikarma, who inhabit the southern districts of India. They procure their livelihood by priesthood, agriculture, and other occupations in this parganah.

Almost all the villages in this parganah are populated by Rajputs. Kunbís are comparatively fewer here than elsewhere. Most of them have the honorary distinction of Singh affixed to their names, like the Chattrís. Somewhere they are reckoned among Sudras, *i.e.*, lower caste.

Koerís cultivate the land and deal in vegetables. Koerís and Kunbís are acquainted with the principles of agriculture.

This parganah is very thinly peopled with Kahars and Hajjáms (barbers).

In certain villages and markets Lohars, Barahís, Mochís, Banneahs, etc., are inhabited.

There are two tribes of Gaharwárs here, viz., Hindu and Musulman.

TEHSÍLDAR OF KONRH.

From enquiry it appears that among the high castes Brahmans have settled here in great numbers. It seems that they came and settled here before the reign of Shahabu'd-dín Gorí. As this parganah is in the centre of Benares and Allahabad, and close to Bindachal, which are all notable places for Hindu worship, the Brahmans leaving their native countries—viz., Sarwar, Kanauj, etc.—came and settled here. When the Bhars ruled over this country, they began to treat their subjects with tyranny and oppression, so much so that they forcibly abducted Brahmaní women. One of the oppressed Brahmans went to complain to Raja Ram, a Maunas, who then came from Umargarh, taking his family along with him on a pilgrimage to Allahabad. This said Maunas, on hearing the grievances of the injured Brahman, took his retinue, and, marching *viá* Sarai Jangau road, came up to Rajpúra, where the Bhars were then residing, and fought a battle with them. After a serious conflict the Maunas' party was victorious, and the Bhars were totally routed. No trace is now found of them in this parganah. The few that still exist are quite unknown; they earn their livelihood by labor, and have now mixed themselves with the Passís.

The Maunases then became owners of the country for a period of 250 years. Subsequently, when Mahárája Balwant Singh obtained possession and governed the country, Chattrís of various sects, such as Baghails, Rajkúmars, Bais, Gaharwárs, Bísains, Nanwogs, etc., in order to have an interview with the Maharaja, and in consideration of the relationships which existed between them and the Maunases, came and settled here. In the Census taken in 1865, Brahmans of all kinds in Parganah Bhadohí were counted 64,469; Chattrís of various sects, 17,119. Among the lower castes, Ahírs were reckoned 34,539; Chamárs, 29,117; Kewots, 14,897. Mahomedans and other castes are very few in the parganah. This parganah is more thickly populated since 150 years, owing to the Mahárája Balwant Singh granting lands to new settlers, for cultivation and for planting gardens.

The above castes still retain their primary character, and have undergone no change.

There is a sect of Chattrís Maunas styled Bahádurs, who reside in Mauzah Túlapur, and another sect, said to be the offspring of Hardas, who live in Mauzah Múr and other villages. These differ somewhat in their origin. The tradition extant regarding them is that there was a king known by the name of Jodh Rai among the Maunas, who brought a handsome young Ahírin from Kantit and made her over to one of his dependants, a Bais Chattrí, by whom she had two children, Lalla and Bahadur, who became very strong and able-bodied men. As they set up a pole in Jodh Rai's tank, which others failed to do, they were rewarded with the honorary distinction of Bahádur for their meritorious achievement.

Now their descendants are allowed to have intermarriages, and to eat and drink with other classes of Chattrís.

This is the story current regarding Hardas, that there was a man known by the name of Pargasroy among the Maunas tribe, who found a newly-born male child in a pond, and brought him home and supported him, and named him Hardas. When he arrived at maturity, he was married by Pargasroy, and joined in his own clan. Now their descendants are celebrated as Maunas, and they have free intercourse and relationship with other sects of Chattrís.

There is a sect of Ditchit Bhuínhars inhabiting Mauzahs Sudhway, etc. Most of them among this class still retain their primary character, and make intermarriages among their own clan : and some of them following the manners and customs of the Sarwaria Brahmans, have mixed with them.

AJMÍR.

Of the Mhairs and Mhairats, the original settlers in the whole of the Mhairwárah tract, and of whom, as being our peculiar and prevalent class, I will give as full an account as possible, we have only the tradition of their Bháts to depend upon. Colonel Hall, who was the first British officer who had any direct dealing with these tribes, took great pains to ascertain the origin of their race from narratives furnished by themselves. All circumstances so elicited have been recorded by the late Commissioner, Colonel Dixon, in his sketch of Mhairwarah, and I cannot do better than give in a condensed form the tradition of these peoples' origin as recorded by that officer in his sketch. He says, "Of the inhabitants of the Magrá or hilly tracts previous to the time from which the present Mhairs date their origin, little seems to be known. It must have been a vast, impenetrable jungle, a refuge for all who had fled from the laws of their country, or had been ejected from castes by their brethren: all these, on seeking the protection of the banditti of the hills were received as brethren. Hence arose the extraordinary melange, dignified by the name of religion, at present professed by the Mhairs and Mhairats. The Chandela Gujars were said to have inhabited the hills in the neighbourhood of the ancient village of Chang, while the caste of Bhatí Rajputs were located in Búrwah, and the hills near Kallinjar, Saroth, and Bhairlan were inhabited by Brahmans. Further to the south-west, Barár and Chetanin, the Todgarh Parganah, were peopled by Daímahs and Dakal Mínahs.

"The Mhairs claim descent from Pirthíraj Chauhan, who reigned in Ajmír early in the twelfth century; he was brother to Khandai Rao, King of Dehli. These two brothers, with other Indian princes, defeated the Afghan invader, Mahomed Ghorí, at the village of Siraurí, on the banks of the Saraswatí, about eighty miles from Dehli. The Afghan army was completely routed, and he marched out of Hindustan. In two years, however, he returned with a large army, and in a contest the Hindus were defeated. Khandai Rao, King of Dehli, was killed, and Pirthí Raj taken prisoner and put to death. Mahomed Ghorí, however, placed Pirthí Raj's son, by name Gola, upon the throne of Ajmír. Pirthí Raj, while reigning at Ajmír, attacked the city of Bundí, then inhabited by the caste of Harra Rajputs, and carried off a girl of the caste of Asawárí Mínehs, by name Sehdeo, and gave her to his son, Jodh-lakhan, by whom she had two sons, named Anhal and Anup. Jodh-lakhan supposed his partner to have been of pure caste until his two sons were reaching manhood. He one night questioned Sehdeo as to her caste, and, when told she was a Míní, his indignation was great, and he turned Sehdeo with her two sons out of his house. The mother and sons went to Chang, in Mhairwárah, and were received kindly by the Chandela Gujars. For five generations the descendants of Anhal and Anup resided at Chang, and are reported to have eventually exterminated the Gujars.

"In the fifth generation, two brothers were born in the family of Anhal, called Kanha and Kála, and from them arose two great castes of Bar and Chítah. Kanha and Kála, though sole masters of Chang, could find no one willing to marry with their children: their progeny were therefore obliged to intermarry amongst themselves, and soon became numerous and powerful. Kála went to Kalwára, in Mewar, and Kanha remained at Chang, and his male descendants began to marry indiscriminately with any woman opportunity threw in their way. Thus Míní, Bhílnís, Dakal Mínís, and others became Mhair matrons. The clan of Chítahs flourished, and from the descendants of Kanha sprung the twenty-four clans of Mhairs, comprehended under the general distinguishing title of Chítah; while the progeny of Kála also formed twenty-four septs, under the common denomination of Bar.

"These forty-eight clans of Mhairs originally professed the Hindu religion. A large family of Mhairats profess the Mahomedan religion.

"We have also castes of Motís and Dakal Mhairs. Of their origin, the following tradition is related:—Bhairlan is shown to have originally been inhabited by Brahmans, and this district had been a thoroughfare for Banjars. It is affirmed that a Banjara woman went to the cell ot a certain Bairagí, who lived in a cave in a mountain, since called Mokat, where she was delivered of twin boys. She declared Rughdass, the Bairagí, to be their father. He was very indignant, and turned her and her children adrift. She was received and sheltered by a Brahman, where she remained a considerable time. The twin brothers, when old enough, were employed by the Brahman to tend his cows at graze. It is related that these boys killed one or more of the sacred cows. The old Brahman was so enraged that he drove the mother and sons out of the place. In the fifth generation of the progeny of these boys, one Mokat was born, who, having conceived a hatred of the Brahmans of Bhairlan for their treatment of his progenitors, waged war against them, massacred nearly all of them, and himself took the district of Bhairlan. This individual is still much venerated by the Mhairs, and the mountain where the Banjaran brought forth the twin founders of his race was named Mokat, after him. He is worshipped especially by the Motís who still inhabit the Bhairlan district. A Brahman who escaped the above slaughter in Bhairlan fled to the village of Barár, then inhabited by Dakal Mínas. He threw aside his caste, and took a girl of the Míní caste as a wife, from whom have sprung eventually the several clans of Dakal Mhair now extant."

I think there can be little doubt that our Mhairs and Mhairats all originally sprung from Rajputs, who from various causes had to seek shelter in the hills. Even to this day the physique of these men closely resembles that of the Rajputs: they are a tall, stout, handsome, and well-made race of men, quite different to the general race of small hill men, such as the Bhíls, etc.

MAJOR A. G. DAVIDSON, *Deputy Commissioner*.

ALLAHABAD.

All enquiry shows that the civilization of this district, and its reclamation from the primitive jungle, was of comparatively recent date—that is, within 450 years. Very few of the Mahomedans claim descent from the followers of Shahábu'd-dín; but few Hindus trace back beyond the reign of Jaichand of Kanauj, whose followers, when defeated by Shahabu'd-dín, populated a portion of this district; but almost all state that their ancestors took possession of those jungly tracts which form their present estates within the period I have mentioned.

East of the Ganges and south of the Jumna the aboriginal ruling race were the Bhars. East of the Ganges no trace of them remains: they were swept away by Hindus from Oudh, by Mahomedan hordes from the north-west, and were finally extirpated in an invasion by the King of Jaunpúr. The invaders seized the Bhar forts, and appropriated the adjoining jungle country, which they speedily partially cleared and populated. The limits of these several conquests can be clearly traced in the talukas existing to this day, and each is mainly inhabited by the direct descendants of the successful invaders.

These have no traditions of further invasion or conquest: they appear to have settled down, and to have remained undisturbed until our times. Perhaps this fact may make their accounts of their remote origin more reliable than they would otherwise appear to be. They escaped those vicissitudes of existence which weaken all family traditions.

North of the Ganges, but little more is heard of the Bhars. There are two reports of the fate of this race—one, that they were almost all cut off by the Jaunpur invaders; the other, that they fled to the east, and received some territory from the neighbouring chiefs (whoever they were) in the Badhoe parganahs. Several bazaars and villages bear the name of the last and greatest Bhar king, the Raja Lílí.

Remains of old Bhar forts and towns are not uncommon in the parganah of Kairagaṛh, south of the Tonse river. This is a wild jungly country, where the Bhars probably remained undisturbed long after they were expelled from the more civilized tracts. They were finally extirpated or driven from these tracts by the ancestors of the present Manda Rajah. There were Bhars also in the Arial and Barah parganahs, but they were dispossessed by Chattrí Hindus from the northern districts of Hindustan, followers and soldiers of the Mahomedan invaders.

Three influential local castes or clans claim an admixture of Bhar blood. These are the Bharors, Garhors, and Tikaits. The two former are not numerous or influential; they are landed proprietors in the southern portions of this district, and appear to be a connecting link between the higher castes, who are generally landed proprietors, and those inferior castes whose lot is servitude.

The Tikaits are numerous, and possess much influence; they are descended from one of the three Chauhán leaders under a Bhar chieftain.

One of these Chauháns carried off his chief's daughter. The descendants from this mixed alliance are Tikaits, and are still proprietors of a portion of that Bhar chief's possessions.

Their relatives, descended from the other two Chauhán chiefs, without the Bhar cross, are Karaits and Pataits. These are simply Chauháns; the origin of their surname is untraceable.

Of Hindu tribes the higher classes all, without exception, claim their descent from Oudh or the northern provinces of Hindustan. Their emigration to this district was in most instances of comparatively recent date; and the cause of their coming was almost always the same,—they were soldiers or adventurers.

Thákurs, Chauhans, and Chattrís are the generic names which include all the various sub-divisions of these Hindu colonists. These are the warrior castes which in former days composed all native armies. The heads of all these clans commanded their own men in the armies of Hindu invaders, or were refugees from the early Mahomedan conquerors, or, in later days, followers of their fortunes. Each clan seems to have settled in its allotted portion of the conquered country, and the ancient limits of each portion are still pretty accurately defined.

Those who claim consanguinity with the Oudh tribes are naturally to be found in the trans-Ganges parganahs, which formed a portion of the Nawábi territory; those who claim a common ancestry with the Rajputs of Mainpúrí and other tribes in the Upper Doáb districts are to be found in the Doáb parganahs.

The southern parganahs are more sparsely peopled than any other portions of this district; but almost every landed proprietor is of one of the foreign clans or castes, aliens from far-off countries.

The most notable Hindu in the district is the Raja of Manda—a direct descendant of Raja Jaichand, of Kanauj. He is a Chattrí. Raja Jaichand was defeated and killed by Sultan Shahabu'd-dín Ghorí in 1193 A.D. Some of his family and followers fled to these southern districts, and settled in portions of what are now Jaunpur, Benares, Mirzapúr, and Allahabad. These large possessions have dwindled down to the estates now held in this district alone.

Akin to the Manda Raja is the Raja of Dyah: he is of the Garwar clan, an influential sub-division of the Chattrí caste. I believe this is purely a local clan. These are Chandarbansí Chattrís, or descendants from the moon, in contradistinction from the Surajbansís, or descendants from the sun. There is rivalry between these two castes, and I believe they have nothing in common. The Súrajbansís and Chandarbansís are as widely known as Hinduism itself.

South of the Jumna is to be found the only colony of Parehar Rajputs. They came from Mainpurí. They are of that caste who murder their female children; and it is certain they must have adhered to this custom of their clan until a quite recent date. It may be as well to notice here that they have been under constant but unobtrusive supervision for the last twenty-five years; and though they may still at heart cherish their old custom, it is certain they have ceased to practice it, for the recent Census shows that their female children bear a just proportion to their sons.

In their neighbourhood, in the Barah parganah, are some Ban Beis families. The "Beis" proper are Oudh Chattrís. These are of that clan also, and the affix "Ban" is to commemorate the fame of their leader in former days, under whom they exterminated the Bhar and Kol residents of the jungle (*ban*), and took possession of their villages.

The Baghel clan are represented by the Rajah of Barah. He claims a common descent with the Maharajah of Rewah and the Chief of Kotah, from a Gujrát chief, by name Baghardeo, who, in Sambat 606 or 1,300 years ago, was a pilgrim from Gujerat to the Hindu shrines in Northern India. The pilgrimage, according to tradition, was abandoned by this famous chief, who seized on Kirwí, Banda, and the southern portions of this district, which formed the original possessions of one of his sons, from whom the Barah Raja claims his descent. The name of Baghardeo, and the name of the clan "Baghel," have a common derivation in the legend—that this famous warrior chief was fed when a child on a tigress' milk. It is the notion of a savage to prefer this to the more natural food of an infant; but the whole clan take great pride in this quaint tradition. A Baghel may not marry but with a Baghel, under penalty of excommunication. The most notorious gang of dacoits who for three generations has infested the south of this district are of this clan, and this claim of consanguinity with the Rewah Maharajah has ensured their constant protection in his territories: and certainly the savage nature of the prototype of their race has pervaded the acts of these noted robbers. Each of their feats has shown the extremes of craft, treachery, and the meanest cowardice. When armed and in numbers they have murdered the single and unarmed; they have beaten women and killed children.

In Parganah Meh there is a caste called "Tassaiyah," whose cognomen is susceptible of explanation. They were Chattrís of Etawah; and tradition has it that the founder of this clan was sent by Timur Shah to take possession of a tract of country from the Bhars: this was was done, and the name Tassaiyah is a corruption of "*Teg Shahigah*," the sword of the King, explanatory alike of the nature of the mission and its originator.

The Chandel is an out-caste Baghel, excommunicated for having intermarried with a Rajput, and having thus disgraced his tribe.

The Brahman caste are few—Misser, Tawarí, Dúbe, Chaube, Sukul,

Pande, and so forth. These came from Kanauj and other noted Hindu cities, either as followers of the fighting castes or by invitation from Hindu chiefs. There is but one family whose prenomen requires notice and explanation. The Chappan Pande are merely the fifty-six (*chappan*) grandsons of one prolific Brahman in the Karrah parganah.

One numerous and influential clan of Brahman landed proprietors are called Chaudrís. This is generally a title, more than a caste name. They have large possessions on the bank of the Ganges. Their story is that their founder was a saint from Gorakhpúr. In a great strait, a Mahomedan king at Jhusí required the prayers of all pious men. This Brahman's prayers were considered of such efficacy that he received in reward eighty-four villages, still peopled by his descendants; but their loyalty has departed from them, for they are a generation of rebels.

The Kayaths are numerous in Parganah Karrah. They seem to have been the marked recipients of favor from the Mahomedan emperors. The Kanungoships of several parganahs, and other possessions, were given to several families of Dehli Káyaths.

There is one family of Káyaths in Karrah who are apostates to Mahomedanism. This was either to obtain or retain a Kánúngoship. The Kánúngoship is gone, but they are still Mahomedans, though they retain the Káyath customs as far as is compatible with their new religion.

There are a few instances of a compulsory conversion from Hinduism to Mahomedanism. In one family the Mahomedan title of *Mallik* was given to an apostate Tassaiya (Teg Shahigah); the others are called Baghel Mahomedans. The cause of Mallik's conversion was simply imprisonment for non-payment of revenue to Dehli. He never paid, but obtained his freedom by apostacy.

The Baghel Mahomedans are descendants of a Rewah chief, a staunch adherent of Akbar Shah. Akbar Shah, in return for his service, gave the Baghel chief whatever country he could obtain from the Bhars across the Ganges; and the Baghel chief, out of gratitude, apostacised.

G. Ricketts, *Collector.*

APPENDIX D.

INTRODUCTORY NOTE.

As the six districts of Dehli, Gurgaon, Karnal, Hissar, Rohtak and Sirsa, which were included in the N. Western Provinces at the period of the publication of the first edition of Elliot's Glossary, have since been transferred to the Panjáb Government, it has been deemed advisable to append to the present work an outline of the later statistics of these divisions, and at the same time to incorporate a summary of the Panjáb returns, many of which have an important bearing upon the questions discussed in these volumes.

I.—Table of Population.

District.	1. Square Miles.	2. No. of Masonry Dwellings.	3. No. of all other kinds.	4. Sikhs.*	5. Hindus.	6. Mahommedans.	7. Others.	8. Total.†
Dehli	1,227	59,514	108,876	580	438,886	130,645	36,496	608,850
Gurgáon......	2,016	35,664	121,111	130	480,307	216,147	20	696,646
Karnál	2,352	39,701	93,897	9,295	356,305	151,723	93,349	610,927
Hissar	3,540	16,928	93,117	1,812	373,937	102,928	5,882	484,681
Rohtak	1.823	22,736	114,812	257	465,536	71,118	......	536,959
Sirsa	3,116	1,362	41,769	21,525	77,980	82,120	29,125	210,795
Ambala	2,628	29,830	214,172	56,440	689,333	286,874	1,455	1,035,188
Ludianah ...	1,359	13,744	138,190	95,413	219,371	206,603	61,619	583,245
Simla	18	7,830	50	410	24,794	5,175	934	33,995
Jallandhar ...	1,333	25,629	216,948	117,167	318,401	358,427	23	794,764
Hoshiarpur ..	2,086	16,615	191,435	79,413	415,471	317,967	125,917	938,890
Kangra	2,826	442	146,992	1,308	676,893	48,662	35	727,148
Amritsar......	2,036	49,518	204,018	262,639	191,321	502,348	126,672	1,083,514
Sylkote	1,960	11,240	186,245	50,289	218,771	601,959	132,185	1,005,004
Gúrdaspur ...	1,341	9,391	143,375	39,967	249,813	297,083	68,390	655,362
Lahore	3,624	56,797	144,739	118,360	117,301	468,387	82,054	788,902
Ferozpur	2,692	7,315	112,175	160,487	68,406	245,659	73,767	549,253

* Number of Christians in the six districts: Europeans, 1,023; East Indians and other mixed classes, 128; Natives, 1,604; Total, 2,755. The number of Christians in the whole of the Panjáb is: Europeans, 17,938; East Indians, etc., 1,032; Natives, 2,940; Total, 20,919.

† Average inhabitants per square mile 224, over a total of 14,074 square miles, of which 8,216 are cultivated, 4,238 culturable, 1,620 unculturable. For the whole of the Panjáb the average

District.	1. Square Miles.	2. No. of Masonry Dwellings.	3. No. of all other kinds.	4. Sikhs.	5. Hindus.	6. Mahommedans.	7. Others.	8. Total.
Gujeranwala	2,657	26,714	131,209	38,911	104,156	357,550	49,858	550,576
Rawal Pindi	6,216	4,000	71,579	24,355	60,720	621,169	2,815	711,256
Jhílam	3,910	2,647	110,363	......	62,976	434,157	3,794	500,988
Gujrát	1,785	14,588	141,607	20,653	53,174	537,696	4,775	616,347
Shahpur	4,698	12,783	73,766	3,122	53,590	305,507	6,561	368,796
Multan	5,882	18,255	93,539	907	86,989	360,165	22,218	471,509
Jhang	5,712	2,828	72,158	2,994	57,299	270,819	16,899	348,027
Montgomery	5,577	7,255	65,021	12,216	69,805	277,291	......	359,437
Mozaffargarh	3,022	5,578	59,557	2,571	36,748	249,865	6,333	295,547
Dera Ismail Khan	7,096	2,141	82,959	1,587	48,756	338,387	5,901	394,864
Dera Gházi Khan	2,319	4,255	57,884	1,124	38,467	264,527	4,656	308,840
Bannú	3,150	10	60,627	493	26,222	260,550	240	287,547
Peshawar	1,929	4,848	116,608	2,014	27,408	481,447	8,871	523,152
Kohat	2,838	96	28,543	1,837	6,544	136,565	413	145,419
Hazara	3,000	57	74,117	973	18,563	346,112	1,516	367,218

inhabitants per square mile are 184, over a total of 95,768 square miles, of which 32,432 are cultivated, 23,780 culturable, 39,556 unculturable.

District.	Agriculturists.	Non-Agriculturists.	Prevailing Languages.*
Dehli	270,338	338,512	Urdu.
Gurgáon	399,332	297,314	Urdu and Hindi.
Karnál	305,974	304,953	Urdu, corrupted Hindi, Panjabi.
Hissar	351,395	133,286	Urdu, Jalu, Panjabi, Bagari.
Rohtak	315,904	221,055	Urdu.
Sirsa	149,469	61,326	Urdu, Panjabi, Bagari, Bhatti.
Ambala	501,056	534,432	Urdu, Panjabi.
Ludianah	320,633	262,612	Ditto.
Simla	13,466	20,529	Urdu, Pahari.
Jallandhar	407,970	386,794	Urdu, Panjabi.
Hoshairpur	565,983	372,907	Panjabi.
Kangra	521,303	205,845	Urdu, Panjabi, and Lahaoli.
Amritsar	417,747	665,767	Panjabi, Urdu, Persian, and Kashmiri.
Sylkot	433,617	571,387	Panjabi and Hindi.
Gurdaspur	371,581	283,781	Panjabi.
Lahore	279,362	509,540	Urdu, Panjabi, English, Kashmiri, Persian.
Ferozpur	340,842	208,411	Panjabi.
Gujeranwala	213,153	337,423	Urdu, Panjabi.
Rawal Pindi	475,976	235,280	Urdu, Panjabi, Pushtu, Persian, Kashmiri, English, Gujerati.
Jhílam	302,874	198,114	Panjabi dialect of Urdu.
Gujrát	363,664	252,683	Panjabi.
Shahpur	177,781	191,015	English, Urdu, Panjabi.
Multan	196,381	275,120	Urdu, Multani, Panjabi.
Jhang	119,619	228,408	Panjabi.
Montgomery	153,401	206,036	English, Urdu, Panjabi.
Mozaffargarh	205,799	89,748	Panjabi.
Dera Ismail Khán	215,933	178,931	Pushtu, Panjabi.
Dera Ghází Khán	173,420	135,420	Hindustani, Panjabi, Belochi.
Bannú	204,410	83,136	Pushtu, Hindi.
Peshawar	267,736	255,416	Pushtu, Urdu.
Kohat	100,257	45,162	Pushtu, Urdu, Hindi, Persian.
Hazara	267,434	99,784	Panjabi, Hindi, Pushtu.

* **From Hazara to Dera Ismail Khán the hill tribes are the Pattián or Pushtú-speaking race; southwards of Dera Ismail Khán they are Biloch.**

II.—Statement of Native States in Feudal Subordination to the Panjab Government for 1867.

Name of State.	Area in Square Miles.	Estimated Population.	Caste of Ruler.
I.—*States under the management of British Officers.*			
1. Bháwalpúr	2,483	364,582	Daudputra.
2. Chamba	3,216	120,000	Rajput.
3. Pataoda	The area of the Native States in political relation with the Panjáb Government is given approximately at 197,340 square miles; but there are no reliable statistics showing the proportion of the area brought under cultivation or culturable.	6,600	Afghan.
II.—*States not under the management of British Officers.*			
4. Jammu and Kashmír		1,500,000	Rajput.
5. Patiála		1,586,000	Siddhu Jatt.
6. Jínd		311,000	Ditto.
7. Nábha		276,000	Ditto.
8. Kalsia		62,000	Jatt.
9. Maler Kotla		46,200	Sheikh.
10. Faríd Kot		51,000	Siddhu Jatt.
11. Dojána		6,300	Afghan.
12. Loháru		18,000	Ditto.
13. Kapurthála		212,721	Ahlwalia.
14. Mandi		139,259	Rajput.
15. Sukít		44,552	Ditto.
16. Sarmúr (Náhan)		75,595	Ditto.
17. Kahlúr (Biláspúr)	47,000	66,848	Chandeli Rajput.
18. Hindúr (Nálagurh)		49,678	Rajput.
19. Bussáhir		45,025	Ditto.
20. Keonthal		18,083	Ditto.
21. Bághal		22,305	Ditto.
22. Jubbal		17,262	Ditto.
23. Bhajji		9,001	Ditto.
24. Kumharsain		7,829	Ditto.
25. Kuthár		3,990	Ditto.
26. Dhámi		2,853	Ditto.
27. Baghát		......	Ditto.
28. Balsan		4,892	Ditto.
29. Mailog		7,358	Ditto.
30. Bija		981	Ditto.
31. Taroch		3,082	Ditto.
32. Kunhiar		1,906	Ditto.
33. Mangal		917	Ditto.
34. Darkuti		612	Ditto.

LATEST COMPARATIVE CENSUS OF ALL INDIA.

Analysis of the names, races, and creeds of which our subjects are composed. To these should be added the Parsís, 180,000, East Indians or Eurasians, 91,000, and Europeans 156,000, including the army.

There are some 10,000 Jews and 5,000 Armenians in India. The number of Musulmans, 25 millions, is not so large as is popularly supposed :—

	Census.		Number.
SIKHS	1868	...	1,129,319
MAHOMEDANS :—			
Panjáb	1868	...	9,335,652
North-West Provinces	1865	...	4,105,206
Central Provinces	1866	...	237,962
Berar	1867	...	154,951
Madras	1867	...	1,502,134
British Burmah	1867	...	38,601
Mysore (Estimate)	......	...	172,255
Kúrg (Estimate)	......	...	3,318
Sindh (Old Enumeration)	......	...	1,354,781
Bombay, in twelve out of twenty-one districts	......	...	779,264
Bombay Island	1864	...	145,880
Calcutta	1866	...	113,059
Dakka Division	......	...	2,493,174
The rest of Bengal and Bombay, and Oudh (Estimate)	......	...	5,400,000
Total		...	24,936,237
NON-ARYANS :—			
Madras (not speaking Tamil, Telugu, Kanarese, nor Malayalam —Dr. Caldwell)			650,000
Central Provinces			1,995,663
South Bengal			4,000,000
North-East Bengal (say)			1,000,000
Karens			402,117
Khyens and Yabangs			61,562
Rest of India (say)			4,000,000
Total			12,099,342

Excluding the feudatory States, the following may be roughly accepted as the relative proportions of creeds and races in India :—

Asiatic Christians	1,100,000
Buddhists	3,000,000
Aborigines or Non-Aryans	12,000,000
Musulmans	25,000,000
Hindus	110,000,000

—*Friend of India*, March 2nd, 1869, p. 194.

END OF VOL. I.

Memoirs

on the History, Folk-lore and Distribution of the Races of the

North Western Provinces of India

Being an Amplified Edition of the Original Supplemental Glossary of Indian Terms

SIR HENRY M ELLIOT

EDITED, REVISED AND RE-ARRANGED BY
JOHN BEAMS

In 2 Vols. Bound in One.

Vol. 2

Low Price Publications
Delhi-110052

MEMOIRS

ON THE

HISTORY, FOLK-LORE, AND DISTRIBUTION

OF THE

RACES

OF THE

NORTH WESTERN PROVINCES OF INDIA;

BEING AN AMPLIFIED EDITION OF THE ORIGINAL

SUPPLEMENTAL GLOSSARY OF INDIAN TERMS,

BY THE LATE

SIR HENRY M. ELLIOT, K.C.B.,

OF THE HON. EAST INDIA COMPANY'S BENGAL CIVIL SERVICE.

EDITED, REVISED, AND RE-ARRANGED

BY

JOHN BEAMES, M.R.A.S.,

BENGAL CIVIL SERVICE;

MEMBER OF THE GERMAN ORIENTAL SOCIETY, OF THE ASIATIC SOCIETIES OF PARIS AND BENGAL.
AND OF THE PHILOLOGICAL SOCIETY OF LONDON.

IN TWO VOLUMES.

VOL. II.

LONDON:

TRÜBNER & CO., 8 AND 60, PATERNOSTER ROW.

MDCCCLXIX.

STEPHEN AUSTIN,

PRINTER, HERTFORD.

SUPPLEMENTAL GLOSSARY

OF TERMS USED IN THE

NORTH WESTERN PROVINCES.

PART III.

REVENUE AND OFFICIAL TERMS.

[Under this head are included—1. All words in use in the revenue offices both of the past and present governments; 2. Words descriptive of tenures, divisions of crops, fiscal accounts, and the like; 3. Some articles relating to ancient territorial divisions, whether obsolete or still existing, with one or two geographical notices, which fall more appropriately under this head than any other.—B.]

Ábkár, آبکار आबकार

A distiller, a vendor of spirituous liquors. Ábkárí, or the tax on spirituous liquors, is noticed in the Glossary.

With the initial *a* unaccented, Abkar means agriculture.

Adábandí, ادابندي अदाबंदी

The fixing a period for the performance of a contract or payment of instalments. From ادا performance, and بستن (root بَند) to bind.

Ádhbaṭáí, آدهبٹائي आधबटाई

Division of produce in equal shares; from आधा half, and बटाई division.

Adhelá, ادهيله अधेला

Half a pice, comprising 12½ dams, or 4 damrís, *q.v.* [Also an eight-ana piece, or half a rupee.]

Adhelí, ادهيلي अधेली

Half a Chauthia, *q.v.* A measure used for corn.—Saugor.
Small fractional divisions of land.—Gaṛhwál.
Also an eight-ana piece, or half a rupee.

Adheliyá, ادهيليا अधेलिया

Adhelia, or Ádhia, signifies a proprietor of a half share.

Adhiyár, ادهيار अधियार

A man who passes half his time in one village, and half in another, is said to be adhiyár karná; called adhbar in Rohilkhand. Adhiyár differs from páhíkásht, inasmuch as adhiyár implies that there are two establishments, one in each of the two villages which are visited, [whereas páhíkásht is a man who lives in one village and cultivates land in another].

Adhiyárí, ادهياري अधियारी

A half share. The word आधा half, enters into the composition of all these words.

Adhkachchá, ادهکچا अधकचा

A soil lying between the land named Pahára and the Taráí, in the district of Saháranpúr.

Adhkarí, ادهکري अधकरी

An instalment of eight anas in the rupee, or half of the Government Jama.

Aghaní, اگهني अगहनी

The produce of part of the Kharíf season, or of the month of Aghan, اگهن (November-December).

*** In Behar there are two rice crops, one in Bhádon, the other in Aghan; the produce of the former is less valuable than that of the latter, and is only eaten by the lower classes, and by animals.—B.

Agaur, اگور अगौर

An advance of rent paid by Asámís to Zamíndárs in the months of Jeth and Asarh.—E. Oudh. The word is derived from *áge* آگي, before, beyond.

'Ahd, عهد अहद

An agreement or contract. Ahdnáma عهدنامه is the written document containing an agreement.

'Ahddár, عهددار अहददार

Literally, holder of a contract. An officer of the Mughal Government, who, for a commission of 2 or 3 per cent., engaged for the revenue of a district, and made himself responsible for the balance.

Ajaurí, اجوري अजौरी

Advances, particularly to agricultural labourers.—Eastern Oudh. Agraurihí is used in a similar sense in Baiswara. Both words are, perhaps, derived from *áge*, before, in advance.

Álí, آلي आली

A land measure equivalent to four Bísís. Nine Alí go to a

Júlá.—Gaṛhwál and Kamáon. See further under the articles Bísí and Júlá.

Algí, الگي अलगी

A separate cess levied by Zamíndárs in part of Behar over and above the regular Jama. They generally do this when short of funds.—W.

Áltamghá,* آلتمغا आलतमग़ा

A royal grant, which the British Government have declared to convey a title to a rent-free tenure in perpetuity.

Altamghá is derived from two Turkish words, Al and Tamghá: both of which signify the royal signet. Al in Persian implies also a scarlet colour, سرخ نيم رنگ را گويند, and therefore it has been supposed to mean the Emperor's *red* signet (Gladwin says, "a red patent," and Harington, in his "Analysis," I., 4, "a red seal—from which its name is derived"): but it may be doubted if the Altamghá seal is necessarily a *red* one; and the "Burḥán-i Ḳáti'," the "Farhang-i Jahángírí," and the "Haft Ḳulzam," while they give the meaning of scarlet to Al in Persian, and at the same time mention the Hindí Al, noticed in a separate article, also add that, in Turkish, "it is the seal and ring of the king," without any special mention of its being a *red* seal, or a *red* ring. It would appear, however, from the extract from the "Farhang-i Rashídí," given below, that Altamghá originally meant a *red* seal, and that Al, by itself, was never taken in the sense of signet, except by reason of its having been coupled with Tamghá, to imply that the Tamghá was *red*.

و بتركي مهر بادشاهان كه آنرا التمغا گويند اي مهر سرخ و گاهي
بجهت تخفيف تمغا انداخته تنها آل گويند

* The word is generally written التمغا *altamghá*, not *áltamghá*, in Persian.—B.

"And in Turkish it signifies the seal of the Padshah, which they call Altamghá, *i.e.*, 'red seal,' and sometimes they call it A'l, for short, rejecting Tamghá."

The assertion therefore rests upon which is the best authority —the Burḥán-i Ḳáti', coupled with the Jahángírí, or the Rashídí. The Haft Ḳulzam is a mere copy, and of no weight in such controversies.

It is difficult to say when Altamghá began first to be used in the revenue language of India in the sense either of a seal or grant. In Persia and Central Asia we have notices of its use at an early period. Towards the close of the 13th century the illustrious Ghazan Khan caused the Altamghá, or the imperial seal of state, to be altered from a quadrangular to an oval shape, considered the most auspicious as well as most elegant of all forms, and on this he at the same time directed to be engraved the Mahomedan profession of faith.—Price's "Retrospect of Mahomedan History," Vol. II., p. 612.

Again, Timúr bestows upon the son of Bajazet the Government of Anatolia, under a patent containing the impression of his hand in *red* ink (Ibid. Vol. III., p. 423; and "Sherefeddin," Lib. v., Cap. 60); but it is not stated whether the title of this patent was Altamghá. In the Institutes of this tyrant, we find no mention of anything but Tamghá, and that with a different meaning.

But, with respect to India, the term certainly does not appear to have been in common and practical use in the fiscal language of the country in Akbar's time; though, as we have seen from the extract just quoted, that it is mentioned in the "Farhang-i Jahángírí," which was compiled at his dictation and dedicated to his son; but then it is to be considered that the authority of certain poets is given for its use;—which would of itself seem to imply that the word was a foreign importation, and up to that time had merely found admission into dictionaries and literary compositions. It is not once mentioned in the passage on Sayúrghal, in his Institutes; the perusal of which chapter, by the way, would afford an instructive lesson to those who assert that the Mughal Government never resumed rent-free tenures, for in it we have the very founder of the system enjoining resumption, and getting more and more exasperated at the shameless frauds practised upon the exchequer even by his own officers. Yet, notwithstanding this apparently modern introduction of the word, it is to be feared that some grants, purporting to be Altamghá of his reign, have been released by our officials.

We find frequent mention of the word Tamghá in his time, but so far from conferring a privilege or immunity, it meant only a tax, or tribute, when applied fiscally.

In the following passage Báj باج "tax," is coupled with Tamghá:—"And it was ordered that the Báj and Tamghá were not to be collected except from arms and horses, elephants and camels, cows, sheep and goats and silken cloth, on which a small sum was to be levied in each Suba."

Tamghá is again called a tax which is raised in excess of the land revenue:—"Umr levied a tax on foreigners in three classes . . . . . which they called Jazia, and in every kingdom they demand something from every man's property except peasants, and that they call Tamghá; and in Irán and Turán they take some little in proportion to the wealth of the taxed."

In one of the general Farmáns issued by him in the 37th year of his reign, by which he justly earned the love of his subjects and admiration of posterity, he remits the Tamghá, Báj, and Zikát, on all articles, with a few exceptions.*

و دیگر اشیا و اسباب و امتعه و اجناس که مدار معاش جمهور انام

* It appears that previous to Akbar's time the tamghá had been remitted by Jahángír, and before that by Bábar. Possibly the remission of a tax by any sovereign was considered to hold good only during his reign, and to require a fresh act of remission on the accession of another emperor. Jahángír's veracity, however, is not beyond suspicion.—E. *add.*

و ملاك معيشت خواص و عوام است سواي اسپ و فيل و شتر و گوسفند و بز و اسلحه و قماش كه در تمامي ممالك محروسه تمغا و باج و زكوة و صد يك و انچه از قليل و كثير گرفته اند معاف و مرفوع القلم بوده باشد

"And other goods and chattels which are the means of livelihood of the people in general, except horses and elephants and camels and sheep and goats and arms and silk, which in all my dominions are liable to Báj and Tamghá and Zikát, and that which they took from small and great, are entirely remitted and struck off."

This is differently translated by Dr. Bird in his "History of Guzerat," in which he calls Tamghá "vested interests," and it must be confessed it is used in that sense in one of Akbar's letters to Abdu'llah Khan Uzbek.

In "Timúr's Institutes" (Book II., p. 308) Tamghá is spoken of as pay, or personal allowance of a soldier, and therefore approaches nearer to our modern meaning.—See also "Bábar's Memoirs," p. 354.

In the following passage it also means a stipend, according to "White's Translation," p. 361: or, a body-mark, according to Colonel Galloway's "Law and Constitution of India," p. 87. The context shews that either may be correct:—

و عمر نمودم كه هر مملكتي كه مسخر گردد گدايان آن ملك ر جمع ساخته و ايشان را تمغه كنند كه ديگر گداي را برطرف سازند اگر بعد از تمغه گدائي نمايند ايشان را به بلاد بعيده بفروشند

"And I commanded that whatever country was conquered they should collect the beggars thereof and make them an allowance that they should beg no more, and if, after being allowanced, they should beg again, they should be sold into distant countries," etc. There is apparently no reason to suppose with Galloway that the beggars were to be branded: it is more in consonance with the lavish generosity of an eastern monarch to pension them, as the natural translation of the text says.—B.

These passages serve to shew that the word Tamghá must have somewhat altered its meaning since its first importation into Hindústan; but they do not enable us to determine at what period Tamghá, or Altamghá, grants were first made.

We have already seen that they do not appear to have been introduced up to Akbar's time; and with respect to his successor, Jehangír, we find him in his autobiography, so far from asserting that a *red* seal was exclusively devoted to Altamghás, saying expressly that he changed the seals of Jagír patents from mixed gold and *vermilion* to gold alone.

جاي مهررا بطلا و دورش را بشنگرف ساختند من تمام را بطلا فردا

"Instead of the seal which they made of gold with a rim of *vermilion*, I used one of gold only."

From these remarks it is to be gleaned that the period of the introduction of even the word Altamghá is a problem in Sphragistics which still remains to be solved; and though it appears to have been used in its present sense in Persia and Turkistan before the establishment of the Mughal dynasty in India, yet there seems reason to conclude that some time elapsed before the term was generally introduced into this country; and we are therefore justified in looking on any Altamghá grant older than Shahjahan with strong suspicion.

That it was not necessarily a rent-free grant, the British Government themselves had incontrovertible evidence, in that they stipulated to pay 26 lacs per annum for their Altamghá Farman from Shah Alam, A.D. 1765. It was, nevertheless, proclaimed by our Government that a grant of this nature was rent-free, and conveyed, moreover, an hereditary and transferable right. That the native subordinates of our Government were anxious to persuade us to that effect was naturally to be expected, and that the European functionaries were glad to assent to any opinion uttered by men who professed to have a knowledge of the laws and customs of the country, was also to be expected; but that the same opinion should have been entertained and confirmed when the regulations came subsequently to be enacted, is somewhat surprising, for there was much to make us pause before we committed ourselves to so positive a declaration. In several instances evidence had been given which was opposed to the construction finally adopted by the Government.

In the case of Jalálu'd-dín *versus* Mihru'n-nisá Begam, tried before the Provincial Council of Patna, in September, 1774, the Amánat officer, whose authority should have carried with it some weight, says, "from the reign of the kings of old, the orders of one king have continued valid, but it is now the ancient custom for the possessors of Altamghás and Madad Máshes to be turned out or removed." And we know that Nawwáb Muhammad Raza' Khan resumed several Altamghá grants in the year 1766, after the Diwání was granted to the Company; which he would scarcely have ventured to do, had he not been authorized by the practice of the country.—(See "Colebrooke's Digest," III., 238, and "Extracts from Official Records regarding Máfí," p. 16), It is therefore the more remarkable that we gave such ready acquiescence to representations not only entirely opposed to our own interests, and to the customs, laws, and records of the country, but frequently to the very language and tenor of the documents which purported to be Altamghá.

Amání, اماني अमानी

Land managed by a collector on the part of Government:—called also Kham and Khas. The Regulations have given the word greater currency in the Benares Province than elsewhere.

'Aml paṭṭá, عمل پتّہ अमल पट्टा
'Aml sanad, عمل سند अमल सनद
'Aml dastak, عمل دستک अमल दस्तक

A deed appointing an agent, or granting authority to collect rents. From the Arabic عمل action, practice, rule.

A'ná, آنہ and آنا आना

A native land measure equal to 16 Rúsís. Sixteen Anas go to a Kancha.—Saugor.

The sixteenth part of a rupee—which is usually written by Europeans, *anna*.

Ankbandí, انک‌بندي अंकबन्दी

An adjustment of rents asanúwár by the Malgúzár at the close of each harvest.—See under Ank.

Antarbed, انتربید अंतरबेद

The old name for the Lower Doáb, extending from about Etawah to Allahabad. Occasionally it is used to signify the whole Doáb—thus, Kachwahas are said by the poet Chand to be in Antarbed; and it does not seem probable that they were in any numbers except in the Upper Doáb (see Kachwahas). The word is now seldom used, except by Sanskrit scholars. In that language it bears much the same meaning as Doáb, signifying the level country intervening (*i.e.* between the Ganges and Jumna), from अन्तर within, and वेदि an altar, a hearth, an earthen platform in the courtyard of a house.

A'olí, آولي आओली

Mode of estimating by the ascertained produce of a Biswa that of a Bígha.—E. Oudh. The rule is very simple. Take the number of seers yielded by a Biswa, halve it, and you have the produce per Bígha in maunds. The produce of a Biswah is ascertained from the produce of a Bígha, by doubling the latter, in maunds, and calling the product seers.

Aṛáṛí, اڑاڑي अड़ाड़ी

The old-established measurement of a field. A man says his Aṛáṛí is so much, say two bíghas, and though modern measurement may rate it higher, he will not consent to any change.—Benares. The term is, perhaps, derived from Aṛáṛá اڑاڑا, a high bank of a river or tank, which may therefore be supposed to enclose an unalterable area.

Arází, اراضي अराज़ी

Lands; plural of Arz عرض land. In revenue language, the word is chiefly applied to detached portions of land, which are generally either rent free, or recovered by the recession of rivers. It is therefore nearly synonymous with Chak.

Arsath, ارسٹه अरसठ

A kind of account which the author of the "Zubdatu'l Ḳawánín" says is the same as a monthly Jama' kharch.

ارسٹھ که عبارت از جمعخرچ ماهواري و مجمل وازخام است

"The arsaṭh, which is an expression for the monthly Jama' kharch and abstract of the Wázkhám."

The "Diwan Pasand" also says it is a monthly entry or abstract of several accounts, called Wázkhám, and that it is in reality only another name for Jama' kharch: بطور جمعخرچ که ارسٹه نیز گویند. This is the meaning the word bears in the Printed Glossary, and the word Arsotta (Arsaṭhá), which precedes it, is probably an error.*

* This word is common all over the eastern part of the provinces, and is said to be so called from containing sixty-eight (arsaṭh) columns.—B.

'Arzdásht, عرضداشت अरजदास्त

An address or memorial, so called from its initial words.

Asámí, اسامي असामी

Literally names. A cultivator, a dependant, a culprit—all of which meanings we may suppose to be derived from such persons being entered in registers and tabular forms under the head of Asámí. It has been supposed, as Asámí frequently means a criminal, that it is derived from اثم *ism*, a crime; and the practice commonly adopted by Káyaths of writing the word اثامي with a *se* ث instead of *sin* س, gives some colour to this opinion, Asámí is the plural of the plural of Ism اسم a name (De Sacy, "Grammaire Arabe," II. 275).

There are two words, one with a ث *se* means a criminal, and the one with a س *sin* means a cultivator; but both words are Indian inventions in their present significations, and rather barbarous inventions too, though they have become so common as to be quite indispensable.—B.

An Asámí Chhaparband is a resident cultivator, that is, an Asámí who has a Chhapar چهپر or thatched house.

An Asámí Maurúṣí is an hereditary cultivator, that is, an Asámí who has Irṣ ارث or inheritance.

An Asámí Páhíkásht is a man who cultivates land of a village different from that in which he resides.—See Páhíkásht and Khudkásht.

An Asámí Shikmí is one who cultivates the land of, and pays the rent to, another Asámí.

Asámíwár, اساميوار असामीवार

Including all the names; usually applied to statements, and to revenue settlements made with the proprietors in detail.

Aslí, اصلي असली

A registered village—literally, original, from اصل *asal*, a root.

Dákhilí داخلي is the term applied to hamlets included in the Aslí village. It is not known at what particular time these words originated, but it must have been subsequent to Todar Mal's settlement. Our new settlements have swept away the distinction, which there was no occasion for preserving in the revised register.*

A'wárijá, آوارجه आवारिजा

A diary, a rough note-book, an abstract account of collections, remittances, etc. etc. The "Zubdatu'l Ḳawánín" says the word is derived from Awára, scattered, wandering, unfixed, because the Awárija is a collection of detached notes which would otherwise be dispersed. It is applied generally to an account of any description.

The work above-quoted says—

اوارجه اطلاق و آن در حقیقت جمعخرچ

It would seem, therefore, to be much the same as the Arsath, except that the latter is more strictly confined to a monthly account.

The "Farhang-i Rashídí" also states that the word is derived from Awára, scattered. The same work adds that Abar, Abara, Awára, and Awárija, mean not only an account, but an office of account, an exchequer :—

آواره دفتر حساب که حساب پراگنده دیوان برآن نویسند و اوارجه گویند و بارگاه که دیوان درآن کنند و بهردو معني بغیر مدالف نیزآمده

"Awára, an office of account, so called because they write there the scattered accounts of the Díwán and call them Awárija: also the office in which they transact the revenue business, and in both meanings it is written without *madda* over the *alif*."

* This is not quite correct: the terms *asli* and *dákhili* are still retained in many districts, not merely in the mouths of the people, but on the registers.—B.

See Awerja in the Printed Glossary, which appears a mistake for Awárija, though closely following Awárija Jama Kharch.

Bád, باد बाद

A remission on account of deficient produce. One of the many meanings of the word in Persian is "annihilated," بمعني نابود و هيچ باشد according to the "Burhán-i Káti'" and "Haft Kulzam," and has thus been extended in the revenue language of India to signify remissions occasioned by annihilation (of crops).

Bádsháhí, بادشاهي बादशाही

Literally, royal, from بادشاه a king. In the language of revenue officers it is generally applied to royal grants of rent-free land. Thus we say, "Bádsháhí Sanad," "Bádsháhí Tenures." The conditions of their validity are given in Reg. XXXVI. of 1803, and the corresponding enactments Reg. XIII. of 1795, and Reg. VIII. of 1805: the first being applicable to the Ceded Provinces, the second to Benares, and the third to the Conquered Provinces.

Benáwat, بيناوت बेनाउत

See above, under Benaudha.

Bhábar, بهابر भाबर

The forest under the Sewalik Hills. The tract varies in breadth from ten to twenty miles, and the slope of the ground varies from fifty to seventeen feet per mile, diminishing rapidly after the first few miles. Cultivation is confined only to the vicinity of the rivers issuing from the Himalayan range, but the soil in many parts is good, and consists of a rich black mould at the extreme verges of the tract, north and south. There are occasional patches also free from trees, but covered with high grass, and many spots afford good pasturage. With these exceptions, the Bhábar is a dense forest, but almost destitute of trees valuable for timber; and water is at such a depth below the surface, that all attempts to dig wells have been fruitless.—See "Printed Report on Rohilkhand Canals," p. 107.*

Bhábar is also the name of a light black soil in Baitúl, in Central India.

Bháíbánt, بهائي بانت भाईबांट

A term equivalent to Bhayachara, *q.v.* It is derived from भाई a brother, and बांटना to divide.

Bhág, بهاگ भाग

Tax; duty; share in kind. Also fortune, destiny.

Bhágnar, بهاگنر भागनर

The name given to the rich alluvial lands under the banks of the Jumna.—Central Doáb.

Bhej, بهيج भेज

Rent; a proportionate share; an instalment. Bhej is in common use, but is not noticed in any of the Dictionaries. It may be a corruption of the Sanskrit Bhág, a portion.

Bhej-barár, بهيج برار भेजबरार

A tenure frequently met with in Bundelkhand, in which the shares of the brotherhood are liable to periodical, or occasional, adjustment; and in which balances of revenue and village expenses, occasioned by the fraud or insolvency of a sharer, are made good by a rateable contribution from the other sharers. Strangers are often introduced in over-assessed estates on condition of paying the barár, but their admission by no means,

* See "Selections from Rec. N. W. P.," IV., 374.

as is sometimes supposed, forms a necessary incident of the tenure, of which the chief characteristic is the re-adjustment of the baráṙ. At the late settlement of Bundelkhand it was stipulated in many instances that this liability to re-adjustment should cease; and practically, for some time previous, the re-adjustment had not been demanded, except upon occasions of a new settlement. It is probable that in a short time, as the value of property increases, the Bhej-barár tenure will altogether cease to exist.

Bhúngáí, بهونگاي भूंगाई

Is the name of a tax levied by the Raja of Bijaypúr on part of the forest produce of Tappa Saktísgaṛh, in zillah Mirzapúr. In the Official Report of the Settlement of the Tappa, the word is said to be derived from Bhúnga, a mallet.

Tangáí is another of these taxes; from Tanga, an axe.

Bharaí, بهرئي भरई

A cess levied in the Province of Benares, of which one-half was given to the Amil for charges of remittance, and the other carried to the credit of Government.—See Sec. 6 and 7 of Reg. II. of 1795.

Bharat, بهرت भरत

Amount of revenue paid by an individual or party. The word is chiefly used in Dehli, and is frequently pronounced Bharit and Barat. It is derived from Bharná, to pay.

Bhaṭṭíáná, بهٹیانه भट्टीश्राना

Is the name given to a large tract of land between the Hissar district and the Garra, which is tenanted chiefly by Bhaṭṭí Rajputs. Bhaṭṭíáná, or Bhaṭṭia, is a country of gro ... import-ance, the population and cultivation having greatly increased since our occupation.

It will be observed, by referring to the map of Dastúrs, that the Western boundary of Sirkár Hisár Feroza has been extended only to the bed of the War river, which runs not far to the Westward of the Ghaggar, the new Parganah of Wattu and Bhaṭṭíáná being altogether excluded: for this tract, full of sandy plains and Thals,* seems to have been little known in the time of Akbar, nor, with the exception of Malaud, which was in Múltán, does it appear to be included in any Sirkár of the adjoining Súbahs. It is to be observed, that Abu'l Fazl, in mentioning the breadth and length of the several Súbahs, measures from Hisár in the Dehli Súbah, from Ferozpúr in the Múltán Súbah, from the Satlaj in the Lahore Súbah, and from Bíkanir in the Ajmír Súbah. He appears, therefore, with the above exception, to leave the tract between all these places as neutral ground. To be sure, the Rev. Mr. Renouard, in his article on Dehli in the "Encyclopædia Metropolitana," includes Fattihabad in Ajmír, on the sole authority, apparently, of Hamilton's Gazetteer; but Abu'l Fazl certainly places it in Hisár Fírozá, and it was included in Hisár before his time, as we learn from the 5th chapter of the 2nd book of Shamsi Siráj's Táríkh Fírozsháhí, where he says—

پیش ازین در عهد سلاطین ماضیه آن سمت را در دفاتر دواوین شق
هانسي مي نِشیند چون شهر حصار فیروزه بنا کردند سلطان فروز فرمود
ازین تاریخ باز شق حصار فیروزه نویسند اقطاعات هانسي و اگروه و
فتح‌آباد و سرستي تا سالوره و خضرآباد و اقطاعات دیگر بتمام داخل
شق حصار فیروزه کردند †

* Thal or thar is the name given to the various deserts in Rajputána, and is probably a corruption of the latter half of the word मरुस्थली *marusthali*, or desert region, applied to this tract.—B.

† This passage, as it stood in the original work, puzzled me considerably, and even now, after a comparison of three manuscripts, I am not quite sure how the text should really stand: the reading given above is, however, the most probable. In Sir H.

"Before this, in the times of the ancient kings, that district in the records of the revenue officers stands as Shakk Hánsí. When he built the city of Hisár Fírozá, Sultan Fíroz commanded that from that time forth they should write is as Shakk Hisár Fírozá, and the kitta's of Hánsí, Agroha, Fattihábád, Sirsútí as far as Sálaurah, and Khizrábád, and other entire kitta's, were included in Shakk Hisár Fírozá." This Shakk must therefore have included Akbar's Sirkár of Sirhind, as well as Hisár, for Sálaurá is under the Sewalik Hills and Khizrábád is on the Jumna.*

Elliot's own copy of Shamsi Siráj's work, the first doubtful passage reads دفاترو ابين the last word, though without the diacritical notes, is clearly meant for ائين *áin*; but in MS. No. 1002 of the India Office Library, I find دواسن (also without dots), which is probably for دواوين *dawáwín*, plural of *díwán*, which seems to me the best reading of the two. The copy lately purchased by the India Office at the Marquis of Hastings' sale wants forty or forty-five pages at this point, and the next page begins in the middle of this very quotation. The passage as it stood in former editions went on شق هاسى نوشته and in the author's copy the words are مي هشتد which has no meaning. In MS. No. 1002 we have the correct reading مي نشيند "it sits" (or as we should say "stands"): further on, for the reading of the first edition, اگروه *agroh*, we have in the author's copy اكره *akrah*, in No. 1002 اكروده *akrodah*, and in the Hastings' MS. by an evident error اكرفيروزه *akar firoza*. Lastly, for بنام in the first edition, which made nonsense of the passage, we find in all the other MSS. بتمام *batamám*, "entirely." These variations, though slight in themselves, are noticed here as an example of the very corrupt state in which we find many Persian MSS. of great historical value, and to shew the necessity for a reconstruction of our texts in accordance with principles of sound and enlightened criticism.—B.

* It was from the vicinity of these towns that the famous Fíroz Shah's Lat was taken and placed in its present position in Dehli. A very particular and interesting account of the removal of the Lat, and of the first discovery of Indian osteological remains in the neighbourhood is given by the same author; who, notwithstanding the adulatory tone of his history, gives us more valuable details respecting the condition of Hindústan in his time than any other historian of that or any subsequent period.

Sálaurá and Khizrábád are two places on the road from Ropar to Sirhind. The two places mentioned in the text are quite different, and have nothing to do with the matter.—E. *add.* And as the MSS. generally have تا instead of و there is no reason to suppose that Sálaurá was included.—B.

We may, perhaps, attribute the little knowledge entertained of these tracts by Ábu'l Fazl to the depopulation caused by "the firebrand of the universe," Timúr. There is not a place in these parts which was not the scene of his wanton cruelty. Bhatnír, Ahrúní, Fattihabad and Tohana, all suffered at his hands. Sirsa was also attacked and plundered, if we may be allowed, as there seems reason, to look upon Sirsa as the town of Sirsutí. Indeed, it is still called Sirsútí by men that come from these parts; and Timúr's Sirsútí is represented as being precisely the same distance and direction from Bhatnír, Fattihabad, Tohana and Ahrúní, as Sirsa is. If this really be the old Sirsútí, the town must have changed its name before Akbar's time, as he only mentions Sirsa, stating that Fíroz Shah's canal passes near the town of that name.

It does not appear that the extensive desiccation which this country has undergone, and the further progress of which it is now hoped will cease (our attention being directed to improving the means* of irrigation), had proceeded to such an extent as we now view it, when Timúr invaded India. Mirkhond, Abdu'l Razzák, Sharfu'd-dín, and all the other historians of his time, though they mention that he had to cross one continuous desert from the Satlaj to Bhatnír, yet describe the great populousness of that town in terms which but ill accord with its present state. Sirsútí is also said to be on the banks of the *river* of the same name, so that it had not ceased to flow in those days, and had not yielded to the Ghaggar, by which the dry river bed under Sirsa is now known. A short time before, also, Ibn Batuta,† while he states he had to cross a desert to Abohar,

* One of the first measures should be the opening of the dams in the native states. There are at this time no less than twenty-four Bands on the Sirsúti from Thanesar to Sagara, where it joins the Ghaggar.

† It is much to be regretted that we have not a perfect copy of this enterprising traveller's work. The abridgment translated by Dr. Lee increases the desire to see the entire work as well edited. Professor De Gayangos, in a note to the first volume

"the first city in Hindústan," says of Sirsútí, "It is large, and abounds with rice, which they carry hence to Dehli;" so that neither in his time could the means of irrigation have been deficient. The river, indeed, up to the commencement of Akbar's time, seems to have been flowing, and to have been still called Sirsútí, for in the "Akbarnama" we read that in Humayún's re-conquest of Dehli, he bestowed upon the young Prince Akbar the Government of Hisár, and the provinces on the river Sirsútí; which, had they been the provinces on the modern Sirsútí, would most probably have been called Sirhind. Yet it must be confessed that Abu'l Fazl, in his detailed description of the Súbah of Dehli, gives prominent notice to the Ghaggar river, and he may therefore have considered the Ghaggar and Sirsútí to be the same.

Major Brown, in his survey of Hisár, fell in with a part of that which is now called the old Sirsútí. "The Sirsútí river was come upon quite unexpectedly. The best maps shew this river as joining the Ghaggar, between Murak and Samánah in the Patiála state. As the survey approached Tohanah, the zamíndárs and native officers brought it to notice, and directed

of his "Mahomedan Dynasties in Spain," states that he has obtained a perfect copy, and that he has it in contemplation to publish a translation of it,—a declaration which it is to be hoped he will shortly fulfil. The period of Ibn Batuta's visit to India (A.D. 1332–1342) is highly interesting, and makes us regret the more that the geographical details have been much confused by the epitomator. After leaving Dehli he goes to Biana (Baran ?)—thence to Kol,—thence to Jalalí, a place seven days' journey (?) distant from Kol—back to Dehli—back again to Kol,—thence to Yieh Barah (Mainpúrí ?) thence to the shores of a lake called "the Water of Life" (Talgram ?)—thence to Kanauj,—thence to Merwa (?)—thence to Gwalior. The Chinese Embassy which he accompanied on its return, appears to have come with a view to the restoration of some Buddhist place of worship below the Hills, and perhaps in the district of Sambhal, which had been destroyed by the Mahometans, who "had also prevented the Hindus from cultivating the plains which were necessary to their subsistence." Hence we may perhaps obtain some information of the precise period when the depopulation of the country below the Sewalik Hills commenced; a question which has been cursorily noticed in the article Des.

our enquiries to this subject. It was stated that formerly this river flooded and enriched the lands to a great extent, and that even within the last ten years many villages derived great benefits from it. The bed of the river, however, has for some years been lost sight of altogether, and it was only in a few villages near Hansdaha that any vestige of it could be found; the remainder of its track was laid down from information from the zamíndárs as far as it could be depended upon." (Reports on Projected Canals in the Dehli Territory, p. 120.)

As this bed of the Sirsútí is nearly parallel with the course of the Ghaggar river, and with the Ghaggar Nalla, or Choya, there seems little room for doubt that it combined with the latter, and formed the river of Sirsútí, which was flowing under the walls of Sirsa (Sirsútí) in the time of Ibn Batuta and Timúr. Whether the Ghaggar* and Sirsútí were originally two entirely different streams, or whether they were originally one and the same; or whether, as is the case now, it has always been that the Sirsútí is merely a tributary of the Ghaggar, are questions that would lead us into too long a discussion, and are irrelevant to the present inquiry.

I am aware that it is usual to ascribe the deterioration of this tract solely to the Chalísa famine of A.D. 1783, but there seems sufficient ground for believing it commenced before that period. That the tract to the east of the Hyphasis was a desert at the

* Wilford says that the famous Drishadwati is the name of the Ghaggar, but in the "Tirtha Yatra" of the "Mahábhárat," where it is mentioned as forming one of the boundaries of Kurukshetra, it is said, "those who dwell *South* of the Saraswati and *North* of the Drishadwati, or in Kurukshetra, dwell in heaven." So that if Wilford's surmise is correct, what is now the Sirsútí was formerly the Ghaggar, and *vice versâ*; which would supply us with a fourth subject of enquiry. See further "Vishnu Purana," p. 181.—E.

This river, which Elliot writes Cuggur, is now generally called Ghaggar, and is usually admitted to be the Drishadwati. It is a few miles to the West of Amballa, and is generally dry. See also Edgeworth, "Botanic Agricultural Account of Protected Sikh States."—B.

period of Alexander's invasion, we learn from Diodorus and Quintus Curtius, and though they differ from Arrian in this respect, there is no doubt they represent truly the condition of a great part of this country in the time of that conqueror. Succeeding events must have increased the natural sterility of this region. The first Mahomedan invasions, which were frequently accompanied by extermination of the old inhabitants, may be considered one of the original causes of depopulation. As these occurred for 200 years, more or less, there was ample time for the desert to extend its reign. These were, after a short space, succeeded by reiterated Mughal invasions up to the time of Timúr, who crowned them by his ravages. The tract could have been but little improved up to the time of Akbar, and whatever prosperity it subsequently attained was reversed* by the Chalísa famine. It is perhaps to that period, when the deficiency of water was so grievously felt, that we are to attribute the drying up of many of the streams† which used to flow up to a late period in the Western Desert. It is a curious fact that the stream (Sankar or Sankra) which in 1739 was of sufficient volume to form the Treaty‡ Boundary between

* All notice of the ravages of the Bhattís is omitted, which was of itself no inconsiderable cause of depopulation.

† With respect to the Sirsútí, it may be doubted if at any time it ever reached the Indus or any of its affluents. From the earliest periods it is recorded as being absorbed by the sand. Some of the oldest legends of the country relate to this peculiarity, and allusions are constantly made to it by the ancient poets: "sicut samim arborem, in qua ignis latet, sicut *Sarasvatim* fluvium, cujus aqua sub terra fluit." "Stenzler's Raghuvansa," p. 17.—See also "Harivansa," pp. 507, 509.

‡ The words of the Treaty are—

تا حدیکه دریاي سند و نالهٔ سنکر بدریاي محیط اتصال دارد و آنچه
سایر جات و مهمات در سمت غربي دریاي سنده و نالهٔ سنکر واقع
شدهٔ باشد مخصوص اندولت نادره و ضمیمهٔ ممالک محروسه آن
سلطنت قاهره نمودیم

the possessions of Nadir Shah and Mahomed Shah, has not now even a puddle to moisten its arid bed. The further examination of this interesting question is foreign to the immediate subject of this enquiry, which is to consider the condition of Bhaṭṭíáná in Akbar's time, so as to shew what place it should occupy in the Dastúr Map; and, all circumstances considered, there can be no great error in having limited the boundary of Sirkár Hisár to the neighbourhood of the modern Ghaggar.

Bhaiyáchárá, بهیاچاره भैयाचारा

The definition in the Printed Glossary is for the most part correct.

Bhaiyáchára is a term applied to villages owned by descendants from a common stock. From भाई brother, and आचार usage.

In such villages the whole of the land is occupied by the proprietary brotherhood, and the revenue assessed by a rate, or *bachh*; and if there be non-proprietary cultivators, they are not responsible to the general body, but are introduced by some individual sharer, and pay him rent for land on which he pays by rate, or *bachh*.

In many of these holdings are sub-divisions paying an ascertained amount of Jama, levied by the proprietors of each subdivision among themselves. They are called *thok*, *paṭṭi*, and various other names; but the existence, or non-existence, of the interior sub-divisions does not affect the general character of the holding of proprietors paying by a rate.

There are also various ways of assessing the rate, as on ploughs, on the actual cultivation of each year, on wells, on the amount of cultivation ascertained at the settlement, etc. etc., but the general distinction continues unchanged.—See Par. 199–201 of the Revenue Board's Printed Circular Order on Settlements.

Bhaibat, بهيبت भैबट

See Bhaiwad.

Bhaihissí, بهي حصي भैहिस्सी

Bhaipansí, بهي پنسي भैपंसी

The shares of a brotherhood, especially in the lands of a village or township.

Bhaiáns, بهي انس भैत्रंश

Division of property or interests among brothers.

These three words are chiefly used in Bundelkhand, E. Oudh, Benares, and Lower Doáb.

Bhaiwád, بهي واد भैवाद

To pay and receive on the footing of one of the brotherhood.

Bi'lmuktâ, بالمقطع बिलमुकता

A Patta or lease under which a ryot pays a certain fixed sum at so much per plough or per Bíghá, not being liable to any further demand.

An engagement stipulating to pay a fixed money rent for the lands under cultivation, not subject to enhancement during the currency of the lease. See the Glossary under Bilmugta. The word is Arabic, and means "at a fixed or determined (rate)." It is often used to mean "in a lump sum," or "on the whole."

In Benares it signifies consolidated rate, including Mal and Abwab.—See Reg. LI. of 1795.

Birrábarár, برابرار बिर्राबरार

Collection in kind.—Central Doáb.

The expression seems derived either from Birah برہ separation, division, on account of the crops being divided before appropriation; or from the Birra of the Patwarí's account books, which is applied to the entry of every crop under a distinct head. The proper word in book-keeping is Beora بیورا explanation; detail; knowledge; which is frequently corrupted into Birra.

Birt,* برت बिर्त

A tenure held on condition of the performance of offices, whether religious or secular. Proprietary right. The tenure in Gorakhpúr, under which the Birtías pay a fixed yearly sum equivalent to twenty per cent. of the Government revenue, on account of the Raja or superior; but are the owners of the soil, entitled to the entire management of the Mauzas, not liable to be ousted, holding a hereditary and transferable tenure, and subject to enhancement of the rent only when the Government Juma should be increased.

The Sankalap (सङ्कल्प "expectation of advantage from a holy work." Benfey) Birt is a religious grant made to a Brahman, in order to secure the merit of sacrifices and ceremonies performed by him, and held at first free, but in almost all these cases the necessities of the Raja of Gorakhpúr had compelled him to demand a small rent from the holder.

The Marwat (मर्वत) Birt was a compensation made by the Raja to the family of any man who was killed in his service in open fight, either with a neighbouring chief or in resistance to the Government, and is also called Khún Bahá (*i.e.* "washing away blood," from خون "blood," and بہانا to "wash away"); it was chargeable, according to the custom of the Raj, with half the rent demandable for a regular Birt village.

Jewan (जेवना "to eat") Birt is an assignment made by the Raja of the day to a younger son, of a certain number of villages in the Talúka for subsistance, to be held by such son and his

* From the Sanskrit व्रत *vrata*, a vow, according to some, but Wilson derives it from वृत्ति maintenance.

descendants as Jewan Birt for ever. The assignee was accustomed to take a Patta from the Raja for these villages, paying a certain sum as rent.—See Talúkdar.

The term Birta is applied in Nepal to rent-free land, of which there are four kinds in that principality, Jagír, Manachaul, Bekh, and Birta. By the last a perpetual title is conveyed, and the land is at the absolute disposal of the grantee and his heirs.

Birtiyá, برتیا बिर्तिया

A tenant who holds his land upon a fixed annual assessment which cannot be altered, except on certain conditions previously stipulated; nor can the land held by him be claimed by the donor. The definition in the Printed Glossary is correct.—See Birt.*

Biswábarár, بسوہ برار बिसवाबरार

Collecting by the Biswa.—Central Doáb.

The Biswa, from بیس twenty, is the twentieth part of a Bígha; and besides being a measure of land, is also used to signify the extent of proprietary right in an estate. Each estate or village is considered an integer of one Bígha, which is subdivided into imaginary Biswas and Biswansís, to shew the right of any particular party. Thus, the holder of five Biswas is a holder to the extent of one-fourth of the entire village.

Biswádárí, بسوہداري बिसवादारी

A name given to the tenure of independent village communities holding under a superior Talúkdar; as in Aligarh, Main-

* I am not sure that this definition is correct; in Behar, certainly, a *birt* grant can be resumed. Elliot himself seems to have had doubts on this subject, and refers to Buchanan's "India," II. 546.—B.

púrí, and Gorakhpúr. It is in some places, as in Dehli, used as equivalent to Zamíndárí and Pattídárí. If a man's share in an estate is sold, he says his Biswa is sold. (See Sel. from Rec. N.W.P. i. 119.)

Biswí, بسوي बिसवी

The alienation of land assessed at low rates on the payment of fines in advance.—E. Oudh.

In the North-west it generally means two Biswas deducted from each Bígha cultivated by under tenants, which are taken by the landlord as his right.—See Dobiswí.

Bolá, بولا बोला

The verbal agreement (from بولنا to speak) between the village lessees and the Asámís, either Páhikásht (non-resident) or Khúdkásht (resident). Any agreement between the Lumberdár (head man of the village) and Asámí (cultivator).—Dehli.

Bolans, بولنس बोलंश

Making over one's share to another.—Benares and E. Oudh.

Bolansí, بولنسي बोलंशी

The holder of another's share or inheritance. An adopted heir.—Benares and E. Oudh.

These words are derived from बोलना to speak, and अंश portion, share.

Bolahdár, بولهدار बोलहदार

An occupant of land under a verbal agreement with the proprietor or tillage community. In Hisár the bolahdárs are of two kinds; the *band-bolahdár*, who pays a fixed rent per annum for the land he cultivates, and the *bolahdár bi'l mukta'*, who pays a quit-rent for a certain amount of land whether he cultivates it or not. Both classes are entered in the settlement record or *band*, and both hold their lands at the stipulated rates during the present settlement (Sel. Rec. N.W.P. iv. 15).—W.

Búṛh Gangá, بڑہ گنگا बूढ़गगंा

Búṛh Gangá, from बूढ़ा old, is the name given to the bed of the old Ganges where it has shifted its stream; more especially to the two old courses, of which one is traced below Hastinápúr, and the other below Soron and Kampil. These changes appear to have occurred since the time of Akbar, and I have therefore in the Map of Dastúrs restored the old stream as it probably ran in his time.

This has not been done without cause. The reasons for restoring the Hastinápúr stream, and throwing Tarapúr to the eastern side of the Ganges are the following.

When Timúr marched from Mirath, he is said in the "Matla' us Sa'dín," and "Zafarnama," and other histories nearly contemporary, to reach Ferozpúr, which is distinctly described as being "on the banks of the Ganges." The course of the Ganges, then, in his time must have flowed in the bed of the present Buṛh Gangá. In the "Khulásatu'l Tawáríkh" also, written in the fortieth year of Aurangzeb's reign, copied by Shere Ali Afsos in the "Araish-i-Mahfil" (which professes to be a more original work than it really is), the Ganges is described as flowing under Barha, which would show that at a much later period the Ganges preserved its old course; for this does not mean indefinitely that it flowed under the extensive tract of country in the possession of the Barha Sadat, *q.v.* but literally, under the town of Barha, which was then in a flourishing condition, before it was sacked in A.D. 1748, by the rabble army of Safdar Jang. Moreover, in the Revenue Board's Records of the year 1819, there is a correspondence respecting several villages then within the area of Tarapúr, but included originally in Azampúr Báshta, which is still on the Eastern side of the Ganges.

From the Dastúr Map it will also be seen that the Soron and Kampil branch has been restored, by giving Faizpúr Badaria to Saheswán, and Nidhpúr and Aolái to Badaon: to which I have been led by the following considerations. They may be thought perhaps of no great force, but where, as in Oriental History, we are never indulged with topographical details, and have no accounts of the habits and pursuits of the people, nor of the intercourse and relations of social life, we must be content with the remotest allusions, and rejoice if, after a whole day's perusal of some almost illegible volume, we can extract a single fact worthy of record.

When the heroic Pirthí Raj retreats from Kanauj, he is represented in the "Kanauj Khand," as following the course of the Ganges, till he reaches Soron.

In the somewhat apocryphal biography of Shah Azízu'd-dín, contained in one of the many collections of the lives of Mahomedan Saints, he is represented as being aided by the Emperor Shamsu'd-dín in the capture of Kasba Khor, in a naval battle under the walls of that town with the Raja, who after his defeat fled to Kamaon. Now we know that Khor is on the bank of the Buṛh Gangá, close to Shamsabad, which city was (it is said) built by Shamsu'd-dín from the ruins of Khor. There may possibly be a shadow of truth in this account, which is also preserved in the traditions of the common people; though, as Khor is mentioned later than the time of Shamsu'd-dín, his building Shamsabad may be doubted.

Let us come to a later period, and we find the Emperor Muhammad Tughlak in one of his mad schemes removing his capital to Sargdwárí, "near Kampil and Patiálí on the banks of the Ganges," according to "Ferishta;" and "near Kasba Khor on the Ganges" according to "Ziáu'd-dín Barní." Either way it shows that the course of the river was then unchanged.

Still later, in the reign of Sayyid Khizr Khan, when there was unusual communication with Katehar, or Rohilkhand, we find the following allusions which may assist us in our investigation. Táju'l-mulk, after subduing Rai Harsingh of Katehar, "arrived at the ferry of Sargdwárí, and passing the Ganges, punished the Kafirs of Khor and Kampil."

The same General, after another campaign, marching from Badáon and Etawah, passes the Ganges at Pachlana.

In the same year the Emperor himself, after plundering Sambhal, crossed the Ganges near Patiálí.

نزدیک پتیالي از آب گنگ گذشته

These quotations are taken from the "Tabaḳát-i-Akbarí."

The "Táríkh-i-Badáoní" uses precisely the same expression in two of these instances: and it is important to observe it, for the author was himself a great traveller, and was constantly on the move between Agra, Sambhal, and Badáon. Both he and the author of "Tabaḳát-i-Akbarí" were contemporaries of Akbar, and could not fail, if any changes in the course of the Ganges had occurred up to their time, to give prominent notice of the circumstance.

All the places noted above are on the right bank of the old Ganges, and would most probably not have been mentioned had the Ganges not run under them. At least in these days there are no such ferries as those of Pachlana, Patiálí, and Sargdwárí. But as it may perhaps be said that, notwithstanding the change in the river's bed, the expressions quoted above would not altogether have been inapplicable, other more decisive testimony may be adduced from a document in an old "Dastúru'l-'Amal," in which mention is made of a Mauza in Tappa Aúlái, Parganah Badáon, which, though the document may not be an exact copy of one publicly issued (it being merely inserted as a model for imitation), may yet serve to show without further question, that Aúlái was once an integral part of Parganah* Badáon. If it be remarked that the change in the course of the river is too great to have occurred within the period which has elapsed since the compilation of the A'ín-i Akbarí, it may be replied that in our own time the change is almost every year perceptible, and that the Ganges has shifted its bed so much since the two opposite banks were measured, that although only five years elapsed between the surveys, they cannot be combined with any accuracy.

It is to be hoped therefore that the reasons given above may be considered to justify the innovation which has been ventured in the map.

Bujhárat, بجهارت बुझारत

Adjustment of accounts. From बुझाना bujháná, to cause to comprehend. In some districts it has a special significance.

"This audit of accounts (or Bujhárat as it is called) is a most important process to the whole of the community. The right of admission to the audit is the criterion of proprietary right" (Sel. Rec. N.W.P. iv. 143, from report on Azimgaṛh by Thomason).—B.

Búrá, بورا बूरा

Redeemable mortgage.—Eastern Oudh.

Britá, برتا ब्रिता

A grant, generally of land, to a religious person, or to a tenant on certain stipulations. See Birt, and the Printed Glossary under Burt.

* Moreover, in the book entitled the "Aḥwál-i Subaját," a new Parganah under the name of Nidhpúr, is entered as "in the time of the Sirkár of Badaun." This work was written before the final disruption of the empire, and is a highly interesting memorial of the state of India at the time of its composition. It was obtained from the library of Nawwab Muhammad Mír Khan, whose family has had close connection with the house of Timúr since its decline.

Brittántpattar, برتانت پتر ब्रितांतपत्तर

The record of a decision given by a Panchayet. From वृत्तांत circumstance, narration; and पत्र a leaf, a deed.

Bachhaunṭá, بچھونٹا बछौंटा

Distribution of an aggregate sum on several individuals. (See Behri).—Upper Doáb.

Bahí, بہي बही

An account book; a register; a ledger.

Thus, Bahí Khata is the day book kept by merchants, and Bahí Patwárí, the village accountant's, or Patwárí's register.

Bakár, بکار बकार

Amount fixed by the appraiser.—See Bak.

Bakhshnámá, بخشنامه बखशनामा

A deed of gift: from بخش gift, and نامه a letter, a document.

Bá farzandán, با فرزندان बाफरजंदान

Bá aulád, با اولاد बाऔलाद

Literally, with sons, with children: words inserted in a grant, when it was intended that the land should be inherited by the heirs of the grantee. The opinion of the Supreme Government (in the famous case of Farzand Ali) was that these terms refer to the immediate heirs of the grantee's body, whether male or female, not to descendants generally; and this, no doubt, is correct; but according to the lenient interpretation of the officers concerned in the investigations respecting Maafí tenures, the words are now generally declared to convey an hereditary title, without any restriction.

The Judges of the Sudder Dewanny Adaulat have also ruled

that a Bá farzandan grant is descendable to the heirs general (Reports, Vol. IV. p. 222): being opposed to the opinion of their law officers, who declared that the words in themselves, and apart from other expressions in the grant, created a joint interest with benefit of survivorship in the grantee and his children; or in the event of his having at the time of grant no children, but only grand-children, in the grantee and his grand-children.—(See "Macnaghten's Precedents of Mahomedan Law," p. 332, and pp. 48–52 of "Extracts from Official Records on Maafí Investigations.")

Baith, بیٹھ बैठ

Value of Government share of produce. The amount *settled* on the land, from *baiṭhná* بیٹھنا to sit: thus bearing the same etymological meaning as assessment. The word is used in many varieties of application in commercial transactions; thus, *kitná baiṭhtá* is "how much does it come to" (in reckoning or apportioning various items).

Bájantarí, باجنتري बाजंतरी

Bájantarí, or rather Bájantarí Mahal, was an item of collection under the Mahomedan regime, derived from H. बाजा a musical instrument; Sanskrit वाद्य.

Bák, باک बाक

Bák is used in the North West to signify an estimate of the produce without measuring the field.

There are men who make a profession of this, and it is wonderful with what accuracy they will guess the probable outturn of a crop by merely looking at it. In cases in my own experience it has happened that when the crop has been cut and threshed the valuer has not been more than one or two seers out.—B.

Bakíotá, بقیوتا बकीयोता

A list of arrears of revenue due from farmers.—Behar.

Bálúburd, بالوبرد बालूबुर्द

From بالو sand, and Persian بُرد cut: a term applied to a tract of land which is covered with a deposit of sand after an inundation. An item of remission of revenue on this account.

Bángar, بانگر बांगर

High ground, or uplands. Thus, "Pánípat Bángar," "Sonpat Bángar," are the elevated portions of those parganahs, in distinction to "Pánípat Khadir," "Sonpat Khadir."

Bárah, بارہ बारह

Land next to, or surrounding, the village, generally enriched by manure. The term is chiefly used in Dehli and the Upper Doáb, and is probably derived from بار or باڑ an enclosure.*

Báráni, بارانی बारानी

Unirrigated land; land dependant on the seasons; from the Persian باران *bárán*, rain. Also a coat or cloak for keeping off rain, which Europeans usually corrupt into "brandy."

Barát, برات बरात

*** In addition to its numerous other meanings, it is used in the provinces, under the perpetual settlement, to imply an order to pay issued by a zamíndár on a mustájir ṭhíkadár or lessee. It is in this way:—Say a zamíndar wants to buy a lot of shawls, jewels, or such things, instead of paying the merchant in cash, he gives him a Barát or order on one of his lessees, the lessee pays the merchant, and at the next audit of accounts produces the Barát as a set-off against the rent due from him. In this

* Called Goháu in Oudh, and Goenḍ or Gwenḍ in Behar.—B.

way some of our zamíndárs contrive to anticipate the whole of their rents for several years to come.—B.

Bárbaṭái, بارِبٹائي बारबटाई

Division of the crops by sheaves or shocks, before the corn is trodden out. From the Persian بار *bár*, a load. In Rohilkhand it is more usually called by the Hindí synonym of Bojh-baṭái.

Bárambá, بارنبه बारंबा

Literally, fruit of mangoes. Revenue derived from the lease of mangoe-groves. From بار fruit, and آم a mangoe.*

Bágam, باگم बागम

Said, in the Printed Glossary, to be the most productive lands in the Southern Division of Dehli, situate on the banks of canals; but this must be a mistake, as there are no canals in the Southern Division. The word, whatever it is, is most probably derived from *bágh*, a garden, or any richly cultivated and irrigated spot.

Ba'zí zamín daftar, بعضي زمين دفتر बाजी जमीन दफतर

An office established in A.D. 1782, before the enactment of the Regulations, for the purpose of enquiring into improper alienation of land. Literally, "the office of certain lands." The plan for the institution of this office is given at p. 224 of "Colebrooke's Digest of the Regulations," Vol. III.

Bebáḳ, بےباق बेबाक

Without arrears; paid up in full.—See Baḳí.

Biáj, بياج बिआज

Interest on money. Biájú is the capital put out to interest.

* This would be more correctly written as two words.—B.

Bídh bandí, بيڈّه بندي बीढ़ बन्दी

This is a peculiar system of calculating the amount to be paid by a cultivator. It is peculiar to Chibráman, a parganah of Farrakhabad, in the Central Doáb. It is thus described by Mr. Wynyard, the settlement officer, "By this system the Asámí pays his rent for the land in the aggregate, no matter whether he cultivates it or not." Kali Rai calls it बीढ *biḍ*.—E. *add.*

Bídhá, بيدها बीधा

Synonymous with Bandobast. Determination of the amount to be paid as Government revenue.—Upper Doáb and Rohilkhand.

Bíghá, بيگها बीघा or बीगहा

A measure of land, subject to local variation. In the Upper Provinces it is usually considered in the English surveys to be 3,025 square yards, or $\frac{5}{8}$ths of an acre. In Bengal it is 1,600 square yards, or little more than $\frac{1}{3}$rd of an acre. A Kachcha Bíghá is in some places $\frac{1}{3}$rd, in others $\frac{1}{4}$th, of a full Bíghá.

Akbar's Bíghá contained 3,600 Ilahí Gaz (see that article).

The following are some of the local variations of the Bíghá in the Upper Provinces:—

		BIGHAS.	B.	C.
In Farrakhabad, 100 acres,	=	175	12	0
In the E. and S. parts of Gorakhpúr,	=	192	19	7

In the W. and N. parts the Bíghás are much smaller.

In Allahabad and part of Azimgaṛh,	=	177	5	15
In part of Azimgaṛh and Ghazipur,	=	154	6	8
In Bijnor,	=	187	19	15

In the Upper Doáb it was found that the average measurement of the side of a Bíghá, deduced from the paces of 148 zamíndárs, who were accustomed to practice this kind of mensuration, amounted to 28 $\frac{834}{1000}$ English yards; making the local (kachcha) bíghá equal to 831$\frac{4}{10}$; and 100 statute acres equal to 582 kachcha bíghás, 3 biswas.

It is needless to continue the comparisons; but see for further information "Prinsep's Useful Tables," p. 89.—E.

*** There seems to be some connection between the size of the kachcha, or local, bíghá and the value of land in different districts. The official bíghá consists of twenty cottahs or biswas, each side of which is measured by a rod of four cubits in length, thus called the chahár dasti, or chár háth ke kattá; but in the remoter parts of Gorakhpúr and the wild tracts bordering on Nepal the bíghá increases in size, till in some places we have it consisting of twenty kattás of as much as ten cubits in length each! and returning from the frontier back again to the more thickly peopled parts of the country, the cottah sinks by degrees to 9, 8, 7, 7½, and 6 háths in the various parganahs.—B.

Bighoto, بگھوتو बिघोतो

The name given to a tract of country bordered by Mewat on the East, Lohárú on the West, Hariána, Dhundhotí, and Chandán on the North, and Rath on the South. It includes Rewarí, Bawal, Kanon, Patodí, Kot Kasim, and a great part of the Bahraich Jagír. The word is only of local application, and does not appear to be known much beyond its own limits.

बिघोतो को द्वो धनी खोरो और चौहान

That is, "Bighoto has two lords, Khoros (amongst Ahírs), and Chauháns (amongst Rajputs)."

The name of Bíghoto, or Bíghota as it is sometimes called, is derived from Bígha Raj, a worthy descendant of the illustrious Chauhán, Pirthí Raj.—See Dhundhotí and Chauhán.

Bigahṭí, بگہٹی बिगहटी

Rent fixed on lands per bíghá. The same as Bigoṭi in the Glossary, which is also correct.

Bíjak, بيجك बीजक

A memo. deposited with grain when stored, specifying its amount; an invoice, a list; also an inscription.

The derivation is probably वेदयक, the causal form of the Sanskrit विद to know.

Bísí, بيسي बीसी

A term peculiar to Kamáon.

Mr. Trail, the English Commissioner of the Province, reduced all the miscellaneous measures of quantity of land to nominal (not actually measured) Bísís. The Bísí is equal to twenty Pathas of Gaṛhwál, or twenty Nalís of Kamáon. The Patha, or Nalí, represents a measure of seed with a capacity of about two seers, and the number of Pathas in any area is estimated by the quantity of seed (generally wheat) required to sow it. The actual extent varies according to the quality and position of the land. The grain is sown much wider in the poor Uparáṅw lands near the summit, than in the rich Taláṅw lands near the base.—See As. Res., xvi., 178.

Behrí, بيهري बेहरी

A subscription; an assessment on a share. Instalments paid by under tenants to the landlord. Distribution of an aggregate sum on several individuals. A monthly collection according to their respective circumstances. Term given to a division of a Bhayachara estate. The share or interest of one of the brotherhood in an estate. The Persian Bahra has the same meaning, and is probably the origin of the word.

Behrídár, بيهري‌دار बेहरीदार

Holder of a share, denominated Behrí.—See Glossary, Beraidar.

Benaudhá, بنودها बेनौधा

A name commonly given by the natives to the country between Allahabad and Sarwar, *i.e.* Sarjúpar, the other side of the Sarjú (ancient Sarayu), the present district of Gorakhpúr; and between the Ganges and the Chhúab Nala, by which it is separated on the North-West from Baiswara. Benaudha appears to include the Western parts of Jaunpúr, Azimgaṛh, and Benares, and the Southern part of Oudh. Indeed, some authorities make it extend from Baiswara to Bijaypúr, and from Gorakhpúr to Bhojpúr. The common saying is that Benaudha, or Benáwat as it is sometimes called, contained twelve Rajas, who comprised one Paut, and were considered to have common interests. 1st, the Gaharwár of Bijaypúr; 2nd, the Khánzada Bachgotí; 3rd, Bais; 4th, Sarnet; 5th, Haiobans of Hardí; 6th, Ujjain of Dúmráṅw; 7th, Rajkumar of Teorí Bhagwanpúr; 8th, Chandel of Agorí; 9th, Kalhans of Sarwár; 10th, Gautam of Nagra; 11th, Hindú Bachgotí of Karwar; 12th, Bisen of Majhaulí. These dimensions would imply that Benaudha was an extensive province, including the whole of Benares and Eastern Oudh; but I believe the limits first mentioned are the correct ones, and out of this narrower space it would be easy to construct the fifty-two parganahs, of which Benaudha is said to consist.

Bakhshíát, بخشیات. बखशीआत

The name of a division of the Jaunpúr Sirkár mentioned in Regulation II. of 1795. This Parganah no longer exists as a separate division. Its former history and the derivation of its name are very obscure; apparently, however, the designation of "Bakhshíát," or "Dihát Bakhshígarí," prior to the Cession, applied only to certain villages which were assigned to the Bakshí of the Fort at Jaunpúr, for repairs and other necessary expences, and it was not till after we got possession of the country, that the Talúkas of Soetha, Kariáwan, Nawái, and Bhadí, all of which are Peshkashí Mahals, were included in the Parganah called Bakhshíát. Under these circumstances, there was no objection at the late settlement to absorb the sub-division in the manner most convenient, and the villages were accordingly distributed between Ghisuá, Havelí, Karákat, and Angli Mahul.

Baldiháí, بلدهائي बलदहाई

Compensation for pasture ground.—Rohilkhand.

It is usually called Bardaihí to the Eastward.—See Ang.

Balkat, بلكٹ बल्कट

Rent taken in advance.—Lower Doáb, Bundelkhand, and Benares.

The word is also applied to the cutting of ears of corn without going through the usual process of reaping. Katáí is likewise used in this sense in Benares.

From this word is derived the name of the old Mahomedan tax bálkaṭí, which used to be demanded on commencement of reaping. From बाल an ear of corn, and काटना to cut.

Bandbehrí, بندبيهري बन्दबेहरी

Statement of the amount of each money instalment or share of a village. The word Band is used in many other combinations in the sense of statement, account, ledger; thus Bandbardasht or Bandbatáí is a statement of the amount of each instalment in grain. Band-hisáb is an abstract account. Bandphántah is a paper like the Bandbehrí which shows the liabilities of each sharer of a village.

Bapans, بپنس बपंश

Father's share.—Benares and Eastern Oudh.

Bapautí is more usual in the N. West and Bundelkhand.

The word is derived from बाप a father, and अंश share.

Bakáyá, بقايا बकाया

Old balances of Revenue; plural of the Arabic باقي an arrear, a residue.

Barárí, براري बरारी

A shareholder paying his portion of the Jama according to the Barár.

Baráwurd, برآورد बरावुर्द

An estimate; calculating; casting up. From the Persian بر above, and اوردن to bring.

Baṛhí, بڑھي बढी

Profits, a corruption of Baṛhotarí: from بڑھنا to increase.

Barmhotar,* برمهوتر बरमहोतर

A free grant given to Brahmins for religious purposes.

Batnan-bád-batnan, بطنا بعد بطنا बतनन बाद बतनन

Literally, "body after body,"—words frequently inserted in grants, after the corresponding expression of Nasalan ba'd Nasalan, to signify that the tenure is heritable by lineal descendants in the male line. Under the present interpretation of the resumption laws, the expression is construed to convey the right of perpetuity, without this restriction.

Baṭṭá, بٹّا बट्टा

Difference of exchange; anything extra; an extra allowance; discount on uncurrent or short weight coins: usually called Batta. The word has been supposed to be a corruption of Bharta, increase, but it is a pure Hindí vocable, and is more usually applied to discount than premium.

Baidár, بيعدار बैदार

A proprietor by purchase; from the Arabic بيع selling. Hence Bainâma, a deed of sale.

* Also spelt ब्रह्मोत्तर and बम्हौतर.

Bai'bi'l wafá dár, بيع بالوفادار बैबिलवफादार

A person having the possession and usufruct of a property on its conditional sale to him; the stipulation being that if a sum of money borrowed from him be not repaid by a fixed period, the sale shall become absolute; from بيع sale, and وفا performance of a promise.

Cháhí, چاهي चाही

Lands irrigated from wells (from the Persian Cháh چاه a well), as distinguished from باراني Báráni, or land dependent on rain for its moisture; Cháhí land pays a higher revenue than Báráni, because it has a certain supply of water, while the supply from rain is of course uncertain.

*** The extreme uncertainty of the supply of rain is the cause of the terrible famines to which India is peculiarly subject; and which it is now proposed to combat by a larger system of irrigation derived from canals. The system of irrigation from wells is defective in many ways. It necessitates the keeping by each cultivator of extra bullocks to work the well. Besides which to dig a well is a costly operation, and can therefore only be done by rich men or by the joint act of the community. A well is like an estate, the joint property of a large body of men, each of whom has his stated number of hours in the week for using the water. In the hot weather the necessity of getting water for the fields is so great that the wells are kept at work all day and all night, the water being led along conduits of earth sometimes for miles. When worked so incessantly the well will sometimes dry up for a time, because the water is taken out faster than it runs in, and the ryot has to stop working till it fills again. All the uncertainty, expense, and other inconveniences of the cháhí system will be obviated by canals.

In many parts of Behar there are no wells for agricultural

purposes, and the people are entirely dependent on rain or tanks.

It is curious to observe how the wells vary in size in different parts of the country. In the Panjáb the wells are often from fifteen to twenty feet in diameter, there is one at Amritsar which admits four rahaṭs or Persian wheels at once. Lower down, in the N.W. Provinces, six or seven feet is the average diameter, and the well is generally worked by the charas or charsá, a large leathern sack, which is drawn up by bullocks walking down an incline. This requires two men to work it, one to drive the bullocks and another to tilt the charas when it comes up; whereas the rahaṭ requires only a man or boy to drive the buffalo round (*v.* Arhaṭ).

Lower down again in Behar the wells diminish to two or three feet in diameter, and are worked by a kuṅr or small bucket of iron or earth, fastened by a long rope to a pole, the pole works on a pivot in a post four or five feet high and is balanced at the other end by a heavy log or mass of earth. This also requires only one man to work it. It is chiefly used by Koerís (or Kachhís) to irrigate their fields of poppy or other rare and costly crops. The labour of using it is hard, and the amount of water raised is less than by any other process; but in Behar, especially in the eastern parts of it, the soil is often so loose that a permanent well cannot be made, and the little temporary wells are therefore more economical. In Purneah they are very small, often not above a foot across, and are supported by rings of burnt clay called páṭ. A well of this kind costs two rupees only, and lasts a couple of years.

It is the western part of these Provinces and in the Panjáb that canal irrigation is peculiarly needed; in the eastern districts and in Bengal the land is low and full of marshes, tanks, and rivers, and the main staple is rice, which grows in three or four feet of water, and during the rainy season, when the country is generally submerged; but in the upper provinces the land is high and dry, and the wheat and other staples require constant irrigation to make them grow at all.—B.

Chákarí, چاکري चाकरी

Grant for personal services in the village; from چاکر a servant.

Chhír, چهير छीर

The lessee's own cultivation; corrupted from Sír.—Saugor.

Chhuṭautí, چهٹوتي छुटौती

Remissions allowed either on the Bíghá, or in rupees, by Malgúzárs, after forming an estimate of a field. Also, generally, any remission of Revenue by Government; from छुटना Chhutná, to be dismissed, to escape.

Chhut, Chhut Má'fí, or Mujrái, are terms specially applied in Benares to the reductions which have been made in the assessment of 1197 Faslí. Some of these have been authorized by the Government, but most of them have been granted without any such authority. Some of those in the former category are alluded to in Sect. 22, Reg. II. of 1795.

Chhorchiṭṭhí چهوڑچٹهي छोडचिट्ठी

A deed of release, from छोडना chhoṛná, to abandon, and चिट्ठी chiṭṭhí, a note.

Chiṭṭhí, چٹهي चिट्ठी

A note; a paper containing an order or demand. From this word are formed chiṭṭhí talab or talab chiṭṭhí, meaning a process or precept; a summons; from the Arabic طلب search, demand; and Chiṭnavís (written Chiṭnís in the Printed Glossary), a writer of notes or precepts; a secretary; from the Persian نوشتن to write.—E.

Chiṭṭhí taksim is a note or memorandum of allotment or partition of an estate by Baṭwára.—W.

Chiṭṭhí tankhwáhí, is a note containing a demand for payment of rent; also the same as Barát *q.v.*—W.

Chukárá, چکارا चुकारा

Customs duty.—Saugor.

Chukautá, چکوتا चुकौता

Field rates of rent; money rate; from चुकाना Chukáná, to settle or complete. Also an agreement for the delivery free of cost of a stipulated share of an estimated crop to the principal shareholder on the part of the rest.—Moradabad.—W.

Chukrí, چکري चुकरी

A fractional division of land.—Garhwál and Kamáon.

Chukat, چکت चुकत

A settlement; from चुकाना Chukáná, to settle.—Dehli and Upper Doáb.

Chungí, چنگي चुंगी

Illegal abstraction of handfuls of market produce. It is frequently, however, given voluntarily as a sort of rent for the use of market conveniences, such as booths, sheds, etc.; and in this sense is equivalent to the Baitak of the Deccan.

Chungí is also sometimes given to Fakírs, Zamíndárs, or Banias, for the establishment of new markets.—E.

In the Panjáb it is the name of a tax levied in kind on all produce that enters the city gates, an octroi in fact; and has been continued under British government.—B.

Chungí mahál, a place where grain may be landed from boats and stored on payment of a portion of it to the owners of the ground.—Behar.—W.

Chaubáchhá, چوباچهه चौबाछा

A levy of Revenue on four things, under the ancient regime, in the Dehli territory; namely, *pag, tag, kori,* or *kudi,* and *púnchhi:* i.e. *pagṛi,** a turban, *tag,* a rag or thread worn by a child round its waist, *kori,* a hearth, and *púnchhi,* animals' tails, as of buffaloes, bullocks, etc.

As *tag* may be considered to be included in *pag,* another tax is substituted for it according to some authorities. Thus *palkaṭi* a cess on the *pala* cuttings (see Jharberí), or a cess on the *daranti* or sickle, or on the *khurpa* or grass-scraper; but the insertion of *tag* is correct, for the tax upon the *pag,* or men, was double of that upon the *tag,* or children.

Chaubísá, چوبيسه चौबीसा

From Chaubís, twenty-four; is a name applied to a tract of country containing that number of villages in the occupation of a particular tribe. There are several of them scattered over our Provinces, but they may perhaps be considered more frequent in the neighbourhood of Mathurá than elsewhere. Thus, we have within a circuit of about thirty miles round that city—

A Chaubísa of Jaes Rajputs.
A Chaubísa of Jadon Rajputs.
A Chaubísa of Bachhal Rajputs.
A Chaubísa of Kachhwáha Rajputs.
A Chaubísa of Jaiswar Rajputs.—See Chaurásí.

Chaudharáí, چودهرائي चौधराई

The jurisdiction of a Chaudharí, whose occupation has been correctly described in the Printed Glossary.

* Called by our early travellers *puckery.* "To scold lustily and to pull one another's *puckeries* or turbats off, being proverbially termed a banyan fight."—"Fryer's Trav." Lett. III. Chap. 3.

Chaudharáít, چودهرايت चौधराइत

A Chaudharí's fees of office.

Chaugaḍḍá, چوگڈا चौगड्डा

The place where the boundaries of four villages meet. It is known also by the names of Chauhadda, Chausinghá, Chaukhá, Chauráha, and Chompta.

Chaumás, چوماس चौमास

Lands tilled from Asarh to Kúar, that is, during the Chaumása (four months), or rainy season, and prepared for the Rabí sowings.

Chaumásá, چوماسا चौमासा

The Indian seasons are, according to the Shasters, six in number, each comprising two months. These divisions are more fanciful than real; and the common people are content to adopt the more definite division of three. Chaumása, or Barkha, constitutes the four months of the rainy season. The rest of the year is comprised in Syálá, Járá, or Mohása, the cold season; and Dhúpkál, or Kharsá, the hot season.

Chaumasiyá, چومسيا चौमसिया

A ploughman hired fo- the season.—Saugor.

Chaur or Chaunr, چونر चौंर

A long low marsh lying between high banks, fit for growing rice, and generally full of water in the rains.—Behar.—B.

Chaurásí, چوراسي चौरासी

The word means, literally, eighty-four: and is territorially applied to a sub-division of a parganah, or district, amounting to eighty-four villages. Tod, in his "Annals of Rajputana," where Chaurásís are numerous, remarks that they are tantamount to the Saxon Hundreds (Vol. I. p. 141). This may be the case in some respects, but it is evident that Hundreds rarely contained a hundred *villages*, and sometimes not even half a hundred. Spelman, in his Glossary, says, "*Nusquam quod scio, reperiuntur* 100 *villæ in aliquo Hundredo per totam Angliam. Magni habentur qui vel* 40, *vel* 30, *numerant. Multi ne* 10 *: Quidam duas tantum.*" Hallam also observes ("Middle Ages," Vol. II. p. 390), that the great divisions of the Northern counties had originally a different name, and that in course of time many of them have *improperly* acquired the name of Hundreds, which is conjectured to be a mere political division more peculiarly belonging to the South of England. Lingard also (Vol. I. p. 335) gives an extract from Doomsday Book to show how little uniformity prevailed with respect to the area and number of manors contained within each Hundred. Thus we see that Hundreds were never originally equally partitioned, and in this respect they differ from Chaurásís; for there is no Chaurásí, even though it may have dwindled down to ten or twelve villages, of which every originally component village could not, according to local tradition, be pointed out by the neighbouring zamíndárs; so that Chaurásís once comprised—theoretically, however inexactly in certain cases,—as the name implies, eighty-four villages.

I took occasion, when reporting the Mírat Settlements, to remark that I had discovered some Chaurásís in that district, and expressed my surprise that their existence had not been previously observed. The assertion, I well remember, was received with some degree of incredulity, and the existence of Chaurásís in any part of these Provinces was altogether denied. I have therefore taken some trouble to ascertain if I was deceived, and the following list, which is the result of my enquiries, will perhaps be considered to establish their existence beyond a question, not only in Mírat, but in almost every district in this Presidency.

In Deolí, now included in the Parganah of Bíbamíyú in Etawah, there is a Chaurasí of Tilokchandi Bais Rajputs.

The Parganah of Kuraolí, in Mainpúrí, constitutes a Chaurásí of Rathor Rajputs.

In Jewar of Bulandshahr, the Chaukarzada Jadon Rajputs have a Chaurásí.

In the Parganah of Chandaus in Aligaṛh, there is a Chaurásí of Chauhán Rajputs.

In Parganah Kantit, of Zillaḥ Mirzapur, there is a Chaurásí of Gaṛhwár Rajputs, of which most of the villages are now in the possession of Brahmans.

In Parganah Khairabad, of Zillah Allahabad, there is another Chaurásí of Gaharwár Rajputs.

The Loháín Játs have a Chaurásí in Hariána.

One of the Tappas in Atraulí of Aligaṛh is a Chaurásí.

The Parganahs of Malaut and Bharangí in Bhattíána are each a Chaurásí.

There is also in the neighbourhood of Karsána, Sirpána, and Sahával a Chaurásí of Balde Brahmans, and in Saheswan and Ujhani one of Tuar Rajputs.—See also article Janghára.

The Solankhí Rajputs have a Chaurásí in Nidhpúr and Sahával, on the borders of the Mainpúrí and Badáon districts. They are the descendants of the princes of the sacred Soron, before the Rathors conquered Kanauj.

From Allahabad to Karra there is a Chaurásí of Johya Rajputs, who have been for a long time converted to Mahomedanism.

In the Parganah of Hansi there is a Chaurásí of Játs, comprising the Gots of Seil, Rongí, Bora and Satraungí.

In Parganah Sheolí of Cawnpore there is a Chaurásí of Chandel Rajputs.

In Oudh, opposite to Sheorajpúr, there is a Fattihpúr Chaurásí tenanted by Bisen Rajputs.

There is a Chaurásí of Chandel Rajputs in Kariat Dost, in Zillah Jaunpúr.

There is a Chaurásí of Tuar Rajputs in Dasna and Jalalabad, Zillah Mírat.

There is half a Chaurásí of the same tribe in Puth, in the same district.

The Nagrí Gújars have a Chaurásí in Dankaur, Zillah Bulandshahr.

The Parganah of Loni was formerly a Chaurásí.

The Parganah of Ghazipur, in Fattihpúr, was formerly a Chaurásí.

In Mahomedabad Gohna, of Zillah Azimgaṛh, there was also formerly a Chaurásí.

The Baláín Játs, the Salakláín Játs, and the Kalsean Gújars, have each a Chaurásí in the Western Division of the Muzaffarnagar District.

The Nirwal Játs have a Chaurásí to the South of Dehli.

In Baghpat the Gaur Tagás had a Chaurásí, of which but few villages now remain in their possession.

Garra Kota in Damoh of Saugor is a Bundela Chaurásí.

In the same Parganah the Deswal Ahírs had half a Chaurásí.

Parganah Jhillo in Saugor is a Chaurásí.

The Títwal Tagas of the Upper Doáb had formerly a Chaurásí.

There is a Talúka Chaurásí to the North of the Son (Soane), in Agorí Barhar of Mirzapur.

There is a Chaurásí of Baḍgújar Rajputs in Mahendwar, the local name of a tract of country between the Mewat Hills and the Jumna.*

There is also a Chaurásí of the same clan of Rajputs, now Musulman, on the banks of the Hindan, to the South West of Muzaffarnagar.

This branch of Rajputs had also a Chaurásí in Rajpúra, and in Neraulí, Parganahs of Rohilkhand, and another on the opposite side of the Ganges at Anúpshahr. These, however, are

* More correctly the name of a small river now dammed up.—E.

only sub-divisions of the much more extensive possessions they had on either side of the Ganges.

There is a Chaurásí of Rangars in Parganah Kata of Seharanpúr.

There is a Chaurásí of Khúbar Gújars in Rampúr in the same District.

The Bunáphar Rajputs have a Chaurásí in Garra Mandla.

There is a Chaurásí of Gautam Rajputs, now Musulman, in Tappa Jar, Zillah Fattihpúr.

There is a Chaurásí also in Hatgaon, in the same District.

The Mahesara Tagas have a Chaurásí in Kithor, Zillah Mírat.

The Basían and Datean Tagas have each a Chaurásí in Puth and Síana, on the borders of Bulandshahr.

There is a Chaurásí of Sakarwal Rajputs in Parganah Chainpúr of Arrah.

The Parganah of Rohtak is a Chaurásí.

The Parganah of Tezgarh, in Damoh, is a Chaurásí.

There is a Chaurásí of Chauháns in Aonla, a Parganah of Bareilly.

There is a Chaurásí of Thukarel Játs in the Western parts of Aligaṛh.

There is a Chaurásí near the Cantonment of Urái in Jalaun.

The Sabaran Brahmans have a Chaurási in Parganah Etawah.

The Ahírs have a Chaurásí in the Northern parts of Shekohabad, in Mainpúrí.

There is a Chaurásí near Bhojpúr, at a short distance from Farrakhabad, known generally by the name of the Chaurásí of Siraulí.

There is a Chauhán Chaurásí of Jhilmilí in Sirgúja.

There is a Chuk Chaurásí between Ghiswa and Jaunpúr.

There is a Chaurásí of Palwar Rajputs in Anaula of Gorakhpúr.

There is also another kind of Chaurásí in Anaula. When Chandersen, the Sarnet Raja, divided his acquisitions among his three sons, he gave a Chaurásí (in Koss) to his eldest son, constituting the Raj of Gorakhpúr; half a Chaurásí (in Koss) to his second, constituting the Raj of Hasanpúr Maghar; and a quarter Chaurásí (also in Koss) to the third, constituting the Raj of Anaula.

There are two Chaurásís in Parganah Chandpúr, Zillah Bijnor.

There are also two Chaurásís of Mewátís, one called the Kamú Chaurásí in Bhurtpúr, and the other the Dehli Chaurásí, near Sonah.*

Súrajpúr, in Ghosí of Azimgaṛh, is a Chaurásí Talúka, belonging to Kurhanya Bhúínhars.

The Suksena† Kayeths had formerly a Chaurásí around Sankisa, on the Kalínadí, between Mainpúrí and Farrakhabad.

* The existence of this Sonah Chaurásí is doubtful.—E. *add.*

† The Suksena Kayeths have now entirely deserted Sankisa (Sankasya). From this place have also sprung the Suksena Naís, Kachhís, and Bharbhúnjas; and it is highly interesting as being mentioned in the Rámáyana, and by the Chinese traveller Fa-Hian (A.D. 400), who speaks in terms of high approbation of Seng-kia-shi and its neighbourhood.

"Ce royame est fertile et abondant en toutes sortes de productions. Le peuple y est nombreux, riche, et sans comparaison plus joyeux que partout ailleurs" (p. 126). There is nothing in the present appearance of the country to warrant this high eulogium. In the 14th Number of the Journal of the Royal Asiatic Society, there is an interesting account of a visit paid to Sankisa by the Múnshí of Lieutenant Cunningham, Bengal Engineers, which seems to call for a few remarks. The ruins of Sankisa (not called now Samkassa) can enter into no comparison with those of Kanauj, even if we include the ancient khera of Saraí Agath. The Gosaín's Temple, moreover, can scarcely be said to be built of the ancient large bricks; as there are but very few in the whole structure. There is also an important misapprehension to be corrected, as Lieutenant Cunningham and Colonel Sykes both lay too much stress upon it. It is stated as an extraordinary fact that the worship of the identical Naga mentioned by Fa-Hian is still annually performed; but the truth is, that the mound where this worship takes place is nothing more than the common heap of bricks, or earth, which we see in every village, erected for worship during the Nag-Panchamí. The only local Deity of Sankish is Bisarí, whose favour is supposed to be efficacious in removing diseases of the eyes.

The Elephant, mentioned at page 242, is the most interesting object at Sankisa. It is carved out of precisely the same description of stone as the Lat of Dehli and Allahabad. The body, which is about three feet high and on a pedestal sunk into the ground to the same depth, is well formed, but the snout has been knocked off by some

There is a Chaurási of Chauhán Rajputs in Bhopal.

There is a Chaurási of Sakarwal Rajputs in Pahargarh in Gwalior.

There is a Chaurási of Jatraní Játs in Khera Bijwasan.

There is a Chaurási in the Northern parts of Gadarpúr, Zillah Bareilly. It belonged to the race called Gobrí; but the space is, perhaps, too small to have comprised a Chaurási of villages, and it may therefore have represented a Chaurási of

zealous iconoclast. It bears inscriptions, or rather scratches, on its two flanks, and on the front of the right thigh.

The outer wall of the town, which does not appear to have a greater circuit than five miles, has been washed down, and nothing of it is now left but a succession of sloping mounds with several large gaps, which appear to represent the old gates. Saraí Agath, which is indebted for its name to the famous Muni Agastya, the fabled regenerator of the Dekkhan, is about a mile to the North of Sankisa, and has every appearance of being equally old. In 1843 about 20,000 rupees worth of coins were found at Saraí Agath, but there were none among them of any type previously unknown. Saraí Agath appears to have been an outwork of Sankisa, for it is beyond the wall above-mentioned. There are mounds beyond the wall in the same direction, which seem to have been rather fortifications than Stupas, though it is not improbable that close search will reward the enquirer with Buddhist remains. Several images of Bodhisatwas, and beautiful specimens of double-glazed pottery, strew the ground in various directions. It was in a vase of this description that the coins lately discovered were enclosed. Lieutenant Cunningham is probably correct in thinking that Sankisa was destroyed in the wars between Prithí Raj and Jaichand, but there seems reason to conclude that the town must have belonged to the latter when it was captured, for it is to the East of the Kalínadí, and is familiarly known as one of the gates of Kanauj. Hence, perhaps, we derive the story of the area of Kanauj being so large as to contain 30,000 shops of betel-sellers.

As the determination of the site of Seng-kia-sḥi confirms the truth of Fa-Hian's narrative, the European public are much indebted to Lieutenant Cunningham for his communication. It is only strange that Professor Wilson, who must have travelled close to, or over, its remains, and must have heard of the Suksena division of Káyeths and their original abode, should have doubted at all respecting its position, for Sankisa is generally recognized amongst the learned natives of these provinces to be the site of the Sankasya of the "Rámáyana;" and it is not unimportant to add that, when any inhabitant of Sankisa visits Nepal or Kamáon, he is treated with marked respect by the Paṇḍits and men of influence, as a traditional story of some original connection with this ancient city is still preserved in those remote regions.

tanks, which are in that spot very numerous. There is one village in the tract which still goes by the name of Chaurásí. But here we appear to have a Chaurásí within a Chaurásí; for the whole tract from the Píra Naddí to the Sardah, when it was under Hill-jurisdiction, was called the Chaurásí Mal (*i.e.* sub-montane region—see Des), because it extended eighty koss in length and four in breadth, or, according to some authorities, because it extended eighty-four koss in length.

The old Parganah of Alamgúpúr, in the district of Amballa, in the Cis-Satlaj states, of which the modern district of Mani majra was a portion, was a Chaurásí.

The Parganah of Gohana, in the Dehli Territory, constitutes a Chaurásí.

Kariat Síkhar, in the Province of Benares, also constitutes a Chaurásí.

The Jaurásís have, no doubt, the same origin. There is a Parganah Jaurásí in Seharanpúr, a Jaurásí Khalsa in Panípat, and a Jaurásí near the Maha Balí temple in Gaṛhwál. There is a Jaurásí range in the Himalaya (J.A.S.B. No. 138, p. 469).

In Jaunpúr, the Parganah of Byálsí is an abbreviation of Byálísí, or half a Chaurásí, of Raghubansí Rajputs.

The Parganahs of Kútia and Gúnír in Fattihpúr also form a Byálísí,* or half Chaurasí.

Parganah Dariabad in Oudh contains five Byálísís, of which three belong to Sayyids, Kurmís, and Bisen Rajputs respectively.

Besides those enumerated in the North West, and those which are known to exist in Rajpútana, we find indications of Chaurásís in several distant parts of the country.

There is a Parganah Chaurásí in Surat, and a Síam Chaurásí between the Bíah and the Satlaj.

There is a Chaurásí of Dhákará Rajputs in Fattihpúr of Hoshangábád, and in Sobhapúr of the same district there is one of Gújars.

* From ब्यालीस "forty-two."

Chaurásí is one of the seven districts into which the hill state of Sukat is divided.

The Kyarda Dún is said formerly to have contained eighty-four villages.

The Upades prasád says there are eighty-four cities in Gújar Das, or Guzerat.

In the Dekkan, eighty-four villages constitute a Desmukh, or Parganah. This can scarcely be universal, but it is so stated ("Journ. R.A.S." No. IV. p. 208) on the authority of Colonel Sykes. Elphinstone, on the contrary, says the Dekkan Parganahs contain 100 villages ("Hist. of India," Vol. I. 120).

There is a Chaurásí Jurah in Orissa ("As. Res." XV. 213).

Captain Blunt ("As. Res." VII. 92), in Parganah Mahtin, on his way to Rattanpúr, meets with a Kauhair chief, of whom he says, "All that I could collect from this chief was, that in these mountains there are seven small Districts, called Chaurásís, containing nominally eighty-four villages, but that, in reality, not more than fifteen were then in existence."

There is a Chaurásí marked on the Surveyor-General's Map at a short distance to the South of Kabul, which shews that all vestiges of ancient Hindu occupation are not yet erased from that country.

I proceed now to adduce instances of the existence in these Provinces, or a least the traditionary remembrance, of the still larger division of 360 villages, which number, as will hereafter be shewn, bears an intimate relation to the Chaurásí, and is based on the same principle of computation. I will merely premise here (what is well worthy of remark) that for territorial subdivisions there is no intermediate number between 84 and 360.

Amongst the six Cantons of Játs on the borders of Hariana and Bikanír, there are no less than four which have each 360 villages, viz., Punya, Kassúa, Saran, and Gadarra.

Panípat Bangar and Khadar are considered to constitute 360 villages.

Sonepar Bangar and Khadar are also considered to constitute 360 villages.

In and around Sirsa in the Bhattí territory, there are, or rather were, 360 villages of Chauhán Rajputs.

The Bisen Rajputs have 360 villages in Oudh.

The Parganah of Barah, in Allahabad, is reckoned to comprise 360 villages.

The Parganah of Bhoelí, in the Province of Benares, consisted of 360 villages.

The Ahírs of Bíghoto have 360 villages.—See Bíghoto.

The Parganah of Mírat is said to have consisted of 360 villages.

The Bhattí Gújars have 360 villages in the Western side of the Bulandshahr District.

The Pundír Rajputs, most of whom are now Musulman, have 360 villages in the North East of Saháranpúr.

The Kachhwaha Rajputs had formerly 360 villages in the Northern Doáb.

The Chandel Rajputs in Bithúr and the neighbourhood, formerly had 360 villages.

The Ráthí Gújars are said to have had 360 villages in the Upper Doáb; but though they claim this number for themselves, it is questionable if they ever had so many.

In the old Province called Nardak, to the West of Karnál, the Mundáhar Rajputs (now Musulman) have 360 villages.

In Parganah Katehar, of Benares, the Raghubansí Rajputs have 360 villages.

The Katherya Raja of Madhar, in Serauli, of District Moradabad, claims as the ancient possession of his tribe 360 villages in Rampúr. This, however, could only have been a sub-division, as the Katheryas had many more villages in their possession.

Raja Ram, Baghel, is said to have given 360 villages to the Brahmans of Arail.

The Dhangal Mewatís, who were formerly Kachhwaha Rajputs, have 360 villages.

The Dulaut, and the Sarban Mewatís have also each 360 villages.

The larger division of 1,440, or 360 × 4, such as the Mohils have at Aurínt ("Annals of Rajasthan," Vol. I. p. 627), does not seem to exist anywhere in these Provinces, though it is claimed by the Pundír Rajputs near Hardwar, the Juria Ladhís of Rámgarh in Jubbulpúr, the Gaur Brahmins and the Jutú Rajputs of Hariana, and sometimes by the Bais of Baiswara.—(See Gautam.)

The Konkan or country between the Western Ghats and the sea, in the Bombay Presidency, is said to contain 1400 villages ("As. Res." I. 361).

It is not, however, with respect to the occupation of land only that the numbers of 84 and 360 are regarded with such favour. We find them entering into the whole scheme of the Hindú, Buddhist, and Jain religions, cosmogonies, rituals, and legendary tales; so much so, as to shew that they are not taken by mere chance, as arbitrary numbers to fill up some of their extravagant fictions, but with a designed purpose of veiling a remote allusion under a type of ordinary character.

Thus, within the sacred precincts of Brij there are considered to be 84 Forests ("Smyth's Dict. *v.* Banjatra.")

Chitterkote (Chittor) is the chief among 84 castles, and has 84 bazars (Khaman Rasa).*

The country of Brij is 84 † Koss round Mathura. When Maha-

* See Tod's "Western India," pp. 156, 204, 213, 248, 268, 326.—E. *add.*

† There appears to be a double Chaurásí in Brij. The Parkarma, or annual perambulation, extends in circumference 84 koss, and does not come nearer to Agra than Gao-Ghat: but the "Bhágavata" says that Brij is shaped like a Singhara, or pignut; and the three corners of it are thus given in a familiar couplet,

इत बरहद इत सोनहद उत सूरसेन का गांव
बिर्ज चौरासी कोस में मथुरा मंडिल मांह

That is, the Chaurásí of Brij extends on one side to Sonah; on another to the lake of Barra (on the Isan, near Bijaygaṛh); and on another to Sursen ka Gaṅw, or Batesar.

It is strange, that notwithstanding the mention of Sursen ka Gaṅw in these trite ines, Colonel Tod should so often take credit to himself for being the discoverer of deo stole Sri Krishna's cows, the sportive God created new ones which grazed within this precise limit; and from that period, according to the Indian legend, the boundaries of Brij have been fixed, and to this day they are annually perambulated in the month of Bhadon (Brij Bilas).

The Mercantile tribes are 84 (Tod's "Raj." Vol. I. p. 120).

The Tribes of Sudras are also 84* (Price's "Hindí and Hindústaní Selections," Vol. I. p. 265).

Mount Meru is described as being 84,000 Yojans above the earth (Bhagavata; 5th Khand; and As. Res. Vol. VIII. pp. 273, 353).

The important places of Hindú Pilgrimage are reckoned to be 84. It is the popular belief, which does not appear to rest on written authority.

this capital, which he identifies with the Cleisobaras of Arrian ("Trans. R. A. Soc. Vol. III. p. 145). Even in the "Táríkh-i-Sher Shahí" (and Musulmans are rarely antiquarians) "Surseni, opposite to Raprí," is spoken of as the scene of an important engagement. In the first volume of the "Transactions," Colonel Tod announces his discovery in these words: "By the acquisition of this coin of Apollodotus, I made a double discovery, namely, of the coin itself, and of the ancient capital city. Conversing with the principal disciple of a celebrated Jain priest of Gwalior about ancient cities, he related to me an anecdote of a poor man, about thirty-five years ago, having discovered, amidst the few fragments left of Surapura on the Yamuná, a bit of (what he deemed) glass: shewing it to a silversmith, he sold it for one rupee; the purchaser carried his prize to Agra and sold it for 5,000, for it was a diamond. The finder naturally wished to have a portion of the profit, and on refusal, waylaid and slew the silversmith. The assassin was carried to Agra to be tried, and thus the name of Surapura became known beyond its immediate vicinity. This was a sufficient inducement to me to dispatch one of my coin-hunters, and I was rewarded by an Apollodotus and several Parthian coins. The remains of Surapura are close to the sacred place of pilgrimage, called by us "Batísur," on the Yamuná, between Agra and Etawah. Tradition tells us that it was an ancient city, and most probably was founded by Surasena, the grandfather of Krishna, and consequently the capital of the Suraseni of the historians of Alexander."—See also Vol. II. p. 286.

* I know no other authority for this statement than the one quoted, which is very poor. The whole Jatimala in the "Selections" is entirely wrong; and though it must be confessed that it would be no easy matter to compile a correct one, yet the more obvious errors should be expunged, as the work is intended to be educational.

Vallabha, the founder of the Rudra Sampradáya sect, had 84 followers (As. Res. Vol. XVI. p. 95).

There are 84 Gurus, or spiritual chiefs, of the sect of Rámánuj (Buchanan's Mysore).

There is an ankle ring called a Chaurásí, from that number of bells upon it (Kánún-i Islám).

The same name is given to the bells on an elephant's howdah cloth (A'ín-i Akbarí).

The temples of Mahadeo at Ujjayin are 84 (Journ. A. S. B. Vol. VI. p. 289).

The Hindú Hell is called Chaurásí, signifying that 84 places of punishment exist in Narak lok.*

The grand palace at Dattiah, which was built by Nar Singh Deo, was a series of ascending Chaurásís (on pillars). (Badshanama, by Abdú'l Hamíd Lahorí : 9th Jalús).

A Chaurásí of minor fortifications is said to have been contained within Rhotas (Jehangírnama, Vol. I).

The different postures of Jogís are 84 (As. Res. Vol. XVII. p. 184). These are called Asan; and the same name and number is given to the attitudes illustrated in the Koh Shastras (Tohfat-ul Hind).

The perfect Jogís, or Siddhas, are 84 (As. Res. Vol. XVII. p. 191).

The Gotras of the Gújars are 84 (Bansaolí).

The Gotras of the Ahírs are 84 (Tashríh-ul Akwám).

There are reckoned to be 8,400,000 species of animals; and these are comprised in four grand divisions, containing each a

* This is the popular belief; but it is not confirmed by the Shasters. In the "Vishnu Purana," p. 207, a list of twenty-eight Narakas is given. The "Bhágavata" also enumerates twenty-eight, but the names differ from those of the "Vishnu Purana." In the "Márkandeya Purana" and in "Menu" (B. IV. V. 88-92) a list of twenty-one is given, *i.e.*, a quarter Chaurásí. In the same Puranas a list of forty-two is given, or half a Chaurásí. Wilson, in his "Sanskrit Dict." Art. नरककुण्ड, says there are eighty-six pits in Tartarus, and the same is asserted by Radha Kanta Deo in the "Sabda Kalpa Druma," on the authority of the "Brahma Vaivartta Purana."

quarter Chaurásí, or 2,100,000—viz. *jaráuj,* those which are produced from the belly; *andaj,* from eggs; *seodaj,* from perspiration; and *udbhid,* from the earth (Garuda Purana,* Pret Khand).

The third grade of Bengal Brahmans is divided into 84 families (Colebrooke's Misc. Essays, Vol. II. p. 188).

There is also a Chaurásí division among the Gaur Brahmans.

There are 84 different sects of Brahmans in Central India (Malcolm's Central India, Vol. II. p. 122).

The Bháts have a Chaurásí sub-division.

There is a Chaurásí sub-division also among the Hindu Kambohs of Upper India.

The Kahars, or bearers, of Parganahs Khair and Koel constitute a Chaurásí.

There are 84 Nayat, or families of Brahmans, in Guzerat (Enc. Metrop. Vol XXIII. p. 33).

There is a Chaurásí sub-division among Tambolís (Martin's Buchanan, Vol. I. p. 164).

There is a Chaurásí sub-division also among Baráis, or betel-sellers (Ib. p. 165).

There is another among Koerís (Ib. Vol. II. p. 470).

Amongst the 12 divisions of Káyeths, the Mathur and Bhátnagar have each 84 sub-divisions. The Siríbastam say they also have 84, but this is not confirmed.

Siva has, like Krishna, 1008 names, *i.e.* 12 × 84 (Linga Purana).

In the Vayu Purana we are told that the water of the ocean, coming down from heaven on Meru, encircles it through seven

* The usual sub-division is somewhat different—9,00,000 fish, 10,00,000 birds, 11,00,000 reptiles, 20,00,000 plants, 30,00,000 quadrupeds, and 40,00,000 different species of men. This division is confirmed in popular credit by the following memorial verses:

नौलाष जीव जल मैं बसै दश पक्षी परिवारा
ग्यारह लाष कीट करम बीस अस्थावर विस्तारा
तीस लाष पशु जीव चारि लाष नर प्राणी ॥

channels for the space of 84,000 Yojans (As. Res. Vol. VIII. p. 322; see also p. 353).

One of the four Vikramas lived, or reigned, 84 years* (As. Res. Vol. X. p. 43).

The following Musical Chaurásí may be considered more artificial than natural, notwithstanding Sir W. Jones' opinion to the contrary.

"Now, since each of the tones may be divided, we find twelve semitones in the whole series; and, since each semitone may in its turn become the leader of a series formed after the model of every primary mode, we have seven times twelve, or *eighty-four*, modes in all, of which seventy-seven may be named secondary; and we shall see accordingly that the Persians and the Hindus (at least in their most popular system) have exactly *eighty-four* modes, though distinguished by different appellations and arranged in different classes: but, since many of them are unpleasing to the ear, others difficult in execution, and few sufficiently marked by a character of sentiment and expression, which the higher music always requires, the genius of the Indians has enabled them to retain the number of modes which nature seems to have indicated, and to give each of them

* Col. Wilford considers this Vikramaditya to be the same as the Sálivâhana mentioned below; and adds, "It is not obvious at first why Sálivâhana is made to have lived *eighty-four* years; but it appears to me that this number was in some measure a sacred period among the Christians, and also the Jews, and introduced in order to regulate Easter day; and it is the opinion of the learned that it began five years before the Christian era, and the fifth year of that cycle was really the fifth of Christ, but the first only of his manifestation to the world, according to the Apocryphal Gospels: and it was also the first of the Christian era. In this manner the cycle of *eighty-four* years ended on the seventy-ninth of the Christian, which was the first of Sálivâhana's era, and was probably mistaken for the period of his life. It is mentioned by St. Epiphanius, who lived about the middle of the fourth century."—(As. Res. Vol. X. p. 93.)

It is scarcely to be wondered at that this imaginative writer should have noticed the very questionable existence of Chaurásis amongst Christians and Jews, and should have altogether passed over their obvious prevalence amongst the Hindus.

a character of its own by a happy and beautiful contrivance" (Sir W. Jones on the Musical Modes of the Hindus).

It may not be unimportant to add, with reference to the particular purposes of our enquiry, that the year is distributed by the Hindus into six Ritus,* or seasons, each consisting of two months, *i.e.* two Springs, Summer, Autumn, and two Winters; and an original Rag, or God of the mode, is conceived to preside over a particular season. "By appropriating a different mode to each of the different seasons, the artists of India connected certain strains with certain ideas, and were able to recal the memory of autumnal merriment at the close of the harvest, or of separation and melancholy during the cold months; or reviving hilarity on the appearance of blossoms, and complete vernal delight in the month of Madhu, or honey; of languor during the dry heats, and of refreshment by the first rains which cause in this climate a second spring. Yet farther: since the lunar year, by which festivals and superstitious duties are constantly regulated, proceeds concurrently with the solar year, to which the seasons are necessarily referred, devotion comes also to the aid of music, and all the powers of nature, allegorically worshipped as gods and goddesses on their several holidays, contribute to the influence of song on minds naturally susceptible of religious emotions. Hence it was that Pavan, or the inventor of his musical system, reduced the number of original modes from seven to six" (Ibid.). And here we cannot but invite attention to the assertion of Dion Cassius, that the planetary theory from which the denomination of the days of the week has been derived (see note to p. 73) is itself founded upon the doctrine of musical intervals. A highly curious exposition of this idea has been given in the "Mémoires de Trévoux," A.D. 1770 and 1771.

The following are a few instances of the use of 360.

* See Chaumasa; and note to p. 53 of Babington's "Guru Paramartan."

The Sun's car is 3600000 Yojans long, and the yoke is a quarter of that amount (Bhagavata, 5th Khand).

Revati, the wife of Bala Ram, was so tall that her stature reached as high as the hands clapped seven times could be heard, and her age at the time of her marriage was 3,888,000 years. Her age, therefore, was 360 × 10800 years (Coleman's Hind. Myth. p. 49).

The wives of Sálivâhana, the founder of one of the most noted Indian eras, were 360.—See Bais.

There are 360 chief places of pilgrimage at Gya (Gya Mahatmya).

There are 360 chief places of pilgrimage at Misrakh Nímkhar, Oudh (Nímkhar Mahatmya).

There are also 360 at Sambhal, in Moradabad (Sambhal Mahatmya).

The respirations of a healthy man are said by the Jogís to be 360 in the course of a Gharrí (Muâlijât-i Dara Shekohí; and Sarode, 1st Khand).

A Chakravartí Raja has 360,000,000 cooks in his dominions, and 360 for his special use (A'ín-i Akbarí).

Raja Bikramajít is said to have raised 360 temples near Ajudhya on the places sanctified by the extraordinary actions of Rama (Buchanan's Eastern India, Vol. II. p. 334).

In the Mahábhárata we read, "Oh twin Aswinas! There are 360 milch cows. There is a wheel without an axis, which revolveth without decay. It hath one name, and its felloes are fixed 720, *i.e.*, 2 × 360, spokes" (Annals Or. Lit. p. 287).

Again, "In this wheel, furnished with twenty-four critical divisions, and turned in perpetual motion round about this axis by six boys, are placed in the midst of it 360;" (ib. 294), which is afterwards (p. 450) explained to mean, that the wheel with twelve spokes, turned by six boys, signifies the year divided into six seasons.

Rama's auxiliaries, in his attack on Lanka, amounted to 360,000 monkeys (Rámâyana).

But, to revert to Chaurásís:* amongst the Buddhists there is a still more systematic use of them than we have seen to prevail amongst the Hindus.

Thus, in a translation by the Honorable Mr. Turnour (Journ. As. Society for 1837, p. 526) we read, "How does it by the Dhamma Khando division consist of 84,000 portions?"

"It comprises the whole of Buddho. It has been said by Anando, I received from Buddho himself 82,000, and from the *bhikkhus* 2,000; these are the 84,000 Dhamma maintained by me. By this explanation of the Dhamma Khando it consists of 84,000 divisions." Again (at p. 792), "Having learned that there were 84,000 discourses on the tenets of Buddha, I will dedicate a *viharo*, or monastery,† to each."

"Then bestowing 6,000 Kotis of treasure on 84,000 towns in Jambudipo, at those places he caused the construction of temples to be commenced by the Rajas" (Ibid. p. 792).

Again, "From 84 cities despatches were brought on the same day, announcing that the *viharos* were completed" (Ibid. p. 793).

Asoko raised also 84,000 columns throughout India. These are supposed by M. Remusat to have been the same as the *viharos* above-mentioned; but the two seem quite distinct (Nouveau Journ. Asiatique, Tom. XII. p. 417; Fa Hian, Ch. XXIII. and XXVII. and As. Res. Vol. VII. p. 423).

* It is extremely doubtful whether the Chaurásís mentioned in the text did always consist of exactly eighty-four villages. In the cases of which I have had personal cognizance, I have had reason to doubt the fact. I think the most reasonable supposition is that as the territories of some powerful clans did really contain eighty-four villages, it grew to be a habit with others who had a large settlement in one place to call it a Chaurásí also.—B.

† Viharo is rather a temple or pleasure ground than monastery. See a definition by Wilson (Journ. R. A. S. No. IX. p. 110); by Mr. Joinville (As. Res. Vol. VII. p. 422), and by B. Hodgson (Trans. R. A. S. Vol. II. p. 246). This word Viharo is the origin of the name of the city at Behar, an important seat of Buddhism (see Sadik Isfahani, p. 24).

In the extracts from the Dípavansa, we read:

"The last of these was Ajitajano; his descendants, 84,000 in number, ruled in Kapilanagaram" (Journ. Asiat. Soc. Vol. VII. p. 926).

The descendants of Makhádeva were 84,000 monarchs, who reigned supreme at Mithilá (Ibid. p. 926).

Asoko's descendants were 84,000 rulers, who reigned supreme in the capital Báránasí (Ibid. p. 927).

In the opinion of Buddhists the life of man reached at one period 84,000 years. This was the highest it attained after successive augmentations (Enc. Jap. Cap. IV. p. 32. See also note 14 by M. Landresse to Ch. XXXIX. of Fa Hian's Travels).

Maitreya was to live 84,000 years, and the law which he was to deliver after his *nirvan* was also to endure for 84,000 years (Ibid. Ch. VI. note 8).

In the third heaven they lived to the number of 1344,000,000 years; *i.e.* $16 \times 84,000,000$ (Alphab. Tibet. p. 484, and Journal Asiatique, Tom. VIII. p. 44).

The life of other gods in the Buddhist mythologic hierarchy was equal to 360,000,000 years (Ibid.; and As. Res. Vol. VI. p. 210).

Buddha had 84,000 wives (Sieon hing pen kei King, quoted by Remusat).

The Buddhists assign to Brahma a life of 1008,000,000 years; *i.e.* $12 \times 84,000,000$ (Foe-tsou-toung-ki, quoted also by Remusat in the Foe koue ki).

The fourth kind of Arúpa, a species of spirit residing in the uppermost heaven, live 84,000 Mahákalpas (Trans. Royal A. S. Vol. III. p. 91; and As. Res. Vol. VI. p. 214).

The Cingalese historians say that 84,000 rocks encircle the great rock Mahámeru. The height of this rock is 168,000 (*i.e.* $2 \times 84,000$) Yadúns (Annals of Orient. Lit. pp. 385, 386).

Meru is generally considered with the Cingalese, as with the Hindus, to be 84,000 Yojanas high, and its ranges, according to the following progressive scale, shew the value attached even to sub-divisions of the Chaurásí.

	Sumeru, or Meru, is in height	84,000	Yojanas
1st.	Yokhunthara, the first hill, is in height	42,000	,,
2nd.	Isinthara, the second ditto	21,000	,,
3rd.	Káraveka, the third ditto	10,500	,,
4th.	The Hill Sudhatsana	5,250	,,
5th.	Ditto Nimethara	2,625	,,
6th.	Ditto Vimantaka	1,312	,,
7th.	Ditto Atsakána	656	,,

(Trans. R.A.S. Vol. III. p. 78.)

The Cingalese fabulous histories also treat us with periods regulated according to this mysterious number. The "Rajavali" says the most powerful king amongst them was called Mahá Dewa, who remained in the wilderness for 84,000 years. There were also, notwithstanding this pre-eminence, 84,000 kings who had this title (Annals of Or. Lit. p. 392).

Four brothers of king Mahálinde had 84,000 children and grandchildren (Ib. p. 391).

Amongst the Burmese also, the mountain Mienmo is 84,000 *jazína* high. The Jagánto is also 84,000 high, and the first river 84,000 *jazínas* wide and deep. The seas, in the midst of which the great islands lie, have a depth of 84,000 *jazínas*. The seats of the Nát are placed one above the other at the distance of 42,000 (84,000 ÷ 2) *jazínas*. The second chain of mountains is 42,000 *jazínas* high, and the second river 42,000 *jazínas* wide and deep. The eastern and western islands are each 21,000 (84,000 ÷ 4) *jazínas* in circumference, and so on (Tandy's Birman Empire, Chap. 2 and 3; and As. Res. Vol. VI. pp. 175–186).

The Buddhists of Nepaul assert that the original body of their sacred Scriptures amounted, when complete, to 84,000 volumes (As. Res. Vol. XVII. p. 42).

The Shastras, or brief aphorisms of Buddha, comprise half a Chaurásí, or 42; and the book in which they are contained is the first which was translated from the Sanskrit into Chinese (C. F. Neumann's Catechism of the Shamans, p. 150).

This is, perhaps, the Book of Foe, contained in forty-two chapters (Foe koue ki, pp. 44 and 263).

In the Jain religion, also, the prevalence of Chaurásís is surprisingly great. Thus, Rishabdeo sent 84 teachers to instruct other countries in the principles of his faith (Ward's Hindús, Vol. II. p. 244).

Near him were 84,000 Jains (Ibid. p. 244).

The Boy Buddha taught 42,000 boys, *i.e.*, 84,000 ÷ 2 (Ibid. p. 261).

The same holy personage retained 84,000 concubines (stated above to be wives), and he lived 84,00,000 great years (As. Res. Vol. XVIII. p. 250).

Sakra, the regent of the north in the Jain Mythology, has 84,000 fellow gods (Ibid. p. 275).

In their cosmogony also, as in the Cingalese, the height of the mountains bears an evident reference to this mystic number. Himavat is twice as broad as Bharata varsha (*i.e.*, omitting fractions, 1052 yojanas): the valley beyond it is double its breadth (2105); the mountain Mahá Himavat is twice as much (4210); its valley is again double (8421); and the mountain Nishadha has twice that breadth (16,842). (Colebrooke's Misc. Ess. Vol. II. p. 223.)

The Swetambaras have 84 Siddhántas (As. Res. Vol. XVII. p. 242).

There are 84 points of difference between the Digambaras and Swetambaras, regarded as of infinite importance (Ibid. p. 289

They have 84 Gachchos, or Gotes, of which a list is given in detail (Ibid. p. 293; and Trans. R.A.S. Vol. III. p. 337).

Mahavira, in one of his births, reigned victoriously 84,00,000 years (As. Res. Vol. XVIII. p. 251).

Rishabdeo lived 84,00,000 great years (Colebrooke's Misc. Essays, Vol. II. p. 208).

The ages of many other Jinás, besides Rishabdeo and Mahávira, are based on the number 84. Thus, the eleventh lived 84,00,000 of common years; the eighteenth lived 84,000; the nineteenth was deified 65,84,000 years before the close of the fourth age; the twentieth 11,84,000 ditto; the 21st 5,84,000 ditto; the 22nd died 84,000 years before the close of the fourth age (Ibid. pp. 310–312).

It is to be hoped that these many instances of the use of 84 will not be considered to rank with the Trinads, Septads, and Enneads of Varro, Bungus, Fabritius, Morel, and a host of other laborious triflers, who have occupied themselves in philosophising about the properties of numbers, and have exercised their time and talents in endeavouring to prove that *Numero Deus impare gaudet*. The thought may not improbably occur to some, that if works on Indian History and Antiquities were ransacked, it would be as easy to trace a predilection for any other number as for 84; but a little examination would soon end in disappointment. *Seven* and *twelve*, as might reasonably be expected, and will be hereafter shewn, come in for a good share of attention; but any higher numbers it would be in vain to look for. Popular sentiment has, to be sure, invested the numbers 24, 32, 52, 60, and 64* with some slight degree of favour, and a

* There is also a very remarkable use of seventy-four in epistolary correspondence. It is an almost universal practice in India to write this number on the outside of letters; it being intended to convey the meaning that nobody is to read the letter but the person to whom it is addressed. The practice was originally Hindu, but has been adopted by the Musulmans. There is nothing like an intelligible account of its origin and object, but it is a curious fact that, when correctly written, it represents an integral

commune of villages comprising one of these numbers is occasionally to be found, but very rarely; and there are also two instances of 87; that is, if the large tracts of Satásí in Badaon and Gorakhpúr derive their names from that number, which may be doubted; but to get any number that can be at all considered to rival 84, it must be shown that it pervades not only the tenures of land, but the mythology, theogony, and literature of India. That this is the case with 84, must be considered sufficiently established from the concurrent proofs collected from different parts of India. It is evident from the frequency of its adoption that these manifold coincidences are anything but fortuitous; and we cannot therefore resist the cumulative evidence here adduced to show that they must have had some esoteric meaning, and been designed with a view to impress the initiated with peculiar veneration for this number.

It becomes, then, a question to consider what is the cause of the selection of the number 84 for such a marked preference; and in doing so it will first be necessary to revert to the number 360, with which it stands in a kind of reciprocal relation.

It is evident that the selection of 360 rests upon astronomical considerations, and it is important to observe what a clue this interpretation affords to unravel some of the chief difficulties of Hindu chronology, which so perplex the student at his first contemplation of the subject, as frequently to deter him altogether from the further prosecution of his enquiries.

number of seventy-four and a fractional number of ten; thus, ७४ ॥ = .* These additional strokes being now considered, except by well-educated men, merely ornamental, we find it frequently written ॥ ७४ ॥. The Musulmans usually write the seventy-four with two strokes across, or after, the number, with the addition of the words بديگران *ba digarán*, which makes it assume the form of an imprecation. May not, then, after all, this seventy-four and ten have been originally intended to convey a mystic symbol of Chaurásí?

* These four lines represent ten anas in the Hindu mercantile system of notation, the two upright strokes stand for four annas each, and the two horizontal ones for one anna each.—B.

Thus we have the following astounding numbers assigned to the four ages:—

Satya Yug	17,28,000	years.
Treta	12,96,000	„
Dwapara	8,64,000	„
Kali	4,32,000	„
Making a Mahayuga of...	43,20,000	

But it has been declared (Manu, Chap. I. 67 to 71) "That a year of mortals is a day and night of the gods." Hence, if we divide each of the numbers mentioned above by 360, we obtain the following more rational periods.

Satya Yug	4,800
Treta	3,600
Dwapara	2,400
Kali	1,200

which gives a regular decrement in arithmetical progression, according to the notions of diminishing virtue in the several ages (Wilson's Note to Mill's India, Vol. I. p. 157).

Here the actual divisor* is evidently based on the days comprised in the lesser equal year, which was adopted by most eastern nations,† and founded, as Scaliger‡ conceives, on the natural lunar year, before the exact period of a lunation was fully understood. It is true that the Indians were acquainted with the equinoctial year, but, in their arbitrary and fanciful

* F. Schlegel is of opinion that the numbers in the Yugs decidedly possess an astronomical import (Philosophy of History, Vol. I. p. 98). Wilson, however, says it does not seem necessary to refer the invention of these periods to any astronomical computations, or to any attempt to represent actual chronology (Vishnu Purana, p. 24).

† The great year of these nations was also, according to Anquetil du Perron, composed of 360 ordinary years. "Or les Astronomes Arabes, particulièrement Albumasar, comme les Chaldéens, les Grecs, reconnoissent de grandes années du Monde, composées chacune de 360 années solaires; celles-ci n'en faisant alors qu'un jour" (Antiquités de l'Inde, Introd. XXII. See also pp. 549, 589).

‡ (De emendatione Temporum).

computations, they might, nevertheless, on account of the roundness of the number, and its possessing so many convenient divisors, have adopted the luni-solar, the first approximation to a true solar year, and the one with which they first became acquainted; particularly as they had divided the circle into 360 degrees,* and had assigned a degree, or Mandala, to each day of the year (Maurice's History of Hindústán, Vol. I. p. 91). In other countries, besides India, we find the concurrent use of these two years; and occasionally we find one used to the supersession of the other, either by interpolation, or by some other mode available to those in search of the means of correction.

A remarkable instance of the endeavour of the Chaldeans to reconcile the periods of the two years is given in the second Book of Diodorus Siculus, and shows how astronomical periods influenced even the architectural designs of the early ages. He says that Semiramis is stated to have built the walls of Babylon of the extent of 360 stadia, to mark *the number of days of the year.* Yet he states that, in Alexander's time, the circuit of the walls was 365 stadia; shewing that a subsequent correction had been applied, after the annual revolution had been more accurately ascertained.

Another curious instance of this system of accommodation occurs in the Egyptian year. A fable respecting the birth of

* It must be borne in mind that this division of the circle is a matter purely conventional, and the 360 parts into which it was divided by the Indians, as well as the Greeks, are evidently dependent on the number of the days of the early year; just as the Chinese, with a more perfect knowledge, divide their circle into 365 parts and one-fourth. "The division of the circle into 360° seems to have been pointed out to the earlier astronomers, by its being an articulate number nearly equal to the days in the year; and consequently one of the degrees was nearly equal to the portion of the ecliptic described by the sun in one day. Whatever, however, were the grounds on which this division was adopted in the first instance, it was adhered to afterwards in the most improved methods of ancient and modern astronomy, from a sense of the convenience presented by the number 360 in the great number of its divisors."—"Peacock's Arithmetic" (39).

three gods and two goddesses was devised, in order to account for the insertion of the five intercalary days, which were superadded to the 360 contained in the old year of twelvemonths.* We may therefore readily admit the supposition that the knowledge of the true year is not incompatible with the occasional application of the lesser year in such instances as those under discussion.

After this instance from Jablonski, it may be needless to add that the Egyptian theology was replete with these allusions to siderial revolutions; and the Gnostics, who frequently borrowed from the Egyptians, apply the mystic numbers of their predecessors, without, probably, being aware of the original purpose for which they were framed. Thus, in the system of Basilides the number of primary Æons is, as in the Persian system, seven; these went on producing and multiplying, till they reached the number 365.† The total number formed, according to the Grecian numeration, the cabalistic‡ word *Abraxas* (Milman's History of Christianity, Vol. II. 116). This number has evidently an astronomical reference, as much as the 360 has in the Indian System. In the system of Bardesanes, there were 36 Decani, who ruled the 360 days of the year (Ib. 125). Other instances need not be adduced to shew the value attached to 360, in consequence of its being connected with the supposed period of the year, and therefore based on siderial computation. Let us now see whether the mystical number 84 may not be found to rest on a similar foundation.

* "Jablonski Panth. Ægyp." Lib. II. C. I. p. 143.

† This is not an exact multiple of 7, but 7 is more nearly than any other short term an aliquot part of 365.

‡ The Romans adopted a strange conceit of representing the period of an annual revolution by indigitation. Pliny tells us the image of Janus was so placed as to indicate with his fingers the number 365.

Janus geminus a Numa rege dictus, qui pacis bellique argumento colitur, digitis ita figuratis, ut trecentorum sexaginta quinque dierum nota per significationem anni temporum et ævi se Deum indicaret.—"Hist. Nat." Lib. XXXIV. 7.

As 360 is the multiple of the number of months in a year, with the number of days in a Savana, or solar, month, or the number of lunations, or tithis, in a Savinya, or lunar, month; so is 84 the multiple of the number of months with the number of days in the week;* the multiple of the number of the planets with the signs of the zodiac; or the multiple of the days of a quarter lunation (in which period the moon passes through seven Nakshatras, or asterisms) with the years of Jupiter's siderial revolution (Bentley on Hindu Astronomy, p. 129). That this is no extravagant supposition may be seen in Colonel Warren's "Kala Sankalita" (212), where he says, "In the cycle of 60 years are contained 5 cycles of 12 years each, sup-

* We are so accustomed to regard the week as a natural division of time, that, if there were room, it would be useful to consider the speculations of the learned on its origin. The question is not unimportant as regards the time of the introduction of Chaurásis, and it may therefore be as well to mention that it is to the quarter lunations that Bailly ascribes the origin of the Indian week. Prof. Wallace, on the contrary, says it was most probably fixed with relation to the number of planets." "British India," III. 79. The following passages from A. W. Schlegel's Preface to "Prichard's Egyptian Mythology" are also subjoined for consideration:—

"Among the Greeks and Romans the observation of the days of the week was introduced very late: although the custom had made some inroads even before the Christian era, through the influence of Egyptian and Chaldee astrologers, and also of the Jews, who were dispersed here and there throughout the Roman Empire. Ideler, in his excellent Manual of Chronology, remarks that the week had a natural origin in the accidental duration of the phases of the moon. Ideler passes over the Indians, and with good reason; for they had not the week, and could not have had it, since they divided the *nychthemeron* into thirty hours."

"Besides the twelve signs of the zodiac, the Indians had also from early times another division of it into the seven-and-twenty *Nakshatras*, or houses of the moon. In order to fill up the breach, which had been neglected, they were increased, as often as was necessary, to eight-and-twenty by an intercalation."

It may be also proper to add that the order in which the names of the days of the week follow each other is dependent, not upon the size, period, or distance of the planets respectively, but solely upon an astrological conceit. The doctrine was that a planet presides over each of the hours, according to the natural order from Saturn down to the Moon, and that planet to which the first hour belonged was also regent of the whole day.

posed equal to one year of the planet Jupiter:" shewing that Jupiter's revolution was used in counting cyclar periods.

It is needless to particularize all the instances in which the partiality of the natives of India for the numbers 7, 12, and 30 is shewn.* It will be sufficient to adduce in detail only two instances of the allegorical uses to which the numbers 7 and 12 are applied.

In Masudi's valuable Historical Encyclopædia, entitled "The Meadows of Gold and Mines of Gems," he says, "In the reign of Bálkít, king of India, the game of chess was invented. He studied the numbers (of the product of the squares) of this game, and wrote a work on the subject for the Hindús, which is known under the title طرق حنكاتيدا. He laid also an allegory of the higher bodies in the chess, that is to say, of the stars of the heavens, observing the numbers 7 and 12. Every piece was consecrated to a star." . . . . . "He preferred it to backgammon (النرد), in which game the 12 points of the tables answer to the 12 months of the year, and the 30 tablemen are expressive of the 30 days of the month." Here, then, we have not only a Chaurásí on a chess-board, but the larger symbolical number of 360 on a backgammon board. Masudi wrote in the early part of the tenth century, and as he frequently exercises a critical acumen which is highly commendable, his statements may be received with confidence, though it is not quite evident what potentate may be meant by Bálkít.

Let us take also the emblematical figure of Surya, the Indian Sun. He is represented with 12 spokes to his wheel, indicating, as the Bhágavata expressly says, the number of months, and

* See "Ward's Hindus," Vol. I. Preface 98, and pp. 55, 56, 266; Vol. II. pp. 70, 74, 75; Vol. III. Proleg. p. 24, Introd. Rem. p. 4, and pp. 7 and 40; and Vol. IV. pp. 17, 20, 315, 457. "Coleman's Hindu Mythology," pp. 196 and 209. "Moor's Pantheon," p. 303. "As. Res." Vol. VI. p. 210; VII. p. 274; and VIII. pp. 289, 290. "Foe Koue Ki," pp. 125, 150, 165, 176, 186, 238. "Wilson's Oxford Lectures," p. 55. "Vishnu Purana," Book II. c. 2 and 4; Book III. c. 1 and 2, and pp. 214, 233, 236.

sitting under a canopy formed by the 7 heads of the Coluber Naga. He is also represented driving 7 steeds, or one steed with 7 heads, and also has 12 titles, forms, or manifestations, which denote his distinct powers (*Ádityas**) in each of the 12 months throughout his passage through the ecliptic. (See As. Res. Vol. I. p. 263, and "Brahma Puran," quoted by Vans Kennedy in his Ancient and Hindu Mythology, p. 349). The allegorical import of this Chaurásí is so evident, that we need go no further to assign causes for the selection of this multiple of 7 and 12, to represent territorial sub-divisions in India: no numbers being considered more appropriate for that purpose than those which bear reference to the motion of the earth, the revolving seasons, and the succession of seed-time and harvest; especially † among

* आदित्य m. sol. (Aut ab आदि et त्य, aff. quo adjecc. formantur e præposs. et adverbb. localibus, ita ut sit initium anni faciens vel a cujus constellatione anni initium factum sit; pro mensium enim numero sol duodena nomina accipit, et in duodenos *Aditjas* discernitur; primus *Aditjas* धातृ est, quo nomine Brahmâ, primigenius deorum, dicitur; Mahâbhâr: I., v. 2524, hunc deum solarem ab initio *Aditjam* dictum fuisse suspicor, nomine ad ceteros posthac extenso; aut vera est Indorum derivatio ab अदिति quæ est cunctorum deorum mater; est आदित्य etiam deus in universum).—Lassen's "Anthologia Sanscritica," p. 172.

† That this multiplication of numbers having in themselves a rational basis, and founded on observation, is at the root of all the extravagant epochs of the Hindus, has been well shewn in an article on their Astronomy in No. II. of the "Calcutta Review." In shewing that the factors which enter into the period of the *Kali-Yug* are derived from the cycle of precession, the author observes:—

"The amount of this precession is, according to the best modern observations, somewhat more than 50″ annually; but, according to the Hindu system as stated by Bailly and all other writers on the subject, it is taken as 54″. Whether this is owing to any actual change in the amount since their epoch, or is due to errors in their observations, we shall have to consider immediately; at present we have only to do with the fact. This precession being observed, it would naturally occur to every astronomer to enquire into the length of the period in the course of which this point would make a complete revolution of the whole equinoctial circle. At the Hindu rate of precession this period will be immediately found to be 24,000 years, the quotient resulting from dividing the whole circle, or 360° by 54″, the assumed precession for one year. Now, the duration of the Kali-Yug is just 18 times this period of 24,000 years; or the Kali-Yug is the period during which the equinox will have been 18 times at each point of the a people whose worship was directed towards physical objects, and the manifold powers and departments of nature; and who in their contemplative moments were fond of marking

"The mighty hand
That, ever busy, wheels the silent spheres;
And as on earth this grateful change revolves,
With transport touches all the springs of life."
—*Thomson's Seasons.*

equinoctial circle. Why 18 should have been chosen as a multiplier rather than any other number, we are not able positively to determine. It might have been chosen arbitrarily, merely on the ground that 24,000 years being too short a period to satisfy Hindu notions, some number must be chosen as a multiplier; or it might be selected as being the greatest common measure of 360 and 54; or it might be for the following reason:—The position of the moon's node, or the point in which her orbit cuts the ecliptic, goes round the ecliptic in a little more than 18 years, just as the intersection of the earth's equator with the ecliptic goes round it in about 25,700 years in reality, but according to the Hindu estimate of the precession, in 24,000 years. If, then, the Hindu rate of precession were correct, and if the period of the revolution of the moon's node were 18 years, instead of about 18 years and 7 months, then if the sun and moon were in conjunction at any point in the ecliptic, they would be in conjunction again at the same point in the ecliptic after a period of 432,000 years. . . . . . The length of the Kali-Yug being thus determined, a short process would lead to the assignment of its commencement. If a point was assigned from which to measure the precession, as we measure it from the first point of Aries, the commencement of the epoch would be at once determined by dividing the distance between that first point and the actual position of the equinox at the period of observation by the annual precession, say 54″. Now it is obvious that any point might be assumed arbitrarily as the first point of the zodiac, or the astronomer might be led by some peculiar coincidence to fix upon some particular point in preference to all others. The latter was the fact in the actual case before us. On calculating backwards the position of the planets, they found that on a particular day in the month of February, in the year 3102 B.C., the Sun, Moon, Saturn, Mars, Jupiter, and Mercury were, not indeed in actual conjunction, but at least in the same quarter of the heavens, the greatest distance between any two of them probably not exceeding 17° or 18°. . . . It is true that at this period Venus was in a different quarter of the heavens, being about 62° in longitude apart from Saturn; but what theorist would allow a single planet to stand in the way of the establishment of so grand an epoch? Not, certainly, the framers of the Hindu Astronomy; and accordingly they did determine that, at the commencement of the Kali-Yug, all the planets were in conjunction at the first point of the zodiac, and thus was the famous epoch fixed."

This is not the place to enter, as fully as the interesting nature of the subject demands, into the enquiry when Chaurásís were first introduced into the mythology and administrative details of India; but it is obvious to remark that the Buddhists and Jains are more partial to the number than the Brahmans; and that the Rajputs, of whom the Agnikula portion appear to have been supporters of the Buddhist doctrines (see Gaur Taga), as well as their congeners, the Gújars and Játs, more particularly affect that number than any other tribes at present found in occupation of the soil. It does not necessarily follow that the Buddhists introduced Chaurásís; but it may fairly be conceded that, if we deduct from the Chaurásís mentioned above, those which may perhaps be considered exclusively Brahmanical, the greater part may be ascribed to Buddhism, and may have been readily adopted and incorporated at some subsequent period by the Hindus, according to the usual accommodating spirit of polytheism. Even the emblematical solar Chaurásí may have been a subsequent importation, as it is questionable if Súrya's chariot is represented in the Vedas* as it is in the Puranas.

It is, moreover, very remarkable that Manu (VII. 115) uses

* It must be confessed, however, that the Sun has 7 steeds and 7 rays, according to the Rig Veda. "Seven yellow mares bore thee in a chariot, Oh shining Sun!" (Chap. IX. Hymn VII.)—according to the numbering in Dr. Rosen's translation of the Rigveda Sanhita. Again, the Sun has seven rays, "These are the seven rays of the Sun, and my abode is in the midst of them" (C. XV. H. XII.). There is also possibly some indication of a quarter Chaurásí in an address to Agni. "Thrice seven secret names the priests have found in thee" (C. XII. H. VIII.). According to the Vedas, also, 21 pieces of Pulas wood are to be got ready against a sacrifice (Stevenson's "Sanhita of the Sáma Veda," p. vii. and "As. Res." VII. 274). A fast of 21 days also is enjoined as an austerity previous to singing the Sama Veda (Stevenson's Sanhita, p. ix.), and 21 milch cows "yield the true milk in the super-excellent place of Sacrifice" (Ib. p. 217). See also another instance of a quarter Chaurásí from the Vedas, in "As. Res." VII. p. 252. In the Puranas, as might be expected, the number is very common (See Langlois' Harivansa, I. p. 112, and II. pp. 68, 440; Stenzler's Raghuvansa, C. II. 25; and Surya Narayan Upanishad, quoted by Vans Kennedy, in his "Ancient and Hindu Mythology," p. 346).

only the *decimal* division when speaking of the civil administration. "Let him appoint a lord of 10 towns, a lord of 20 towns, a lord of 100, and a lord of 1000."

It must not be forgotten also, in the attempt to fix the time of the introduction of Chaurásís into India, that in the compilation of Parásara, who, by the position of the colures recorded by him, is ascertained to have lived not earlier than 1200 years before Christ, the estimate of the lunation is erroneous, nor is any mention made of the days of the week, or of the twelve signs, which seem to have been introduced into India at a much later period; so that if Chaurásís do depend on the astronomical basis which has been assigned to them, they could not have existed in his time.

As, therefore, neither in the time of Parásara, nor in that of Manu, who is supposed to have flourished about three centuries after Parásara, or in the ninth century before Christ, is there anything which can be construed into the remotest allusion to Chaurásís, we must look for their introduction to some subsequent period; and in the midst of so much uncertainty, it seems lawful at least to conjecture, that the most probable date is that, when the Buddhists from Scythia, following that tide which from the earliest ages has been setting in towards the South East, immigrated to India, and became incorporated with the tribes who were in previous occupation of the country.

Chaus, چوس चौस

Land four times tilled.—Rohilkhand.

Chausinghá, چوسنگها चौसिंघा

A raised mound indicating where the boundaries of four villages meet.—See Chaugadda.

Chauthiyá, چوتهیا चौथिया

A measure in general use for grain, and about equal to a seer of wheat; Chaukarí is a quarter, and Adheli is a half, Chauthiyá. Five Chauthiyás are equal to a Kuro or Pasera (*i.e. pánch ser*, five seers), and twenty Kuros to one Khanṛí. These words are equally used in superficial measures. Thus, an area which would require five Paserí of seed to sow it, is about equal to a Bígha (which in Hoshangabad is a little more than a statute acre, being 4,900 square yards), and was rated at about a Rupee of revenue. A Khanrí would be about equal to four rupees, and a Mání to twice that amount.—Saugor. See Bísi and Jaríb.

Chak, چک चक

A portion of land divided off. It is applied to detached fields of a village, and to a patch of rent-free land. In old revenue account books it is the name given to that part of the township which is taken from the residents of the village and assigned to a stranger to cultivate. A passage in the "Zubdatu'l Ḳawánín" runs as follows:—"And in a village the whole of whose area is not really cultivated by the máliks and mustájir, they leave them as much as they can manage, and make the rest into a 'chak' under a complete sanad, giving it into the possession of some one else to cultivate."

Chak bandí, چک بندي चकबंदी

The fixing or registering the boundaries of a chak, showing the corners or points where it abuts on other lands.

In Dakhiní Hindí the equivalent is चतुसीमा or "four boundaries" (see Journal R.A.S. VI. 368).

Chakbarár, چک برار बकबरार

Collecting rents according to the size or productiveness of chaks.—Central Doáb.

Chakkat, چکّت चक्कत

The loss of a whole plot of ground by diluvion: the contrary of *ritkat*.

Chaklá, چکله चकला

A Chaklá is a sub-division of a Sirkár, comprising several parganahs. The only Chaklás familiarly known in these Provinces are those of Azimgarh and Korah. The designation is not uncommon in Oudh.

Chaklás were first instituted in the reign of Shahjahán, by Sa'dullah Khan, the minister (see Karorí), and therefore there is reason to apprehend that the Sanads given at p. 253, Vol. III., of "Harington's Analysis," are forgeries. Much stress was laid upon these documents at the time of their publication, but as they purport to be of the time of Akbar, and at the same time mention Chaklás, they are open to dispute.

Chaknámá, چکنامه चकनामा

A deed, or statement, shewing the area and boundaries of a Chak. The word is as old as the time of Akbar. It is mentioned in his instructions to Amilgazars.

Chalán, چلان चलान

An invoice; an announcement of despatch (from चालाना to cause to go).

Chanchar, چانچر चनचर

Land left untilled for one, two, or three years.

Chaniyádá, چنیاده चनियादा

Land under a crop of Chana, or gram.—Rohilkhand. In Dehli the same is called Chanial and Umri, and in some other Provinces Chanara; in Lower Doáb, Oṅr.

Charhwí, چڑھوی चढवी

Raising rent (from चढाना to raise).

Dáin, داين दाइन

The eight Dáins in the Dún are hill estates, each containing a certain number of hamlets, of which the fields and the lands of one adjoin to, and mix with, the fields of another. The Mokaddams of these Dáins are probably the ancient zamíndárs of the Dún.

Dákhilá, داخله दाखिला

A receipt (from the Arabic دخل *dakhl*, arriving, entering). In the Printed Glossary it is called Dachela, as well as Dakhila.

Dákhilnámá, داخلنامه दाखिलनामा

A warrant of possession; also derived from دخل *dakhl.*

Dám, دام दाम

The Dám in the "Áín-i Akbarí," and consequently in most revenue accounts, is considered to be the fortieth part of a rupee; but to the common people it is known as the fiftieth part of a Taka: twenty-five therefore go to a Paisa, and twelve and a half to an Adhela.—See Damrí and Chhadam.

Dámí wásilát, دامي واصلات दामी वासिलात

Gross assets of a village (from the Dám of account, mentioned above, and the Arabic root وصل, joining, arriving).

Dánabandí, دانهبندي दानाबन्दी

Cursory survey, or partial measurement, or weighment, to ascertain the produce of each field. The usual method of Dánabandí, under the Native Governments, was to divide the crop into three or four kinds, and then for the Government Officer to select from each kind a biswa of the best looking crop, and for the cultivator to select a biswa of the worst looking crop. The produce of the two was carefully cut and weighed, and the average produce estimated accordingly. This would go on as long as there was any variety of crop, or quality of produce, which could occasion dispute.

زرعتِ آنجا چهار قسم سازد اول دوم سوم چهارم بعد ازان بموجه رعایا از یک قسم یک بسوه بهتر خود بگیرد و رعایا از همان قسم یک بسوه که زبون دانند خود بگیرند * (Kitáb-i Ḳánún)

"Let him divide the cultivated land into four kinds, first, second, third, and fourth, after that in presence of the ryots let him select himself one biswah of the best of one kind and let the ryots themselves select from the same kind one biswah which they consider worst."

Dánadár, دانه‌دار दानादार

Apportionment of Jama, or of any other contribution, according to the actual produce.—Benares.

Dánpattar, دان‌پتر दानपत्र

A deed of gift by which land is conveyed to Brahmans.

Dánpattardár, دان‌پتردار दानपत्रदार

Grantee of Brahman caste, to whom lands have been assigned for religious purposes.

Dastúr, دستور दस्तूर*

As this word, which is perhaps a mere abbreviation of Dastúr ul 'Aml, has been fully explained under Sirkár, this article will be devoted to a detailed consideration of the Map

* The author's principle of keeping strictly within the limits of the North-Western Provinces as then constituted, renders this article imperfect, as it refers to an earlier political division of the country. The map will be found in some cases not to tally with the lists given in the article. For instance, under Sirkár Agra, we are told that it contains four Dastúrs, but in the map only three are given, the fourth, that of Mandáwar, not being in the N.W.P., but in a native state.—B.

of Dastúrs, and of the territorial changes which have occurred since Akbar's time.

SU'BA AGRA.

Sirkár Agra.

حويلي آگرا	1 *Havelí Agrá.*	دهولپور	17 *Dholpúr.*
اٹاوه	2 *Eṭáwah.*	راپري	18 *Rápri.*
اود	3 *Od.*	رجوهر	19 *Rajohar.*
اودهي	4 *Odhí.*	سونکهرسونکهري	20 *Sonkhar - Sonkhrí.*
اول	5 *Ol.*	فتح پور	21 *Fattihpúr.*
بجواره	6 *Bajwárah.*	کهتومر	22 *Khatomar.*
بيانه	7 *Biánah.*	مهابن	23 *Mahában.*
باري	8 *Bárí.*	متهرا	24 *Mathurá.*
بهوساور	9 *Bhosáwar.*	مهولي	25 *Maholí.*
بناور	10 *Banáwar.*	منگوٹله	26 *Mangoṭalah.*
توده بهيم	11 *Todah Bhím.*	منداور	27 *Mandáwar.*
بهسکر	12 *Bhaskar.*	وزيرپور	28 *Wazírpúr.*
جليسر	13 *Jalesar.*	هندون	29 *Hindaun.*
جنوار	14 *Janwár.*	هتکانت	30 *Hatkánt.*
چوستهه	15 *Chausaṭh.*	هيلک	31 *Hílak.*
خانوه	16 *Khánwah.*		

This Sirkár is said to contain thirty-three Mahàls, but none of the copies of the "A'ín-i Akbarí" give the names of more than thirty-one. The discrepancy is cleared up by referring to the Dastúr Statement, where we find the Baldah and Havelí Agra, and the Baldah and Havelí Bianah, given each as two Mahàls.*

* Havelí and Baldah mean respectively "home" and "abroad," or literally, "house" and "country:" the former alludes to the district close to the capital, and the latter to that at a distance.—B.

There are four Dastúrs in this Sirkár, viz., Havelí Agra, Etawah, Bianah, and Mandáwar, of which the only perfect one which we retain is Etawah.

It will be observed that there are in this list several names of which we have now no knowledge, and Agra is consequently a very difficult Sirkár to restore. The changes which have affected Agra more than other Sirkárs are attributable to the different dynasties to which this portion of the country has been subjected. Játs, Imperialists, and Maráṭhas have at different times imposed names of their own creation on their acquisitions, and have served thus to confuse the records of Akbar's reign.

After excluding the Parganahs which belong to the now foreign* territories of Bhartpúr, Jaypúr, and Dholpúr, we have in our own dominions the following of which the name no longer exists—Numbers 1, 5, 14, 16, 18, 25, 26, and 30.

1.—Havelí Agra was divided by the Játs into several Chaklas, the distribution of which will be explained hereafter. Many of them appear as separate Parganahs in the records of our first settlements.

5.—Ol is a large village in the Parganah of Farrah, held rent-free with others in the neighbourhood, in virtue of a Sanad given by Maharaja Daulat Rái Sindhiá to Múnshí Chait Singh. This tenure is sometimes known as Parganah Berí. Ol no longer gives name to a Parganah, Farrah having succeeded to its importance, as Súraj Mal removed the Tehsíldarí Katcherry to it, after he had plundered Ol, on account of the opposition he experienced from the Zamíndár of that place. A portion of the Parganah of Ol is included in the Bhartpúr territory.

* By this expression must be understood those states which formed part of the Mughal empire, but are now ruled by native feudatories, and whose internal affairs are not managed directly by British officials.—B.

14.—Janwar. All the copies concur in writing the word thus, but there can be no question that it is properly Chandwár.. It has been succeeded as a Parganah by Ferozabad. Chandwár was built among the ravines of the Jumna by Chandar Sen, a Chauhán, whose fort is still to be seen on the banks of the river, and is early conspicuous in Musulman annals. The "Táju'l Ma'áṣir"* tells us that it was near this place that Jay Chand encountered his fatal defeat. Shortly after the invasion of Timúr, we find the Chandwár Rajputs in occupation of Jalesar, from which they were not expelled again till A.D. 1413. The precise date of the decline of Chandwár cannot be ascertained. The legends of the neighbourhood are completely contradicted by authentic history.

16.—Khánwah. The greater part of Khánwah is in Sirhindí, but the town of Khánwah is in the Bhartpúr territory. As the Ját 'Amil resided at Sirhindí, the name of that town was imposed on the Parganah.

18.—Rápri has been superseded as a Parganah by Shikohabad, its position on the Jumna being more calculated for defence than for controlling collections. In all the copies of the "Áín-i Akbarí," Rápri is recorded as in the Dastúr of Biánah; but as this is impossible, on account of the intervention of Chandwár and Hatkánt, we must presume it is a mistake; more particularly as a Dúmrí is inserted in the Etawah Dastúr, which should of course be Rápri. In the early Mahometan History of India, Rápri obtains frequent notice, and appears usually to have been united with Chandwár under one government. The ruins of Rápri opposite to Batesar still remain to testify its former importance, but they are more of a Mahometan than a Hindu character.

25.—Maholí is now included in the Parganah of Mathurá

* There is some doubt as to this reference. It is probably a mistake for "Tabaḳát-i Násirí.—E. *add.*

(Muttra); and the village of Maholí is still extant about four miles to the South of that city.

26.—Mangotlah is still the site of a Thana in the Southern angle of Aríng. The Talúkas of Sonk and Sonsa were included in it.

30.—Hatkánt is on the left bank of the Chambal, and has been noticed in the article Bhadauria. On account of its inconvenient situation, the Játs removed the Tehsíldarí Katcherry to Bah.

The Parganahs now included within the boundaries of Sirkár Agra, and of which no mention occurs in the "Áín-i Akbarí," form an unusually long list.

سعد آباد	1 *Sa'dábád.*	بیبامو	13 *Bíbámau.*
فتح آباد	2 *Fattihábád.*	باہ پناہت	14 *Báh Panáhat.*
ارادت نگر	3 *Irádatnagar.*	فیروز آباد	15 *Fírozábád.*
حضور تحصیل	4 *Hazúr Tahsíl.**	مصطفی آباد	16 *Mustafábád.*
کھندولی	5 *Khandauli.*	ارینگ	17 *Aríng* (part).
فرح	6 *Farrah.*	سونئی	18 *Sonei.*
سیکری	7 *Síkri.*	رایا	19 *Ráyá.*
جانب راست	8 *Jánibrást.*	ہاتھراس مڑسان	20 *Háthras Mursán.*
لکنان	9 *Laknán.*	ماٹ	21 *Mát.*
شکرہ آباد	10 *Shikohábád.*	سرہندی	22 *Sirhindi.*
گھرور	11 *Gihror.*	سہپو	23 *Sahpo.*
کرہل	12 *Karhal.*		

* It is perhaps hardly necessary to explain that in all districts in the N.W.P. the Hazúr Tahsíl is that in which the chief town of the district lies, and which is therefore in the Hazúr, or "presence," of the Collector and other Government officials. It is sometimes also called the Sadr, or "chief," Tahsíl.—B.

Sa'dabad.—In the time of Sa'dullah Khan, Wazír, who has acquired notoriety for his proceedings in Afghanistan, and the general ability of his administration during the reign of Shahjehan, this Parganah was formed from about 200 villages of Jalesar, and eighty from Mahaban, with a few from Khandaulí; and a town was built in the centre of them, which he called after his own name, Sa'dabad.

Fattihabad, known also by the name of Zafarnagar, was included in the Havelí of Agra, and formed part of the Tappa of Shamsabad. The town and saraí of Fattihabad were founded by Aurangzeb in 1067 A.H., in commemoration of the victory obtained by him over his brother Dara Shikoh.

Iradatnagar is formed from part of Shamsabad, and from Sanya, one of the Tappas of Havelí Agra. The towns of Sanya and Shamsabad are both within the Parganah.

Hazúr Tahsíl is formed from part of Gaoghat and of Kakáraul, or Paltaura, and from Merhakar, Tappas of Havelí Agra.

Khandaulí was one of the Chaklas, or Tappas, of Havelí Agra. It is frequently entered in the old records as little Kábul, or Tappa Kábul Khúrd. More than half of the present Parganah of Khandaulí has been taken from Chandwar.

Farrah is formed from Ol and part of Gaoghát, a Tappa of Havelí Agra. Achnera, one of the many Parganahs intermediately formed from Havelí Agra by the Játs, is included in Farrah.

Síkrí, or Fattihpúr Síkrí, contains the Parganah of Fattihpúr, and parts of Karaulí and Karahra, Tappas of Havelí Agra. It is a mistake to suppose that Síkrí was a mere village before Akbar built his palace there. We find mention of Governors of that place long before his time. Thus, in the "Tawáríkh-i-Mubárik Sháhí" we find Malik Khairu'd-dín Tuḥfa recorded as Governor of Síkrí, even as early as the time of Sayyid Mubárik; and we find it also mentioned in that voluminous compilation, the "Akbarnama," that shortly before the battle of Khanwa, which established the empire of the Mughals, Bábar, having obtained in the neighbourhood of Síkrí some important advantages over Rana Sanka, directed that the name should be changed from Síkrí to Shukarí, or "place of thanks." It is strange that the addition of Fattihpúr should have been imposed upon it by his son on similar grounds.

Janibrast.—This Parganah, so called from being on the right bank of the Jumna, and known also as Barcipúra, comprises other inferior Pattís and Talúkas. Kamait Pattí, opposite the town of Etawah, and Chakarnagar were included in Indawa and Bakípúr, Tappis of the Havelí of Etawah. The Talúka of Sandaus, known also as Parhára, will be treated of under I'rij.

Laknan remained attached to Etawah up to the time of Govind Pandit. It was separated when this tract of country came into the hands of the Nawab Wazír. The Havelí of Etawah comprised seven Tappas—1, Khás Havelí; 2, Sataura; 3, Indawa; 4, Bakípúr; 5, Dehli; 6, Jakhan; and 7, Karhal. Laknan is composed of portions of the two Tappas of Indawa and Bakípúr. Sataura, as well as Havelí Khás, are included in the present Parganah of Etawah.

Shikohabad is composed of Rápri and parts of Tappas Dehli and Jakhan in Etawah. Shikohabad was not founded till the time of Dara Shekoh, the eldest brother of Aurangzeb.

Gihror, now a Parganah of Mainpúrí, was included in Rápri.

Karhal, also a Parganah of Mainpúrí, was one of the seven Tappas of Havelí Etawah.

Bíbamau is composed of parts of the Tappas of Dehli and Jakhan in Havelí Etawah. Bíbamau (Bibameyú), where the Tahsíldar's Katcherry is fixed, is a small village situated on the Sarsú river, in the Parganah of Jakhan. Dehli (Deolí) lies between the Sarsú and the Saingur Naddís. Jakhan is now uninhabited, but the ruins of the Khera are on the Jumna. I should have been disposed to give the whole of Jakhan to Rápri, in which it certainly was included before the time of Akbar, for we find it expressly said to be a Parganah of Rápri at p. 336 of "Bábar's Memoirs," but the local records distinctly state that Jakhan has been from time immemorial considered a Tappa of Havelí Etawah.

Báh Panáhat was originally Hatkánt.* Báh and Panáhat were rated as two separate Parganahs during the early period of our administration.

Ferozabad succeeded to Rápri, being in a more convenient position to control the collections. It was built in the reign of Shah Jahan by a nobleman called Feroz Khan, on the lands of the five Mauzas, Pempúr, Rasúlpúr, Dataulí, Muhammadpúr, and Sukhmalpúr; and the Játs subsequently raised a fort here to the South of the town,—one of the bastions of which has now been converted into a Trigonometrical Survey Tower.

Mustafabad, sometimes called the second division of Shikohabad, forms part of Rápri.

Aríng (part).—About one-third of the present Parganah of Aríng was originally included in Mangotlah. The remainder has been noticed under Sirkár Sahar.

Soneyí was originally a portion of Mahaban,—or Mahâwan, as it is generally written by the Musulmans.

Raya.—The same remarl. applies. Both these Talúkas were subsequently included in the Mursan Talúka.

Hathras and Mursán were detached from Jalesar chiefly. They were till lately considered as two separate Parganahs.

Mát formed part of Mahaban.

Sirhindí has been formed from portions of Khánwah and Havelí Agra.

Sahpo formed part of Jalesar. It has lately been increased by annexations from Sa'dabad.

* For Hatkánt, see article Bhadauriá in Part I.—B.

Sirkár Kanauj.

بهويگانو 1 *Bhúígáńw.*	سورکهه 17 *Saurakh.*
بهوجپور 2 *Bhojpúr.*	سکندر پور اودهو 18 *Sikandarpúr Údhú.*
تال گرانو 3 *Tálgráńw.*	بيرور 19 *Bírwar.*
بٹهور 4 *Biṭhúr.*	سکندر پور اتريجي 20 *Sikandarpúr Atrejí.*
بلهور 5 *Bilhúr.*	شمس آباد 21 *Shamsábád.*
پٹيالي 6 *Paṭiálí.*	چهبراموُ 22 *Chhabrámau.*
پٹي علي پور 7 *Paṭṭí 'Alípúr.*	ديوها 23 *Deohá.*
پٹي نکهت 8 *Paṭṭí Nakhat.*	کنوج با حويلي 24 *Kanauj ba Havelí.*
برنه 9 *Barnah.*	کنپل 25 *Kampil.*
پهپهوند 10 *Phaphúnd.*	کراولي 26 *Karáolí.*
سکيت 11 *Sakít.*	ملکونسه 27 *Malkonsah.**
سونج 12 *Sonj.*	نانامو 28 *Nánámau.*
شيولي 13 *Sheolí.*	بارا 29 *Bárá.*
سکت پور 14 *Sakatpúr.*	
سکرانو 15 *Sakráńw.*	
سهار 16 *Sahár.*	

سهاور 30 *Saháwar.*

Sirkár Kanauj contains 30 Mahals, and is divided into the three Dastúrs of Kanauj, Bhúígáńw, and Sakít.

The Parganahs of which there is now no longer any mention are—Numbers 8, 18, 20, 23, 27, 28, and 29.

8.—Pattí Nakhat is now included in the North of Parganah Uriyá, and was considered a separate Parganah till the commencement of our administration. The chief town was Babarpúr, near Saráí Ajít Mal.

* Kali Rai writes this مالکون سا *mālkon sá*, in two words.

18.—Sikandarpúr Udhú is now included in Chhabrámau, and is mentioned as a separate Parganah in the reports of the three first Settlements. The town of Sikandarpúr still exists.

20.—Sikandarpúr Atrejí, which one copy says was called also Malikpúr Sikandarpúr, was subsequently known by the name of Karsanah, and is now included in Sahâwar. The remains of Atrejí still exist in Parganah Marehra on the right bank of the Kálí Nadí; and Sikandarpúr on the opposite bank is now known as Sikandarábád. It is reported in the neighbourhood, that in consequence of some quarrel between the Zamíndars, a Government Officer was sent from Dehli to institute enquiries into the cause, and the result of his mission was that 60 villages of Solankí Rajputs were detached from Sahâwar, and made into a separate Parganah by the name of Sikandarpúr Atrejí.

23.—Deoha is included in Bilhaur, and was mentioned in the early Settlements as a separate Parganah, under the name of Dewa. The town of Dewa still exists near Bilhaur.

27.—Malkonsá is the old name of Rasúlabad. The names are still frequently united, as Rasúlabad Malkonsá.

28.—Nánámau is on the Ganges, and was the head town of a Parganah, till it was included in Bilhaur by Almas Ali Khán.

29.—Bárá is now included in Akbarpúr.

The new parganahs within the old Sirkár of Kanauj are—

ترروا 1 *Tirúá.*	بيله 6 *Belah.*
تهتّيا 2 *Thaṭṭíá.*	اكبرپور 7 *Akbarpúr.*
رسول آباد 3 *Rasúlábád.*	كشني نبي گنج 8 *Kishní Nabíganj.*
شيوراج پور 4 *Sheorájpúr.*	پيپرگانو 9 *Pípargánw.*
اوريا 5 *U'riyá* (part).	محمد آباد 10 *Muḥammadábád*

تپہ پہارا 11 *Tappa Pahárá.*	مہرآباد 15 *Mihrábád.*
حضور تحصیل 12 *Hazúr Tahsíl.*	بان گانو 16 *Bángánw.*
قایم گنج 13 *Káimganj.*	اسلام گنج 17 *Islámganj.*
سونہار 14 *Sonhár.*	اعظم نگر 18 *A'zamnagar.*

Tirúá and Ṭhaṭṭia.—These were not rated as separate Parganahs till the commencement of our administration, and have now been thrown again into a single Parganah. They were formerly within the Parganah of Talgrám, or Talgráṅw (the village of lakes).

Rasúlabad has been explained under Malkonsá.

Sheorajpúr was formerly within the area of Bithúr.

Uriyá (part) has been explained under Pattí Nakhat.

Belah was originally merely a village of Sahár, and was for a long time the seat of a Sub-Collectorship.

Akbarpúr gave name to a Parganah, when it was made the chief town of Sirkár Shahpúr; and now frequently goes by the name of Akbarpúr Shahpúr, in consequence. See further, under Shahpúr, Sirkár Kálpí.

Kishní Nabíganj was formerly in Bhúigáṅw. As on the British accession it was held by Chandharí Uday Chand under a different tenure from the rest of Bhúigáṅw, it was constituted a Parganah, and has so remained.

Pípargáṅw.—The villages included within Pípargaṅw were given in Jagír by Mahomed Khán Bangash to his wife, and detached for that purpose from Shamsabad. On her death they continued under separate management, and so remained till the British accession, when they were permanently formed into the separate Parganah of Pípargaṅw.

Muḥammadabad, usually pronounced Moḥamdabad, was also a Zillah of Shamsabad.

Tappa Pahara, within which the City of Farrukhabad (Farrakhabad) and Station of Fattihgarh are situated, was originally a portion of Bhojpúr, from which it was detached by Mahomed Khán Bangash, and its revenue assigned for the expenses of his Zenana.

The Hazúr Taḥsíl is a large tract, detached in the year 1217 Faslí, for the convenience of collection, from Shamsabad, and united with Píparganw, Muhammadabad, Bhojpúr, and Tappa Pahara under the charge of a separate Tahsíldar.

Káímganj.—Part of Kampil and part of Shamsabad were taken to make this Parganah. Certain villages of these two Parganahs were held in farm by Jahán Khán, and other Patháns of Maú and Káímganj (called after Káím Jang, the son of Mahomed Khán Bangash); and as these villages had thus for a long time been held separate from the other two Parganahs, they were formed into the Parganah of Káímganj, when the British administration commenced.

Sonhár formed at one time a portion of Barna. It is said in the annals of the Rathors, that on Jay Chand's defeat by Mahomed Ghorí, the remnant of his family, which chose not to seek their fortunes in Rajputana, took up their abode in Barna, and after residing there for several generations, gave the present Parganah of Barna as a Sankalap (or grant for the performance of religious ceremonies, *v.* Birt) to Brahmans, and making Sonhár their residence, it became in course of time a separate Parganah.

Mihrabad was formerly included in the large Parganah of Shamsabad. Its name is said to be derived from Mihr-Parwar, the wife of Shamsu'ddín, King of Dehli.

Bángánw was a Zillah of Mihrabad, and therefore originally in Shamsabad.

Islámganj was also formerly a Zillah of Mihrabad.

A'zamnagar* was constituted a Parganah at the commencement of the British administration. It was formerly a Tappa

* Kali Rai calls this Aliganj, and it is so called in the map of zamíndárí possessions.

of Shamsabad, and was for some time the residence of the Amil of that Parganah.

SIRKÁR KÁLPÍ.

اورئي 1 *Urai.*	سوگن‌پور 8 *Súganpúr.*
بلاسپور 2 *Bilásprúr.*	شاه‌پور 9 *Sháhpúr.*
بهدهيک 3 *Bhadhek.*	کالپي 10 *Kálpi.*
ديراپور 4 *Derápúr.*	کنار 11 *Kanár.*
ديوکلي 5 *Deokali.*	کهنڈوت 12 *Khunḍaut.*
راٹهه 6 *Ráṭh.*	کهريله 13 *Khurela.*
راي‌پور 7 *Ráipúr.*	محمدآباد 14 *Muhammadábád.*

همیرپور 15 *Hamírpúr.*

The Sirkár of Klápí contains 16 Mahála, the Havelí and Balda of Kálpí being divided in the Dastúr Table into two Mahála. These constitute only one Dastúr. It is strange that the area is omitted from No. 7 to 12, but as there is no doubt about their present position, the omission is of no consequence.

It will be observed that in the list above given, there are but few which are recognized in the present day in our own Provinces; the missing ones being Numbers 1, 2, 3, 4, 5, 7, 8, 9, 11, 12, 13, and 14.

1.—Uraí is in Jalaun, and the site of a British cantonment.

2.—Bilaspúr still exists on the banks of the Jumna, about six miles South from Sekandra. The Parganah of Bilaspúr is now generally known as Sekandra, or Bilaspúr Sekandra.

3.—Bhadhek now forms a portion of the Parganah of Kalpí, and is included in part of the long strip of lnd which runs between Jalaun and the Jumna. The word is difficult to read in all the copies I have consulted. It assumes the various forms of Badhalsa, Badhasabad, Babban, Badangola, and Badhatasta.

4.—Derapúr forms part of Dera Mangalpúr in Cawnpore.

14.—Muhammadabad is a Parganah of the Jálaun District, skirting the northern bank of the Betwa.

The Parganahs of which we have no trace in the "A'ín-i Akbarí" are—

بهوگني پور 1 *Bhognípúr.*	سكندره 4 *Sikandrah.*
منگل پور 2 *Mangalpúr.*	جلال پور 5 *Jalálpúr.*
أوريا 3 *U'riyá.*	كهركه 6 *Kharka.*

پنواري 7 *Panwárí.*

Bhognípúr was formerly contained within Sháhpúr. It was constituted a Parganah at the commencement of our administration, and now includes within its area another new Parganah, called Músánagar.

Mangalpúr was formerly a village called Nera in Parganah Bilaspúr. It was bestowed along with fifty-two villages upon Mangal Khan, by Muhammad Ahmad Khan, the Jagírdar of Sirkár Sháhpúr. Mangal Khan changed the name of Nera to Mangalpúr, and thenceforward the fifty-two villages constituted a separate Parganah. In the year 1216 Faslí, it was united with Derapúr into one Parganah, now known as Dera Mangalpúr.

U'riyá. About two-thirds of U'riyá are in this Sirkár, containing the two Parganahs of Súganpúr and Deokalí. The remainder of U'riyá formed Pattí Nakhat in Sirkár Kanauj. The three were united into the Parganah of U'riyá in 1216 Faslí.

Sikandrah was formerly Bilaspúr.

Jalálpúr, sometimes called Jelálpúr Kharela, contains two old Parganahs—Khandaut on the North, and Kharela on the South. The town of Jalálpúr, which is called after Jalál Shah, a Fakír, who lies buried there, is built within the lands of Khandaut.

Kharkah was formed from parts of Muhammadabad, U'ráí, Khandaut and Rath.

Panwárí was a portion of Rath, which has an area of no less than 580,000 Bíghas. But no certain information respecting this Parganah can be gleaned, except that it was originally called Parhárpúr; still, this gives us no clue to its position, unless we assume it to be the Parihár in Sirkár Írij. But the probabilities are in favour of its having been a part of Rath.

SIRKÁR KOL.

اترولي	1	*Atraulí.*	خورجه	11	*Khúrja.*
اكبرآباد	2	*Akbarábád.*	دبهائي	12	*Dabhái.*
اهار	3	*Ahár.*	سكندرا راو	13	*Sekandrá Ráo.*
پهاسو	4	*Pahású.*	سورون	14	*Soron.*
بلرام	5	*Bilrám.*	سيدهوپور	15	*Saidhúpúr.*
پچلانا	6	*Pachláná.*	شكارپور	16	*Shikárpúr.*
تپل	7	*Tappal.*	كول	17	*Kol.*
تهانه فريدا	8	*Thána Farídá.*	گنگيري	18	*Gangerí.*
جلالي	9	*Jalálí.*	مارهره	19	*Márehra.*
چندوس	10	*Chandaus.*	ملكپور	20	*Malikpúr.*

نوح 21 *Noḥ.*

This Sirkár contains 21 Mahals, divided among the four Dastúrs of Kol, Márehra, Akbarábád, and Thána Farídá.

There are but few lost names in the above list, viz., Numbers 6, 15, 18, and 20; and three even of these have only very lately been absorbed into other Parganahs.

6.—Pachláná forms the eastern portion of Atraulí.

15.—Saidhúpúr.—There has been great difficulty in restoring this Mahál, but it appears to be no other than Siṛhpúra. In some copies, indeed, it is written Siṛhpúr.

The chief objections to consider Saidhúpur as Siṛhpúra, arise from its being separated from the rest of the Dastúr of Márehra by Sikandarpúr Atrejí and part of Sakít; and from its being combined with Pachláná, the most distant Parganah of the Dastúr, as two Mahâls; but on closer examination it is found that only by taking a portion of Sakít into Márehra and Siṛhpúr, can the true area of all the neighbouring Parganahs be restored according to the "A'ín-i Akbarí;" and when this is done the old status is represented with surprising correctness. The second objection vanishes when we find other distant Parganahs, about which we can entertain no doubt, grouped as two Mahâls; as in the instance of Tilbegampúr and Jelálpúr, Sirkár Dehli, and Seohára and Jhalú, Sirkár Sambhal. Under these circumstances, coupled with the consideration that Saidhúpúr has Solankhí Zamíndárs, we may safely assume Siṛhpúra to be in the Dastúr of Máṛehra.

There was another cause of hesitation. In the Sirkár of Kanauj, Birwar (بيرور) occupies the alphabetical place of, and is written like, Sarwar (سرور); and had there not been other instances in that Sirkár of the alphabetical arrangement being disregarded, we might have supposed that Siṛhpúra was meant.

18.—Gangerí forms the South-Eastern portion of Atraulí. Gangerí and Pachláná have been absorbed since the last Settlement.

20.—Malikpúr has now been converted into Anúpshahr. The village of Malikpúr is about five miles South-West from Anúpshahr. In the first few Settlements it is spoken of as a Parganah, generally in conjunction with Ahár.

The new Parganahs are also few—

كهير 1 *Khair.*	گورئي 3 *Goraí.*
حسن گڑه 2 *Hasangaṛh.*	انوپ شهر 4 *Anúpshahr.*

Khair, Hasangaṛh, and Goraí have been detached from Kol.

Anúpshahr.—The town and fort of Anúpshahr, after which this Parganah is called, were built by Anúp Singh, who was honoured with the title of Raja Aní Raí Singh Ahmad Khání, by Jahangír, and invested by him with a Jagír of 84 villages on each side of the Ganges, tenanted by Badgújars of his own tribe. Raja Aní built Jahangírábád also, and called it after the name of his royal patron, as well as Ahmadgaṛh in Pítámpúr, in honour of his dignity of Ahmad Khání. The present incumbent has succeeded to the title, but not to the extensive possessions of his ancestors; for Rája Sher Sing, who was the incumbent at the time of the cession, sold nearly the entire Estate, except the Talúkas of Jahángírábád and Ahmadgaṛh, which were then possessed by another branch of the family. Anúpshahr was formed from the area of Malikpúr, but it is only of late years that the entire area of Malikpúr has been absorbed into Anúpshahr, for in the first Settlements of Aligaṛh and Moradábád we find them recorded as separate Parganahs.

SIRKÁR TIJÁRAH.

اندور	1 *Indor.*	بیگوان پور	4 *Begwánpúr.*†
اوجینه	2 *U'jina.*	بیسرو	5 *Bisrú.*
اومري اومرا	3 *U'mrí U'mrá.**	بهسوهرا	6 *Bhasohrá.*

* Mr. C. Gubbins says Umrí Umrá are in the Noh according to the old arrangement, but in the map they are in Hatín.—E. *add.*

† There is some confusion in the text, not only in the spelling of certain names, but also as to the situation of the mahals. Begwánpúr is an anomalous looking word, and is probably a corruption of Bangwán, a mistake which might easily occur in Persian writing (بنگوان and بیگوان). The termination *púr* does not belong to the word, which, on the authority of Mr. C. Gubbins, should be Paningwán (پننگوان). "It is an old city surrounded by ruins and tombs and tamarind groves and fine old wells. It used to be one of the chief head-quarters of the Khanzádas. The houses there are roofed for the most part with slate set on edge." It is not in Hatín but in Púnáhána.—E. *add.*

تجاره 7 *Tijárah.*	فتح پور مونگرتا 13 *Fattihpúr Múngartá.*
چمراوت 8 *Chamráwat.**	کوتله 14 *Kotila.*
خانپور 9 *Khánpúr.*	گهاسیره 15 *Ghásera.*
ساکرس 10 *Sákras.*	کهوا کاتهانا 16 *Khawá Káthána*
ساتهاداري 11 *Sáthádári.*	نگینان 17 *Naginán.*
فیروزپور 12 *Fírozpúr.*	

This Sirkár consists only of one Dastúr. It contains 18 Mahâls; but the name of one between Tijárah and Chamráwat remains blank in all the copies which have been consulted. By referring, however, to the Dastúr table, it appears that the name of the omitted Mahál is Púr, which, as it is not within our territory, requires no further notice.

Of the old Tijárah Parganahs within the district of Gurgáńw there are eight which no longer exist, viz., Numbers 1, 2, 4, 5, 10, 14, 15, and 17.

1.—Indor is a Parganah of which the chief town still exists on the Western brow of the Mewat Hills, near the source of the Indorí river, one of the streams which fall into the Sábí. It lies between Noh and Kotila. The area is represented as containing 1,30,450 Bíghas, of which the British portion is included in Parganah Noh, the remainder in the Tijárah country.

2 and 4.—Új́ina and Begwánpúr are included within Hatín.

5.—Bísrú is included in Púnáhána.

10 and 17.—Sakras and Nagína (Nagínán) are included in Fírozpúr; but were considered separate Parganahs till the lapse of the Fírozpúr Jagír to Government.

14.—Kotila contained 71,265 Bíghas, of which the greater part has gone to form the Parganah of Noh, and the remainder to form the Parganah of Hatín. Kotila still exists, eight miles South from Noh, but scarcely ranks above an ordinary village.

* Or Jhimráwat.

It was formerly a place of very considerable importance, and was one of the chief strongholds of the turbulent Mewatís. We learn from the "Tawáríkh-i Mubarikshahí" that it was taken and destroyed by the Sayyid King, Khizr, in A.D. 1421.

15.—Ghasera has been thrown into Noh. It is still a respectable town, encircled with a strong wall with bastions.

The present Parganahs included within this area, and not mentioned in the "Áín-i Akbarí," are—

نوح 1 *Noh.*	هتين 2 *Hatín.*

پوناهانه 3 *Púnáhánah.*

Noh was formerly a Mauza within the area of Parganah Indor. In A.D. 1764 the Ját chief, Súraj Mal, after killing Rao Bahádúr Singh, who had previously seized upon the Parganahs of Indor and Kotila, and after plundering the town of Ghasera, established his own Amil in Noh, and placed under his charge the collections of Indor, Ghasera and Kotila; since which time it has remained a separate Parganah.

Hatín, which lapsed to the British Government in 1231 Faslí, on the death of Faizulláh Beg Khan, was originally named after a Mauza of Bhagwánpúr, and now includes within its area Ujína and Bhagwánpúr,* and parts of Sonah and Kotila. In the time of Mohamed Shah, Rao Badan Singh, the father of Súraj Mal, held a lease of this Mahál from the Jagírdars in possession. His son, taking advantage of the weakness and decline of the Mahomedan Government, refused to fulfil the conditions his father had entered into, and maintained by force of arms possession on his own account: and building a mud fort in Hatín, included his acquisitions within a new Parganah of that name, which has been retained to this time.

* Or Paningwán.

Púnáhánah, which was formerly included in Nawwab Shamsu'd-dín's Jagír, was originally a small Mauza in Parganah Bisrú. In A.D. 1717 Súraj Mal built a mud fort in Púnáhánah, and established it as the head quarters of a new Parganah, formed out of Bisrú and parts of Chamráwat and Paháṛí.

SIRKÁR I'RIJ.

The only Parganahs of I'rij in our territory (excluding Jalaun, which, having lately lapsed to us, I have not considered), are—

كونچ 1 *Kúnch.*	پريهار 2 *Paríhár.*

Kúnch retains its name in the district of Hamírpúr, and is isolated by Parganahs of the Jalaun territory.

Parihár, so called from the tribe of Rajputs who are its zamíndárs, includes in a portion of its area the Talúka of Sandaus, now contained in the Parganah of Janibrast in Etawah. Its position in the midst of the ravines of the Kúárí and Chambal has always fostered the turbulence of the zamíndárs, and in the early period of our administration a military party sent out to control them was severely handled, and the officer in command lost his life.

SIRKÁR SAHÁR.

پهاري 1 *Pahárí.*	كامه 4 *Kámah.*
بهدولي 2 *Bhadaulí.*	كوه مجاهد 5 *Koh Mujáhid.*
سهار 3 *Sahár.*	نون هيره 6 *Núnherah.*

هوڈل 7 *Hoḍal.*

This Sirkár, which is sometimes called Pahárí, contains seven Maháls forming one Dastúr; but in some copies Núnhera is recorded as a separate Dastúr. Only two of these Parganahs

5.—Deokalí is now contained within Uriya. The old town is about two miles South from Uriya, on the bank of the Jumna.

7.—Ráípúr is on the right bank of the Jumna, and extensive ruins proclaim its former importance. Only a small portion is included in the Hamírpúr District, the rest is in Jalaun.

8.—Súganpúr is now in Uriya, between Deokalí and Pattí Nakhat. Súnganpattí still exists in the centre of Uriya.

9.—Shahpúr is now a deserted village in Bhognípúr, on the bank of the river Jumna, a short distance South-West from Bhognípúr. It was formerly the residence of the Amil, till the Nawab of Oudh removed it to Akbarpúr. In the Registers of the later Empire, as in the "Hakikat-i-Jama" of Hardí Rám Kayath, we find Sháhpúr giving name to a separate Sirkár, which comprised 25 Mahály, among which were the Parganahs of Pattí Nakhat, Súganpúr, Bilaspúr, Derapúr, and Mangalpúr. The Sirkár was frequently held in Jagír by a prince of the royal family. When Sháhpúr was much injured by the encroachments of the Jumna, the chief station was removed to Hajípúr on the Sengár, and in the course of time, in consequence of alarms inspired by the malice of a sprite called Bhúra Deo, it was removed to Akbarpúr. Hence it has retained the name of Akbarpúr Shahpúr; but at the commencement of our administration, Bhognipúr was separated from Akbarpúr, and formed into a separate Parganah.

11.—Kanar is a large Parganah of Jalaun. The old town of Kanar, being now in ruins, is called Kanar Khera. As Jagmohanpúr is built near the site, the chief of the Sengár Rajputs is frequently known as the Raja of Kanar Khera.

12.—Khandaut is included in Jalálpúr, in the Hamírpúr district. The village is on the south bank of the Betwa, about two miles west of Jalálpúr.

13.—Kharela is also in Jalálpúr, and the town is at the southern extremity of that Parganah.

are in our territory—numbers 3 and 7,—but the dimensions of the former are much curtailed, on account of the formation of other Parganahs from part of its large area. We find it stated in the history drawn up by Sarúp Chand, for the use of Sir J. Shore, that Shahjahán, in the twentieth year of his reign, gave Kámah, Pahárí, and the other Parganahs of this Sirkár, to Kírat Singh, the father of Raja Jai Singh, as the imperial authorities were not strong enough to control the turbulence of the Mewatís; but I do not find it mentioned among the transactions of that year in the "Shahjahán-náma."

The new Parganahs within this area are—

شیرگڑه 1 *Shergarh.* | کوسي 2 *Kosí.*

ارینگ 3 *Aring (part).*

These three Parganahs were formerly included in Sahár. The two first were separated by the Játs, but for a long time retained the single name of Kosí, and the latter, at the commencement of our administration; since which time the three have continued separate Parganahs. Aríng includes also the Parganahs of Govardhan and Sonsa; and Kosí includes that of Shahpúr; but as they were intermediately formed, and no mention is made of them in the "Áín-i Akbarí," they require no notice.

In the Hakíkat-i-Jama of Hardí Rám Káyath, which was written about the time of the decline of the empire (the precise year is not mentioned), there is no such Sirkár as that of Sahár, and we find it succeeded by Islampúr (called by Aurangzeb, Islamábád) Muttra (Mathurá), containing 12 Mahály. There is also the new Sirkar of Biana Hindaun formed according to the same work, containing 29 Mahály, while the Sirkár of Agra is reduced to the mere Havelí round the city.

II.—*SÚBA ILAHÁBÁS.*

Sirkár Iláhábás.

الاباس با حويلي	1	*Ilahábás bá Haveli.*	سكندرپور	6	*Sikandarpúr*
بهدوي	2	*Bhadoí.*	كنتت	7	*Kantit.*
جلال آباد	3	*Jalálábád.*	كيواي	8	*Kewáí.*
سورانو	4	*Soránw.*	كهيراگڑه	9	*Khairágarh.*
سنگرور	5	*Singraur.*	مهه	10	*Mah.*
			هادي آباس	11	*Hádíábás.*

This Sirkár is said to contain only 11 Maháls, though Jalálábád is reckoned as 4. They are divided among the three Dastúrs of Ilahábás, Bhadoí, and Jalálábád.

The Parganahs now no longer extant are Numbers 1, 3, 5, and 11.

1.—Ilahábás.—The name of the fort and Parganah were subsequently, according to the Chár Gulshan and several other authorities, changed by Shah Jahán to Ilahábád, as the termination of *bás* was presumed to savour too much of Hinduism.* The Parganah is now known by the name of Chail, which is itself a place of some antiquity, as it is mentioned in the "Latáif-i Ashrafí."—See Harbong ka Raj.

3.—Jalálábád, or Jalálábás, is the name of Arail, which was imposed on it by Akbar, in commemoration of his own title of Jalálu'd-dín.—See note to Harbong ka Raj.

During the time of the Nawwáb Wazír's Government, Arail was included in Sirkár Tarhár,† and is so mentioned in the

* It is far more probable that the name Ilahábád was the original name as imposed by the Musulmans, and that the final syllable "bád," which they did not understand the meaning of, was changed by the lower orders to "bás," as it is to this day always pronounced "Ilahbás" by them."—B.

† Sirkár Tarhár appears to have occasionally varied its bounds. It seems at one

Schedule of Revenues given in the "Appendix to the 5th Report." It is strange that we find this Parganah, which forms a separate Dastúr, intervening between the Parganahs which form the Dastúr of Havelí Ilahábás. The position of Bara would point it out as a component part of Jalálábád, but, for the considerations given in the article Ghora, I have recorded it in that Sirkár. There is no measurement to guide us in this case, but the Revenue yielded is so small—being 7,37,220 Dams, with the small contingent of only 10 Sawárs and 400 Infantry—that it does not admit of the addition of Bara.

5.—Singraur is the old name of Nawábganj. Singraur is a very ancient place, and is spoken of in the "Rámáyana," as Sringavera.* The town of Singraur is still extant on the left bank of the Ganges, a few miles above Allahábád.

11.—Hadíábás was the name of the Parganah now called Jhúsí.—See Harbong ka Raj.

The new Parganahs are—

اريل 1 *Arail.*	تپه كون 5 *Tappah Kon.*
نواب‌گنج 2 *Nawábganj.*	تپه چوراسي 6 *Tappah Chaurási.*
جهوسي 3 *Jhúsí.*	تپه اوپرودھ 7 *Tappah Upraudh.*
چايل 4 *Cháil.*	سكتيس‌گڑھ 8 *Saktísgarh.*

Arail.—See Jalálábád.

Nawábganj.—The Parganah of Singraur received its new name of Nawábganj from Nawáb Mansúr Ali Khan, who built a ganj and town near Singraur, which he established as the chief station of the Parganah.

time to have included part of Chanár. In the "Ahwál-i Súbaját," mentioned in the article Budhganga, Sirkár Tarhár is said to contain nine mahâls, amongst which are to be recognised Jalálábás and Chaukandí.

* Wilson, "Theatre of the Hindús," I. p. 300; "Rámáyana," I. i. 28; Carey and Marshman, Vol. III., p. 247.—E. *add.*

Jhúsí.—See Hadíábás.

Cháil is the old name of Ilahábás bá Havelí. The town of Cháil is situated in the centre of the Parganah.

Tappah Kon is a portion of Bhadoí, from which it was detached when Sakat Singh married the Maunas Raja's daughter, to whom it was given in dowry, and thenceforward became a Tappah of Kantit, to which it did not belong when the "Áín-i Akbarí" was written.

Tappah Chaurásí is a portion of Kantit. Probably but a very small portion of this Tappah was known in Akbar's time, but we have no measurement to guide us.

Saktísgaṛh. This, too, was in Kant t, and was also, perhaps, mostly unknown. The country was previously called Kolana, in consequence of the residence of the Kols in this neighbourhood; and it was not till Raja Sakat Singh of Kantit destroyed their stronghold, and built Saktísgaṛh on its site, that the Tappah obtained its new name.

The Talúka of Mirzapúr Chauhárí, which is in the Allahábád district, was formerly in the Parganah of Jalálpúr Bilkhar in Sirkár Manikpúr, the rest of which Sirkár is in Oudh. It has been included in Allahábád since the time of Raja Madárí Lál, Ámil.

Sirkár Karra.

اینچهي	1 *Enchhí.*	کوتله	8 *Kotílah.*
اتهربن	2 *Atharban.*	کونرا عُرف کرسون	9 *Kuńrá,* alias *Karsoń.*
اياه ساه	3 *Ayáh Sáh.*	فتحپور هسوا	10 *Fattihpúr Haswá.*
حويلي کرا	4 *Havelí Karrá.*	هتگانو	11 *Hatgánw.*
راري	5 *Rárí.*	هسوا	12 *Haswá.*
بلده کرا	6 *Baldah Karrá.*		
کراري	7 *Karárí.*		

This Sirkár has 12 Mahál s comprised in one Dastúr.

The numbers which are obsolete are 1, 4, 5, 6, and 9.

1.—Enchhí.—This Parganah is now represented by Ghazípúr. The modern histories of India convey to us this information by calling the famous rebel Bhagwant, Khíchar, a Zamíndár of Parganah Enchhí (see further under Gházípúr). The village of Enchhí is still extant on the bank of the Jumna. The old fort, which is the theme of popular story, is not to be seen, but the people of the neighbourhood delight in telling a marvellous tale how Raja Palbhan Deo was slain in it, with all his family, by a demon called Brimha Dano; from which time it has been deserted; but the site is visited during the Dahsehra, when the superstitious villagers come from afar to make their annual offering at the shrine of the demon.

4 and 6.—Havelí Karrá and Baldah Karrá. The distinction has now been lost between them as separate Parganahs. They are both included in Parganah Karrá.

5.—Rárí has now been changed to Ekdalla, in which place Nawwáb Shuja'ud-daulah established his Tahsíldarí, but the Parganah retained its name of Rárí till the cession. The town of Ekdallah is on the Jumna, about two miles to the West of Rárí. Dhátah is also a Zillah of Rárí.

9.—Kúṅrá, *alias* Karson.—This is the old name of Mutaur, which it appears to have acquired from the course which the Jumna takes in this neighbourhood. The projecting patches of alluvial land which are formed near the banks of the river are called by the Zamíndárs Kunda, probably from their shape, which they might have conceived to bear some resemblance to a Kuṇḍa,* a vessel for kneading bread in; a platter. The Mauza of Kunda, or Kunra, still exists on the bank of the Jumna, at the North-Western angle of Parganah Mutaur.

* See "Dabistán," II. 79.—E. *add.*

The new Parganahs included within Sirkár Karrá are—

ایکدله 1 *Ekdallah.*	غازي‌پور 3 *Ghâzipúr.*
دهاته 2 *Dhátah.*	متور 4 *Mutaur.*

Ekdallah.—See Rárí.

Dhátah.—In consequence of the disturbances which arose between two parties of Kurmís in this neighbourhood, the Nawwáb Wazír was compelled to establish a separate Zillahdar in this place, in the year 1197 Faslí, and about fifty villages taken from Rárí were placed under his charge. Since the cession, Dhátah has been considered a separate Parganah.

Gházípúr may be considered to have been established as a Parganah in lieu of Enchhí, from the time that Bhagwant Rai Khíchar built his fort here, and killed Ján Nisár Khan, the general of Muhammad Shah; of which a full account is given in the "Taríkh-i Muzaffarí," and most other modern histories of India. The "Hadíkatu'l Akálím" assures us that he retained possession of the entire Sirkár of Kora for several years, and was only at last subdued by the strenuous efforts of Nawwáb Sa'ádat Khan. Dunyápat, the worthy descendant of the family, opposed our government shortly after its accession, but did not lose much by it, as he was subsequently rewarded with a handsome pension. After the death of Bhagwant Rai, the Amil continued to reside in Gházípúr; but Gházípúr was not recognized as a Parganah till the commencement of our administration in 1803, when for the two first settlements it is recorded as Enchhí, 'urf Gházípúr.

Mutaur.—Nawwáb 'Abdu's Samad Khan, who performed a conspicuous part in the time of Aurangzeb, was presented by that monarch with the Jagír of Kuṅra. Shortly after his investiture, he built a fort and dug a handsome tank at Mutaur, which succeeded to the importance of Kuṅra; but Wásilbáḳí papers are in existence which show that the Parganah retained its old name to as late a period as 1188 F.S.

SIRKÁR KORÁ.

جاجمو 1 *Jájmau.*	کوتیا 5 *Kútiá.*
کورا 2 *Korá.*	گنیر 6 *Gunír.*
گهاتم‌پور 3 *Ghátampúr.*	کیرت‌پور کنانده 7 *Kíratpúr-Kanánda.*
مجهاون* 4 *Majháwan.*	

محسن‌پور* 8 *Muhsanpúr.*

This Sirkár has eight Mahals, divided into the three Dastúrs of Korá, Kútiá, and Jájmau.

The missing Parganahs are numbers 4, 7 and 8.

4.—Majháwan, which is reported as a separate Parganah during our first settlements, is now included in Jájmau and Saṛh-Salímpúr. The town of Majháwan is still extant on the Pandu river, in the South Eastern angle of Jájmau.

7.—Kíratpúr-Kanánda is the old name of Parganah Bindkí.

8.—Muhsanpúr, called also Rawatpúr Muhsanpúr, is now included in Saṛh-Salímpúr, and is reported as a Parganah in our first settlements. The village of Muhsanpúr is still extant near the Arind river, in the Southern angle of Saṛh-Salímpúr. Its position is pointed out in the interesting letters of Naunít Rai, who styles himself "one of the Amlá of Muhsanpúr, a Parganah of Kora."

The new Parganahs are—

تپه جار 1 *Tappah Jár.*	بندکي 2 *Bindkí.*

ساره سلیمپور 3 *Sarh-Salímpúr.*

Tappah Jár belonged to Parganah Kora, from which the Wásilbáḳís show it to have been separated from the year 1180 F.S.

Bindkí.—See Kíratpúr Kanánda.

Saṛh-Salímpúr.—This Parganah has been formed from Muhsanpúr and Majháwan. There have been several intermediate changes in the size and constitution of all these Parganahs, owing to the various jurisdictions to which Sirkár Korá has been subject; but there is no occasion to record them here, as they have no concern with the comparison on which we are at present engaged.

Sirkár Kálinjar.

اوگاسي 1	*Ugási.*	رسن 6	*Rasan.*
اجيگڑه 2	*Ajaigaṛh.*	كالنجر 7	*Kálinjar.*
سهوندا 3	*Sihondá.*	كهنده 8	*Khandeh.*
سموني 4	*Simauní.*	مهوبا 9	*Mahobá.*
شاديپور 5	*Shádipúr.*	مودها 10	*Maudhá.*

This Sirkár contains eleven Maháls, Kálinjar ba Havelí being counted as two. It comprises a single Dastúr.

The Parganahs either extinct or beyond British Bundelkhand are the following—Numbers 2, 5, 6, 7 and 9.

2.—Ajaigaṛh.—This Parganah lies to the South of Kálinjar. The fort is garrisoned by British troops.

5.—Shádípúr is the old name of Parganah Pailání. The large village of Shádípúr is still extant on the bank of the Jumna. When the Bundelás built their fort in Pailání, and made it the residence of their Tehsíldar, the name of Pailání was gradually substituted for Shádípúr. From the Sanad appointing Bhím Sen Chaudharí of the Parganah, it appears that in the year 1121 F.S. the name of the Parganah was Shadípúr Pailaní.

6.—Rasan is the old name of Parganah Badausa. The town still exists about seven miles to the South of Badausa. Tieffenthaler gives us a clue to this Mahál by telling us it is seven miles N.E. from Kálinjar.

7.—Kálinjar ba Havelí.—See Badausa.

9.—Mahoba is in the Jalaun territory.

The new Parganahs are—

بدوسا 1 *Badausá.*	باندہ 3 *Bándah.*
پيلاني 2 *Pailání.*	سميرپور 4 *Sumerpúr.*

Badausá.—See Rasan. This was established by the Bundelas as the site of a new Tehsíldarí, in consequence of Hardbans Raí, a Raghubansí Rajput, being in independent occupation of Rasan. The greater portion of Kálinjar is included in Badausá.

Pailání.—See Shádípúr.

Bándah was originally a portion of Sihonda, but has been considered a separate Parganah since the time that Raja Gumán Singh, the Bundela, took up his residence here. Briggs, in his translation of Ferishta, says that Sikandar Lodi penetrated to Bándah,—which would imply that the town was older than the time of Akbar; but "Bándah" has been written by mistake for "Bándhú," or "Bándúgaṛh," as is evident from the "Táríkh-i Afághana," where a more detailed account of this difficult and unsuccessful expedition is given.

Sumerpúr was originally a portion of Maudha.

SIRKÁR BHATGHORA.

See Ghora in a separate article.

SIRKÁR JAUNPÚR.

الديمَو 1 *Aldímau.*	جونپور 6 *Jaunpúr.*
انگلي 2 *Anglí.*	چاندي پور برهر 7 *Chándípúr-Birhar.*
بهتري 3 *Bhitarí.*	چاندہ 8 *Chánda.*
بهدنو 4 *Bhadanw.*	چريا كوت 9 *Chiria Kot.*
تلهني 5 *Tilhaní.*	

چکیسر	10	*Chakesar.*
خرید	11	*Kharíd.*
خاص‌پور تانده	12	*Kháspúr Tánda.*
خانپور	13	*Khánpúr.*
دیوگانو	14	*Deogánw.*
راري	15	*Rárí.*
سجهولي	16	*Sajhaulí.*
سکندرپور	17	*Sikandarpúr.*
سگري	18	*Sagrí.*
سرهرپور	19	*Surharpúr.*
شادیاباد	20	*Shádiábád.*
ظفرآباد	21	*Zafarábád.*
قریات متو	22	*Ḳariát Mittú.*
قریات دوست‌پور	23	*Ḳariát Dostpúr.*
قریات مینده	24	*Ḳariát Menda.*
قریات سویتهه	25	*Ḳariát Soethah.*
کوله	26	*Kolah.*
گهسوا	27	*Ghiswá.*
گهوسي	28	*Ghosí.*
گڑواره	29	*Gaṛwárah.*
کوڑیا	30	*Kauṛiá.*
گوپالپور	31	*Gopálpúr.*
کراکٹ	32	*Karákaṭ.*
مریاهو	33	*Mariáhú.*
محمدآباد	34	*Muhammad-ábád.*
مونگرا	35	*Múngrá.*
مجهورا	36	*Majhaurá.*
مو	37	*Mau.*
نظام‌آباد	38	*Nizámábád.*
نیگون	39	*Negún.*
نتهوپور	40	*Nathúpúr.*

The Sirkár of Jaunpúr has 41 Mahāls, Jaunpúr bá Havelí being considered as 2; and 2 Dastúrs, which in size are very disproportionate—one comprising only the 2 Mahāls of Múngrá and Garwárah.

This large Sirkár has descended to us in a more perfect shape than any other which we have to examine. Exclusive of those within the Oudh territory, namely, Aldemau, Chandípúr Birhar, Chándah, Kháspúr, Tándah, Sajhaulí, Surharpúr, and Majhaura, the only Mahāls not now extant within British jurisdiction are Numbers 10, 25, 26, and 39.

10.—Chakesar was in existence till the late settlement; when, under the arrangements then made for improving Parganah Boundaries, it was included, with a newly-formed Parganah, called Surajpúr, in Ghosí; where the two united still constitute the Tappah of Chakesar.

25.—Ḳariát Soethah is now included in Parganah Anglí of Jaunpúr. It formed one of the Talúkas of Bakhshíat, which was broken up and distributed amongst several Parganahs at the late settlement.

26.—Kolah is the old name of Kol Aṣlá.

29.—Negún is included in the modern Parganah of Máhul.

The new Parganahs are also very few.

ماهل 1 *Máhul.*	گذارا 4 *Guzára.*
اترولي 2 *Atraulí.*	كول اصلا 5 *Kol Aṣlá.*
پادشاهپور 3 *Pádsháhpúr.*	سنگرامو 6 *Singrámau.*

Máhul is formed from Parganah Negún, and parts of Anglí and Surharpúr. Although at the time of the cession Máhul is entered in the registers as one of the four portions into which the province of Gorakhpur was divided, it received no higher denomination than that of Talúka, which has been changed by us into Parganah. In the middle of the last century, two Sayyids of the name of Sher Jehan and Shamshád Jehan, acquired possession of Negún and parts of Surharpúr and Anglí, as well as a few villages of Jaunpúr, and taking up their abode in Máhul Khás, gave their usurpations the name of Talúka Máhul. The town of Negún is now known as Ḳasba Khas, on the Eastern border of Máhul.

Atraulí was a Parganah formed a short time previous to the cession out of Balwant Singh's acquisitions from Tilhaní, but was originally included in Kauria. It has now been included again in Tilhaní, and the Parganah goes by the united name of Atraulí Tilhaní.

Badshahpúr is another name for Múngra. The Parganah is also known by the name of Múngra Badshahpúr.

Guẕára.—Tappa Guẕára, including Bhainsa, was originally in Karakat; and Sultánípúr, which is in the western angle of Bhainsa, is a Talúka of Katehar.

Kol Aṣlá ís the modern name of Kolah, derived from the village of Aṣlá, which was formerly the site of a Tehsíldarí Katcherry.

Singramau is a Talúka of Parganah Chanda, the rest of which is in Oudh.

See further under Sirkár.

SIRKÁR GHÁZÍPÚR.

بليا	1	*Balliá.*	قريات پلي	11	*Kariát Palí.*
پچوتر	2	*Pachotar.*	كوپا چيت	12	*Kopá Chít.*
بلهابانس	3	*Bilhábáns.*	گڑھا	13	*Gaṛhá.*
بهرياباد	4	*Bahríábád.*	كرينده	14	*Karendah.*
برايچ	5	*Baráich.*	لكهنيسر	15	*Lakhnesar.*
چونسا	6	*Chaunsá.*	مدن بنارس	16	*Madan Benares.*
دهمه	7	*Dihmah.*	محمدآباد پرهاباري	17	*Muhammadábád Parhábárí.*
سيدپور نمدي	8	*Sayyidpúr Namdí.*			
ظهورآباد	9	*Zahúrábád.*			
غازيپور	10	*Gházípúr.*			

Sirkár Gházípúr comprises only one Dastúr. It has nineteen Mahàls, Havelí Gházípúr and Muhammadábád Parhábárí being each counted as two.

This Sirkár, after all the ill-written names have been verified, is also found to have descended to us in a perfect shape. In the above list we miss now only the following Parganahs, viz., 5, 6, 11, and 16.

5.—Baráich.—This Parganah has caused more doubt than any other; but I believe it to be represented by the present Mauza Baráich in the Mahál of Bhataulí on the Gangí Naddí, which falls into the Ganges between Karendah and Gházípúr. Baráich is a small Parganah, containing only 2,000 Bíghas, and the place I have assigned to it is not altogether an improbable one for a Parganah.

6.—Chaunsá is in the Shahábád district in the Bengal Presidency, noted for being the place where two battles have been fought which have decided the fate of India, viz., that of Buxar in 1765, and the one which led to the expulsion of Humáyún from India; in describing which, by the way, some translator or compiler, whose name I do not now remember, has been led into a ludicrous mistake. In translating Ni'amat ullah, he says Humáyún when retreating from Chaunsá across the Ganges recognized Nizám, his water-carrier, by a strong smell of *musk*, whereas the original merely informs us that he saved the emperor by seating him on an inflated mashak (a leather water bag).

11.—Kariát Palí was included at the late revision of boundaries in Muhammadábád Parhábárí.

16.—Madan Benares is the old name of Zamania.

There is only one new Parganah in this Sirkár.

زمانيه 1 *Zamánia* (now generally written and pronounced زِمَنيه).—B.

Zamánia has succeeded to Madan Benares. During the decline of the empire we find it combined with Gházípúr in giving name to the Sirkár. Thus, "Sirkár Ghazípúr Zamánia, 17 Maháls."

Doába is a Tappah of Parganah Fattihpúr Bahia, which is recorded as being in the Sirkár of Rohtas, and the Súbah of

Bihár. It has only been noticed here because its position would appear to point it out as a portion of this Sirkár.

Sirkár Benáres.

افراد 1 *Afrád.*	پندره 4 *Pandrah.*
بنارس با حويلي 2 *Benares bá Havelí.*	كسوار 5 *Kaswár.*
بيالسي 3 *Byálisi.*	كتيهر 6 *Katehar.*
	هرهوا 7 *Harhúá.*

This Sirkár, which comprises only one Dastúr, has 8 Maháls, Havelí Benáres being counted as two.

The extinct Parganahs are Numbers 1, 2, and 7.

1.—Afrád (*i.e.* pieces) consisted chiefly, as the name would imply, of several detached Mauzas in different Parganahs, and had therefore, perhaps, no determinate boundary. There are Mauzas, for instance, in Katehar and in Kaswár, which are still recorded as having been once in Parganah Afrád. I have assigned to Afrád a position between Katehar, Kaswár, Benares, and Kola, but the greater portion has been taken from Kaswár, in which Afrád Khas is situated.

2.—Benares bá Havelí contained the modern Parganahs of Lotha, Dihát Amánat, and Sheopúr, the two former to the South, and the latter to the North, of the little river Barná.

7.—Harhúá is the old name of Aṭhgáṅw. The village of Harhúá is still extant in this Parganah, on the high road from Benares to Jaunpúr. It is said that there were formerly only eight villages in Harhúá, and hence the name of Aṭhgáṅw.

The new Parganahs within Sirkár Benares are—

جالهوپور 1 *Jálhúpúr.*	مجهوا 4 *Majhowá.*
شيوپور 2 *Sheopúr.*	اتهگانو 5 *Aṭhgáṅw.*
لوتها 3 *Lothá.*	دهات امانت 6 *Dihát Amánat.*

Jálhúpúr is a Talúka detached from Katehar by Raja Balwant Singh.

Sheopúr was originally in Havelí Benares, from which it was detached by Raja Chait Singh.

Lothá is a portion of Havelí Benares. It was subsequently included in Dihát Amánat; but is now considered a separate Talúka.

Majhowá is a Talúka of Kaswár.

Aṭhgáṅw.—See Harhúá.

Dihát Amánat was originally in Havelí. It comprehends the city of Benares and the tract immediately around it.

It is strange that in the Benares Mahális, Bhúínhárs are not mentioned as Zamíndárs by Abu'l Fazl. The difference between them and Brahmans does not appear to have been fully comprehended; for that it did not exist two hundred and fifty years ago, it is difficult to suppose.

Sirkár Chanár.

اهيرواره	1	*Ahirwárah*	قريات اين روي اب	8	*Kariát in rúi áb.*
بهويلي	2	*Bhúolí.*	مجهواره	9	*Mujhwára.*
بڑهول	3	*Baṛhaul.*	مهايچ	10	*Maháich.*
تانده	4	*Tánda.*	مهواري	11	*Mahwárí.*
چنار با حويلي	5	*Chanár bá Havelí.*	موئي	12	*Mawaí.*
دهوس	6	*Dhús.*	نرون	13	*Narwan.*
رالهوپور	7	*Rálhúpúr**	هنوا	14	*Hanwá.*

There is only one Dastúr in Chanár, comprising 14 Mahális;

* This is entered in the best copies as Rághúpúr راگهوپور. It is certainly now written and pronounced Ráhúpúr.

though the Parganah tables concur in saying there are only 13 Mahál̤s. The two last are omitted from most of the copies of the "Áín-i Akbarí," but are requisite to complete the Sirkár. In those copies, indeed, in which they are entered they are nearly illegible.* It is evident from history that this part of the country was but little known, and we must therefore allow for some error and confusion.

We retain the names of all the Parganahs in the above list, except those of Numbers 1, 4, 8, and 14.

1.—Ahírwárah, so called after the original Zamíndárs of those parts, has now been corrupted and abbreviated into Ahrora.

4.—Tándah is the old name of Parganah Barah. The Mauzas of Tándah Kalán and Tándah Khúrd still exist on the right bank of the Ganges, at a short distance from each other.

8.—Ḳariát ín rú-i áb (*i.e.* the villages on this side of the water) is now known as Ḳariát Síkhar.

14.—Hanwá.—See Bhagwat.

The new Parganahs, of which we find no mention in the "Áín-i Akbarí" as belonging to this Sirkár, are—

برہ 1 *Barah.*	بھگوت 3 *Bhagwat.*
قریات سیکھر 2 *Kariát Síkhar.*	اھرورہ 4 *Ahrorah.*

کیرامنگرور 5 *Kera Mangror.*

Barah.—See Tándah.

Ḳariát Síkhar.—See Ḳariát ín rú-i áb. It does not appear when the name of the Parganah was changed, or for what particular reason the strange title of Ḳariát ín rú-i áb was given originally to this Parganah.

Bhagwat.—This Parganah, previous to the conquest effected

* In them, moreover, they are entered as being entirely Siyarghal, or rent-free, which may be perhaps the cause why they are omitted in so many copies.

by the Gautams, was held by Jamí'at Khan, Gaharwár, whose defence of the fort of Patíta is a favorite theme with the people. The old name of this Parganah was Hanoa, which was extinct before the time of Jamí'at Khan, when it was known only as Bhagwat.

Ahrorah.—As much of this Parganah as was known in Akbar's time was called Ahírwára.

Kera Mangror.—Mangror is entered in the "Áín-i-Akbarí" as a Parganah of Sirkár Rohtas, Súba Behar, and in the later periods of the empire, as belonging to Sirkár Shahabad, which is now the district of Shahabad in Southern Behar, under the Lieutenant-Governor of the Lower Provinces.

SU'BA OUDH.

Sirkár Gorakhpúr.

اترولا	1	*Atraulá.*	رسولپور غوث	11	*Rasúlpúr Ghaus*
انہولا	2	*Anhaulá.*	رام گڑه گوري	12	*Rámgarh Gaurí.*
بنايكپور	3	*Bináikpúr.*	گورکهپور	13	*Gorakhpúr.*
بمہني پاره	1	*Bamhnipárah.*	کٹہلا	14	*Kaṭihlá.*
بہاواپاره	5	*Bháwápára.*	رهلاپاره	15	*Rihlápára.*
تل پور	6	*Tilpúr.*	مهولي	16	*Mahaulí.*
چلوپاره	7	*Chilúpára.*	مندوا	17	*Mandwá.*
دهرياپاره	8	*Dhuriápára.*	منډله	18	*Mandla.*
دهيواپاره کہانا	9	*Dhewapára Kuháná.*	رتن پور مگهر	19	*Ratanpúr Maghar.*
رهلي	10	*Rihlí.*			

This Sirkár forms only one Dastúr, containing twenty-four Mahále; Gorakhpúr bá Havelí, Rasúlpúr Ghaus, Ratanpúr

Maghar, Binaikpúr, and Rámgaṛh Gaurí, being each reckoned two Maháls.

This is a difficult Sirkár to restore, and, even after verifying all the illegible names, we have in the list of extinct or foreign Parganahs numbers 1, 4, 9, 10, 12, 14, 15, 17 and 18.

1.—Atraulá is in Oudh.

4.—Bamhnípárah.—This is the South-Eastern angle of Parganah Nawwábganj, which we gave up to Oudh in 1817.

9.—Dhewápára Kuhána is the old name of Salímpúr Majhaulí, Shahjahánpúr, and Sidhoa Jobna, which were part of the great Majhaulí Raj. In some old writings the name of the Mahál is entered Nawápár Kuháná Dhewápár. The popular name of the village of Salímpúr is Nawápár; (Buchanan, "Eastern India," Vol. II. p. 361, says Nagar); and the Parganah would have been restored as Kuháná Nawápár, had it not been for the alphabetical arrangement requiring an initial *d* in this place. The name Dhewápár is now nearly extinct. Nawápár is common.

10.—Rihlí is the Northern and Western part of Nawwábganj, ceded to Oudh.

12.—Rámgaṛh Gaurí—We are assisted in this name by being told it is on the Raptí. It is the old name of Balrámpúr, in Oudh.

14.—Katihlá is the old name of North Bansí. When the Katihlá Raja was defeated and slain by the Bansí Raja, the old name of the Parganah became extinct. Bansí, South of the Raptí, was called Ratanpúr, which Mahál is combined with Maghar in the "Áín-i Akbarí."

15.—Rihlápára.—At the suggestion of Mr. Reade, the late collector, I have entered this Parganah as the old name of Aurangabad Nagar; but I confess some doubt on the subject, for all the copies give distinctly Kihlápára, and the substitution of the *r* for *k* displaces the alphabetical order usually preserved.

17.—Mandwá is the ancient name of Bastí.

18.—Mandla.—No trace can be had of this Mahál. Mr. Reade suggests that it may be the old name of Amorha; but Amorha is itself an old Parganah, and is included, in the "Áín-i Akbarí," in Sirkár Oudh.

The new Parganahs in Sirkár Gorakhpúr are—

سليمپور مجهولي	1	*Salímpúr Majhaulí.*	منصورنگر بستي	5	*Mansúrnagar Bastí.*
سدهوا جوبنا	2	*Sidhuá Jubná*	اورنگاباد نگر	6	*Aurangábád Nagar.*
شاهجهانپور	3	*Sháhjahánpúr*			
سلهت	4	*Silhet.*			

Salímpúr Majhaulí.—This is a portion of the old Parganah of Dhewápára Kuháná.

Sidhuá Jubná.—Ditto.

Sháhjahánpúr.—Ditto. I have somewhere seen it mentioned that these Parganahs were in Sáran, but the statement appears to rest on no authority.

Silhet was detached from Parganah Havelí about the year 1633 by the Majhaulí Raja, and was recovered by the Satásí Raja about fifty years afterwards. It has since this period been rated as a separate Parganah.

Mansúrnagar Bastí.—See Mandwá.

Aurangábád Nagar.—See Rihlápára.

Sirkár Oudh.

Amoṛha (Amoḍh) is the only Parganah of this Sirkár in British territory. It is in the Dastúr of Havelí Oudh.

Sirkár Khairábád.

The only portion of this Sirkár in our jurisdiction is Khákatmau, which probably included also the modern Parganah of

Paramnagar, although the local officers are unanimous in representing that Paramnagar was originally a portion of Shamsabad. Kháhatmau is in the Dastúr of Palí.

III.—*SÚBA DEHLI.*

SIRKÁR DEHLI.

اسلام آباد پاکل	1	*Islámábád Pákal.*
اڈہ	2	*Aḍh.*
پاني پت	3	*Pánípat.*
پالم	4	*Pálam.*
برن	5	*Baran.*
باغپت	6	*Bághpat.*
پلول	7	*Palwal.*
برناوہ	8	*Barnáwah.*
پوتهه	9	*Púth.*
دوبلدهن بيري	10	*Dobaldhan Berí*
تلپت	11	*Tilpat.*
تانده پهوگانه	12	*Tánda Phúgánah.*
تل بيگم پور	13	*Tilbegampúr.*
جهجهر	14	*Jhajhar.*
جهارسه	15	*Jhársa.*
جيور	16	*Jewar.*
جهنجهانه	17	*Jhinjhána.*
چهپرولي	18	*Chhapraulí.*
جلال آباد	19	*Jalálábád.*
جلال پور بروت	20	*Jalálpúr Baraut.*
حويلي قديمي	21	*Havelí Ḳadímí*
حويلي جديدي	22	*Havelí Jadídí.*
دارالملک دهلي	23	*Dárú'lmulk Dehlí.*
داسنه	24	*Dásnah.*
دادري طاها	25	*Dádrí Táhá.*
دنکور	26	*Dankaur.*
روهتک	27	*Rohtak.*
سونيپت	28	*Sonípat.*
سفيدون	29	*Safídún.*
سيکندرآباد	30	*Sikandarábád.*
سراوہ	31	*Saráwah.*
سينته	32	*Sentah.*
سيانه	33	*Siánah.*
شکرپور	34	*Shakarpúr.*
کرنال	35	*Karnál.*
گنور	36	*Ganaur.*

گڑه مکتيسر 37 *Gaṛhmuktesar.*	لوني 43 *Loni.*
کتانه 38 *Kutánah.*	ميرتهه 44 *Mírath.*
کاندهله 39 *Kándhlah.*	ماندوتهي 45 *Mándauthí.*
کاسنه 40 *Kásnah.*	مسعودآباد 46 *Masa'údábád.*
کهرکهوده 41 *Kharkhauda.*	هستناپور 47 *Hastinápúr.*
گنگيرو 42 *Gangerú.*	هاپور 48 *Hápúr.*

The Sirkár of Dehli consists of forty-eight Mahåls, divided into the seven Dastúrs of Havelí, Pánípat, Baran, Mírath, Jhajhar, Rohtak and Palwal.

This large Sirkár has descended to us in a very perfect form. Excluding the foreign Parganahs of Jhajhar, Dádrí Táhá, and Safídún, we miss in the above list only numbers 11, 12, 21, 22, 23, 32 and 46.

11.—Tilpat.—The greater part of Tilpat was included by Nawwáb Faríd Khan, a nobleman of Jehangír's time, in Farídabad, now a Parganah of the Balamgaṛh Jagír; but the town of Tilpat is included in the Southern Parganah of Dehli. It is a place of great antiquity, and is one of the five towns demanded by the Páṇḍava brothers, the refusal of which was one of the causes of the "Great War." Authorities do not concur in the names of the five towns, but Tilaprastha (Tilpat) is generally one ("Wilson's Hindu Theatre," Vol. II. 337).

12.—Tánda Phúgánah.—This Mahál is generally written Tánda Bhagwán, and we are led to the identification of it by learning that it has a fort on the Jumna. There is a Tánda on the Jumna, and the Parganah attached to it, although it consisted of only four or five villages, was considered a separate one till the late revision of Parganah boundaries, when it was aborbed into Chhapraulí. Tánda and Phúgánah continued to form one Parganah till the time of the Maráṭhas, when Phúgánah was separated, and given in Jagír to Nijábat Ali Khan, Bahraich.

21, 22, and 23.—The three next Mahâls comprise the environs of Dehli, and the names sufficiently point out their relative position.

32.—Sentah is the old name for Parganah Agauta in Bulandshahr. It would have been difficult to identify this, had not Agautá been called a Chauhán Battísá, or commune of thirty-two villages of Chauháns. There are now not very many Chauhán Zamíndárs here, and as the Parganah of Sentah is represented in the "Áín-i Akbarí" to have Chauhán Zamíndárs, I was disposed to think that it was meant for Somna in Aligaṛh; and in many copies the word more resembles Somna than Sentah; but this local designation of the Battísá establishes that Sentah is the proper reading. Sentah, moreover, is considered in the neighbourhood to have been the chief town of the Parganah.

46.—Masa'údábád.—The old traveller, Ibn Batuta, has helped me to verify this, as he mentions at p. 110, that he stayed at Masa'údábád on his way from Hánsi to Dehli, reaching it after two days, and receiving there a complimentary visit from the minister. Now, Masa'údábád on that road is the old name of Najafgaṛh, which is a late erection, being built by Ghulám Husain Khan, and called after his patron Najaf Khan. Masa'údábád had, however, previously changed its name to Afzalpúr, which was built by Chaudharí Afzal Khan in the time of Alamgír. The old mud fort of Masa'údábád is still to be traced about a mile to the East of Najafgaṛh.

The new Parganahs included within Sirkár Dehli are the following:·

دادري	1 *Dádrí.*	بہادرگڑہ	5 *Bahádurgaṛh.*
اگوتا	2 *Agautá.*	سنبہالکا	6 *Sambhálká.*
فريدآباد	3 *Farídábád.*	کہور	7 *Kithor.*
پالي	4 *Pálí.*	گوره	8 *Gorah.*

اجراره 9 *Ujrárah.*	دهلي پرگنه جنوب 11 *Dehlí S. Parganah.*
دهلي پرگنه شمل 10 *Dehlí N. Parganah.*	بهواني 12 *Bhiwání.*

Dádrí was not formed into a Parganah till 1231 Faslí, when Rao Dargahí Singh of Chatahrá, a Bhaṭṭi Gújar, who was appointed Faujdár of Dásna, Sikandarábád, etc., under Najíbu'd daulah, took advantage of the disorganization of the country during the decline of the Moghul monarchy, to obtain possession of certain villages of Sikandarábád, Kásna, Tilbegampúr, and Dásna, of which 70, including Dádrí Khás, were acquired from Kásna alone; and his family were retained in possession on a Mukarrarí Jama when our rule commenced. The Talúka lapsed to Government on the death of Rao Ajít Singh.

Agautá has succeeded to Sentah, which still exists as a village on the right bank of the Kálí Naddí, about four miles West from Agautá. Before the establishment of the name of Agautá, the Parganah was known by the name of Sentah Partábpúr: Partábpúr being a large village in the Northern angle of the Parganah.

Farídábád has been explained under Tilpat. The Parganah is in the Balamgaṛh jurisdiction. Balamgaṛh is itself only a modern fort, having been built by a Ját, called Balú, *alias* Bilram, a relative of Súrajmal of Bhartpúr, within the boundary of his own village of Sahípúr, in Tilpat.

Pálí is included within the area of Pákal, or Islámábád Pákal, as it is called in the "Ãín-i Akbarí." The united Parganah is now generally known as Pálí Pákal.

Bahádurgaṛh.—This Parganah is composed of about an equal number of villages from Pálam and Jhajhar, which the Emperor Muhammad Shah, in A.D. 1728, bestowed upon Bahádur Khan, Beloch, who built the fort of Bahádurgaṛh within the area of Sharifábád, a village of Pálam. Bahádurgaṛh is still held in Jagír.

Sambhálká was detached from Pánípat in the fourth year of the reign of Farúkhsír, and held as a royal demesne for his own private expenses. It continued subsequently to be held as a Jagír, and when on the death of the last incumbent it escheated to Government, it was again included in Pánípat.

The Parganah of Sambhálká was more usually known amongst the natives as Farrukhnagar.

Kithor was originally a Tappah of Siráwá, from which it was detached in the time of Najíb Khan by Jít Singh Gújar, the founder of the Gújar family of Príchatgaṛh.

Gorah was formerly in Hápúr. The Gújar Raja of Paríchatgaṛh, Nain Singh, formed it into a separate Tappah.

Ujrárah was also detached from Hápúr. Fattih Ali Khan, the ancestor of Khwájah Basant, in whose Jáidád it was comprised, formed it into a separate Tappah, and it now, small as it is, ranks as a Parganah.

Dehli, Northern Parganah. This Parganah was formed in the year 1838. It includes part of Havelí and Pálam. The Parganah of Báwana, or Boana, which is included in it, was itself a new formation from villages of Palam, which Aurangzeb detached for the purpose of paying certain expenses of the Royal household, and as they comprised fifty-two villages (Báwan) the tract, as well as the chief town within it, was designated Báwana.

Dehli, Southern Parganah, was also formed in 1838. It includes a part of Palam, Havelí, and Masa'údábád, and a few villages of Tilpat. Najafgaṛh, which has been already mentioned, was subsequently formed from Masa'údábád, and included, besides the villages of that Parganah, twenty-four villages from Jhajhar, and twelve from Jharsa. The two modern Parganahs of Dehli, therefore, comprise the old Parganahs of Havelí Ḳadím, Havelí Jadíd, Dáru'l-mulk Dehli, Pálam and Masa'údábád. The three first were subsequently united into the Parganah of Havelí, and when Palam was afterwards added, it was known as one Parganah under the name of Havelí Palam. This name it retained under our administration, till the new division took place, which has been particularized.

Bhiwání was originally a portion of Dádrí Táhá.

Sirkár Rewárí.

باول	1	*Báwal.*	رتاي جتاي	6	*Ratáí Jatáí.*
پاتودهي	2	*Pátaudhí.*	كوٹ قاسم علي	7	*Koṭ Ḳásim Alí.*
بهوره	3	*Bhorah.*	گهلوت	8	*Gahlot.*
تاورو	4	*Táoru.*	كوهانه	9	*Kohánah.*
ريواري با حويلي	5	*Rewárí ba Havelí.*	سهنه	10	*Suhnah.*
			نيمرانه	11	*Nímránah.*

This Sirkár contains eleven Mahála, divided into four Dastúrs. Only four of these Mahála are in British territory, and as they retain their ancient names, they require no notice, except to observe that Sonah (Suhnah) is out of its place in the alphabetical list, and might therefore give rise to some suspicion of its correctness, but Abu'l Fazl mentions it also in the text, in such a manner as to enable us to identify it as the Sonah which still gives name to a large Parganah.

The only new Parganah within this Sirkár is,

شاه جهان پور 1 *Sháhjahánpúr.*

This small Parganah, containing only eight villages, is isolated from the rest of Gurgáṅw by territory belonging to the Tijara Raja. The popular story runs that it was formed by Sháhjahán, in compliance with a vow which he made when he was retiring in anger from his father. He met with favorable omens in this neighbourhood, and vowed, if they were accomplished, he would raise a town and constitute it the head of a Parganah.* The new Parganah was taken chiefly from Lohana, and in the "Aḥwál-i Súbaját" the Parganah is entered as Lohana, 'urf Shahjahánpúr Chaubára.

Sirkár Sahárańpúr.

اندري 1 *Indrí.*	چرتهاول 15 *Charthácwal.*
امبهته 2 *Ambihtah.*	حويلي 16 *Havelí.*
بدهانه 3 *Budhánah.*	ديوبند 17 *Deoband.*
بدولي 4 *Bidaulí.*	رام‌پور 18 *Rámpúr.*
بهت كنجاور 5 *Bahat Kanjáwar.*	روركي 19 *Rúrkí.*
بهوگپور 6 *Bhogpúr.*	راي‌پور تاتار 20 *RaípúrTátár*
پور چپار 7 *Púr Chapár.*	سيكري بهوكرهيري 21 *Síkrí Bhuk-arherí.*
بهومه 8 *Bhúmah.*	سرساوه 22 *Sarsáwah.*
بگهرا 9 *Baghrá.*	سروت 23 *Sarwat.*
بنت 10 *Banat.*	سردهنه 24 *Sirdhanah.*
تهانه بهيم 11 *Thána Bhím.*	سنبل‌هيرا 25 *Sambalherá.*
تغلق‌پور 12 *Tughlakpúr.*	سورن پلري 26 *Soran Palrí.*
جوراسي 13 *Jaurásí.*	كهاتولي 27 *Khátaulí.*
جولي 14 *Jaulí.*	

* Another origin is ascribed to Sháhjahánpúr, which is perhaps more probable than the one mentioned above. Ihlád Sing, a relative of the Chauhán chief of Nímranah, was held in high consideration in the Court of Sháhjahán, and obtained leave from the Emperor to rebuild Lohana, which had been destroyed in consequence of its harbouring notorious robbers. Ihlád Sing called the new town after the name of his patron.

If Sháhjahán was himself the founder, and ever occupied the spot, it was most probably visited by him when his army was encamped at Belochpúra in A.D. 1623, and was in possession of the passes of the Mewat Hills.

كهودي 28 *Khúdi.*	مظفرآباد 32 *Muzaffarábád.*
كيرانه 29 *Kairána.*	منگلور 33 *Manglaur.*
گنگوه 30 *Gangoh.*	ملهي پور 34 *Malhaipúr.*
لكهنوتي 31 *Lakhnauti.*	نكور 35 *Nakor.*

نانوته 36 *Nánautah.*

This Sirkár contains thirty-six Maháls, divided into four Dastúrs—Deoband, Kairána, Sirdhanah and Indrí. The last is on the right bank of the Jumna, and is not within British jurisdiction, its villages being distributed amongst the Sikh lords of Jagadrí, Ladhoa, Thanesar, etc. etc., while Indrí Khas is included within the Kanjpúra Nawwáb's 'Iláka.*

The Parganahs in the above list, which are no longer recorded as such, are Numbers 5, 6, 8, 11, 12, 16, 20, 23, 28, 31, and 36.

5.—Bahat Kanjáwar was in the time of Sháhjahán converted into Sultánpúr Bahat. In the time of Najíbu'd daulah, Bahat and Sultánpúr became separate Parganahs, and have so remained since. The Mauzá of Kanjáwar is in Muzaffarábád.

6.—Bhogpúr is on the Ganges, and the Parganah comprised the Eastern portion of Jawálapúr, including Hardwár. Bernoulli states, indeed, that Bhogpúr is another name for Hardwár, but this is, I believe, not correct. At any rate there is a Bhogpúr about ten miles South of Hardwár, which is no doubt the head town of the old Parganah of the same name.

8.—Bhúmah has only within the last ten years lost its name as a separate Parganah. Baisúmhah has now succeeded to it, but Bhúmah is still a very respectable town, and in Akbar's time is spoken of as chief of the Barha Sadat villages.

11.—Thánah Bhím.—All the copies concur in writing it Bhím, which is the name derived from the founder of the town,

* This territory is now part of the Ambála district of the Panjáb. As much of Súba Dehli as lies to the West of the Jumná is also under the Government of the Panjáb.—B.

who is represented to have been a mace-bearer to the king. In later times, the place has been known by the name of Bhaun, so called from a famous Bhaun (Bhawan), or temple, of Deví, near the town.

12.—Tughlakpúr.—The Timúrnáma mentions that Tughlakpúr, where the Indians opposed the conqueror in naval combat, is situated twenty-five koss above Ferozpúr (in Hastinápúr). Tughlakpúr still exists in Núrnagar, and was formerly the chief town of a Parganah, to which Núrnagar has now succeeded.

16.—Havelí has become the Parganah of Saháranpúr.

20.—Raipúr Tátár.—Within the area of Faizábád, in the old Parganah of Raipúr Tátár, Shahjahán built his palace of Bádsháh Mahal, and changed the name of the Parganah to Faizábád. The Mauza of Raipúr still exists on the banks of the canal.

23.—Sarwat is the old name of Parganah Muzaffarnagar, and the village of that name still exists about a mile N.E. from Muzaffarnagar.

28.—Khúdí is the old name of Shikárpúr, which is not yet altogether dropped by the common people. It is said to be the name of the Raja who founded the town.

31.—Lakhnautí.—The greater part of Lakhnautí has within the last three years been thrown into Gangoh, and part into Bidaulí.

36.—Nánautah.—The greater part of Nánautah was at the same time thrown into Gangoh, and parts of it into Rámpúr and Thánah Bhaun.

The new Parganahs present a long list, chiefly owing to the changes effected by Najíbu'd daulah and the Gujar Talúkdars.

کهیري	1	*Kheri.*	جوالاپور	5	*Jawálápúr.*
سکرودہ	2	*Sakraudah.*	فیض آباد	6	*Faizábád.*
نورنگر	3	*Núrnagar.*	پتیہر	7	*Patehar.*
جمال گڑہ	4	*Jamálgaṛh.*	جہانگیرآباد	9	*Jahângírábád.*

سلطانپور 9	*Sultánpúr.*	تهانه بهون 12	*Thánah Bhaun.*
مظفرنگر 10	*Muzaffarnagar.*	شاملي 13	*Shámlí.*
كاتهه 11	*Káthah.*	جانسته 14	*Jánsath.*

بيسومها 15 *Baisúmhá.*

Kherí.—This was formed into a separate Tappa in the time of Zabit Khan, through the influence of the Púndír Zamíndárs, who are Rajputs converted to Mahomedanism. It was formerly a part of Rurkí.

Sakraudah was originally in Jaurásí, and formed into a Parganah by Rao Kutbu'd dín, in the time of Zabit Khan.

Núrnagar is called after the famous Núr Jahán Begam, who took up her abode there for some time. Núrnagar, or rather Govardhanpúr—by which name the Parganah is now more generally known, since Núrnagar Khas has been transferred to Saháranpúr—has succeeded to the old Parganah of Tughlakpúr.

Jamálgaṛh, or Jamál Kherah, was originally in Gangoh, and was formed into a Parganah by Jamál Khan, the Amil of Gangoh in the time of Najíb Khan. By late arrangements Jamálgaṛh has been thrown into Nakor.

Jawálápúr.—This is the new name of the greater part of Parganah Bhogpúr. In records written previous to the British accession, the Parganah is denominated Bhogpúr, 'urf Jawálápúr, but is now known only as Jawálápúr.

Faizábád.—See Raipúr. In the time of Shahjahán Faizábád became a place of great importance, and gave name to an entire Sirkár. In the "Hakíkat-i Jama," by Hardí Rám Káyeth, it is said to contain 24 Mahál; while Saháranpúr was reduced to 17.

Patehar.—Anwar Khan, an Afghan of Patehar, in the time of Najíb Khan, established this as a separate Tappa, or Parganah. It was a part of Bahat Kanjáwar.

Jahángírábád was originally in Ráipúr Tátár, and was formed into a Parganah at the same time as Faizábád.

Sultánpúr.—See Bahat Kanjáwar.

Muzaffarnagar.—See Sarwat.

Káthah was originally included in Deoband, from which it was detached by Najíb Khan, who was compelled to establish a separate collector in Badgáṅw, on account of the turbulence of the Zamíndárs of the neighbourhood.

Thána Bhaun.—See Thana Bhím.

Shamlí was originally a portion of Kairana. We learn from the collection of letters of Nand Ram Mukhlis* that a village in Kairana, called Mahomedpúr Zunárdar, was included in the Jagír bestowed by Jehángír upon Hakím Muḳarrab Khan. A Chela of the Nawwáb's (Shaman) built a ganj, or market, in the village, and after otherwise improving it, called it after his own name, Shamlí. The Jagír remained in the family of Muḳarrab Khan till it was resumed by Bahadur Shah, who also formed Shamlí, with a few other villages, into a separate Tappa, which in course of time has acquired the title of a Parganah.

Jánsath is now included with Jaulí in one Parganah, called Jaulí Jánsath. It was formed into a separate Parganah in the time of Farrukhsír, through the influence of the famous ministers Hasan Ali Khan and Abdullah Khan.—See Barha Sadat.

Baisúmhá has attained the dignity of a Parganah, by the town of Baisúmhá having been one of the head-quarters of the Gújar confederacy in the time of Raja Gulab Sing. The old Parganah of Bhúmhá is included in it.

SIRKÁR HISSAR FEROZA.

اگروهه	1	*Agrohah.*	بهنگيوال	4	*Bhangíwál.*
اهروني	2	*Ahroní.*	پونيان	5	*Púnián.*
اتهکهيره	3	*Aṭhkheṛa.*	بهارنگي	6	*Bhárangí.*

* I doubt if this is the correct authority. I think it is in the "Jahángír-náma."—E. *add.*

بروالا	7	*Barwálá.*	سرسا	17	*Sirsá.*
بهتو	8	*Bahtú.*	شیورام	18	*Sheorám.*
بروا	9	*Birwá.*	سیدهمکه	19	*Sidhmukh.*
بهتنیر	10	*Bhaṭner.*	سیواني	20	*Sewání.*
توهانه	11	*Tohánah.*	شانزدهدهات	21	*ShánzdahDihát*
توشام	12	*Toshám.*	فتح آباد	22	*Fattihábád.*
جیند	13	*Jínd.*	گوهانه	23	*Gohána.*
جمال پور	14	*Jamálpúr.*	کهانڈه	24	*Khánda.*
حصار	15	*Hissár.*	میهم	25	*Míhim.*
دهاترت	16	*Dhátrat.*	هانسي	26	*Hánsí.*

There are twenty-seven Mahàls in this Sirkár (Hissár being counted as two), and four Dastúrs—Havelí Hissár Feroza, Gohána, Míhim, and Sirsá. There are, however, several Parganahs excluded from the Dastúr list, for what reason does not appear.

Of these Mahàls, those which do not retain their old name in our territory are numbers 2, 3, 4, 5, 6, 8, 9, 10, 11, 13, 14, 16, 18, 19, 21 and 24.

2.—Ahroní is partly in Ratiyah and partly in Fattihabad. The historians of Timúr point out its position, by saying it is on the road from Fattihabad to Tohana. The place was burnt and pillaged by the conqueror, merely because the inhabitants did not come out to pay their respects (مراسم استقبال بجا نیاوردند). Ahroní has now reverted to its original name of Ahírwan; whereas in Sirkár Chanár, Ahírwara, which derived its name from the same tribe, has now been corrupted into Ahrora.

3.—Aṭhkhera is under the Raja of Jhínd, and is known now by the name of Kasonan.*

* Aṭhkherá is in the Parganah of Mirwána, in Patiála, and Kasonan or Kasun is four miles off, in Jhínd.—E. *add.*

4.—Bhangíwál, so called from the tribe of Játs which inhabited it, is the old name of Darbah, in which place the officers of the Raja of Bíkaner built a fort, and thenceforward it came to be considered the chief town of a Parganah.

5.—Púnián, called also after a tribe of Játs, is in Bíkaner, but is now included in another Parganah.

6.—Bharangí is also in Bíkaner.

8.—Bahtú is partly in Fattihabad and partly in Darbah. Bahtú Khas is in the former Parganah.

9.—Birwá is the protected Sikh territory.

10.—Bhaṭner.—The old town of Bhaṭner is in Bíkaner, but part of the Parganah is now included in Raniyah.

13.—Jhínd gives name to one of the protected Sikh states.

14.—Jamálpúr is included in the late cession from Patiála. The old town of Jamálpúr is near Tohana.

16.—Dhátrat was in Jhínd, but is now in British territory.

18.—Sheorám is in the Bagar country, in the Jagír of Nawwáb Amír Khan. Two-thirds of Sheorám are now in Loharú, the remainder in Dadrí.

19.—Sídhmukh is in Bíkaner.

21.—Shánzdah Dihát, or Ḳariát (*i.e.* the sixteen villages), is included in Ratiyah Tohana amongst the late cessions from Patiála. The Ilaka is generally known by the name of Garhí Rao Ahmad. I have heard it stated that it is in Jhínd, and not in Ratiyah Tohana.

24.—Khanda is in Jhínd.

The modern Parganahs are—

بهل 1 *Bahal.*	رتيه 3 *Ratiyah.*
رانيه 2 *Rániyah.*	دربه 4 *Darbah.*

Bahal was originally in Sewání, from which it was separated in A.D. 1758 by Jawání Singh, a Rajput, who built a mud fort at Bahal, and maintained possession of a few neighbouring villages.

Rániyah was in Bhaṭner. The old name of the village was Rajabpúr. The Rání of Rao Anúp Sing, Rathor, took up her abode here, built a mud fort, and changed the name of Rajabpúr to Rániyah, which it has since retained.

Ratiyah is now included in one Parganah with Tohana. It was composed of villages from Ahroní, Jamalpúr, and Shánzdah Ḳariát.

Darbah.—See Bhangíwal.

Some considerations respecting the Western boundary of this Sirkár have been offered in the article Bhaṭṭíáná.

Sirkár Sambhal.

امروهه	1	*Amrohah.*	جهالو	15	*Jhálú.*
اعظم پور	2	*A'zampúr.*	جدوار	16	*Jadwár.*
اسلام پور بهرو	3	*Islámpúr Bahrú.*	حويلي سنبهل	17	*Havelí Sambhal.*
اوجهاري	4	*Ujhárí.*	ديوره	18	*Deorah.*
اكبرآباد	5	*Akbarábád.*	ڈهاكه	19	*Dhákah.*
اسلام پور درگو	6	*Islámpúr Dargú.*	دبهارسي	20	*Dabhársí.*
اسلام آباد	7	*Islámábád.*	دوديله	21	*Dúdílah.*
بجنور	8	*Bijnor.*	راجپور	22	*Rájpúr.*
بچهراون	9	*Bachhráon.*	رجب پور	23	*Rajabpúr.*
بروي	10	*Biroí.*	سنبهل	24	*Sambhal.*
بساره	11	*Bisárah.*	سيوهارا	25	*Seohárá.*
چاندپور	12	*Chándpúr.*	سرسي	26	*Sirsí.*
جلال آباد	13	*Jalálábád.*	سهسپور	27	*Sahaspúr.*
چوپله	14	*Chauplah.*	سرساوه	28	*Sirsáwah.*

شيركوت 29 *Sherkot.*	لكهنور 38 *Lakhnor.*
شاهي 30 *Sháhí.*	لسوه 39 *Liswah.*
كندركهي 31 *Kundarkhí.*	مغل پور 40 *Moghalpúr.*
كيرت پور 32 *Kíratpúr.*	مجهوله 41 *Mujhaulah.*
كچهه 33 *Kachh.*	منداور 42 *Mandáwar.*
گندور 34 *Gandaur.*	نگينه 43 *Naginah.*
كابر 35 *Kábar.*	نهتور 44 *Nahtaur.*
گنور 36 *Ganaur.*	نيودهنه 45 *Neodhanah.*
كهانكري 37 *Khánkarí.*	نرولي 46 *Nerauli.*

هتمنه 47 *Hatmanah.*

This Sirkár contains forty-seven Mahals and three Dastúrs—Chándpúr, Sambhal, and Lakhnor.

The missing Parganahs exceed those of any other Sirkár, amounting to more than half of the entire number, viz., Numbers 3, 4, 6, 7, 9, 10, 11, 13, 14, 16, 17, 18, 19, 20, 21, 22, 23, 33, 34, 36, 37, 38, 39, 41, 45 and 47.

3.—Islámpúr Bahrú is now contained in Thákurdwara. The town is still is existence. The Jesuit Tieffenthaler leads us to this information by giving its name correctly, which cannot be said of any other copy which I have consulted. Salímpúr Bahrú, by which name it is now more usually known, has the credit in the neighbourhood of having been the head town of a Parganah.

4.—Ujhárí has only lately been absorbed into Hasanpúr.

6.—Islámpúr Dargú is now included in Bachhráon, one of the Parganahs of Hasanpúr. In the revenue accounts of 1166 F.S. it is recorded as Islámpúr Dargú, shamil Bachhráon.

7.—Islámábád.—This Parganah was retained till the year 1209 F.S., and was absorbed into Nagína at the commencement of our administration. The village of Islámábád is abandoned.

9.—Bachhráon is now in Hasanpúr.

10.—Biroí is in the Rámpúr Jagír.

11.—Bisára is also in Rámpúr.

13.—Jalálábád.—This is the old name of the Parganah of Najíbábád. The town of Jalálábád is still in a flourishing condition.

14.—Chauplah is the name of Morádábád. Rustam Khan, Dekkání, founded Rustamnagar in this Parganah, which in the time of Farrukhsír was changed to Morádábád, and the name of Chauplah became extinct. Sirkarah was also formed from Chauplah.

16.—Jadwár remained as a Parganah till 1153 F.S. Part of Jadwár is included in Bahjoí, and part in Islámnagar and Asadpúr. The village of Jadwár is in the Southern angle of Bahjoí.

17.—Havelí Sambhal is included in the Parganah of Sambhal.

18.—Deorah is the old name of Seondarah, and the village of Deorah is about five miles to the south of Seondarah. Seondarah was occupied by a Tehsíldárí Katcherry before the time of the Patháns, but the name of Deorah was preserved till the cession, and began to be called Deorah Seondárah only in the Second Settlement. The name of Deorah is derived from the Dor Rajputs, who were the Zamíndárs of the Parganah.

19.—Dhákah, } These two Parganahs have also lately been
20.—Dabhársí, } absorbed into Hasanpúr—the intermixture of villages being so great as to render this arrangement convenient.

21.—Dúdílah is in Rámpúr.

22.—Rájpúr is also in Rámpúr.

23.—Rajabpúr is now included within Amroha, and is held chiefly in rent-free tenure. The village of Rajabpúr is about ten miles to the S. W. of Amroha.

33.—Kachh is the old name of Parganah Tigrí, now included in Hasanpúr.

34.—Gandaur is the old name of Bashta, which is now combined with Asampúr. Bashta, indeed, used frequently to be called Gandaur Bashta.

36.—Ganaur.—The town of Ganaur still exists in Asadpúr. The greater portion of the Parganah is in Asadpúr—a part is in Rajpúra.

37.—Khánkarí is in Rámpúr.

38.—Lakhnor is also in Rámpúr, and is more generally known as Shahábád on the Rámganga. This, being the seat of the old Katherya Rajas, may be considered the capital of the country, and is so spoken of by the ancient historians. As the place is now but little known, transcribers generally confound this town with the more celebrated Lakhnau, and English translators have not been free from the same error. Bernoulli gives Lakhnor as a separate Sirkár, and alters its dimensions greatly from those given to the Dastúr in the "Áín-i Akbarí."

39.—Liswah is included in Rámpúr.

In these, and other similar instances I have not attempted to verify the names. It was sufficient for me to find these Mahâls in the Dastúr of Lakhnor to make me include them in the Rámpúr territory. All that we have of Lakhnor is easily identifiable, and as nothing is wanting to complete our boundary, and as it will be observed from the Map there is ample space in Rámpúr, we may fairly presume the missing Mahâls to be in that Jagír.

41.—Majhaulah.—The greater part of Majhaulah is now included in Bahjoí—part is in Rájpúra and Islámnagar. Majhaulah Khás is still a large village, about five miles to the East of Bahjoí.

45.—Neodhanah is the old name of Islámnagar. Here again we are assisted by Tieffenthaler, when all Persian copies fail. He calls it Neudhana (Bernoulli I. 133). The two instances mentioned in this Sirkár are almost the only ones where I have found this enterprising Jesuit traveller of any use; and it is strange it should be so in Sambhal, for his list of that Sirkár is the worst he has given, being filled with names which have either been ill-transcribed, or fabricated. It does not appear that he ever visited these parts himself, but sent natives to pick up information. The name of Neodhanah being given correctly we are able to connect it with the traditions of the Gautam Rajputs of Núrpúr in Islámnagar.

47.—Hatmaná has gone to form part of Richhá and Chaumahalá. Hatmaná Khás is in Chaumahalá.

The following list shows the new Parganahs of Sirkár Sambhal—

دارانگر	1	*Dáránagar.*	سیوندارہ	9	*Seondárah.*
نجیب آباد	2	*Najíbábád.*	تهاکر دوارا	10	*Thákurdwárá.*
رجپورہ	3	*Rajpúrah.*	تاراپور	11	*Tárápúr.*
اسد پور	4	*Asadpúr.*	رچها	12	*Richhá.*
بهجوئي	5	*Bahjoí.*	حسن پور	13	*Hasanpúr.*
اسلام نگر	6	*Islámnagar.*	چومحله	14	*Chaumahalah.*
سرکرہ	7	*Sirkarah.*	باشته	15	*Báshtah.*
مراد آباد	8	*Murádábád.*	افضل گڑہ	16	*Afzalgaṛh.*

Dáránagar.—This Parganah was formed from portions of Bijnor and Jhálú by Ráo Jet Singh, Ját, in the time of Muhammad Shah.

Najíbábád.—The town of Najíbábád was founded by Najíb Khan, within the Parganah of Jalálábád, the name of which has now been superseded by Najíbábád.

Rajpúrah is formed from parts of Majhaulah and Ganaur.

Asadpúr is formed from parts of Ganaur and Jadwár.

Bahjoí comprises parts of Majhaulah and Jadwár.

Islámnagar is formed from Neodhanah and parts of Jadwár

and Majhaulah. The name of Islámnagar is said to have been given to Neodhanah by Rustám Khan, Dekkání.

Sirkarah was originally a portion of Chauplah, but it does not appear when it was established as a separate Parganah.

Murádábád (Morádábád).—See Chauplah.

Seondárah.—See Deorah.

Thákurdwárá.—This Parganah was established about the time of Muhammad Shah, by Katheryas, of the name of Mahandí Singh and Surjan Singh. The greater part of Thákurdwárá has been obtained from Islámpúr Bahrú. The Northern portion was originally within the jurisdiction of Kamáon. In Thákurdwárá are also included about fifty villages of Seohara, and nearly 150 of Moghalpúr.

Tárápúr.—This Parganah has been restored to the Eastern side of the Ganges.—See Budhganga.

Richhá.—Part of this Parganah is formed from Hatmaná; but the greater portion we may presume to have been under the jurisdiction of Kamáon. Part is also taken from Baláí.

Hasanpúr* was originally in Dháká; but now comprises six old Parganahs—Kachh, Bachhraon, Dháka, Dabhársí, Ujharí, and Islámpúr Dargú.

Chaumaḥlá is a modern Parganah, formed by Nawwáb Faizullah Khan from the four Parganahs of Sirsawa, Richhá, Kabar and Rudrpúr. The old Parganah of Hatmaná, which was extinct before this Parganah was formed, is for the most part comprised in the Northern angle of Chaumaḥlá.

Báshtah is the new name of Gandaur.

Afzalgaṛh.—I have restored Afzalgaṛh to Sherkoṭ and Nagína,

* An Altamgha grant, said to have been given by Shahjahán in favor of Mubariz Khan, ancestor of the present Zamíndárs of Hussainpúr, places Hussainpúr in Havelí Sambhal, but it is not easy to conceive how that Parganah could have penetrated through Dhaka and Ujharí. The grant, therefore (it was resumed by the Pathans), must either be a forgery, or Sambhal is alluded to rather as a Sirkár than a Parganah.

as far as the Ramganga. The rest has been concluded to have been within hill jurisdiction; though it is usual to consider the whole of Afzalgaṛh and Rehar as belonging to Sherkoṭ.—See Des.

SIRKÁR BADÁON.

اجاؤن	1 *Ajáon.*	بلئي	7 *Balaí.*
انوله	2 *Aoṅla.*	سهسوان	8 *Saheswán.*
بداون با حويلي	3 *Badáon bá Havelí.*	ستاسي منديا	9 *Satásí Mundiyá.*
		سنيا	10 *Suneyá.*
بريلي	4 *Barelí.*	كانت	11 *Kánt.*
برسير	5 *Barsír.*	كوت سالباهن	12 *Koṭ Sálbáhan.*
پونر	6 *Púnar.*	گوله	13 *Gola.*

This Sirkár consists of thirteen Maháls, which constitute only one Dastúr.

The extinct Mahals are numbers 5, 6, 7, 9, 11 and 13.

5.—Barsír is the old name of the Parganah of Saraulí, which it retained till the time of the cession. The village of Barsír, which is still inhabited, is about six miles to the South of Saraulí, and is on the borders of Aoṅla. Saraulí is still called by the common people Barsír.

6.—Púnar.—Púnar Khas is a deserted Mauzah in Púranpúr Sabna. Púnar forms only a small portion of the present Parganah of Púranpúr Sabna, since it is represented as containing only 5,749 Bíghas.

7.—Balaí.*—When Mírak Ján, Amil in the reign of Shahjahán, founded Jehanabad, the name of the Parganah was changed from Balaí to Jehanabad, in honor of his new town. The Khera of Balaí is still to be seen near Jehanabad.

* Also called Bilahtí.—E. *add.*

9.—Satásí Mundiyá.—This is a very difficult Parganah to restore. It assumes all kinds of shapes in the various copies,—Mokudduma Sunas, Munala Sunasun, Sunanut Mudrusa; and Bernoulli increases our doubts by calling it Mandia, *surnommée* Saniassi. If it had not been for the present existence of the Parganah of Satásí, on which word many of the changes seem to ring, we might not have been able to identify it at all; and even now it might be considered open to suspicion, because the Mahál is said to have Tagá Zamíndárs, whereas Satásí has none; but then neither is there a single Tagá Zamíndárí throughout the district of Badáon, and scarcely any in its immediate neighbourhood,—so that this is no real objection. It only shows that the Tagá Zamíndárís have become extinct. The ruins of Satásí are said to be near Bírkhera, four miles to the South of Bisaulí, and Mundiya is a large inhabited village about six miles to the North West of Bisaulí. The position of the two chief towns renders it very probable that they were combined into a single Parganah. I was at one time disposed to call it Satásí Manaunah, because Manaunah was the seat of a Native Collector at one period, but its close proximity to Aoṅla, which is itself the head town of a Mahál, would not admit of this construction. Guided by all these considerations, I believe I have not been wrong in calling the Mahál Satásí Mundiyá.

11.—Kánt.—This was originally the name of Shahjahánpúr. When that city was founded by Bahadur Khan, in the time of Farrukhsír, the name of Kánt became extinct. Tilhar is also formed from Kánt.—See Bachhal.

13.—Gola has been considered in its alphabetical place.

The new Parganahs within this Sirkár present a list of unusual length.

بسولي 1 *Bisaulí.*	بليا 3 *Baleá.*
كرور 2 *Karor.*	جهان آباد 4 *Jahánábád.*

نواب‌گنج 5 *Nawwábganj.*	جلال پور 15 *Jalálpúr.*
بيسلپور 6 *Bisalpúr.*	كهيرا بجهيرا 16 *Kherá Bajherá.*
شاهجهان پور 7 *Sháhjahánpúr.*	كتره 17 *Katra.*
پيلي بهيت 8 *Pílíbhít.*	پواين 18 *Pawáin.*
سليم پور 9 *Salímpúr.*	بڙاگانو 19 *Baṛágánw.*
اوجهاني 10 *Ujhání.*	پورن پور سبنا 20 *Púranpúr Sabná.*
فريدپور 11 *Farídpúr.*	كهوتار 21 *Khotár.*
اوسهت 12 *Usahat.*	فيض پور بدريا 22 *Faizpúr Badariyá*
تلهر 13 *Tilhar.*	ندهپور 23 *Nidhpúr.*
نگوهي 14 *Nigohí.*	اولاي 24 *Aúlái.*

Bisaulí is a portion of Satásí Mundiyá, the remainder being represented by the present Satásí, with the addition of Tappa Rotah of Badáon.

There seems no reason why Bisaulí should not have given name to a Parganah in Akbar's time. It is an old town, and though it is indebted for its chief improvements to the generous and gallant Nawwáb Dúndí Khan, who lies buried, as well as many other members of Ali Mahomed's family, at Bisaulí, yet it had been for a long time previous a place of some consideration. In our eyes it possesses interest as being the first cantonment of a British brigade in Rohilkhand.

Karor is included in the old Mahál of Bareilly.

Baleá was originally in Saneyah, but subsequently in Karor, from which it was detached at the fourth settlement.

Jehánábád.—See Balyí.

Nawwábganj was originally a portion of Bareilly. It was not formed into a new Parganah till the fourth Settlement, when a Tehsíldárí was established at Nawwábganj. The town was founded on the lands of Bichorea, in the time of Nawwáb Asofud-Daulah.

Bísalpúr was also in Bareilly. It derives its name from an Ahír of the name of Bísú, who lived in the time of Sháhjahán.

Sháhjahánpúr.—See Kánt.

Pílíbhít, or as much of it as was known in the time of Akbar, was taken from Balyí.

Salímpúr was originally in Saneyah.

U'jhání.—From the old settlement records we find that when the Parganah of Badáon was annexed at the fourth settlement to Bareilly, it comprised seven Tappas. U'jhání comprises Tappa Jalálpúr, and is separated from its parent Parganah, along nearly its entire Eastern border, by the river Sot.* The

* Sot means any small stream in Rohilkhand.—E. *add.*

The same word is applied in Gorakhpúr and the adjoining parts of Bahár to the old bed of a river in which there is only a small quantity of water with a feeble current. It is probably derived from the old Hindi स्रुत, which means trickling, oozing; connected with which are the Maraṭhi words स्रव, स्राव, स्रवण, etc., with a similar meaning, from the Sanskrit स्रु to trickle, ooze.—B.

This river is now generally known by the name of Yárwafádár, or "the faithful friend." As various origins are ascribed to this name, it may be as well to subjoin the correct one from the "Táríkh-i Muhammad Sháhí" of Khushḥál Chand:—

از مضافات سنبهل بصوب سرکار بدایون لواي فیروزي انتماے متوجه
گشتند دراثناء راه بسبب اشتداد تموز و کمیابي آب روزے چند
تکالیف بر عسکر منصور میگذشت وعالمے بعلت حرارت وامراض دیگر
مبتلا گشته وپیکر عنصري حضرت جهانبانے نیزتکسل کشیده بارے
درین راه سوت نام دریاچه که پیچ درپیچ میگذرد همراهي رکاب
سعادت نموده در هر منزل خدمت آبداري لشکر بحر پیکر بجا آورده
ابروے تمام حاصل نموده حضرت آنرا بنام یار وفادار موسوم فرموده
چون چشمه سلسبیل شهره افاق فرمودند

On their way from Sambhal to Badáon His Majesty and the royal army suffered much from heat and thirst, till they came to the little river Sot, which kept winding in and out by the side of the road, and supplied them with water at each stage. In gratitude for this service His Majesty honored it with the name of "Yár-i Wafádár," or "the faithful friend."—B.

village of Jalálpúr is about ten miles to the South of U'jhání. When Rohilkhand was under the administration of the Patháns, U'jhání became the residence of Nawwáb 'Abdullah, and thenceforward it was constituted the chief town of a Parganah.

Farídpúr was originally a portion of Bareilly, known as Tappah Khalílpúr.

U'shat, or U'sahat, includes Tappah Mahánagar of Badáon.

Tilhar was a portion of Kánt. When Raja Tilok Chand, a Bachhal Rajput, founded Tilhar, he included the surrounding villages in a new Parganah.

Nigohí.—This Parganah was originally a portion of Golah.

Jalálpúr was a portion of Bareilly, known as Tappah Charkholah. The town of Jalálpúr was founded by Raj Deo, son of Raja Básdeo, Katherya, who lived subsequent to the time of Akbar.

Kherá Bajherá.—This Parganah was formed from portions of the new Parganahs of Jalálpúr, Tilhar, and Farídpúr, and therefore was originally a part of Kánt and Bareilly.

Katrah was originally in Bareilly, and it was not till the time of Kamál zaí Khan, the son of Muzaffar Khan, who in the time of 'Alamgír founded Katrah on the ruins of the old town of Míránpúr, that the Parganah of Míránpúr Katrah was established.

Pawáin was originally a portion of Golah. The old village of Golah is in this Parganah, and is still inhabited.

Barágáṅw was also a part of Golah.

Púranpúr Sabná.—Púranpúr is the chief town of the Parganah. Sabná, which was taken by the Rohillas from the Dotí Ilaka, which has been carried away by the Sardah.

Parganah Púranpur is formed from parts of Golah and Púnar, and the village of Púranpúr was in the former Parganah. The portion near the Sardah was not known in Akbar's time, and has therefore been excluded from the map.

Khotár was originally a portion of Golah, but the greater

part has been excluded from the map for the reasons stated under Golah.

Faizpúr Badariya was originally included in Saheswán.

Nidhpúr was a portion of Badáon.

Aúlái was also a portion of Badáon.—See Budganga for further information respecting the boundary of this Sirkár.

Dahsanní, دهسني दहसन्नी

Belonging to ten years. A book comprising the collections, accounts, registers, etc., of ten years.

The book generally known as the "Dahsanní Kitáb" was compiled in the year 1210 F.S. with the aid of the Kánúngoes, Mútawallís, and Ḳázís, assembled at Bareilly for the purpose of shewing the quantity of land in occupation of the Mafídárs. In it the name of the occupant was sometimes recorded, sometimes that of his son, and sometimes, when neither could be ascertained, the name of the original grantee.

The "Dahsanní Kitáb" was compiled with a view of meeting the changes of property attendant on two revolutions: the usurpation of the Rohilla Patans, and the conquest by the Nawwáb Wazír. Two columns of this register exhibit, under the description of Málik Ḳadím and Málik Hál, the ancient proprietor known to the Kánúngo records, and the more recent occupant.—"Bengal Revenue Sel." Vol. I. p. 319.

Da'wí, دعوي दावी

A demand; a claim; a plaint.

Ḍeoṛhá, ڈيوڑھا डेवढा

One-and-a-half; used to express interest in kind on grain, at the rate of 50 per cent.—See under Bengat.

Des, ديس देस

Literally country; a term applied in Rohilkhand to cleared

villages on the borders of the Taráí. In the Dekkan it is used much in the same way to signify a champaign country. See "Journal R.A.S." Vol. II. p. 212, and the Printed Glossary, under Des and Desh.

It will be seen by referring to the map of Dastúrs, that a large tract has been excluded from Sirkárs Sambhal and Badáon which might be supposed to have belonged to them. The fact is, that the districts on the Northern boundary either belonged to Kamáon, or were altogether unknown. Even those which are entered in the ancient Registers as being in Sirkár Kamáon, have no recorded area: such as Gadarpúr; Sahajgír, now Jaspúr; Dauázda Kot, now Kota; Chinkí, now Bilherí and Sabna; Bhuksár, now Kilpúrí and Rudarpúr. A great portion of this tract was included in the Chaurásí Mál, of which the boundaries are given in the article Chaurásí. It was known also as the Naulakhí Mál;* but what portion of the present Des was included in, or excluded from it, is very doubtful. The idea of this tract ever yielding, as its name implies, nine lacs of rupees, is surprising to us who view it in its present state; and the name of Naulakhí Mál notwithstanding its avowed prosperity from the time of Akbar to Aurangzeb, particularly in the reigns of Tremal Chand and Báz Bahadur, may with some reason be deemed an exaggeration.

That these wild regions yielded, not long before our accession, more revenue than they do at present, is easily accounted for by the intestine troubles of Kamáon on the North, and of Rohilkhand on the South, which induced a large refugee population to resort to them for security; and that they have somewhat deteriorated of late years may be accounted for by our early assessments having been too high, which has necessitated present deductions; and by a withdrawal of some portion of its popula-

* I suspect this to be a corruption of Mahál, "estate," but not being personally acquainted with the district in question, I hesitate to alter it on a presumption.—B.

tion, which has been induced by the quiet and security which prevail in more favoured spots in the neighbourhood. Notwithstanding, however, their apparent deterioration, there can be little doubt that the Des is gradually encroaching upon the Taráí, and that there is prospect of further improvement by a judicious application of the abundant means of irrigation which nature has placed at our disposal.

We may be pretty certain that, even in the most palmy days of the Naulakhí Mál, the Des had not advanced into the Taráí so far as it now has, and that it was chiefly the Northern portion of the Taráí which was so prosperous under the rule of the Kamáon Rajas.

The fact of the Mahomedans not being able to extend their dominions to the foot of the hills, proves that the portion beyond the Des must have been nearly, if not quite, as inhospitable and insalubrious as it is now; for we cannot but conceive, that nothing would have protected it against aggression but a thick belt of jungle on its Southern border, which would have invested that tract with more terror than thousands of armed men. That there was no indisposition to acquire territory in that direction we know from two invasions of the time of Akbar, though he professed to have given a Sanad to the Kamáon Raja, Rudar Chand;* and that there was no strength in the Kamáonís to oppose them, if the Mahomedans had determined on it, we know from their appeals to Rustam Khan for assistance against the Katheryas; from the easy occupation which was effected for a short time by the Imperial general, 'Azmatullah Khan; from the purchased retreat of the Rohillas after their first invasion; and from the feeble resistance offered at a later period to the Gorkhas. Indeed, from the establishment of the Mahometan Empire down to the present time, we cannot contemplate any period when the Des, or the cleared plain, was

* Rudar Chand was the son of Kalyán Chan', who established Almorah as the capital. Rudarpúr was founded by Rudar Chand.

cultivated so far North as it now is. What the Taráí may have been in olden time it is not possible to say; but there are many symptoms of the tract having enjoyed a prosperous state long antecedent to the times of the Chand dynasty, when there was probably no Taráí, but what was marked by rich cultivation and populous abodes of man.

The occasional remains of ancient buildings and aqueducts assure us that it enjoyed an early period of prosperity, and the allusions in the drama of Sakuntalá to the scenery in the neighbourhood of the Málin, which falls into the Ganges near Bijnor, could scarcely have been applicable, had the features of the country not been greatly changed since the time that Kálidása wrote. We cannot be far wrong in supposing that it followed the fate and fortunes of the Gorakhpúr jungle, which from the Chinese Travels lately published, we know to have been the site of flourishing towns before the fourth century, and to have presented signs of growing deterioration in the seventh, when the Buddhist religion was approaching the period of its extermination in India. From this time to the occupation of the Mahomedans, the history of India is a complete blank, and scarcely can we extract a single fact from the voluminous Puranas, which, notwithstanding Colonel Vans Kennedy's emphatic denial, are now pretty well acknowledged to have been compiled at this comparatively late period.

In the Mahomedan histories the gloom is but little dispelled; but whenever we have allusions to these districts, we find every cause to suppose that the country was at least as wild as it is now. All beyond Amroha, Lakhnor, and Aonla is spoken of as a desert, which the Imperial troops fear to penetrate.

The most northerly position ever mentioned is that of Kábar, when it is marked as the boundary of cultivation at the close of the thirteenth century, in allusion to some revenue reforms introduced by Jalálu'd-dín, the first of the Khiljí dynasty. But, beyond this, there is not anywhere to be found the remotest allusion to crossing even the Ramganga; except when Feroz Shah is represented to have come for several successive years to Sambhal, to carry his inroads into the country of the Katheryas; and, in another instance, when we hear of an Imperial commander having pursued the Katheryas from Badáon to the hills, but not till they had endeavoured to secure their safety in the Jungles of Aonla, which are said by Abdu'l kádir Badáoní to extend round that place *no less than twenty-four Koss.** The exaggeration is evidently great, but if the statement is even partially true with respect to Aonla, we may be sure that the country under the hills was not in a much better condition.

We then come to the period alluded to at the beginning of this article, when, during a few years of the Moghul dynasty, the prosperity of the tract in some measure revived; but it was not long before it again declined, for even in the time of Muhammad Shah, we find the neighbourhood of Kashípúr thus described by Shaikh Yar Muhammad, an acute observer, who wrote an amusing account † of his embassy of condolence to the Kamáon Raja, Deví Chand, in A.H. 1130:

هر آینهٔ از صعوبت راه و رنج صعود و نزول گهاتي و شعب جبل و دامنگریهاي خار زار و کوه و بیابان چگویم این همه شورش و مستي و جرش و خروش آغاز مشغولي که شاهصاحب بملاحظه آن سیر کوهستانرا تجویز فرموده بودند فرو نشست لیکن ذوق شوق بار و باد پیوست در عرصه چهار روز الموره کمایون منزل گاه شد *

* جنگل انوله که تا بست و چهار کروه محافظ آنست

† This appears in a collection of letters entitled "Insha-i Kalandar," which has been printed in quarto in Calcutta, under the title of "Dasturu'l Insha." There are some interesting allusions in this work to the early progress of the British in India I cannot find this in the India Office Library.—B.

Not long after this, we find the Jesuit Tieffenthaler thus describing the commencement of the route from Rudarpúr to Almorah—"On traverse d'abord *un desert long de* 20 *milles*, dans le quel on trouve des arbres extrèmement hauts," etc.

So that, after all, these districts do not present a very unfavourable contrast with their condition under the preceding administration. Enough, at any rate, has been adduced to shew, that there was no occasion to place the Des boundary of Badáon and Sambhal in a more advanced position than has been represented in the map.

Dhálá, دھالا धाला

Collections levied from Asámís to cover village expenses, generally at the rate of one anna to every rupee, or a seer of grain to every maund of actual produce.—Rohilkhand.

In the Central and Lower Doab and Saugor it is generally used in combination with Jama, as Jama-Dhala, and is synonymous with Dhár-báchh, *q.v.*

Dhárbáchh, دھارباچھ धारबाछ

Dhárbáchh means any even or general distribution; but the term is chiefly in use in the central portion of these provinces to denote an imperfect Pattídarí tenure, in which part of the village lands is held in common, and part in severalty; the profits of the land held in common being first appropriated to the payment of the Government revenue and village expenses; and the balance, whether under or above, being distributed among the proprietary body according to the extent of their respective holdings.

Dhárbáchh, in short, is synonymous with the meaning most generally given to Báchh in the Western Provinces, and Bíghádam in the Eastern: under which latter term the tenure has been properly described in the Printed Glossary.—See Dhála and Dhár.

Dhárdhúrá, دھاردھورہ धारधूरा

The boundary formed by a stream. The changes in the course of streams form a frequent subject of disputes, which are settled on this principle, especially in Rohilkhand, by determining where the deep stream flows; from *dhár*, or *dhála*, a stream, and *dhúrá*, a boundary.

The principle is very good where land is gained by gradual accretion, but is open to objection where the lost lands are capable of identification, and is opposed not only to the sensible maxim, "*Quod vis fluminis de tuo prædio detraxerit et vicino prædio attulerit, palam tuum remanet*"—but to Regulation XI. of 1825, which was based on the decisions of the Sudder Dewanny Adawlat, and the replies of the law officers, and which regulates the principle to be observed in such disputed cases, wherein a law of immemorial usage does not prevail. The consequence is, that even where the Dhárdhúrá law is acknowledged, the decisions in these extreme cases are not found to be uniform. Note to p. 251, Vol. III. of "Harington's Analysis;" and p. 146 of "Notices of Suits," by Maulavi Muhammad Bakar.

Dhonchá, دھونچا धोंचा

Four-and-a-half. The word is found in arithmetical tables of the multiplication of fractions, which are in constant use with our surveying Amíns, when reducing their linear measurements to Bíghas. The words used by them in fractional multiplication are—

Ḍeorhá,	डेवढा	ڈیوڑھا	1½
Dhamá,	धमा	دھما	2½
Hontá,	होंटा	ہونٹا	3½
Dhonchá,	धोंचा	دھونچا	4½
Ponchá,	पोंचा	پونچا	5½

Khonchá,	खोंचा	کھونچا	6½
Satonchá,	सतोंचा	ستونچا	7½

The size of the fields rarely requires Amíns to go beyond this.

Dhúr, دهور धूर

The twentieth part of a Biswa, and therefore equal to a Biswání. The word is little used in the Upper Provinces, except in Benares; but is common in Behar.

Dhurá, دهرا धुरा

A boundary. The word is used chiefly in the Doáb and Rohilkhand, and is sometimes pronounced Dhúra.—See Dhárdhúra.

Dhúrkaṭ, دهورکٹ धूरकट

An advance of rent paid by Asámís to Zamíndárs in the month of Jeth and Asarh.—Benares and E. Oudh.

Dhaurí, دهوري धौरी

A corruption of Adhaurí (from *adha*, half); a bull's hide cut into two pieces.—Dehli.

Dharah, دهره धरह

A percentage on all weighments of goods imported into the city. The word is peculiar to Núrpúr, in the Panjáb.

Dhaṛí, دهڙي धडी

A measure of five seers.

Dharaukí, دهروکي धरौकी

To ascertain by guess, in case of a dispute, as to the quantity of land in actual cultivation, on which to estimate the Jama.—Eastern Oudh.

Dhartá, دهرتا धर्ता

Discount and commission. Applied to increase of demand upon land; also to an item entered according to usage by bankers in excess of cash advanced; being generally about three per cent.—Saugor.

Dishṭbandhak, دشتبندهک दिष्ठबनधक

The pledge of real property, being that which the debtor can keep in view, such as land, houses, etc., from Sansk. दृष्टि *drishṭi*, sight, and *bandhak*, pledge. Hypothecation. It is not much used in the North-West, except in Benares.—See Bhogbandhak.

Dubsí, دبسي दुबसी

The percentage allowed to Government farmers on the revenue paid to Government; formerly 10 per cent, *i.e.* two *biswas'* produce out of twenty—Saugor.—See Dobiswí, from which it is contracted.

Dofaslí, دوفصلي दोफसली

Land producing two crops a year. It is also known by the names of Dobar, Dosáí, Dosáhí, and Juthelí.

Ḍúhí, ڈوهي डूही

Alluvial formations. A mark of village boundaries.—See Dúdha.

Dobiswí, دوبسوي दोबिसवी

An allowance, reduction, or cess of two Biswas out of twenty; or ten per cent. The right of the Zamíndár in land, as Malikana is in money. Dobiswí is frequently given by Mafídars to Zamíndárs, particularly when they are not confident of the validity of their tenure.

Dohlí, دوهلي दोहली

Service land; applied in the Dehli territory as Baunda in the Doáb.—See Bhúndarí. But in many places within that territory it is only that land which is given to Brahmans. Dohlí, or Dohrí, is also applied there to the perquisite of Fakírs at harvest time.

Ḍaul, ڈول डौल

Estimate of assets for the purpose of assessment. Daulnama was the name given to the extract from this estimate, which was made over as a *Potta* to the party who was to pay the revenue.

ڈولنامه كه آنرا پٹه گويند برعايا بدهد و قبوليت از رعايا بگيرد

—Extract from the "Kitáb-i Ḳánún."

Ḍaul properly means a form, and is used in parts of Behar to express the formal application made by a ryot to a Zamíndár for permission to cultivate land. This application, with the word "granted," or the signature of the Zamíndár alone written on it, is given back to the ryot, and does duty for a *Potta*.—B.

Don, دون दों

A fractional division of an estate.—Gaṛhwal.

Dungání, دنگاني दुंगानी

A small fractional division of an estate.—Kamáon.

Dar, در दर

A rate; whence Darbandí, used to express the rate of rent of each field in the township.—See Darbandí.

Dariyáburd, دريابرد दरियाबुर्द

Dariyáshikast, درياشكست दरियासिकस्त

Lands cut away by encroachments of a river; from *daryá,* a river, and *burdan,* to bear away, and *shikastan,* to break.

Dariyábarámad, دريابرآمد दरियाबरामद

Alluvion. Lands reclaimed from a river; from *daryá,* a river, and *barámadan,* to accrue, to come up.

Dariyábarár, دريابرار दरियाबरार

See Dariyabaramad.

Dahotará, دهوتره दहोतरा

Tithes. An allowance, or tax, of ten per cent.; from *dah,* ten.—See Dahaik.

Darámad, درآمد दरामद

A term in keeping the *Itlák;* an account of fees paid for serving processes; the return of a process: from the Persian درامدن to come in.

Darbandí, دربندي दरबंदी

A statement of the different rates of a village; also, assessing the price or value of crops or produce.

Dastúru'l-'aml, دستورلعمل दसतूरउलअमल

A body of instructions and tables for the use of revenue officers under the Native Government. Notwithstanding the frequent appeal by Ḳánúngoes and our early European officials to the Dastúru'l-'aml, no two copies can ever be found which correspond with each other, and in most respects they widely differ. Those which profess to be copied from the Dastúru'l-

'aml of Akbar, are found to contain on close examination sundry interpolations of subsequent periods.

Besides the Dastúru'l-'aml, another book, called the 'Aml Dastúr, was kept by the Ḳánúngoes, in which were recorded all orders which were issued in supersession of Dastúru'l-'aml. It is probable that the Dastúru'l-'amls in use, shortly before our administration, were compiled from both these books, and hence have arisen the variations noted above.

Fárighkhatána, فارغخطانه फारिगखताना

A fee on writing a Fárigh-khattí, sometimes taken by Patwárís. The term Fárigh-khattí is correctly explained in the Glossary to signify a written release or acquittance.

Fárigh-khattí means a receipt given at the close of the year by the Zamíndár to the ryot, stating that all rent and demands of all sorts have been paid for that year.—B.

Fautínáma, فوتي نامه फौतीनामा

A document reporting the death of an incumbent and the names of his heirs; from the Arabic فوت *faut*, death.

Fard, فرد फर्द

A list, a sheet, a statement. Thus Fard-i-Kásht is a statement of a ryot's cultivation, from *kásht*, cultivation; and Fard-i Tashkís is a settlement record, from *tashkis*, specification, assessment.—See Fird in the Printed Glossary.

Farmán, فرمان फरमान

A royal mandate; an order; a patent. In English it assumes various shapes, as Firman, Pharmaun, and Phirmand.

Farod, فرود फरोद

Literally down, descending, alighting. A term used in the

customs' department to express the arrival and deposit of goods within certain defined limits.

Faryádí, فريادي फरियादी

A plaintiff; from فرياد *faryád*, a complaint, lamentation.

Fasl, فصل फसल

A season, crop, harvest; and hence the term *fasli* is applied to the era established with reference to the harvests of Hindústán. These harvests occur twice in the course of the year; one is known by the name of Kharíf, and the other by the name of Rabí'. The former is correctly explained in the Printed Glossary, under "Fusly Kheruf," to signify the autumnal harvest of rice, millet, etc.

Rabí' signifies the spring crop, or dry harvest, comprising peas, wheat, barley, gram, etc. The common people sometimes denote these harvests by other names.—See Asarhí.

Kharíf is derived from the Arabic خرف, the falling of autumnal rains, the gathering of autumnal fruits; and thus it came generally to mean the gathering of harvest: whence the term Al-Mukhárif (not noticed by either Golius or Richardson) a tribute gatherer.

Rabí' literally means spring (Pocock, Spec. Hist. Ar. p. 181), and it may therefore appear strangely applied to a Muhammadan lunar month, which in course of time makes a revolution of all the seasons, occurring sometimes in winter, sometimes in summer, sometimes in spring, sometimes in autumn. But the false prophet cared little for chronological propriety, and adopted in his new calendar the names of the old Arabian months of the solar year without any reference to their meaning, or more probably without reflecting that in a short time they would become exceedingly inappropriate. In the same way, Jalálu'd-dín, when he reformed the Persian calendar, introduced similar anomalies, and the names of many of the months, as at present applied, depart widely from their original meaning. Mardád, for instance, is the presiding angel of winter (Farhang-i Jahángírí), but the present month of Mardád is July.*

With respect to the period during which the harvests last, authorities are by no means agreed; some, like the Díwán Pasand, give eight months to the Kharíf, and four to the Rabí'; others, like the Zubdat-ul ḳawánín, and Raj Rúp,† give six months to each harvest. It is not easy to define the exact period of each, as the occupations of both harvests are, during some months, carried on simultaneously. Thus the sowing of the Rabí' and cutting of the Kharíf, and very frequently the ploughings for both harvests, are carried on at the same time, and it becomes difficult to say to which harvest most labour is devoted.

There is an attempt made to explain the cause of this difference of opinion respecting the duration of the two harvests in the second book of an anonymous Dastúru'l-'aml. The author says, "Some writers assign different periods to the Rabí' and Kharíf. In the Súbah of Bengal the Kharíf has nine months, and the Rabí' three. In Orissa the Kharíf has ten months, and the Rabí' two;" so that, if this be the real cause, we must always regard the country of the writer, when we consider his accounts of the periods of Rabí' and Kharíf.

* And Murdád is always July according to Richardson. The words in the Farhang-i Jahángírí are موکل بر فصلِ زمستان, and Rashídí repeats the statement in the same words, but also says it is the name of the fifth month of the solar year. Perhaps the anomaly may arise from the harvest alluded to being that of the crop which is sown in the winter, and reaped in the summer like the Rabí.—B.

† He observes that the Indians begin their year at the new moon of the month of Mihr, which is the commencement of the rainy season; and their year is divided into two parts: the Kharíf, from the new moon of Mihr (the seventh Persian month—September) to Sipandármuz (the twelfth month—February), 6 months and 178 days; and the Rabí, from the new moon of Farwardí (the first month—March) to Shahriwar (the sixth month—August), 6 months and 187 days—total, 365 days. At the same time he observes that the people of Irán and Turán continue to reckon Rabí first.—B.

Faisala, فیصله फैसला

Adjustment, decision, decree, settlement. It is an Arabic word, derived from the *fasl* mentioned above, which signifies cutting, separating, disjoining; and hence applied to a season. Hence also *faisal* is a judge, because he discriminates between right and wrong, and the decision given by him is a *faisala*. Ibn-i Arab Sháh calls the Day of Judgment يوم الفصل. The word Mufassil, so familiar to our ears, is similarly derived, signifying districts, or territory separated from the seat of Government.

Gachh, گچه गछ

Portion of an estate, held separately.—Purneah, Behár.—B.

Gánwbat, گانوبت गांवबट

A division of a Talúka into separate villages, or of the several Dákhilí Mauzás of an Aslí village: from गांव *gáṅw*, a village, and बटना *baṭná*, to be divided.—See Gátábandí.

Gánw kharcha, گانوخرچه गांवखरचा

Expenses incurred in the municipal administration of a village; from *gáṅw*, a village, and *kharach*, expenditure. This item is called also Malba in the Western part of these provinces. The literal meaning of that term is refuse, sediment, dirt; and is applied, like Ghúrbarár, *q.v.* in the sense of Gáṅw kharcha, on account of the many small items thrown into it, which could not be included under any other more specific head.

In the Panjáb this fund is often applied to the entertainment of travellers in a Musulman village; defalcations not exceeding ten rupees are also paid from it.

Gánwtí, گانوتي गांवटी

Of, or belonging to, a village; especially applied as Gáṅw

kharcha to the several expenses of municipal administration, such as wages of accountants, craftsmen, and police.—Saugor.

Gauhán, گوهان गौहान

A village made over by its proprietors to any person on a permanent Jama, with all the privileges of Zamíndár.—Eastern Oudh.

Gaunṭá, گونٹا गौंटा

Village expenses.—Bundelkhand.—See Gaṅwkharcha.

Gaunṭiyá, گونٹیا गौंटिया

A small hamlet. All these words are derivatives from *gáṅw*, a village.

Gauṭíká, گوٹیکا गौटीका

The head manager of a village, equivalent to a muḳaddam elsewhere.—Sohágpúr.

Gáṭábandí, گاٹابندي गाटाबन्दी

The division of a village by Gáṭás, corresponding with Khetbat. The opposite of Gáṭábandí is Pahábandí.

Gáṭábandí is a peculiar kind of tenure under which the fields of individual proprietors are not found in juxta-position, but scattered through many villages. Thus the boundaries of one village are frequently found to contain lands belonging to other villages, while some of its own fields will be included in the boundaries of another village, and that, perhaps, not contiguous. The tenure assumes various forms of complexity, being sometimes exceedingly intricate. It is found to prevail extensively in the Central and Lower Doab, Bareilly, and Benares. The mode of recording it is detailed in paragraphs 225 to 237 of the Board's Settlement Circular.

We owe the discovery of this kind of complex tenure to late years, when a more perfect system of registration was established at the Settlements made under Reg. IX. of 1833; but it is by no means such a rarity as it was considered when first brought to notice. It is found to prevail over various parts of India.

Gaṭhá, گٹها गठा

The twentieth part of a Jaríb, or measuring chain. Each Gaṭhá contains three Iláhí gáz, *q.v.* The word is derived from गठना *gaṭhná*, to join, to unite by knots.

Gaz, گز गज

A yard. 3 Gaz = 1 Gaṭhá, and 60 Gaz = 1 Jaríb.—See Iláhí gáz, and the Printed Glossary, under Guz and Gudge.

Gayál, گيال गयाल

The land of deceased Biswádárs lying unclaimed; land coming under the management of the Malguzár after an Asamí deserts his village.—Rohilkhand, Dehli, and Upper Doab. It is called also Uṭh; both derived from words signifying departure--the former from गया gone, and वाला a person; the latter from उठना to rise up (and depart).* It is equivalent to the Gatkul of the Dekkán; from the Sanskrit गत *gata*, gone, passed away, and कुल *kul*, family, lineage.

Gáṭewár, گاٹيوار गाटेवार

Is also synonymous with Khetbat.—See Gáṭábandí.

Ghardwárí, گهردواري घरद्वारी

An illegal cess from shopkeepers and householders; from घर *ghar*, a house, and द्वार *dwár*, a door.

* This derivation is from Col. Sykes, in J.R.A.S. No. IV. p. 208, but as the word is sometimes written and pronounced *ghaṭkul*, may it not be from घटना to decrease? —E. *add.*

Ghaṛí, گهڙي घडी

An hour; or the instrument for measuring time. As a revenue word, it is applied to the sub-division of a village; thus, Khandígáṅw in Dehli is divided into 144 Lángrís, each Lángrí containing 8 Ghaṛís.

Gharphánt, گهرپهانت घरफांत

An arrangement made by the manager of an estate, or by the shareholders themselves, for the payment of the Government revenue by each village, when more than one is included in a lease.—Kamáon.

Gharpattí, گهرپتي घरपत्ती

A house-tax, now abolished.—Kamáon.

Gharwára, گهرواره घरवारा

The local name of a sub-division of a portion of Bundelkhand, extending from about Tirohan to the Jumna, said to have been bestowed rent-free on Kanaujiya Brahmans by Raja Ram, Baghel. It may perhaps be derived from the Ghora mentioned above, *q.v.*

Ghair mazrú'ah, غيرمزروعه गैरमजरुआ

Uncultivated land; from the Arabic غير *ghair*, not, and مزروعه *mazrú'ah*, cultivated.

Ghátạní, گهاٹاني घाटानी

The name of a toll levied on crossing rivers or hill-passes; from Ghát̤, a pass or ford.

Ghíkar, گهيكر घीकर

A tax for pasturage in the hills, chiefly in use in Kilpúrí; equivalent to Gobal in the plains.

Ghúnt, گھونت घूंत

Rent-free lands, assigned as endowments of religious establishments.—Gaṛhwál and Kamáon.—See Gúnth.

Ghúrbarár, گھوربرار घूरबरार

Dues levied on every sharer and under-tenant in proportion to the whole expenses incurred during the year.—Bundelkhand. The word is derived from Ghúra, a dunghill, or sweepings; as all kinds of miscellaneous items are included.—See Gaṅw-kharcha.

Ghorá, گھورا घोरा

Ghorá, or Bhatghorá, subsequently known as Ahmadabad Ghorá, is the name of an old and extinct Sirkár, which, according to the register in the "Áín-i Akbarí," contained 39 Mahàls, and yielded a revenue amounting to 72,62,780 Dams. But it is evident that this Sirkár was almost entirely unknown, for the names of the Mahàls are not given, nor is there any record of measurement; nevertheless, we may fairly presume that Tirohán, Chíbúmau, Darsenda, and Bara, and the greater part of the Rewah territory, were included in Ghorá. It might have been supposed that the Parganahs below the Ghats, bordering on the Jumna, would have had separate names and areas in the Imperial Records, but it appears from an examination of an ancient grant conferring rent-free lands on the Ḳáẓí of Darsenda, that the Parganah of that name is distinctly said to be included in Ahmadabad Ghorá. Bara, also, we know from the authentic records of our own history, was under the Rewah Raja till the time of Asafu'd Daulah, and the present Zamíndár of the Parganah is a Baghel, connected with the Rewah family.*

* "I have stated that Parganah Barah was included in the Sirkár of Bhatghora, on the authority of Sir H. Elliot's Glossary; but even that work does not contain much information respecting the territorial divisions connected with this Parganah.

Ghorá, moreover, still exists under the name of Ghorá Khás, on the borders of Tirohán and Chíbúmau. The patent above alluded to was issued by 'Alamgír in A.H. 1095. From about this period to the decline of the monarchy, Ghorá was better known, and even Singraulí is said to have been added to it. An Amil also was established in Tirohán, who used to reside in the fort built by Basant Rái, but the whole Sirkár was subject to constant annexations and separations, according to the extension or diminution of Mahomedan influence in these wild parts.

If anything were wanting to show how little this part of the country between the hills and the Jumna had been subdued by the Mahometans up to the time of Akbar, we might satisfy ourselves by finding the Afghan emperors attacking Kantit, which is said to be "a dependency of Panna." Here, also, as in the case of Bandá, we have another mistake respecting names, which we can only correct by referring to other histories of the same period. Briggs, in his translation of Ferishta, speaks of

In fact, there are few parts of these Provinces regarding the early history of which less is known. In the "Áín-i Akbarí" the gross revenues and the number of mahâls in Bhatghora are merely given, the names of the mahâls are not specified. If Barah was included in this Sirkár, it must have ceased to belong to Rewah, especially if the latter territory were ma'f. But, at all events, after the downfall of the Empire, it would seem that Barah reverted to Rewah. . . . . It is generally believed in the Parganah that the Nawwáb Vazír's authority was established there previous to the time of Asafu'd-daulah, and that the Barrah Baghels, wishing to throw off their allegiance to Rewah, and to secure to themselves proprietary possession, sided with the Nawwáb Vazír, and offered to pay a small tribute. The Nawwáb accepted this offer, protected them from Rewah, confirmed them in their Zamíndárí position, and subsequently augmented the small tribute into a regular jama'. However this may be, there are complete accounts of the contest between Asafu'd-daulah and the Rewah Raja, from which it would seem that Barah was then for the first time fairly annexed to the Oudh dominions."—Mr. R. Temple's Report on Barah, Sel. Rec. N.W.P. Vol. IV. p. 412. He states in another place (p. 400) that, in 1778, when the Nawwáb's force, commanded by Mr. Osborne, proved victorious over the Raja, the Parganah was farmed out to Mr Osborne himself, and subsequently, in 1801, ceded to the British.—B.

"Balbhaddar Ray, Raja of Kutamba, a place dependent on Patna," instead of "Kantit, dependent on Panna," as it should be. Now, if Kantit was at that time dependent on Panna, even according to the shewing of Musulman histories, we must not be surprised if Chíbúmau, Darsenda, etc., were also little known till the time of 'Alamgír.

In a Dastúru'l-'aml of the later Empire, Panna is entered as containing 115 Mahále, and Ahmadabad as containing nine Mahále, and at this time there was a specification of Parganahs, which we do not find in Akbar's register.

The "Ḥadíḳatu'l Akálím" describes Tirohán as dependent on Sirkár Arail, or Tarhar (six Mahále); but this was at a period long subsequent, when Allahabad was under the Government of the Nawwáb Wazír.

Under all circumstances, we may perhaps consider that the limits which have been assigned to Ghorá in the Dastúr Map are not far wrong, but it is not easy to speak with confidence on the subject, as this part of the country was rarely, or never, visited by the Imperial generals, and we can only take advantage of such slight and incidental allusions as can be obtained in the absence of more satisfactory information.

Ghumáo, گهماو . घुमाउ

A term applied to as much land as can be ploughed by one pair of bullocks in a day.—Dehli.

The Ghumáo, however, has in many places lost its original meaning, and is used as a measure of land of varying extent. In Jalandar it is stated to be one-fifth of a bigha only, while in Wadin it is three-fourths of an acre. Eight kanále make a ghumáo, and two kanále are rather more than one bígha.

Ghair mumkin, غیر ممکن गैरमुमकिन

Barren waste; unproductive land; not capable of cultivation

(contracted from غیر مُمکِنُ الزَراعة *ghair mumkinu'l zará'at*, i.e., "whose cultivation is not possible").

Girdáwarí, گرداوري गिर्दावरी

Patroling, inspecting, going the rounds (from the Persian گرد *gird*, circuit, circumference, and آوردن *áwardan*, to bring).—See Girdáwar.

Grihasth, گرهسته गृहस्थ

A householder, a villager, a ryot. This word formerly indicated that stage in the life of a Brahman when he lived in a house discharging the ordinary duties of life; but is now applied to agriculturists generally, in which sense it is the equivalent of किसान peasant (from Sansk. गृह house, and स्था domain).

Grihasthí, گرهستهي गृहस्थी

Husbandry.—From the above.

Gola, گوله गोलह

The name of a tract of country which once comprehended a great part of the present district of Shahjahánpúr. It is said to have contained 1484 villages, and, before the time of the Rohillas, to have comprised ten Tappas.

Havelí. 268 Villages.	*Islamabad.* 277 Villages.	*Aurangabad.* 34 Villages.
Pilkhana. 70 Villages.	*Chakidpúrí.* 347 Villages.	*Godarna.* 103 Villages.
Nigohí. 112 Villages.	*Majhwa.* 135 Villages.	*Matí.* 139 Villages.
	Murtazábad 'urf Jíwan. 103 Villages.	

Ṭhákúr Uday Singh of Pawáin seized upon the Tappas of Islamabad, Jíwan, Aurangabad, and part of Havelí, and formed the Parganah of Pawáin. Godarna, Nigohí, and part of Havelí went to form Nigohí. Baṛágaon was formed from Pilkhana and part of Havelí. Chakídpúrí and part of Majhwa went to form the Southern part of Púranpúr; and Matí and part of Majhwa went to form Khotar. I have been particular in my enquiries respecting this Mahál, both from its intrinsic interest as a "terra incognita," and because it cannot be concealed, that if so many large districts have been formed from Gola, the "Áín-i Akbarí" gives it a very inadequate area—only 24,540 Bíghas. The above sub-divisions are taken from a Zillabandí, dated as far back as 1119 Faslí, which is in the possession of the Ḳánúngoes. It is not easy to discredit this return, and we must presume, as is of course highly probable, that the greater portion of this modern Gola must have been uncultivated in Akbar's time, and that, the Northern and Eastern boundaries being undefined, new clearances, as they were made, were added to the original Mahál of Gola; so that when the Zillabandí was subsequently made, its limits had increased to an extent utterly inconsistent with the entry in the "Áín-i Akbarí." The greater portion of Khotar, and parts of Baṛágáṅw and Pawáin, have, therefore, been excluded from the Dastúr Map, as serving to represent more accurately the limits of Gola as known in Akbar's time.

It has been supposed that the first historical mention which we have of this remote region is in the "Akbarnáma," where that strange madman, Kumber Díwána, is represented as extending his ravages into Kant* Gola, until he was defeated by Rukn Khán; but it was in truth mentioned before this period, for it is evident that Gola is meant, when it is stated in Ferishta that Ḥisámu'l Mulk was, in A.D. 1377, appointed to the Government of Oudh, Sambhal, and Korla. His work was written subsequent to the "Akbarnáma," but, in writing of

* The name of this Mahál is frequently coupled with Gola in old histories.

past times, he never adopts modern territorial divisions, and, therefore, there is no reason to suppose that Gola was not in existence in the year mentioned;—in fact, we have positive proof of its existence before that period, for Zíáu'd-dín Barní distinctly mentions Gola in the reign of 'Aláu'd-dín Khiljí, A.D. 1296 to 1316.

We may also be allowed to indulge in the speculation that Gola is perhaps mentioned by Fa-hian (A.D. 399) under the name of Ho-li, in the following passage of the French translation:—"En passant la rivière *Heng*, et se dirigeant au midi l'espace de trois *yeou yan*, on arrive à un forêt nommée *Ho-li*."

Now, as *g* is changed by the Chinese traveller into *h*—as in the instance of Gang (the Ganges) into Heng,—it would be no extravagant supposition to conceive that Gola is represented by the forest of Ho-li, notwithstanding that its position is not very correctly represented. Indeed, all his bearings between the Ganges and Gogra appear to be wrong.

Gonṭiyá, گونٹیا गोंटिया

The chief manager of a village; a Potel. In some places the term is applied only to Brahmans who have the management of villages.—Benares and Saugor.

Gunjáish, گنجایش गुनजाइस

A Persian word signifying capacity, and applied in fiscal language to the capabilities of a village, particularly with reference to a proposed increase of revenue.

Gurdachhná, گردچهنا गुरदछना

Rent-free land given to a spiritual teacher; from Guru, a teacher, and Dachhná, a fee or homage.

Gurkhaí, گرکهئي गुरखई

The name applied to a mortgage in Bundelkhand, which is

attended with the peculiar condition of leaving the mortgager to pay three-fourths of the revenue of the mortgaged land.

Gaṛá baṭáí, گڑابٹاي गड़ा बटाई

A division of produce previous to the threshing, effected by stacking the sheaves in proportionated shares; from गड़ा a sheaf.—Rohilkhand.

Gaṛhíband, گڑھي بند गढ़ीबन्द

A description of Má'afí tenure in Bundelkhand, by which lands are held on paying a stipulated yearly tribute; but not one-fifth the amount which ought to be paid. These favourable terms have been made by the Gaṛhíbands themselves during the imbecile state of the former Government, which had not power or force sufficient to compel them to pay their proper quota. On its being demanded, they shut themselves up in their forts—hence the name—and if not the stronger party, were at any rate sufficiently powerful to withstand any attack on the part of the Government. After standing a siege for weeks, the Government were glad to come to terms, and let them off their revenue for a stipulated yearly sum. The title dates from the first advent of the Maraṭhas into Bundelkhand, when they found a large portion of the lands ceded by Chattarsál to the Peshwa, held by these petty Ṭhákúrs, related either by blood, or caste, to the numerous local Rajas, then in the country, to whom they were bound to pay a light quit-rent, or to perform military service when called upon. Some of them were younger branches of the reigning family, and others took advantage of the anarchy which followed the demise of Govind Pandit, to seize upon adjacent villages, and fortify them.

When the power of the Maráṭhas became consolidated, they soon perceived that the Gaṛhíbands were difficult to deal with in every way; slow and irregular in their payment of revenue; ready to take offence at the slightest insult which they might fancy had been cast on them, and capable, from their numerous ties of brotherhood and caste, of raising a formidable, and often successful, opposition to the Government, and making common cause whenever it was attempted to coerce even the weakest individual of their body. A continual struggle was therefore maintained between the Government and the Gaṛhíbands, which generally ended to the advantage of the latter; and hence we still find them in full occupation of the territory which they usurped, and from which they could not be dislodged (Public MSS).

Guzashta dár, گذشته‌دار गुजस्तदार

A ryot who holds his lands by prescriptive right—literally, "from time past," *az sálhá-i guzashtah.*—W.

Hál, حال हाल

Literally, the present state. The word is used in revenue accounts to represent the existing state of Collections [chiefly those of the current year, as opposed to *baḳáyá* بقايا, those of past years].—See Hál Tauzí'.

Hálá, حالا हाला

An instalment of revenue.—Dehli.

Hálí, حالي हाली

The Government assessment.—Dehli.

Hál tauzí', حال توزيع

An account of Collections for the current period.

This word is also written توجيه *taujíh,* in which case it would mean "examination." I am unable to say which is correct, both are used in the same technical sense.—B.

Hár, هار हार

A sub-division, or part of an estate. In Saugor it means the cultivated space immediately round a village, which is quite opposed to the meaning it generally bears in the North-West, where it is applied to the land most distant from the site of the village, *i.e.* beyond the *manjha*. In Bundelkhand, and some other places, it signifies a tract of land, but the term in no way indicates separate possession of the tract designated. All the sharers may hold land in one Hár. In the first and last sense, the word may be supposed to be derived from *hár*, a necklace, a chaplet; in the second, from *harná*, to tire out. However fanciful this latter derivation may be, the most unimaginative cultivator in Hindustan will declare that it is so called because both bullocks and men get fatigued (*har játe*) before they reach it.

Házir zámin, حاضرضامن हाजिर जामिन

The person who becomes security for the appearance of another.

Habúbát, حبوبات हबूबात

Articles formerly furnished gratis to men in authority, consisting of sheep, milk, eggs, blankets, hides, etc. The system of Habúbát is not yet extinct, where European functionaries are negligent in the control of their establishments.

Had, حد हद

A boundary.

Hadbandí, حدبندي हदबन्दी

The settling and demarcation of boundaries. This has been most carefully done in the N.W.P. preliminary to the late Settlement. When they were not pointed out by the parties concerned, they were adjusted by arbitration. Wherever disputes were likely again to arise, it has been usual to bury some imperishable material in the earth, according to the instructions of the Hindu lawgiver Manu (Chap. VIII. 249–251). "The persons concerned reflecting on the perpetual trespasses committed by men here below, through ignorance of boundaries, should cause other land-marks to be concealed under ground. Large pieces of stone, bones, tails of cows, bran, ashes, potsherds, dried cowdung, bricks and tiles, charcoal, pebbles and sand, and substances of all sorts which the earth corrodes not, even in a long time, should be placed in jars not appearing above ground on the common boundary."—See also the "Mitákhshará" on the same subject.

Halbandí, هلبندي हलबन्दी

Is occasionally used in the sense of Halbarár and Halsarí, *q.v.* Also a tenure in Ajaon, Sirsawah, and the North Western parts of Bareilly, in which a few Bíghas are assigned to each Asámí who has a plough, for the cultivation of cotton and Indian corn, for which he pays at the rate of one rupee per Bígha: for all other land in his occupation he makes payment in kind.

In Kamáon, Halbandí is applied, as Jot is in the plains, to signify the quantity of land under cultivation by any party.

Halḳa, حلقه हलका

A village circuit. A boundary line which comprises the lands and dwellings of a Mauza. The word, in Arabic, literally signifies a ring. Halka, says De Sacy in a note to his "Excerpta ex Abulfeda," p. 539, "proprie est annulus. Temporibus recentioribus Halḳa dicti sunt milites pretoriani, qui apud Sultanos Ægyptiorum corporis custodiæ inserviebant."

Halsárí, هلساري हलसारी

Sub-division and apportionment of revenue on ploughs. The

assessment of a certain amount on each plough in a village. The word is synonymous with Halbandí and Halbarár.

Haḳḳ, حق हक

Share or right.—See Haḳḳ Malikána in the Printed Glossary. This word enters into the composition of the seven following articles.

Haḳḳ bhenṭ, حق بھینٹ हक भेंट

Presents frequently made half-yearly by the Malzugárs to native officers in authority.

भेंट means "meeting:" and the presents were made on meeting the great man who received the rent.

Haḳíyat, حقیت हकीयत

Right, share, proprietorship.

Haḳḳ hawáladár, حق حوالدار हक हवालादार

Haḳḳ Hawáladár, or correctly, Haḳḳ-i Hawáladár, is the grain given to Shahnas, generally at the rate of a seer and a half to every maund.—Rohilkhand.

Haḳḳ kamínchárí, حق کمین چاري हक कमीनचारी

Haḳḳ siyánchárí, حق سیان چاري हक सयानचारी

Haḳḳ thokdárí, حق تھوک داري हक थोकदारी

Dues and fees to Kamíns, etc., derived, according to old custom, from the inhabitants of villages, and varying in every Pattí, but generally equivalent to about three per cent. on the Government revenue.—Kamáon and Gaṛhwál.

Kamín in the plains is applied to village servants, but in Kamáon it is used synonymously with Búrha, to signify a superintendent of village management, whose office is in the gift of Government, and generally hereditary. Seana bears the same meaning in Gaṛhwál.

Hakk zamíndárí, حق زميندارى हक जमीनदारी

A Zamíndár's proprietary right.

Hariyánw, هريانو हरियांव

A division of a crop, in which the ryot retains nine, and the zamíndár receives seven, parts. The word is derived from Har, a plough, because the ryot retains a ploughman's share (one-eighth) more than the half.

Harhamesh, هرهميش हरहमेस

The insertion of this barbarous expression into a grant is considered to imply perpetuity. The literal meaning of the word is "every always," *i.e.* for ever and ever.

Hasho minhái, حشو منهائي हसो मिनहाई

That which, after being deducted, is entered in the Hasho and excluded from the rent-roll. The term is therefore applied to rent-free, Nankar, or other assigned lands.

و انچه از جمله مواضع در وجه نانكار و معافي ايمه وغيره بوده
باشد منها كرده باقي را در مقام حشو قلمي سازند

See Bariz for a description of the Hasho.

Hastobúd, هستوبود हस्तोबूद

The learned translator of the Institutes of Timúr says, at p. 367, that the meaning of this expression is not understood by him. It signifies a calculation on the data of the present (هست "is") and past (بود "was"). An estimate of the assets of a tract of land. Also, when corrupted into Hastnabúd, it signifies a remission granted by Zamíndárs for the portion of land failing in produce. The meaning of Hastobúd has been well explained in the Printed Glossary, under Hastabúd.*

Hawáladár, حوالدار हवालादार

One employed to protect the grain before it is stored; a steward or agent employed for the management of a village; corrupted by the English into Havildár.—See the Printed Glossary under Huwáludár and Havildár.

Hibadár, هبه‌دار हिबादार

A possessor of property by deed of gift; from *hiba*, a gift.

Hibanáma, هبه‌نامه हिबानामा

A deed of gift.

Hissadárí, حصه‌داري हिस्सादारी

Co-partnership; applied to a village in which a number of sharers have a proprietary right in the land. From *hissa*, a share, which has been explained in the Printed Glossary.

Hissa hákimí, حصه‌حاكمي हिस्साहाकिमी

The share of produce to which the king, or ruler, is entitled. It is needless here to enter on the controversies on this subject, respecting the amount, under the old law, Hindú and Muhammadan, to which he was entitled. It is pretty certain, however, that, even in the most favourable periods of Hindú rule, when they had to pay twenty other taxes besides that on land, less was never taken from the ryots than they are now called upon to pay—at least, in these Provinces.

Hissa hálí, حصه هالي हिस्सा हाली

A ploughman's share, or wages in kind; generally amounting to about one-eighth of the produce.

* In Purneah it supersedes the village Jama'bandi entirely.—B.

Hissa kashí, حصه كشي हिस्सा कशी

The distribution and apportionment of shares according to strict genealogical succession. Several collectors, during the time of the Settlement, used to make out laborious statements of this nature, under a misapprehension of the particular course of enquiry enjoined by Reg. VII. of 1822, for the purpose of registering and securing the rights of inferior sharers.

Hissait, حصيت हिस्सैत

A shareholder.

Ínch, اينچ ईंच

Security.—Dehli.

Ikbáchhí, اكباچهي इकबाछी

Distribution of any sum or cess, levied upon all lands at an equal rate.—Central Doáb.

Ikotrá or Ekotrá, يكوترا इकोत्रा or एकोत्रा

Ekatrá, يكترا एकत्रा

The sum total.—Bundelkhand.

It is also applied generally to signify the numeral 101, as well as interest at the rate of one per cent. per mensem.

Ijmálí, اجمالي इजमाली

A tenure in which several persons hold an estate in common, each receiving a certain share of the rents, without actual division of the land.—B.

Iláhí gaz, الهي گز इलाही गज

The standard Gaz, or yard, of forty-one fingers, instituted by Akbar. After much controversy respecting its length, it was authoritatively declared by Government to be thirty-three inches long; and the declaration has been attended with considerable convenience to revenue officers, as a bígha measured by this yard constitutes exactly five-eighths of an acre. The several opinions respecting the length of the Ilahí Gaz, and the means instituted for determining the point, will be found given in detail in Thomas's "Prinsep," Vol. II. p. 88, and the Journal of the B.A.S. vol. VII. p. 42.—See Kos and Bígha.

'Ilákadár, علاقدار इलाकादार

The person who enters into engagements at the Settlement.—See Lumbardar, and Malguzar.

Inglis, انگلس इंगलिस

A pensioner.

Isti'mál, استعمال इस्तेमाल

Custom, usage. This word is employed to denote the peculiarities in the use and pronunciation of Persian words which occur in the official documents of the courts of India.

"I subjoin a few notes on the *Isti'mál i Hind.* Those who wish to study this important subject, ought to make themselves acquainted with the writings of Mírzá Qatíl, entitled چهار شربت, شجرة الاماني and نهر الفصاحة; and a treatise by Anwar 'Alí on the spelling of Persian words, entitled *Risálah i Imlá i Fársi.* These works have been lithographed, and are easily obtainable.

"The *change* in spelling, form, meaning, and construction, which an Arabic word, apparently without any reason, undergoes in Persian, or which an Arabic or a Persian word undergoes in Hindustani, is called تصرف *taçarruf.* The taçarrufát of Persian words are included in the استعمال فرس *isti'mál i furs,* the usage peculiar to the Persians, and the taçarrufát of the Hindustani language, and of the Persian written in India, in the استعمال هند *isti'mál i hind.* A knowledge of the latter is of great importance, not only for those who read Persian books written or printed in India, but also for every Hindustani scholar; for although the Isti'mál i Hind is looked upon with suspicion by learned natives, we have to bear in mind that its peculiarities are *generally adopted*, and therefore correct. So at least for the Hindustani, according to the proverb غلط عام صحیح و فصیح.

"In its relation to Persian the Isti'mál i Hind will, of course, in most cases, appear as something faulty; for the peculiarities may no longer be a natural form of development, or a غلط عام, but the result of ignorance, a غلط عوام کالانعام. Nevertheless, the Isti'mál i Hind is visible in every Persian book written by Indians, from the works of their excellent historians down to a common dinner invitation (ضیافتنامه) of the daily life. Even the works of a writer like Abulfaszl, "the great Munshí," shew traces of it. Hence the truth of Mons. Garcin de Tassy's remark that every Persian scholar ought to be acquainted with Hindustani. If this be true for the Persian scholar, it is much more true for the compiler of a Persian dictionary; for a good dictionary ought to be based upon a thorough knowledge of the language in all its forms of development, and must be a history of the language as well as a vocabulary.

"But if we only understand by Isti'mál i Hind the influence of the Hindí and Hindustani upon the Persian, we would almost identify the term with "the usage of the Persian writers since the establishment of the Mogul dynasty." This would be wrong; for the Isti'mál i Hind includes peculiarities which once belonged to the Persian, as spoken in Persia, but which the modern Írání, in the course of its progress, has entirely discarded. In early times Persian had become the court language of Túrán, and from Túrán it was carried to India by the waves of the Túránian immigrants and invaders. Hence on the whole, the Persian of India is Túránian. As Latin in the Middle Ages, so was the Persian in Túrán, and subsequently in India the language of the learned. The works of the pre-classical and classical periods were studied and imitated, and peculiarities have thus been preserved which have long since disappeared in the Írání Persian.

The difference between the pre-classical and the modern Persian is, of course, not so great as between Latin and any of the Romanic languages; because the pre-classical Persian had already attained that logical simplicity to which our modern European languages happily tend; and though representing the growth of the Persian language during nine centuries, it is scarcely greater than the difference between the English of Fletcher and Beaumont and the English of our century. The Persian language has been compared to a bare tree, *stripped of all its leaves.* This stripping process, however, is going on in every spoken language, and shews that the copious and beautiful forms of languages like Sanskrit, Gothic, Greek, and many modern *savage* languages, are as many illogical incumbrances. The sequences of events and the order of things which the imitative genius of the modern languages expresses by the order of the words, are expressed in the ancient languages by the annexation of words and particles rather than by a logical order of the words, as if the speaker was afraid that the hearer could only understand those ideas for which there was an audible equivalent. Whilst many are apt to look upon *stripping off the leaves* as a matter of regret, I would consider it as a step towards delivering the human mind from the fetters of form. Perhaps I tread upon contestable ground. But a fact remains: it is this, that of all nations whose languages are preserved to us, the Persians are the first Arians that pitched the tent of speech on the elevated table-land of logical thought.

"Simplified, then, as the Persian language is, further change in terminations being impossible, the growth, as in modern English, is only visible in the pronunciation, the spelling and the meanings of words. For the study of this development a comparison of the works of the older writers with those of the modern, is essential; and as the Persian written and studied in India has hitherto been imitating the pre-classical and classical Persian of the early invaders, the importance of the Isti'mál i Hind is easily recognised.

"The following peculiarities are said by native writers to be common to the Persian of Túrán and India.

"*a.* Many words end in the Túránian Persian in ک (kaf) whilst the

I'ránian has a گ (gáf); as کبگ a kind of partridge, in Túr. کبک; مشگ *mishg*, musk, in Túr. مشک *mushk*; اشگ a tear, in Túr. اشک; سرشگ a drop, in Túr. سرشک. Similarly, بزشگ a doctor, رشگ jealousy, خلشگ, etc., in Túr. with a final káf.

"*b.* Also in the beginning of certain words: as گشادن, in Túr. کشادن (as every Muhammadan in India pronounces); گشنیز coriander seed, in Túr. کشنیز.

"This difference between the Túránian ک and the I'ránian گ becomes very apparent in dictionaries arranged according to the first and last letters. Thus in Surúrí اشگ stands in the فصل الف مع کاف فارسي, whilst in the Madár in the فصل الف مع کاف تازي.

"*c.* The Túránian has preserved a clear distinction between the واو and یا, when مجهول (ó, é) and معروف (ú, í). The modern I'ránian has only معروف forms (í, ú). The *words* which have a majhúl letter must be learned from the dictionaries; Indian Persian grammars specify the cases, when the *ending* ي is pronounced معروف.

"*d.* The Túránian has in all cases preserved the نون غنه. The I'ránian has given it up in some, especially after an alif. Thus, forms like ماندم, راندم, آن گاه, هرآنچه, etc., are pronounced in I'rán *mŭndam, rŭndam, ŭngáh, harŭnchi*, but in India still *mán̲dam, rán̲dam*, etc.

"*e.* The Túránian never adopted the interchange of *dál* (د) and *dzál* (ذ).

"*f.* Certain words are peculiar to the Túránians. Examples—وي *he*, for the I'ránian او; پور *son*, for پسر; سو *side*, for طرف; شو *husband*, for شوهر; پگاه *dawn*, for صبح; بیگاه *evening*, for شام; اري for بلي; یزنه *brother-in-law*, for شوهرخواهر; ینگا or ینگاه *sister-in-law*, for برادر زن; دادر *brother*, for برادر; خوش دامن *mother-in-law*, for مادر زن; خسر *father-in-law*, for پدر زن; خسر پوره for برادر زن; پالیدن and کافتن *to search*, for جستن; تیر را برتافتن *to throw the arrow*, for انداختن تیر را; شستن *to sit*, for نشستن; خاستن *to rise*, for برخاستن; دینه روز (cf. شبانه روز) *yesterday*, for دیروز; آب سوار شدن *to swell (water)*, for آب زیاده شدن; روز سوار شدن *to pass away (day)*, for گذشتن روز;

فوت شدن *to die;* پائیدن for قرار نمودن ; خسپیدن *to sleep,* for خوابیدن ; رفتن, the same as شدن, *e.g.* قربانت روم *I am thy sacrifice;* پائین شدن for فرود آمدن ; خلانیدن for گائیدن ; ماندن 1. the same as نهادن *to put;* 2. the same as گذاشتن *to leave behind,* e.g. چیزرا بر طاق ماندوام *I have left the thing on the shelf,* where ماندو is a Túránian form for ماندە ; or این خانەرا بمانید *leave this house* (بگذارید) ; 3. the same as طلاق دادن *to divorce*; 4. the same as نهادن ; گائیدن *to leave behind;* etc.

"Although several of those words do occur in Iránian authors, yet we generally find them used in peculiar places, as in rhyme, where it was difficult to avoid them; or in order to prevent repetitions, etc.

"The following peculiarities appear to be limited to the Persian spoken and written in India.

"*a.* Words have peculiar meanings. Examples—آسودە, the same as سیر *satisfied;* پس خوردە *leavings;* پس غیبت *absence,* for غیبت ; مثل misl, *a set,* the same as ردە ; جامە *a* (made up) *coat;* حلال خور, the same as کناس or خاکروب *a sweeper;* برف *baraf,* often pronounced *barf,* ice (for *snow*); داماد, *vide* Vull. Dict.; خلیفە a flattering title applied to cooks, tailors, etc.; سبزي *hemp,* for بنگ ; سەپهر *afternoon;* ناچار for لاچار ; مایوس *despairing;* جاي‌ضرور *a closet,* for ضروري ; ولایت Kábul and Persia;* خالصە the royal exchequer; جارجە and ترک *tark,* the catch-word at the bottom of the page of a manuscript; سرکار, *vide* Vull. Dict.; جاگیر, *vide* Vull., *also* board given to a poor student who is to teach children in return; صوبە 1. a province, 2. the same as صوبەدار an officer in charge of a province; رسالە, the same as رسالە دار an officer commanding a troop; آبکاري *vide* Vull.; مخواە خواە without reason.

* Vullers has at least half a dozen blunders in his dictionary, all arising from his ignorance of the meaning of this word. Thus, under اصول, in his Corrigenda II. p. 1558, No. 2, in regione Kashmír کشمیر ولایت, a blunder for کشمیر و ولایت Kashmír and Persia; also sub جیقە جیقە کردن I. p. 546; s. چل دختران I. p. 578, etc. Now-a-days, in India, ولایت means *Europe,* esp. *England.*

"*b*. The word كه is pronounced *ké*, not *kĭ*. This seems to be the old form كے, still preserved in كاشكے. The Iszáfat is pronounced *ĕ*, not *ĭ*, and *é* in cases of words ending in ه, *e.g.* خانۂ من khanah *é* man. The word بادشاه is pronounced بادشاه *bádsháh*, as پاد *pád* in Hind. means *crepitus ventris*. Similarly do the Persians use the form انكژ (a prick to urge on an elephant), in order to avoid the Hind. انكس which sounds, as Rashídí observes, like آن كس. Other Indian pronunciations are—پلك *palk* and *palak*, for *pilk*, an eyelid; فغان *fighán*, the same as ناله, for *fughán;* قائزه for قيزه, already observed by Abul-Faszl in the *Aín* i Akbarí. Words of the same class as عفو *e.g.* سهو a mistake, هجو a satire, وحي a revelation, سعي exertion, have lost the jazm and are pronounced *'afó, hafó* with the واو مجهول, the accent being on the penultima, but *sa'ĭ, wahĭ* with the accent on the ultima.

"*c*. Peculiar forms are يارش ,زيبايش ,پيدايش (the first and last occur in Abulfaszl), for ياري ,زيبائی ,پيدائي, the ending *ish* being properly restricted to nouns derived from *verbs;* ترشائي for ترشي acidity; كسائي (derived from كس), for آدميت humanity; سائس, سئيس, or سائيس a groom, for سائس; a plural اجنه *ajinnah*, ghosts; گنجيفه *a pack of cards*, for گنجفه; سنجاف for سجاف, *vide* Vull.; درستگي ,مهربانگي ,سختگي, (Abulfaszl), for درستي ,مهرباني ,سختي, the ending گي not leading to an adject. form in ه; دوغله and دوخله *a mongrel;* اسپ ماديه for اسپ ماده; الا نه for الا; باد الله for عباد الله, a proper noun; پتيله for پاتله; تالاش for تلاش; جامداني *a wardrobe*, for جامدان; جريبانه *a fine*, for جرمانه; ربيع الثاني for ربيع الآخر; جماد الاول and جماد الآخر for جمادي الاولى and جمادي الاخرى; دوات for داوات; دروغه for داروغه; دوكان for دكان *a shop;* دوانين for دواوين; شوله for شلە *a certain dish;* ريشم for ابريشم; صميمي *pure*, for صميم; لازمي for لازم; كمخواب for كمخاب; معه for مع; مفروغ for فارغ; هرج for حرج.

d. In words beginning with آ, the Madd is often omitted; as اچار

pickles, استر *lining,** استين *sleeve,* ابفت *canvass,* اماده *ready,* التمغا *a royal order,* ابكار *a distiller,* for آچار ,آستر ,آبفت ,آماده ,آلتمغا, آبكار.

e. After a long vowel we often find a vowel elided; as آفرين *áfrín,*† for the I'ránian *áfarín;* مولوي *maulwí,* for *maulawí;* امادگي *ămádgí,* for *ámádagí;* پوشيدگي *póshídgí,* for *póshídagí;* خالصه *khálçah,* for *kháliçah;* آژدن *ázhdan,*† for *ázhadan.*

"*f.* Two Sákins are avoided; as ارجمند *arjamand,* for *arjmand.*

"*g.* The Persian letters گ ,چ ,پ, are used instead of the Arabic ك ,ج ,ب; as in شگافتن ,شگوفه ,افگندن, for شكافتن ,شكوفه ,افكندن; اسپ ,تپ, for اسب ,تب; غنچه for غنجه; ديباچه for ديباجه; خرچ for خرج.

"*h.* The Tashdíd of many Arabic words falls away, as نواب *nawáb,* for *nawwáb,* an (Indian Nawáb); ذره, pl. ذرات *an atom.*‡

"*i.* The following pronunciations are very common, though generally *prohibited* in the dictionaries—خزان *khizán,* autumn, for خزان *khazán;* دراز *diráz,*§ for the Persian *daráz,* long; شنبه *shambah,* and even *shumbah,*‖ Saturday, for شنبه *shambih;* پلاو *puláw,* and even پولاو, a well-known dish of rice, meat, and spices, for پلاو *paláw.* The modern Persian and Turkish have پلاو *piláw.* درويش *durwesh,*¶ for *darwísh,* a beggar; نمك *nimak,* salt, for *namak;* نمكين *nimkín,* adj., for *namakín;* گواه

* Entered by Vullers as Persian. It is Indian.

† So in many Persian Dictionaries written by Indians.

‡ There is a curious mistake in Vull. Dict. I. p. 378. Burhán, whom Vullers copies, has پنده بمعني نقطه و ذرات هم بنظر آمده است; but Vullers does not observe that نقطه and ذرات (the Indian printer of the Burhán left out the Tashdíd) are synonymous, reads ذرأت for the A. ذرءت, and translates *canities in anteriore capitis!*

§ Vull. also has *diráz,* although Burhán gives clearly بروزن نماز *namáz.*

‖ Vull. also has پنجشنبه *panjshambah,* I. 375, b., and سه شنبه *sihshambah,* II. p. 354, whilst in other places he has correctly *shambih.*

¶ Adopted by some Indian Dicts., as the Ghias, on a mistaken etymology.

gawáh, a witness, for گواه *guwáh;* گره *girah*, a knot, for *girih;* مزدور *mazdúr*, wages, for *muzdúr;* کاغذ *kághidz*, paper, for کاغذ *kághadz*.

"*k.* A great number of Arabic words are universally pronounced wrongly in India; as قلعه *qil'ah*, a fort, for *qal'ah;* قیامت *qaiámat*, the resurrection, for *qiyámat;* قطعه *qat'ah*, for *qit'ah;* عروس *'urús*, a bride, for *'arús;* هجر *hijr*, separation, for *hajr;* عجز *'ijz*, weakness, for *'ajz;* رجا *rijá*, hope, for *rajá;* فضا *fizá*, space, for *fazá;* رضا *razá*, contentment, for *rizá;* جیب *jéb*, a pocket, for *jaib;* غیاث *ghaiás*, for *ghiás*, help; شهاب *shaháb*, for *shiháb*, a meteor; عصمت *'açmat*, chastity, for *'içmat;* موقع *mauqa'*, for *mauqi';* موسم *mausam*, a season, for *mausim;* خیمه *khímah*, a tent, for *khaimah;* شجاعت *shujá'at*, bravery, for *shajá'at;* حماقت *himáqat*, for *hamáqat*, folly; قصور *qaçúr*, a fault, for *quçúr;* عقوبت *'aqúbat*, for *'uqúbat*, punishment; حشمت *hashmat*, pomp, for *hishmat;* جنت *jinnat*, paradise, for *jannat*.

"*l.* Peculiar spellings; as ازدهام for ازدحام ; پیکار for تعویز ; for تعوید. Proper nouns are often written together, as حسینعلي for حسین علي. Similarly, صاحبدل for صاحب دل ; انشاء الله تعالیٰ* for ان شاء الله تعالیٰ ; مشتملبر for مشتمل بر consisting of; آنحضرت for آن حضرت ; عنقریب ,علیحده, ذ یحجه, ذیقعده, for عن قریب, ذي حجه, etc. Reversely, خانه‌ها ,ساده‌لوهي‌ها, for خانها ,ساده‌لوحیها. Also, موسا for موسیٰ ; خورم happy, for خرم *khurram;* رحمان for رحمن.

m. Barbarous forms; as دار الکچهري ,پرگنات ,بهیات books, for کتابها ; مرفع الحال for مرفه الحال ; مچرب *mücharrab*, greasy; شب لیلة القدر, as we say, *the strait* of *Bab* el Mandeb; فریسد *firísad*, for فرستد he sends; قلف *qulf* for قفل *qufl*, a lock; قطع for قطعه ; نماز خواندن, Hind. نماز پڑهنا, for نماز کردن."—From an Article by Mr. Blochmann, on "Contributions to Persian Lexicography," in J.A.S.B. Vol. XXXVII. Part I. p. 32.—B.

* Thus also in Persian MSS.

Itlák, اطلاق इतलाक

The term is applied to the office and records of Dastaks (demand, or summons), and Talabana (fees for the service of processes). It literally means freeing, liberating; and it is therefore difficult to say why it is so applied in revenue accounts; except it may be in the sense of forwarding, issuing, striking off.

Itlák navís, اطلاق نویس इतलाक नवीस

The person who keeps the Dastak accounts.

Jáedád, جايداد जाएदाद

Jáedad signifies a place; employment; also, assets, funds, resources. It signifies likewise the ability of any district or province in respect to its revenue; an assignment on land for the maintenance of troops, or of an establishment.

Jáedad now generally means, at least in Behar, landed property generally, also the crops as they stand.

Jeṭh ra'iyat, جیٹھہ رعیت जेठ रइयत

The head ryot who conducts the village business, and acts as Chaudharí of the village; from Sanskrit *jeshṭha*, eldest, chief. The meaning is correctly given in the Printed Glossary. Where there is a Mukaddam, the Jeṭh-ryot ranks below him, and is often known by the name of Chukaddam; but it is most usual to consider Mukaddam, Jeth-ryot, Mahtoṅ, Mukhya, Mahetya, and Basít as synonymous terms.

Jewan* birt, جیون برت जेवन बिर्त

A stipend allowed to the family of an old deceased servant.—Eastern Oudh and Benares.—See Birt.

Jhánsá, جهانسا झांसा

An assessment formed without specific ground, and only by

* From जेवना *jewnd*, to eat, a word of the Bhojpuri dialect.—B.

general estimate.—Saugor. The word is, perhaps, derived from *jhansná*, to cozen, to flatter, to deceive.

Jhúndí, جهونڈي झूनडी

A clump of grass. It is also applied in Dehli, as Khewat is elsewhere, to signify the amount due from each sharer in a Bhayachara estate.

Jins-i-kámil, جنس کامل जिन्सकामिल

First-rate crops. The best crop that a field can produce.

Jinswár, جنس وار जिन्सवार

(A statement) relative to crops.—See Jamabandí.

Jiziya, جزيه जिजिया

A tax on infidels. Applied in Saugor to a house-tax on the inhabitants of towns not engaged in tillage, which is also called Pandrí, *q.v.*—See Jazea.

Júla, جوله जूला

A tract of land containing four Alí, or sixteen Bísís.—Gaṛhwál and Kamáon.—See Bísí.

"In Gaṛhwál, as in Kamáon, there are numerous denominations of land, but the Júla was, and is, the chief measure, differing in value according to local usage, and the various classes of landholders, but in every instance exceeding in quantity one Bísí, and measurable by it."—Gaṛhwál Settlement Report.

Jama', جمع जमा

The whole; total; revenue generally, and the Government demand in particular; amount assessed.

Jama'bandí, جمع بندي जमाबन्दी

A village rent-roll. A statement of the rents fixed on every field in the township. In Madras it signifies the annual settlement of the revenue, and bears this meaning in the Printed Glossary.

The term is very comprehensive, and, indeed, admits of so many meanings, that it is found to change, so as to accommodate itself to the prevalent system of revenue management. About fifteen years ago, a Jama'bandí was most commonly known as a daul, or estimate, on which to base an assessment. It is now applied chiefly to the annual rent-roll furnished by the village accountants. It is also used variously in villages, as well as in Government records. Jinswar Jama'bandi, for instance, is usually a detailed statement of the rent levied upon each kind of crop. In Brij it is more specially applied to a kind of tenure found in parts of that tract.*

Jama' jhartí, جمع جهرتي जमा झर्ती

A statement of receipts and expenditure. Periodical account of either cash or grain.—Saugor.

Jama' kharch, جمع خرچ जमा खर्च

Debit and credit. Cash account.

Jama' wásil báḳí, جمع واصل باقي जमा वासिल बाकी

An account of the revenue of Government, with entries of payments and arrears.

Jamnauṭá, جمنوٹا जमनौटा

Jamnauṭyá, جمنوٹیا जमनौटिया

A certain consideration given to a Zámin, or security; generally amounting to about five per cent.†

* The Jama'bandí in the Provinces under perpetual settlement is a very lengthy statement of each ryot's holding, his rent and other dues, the amounts paid, remitted, or due, and many other particulars. It is, in fact, the rent-roll of a whole village.—B.

† A Hindi derivative from the Arabic ضامن.

Jamog, جموگ जमोग

Transfer of liabilities by mutual consent. A conditional mortgage.—Benares, Eastern Oudh, and Lower Doáb.

Jamogdár, جموگدار जमोगदार

A person who lends a landed proprietor a sum of money, and recovers that money from the Ryots.—Benares, E. Oudh, and Lower Doáb.

Jaríb, جريب जरीब

A measuring chain or rope. Before Akbar's time it was a rope. He directed it should be made of bamboo with iron joints, as the rope was subject to the influence of the weather. In our survey measurements we use a chain. A Jaríb contains sixty Gaz, or twenty Gathas, and in the standard measurement of the Upper Provinces, is equal to five chains of eleven yards, each chain being equal to four Gathas. A square of one Jaríb is a Bígha. Till the new system of survey was established, it was usual to measure lands paying revenue to Government with only eighteen knots of the Jaríb, which was effected by bringing two knots over the shoulder of the measurer to his waist. Rent-free land was measured with the entire Jaríb of twenty knots.

A Jaríb, in Hebrew and Arabic, signified originally only a measure of capacity, equal to four Kafíz, or 384 Mad, and in course of time came to signify the portion of land which required as much to sow it as a Jaríb would contain (Asása-l-lughát). The Patha and Nalí of Gaṛhwál and Kamáon have a similar origin.—See Bísí. This use of the term must have altered before the reign of Timúr, for in the Institutes we have the following injunction, which is evidently the foundation of Akbar's division of soil into three classes:

واگر رعيت بحاصل و قسمت سه توده راضي نشود اراضي مضبوط را
اول و دويم و سيوم جريب نمايند و جريب اول را سه خروار و

جریب دویم را دو خروار و جریب سیوم را یک خروار جمع بربندند و نصف را گندم و نصفی را جو اعتبار کنند وانچه جمع شود دو یک مال بگیرند

Jaziya, جزیه जज़िया

From the Arabic جزا subjugation; conquest; compensation. A capitation tax levied by the Muhammadans on their subjects of another faith. The correct word is Jizyat, but it seems usual in Hindústan to pronounce the word Jazya.—See Jazziah, Jezia, and Jaizeyeh in the Printed Glossary.

From the passage quoted from the "Á'ín-i Akbarí," in the article Altamgha, it appears that the Khalífa Umar laid an annual tax upon every one who was not of the Muhammadan religion. A person of high condition paid forty-eight dirhams, one of moderate means twenty-four, and one in an inferior station twelve dirhams.—See "Hedaya," Book IX., cap. ii. and viii.

It does not exactly appear when this tax was instituted in India. Tod ("Annals of Rajasthan," vol. i. p. 403) thinks it was imposed by Babar in lieu of the Tamgha which he solemnly renounced on the field of battle, after the victory which gave him the crown of India; but we read of it long before this, for as early as the time of Alá-ud-dín, only a century after the final subjugation of Hindústan, we find it spoken of as an established tax. Thus, in the dialogue recorded by Ziáu'd-dín Barní and Ferishta, between that tyrant and Kaẓí Mughíṣ-ud-dín, we read, "From what description of Hindús is it lawful to exact obedience and tribute?" To which the obsequious Kazí replies, "The Imam Haníf says that the Jazya, or as heavy a tribute as they can bear, may be imposed instead of death on infidels, and it is commanded that the Jazya and Khiraj be exacted to the uttermost farthing, in order that the punishment may approach as near as possible to death." "You may perceive," replied the king, "that, without reading learned books, I am in the habit of putting in practice that which has been enjoined by the prophet."

But it would appear that up to the time of Fíroz Shah, Brahmins were exempted from the tax, for in a very interesting chapter of Shams-i-Siráj's work we find that monarch imposing it for the first time on this influential class.

ودر عهد سلاطين پيشين البته از طايفه زناردارٰان جزيه نستيده جزيه ايشان معاف كرده بود هيچ وقتي اين طائفه بكسي جزيه نداده سلطان فيروز شاه بتوفيق حضرت الله جميع علماء دين‌دار و مشايخ نامداررا بدرگاه خود جمع كنانيده بگوش ايشان رسانيده كه اين غلط عام افتاده كه از طائفه زناردار جزيه نستد و سلاطين گذشته كه درين كار كوشش بسيار نكرده از سبب انكه كاركنان و غلامان انزمانه هوا خواهان يگانه غفلت ورزيده بر ايشان آگاهي نداده چون طائفه زناردار كليد حجره كفر اند و كافران بر ايشان مستقل اند اول از ايشان جزيه بستانند و معاف ندارند

"In the time of the former Sultáns certainly the Jazya was not taken from the tribe of thread-wearers (Brahmins), their Jazya was remitted, and at no time has this tribe ever paid Jazya to any one. Sultán Firoz Shah, by the divine guidance, collected all the Ulemá and Shaikhs into his darbár, and represented to them that this was a common fault into which all his predecessors had fallen, being misled by their servants, who were negligent and did not inform them of the omission, and that now as the thread-wearers were the chief of the infidels, they were the first from whom Jazya should be levied."

On this occasion, which was so much at variance with his usual spirit of conciliation, the Brahmins thronged him in his hunting-palace, and threatened to burn themselves alive before him; and at last were only dissuaded from their purpose by the other Hindús of Dehli taking upon themselves to pay the Jazya of the Brahmins. In his time, the highest class of Hindús was rated at forty, the second at twenty, and the third at ten Tankas per head; and these remonstrances had the effect of inducing the king to admit the Brahmins to the favorable terms of the lowest class.

After the death of Ratan Chand, the capitation tax was once more levied, as it is stated in the Tawáríkh-i Muhammad Shahí to have been again repealed by Muhammad Shah, at the intercession of Maharaja Jay Singh and Girdhar Bahadur.

Since that period, no Emperor was possessed of sufficient authority to enforce the Jazya, and this odious tax became extinct for ever; but not till it had operated as one of the most effectual causes of the decline of the Muhammadan power, by alienating the affections of the Hindú population, which the early Moghul Emperors had courted, and in some measure obtained.

We again learn that it was enforced with great severity in the time of Behlol and Sekander Lodi, which was perhaps no inconsiderable cause of the facility with which the empire was wrested from the hands of that family.

The tax was abolished by Akbar in the ninth year of his reign, and was not imposed again till the twenty-second of Aurangzeb, who with his wonted intolerance, directed that its levy should be attended with every circumstance of contumely which his ingenuity could devise.

A passage in the Zubdatu'l Akhbárát states that he ordered that the Jazya should be brought to the collector by the payer himself and on foot, and that the collector should sit, while the payer stood, the collector should put his hand *over* that of the payer and lift the money out of it, and that the tax must not be sent to a collector by a messenger, but brought in person. The rich were to pay the whole year's tax in one instalment, and the middle classes in two, the poorer in four. The Jazya is remitted on conversion to Islam or death.

It was at this time that admirable letter is said to have been written which is ascribed by Orme to Jaswant Singh, by Tod to Rana Raj Singh, and by the Mahrattas to Sevaji (Grant Duff, vol. i. p. 219, and Elphinstone's India, vol. ii. p. 458). Stewart (Hist. Bengal, p. 308) says that Shaista Khan, in A.D. 1679-80, enforced the Jazya in Bengal at the rate of 6½ per 1000 on all property, and that Christians paid one and a half per cent. additional duty on their commerce. The sick, lame, and blind were excused.

From this period it appears to have been regularly levied, and with particular severity in the time of Farrukhsír (in consequence of the appointment of Ináyat Ullah as financial minister, who had been secretary to the bigoted Aurangzeb), until the time of Rafíu'd-darját, when the Barha Sayyids abolished it, and the Hindús again recovered their consequence, Rattan Chand, a Hindú, being appointed financial minister, and being possessed even of such influence, as to be empowered to nominate the Mohamedan Kazís of the Provinces.*

Kúdá Bíghá, کودا بیگها कूदाबीगहा

A Bígha measured after a curious fashion in some of the Eastern parts of Rohilkhand. The Malguzar measures the breadth by the rope, or by the ordinary Kadams (steps), and then the cultivator, running by springs as great a space each time as he can stretch, measures the length: each spring being counted half a Kadam. The result is the area. The Bígha of this mode of measurement varies from 2½ to 3½ Kachha Bígha.

* Colonel Galloway (Law and Constit. of India, p. 27), states this on the authority of Ferishta: but Ferishta died more than a century before this period.

The meaning of the words is a Bígha measured by leaps, from کودنا Kúdná, to jump.

There is another curious Bígha of these parts, measured by the paces of a woman eight months gone with child.

Kos, کوس कोस

The itinerary measure of India, of which the precise value has been much disputed, chiefly on account of the difficulties which attend the determination of the exact length of the Gaz, or yard. The "Áín-i Akbarí" lays down distinctly that the Kos consists of 100 cords (طناب tanáb), each cord of 50 Gaz; also of 400 poles (بانس báns), each of 12½ Gaz: either of which will give to the Kos the length of 5000 Gaz. The following particulars relative to the distances between the old Minars, or Kos pillars, may be interesting, and may be considered to afford an approximately correct means of ascertaining the true standard.

	Road distance in English yards.	Direct distance in ditto.
Octagonal Minar to Nurelah in Delhi ...	4,513	4,489
Minar between Nurelah and Shápúrgaṛhí	4,554	4,401
Minar opposite Alípúr	4,532	4,379
Minar opposite Siraspúr	4,579	4,573
Ruins of Miṇar opposite to Shalimar......	4,610	4,591
Average....................	4,558	4,487

Length of the Kos = 2 miles 4 furlongs 158 yards.

It is important to observe that the length of the Ilahí Gaz deduced from these measurements is $32\frac{818}{1000}$ inches, showing how very nearly correct is the length of 33 inches assumed by the British Government (See Ilahí Gaz).

The measurements taken to the South of Dehli, between the Minars in the Muttra district, closely correspond. Out of twelve distances it is found that eight give 2 m. 4 fur. 19 p. 1 yard, three give 2 m. 4 fur. 25 p. 3 yards, and one gives 2 m. 4 fur. 38 p. 2 yards.

It may be proper to remark that it is frequently supposed that the Minars are set up every two Kos, and that the Kos contained 2,500 yards; but the "Áín-i Akbarí" appears sufficiently explicit on the point. The same work gives the values of the local Kos. It says, the Guzerat Kos is the greatest distance at which the ordinary lowing of a cow can be heard, which is determined to be 50 Járíbs, or 15,000 Gaz. This Kos resembles the Chinese lih, *i.e.* the distance which can be attained by a man's voice exerted in a plain surface, and in calm weather. Another in Bengal is estimated by plucking a green leaf, and walking with it till it is dry. Another is measured by a hundred steps made by a woman carrying a jar of water on her head, and a child in her arms. All these are very indefinite standards.

The same may be remarked of the Oriental míl, as well as the European mile and league. The two former evidently derive their name from the Roman *milliare*, and the difference of their value in different places proves that the mere name was borrowed, without any reference to its etymological signification. According to the "Kamoos," the Oriental míl is a lax and vague measure, but it has been considered by Dr. Lee to be to the English one, as 139 to 112.

Kos is an Indian word: the equivalent word in Persian is Karoh, the same as the Sanskrit Krosa, of which four go to the yojan; about the precise value of which different opinions are held. Bopp ("Nalus," p. 213) says it is equal to eight English miles. Professor Wilson ("Sanskrit Dictionary," p. 689) estimates it at nine miles, and says other computations make it about five miles, or even no more than four miles and a half, and, in his commentary on the Chinese travels, estimates it at no higher than four. But these travels enable us to fix the distance with tolerable precision. By following Fa-Hian's route between places of which the identity is beyond question, as between Muttra and Kanouj, and between Patna and Benares, we find the yojan in his time to be as nearly as possible seven

English miles; and this agrees much better with what we find the yojan to be, if we resolve it into its component parts. Eight barley-corns equal a finger, twenty-four fingers equal a Dand, one thousand Dands equal one Krosa, and four Krosa one Yojan. Now, estimating the fingers' breadth at eight barley-corns, this makes the yojan equal to six miles, one hundred and six yards and two feet.*

Kror, کرور करोड़

Ten millions. The names of the higher numbers are thus given in the "Zubdatu'l Kawánín." 100 Kror = 1 Arab. 100 Arab = 1 Kharab. 100 Kharab = 1 Níl. 100 Níl = 1 Padam. 100 Padam = 1 Sankh. 100 Sankh = 1 Ald. 100 Ald = 1 Ank. 100 Ank = 1 Padhá.

The three last names are rarely met with in other account books, but Colebrooke (Hindú Algebra, p. 4) assigns names to seventeen orders of superior units in the decimal scale, ending with Parárdha. In one work, the name of which I cannot now

* **क्रोश:** In Böhtlingk and Roth two definitions are given. One is = 1000 daṇḍas = 4000 hastas = ¼ yojana; the other = 2000 daṇḍas = 8000 hastas, but still = ¼ yojana, showing that the values of the daṇḍa and hasta were undefined.

The actual kos of the present day in India is equal to two English miles in most places, but in the Panjab it is seldom more than a mile and a half or a mile and one-third. The further east the longer the kos, so that in Bengal it exceeds two miles; and I am told that in Bundelkhand it is as much as four miles. In Bahár and Gorakhpúr, and many other parts of India, there is also a kachá kos, which is not much more than a mile, and sometimes even less.

The calculations in the text are not exact. The table should stand apparently—

8 barley-corns = 1 finger.
6 fingers ...... = 1 hasta or hand (which is omitted in the text).
4 hastas ...... = 1 daṇḍa or rod.
1000 daṇḍas ...... = 1 kos.
4 kos .... = 1 yojan.

The other computation makes 8 hastas = 1 daṇḍa. It is probable that the lower amount of 4 hastas to the daṇḍa represents the kachá kos so prevalent in India, and the larger, the pakká or official kos. The same double system of pakká and kachá pervades all the weights and measures of India.—B.

remember, the grades in the ascending scale are carried much higher, and the names differ in some respects from those of Colebrooke. Thus 100 Sankh = 1 Udpada. 100 Udpada = 1 Maha Udpada. 100 Maha Udpada = 1 Jald. 100 Jald = 1 Madh. 100 Madh = 1 Parárdha. 100 Parárdha = 1 Ant. 100 Ant = 1 Maha-ant. 100 Maha-ant = 1 Shisht. 100 Shisht = 1 Singhar. 100 Singhar = 1 Maha-singhar. 100 Maha-singhar = 1 Adant-singhar, which in numerals amounts to 1,000,000,000,000,000,000,000,000,000,000,000,000,000. But it is evident that this advance should have been made by tens, and not by hundreds; by which the numerals would be reduced to twenty-four places—100,000,000,000,000,000,000,000. This luxury of names for numbers is without example in any other language, ancient or modern, and implies a familiarity with their classification according to the decimal scale which could only arise from some very perfect system of numeration; at a period, moreover, when the most scientific people of the Western world were incapable by any refinement of arithmetical notation of expressing numbers beyond one hundred millions.—See "Enc. Metrop." Arithmetic (12), and "Vishnu Purana," p. 631.

Karoṛí, کڙوڙي काड़ोड़ी

When Akbar introduced his revenue reforms, he appointed a collector for every Karoṛí of Dams (*i.e.* 2,50,000 Rs.) whom he designated by the title of Amil, or Amilguzar, and to that functionary the instructions are directed in the "A'ín-i Akbarí," the designation of Karoṛí being of subsequent introduction. This sum, which was placed under his management, agrees with the amount at present established under the resolutions of Government, dated 30th October, 1837, as that which should form the charge of a Tahsíldar.

A Karoṛí, however, on his first appointment had somewhat more power than is invested in our Tahsíldars. He received eight per cent. on the amount of his collections, besides perquisites: he was directed to see that lands were not suffered to fall out of cultivation; to scrutinise the rent-free grants; to report upon the condition of the Jágírdárs, and of the subjects generally in his neighbourhood; to forward an account of all remarkable occurrences; and to perform the duties of kotwal, if none were appointed within his jurisdiction; and whenever, on account of drought or other calamity, he thought it advisable to depute any one for local enquiries, he could avail himself of the services of the Amín of the Súbah. This system lasted till A.D. 1639, in the reign of the Emperor Shah Jahán, when his minister, Islám Khan, deputed a separate Amín to every Parganah for the purpose of fixing the Jama, and the Kaṛoṛí was left in charge of the collections, to which the duties of Faujdar were added, with an allowance of ten per cent. on the collections. But it was found that the powers of the Faujdar and Kaṛoṛí were too great to be united in one person, and to check the abuses which began to be prevalent, Raí Ráyán Jíswant Ram, the Peshkar of Islam Khan, suspended for a time the power of the Kaṛoṛís, and appointed subordinate collectors for each village, who were ordered to take exact account of the collections of the Kaṛoṛís, and the purposes to which they had been applied, to check all the fraudulent exactions of which they and their dependents had been guilty, and to resume all the extra cesses which they had illegally demanded from the people.

When that excellent minister Sa'dullah Khan succeeded Islam Khan, he combined the duties of Amín and Faujdar in one person, and appointed him superintendent of a Chakla of several Parganahs (see Chakla); and placing the Kaṛoṛí entirely under his orders, established five per cent. on the collections as the amount of the Kaṛoṛí's allowance, and of this, one per cent. was subsequently deducted. The business of assessment and settlement was left entirely to the Amín—with that the Kaṛoṛí had no concern, but it was his business to encourage agriculture, to make advances, station watchmen over the ripening crops, and report when any indulgence and leniency appeared expedient.

This system lasted during the time of Aurangzeb, and till the dissolution of the empire.

The following extract, taken from the patent of the Amín-Faujdar, written at the beginning of last century (the title *خلد مكان proves that the document is subsequent to Auranzeb's reign), will show how much the power of the Karorí had declined since his original appointment.

و زريكه از سنه چهل و دوعهد حضرت خلدمكاني نزد رعايا باقي
باشد بكروري قدغن نمايد كه سريصد پنجروپيه برجمع حال كه به
تشخيص درآيد درهر فصل تا وصول آن به تحصيل درآورده و انچه
بصيغهٔ تقاوي درسالگذشته برعايا تنخواه شده باشد آنرا باباقي سالمذبور
در اول توزيع سال حال بگيرد كه درصورت اهمال بازخواست ازو
خواهد شد و احتياط بكار برد كه كروري جرات باخذ ملبه و وجود
ممنوعه بارگاه والا نكند

* * * * * * *

و برطبق قاعدهٔ معين از وجه حق التحصيل كروري يكروپيه عوض

* The lakabs or titles of honour of the six greatest Mughal Emperors are as follows :—

BABAR	A.D. 1526	فِردَوس مكاني	Firdaus Makání.
HUMÁYÚN	1530	جنت آستاني	Jinnat Ástání.
AKBAR	1556	عرش آشياني	'Arsh Áshyání.
JAHANGÍR	1605	جَنت مكاني	Jinnat Makání.
SHÁHJAHÁN	1627	فردوس آشياني	Firdaus Áshyání.
AURANGZEB	1658	خلد مكانى	Khuld Makání.

They are always mentioned after death by t e titles in official and literary documents.—See J.A.S.B. Vol. XXXVII. Part I. [illegible] —B.

برآمد موقوف داشته داخل درجمع نماید که ثاني الحال در برآمد کروري مجرا خواهد شد و مابقي را بموجب سند حضور ماجمله زر بقایا و تقاوي که بوصول رسد بتصدیق خود بکروري تنخواه میداده باشد و بر تقدیریکه زر مسطور به تنخواه حق التحصیل وفا نکند قدر زاید را ازتحصیل سالحال تن نماید

"And as to the money which is still owing by the ryots from the forty-second year of his late majesty's reign, the Kaṛoṛí is charged to collect at every harvest five per cent. in excess of the present jama', according to assessment until the whole be collected; and the sums which were allowed to the ryots under the head of "takávi" in the past year are to be realised, together with the arrears of the said year, at the first audit. In case of negligence he will be held responsible, and let him beware of venturing to collect any sum on account of village expenses, or under any head prohibited by the government." . . . .

"And according to the established rule the Kaṛoṛí may keep back one per cent. as his haḳḳu'l tahsíl (*i.e.* his fee or allowance for collecting) but must enter it in his accounts under the head of jama', and credit will be allowed him subsequently to that extent; and the rest that he shall collect under his majesty's warrant under the heads of taḳávi and arrears is granted to him as salary; if it do not amount to what he is entitled to, he may make good the deficiency out of the collections for the current year."*

Kachwánsí, کچوانسي कचवान्सी

The twentieth part of a Tiswansí, of which twenty go to a

* The second passage I have translated freely, as it appears to have been incorrectly copied or carelessly worded by the original scribe, or both. I think, however, I have succeeded in catching the general import. The document itself is not in my possession, and no clue to its whereabouts is given by the author.—B.

Parganahs as they stood in the time of the Emperor Akbar. The copies of the "Áín-i Akbarí" vary so much, and such ignorance is frequently exhibited by the transcribers, that to verify the names of Parganahs has been a work of great labour, which is by no means to be estimated by the ease with which the eye runs over a coloured map.

The Parganahs which retain their own names have frequently occasioned as much doubt as those which have undergone a complete change. The annoyance may be easily estimated by those who know what various phases Oriental alphabets can assume; and those who do not, may be convinced by learning that in a single Sirkár one copy presents you with such complete disguises and metamorphoses as Kathal for Kampil, Sanani for Patiali, and Saniwarbarka for Saurakh; and the difficulty does not cease when, after freqúent conjectures and comparisons, the name has been verified; for the adjustment of areas to meet those represented in the "Áín-i Akbarí," has frequently been the source of much perplexity. But it is in separating the Sirkárs into Dastúrs that the ignorance of the copyists has been chiefly exhibited, for all the Parganahs are frequently mixed together, s if there were no meaning at all attached to Dastúr. It has been therefore thought proper to explain in some detail the principle of the construction of the map, premising that several :opies of the "Áín-i Akbarí" have been consulted for the occasion.—See Dastúr.

EXPLANATION OF THE SYSTEM ADOPTED IN THE ARRANGEMENT OF THE MAPS.

Should it be desired to ascertain the position and names of he Parganahs as at present constituted, they may be learnt by eferring to the Modern Ethnographical Map, which has been drawn up for the purpose of illustrating several articles in this Supplement.*

* *Note.*—The Maps will be found in the fold of Vol. I.

An endeavour has also been made to represent the state of Zamíndárí possession in the time of Ạkbar—but in comparing the difference of colour in the modern and ancient map, it is not to be inferred that it is entirely occasioned by change of possession. There is reason to apprehend, as Abúl Fazl generally enters only one tribe as in possession of the Parganah Zamíndárí, and seldom more than two, that he has only mentioned those which had a predominance or clear majority; omitting all consideration of the others, whose number was inferior: now, the map of modern possession has been drawn out with a view of shewing as far as the scale would admit, all tribes of importance, so that if one particular class is found in possession of but a small part of a Parganah, it has been entered under its appropriate colour. As even in the same Parganah, the villages of each tribe are much intermixed, the colours of course represent the proportions, and not the positions, of each.*

The boundaries of the old Sirkárs appear for the most part well rounded off and defined. There are some which are somewhat doubtful, as will be seen by referring to the articles Bhattiana, Budhganga, Des, and Ghora. There is only one which appears to require notice in this place.

It will be observed from an inspection of the map of Sirkárs and Dastúrs, that the Parganahs of Sirkárs Gházípúr and Jaunpúr are strangely locked into each other near the confluence of the Gunti and Ganges. The fact of Sayyidpúr Namdí being in the old registers entered in the Sirkár of Gházípúr, while Bhítarí, which is between Sayyidpúr and Gházípúr, is entered in the Sirkár of Jaunpúr, would seem to show that the proper reading is Sayyidpúr Bhítarí, and that Bhítarí has been entered separately by mistake; but Sayyidpúr used formerly to be called Namdí; so that solution does not help us. The fact is,

* The original maps were on a large and legible scale; but it was found necessary to reduce them for the press; which could not, of course, be accomplished without throwing many of the limited tribes into the *miscellaneous* colours.

that Sayyidpúr and Bhítarí, which habit induces us now to couple together, were originally two distinct Parganahs, and in two different Sirkárs; nor were they regarded in any other light than as two distinct Parganahs, till they were given in Jágír to Babu Usan Singh, from which time as they were held under one Sanad (see the "Balwant-náma"), they began to be spoken of as one Parganah, and are so entered in the Regulation of 1795. In the Parwanah appointing Shaikh Abdullah Amil of Ghazípúr, amongst the twenty-two Parganahs mentioned in his Sanad, Sayyidpúr and Bhítarí are given separately; and this consideration throws much suspicion upon the Zamíndarí Sanad given in the Azimgarh Settlement Report, printed in the "Journal of the Asiatic Society" for 1838, and which might otherwise have been of some service in unravelling the difficulty. Sayyidpúr and Bhítarí are written together in the Persian Ziman, and (though they certainly appear to be enumerated as two) yet they occur without the intervention of the word Parganah; and in a manuscript copy of the Sanad, the entry of Sayyidpúr Bhítarí as one Parganah is beyond question. The same is observable in Kauria Tilhaní. Now, these are modern combinations, and could scarcely have been used in the fourth year of Jahangír, within twenty years after the compilation of the "Áín-i Akbarí," where they are entered with such marked distinction. Kauria and Tilhaní being in all respects separate Parganahs; and Sayyidpúr and Bhítarí not only separate Parganahs, but in two different Sirkárs. The entry of Maunát and Bhanjan as two separate Parganahs in the same Sanad, which are entered simply as Mau in the "Áín-i Akbarí" is also suspicious. These considerations, coupled with the loose wording of the document, lead us to put little faith in it as evidence respecting the mode in which Sayyidpúr and Bhítarí were entered at an early period in the imperial records, and justify the implication conveyed in that report, that the document is not authentic.

We must, therefore, notwithstanding the irregular appearance which this part of the map presents, consider that the entries are correct, and that the division was intentional.

PART IV.

TERMS ILLUSTRATIVE OF RURAL LIFE.

[Under this head I have thrown together all words which do not properly fall under the three preceding heads. This Part therefore is a very heterogeneous one. Names of trees and plants, rustic tools and implements, descriptions of soil when they have reference merely to agriculture and not to revenue purposes, and many other matters are here included.—B.]

A'bád, آباد आबाद

Literally, as stated in the printed Glossary, "abode, residence;" but more frequently used in the N.W. Provinces, as cultivated, flourishing, populous.

A'bádán is used in the same, but, as the "Farhang-i Rashídí" observes, in a somewhat intensive sense.—A'bádání signifies prosperity, population.—A'bádkár is a settler on waste land.

A'bád is frequently used in combination with a proper name to denote a city, as Haidar-ábád, Shahjahan-ábád. When used in construction with a Hindú name or vocable, it generally denotes that the termination has been changed from bás باس to A'bád آباد. Thus the Brahminábád, mentioned in the "Chachnama," and "Tuhfatu'l Kirám," was originally Brahminbas, or Bamanwas.—See Harbong ka Raj.

Ábpáshí, آبپاشي

Irrigation of fields, from P. آب water, and پاشیدن to sprinkle.

Ábí, آبي आबी

Irrigated land; from آب water. The word, though of general application, is more exclusively applied in Central Doáb to land irrigated from tanks, jhíls, and streams. As the supply of water is generally precarious, the rent paid for such land is about one-half of that which is paid for land irrigated from wells.—See Cháhi, Part III.

Abíj, ابيج अबीज

Grain that does not germinate; the same as Nirbíj. From अ a, or निर nir, priv. and bíj बीज seed.*

Adhikárí, ادهكاري अधिकारी

Proprietor; holder of a right or privilege.

Ágal, آگل आगल

A long and heavy piece of wood to which the hill-men tie their buffaloes. The Ghikar, or grazing-tax, *q.v.* was formerly levied "fí ágal," or so much per log.—E. *add.*

Agar, اگر अगर

Aloe wood; lignum aloes (*Aquilaria agallocha*, Roxb.). It emits a pleasant odour when burnt, and forms one of the chief ingredients of native pastils.

* A distinction is sometimes drawn between these two words. Abíj being used to signify grain which has been produced in a withered and worthless state in the ear, while Nirbíj implies that which, though produced healthy, has been subsequently destroyed by weevil or damp, etc.—B.

Ágar, آگر आगर

A salt pit. Áharí is the name of the small compartment within it.

It is stated by some authorities that this word is the origin of the name of the imperial city of Agra, and from the brackish nature of the soil and water, there is no improbability in the statement; but Ni'mat ullah, in his History of the Afghans, gives a very different account. He says that Sultán Sikandar Lodi, after getting on board a boat at Mathura (Muttra), asked his steerer which of the two heights before them was fittest for building. On which the steersman replied, "That which is a-head (Agra) is the best." At this the Sultán smiled and said, "The name of this town, then, which I design to build, shall be Agra." This must be altogether an imaginary dialogue; besides which, it is not likely the steersman would speak Sanskrit to the Emperor. It is evident, moreover, that Sikandar was not the founder of Agra, as is generally reported, though he may have built the fort of Bádalgaṛh; for the capture of it is celebrated in the verses of a Ghazni poet in the time of Masa'úd, the son of Ibrahim, the grandson of the great Mahmúd; and it is even acknowledged to have been an old city before the time of the Afghans, in the autobiography of Jahangír, whose veracity need not be impeached in passages where he has no occasion to indulge in the "Ercles' vein" respecting the achievements of himself or his ancestors. There is in Ferishta mention of the conquests made in India during the reign of Masa'úd.

"In his reign Hajib Toghantagín proceeded in command of an army towards Hindústan, and being appointed Governor of Lahore, crossed the Ganges, and carried his conquests further than any Mussalman had hitherto done, except the Emperor Mahmúd. Like him he plundered many rich cities and temples of their wealth, and returned in triumph to Lahore, which now became in some measure the capital of the Empire."—Briggs' Ferishta.

Ágarí, آگري आगरी

A manufacturer of salt. See Ágar.

Agayá, اگيا अगया

A disease which affects rice, in which the whole plant is dried and burnt up, from Ág آگ fire. See Khaira.—E.

Also in Bahár, the lemon-scented grass (*audropogon muricatum*) which is used as a specific in some diseases of cattle, such as goti or small-pox.—B.

Agaund, اگوںد अगौंद

The top of the sugar-cane cut up for seed; in distinction to Bel ka bíj, in which the whole cane is cut up into six or seven pieces. The division of the cane is much more minute in some places. Păt comprises the leaves at the top. Ag, Agáo, Agaurá, Agin, and Gaundí are the names given to a few inches below the Pát. Kánchá, called also Gulli, Palwa, and Phungí, consists of about a foot below the Ag, and is chiefly used for seed. The rest of the cane is called Gánde, Gandá and Ganná.

Agor, اگور अगोर

Agor, or Agoraiyá, is a man appointed to keep watch over crops; from agorná اگورنا to watch. The term is used chiefly in Benares, rarely in the North West.

Agwár, اگوار अगवार

The portion of corn set apart for village servants, so called because it is (áge) آگي—the first thing to be taken from the heap. In the East, it is used to signify the perquisites of ploughmen in kind. See Jeora and Thápa.

Agwásí, اگواسي अगवासी

The body of the ploughshare.—Eastern Oudh.

A'har, آهر आहर

A'harí, آهري आहरी

A small pond; smaller than a Pokhar and Talú, and larger than a Talaya and Marú. These two last words are chiefly in use to the Eastward. In Dehli, and the neighbourhood, Johar is a large pond, Jharí is a middling sized one, and Let* is a small one, more resembling a puddle. Thus, *Let páni barsá* means, "It has rained but little." Higher proportions are indicated by *Kuṅr páni barsá*, "It has rained a furrow full;" *Kiári bhár*, "To the extent of the bed of a garden;" *Naka tor páni barsá*, "It has rained enough to break the embankments."

Taláo in Dehli is applied generally only to such tanks as are lined with masonry.

In the Doáb and Rohilkhand, the words more generally known are, Ságar, Taláo, Pokhar, Dabrá, And, Liwár, Talárí, and Gaṛhaiya, or Gaṛhela—Ságar being the largest.

Ahar is also a salt-pit, a trough for watering cattle, a drain. —E.

In Amritsar the large pools which abound inside the city walls† are called *ḍáb*, probably meaning "depressions," from *ḍábná*, to press down. Another word used for a natural lake (*taláo* being often artificial) is सर *sar*, which forms the last member of the word Amritsar(= the lake of nectar). A pretty couplet, sometimes quoted in the Panjáb, runs—

ऐ सर हंस प्रीत न कर चोग चुग गहि उड़जाहि ।
कर कमलन सिउ दोस्ती सर सुके मुरझाहि ॥

"Love not the swan, o lake, for he feeds and flies away;
Give to the lotus thy love, tho' he wither and die, he will stay."
—B.

* Probably from *leṭná*, to lie down, to be flat.—B.

† I ought, perhaps, to have written "abounded," because I believe they are now nearly all drained off. At least, the authorities were at work on them so long ago as 1860.—B.

Ahíṭá, اهيتا अहीटा

A person appointed to watch the grain when it is ripe, and see that none of it is carried away before the demand is paid. The word is Hindi.

A'índán, آئين دان आईनदान

From A'ín آئين a law, and dánistan دانستن to know; a man who practises on the simplicity of his neighbours by his knowledge of the regulations of Government.

Aiwára, ايواره ऐवारा

A cow-shed in the middle of a jungle, according to the "Gharíbu'l-lughat" of Khan Arza. The "Tuḥfatu'l-lughát" does not notice it.—E.

The common words are Arár अड़াड़ and Bathán बथान q.v.—B.

Ajmúd, اجمود अजमूद

Parsley *(Apium involucratum)*.

Ajwáín, اجواين अजवाईन

(*Ligusticum ajowan*, Roxb.). Aniseed.

A'k, آک आक

Gigantic swallow-wort *(Asclepias gigantea)*. It is a common shrub all over Upper India, and is celebrated in the Tálíf-i sharíf for its many valuable properties. It is of high repute amongst the Indian practitioners, and at one time much attracted the notice of European physicians. The plant is more commonly known under the name of Madár.

A'k is also a sprout of sugar cane.

Akaiá, اكيّا अकैया

One of the sacks or baskets of a pannier.

Akan, آکن आकन

Grass and weeds collected from a ploughed field.—See Godhar.

A'kás bel, آکاس بیل आकास बेल

The air creeper *(Cuscuta reflexa ?)*. It has no root, or leaves, but grows luxuriantly on the tops of trees. It is from this circumstance that the name is derived—आकाश A'kás meaning in Hindí, the sky, the atmosphere. It is also called अमर बौंरिया Amar bauṇriá, or the undying creeper, and under this name is much used in native medicine as a remedy for rheumatism, and in alchemy is considered very efficacious as a transmuter of metals. It is supposed by Hindús that the man who finds its root will become rich.

A'khá, آکها आखा

A pair of grain bags used as a pannier.

Akor, اکور अकोर

A bribe. Hence it is applied in the North-West to the coaxing a cow or buffalo, which has lost its calf, to eat grain. The same process is called Toria in Benares.

Akor, or Kor, as it is sometimes pronounced, is also applied to the food which a labourer eats in the intervals of work in the open field.

Akrá, اکرا अकरा

A grass, or vetch, which grows in fields under spring-crop, creeping round the stem of the young plant, and checking its growth *(Vicia sativa)*. Akrá, or Ankrí, as it is often called, is something like the Masúr, and it is used as fodder for cattle.

A'l, آل आल

The *Morinda citrifolia.* Its roots give a permanent red dye to the well-known Kharúá cotton cloth. It is said in the Mu'álaját-i-Dárá Shikohí to be the same as Manjít; but the latter is the *Rubia tinctorum*, or, perhaps, more correctly, the *Rubia cordifolia*. The plant, which is very hardy and rarely ever affected by drought, is generally considered not to be productive till the third year of its growth. It is cultivated in several provinces of India. In the Peninsula, the best quality comes from Maisúr. In the North-West Provinces, the Ál of Hattá and Bundelkhand is the most prized; and the chief emporium of its sale is Músánagar in the Doáb. It is grown only in Már and Kábar soils, and, when ripe, is dug out of the ground with narrow pickaxes; every care being taken to prevent the small roots sustaining injury, from the bark of which the most valuable portion of the dye is extracted. It is not an exhausting crop, and is usually followed by gram.

Ál is also sometimes used in the North-West for a Páná, or division of a village.

A'lá, آلا आला

Wet; moist; land saturated with water, especially with rain water. This is the correct word, but it is provincially pronounced Al, Ahal, Alí, and Ael.—E. Also in the Eastern districts for the ridge separating fields, especially in land irrigated from tanks, or which depends on rain water for its moisture. It is sometimes written आईल *áil*, and under the forms *ahal* and *ali* is occasionally, though incorrectly, applied to the fields themselves.—B.

Almárí, الماري अलमारी

A chest of drawers; a book-case. The word is derived from the Portuguese *almario*, which comes from the Latin *armorium*, an armoury, or cupboard for keeping arms and clothes in; in old English *aumbry*.—B.

Álo, آلو आलो

The word is in use in Benares in the same sense as Dadrí, *q.v.* to signify a portion of unripe corn.

Áltá, آلتا आलता

Was formerly on our tariff. It consists of balls of cotton impregnated with lac dye, and manufactured in all large towns where jungle produce is procurable. It is more generally known by the name of Mahâwar.

Anárdána, انار دانه अनारदाना

A species of millet, so called from its resemblance to the seed of the pomegranate.—See As. Res. XV. 473.

Andhị, آندهي आंधी

A hurricane, or storm. The word is pure Hindí, and extremely common everywhere in India; but M. Langlès in an amusing note on the travels of Mr. Hodges, presumes that the word is a corruption from the French. "Aoundy, *ouragans.* J'ignore l'origine de ce mot sur lequel toutes mes recherches ne m'ont procuré aucun renseignement. Je serais tenté de croire qu'il y a erreur de la part de M. Hodges; car plusieurs savans voyageurs que j'ai consultés m'ont avoué ne point connaitre ce mot, et ne se rappelaient pas l'avoir entendu prononcer dans l'Inde; peut-être est-ce une corruption du mot Francais *ondée!!*"

Áng, آنگ आंग

Signifies the demand on each head of cattle for the right of pasture.—Dehli. This is paid to the proprietor of the land. Bít is that which is paid per head to the cowherd.

Angaḍḍiyá, انگڈيا अंगड्डिया

Said in the Glossary to be applied to persons in the Northern

Provinces, who carry money concealed in their quilted clothes. The word may, perhaps, therefore be derived, or somehow corrupted, from Angarkha; but it is used, I believe, only in Gujrát, and not in our Northern Provinces, where Rokaria is the term applied to such persons; from *rokar*, money.—E.

*** In Behar it is the name of a class of men who are employed by merchants and bankers to carry remittances of cash from one firm to another. They travel long distances with very large sums of money, and are never known to embezzle or act dishonestly, though they are poorly paid. The facilities for making remittances now afforded by the introduction of the money-order and other systems, will probably, in course of time, lead to the extinction of this trade. The men are, I believe, of no particular caste.—B.

Ańgan, آنگن आंगन

A court yard. An enclosed area near a house—Angná is also used in the same sense.—E. Rather the courtyard, or "patio," as the Spanish call it, formed by the rooms of the house itself, which is usually built round the four sides of a square.—B.

Angwárá, انگوارا अंगवारा

The proprietor of a small portion of a village.—Eastern Oudh and Benares.

It is also applied in the former province to reciprocal assistance in tillage.

Anjan, انجن अंजन

A grass which grows in great abundance in the Upper Provinces, and is largely used as fodder for cattle.

Anjaná, انجنا अंजना

An inferior kind of rice.—See Dhan.

Áṅk, آنک आंक

Figure, unit, number, amount, a share. Hence, Ankdár is used in the Central Doáb to signify a sharer.

The initial *A* is either long or short—both are correct; but the former is most usual in Hindí.

Áṅwlá, آنولا आंवला

(Phyllanthus emblica). A kind of myrobalan. The fruit is acid, and is stated in the "Tálíf-i Sharíf" to be of great use in cutaneous eruptions, and to be known also as بجي *Bijji* and دهابري پهل *Dhábri Phal.*

The tree is worshipped by agriculturists on the 11th of Phagun, which day is therefore known by the name of आओंला एकादसी, and on this occasion libations are poured at the foot of the tree, a thread (generally red or yellow), is bound round the trunk, prayers are offered up for its fruitfulness, and the ceremony is concluded by a Pranám, or reverential inclination of the head to the tree.

Áokán, آوکان आओकान

Straw and grain heaped up.—Benares. See Gantah.

Áokhal, آوکهل आओखल

Land reclaimed from waste, and brought under cultivation. Also spelt ऊखल *úkhal,* especially in the Northern Doáb and Dehli.

Áorí, آوري आओरी

Bank of a pond or rivulet to the water's edge; applied generally to signify a piece of dry land left uncultivated.

Ár, آر आर

Ladle used in sugar factories.—E. Oudh. The same word, or

rather आड़, is applied in Benares as an abbreviation of Arárá, the bank of a pond. And in Hindí generally *Ár* signifies a goad.

Arába, ارابه अराबा

A cart. It is usually spelt with an ع, but the "Burhan-i Káti'" gives it correctly with an ا. The word being purely Persian cannot begin with ع. In the "Farhang-i Rashídí" and in the "Haft Kulzam," the king of Oudh's dictionary, I find no mention of it under either letter, but in the former, under the article Banádar, it is spelt with an ع. Arába is not much used in India, except in writing; but it is in common use throughout the Turkish empire. Richardson describes it as a two-wheeled carriage; but in Constantinople it has four wheels.

Arah, اره अरा

Cross-ploughing. The straight furrow is *khaṛá*, and ploughing from corner to corner is *nok-náka*. This is only when fields require three ploughings.—E. *add.*

Aṛár, اڑاڑ अड़ाड़

Outsheds for cattle; harvest floor for Mahwa blossoms.—Eastern Oudh and Benares.—E.

Otherwise a small grass hut in the jungle, where the cowherds pass the night; it is usually on the edge of a cleared patch on which the cattle assemble. Fires are sometimes lighted round them to keep off tigers. See Bathán.—B.

Aṛáṛá, اڑاڑا अड़ाड़ा

Steep bank of a river, pond, or tank.

Araí, ارئي अरई

Goad at the end of a whip. The diminutive of Ar. *q.v.*

'Arak, عرق अरक

Juice; whence we derive our "Arrack."

Arand, ارنڈ अरंड

The castor-oil plant (*Palma Christi*).

Also रेंढ़ी renṛhí, which is more common.—B.

Ardáwa, ارداوه अर्दावा

Ground meal. The mixture now known by the name of Ardáwa comprises equal portions of the chick pea and barley, and forms almost universally, in Upper India, the food of horses kept by Europeans.

Argaṛá, ارگڑا अर्गड़ा

An enclosure, or pound for cattle, in Puráṇiyá (Purneah). Elsewhere called Pháṭak.—B.

Arhar, ارهر अरहर

A species of pulse (*Cytisus Cajan*) called also frequently توار tuár.

The "Mirat-i-Aftabnama" says that tuár or túr, is only amongst the people of Shahjahánabad (Dehlí) synonymous with Arhar, and that elsewhere Túr is another species and larger than Arhar, having a stalk like sugar-cane. It is also called Rahar.

Arhaṭ, ارهٹ अरहट

*** Also and perhaps more commonly रहट rahaṭ. A machine for raising water from a well, usually called by Europeans the "Persian wheel." Its construction is rather complicated and may be thus described. Across the mouth of a well is laid a long beam or láṭh, one end of which projects six or seven feet beyond the edge of the well; this beam serves as an axis to a large heavy double wheel hanging over the well, and has at its other end a small wheel with cogs of wood, which fit into corresponding cogs in a horizontal wheel, whose axis is fixed into the ground below and at the top into a beam supported at either end by walls of mud. To this upright axis is attached a long branch of a tree to which a buffalo is harnessed, having his eyes blinded by little caps of leather. He walks round and round the horizontal wheel and sets the whole in motion. On the wheel that hangs over the well is a long string of little earthen pots called तिंड tinds which going down empty, and coming up full, tilt over at the top and discharge their contents into a trough which carries the water along an earthen conduit or aḍḍá to considerable distances. It is obvious that such a well cannot be worked where the water is very far from the surface, as the expense and difficulty of making a long string of pots or tinds would be very great. Accordingly the Persian wheel is not found much lower down than the Upper Doáb, and is more common on the Jamna side of the Doáb than near the Ganges. It is, however, almost the only kind of well-gear known in the Panjáb. The creaking of the wheels and the splash and sparkle of water, with the old mud walls under a spreading tree, form one of the commonest and most pleasing features in a Panjáb landscape. As regards supply of water it is a question whether the arhaṭ or the *charas* q.v. is the better. My own opinion is in favour of the former, as its supply is continuous, though each tinḍ holds but little water; the huge charas discharges more water, but much time is lost in its descent and ascent. I think it will be found that an arhaṭ worked for twelve hours—other things being equal—delivers more water than a charas worked for the same time. See Cháhí, in Part III.—B.

'Aríat, عاريت आरीयत

Borrowing anything which is itself to be returned—from the Arabic عار. It differs from Karẓ, inasmuch as in the latter, the articles borrowed are not to be identically returned.—See "Hedaya," Book XXIX.*

Arthiá, ارتهيا अर्थिया

A client, a broker, an agent, a dependant.

Arwí, اروي अरवी

A species of Arum, an esculent root called in the Eastern districts a कचालू Kachálú, and घूंइंयां ghuṅiṅyáṅ.

Asharfí, اشرفي अशरफी

A gold mohar.—See "Prinsep's Useful Tables," p. 4.

More correctly Ashrafí. The gold mohar is not now a legal tender in British territory, though there are heaps of them in existence. The ordinary value is 16 Rs., but varies according to the character of the coin.—B.

Ashjár, اشجار अशजार

Trees; plural of the Arabic شجرة.

Ashráf, اشراف अशराफ

Plural of the Arabic شريف *Sharíf,* noble. A class of cultivators in Rohilkhand, and Oudh, and Benares, who designate themselves by this title, and claim certain privileges. The opposite of the term is ارذال, *i.e.* those of low degree, the vulgar.—E.

The term is generally used in speaking of Brahman, Rajput, or Bhúíṅhár cultivators, as opposed to Kurmís, Kachhís, and the like, who are 'razíl. The privileges claimed by the Ashráf are principally that they should be assessed at a lower rate, and have better lands assigned them than the Irzál.—B.

* *e.g.* If you borrow an umbrella it is *'ariat,* if you borrow money it is *ḳarz.*—B.

'Ashrát, عشرات अशरात

Tens; plural of the Arabic عشر ten.

Asíchá, اسيچا असीचा

Unirrigated; from अ not, and सिचना to water.

Aṣíl, اصيل असील

A female servant amongst Mussulmans. It bears also a contrary meaning; as, noble by birth. The origin of both is from the Arabic. The former meaning is derived from a free servant being superior to a Laundí or purchased slave; the second from the stem of an illustrious lineage. It is not uncommon amongst ill-educated people to call a slave Aṣíl, but it is proper to observe the distinction noted above.

Ason, اسوں असों

The current year; the word is not used much in the North-West, but when used is generally pronounced Eson.*

Asthán, استهان अस्थान

An abode, residence. From the Sanskrit स्थान a place.

Asthal, استهل अस्थल

A fixed residence; usually applied to the spot in which Fakírs remain; a hermitage, presided over by a mahant.

Aṭá, اٹا अटा

Aṭárí, اٹاري अटारी

An upper-roomed house; an upper story. The second of these words is a diminutive of the first.

* From Persian اين سنه *in sanna,* this year.

Aṭábú, اتّابو अटाबू

The local name given by the resident Ahírs to a tract of country between the Kálá Naddí and the Ratwá, including the greater part of the Parganah of Márehra.

Aṭhmás, اتّهماس अठमास

Lands constantly ploughed from Asáṛh to Magh for sugar-cane, from आठ eight and मास a month. See Chaumás.

Athmaná, اتهمنا अथमना

The West.—Dehli. The word used in opposition to Athmaná is Ugmana, the East. Athae अथये is also occasionally used to signify the West, but its more correct and universal meaning is "the evening."* Both words appear to be derived from Ast, *q.v.*

Atarpál, اترپال अतर्पाल

Land which has been once under cultivation, and then abandoned. The word is more correctly Antarpal.—Central and Lower Doáb.

Áwá, آوا आवा

A furnace or potter's kiln. A brick kiln is پجاوه pajáwa, a corruption of پزاوه pázáwa, from پزانیدن pazánídan, to cook.

Awásí, اواسي अवासी

A word used in the province of Benares (See Dadrí).—E.

It means unripe corn picked from time to time and brought home to be eaten. In times of scarcity many of the poorer ryots are often obliged to forestall the harvest in this way to the detriment both of their health and pockets.—B.

* Under this sense it is given as a local word of Bundelkhand, in the Vocabulary printed in No. 144 of the "Journal of the Asiatic Society of Bengal;" but it is a common Hindí term, by no means confined to that Province. In the same Vocabulary there are some other words which do not appear to be correctly entered, either with regard to their meaning or local application.

Awáí, اوائي अवाई

A pickaxe.—Eastern Oudh.

Bábú, بابو बाबू

Formerly Bábú was used only as a title of respect; now, especially among Europeans, it is used also to designate a native clerk who writes English, such clerks being chiefly Bengalís, among whom the title of Bábú has a wider acceptation than in Hindústan.

In Gorakhpúr, the descendants of the younger brothers of the Sarneṭ Raja are called Bábú, and there the term, still maintaining its original dignity, is applied generally to any man of family or influence. Crossing the Gogra into Benaudhá, and Benares, we find it applied only to the younger brothers, or near relatives of Rajas. Thus in Reg. VIII. of 1795, Sec. X., Bábús are defined to mean "persons of the (Benares) Raja's blood and family." In the East, Bábú is also applied to Mussalmans, as Bábú Musharraf Ali Khan of Talúka Báz Bahádur in A'zamgaṛh.—E. *add.*

The term Bábú is now very generally used by Europeans and natives alike, especially in Bengal and Behar, as a title of Zamíndárs and native gentlemen of wealth and position who have no other special title. The Zamíndár of Madhoban in Parganah Mehsi of Champáran has the title of "Rájkumár Bábú," to indicate his descent from the family of the Rajas of Sheohar and Maharajas of Betiyá (Bettiah). This title has been confirmed by Government; but in most cases the title of Bábú alone is assumed and conferred at the pleasure of the people themselves.—B.

Bágh, باغ

Bághíchah, باغيچه

A garden. Bághíchah or Bághchah is the diminutive of Bágh.—E.

Baghíchah is generally used as synonymous with फूलवारी phúlwárí, a garden attached to a gentleman's house. Bágh is applied to large orchards and mango groves which pay revenue to Government.—B.

Bágar, باگر बागर

A hedge of thorns or twigs.—Hoshangabad.

Ríndhna is used in the same sense in Benares, and Bár in the rest of the North West.

Báhá, باها बाहा

A watercourse; generally an artificial one, but in Dehli it is applied to a natural one; and Kahál and Khálá which generally signify natural, are there applied to artificial watercourses.

Báhná, باهنا बाहना

To plough. The word is in common use, but is not apparently mentioned in any dictionary, except Gilchrist's.

Báhan, باهن बाहन

Fallow land, from Bahna باهنا to plough.

Báhara, باهره बाहरा

The man who stands at the well to upset the water from the Charas, *q.v.*—Dehli.

Báj, باج बाज

A tax; a toll. Originally, tribute taken by one king from another. The "Burhán-i Káti'" and the "Haft Kulzam" say—

مال باشد که بادشاهان بزرگ از بادشاهان زیردست گیرند

The word is also frequently written باژ. See Altamghá, Part III.

Bájra, باجره बाजरा
Bájrí, باجري बाजरी

(*Panicum spicatum*, Roxb.) (*Holcus spicatus*, Linn.) Bájrá is everywhere cultivated in these Provinces; but very sparingly to the East of Allahabad. The Bájrí is a smaller species of millet than the Bájrá, and ripens a month before it. Village Zamíndárs also comprehend by the term Bájrí, the stalk of the Bájra, used as fodder.—See Jour. A.S. Bengal, 1852, p. 158.

Bákrí, باكري बाकरी

A cow advanced about five months in pregnancy. A small buffalo is sometimes called a Bákrí.

Bákhar, باكهر बाखर

A house; an enclosure. Dwellings contained within an enclosure.

In Dehli the word is applied to cattle sheds.

In Bundelkhand, Saugor, and Malwa, it is an agricultural implement, a sort of bullock hoe, usually employed instead of the plough in the preparation of the black soil of those provinces. It has an iron scythe, in the room of a share, about twenty inches broad and five deep, fixed to the centre of a beam of wood between four and five feet long and six inches broad. This scythe enters about eight inches into the ground, effectually eradicating weeds and grass, and the beam pulverising the earth as it is turned up. The land intended for the Kharíf, or rainy season crop, is once turned by this instrument before the seed is scattered. It is then ploughed to cover the seed, and protect it against the birds. The Rabí land is turned up two or three times with the Bákhar during the rains, and sown with the drill plough about eight inches deep.

Bákand, باكند बाकंद

The proportion of two-fifths of the crop, which is sometimes paid as rent by cultivators to Zamíndárs. It is also known as Pachdo, Pachdoli, *i.e.* do (two) out of panch (five).

Bál, بال बाल

An ear of corn.

Bálá, بالا बाला

A grub which eats the young plants of wheat or barley when they are about six inches high.—Benares.

Bálákhánah, بالاخانه बालाखाना

An upper story; a "balcony," of which word Bálákhánah is the origin.

Bándh, باندھ बांध

An embankment.—See Bandhan.

Bání, بانی बानी

Besides the meanings given ordinarily in the dictionaries it is the name of a yellow earth with which potters sometimes ornament their vessels. In parts of Rohilkhand it is called Kapas.

Bángá, بانگا बांगा

Raw cotton; not confined to one species, as mentioned in the Glossary.

Bánjh, بانجھ बांझ

Barren. From the Sanskrit बन्ध्या. It is sometimes used as an abbreviation of the word Banjar, which owns the same root.

Bánk, بانک बांक

A bend in a river. From the Sanskrit root वृज to be curved.

Bánsá, بانسا बांसा

From بانس Báns, a bamboo; the channel through which the

seed descends in a drilling machine. In Dehli it is generally known by the name of Orna. In the North-West the Bansa is generally fixed to the ordinary plough. The month in which the seed is cast is called Daurá or Nálá in the East, and Waira in the West.—See Haltadí.

In Benares the entire drilling machine is called Tár. It is a separate instrument, and not attached to the ordinary plough.

Báns, بانس बांस

A bamboo. It has not, as far as I am aware, been noticed in any work that the bamboo seldom flowers in Bengal till just before its death. At least, so say the natives, and my own experience confirms the supposition. The flowering of the bamboo is said to bring ill-luck to the owner of it.—B.

Bánsarí, بانسري बांसरी

A weed found in parts of the Doáb near the Jumna, which is very injurious, choking the crops, and most difficult to eradicate from arable land.

Báuní, باوني बाउनी

Seed time, also the act of sowing.—Rohilkhand and Doáb; called Baug in Benares and Behár, and Berá in Dehli.

Báolí, باولي बाश्रोली

In upper India a large well where the water lies deep, and steps and galleries underground are made to give access to it.—E. *add.*

Báklá, باقلا बाकला

A bean; pot-herbs; the kidney bean (*Phaseolus vulgaris*). From the Arabic بقل. From which root is also derived the familiar word Bakkál بقال, the Arabic name of a Banya, or grain seller; but, originally, a person who sells pot-herbs and beans; a greengrocer.

Báṛ, باڑ बाड़

A fence; a hedge; a margin. Also Beṛha.

Bár, بار बार

Bára, باره बारा

Perquisite of the Ahír in milk; generally the milk of every eighth day.—Rohilkhand.

Bára are also the little fibrous roots of trees, which are favorable to transplanting.—E. *add.*

Báráhí, باراهي बाराही

Land, according to the dictionary in the "Tuhfatu'l Hind."

Bárbardárí, باربرداري बारबरदारी

Carriage hire. From the Persian بار bár, a load, and برداري bardárí, conveyance.

Báṛí, باڑي बाड़ी

A plot for sugarcane or other garden produce; an enclosed piece of ground; a kitchen garden; also cotton. From the Hindí باڑ or بار an enclosure.

Báṛhí, باڑهي बाढ़ी

Interest in kind, paid upon seed grain. From بڑهنا baṛhná, to increase, to rise, to advance.

Bárik, بارك बारिक

Rain; according to the Dictionary in the "Tuhfatu'l Hind."

Báriz, بارز बारिज

A term in arithmetic. The page of an account book is divided into two equal parts called Zillah; each Zillah is divided into two Rakans. The right hand Zillah is called the Hasho. The first right hand quarter (some say half) of the left Zillah is appropriated to the Bariz, and the remaining portion is called the Iráda. The Bariz contains the sum finally brought to account, after the necessary deductions have been made from the gross amount in the Iráda and Hasho, *q.v.*, also see Printed Glossary, *s.v.*

Básmatí, باسمتي बासमती

A fragrant kind of rice and millet. From Hindí बास scent. —See Dhan and Jawár.

Bátin, باتن बातिन

A tract of land in Etawah, lying between the river Jumna and the Ghar (which see).

Báwag, باوگ बावग

Seed time.—Eastern Oudh.—See Baoni.

The act of sowing.—B.

Bechirágh, بےچراغ बेचिराग़

Without a vestige: (a village) ruined beyond hope. It means, literally, without a light; بي privative, and چراغ a light.

Biár, بيار बीआर

Seed bed; also air, wind. In the former sense the word is usually spelt with an ژ.

In Dehli, the evening is called Biyár.

In Saugor, it signifies waste land fit for cultivation.

In the Lower Doáb, it is used in the same sense as Pattí is elsewhere; that is, as a sub-division of a village.

Biás, بياس बिआस

Land cultivated, to be sown in the following year; field under preparation for rice cultivation. The word is chiefly used in Rohilkhand.

Bíḍá, بيڈا बीडा

Mounds.—E. Oudh. The word is probably a corruption of بيہڑ uneven, rugged ground.

Bíhaṛ, بيہڑ बीहड़

Sterile land; uneven or cragged land; waste land; land full of ravines.

Bíjmár, بيجمار बीजमार

Failure of germination. From بيج seed, and مارنا to strike, to kill.—See Abij.

Bíjar, بيجر बीजर

A description of soil in which the cereal grains are generally grown.—Lower Doáb.

Bímá, بيما बीमा

Insurance. The word is also written بيمان.

Bínd, بيند बीन्द

A reed; a rush.

Bínḍa, بينڈه बींडा

A kind of rope made of grass or of the fibres of the Arhar plant. The word appears to be derived from بينڈهنا to plait, to braid. Hence بينڈي the hair plaited behind.

Bír, بير बीर

Pasturage. The word is in general use, but is most common in Dehli and the Saugor territory.

Bíṛá, بيڑا बीड़ा

A parcel made up of betel leaves and other ingredients, called Pan sopárí, which comprises betel leaves, areca or betelnut, catechu, quick-lime, aniseed, coriander seed, cardamums and cloves.—Ḳánún-i Islam.

Bírbání, بيرباني बीरबानी

A common expression in the North West, particularly among the Játs, applied to designate a man's own wife. The word बीर víra signifies in Sanskrit a warrior; a man. Báni is derived from the Sanskrit वनिता vanitá, a woman.

Biṭ, بيٹ बीट

A Dehḷi word.—See explanation under Ang.

Begár, بيگار बेगार

Begárí, بيگاري बेगारी

A person forced to work and carry burdens. Under the former regime, he got no pay. Now, though he gets pay, yet if he is ordered to work by any public official, he is still generally called Begár.

In Shakespear's and Smyth's dictionaries these words are represented as Hindí, but they are Persian also, and are entered in all the best Persian Lexicons.

کار فرمودن بے مُزد بود يعني کار بفرمايند و اُجرت ندهند

And the "Haft Kulzam" adds that the word is spelt either Begar or Bekar.

Behnaur, بيهنور बेहनौर

Behan, بيهن बेहन

Nursery for rice plants.—E. Oudh and Benares.—Panír is more commonly used in the North West, and Jáyí in Bundelkhand. Píad in Dehli is used as a nursery, not only of rice, but of any other plant.

Behrah, بيهره बेहरा

Grass kept for pasturage.—Rohilkhand.

The word is probably a corruption of Bír, *q.v.*

Bejhará, بیجھڑا बिझड़ा

A mixed crop, generally of gram and barley.

Bekas, بیکس बेकस

A kind of grass growing in low ground, which resembles the Dúb, but its leaves and stem are larger. It is good fodder for horned cattle, but is reckoned injurious to horses. It grows throughout the North West Provinces.

Beb, بیب बेब

Bábar, بابر बाबर

A grass from which a twine is made, which is much used for native beds. Bábar is also much used for thatching.

Bel, بیل बेल

Bel is the name applied to a spot in which the receiving pans are placed when sugar is manufactured. In most places the pans amount to three, Karáh, Chásní, and Phúlhá, the first being the biggest, and Chásní, which occupies a place between the other two, the smallest. In Dehli, Bojh sometimes takes the place of the Karáh and Karáhí of the Chásní; the Phúlhá being frequently omitted, especially of late years.

Bel is also the name of the thorny quince (*Œgle Marmelos*) and the single Arabian jasmine (*Jasminum Sambac*). Also a creeper, a tendril, a pole for directing a boat, a spade, or hoe.

Belbúṭá, بیلبوٹا बेलबूटा

A bush. From Bel a tendril, and Búṭá, a flower.

Belchak, بیلچک बेलचक

Belchá, بیلچا बेलचा

A small hoe, or spade. Diminutives of Bel.

Belkí, بیلکی बेलकी

A cattle grazier.—Baitúl.

Belak, بیلک बेलक

A small mattock.—See Bel, Belchak.

Bent, بینٹ बेंट

The handle of an axe, hoe, and similar implements. Bent is the correct word; but it is generally pronounced Bítá in Rohilkhand, and Bintá in Dehli.

Byohár, بیوهار ब्योहार

Money lending, or traffic of any kind; a calling; a trade.

In Jabalpúr, the name is applied to a Kanúngo. The Sadr Byohár, besides his salary, holds large rent-free estates. From Sansk. व्यवहार.

Bera, بیر बेर

The lotus of the ancients. J. A. S. B. 1847, p. 235.—See Jharberí.

Berána, بیرانہ बेराना

A grove of Ber trees. The Ber is the *Zizyphus jujuba.*—See Jharberí.

Birár Pándía, برار پانڈیا बिरार पांडीया

In Baitúl and the Deccan, is the Kanúngo of the North West Provinces.

Berhá, بیڑها बेढ़ा

A paling. From Berhná, to enclose with a fence, to surround. See next article.

Berhná, بیڑهنا बेढ़ना

Besides the meaning above given, the word signifies in the Doáb, Bundelkhand, and Rohilkhand, "to drive off cattle by force." In this sense it is used generally in Hindústan, but Khedke lejáná is the equivalent term in the Dehli territory.

Beshí, بیشي बेशी

Increase; surplus: From the Persian بیش more.

Besan, بیسن बेसन

The flour of pulse; especially of Chaná (gram), or the chick pea, used for washing with.

Beṭh, بیٹھ बेठ

Sandy unproductive soil.—Rohilkhand.

Bhánkarí, بهانکري भांकरी

A jungle shrub found in great abundance in the Dehli territory. It differs in no respect from the Gokrú, *q.v.* It is used as a specific in certain complaints, and to attract purchasers its vulgar name is transformed by the druggists into Hasd Singhárá.

Bhát, بهات भात

Advances to ploughmen without interest.—Benares and Eastern Oudh.

Bhantá is used in this sense in Rohilkhand.

Bhát is also the name of a soil to the north of the Ganges that retains its humidity for a long time, and contains a large quantity of nitre. It is a peculiar soil, and is not found West of the Gandak.

In the Lower Doáb and Bundelkhand, Bhát means uneven ground.—See Bhatúa.

Bhíṭ, بهیٹ भीट

An elevation of earth made near a tank for the purpose of planting Pan; mounds of a tank; the vestige of an old house.

Bhelí, بهیلي भेली

A lump of coarse sugar; generally consisting of four or five seers.

Bhis, بهس भिस

The edible root of the Lotus. The correct word is भसींर Bhasínr, but it is provincially corrupted into Bhisendá, Bhis, and Basend.

Bhoí, بهوئي भोई

Used in the neighbourhood of the Narmadá (Nerbudda), to signify a "bearer." The same word is used in the Peninsula, and corrupted by Europeans into "boy." Hence the exclamation of "boy," so commonly used at Madras, is not, as has been supposed, a pure English, but a corruption of Bhoí.

Bhoí is also, to the South of the Nerbudda, applied to designate the head of a Gond village.

Bhúmiyá, بهوميا भूमिया

Landlord; a proprietor of the soil; descendant of the founder of the village. It is derived from भूमि land. In Ajmer it is the title of a village watchman who has land assigned him for maintenance. Tod. i. 497.

Bhúmiyáwat, بهومياوت भूमियावत

A general plundering, or more correctly a fight between neighbouring Zamíndárs about landed property.—Saugor.

Bhúnḍiá, بهونڈيا भूंडिया

One who cultivates with a borrowed plough or hand instrument.—Central Doáb.

Bhúnhará, بهونهرا भूंहरा

A subterraneous dwelling; according to the Dictionary of Khan Arzu.

Bhúṛ, بهوڑ भूड़

A sandy soil. The word is frequently pronounced Bhúḍa. It is in Sahâranpúr the same as the tract called Bhábar in Rohilkhand.

Bhuṛarí, بهڑري भुड़री

A term applied to the corn which remains in the ear after being trodden out.—Rohilkhand and Delhi.

The corresponding word in Benares and the Lower Doáb is Linduri, and in the Upper and Lower Doáb, Dobrí, Pakurí, and Chittí.

These words are applied to the Rabi' grains chiefly, as wheat, barley, etc. To Jawár, Múng, etc. Chanchari, Gúrí, Kosí, Karahí and Thanthí are more commonly applied.

Bhus, بهس भुस

Bhúsá, بهوسه भूसा

The husk of corn; chaff. The English gipsies use Pus in the same sense. (Trans. R.A.S. vol. ii., p. 543).

Bhusaurí, بهسوري भुसौरी

Bhusaulá, بهسولا भुसौला

Bhusehrá, بهسيهرا भुसेहरा

The place in a dwelling house for keeping straw. These terms are in general use; but Obrá اوبرا is also so applied in Dehli.

Bhusrá, بهسرا भुसरा

An inferior kind of wheat, *i.e.* one which yields too great a proportion of bran (भूसा).—Saugor.

Bhuṭṭá, بهٹا भुट्टा

The corn-cob or ear of Indian corn; any large bunch.

Bhor, بهور भोर

Dawn of day.

Bhaḍá, بهڈا भडा

A kind of grass which grows in poor soil, attaining the height of a little more than a foot. It makes excellent fodder.

Bhadbhadáná, بهدبهدانا भदभदाना

Used in the Upper Doáb in the same sense as Bhadáhar (which see). It also means the shaking of fruit from a tree. Shakespear does not give this application of the term in his Dictionary; but bhadbhad and bhadbhadáhat, are said in it to denote the sound which is made by the fall of fruits.

Bhadwár, بهدوار भदवार

Land prepared for sugar cane; land ploughed during the Kharíf, and allowed to lie fallow till cotton is sown; land ploughed from Asárh to Bhadon for the Rabí sowings. The name is derived from Bhadon, apparently because the entire rain of that month is allowed to saturate the field when ploughed. It is called Bhadwár Paṛál, from Paṛná, to lie fallow, in parts of Rohilkhand and the Doáb.

Bhadaí, بهدئي भदई

The produce of the month Bhadon. [Especially applied in Behar to the early rice crop. See Aghani. It is also pronounced Bhadoí भदोई بهدوي].

Bhang, بهنگ भंग

Bháng, بهانگ भांग

In Persian Bang. An intoxicating drink made from the leaves of the *Cannabis sativa*. The plant from which it is made has female flowers; the male being the Gánja plant, which is also applied to the purpose of intoxication, and is usually inhaled from a pipe. It is commonly considered that there is no difference between the plants which produce Bhang and Gánja, but natives generally recognise the distinction of the male and female plant noted above.

O'Shaughnessy says that Bang, or Sidhí, or Sabzi, consists

of the large leaves and capsules without the stalks, but makes no allusion to Bhang being produced from a plant different from that which produces Gánja.

The best Bhang of the N.W. Provinces comes from Bahráich and its neighbourhood, and from Dandwári in Kanauj; the best Gánja, from Rajsháhí, in Bengal. Bhang is also known by the name of Bijaya (See Gánja).

Bhangela, بهنگیله भंगेला

A sack or pannier made from the fibres of the Bhang plant. It is not so coarse or strong as the Gon.

Bhangra, بهنگره भंगरा

A small creeping herb with minute flowers which grows in a wet soil (*Verbesina prostrata*). There are said to be two species, the white and the black. The white is very common, and is much used in medicinal preparations; the black is unknown, but is much sought after by alchymists, and is reputed by native practitioners to be a panacea.

Bhare, بهرے भरे

A grass which grows in the jungles to the height of about nine feet, and is used for thatches and tatties. Its canes are known by the name of Núnre.

Bharná, بهرنا भर्ना

To give property in re-payment of a debt, literally, "to fill up."

Bharauná, بهرونا भरौना

A load of wood.—Gharáibu'l Lughát.

Bhattiyá, بهٹیه भटिया

The poorest kind of land in the Saugor territory and Bundle-khand. It is of a reddish colour, and has Kankar and other stones mixed up with it. It is very shallow in depth, and generally exhausted at the end of the third year, after which it requires a fallow of four years to restore it. Only Kodo and Kutkí, and the poorest sort of corn can be raised on this kind of land. It is more generally called Bhattí and Bhatua in Bundelkhand.—See "Spry's Mod. India," II. 276.

Bhaṭkaṭaiyá, بهتکتیا भटकटईया

(*Solanum Jacquini*). There are two kinds of this herb according to the "Talíf-i Sharíf;" the white is usually called the Katáí, and the large and red kind the Barehta. The flower is called Gulkhár *i.e.* "rose-thorn." It may be doubted if this statement is quite correct. There are generally reckoned to be four kinds of Kaṭaiya, of which the Bhaṭkaṭaiyá, frequently miscalled the camel's thorn, is one, and the common people, who see these weeds growing wild, do not acknowledge that there are two kinds of Bhaṭkaṭaiyá. The only Bhaṭkaṭaiyá which they know is much used in veterinary practice, particularly in diseases which affect horned cattle. It is also devoutly believed that if the roots of the Bhaṭkaṭaiyá, are shown to a man bitten by a snake, he immediately recovers.—(See Jawasa).

The other three kinds of Kataiya are the following.

Bang Kataiya. This resembles a common thistle, and is not applied to any useful purpose. It is known also by the name of Satyánásí, and found in all parts of the country.

Gol Kataiya. This is not so erect as the others, but spreads more over the surface of the ground. It has purple flowers and produces a round berry. It is frequently used in native prescriptions.

Kataiya proper. This is the largest of the four, and is more frequently found in jungles than near the abode of man. It is a prickly shrub, growing to the height of ten or twelve feet, and does not at all resemble the other Kataiyas.

Bhaṭolar, بهٹولر भटोलर

Lands allotted to Bhats or Bards.

Bhaṭulá, بهٹلا भटुला

The name given to bread made from the grain of Arhar, Chaná and Múng. It is called also Gánkar. It is notorious for its hardness, and is therefore seldom eaten by those who can afford to grow or purchase the better grains.

Bhaṭulá is said to have been the cause of the elevation of the Bhadauriás, and the story, absurd as it may appear, is commonly believed in the neighbourhood of Bhadáwar, and is not denied by the Bhadauriás themselves. One of the Bhadauriá chiefs, Gopal Singh, went to pay his respects to the Emperor Muhammad Shah. The chief had very large eyes, so much so, as to attract the attention of the Emperor, who asked him how he obtained them. The chief, who was a wit, replied that in his district nothing but Arhar was grown, and that from the constant practice of straining at swallowing Bhaṭulá, his eyes had nearly started out of his head. The Emperor was pleased at his readiness, and bestowed on him other Parganahs on which he could produce the finer grains.—See Bhadauriá.

Bhaṭṭhí, بهٹهي भट्ठी

A liquor shop; a distillery.

Bhaṭṭhídár, بهٹهي‌دار भट्ठीदार

A person who manufactures and sells spirituous liquors.

Bhawan, بهون भवन

A house; a temple; a fort.

Bhaiyábánṭ, بهيابانٹ भैयाबांट

See Bhaíbanṭ and Bhaiyáchára.

Bihanḍ, بهنڈ बिहंड

Land cut up by a torrent; according to the Gharáibu'l-lughát.

Bikrí, بكري बिक्री

Sale. From Bikná بكنا to be sold.

Bilahbandí, بله‌بندي बिलहबनदी

The Glossary is correct under Bílabandy; but in the North West, the word is most usually applied to arrangements made for securing the revenue.

Billí-loṭan, بلي‌لوٹن बिल्लीलोटन

Valerian. The name is derived from its reputed effect upon cats, who are said to be so delighted with its fragrance, as to roll about in their ecstasies. From billí بلي a cat, and loṭná لوٹنا to wallow; to roll.

Bilaungí, بلونگي बिलौंगी

A species of grass.

Binaulá, بنوله बिनौला

Cotton seed. It is much used as fodder for cattle, and when steeped in oil makes a capital lamp.

Binauriyá, بنوريه बिनौरिया

The name of a herb which grows about a foot and a half high in fields which have been sown with Kharíf crops. It bears several little flowers of a purple colour, and is given as fodder to horned cattle.

Birhána, برهانه बिरहाना

Lands in which culinary herbs are produced.—Rohilkhand.

Birinjphúl, برنجپهول बिरिंजफूल

A species of rice.—See Dhan.

Birkah, برکه बिर्का

A pond ; a small well.

Birrá, بِرّا बिर्रा

Gram and barley sown in the same field. Bejara and Bejar are the more usual terms.

In Dehli it is applied to Chaná, or gram, injured by wet.

It is also the name of a ceremony connected with the building of a house.—E. Oudh.

Birwá, بروا बिरवा

A tree. In Eastern Oudh it is the name given to the labourer employed upon the Daurí or Berí, *q.v.*

Birwáhí, برواهي बिरवाही

An orchard. From Birwa بروا a plant ; a tree.

Bisátí, بساتي बिसाती

A pedlar. From the Hindí Bisát بسات means ; capital ; stock. The Arabic Bizá'at بضاعت has also the same signification. "Pars opum," says Golius, "quæ impenditur in mercaturam, lucroque exponitur." Bisátí, etc., is sometimes spelt with an Arabic ط but incorrectly ; though, as Bisát بساط means a carpet spread out, there may appear to be some reason in calling بساطي a pedlar ; as in that mode Bisátís usually dispose of their goods at country fairs.

Bishnprítdár, بشن‌پريتدار बिष्णप्रीतदार

Grantees of Brahmin caste to whom land has been assigned in the name of Bishn or Vishnu, from religious and charitable motives by Zamíndárs.—Benares.—E. Oudh.

Bisht, بشت बिष्ट

A provincial term in Kamáon for a kind of Talúkdár, whose office is in the gift of Government.

Biskhapra, بسکهپره बिसखपरा

The name of a grass which is used in medicine (*Trianthema pentandra*). It spreads over the ground, and forms a circle of nearly a yard in diameter.

Bisahrú, بسهرو बिसहरू

A purchaser. From Bisahná بسهنا to buy.

Biṭhak, بٹهک बिठक

Ant hills.—Eastern Oudh and Benares. Literally, a seat or platform, where people meet to converse.*

Bitaurá, بتوره बितौरा

A heap of dried cow dung, called Battaiya in Rohilkhand.

Bitrábandí, بترابندي बित्राबन्दी

The same as Bilahbandí, *q.v.*—Saugor.

Bo, بو बो

Cultivation. It is usually combined with Jot, which signifies the same. Bo is the verbal root of Boná, to sow.

Boárá, بوارا बोआरा

Seed time; sowing. Boáí بواي, Báwag باوگ, and Boní بوني, are also used. From Boná بونا, to sow.

* Also, and perhaps more generally, especially in the second sense it is spelt, बैठक baiṭhak, from बैठना to sit.—B.

Bob, بوب बोब

The sowing of grain by the drill.—Bundelkhand.

The term Jaiyá is so applied in Dehli; and Wair in Rohilkhand and the Doáb.—See Bansa.

Bodá, بودا बोदा

A buffalo.—Saugor.

Bodar, بودر बोदर

A place to stand on for throwing the Daurí or basket by which water is raised to a higher level.—Benares.

Pairá is the corresponding word in Dehli.—See Daurí, Boka, Berí.

Boíbáchh, بوںباچه बोइबाछ

Assessment to be realized on cultivation.—Dehli. From بونا to sow and باچه selection, division. See Printed Glossary under Bach.

Bojh, بوجه बोझ

Literally, a load. In agricultural language it comprises about five Dhokas of corn.—See Dabia and Bel.

Bojhbaṭái, بوجه بٹائي बोझबटाई

A mode of division by stocks, or bundles of mowed corn.—Rohilkhand. It is derived from the preceding word.

Boká, بوکه बोका

A basket, pail, or leather bag, for throwing water to a higher elevation: called also Berí and Daurí (which see). This word is not in Shakspeare's Dictionary, but it would appear to be common in India.

Búd, بود बूद

Literally, existing; being; from the Persian بود "was."

In fiscal language Búd is much used in combination with other words, as Hastobúd, Búd-nabúd.—See Hastobúd.

Búk, بوک बूक

Land recovered by the recession of a river.—Rohilkhand.

Búkárá, بوکارا बूकारा

Bears the same meaning, but is applied only when the land is rendered useless, by a deposit of sand.—Rohilkhand.

Bulandí, بلندي बुलन्दी

High land. From Buland, high.

Bun, بن बुन

Unground coffee. Coffee before it is made into kahwa قهوه.

Búnga, بونگه बूंगा

A stack of Bhús, or straw. It is frequently pronounced Bonga.

Búnt, بونت बूंट

A green unripe gram (*Cicer arietinum*).—See Chaná.
Also used for gram in general.

Burída, بريده बुरीदा

Fields cut by stealth by a cultivator. From the Persian burídan بريدن to cut down.—Rohilkhand.

Burrí, بُرّي बुर्री

Sowing, by dropping seed from the hand into the furrow; instead of sowing broadcast, or with the drill. The words Gurr' Gullí, Sí, are also so applied.

Bora, بوره बोरा

A sack for holding rice.

Boro, بورو बोरो

Marsh rice. The "Fasl," which is added to the word in the Printed Glossary, means the harvest of this rice.

Bauchhár, بوچهار बौछार

Wind and driving rain.

Baulí, بولي बौली

Synonymous with a Khas settlement, according to section 12, Reg. IX. of 1805. The word may be presumed to be meant for Bhaolí. In Behar it is equivalent to Batáí, *q.v.*

Boáí, بوائي बोआई

Sowing. Boní, Bawera and Boara have the same meaning.—See Boara.

Babúl, ببول बबूल
Babúr, ببور बबूर

The name of a tree. Called also Kíkar (*Acacia Arabica*, Roxb.) —See Printed Glossary under Bavalla. The wood is much used in making agricultural implements, such as ploughs, sugar mills, etc., and in the construction of carts. The Babúl produces also a valuable gum, and its bark, being a powerful astringent, is used in tanning by Chamárs.

Bádámí, بادامي बादामी

A species of rice. (See further under Dhan.)

Badbácha, بدباچه बदबाचा

A false or fraudulent Bach or division.—Dehli

Badí, بدي बदी

The dark half of the month; from full to new moon.

Badhiyá, بڈھیا बढ़िया

A disease affecting Jawár, Bájra, sugar cane, and Indian corn, which prevents the head from shooting.

Bagár, بگار बगार

Pasture ground.—Bundelkhand.

Applied generally as synonymous with Banjar.

Bagarí, بگری बगरी

A species of rice cultivated chiefly in the province of Benares. —See Dhan.

Bahera, بہیرہ बहेरा

The Belleric Myrobalan (*Terminalia bellerica*, Roxb.)

Bajídár, بجیدار बजीदार

An agricultural servant in Rohilkhand who takes corn as a recompense for his labour, in distinction to a Mihdar who receives money. The latter is derived from محنت labour, and might therefore apply equally to both.

Bajhwat, بجھوٹ बझवट

Stalk of cereals, without the ear.—Eastern Oudh and Gorakhpúr.

Bakárá, بکارا बकारा

Intelligence forwarded by word of mouth. From Bak باک speech.

Bakel, بکیل बकेल

Twine made from the root of the Dhak tree. The word is chiefly used in the Eastern Provinces, not in the North-West.

Bakhá, بکھا बखा

Grass kept for pasturage.—Rohilkhand.

Bakhár, بکهار बखार
Bakhárí, بکهاري बखारी

A granary or store house.—Khán Arzú spells it بخار.

Bakhar, بکهر बखर

A kind of plough or bullock hoe in use in Bundelkhand, Saugor and Malwa. Its use has been fully described under Bákhar, but the more correct and usual pronunciation is Bakhar.

Bakolí, بکولي बकोली

Name of a green caterpillar destructive to rice crops.

Baláhar, بلاهر बलाहर

A low caste servant; a village guide or messenger. The word is not generally in use to the East of Allahabad. In the "Gharáíbu'l Loghát" it is spelt بلادهر Baládhar. The word is probably derived from bulana بلانا to call; to summons; just as another village menial, the Dauṛáha, is derived from dauṛna دوڙنا to run.

Balbhog, بلبهوگ बलभोग

Taking possession by force of another's right. The word is derived from the Sanskrit Bal बल force, and Bhog भोग possession; wealth; enjoyment.

Bald, بلد बलद

Bullocks; horned cattle. The word is not in the Dictionaries, though Baldiya بلديا is given as a cow-herd, a bullock driver.

Baldeo, بلديو बलदेव

A cow-herd. From the preceding word.

Baluá, بلوا बलुआ

Sandy. The word is used chiefly in Benares.—See Doras.

Balsundar, بلسندر बलसुन्दर

The name of a kind of soil in Azimgaṛh. The origin of all these words is bálú بالو sand.

Bamíṭhá, بميتها बमीठा

A term applied to ant hills in the Lower Doáb. Bámbhí بانبهي which is the correct word, is used in the North West, and Bithak in Eastern Oudh. Also a snake-hole. Probably derived from मर्मि a stinging insect, and स्थानं a place.

Bamhní, بمهني बम्हनी

Light red soil.—Eastern Oudh.

Banbhánṭa, بن بهانٹه बनभांटा

The wild egg plant (*Solanum melongena*).

Banchari, بن چري बनचरी

A high jungle grass, the leaves of which are much like the Jawar. Wild elephants are very fond of this grass, which is known also by the name of Baro.

Bandá, بندا बन्दा

A grain magazine above ground.—Saugor.

Bandhán, بندهان बनधान

A pension.

Bandhán, بندهان बनधान

Bandhíá, بندهيا बंधीया

Raised earthen embankments for flooding lands. Bándh from bándhná باندهنا to bind, is in more general use.—See Bandhwás.

Bandhán, بندهان बंधान

Bandhúr, بندهور बंधूर

Purchase of grain in advance of the harvest.—Saugor.

Bandhwás, بندهواس बनधवास

Land embanked all round, or in such manner as to retain the water. It is also generally applied to level ground; uneven ground being called Tagar, and when surrounded by embankments Tagar Bandhia.—Jabalpúr.

Bandlí, بندلي बनदली

A species of Rohilkhand rice. Called also Raímunia and Tilokchandan.—See Dhan.

Bandrí, بندري बनदरी

A grass which is found in fields of rice and Kodo. It grows to the height of about two feet, and has an ear, but produces no grain. It is used as fodder for cattle.

Bandtál, بندتال बनदताल

Damming a water course for the purpose of irrigation.

Bangá, بنگا बंगा

Is the name given to the white kind of Sarson (*Sinapis dichotoma*, Roxb.) It is also applied locally to well-water, slightly brackish.—Central Doáb.

Bangká, بنگکا बंगका

An aquatic beetle which eats rice plants. It is said to manufacture something like a boat from leaves, and to paddle itself along from plant to plant. It is harmless when the water is let out from the field. It is also called Katua.—Benares.

Bangkí, بنگکي बंगकी

A species of rice cultivated in Benares.—See Dhan.

Bangkaṭaiyá, بنگکٹیا बंगकटइया

See Jawasa and Bhatkataiya.

Bangaunṭhá, بن‌گونٹھا बनगौंठा

Cowdung found in the forests.—See Bankanda.

Bangaliyá, بنگلیا बंगलिया

Literally, Bengali. A species of rice cultivated in the Eastern part of these provinces.—See Dhan.

Banínhár, بنّیہار बन्नीहार

The word is used to signify a ploughman, or labourer, whose services are paid in Banní, or in kind.—Benares.

Banjin, بنجن बंजिन

Land close by the village.

Also the name of a weed about three feet high, which springs up with Kharíf crops. It is much sought after by Fakírs who practice Alchemy.

Bankhará, بنکھرا बनखरा

Lands on which cotton has grown during the past season.—Central Doáb.

The word is derived from ban, cotton, which though very commonly used in this sense, is not in the dictionaries. It is not improbable that it is so applied, because a field of cotton bears resemblance to a ban बन or forest. Baraundha is more commonly used in the same sense as Bankhara, in Rohilkhand and the Upper Doáb; and Múḍí (perhaps from مونڈنا to cut, to shave) in Dehli.

Kapseṭ is also very generally used for a field of cut cotton; from the Sanskrit karpas कर्पास, the cotton plant, or undressed cotton.

Bankaṇḍá, بن‌کنڈا बनकनडा

Cowdung found in a jungle or forest, or dried for fuel. From Ban بن a forest, and Kanḍa کنڈا cowdung. Bangautha is also used in this sense. Arní Kandá is likewise applied to this useful article of Hindu economy; from the Sanskrit आरण्य a forest. In Dehli this is corrupted into Rana, and coupled with گوسا Gosa, *i.e.* a cake of cowdung. The familiar words U'pla and Gobar are applied to that which is collected at home.

Bankar, بنکر बनकर

Spontaneous produce of jungle or forest land, such as gums, brushwood, honey, etc.* It is generally supposed that the person who possesses the right of collecting Bankar, or any tax or cess in lieu of it, holds necessarily a Zamíndárí title in the ground which produces it. But this is an erroneous impression. The Sudder Dewáni Adaulat have ruled that the sale of Bankar does not convey Zamíndárí right. One case is reported in which A. purchased, at a public sale, a portion of a Zamíndárí.—B. purchased another portion, besides the bankar of the whole estate. The Court ruled that the purchase made by B. conveyed to him a right over all the forest timber of the entire estate, though growing on the portion purchased by A. It was declared however that the latter from his right in the soil was permitted to clear away the trees, and to cultivate it; the proceeds of the timber felled appertaining to B.—(See "Reports," Vol. II., p. 105.)

It will be seen also at Section 9, Reg. I. of 1804, that the British Government consider Bankar as a thing altogether distinct from Zamíndárí.

Bankas, بنکس बनकस

A grass used in making ropes.

* See J. A. S. B. for 1845, p. 543.—E. *add.*

Bankaṭí, بنكٹي बनकटी

The right obtained by clearing jungle, and bringing it into cultivation.—Benares.

Banní, بني बन्नी

A portion of grain given to a labourer as remuneration for his services.—Benares.

Bansá, بنسا बनसा

A grass which grows in fields of rice and dál. It is given as fodder for cattle.

Bansí, بنسي बनसी

A kind of wheat with blackish ears.—Hoshangábad.

Bantariá, بنتريا बन्तरिया

A class of wood rangers in some of the northern Parganahs of Gorakhpúr, holding about 20,000 acres granted by the native government in lieu of police services. As the services are no longer performed, the lands have been resumed, and settled at very easy rates with the occupant Bantariás.

Bar, بڑ बड़

The Banian tree; the large Bengal or Indian fig tree (*Ficus Indica*). It is commonly also known as the Bargat बरगत.

Baráhí, براهي बराही

A small species of sugar cane.—Saugor, Lower Doáb, and Bundelkhand.

Barár, برار बरार

Tod says (Annals of Raj. Vol. I. p. 143). "Barrar is an

indefinite term for taxation, and is connected with the thing taxed, as Halbarrar, plough-tax."

An apportionment of Bhyachara Kists (or instalments of rent) according to the agreement of the village community. Generally, any division; bearing much the same meaning as Báchh. The word, though common in the Doáb and Western India, is not found in Hindí dictionaries.

Barban, بربن बर्बन

A North wind according to Khan Arzú.—See Dándwára.

Bardí, بردي बर्दी

Light stony soil. Also Bardár.—Saugor.

Barehṭá, بريهتا बरेहटा

Land of the third quality; also a plot of ground on which sugar cane has been lately grown.—Saugor. See Bhatkataiya.

Barej, بريج बरेज
Bareja, بريجا बरेजा

A betel or pán garden.

Bargan, برگن बरगन

Partition; a share.—Hoshangabad.

Barhá, برها बरहा

A channel for the passage of water from a well to a field, or from one field to another. To the eastward it may be considered the smallest size of watercourse; the size in the ascending scale is indicated by the terms Barhá, Nalkí, Nalí, Narwá and Gúl. But in the West, Barhá is by no means a small water course. The word is probably derived from Baṛhna بڑهنا to increase, though the usual mode of spelling it is against that etymology.

A field in which cows are fed; a rope, or string; especially one by which a harrow is drawn, or one that is thrown over a cart to keep the load from falling or getting injured.

In parts of Central and Upper Doáb, Barhá is the term applied to the land of a township which is farthest from the homestead. Bárá is the nearest to the village; Manjha between both.

Baṛhiyá, بڑھیا बढ़िया

The name of a sugar millstone, extracted from the Chanar quarries.

Baṛhotarí, بڑھوتري बड़ोतरी

See Barhí.

Baṛkuiyán, بڑکویان बड़कुइआं

A Kachha well, *i.e.* one without a cylinder of masonry.—E. Oudh.

Baro, برو बरो

The name of a high jungle grass.—See Banchari.

Baronkhá, برونکھا बरोंखा

A kind of sugar cane with long thin joints.

Baraundhá, بروندھا बरोंधा

Cotton land.—Rohilkhand.

Barroh, بروہ बरोंह

A name given to the uplands in the Parganah of Jánibrast, *i.e.* the right bank of the Jumna, Zillah Etowah.

Barsáná, برسانا बर्साना

To winnow the grain; literally, to cause to rain.

Bartush, برتش बरतुश

Land sown with sugar cane, after a rice crop.—Rohilkhand.

Barat, برت बरत

A disease which affects rice crops.

A leathern girth, or large cable; especially one used for drawing water by a púr, or large well bag.

In the Dehli territory, Barat, or Barit, is also used to signify the Government Jama, or a portion of it.—See Bharit.

Basíkat, بسیکت बशीकत

Inhabited. From Basna بسنا to dwell.

Basít, بسیت बशीत

The head manager in a village; the same as Mahetya or Mukaddam.—Central Doáb.

Basend, بسینڈ बिसेंड

An edible root which is found in jhíls or marshes.

In Rohilkhand the word signifies a Khákrob, or sweeper.

Basgit, بسگت बसगित

Homestead; site of a village residence. From بسنا to dwell. The word is pure Hindí, but is more used in Eastern Hindustan than in Western.

Basúlí, بسولي बसूली

A small instrument for cutting. The diminutive of Basúla, an adze.

Bastah, بستہ बस्ता

A cloth in which papers are bound up; a bundle of papers. From the Persian بستن to bind.

Baswárí, بسواري बसवारी
Basaur, بسور बसौर

A bamboo garden. From बांश a bamboo.

Baṭ, بٹ बट

A partition; division. From بٹنا to be divided.

Baṭái, بٹائي बटाई

Is derived from the word preceding, and signifies the same as the Metayer system of Europe; but it includes not only the literal Metayer, *i.e.* "à moitié fruit," but the "tier franc," or any share into which the crops may be divided. In poor lands a batái of one-sixth only is not unfrequently the extent of the Zamíndár's demand.

Batái [illegible]ya is applied to a division which gives nine shares t[illegible] one party, and seven to another.—Benares.—See Hariáṅw.

Baṭenth, بٹینتهه बटेंथ
Baṭania, بٹنیا बटनिया

Proprietor, or holder of a share.—Central Doáb.—See above, under Baṭ and Baṭái.

Baṭes, بٹیس बटेस

A passage; a pathway. Baṭía بٹیا is in more general use in the same sense. Both are from the Sanskrit Báṭ बाट a road, a highway.

Baṭhán, بٹهان बठान

Pasture ground. From بیٹهنا to sit, to settle, or more probably from बल्द a bullock, and स्थान or ठान a place. Eastern Oudh. —See Baisak; which is also similarly derived. *Abathán* is more usually applied to the little shed erected by cowherds in the jungles to sleep in at night, the cattle being all collected round it. It is also called **अरार** or **अड़ाड़**, *q.v.*

Bathuá, بتهوا **बथुआ**

A herb which springs up with Rabi' crops, and in the neighbourhood of water. It is sometimes cooked as a pot-herb by the poorer classes (*Chenopodium album*).

Bathiyá, بتهيا **बथिया**

See Bitaura.

Batúrí, بتوري **बतूरी**

A name given in Benares to Chaní, or the small kind of Chana, *q.v.*

Baṭolan, بٹولن **बटोलन**

Baṭoran, بٹورن **बटोरन**

Gathering or collecting grain in one place at the time of harvest. From بٹورنا baṭorná, to gather up.

Batar, بتر **बतर**

Land in a state fit for the plough.—Saugor. In the Panjab I have heard watar **वतर** used to signify the rain which falls in January, and by softening the soil enables the young wheat to sprout and grow.—B.

Baṭwár, بٹوار **बटवार**

A custom or police officer stationed on a road.

A tax gatherer, who collects taxes in kind.

Bawáda, بواده **बवादा**

A herb something like the Turmeric. It springs up in the rains, and it is sometimes sown, as it is considered a specific in rheumatism.

Baib, بيب बैब

Afar off—at a distance.—Bundelkhand.

Baijilá, بيجلا बैजिला

A species of black pulse.—E. Oudh.

Baikhaṭ, بيكهٹ बैखट

Sale.—Eastern Oudh and Benares.

Baisak, بيسك बैसक

A spot in a jungle to which cattle are sent out to graze.—Dehli. It is elsewhere called Kharak (a cowshed) and Bathán.—*q.v.* The word is also applied, generally, to old and worn out animals.

Chánda, چانده चांदा

A common station of the revenue survey.

Chák, چاك चाक

A wheel. Especially applied amongst cultivators to the pulley over which the lao, or well-rope passes; called Bhon in Dehli, Chalí and Charkhí in Rohilkhand, Garrí and Garílí in Benares and Bundelkhand. But these four last terms are only applied if the wheel is formed out of one block of wood.

Chák means also a mill; rings of earth for forming a well; a vessel in which sugar is manufactured, after being transferred from the Chásní or Karahí.—See Bel.

Chánṭí, چانٹي चांटी

Cesses levied from artizans and others. From Chánṭná چانٹنا to squeeze, to press.

Cháunrí, چاونري चौंरी

A police station; usually the kotwal's.—Saugor.

Cháp, چاپ चाप

The refuse of the Jharberí after the Pála is beaten from it. Dehli and Upper Doáb.—See Jharberí.

Chápṛe, چاپڑي चापड़े

Cakes of cow-dung. They are also known by the names of Gobar, U′pla, Gosa, Doja, Theprí and Chot.

Chára, چاره चारा

Truss; sheaf; grass; food.

Chásní, چاسني चासनी

A pan in which the juice of the sugar cane is boiled. It is much the same as the Karáhí, except that it is somewhat larger. From the Chásní it is transferred into the Chák, *q.v.*

It is probably a corruption of the Persian چاشني flavour, syrup.

Cháwal, چاول चावल

Rice undressed, but cleared of the husk.

Chíbhar, چيبهر चीभर

Land which remains long moist.—Saugor.

Chík, چيک चीक

Chíkar, چيکر. चीकर

Mud; slime. The name of Chík is consequently given to the turf or rushes on which the water pot of the Dhenklí is made to rest, when it is brought to the top of the well. Párchha and Chilwáí are likewise so applied.

Chíkaṭ, چيکٹ चीकट

Chikṭí, چکٹي चिकटी

Clayey soil.—Saugor.

Chíta, چيته चीता

The name of a creeping herb. It is used in medicine as a cure for leprosy (*Plumbago Zeylonica*).

Chihra, چهره चिहरा

A descriptive roll of a servant or fugitive. Literally, a face.

Chíná, چينا चीना

Canary seed (*Panicum Miliaceum*) (*Panicum pilosum*, Roxb.)

It is sown and reaped in the hot season, after nearly all the rabi' crops have been cut. It requires much irrigation, and is a precarious crop; hence the saying:

चीना जी का लेना
चौदह पानी देना
ब्यार चले तो न लेना न देना

"Take of master Chíná,
Give him fourteen waterings,
Let the wind blow, and you'll have nought to give or take;"

i.e. You may irrigate your Chíná as much as you like, but a blast will destroy it, and you get nothing for your pains.

Chench, چينچ चेंच

A herb which springs up in uncultivated places during the rainy season. Its fruit is frequently called Jonk, from its resemblance to a leech.

Chhaí, چهئي छई

A pad, to prevent laden bullocks from being galled.

Chháj, چهاج छाज

A basket used in winnowing grain.

Chhákná چهاكنا छाकना

To clean the water of a well.

Chháp, چهاپ छाप

A stamp; generally the Potdar, or cashier's, stamp.

In Dehli and the Upper Doáb it is the name applied to a small bundle or heap of thorns about a foot high. When larger, it is called Khewa کهیوا *q.v.**

Chhápá, چهاپا छापा

The village seal used to impress grain with.—See Chank and Thapa.

It also means the heap of refuse corn and chaff which is formed in winnowing. In a heap of cleaned corn there is about four per cent Chhápá. Also, a small heap of grain appropriated to purposes of charity.

Chhápá is likewise in some places the name given to the basket used for throwing water out of a pond, for the purpose of irrigation.—See Berí, Boka, and Daurí.

Chhár, چهار छार

A bank of a river; hence Chharchittí, a permit, or pass, over a river.

Chhedá, چهیدا छेदा

A destructive little animal similar to the weevil (*Calandria granaria*). From Chhed چهید a hole. It is also the name of the disease which the corn sustains when affected by the ravages of this animal.

Chhída, چهیدا छीदा

Thin, not close—according to Shakespear's Dictionary, "said of a person or animal whose legs are much separated." But it is also applied to corn fields, or plantations, in opposition to Ghaná گهنا or Ghinká گهنکا close, thick.

* See J.A.S. Bombay, No. III., p. 119.—E. *add.*

Chhímí, چهيمي छीमी

A pod; a legume.

Chhínká, چهينكا छींका

An ox muzzle.—Dehli; called Múkha, Mushka, and Jalí in Rohilkhand and the Doáb, Khonta in Benares, and Muska in Bundelkhand. Also a net for hanging pots, etc.—(See Jab.)

Chhínṭa, چهينٹا छींटा

From chhínṭná چهينٹنا to sprinkle; a field in which peas and linseed have been sown by broad-casting, while the rice crops are standing on the ground. When the rice is cut, these crops are left to grow, and harvested in the beginning of Chayt. In Dehli, the term Chhánta is applied to throwing more seed amongst a growing rice crop.

The same word is employed in Gorakhpúr to signify lands in which seed has been scattered after a single ploughing; more particularly at the extremities of villages, with a view to secure possession.

Chhíyúl, چهيول छीयूल

A jungle tree; called also Dhak, *q.v.*

Chheoná, چهيونا छेवना

To extract juice from a tar tree. Literally, "to slice," as the bark is sliced off and a pot hung underneath to catch the sap as it exudes.—B.

Chhikáí, چهكائي छिकाई

Bears the same meaning in Rohilkhand as Farighkhatána, *q.v.* The word is perhaps derived from Chhinkwáná چهنكوانا to cancel.

Chhilká, چهلكا छिलका

Bark; rind.

Chhiṭuá, چهٹوا छिटुआ

Sowing broad-cast. From Chhínṭná چهینٹنا to sprinkle.—Benares.

The usual words in the Doáb, Rohilkhand, and Dehli, are Paberí, or Pabar phenk dena, or Jel karna. In Bundelkhand it is called Chhíntab, from the same root Chhínṭná.

Chhitrí, چهتري छितरी

Said in Shakespear's Dictionary to be "a small basket without lid or handle," but it is more generally understood to be a broken basket, or Daliya; one nearly ineffective from being worn out.

Chholá, چهوله छोला

Gram—Saugor and Bundelkhand. Also the title of the man who cuts the standing sugar cane. He strips off the leaves, and lops off the head, which he receives as his perquisite, besides about ten canes per diem during the time he is employed. The name is derived from chholna چهولنا to pare, to scrape.

Chholní, چهولني छोलनी

A scraper.

Chhaur, چهور छौर

A large stack of Juwar or Bajra collected for fodder, comprising several smaller stacks called Syí. In years of plenty this is added to, till the village stock amounts to several hundreds of maunds.—Dehli.

In some districts, as in Rohilkhand, this is known by the name of Garrí; elsewhere by the name of Kundar and Kharaí. —See Garrí.

Chhadám, چهدام छदाम

Literally, six dams; equal to two damrís. The proper

amount is six and a quarter dams, but by abbreviation it is called Chhadám.—See Damrí, Adhela, and Ganda.

Chhahkur, چهكر छकुर

Division of crops where the Zamíndár gets only one-sixth.—E. Oudh.

Chhakṛá, چهكڑا छकड़ा

A carriage. It is built on the principle of a bailí, has no sides like the Garí, but carries burdens on a sort of platform. It is much used for the conveyance of cotton, to which its construction is well adapted. The names of some of its component parts are Nasaurí, Goriá, Tuláwa, Akarí, Koṛha, Phar, Shagún, Ank, Típh, Dántuá, Chaukhará and Bichuá, the uses of which it is needless to particularise.—See Garí.

Chhaṭáo, چهٹاو छटाव

Clearing rice from the husk.

Chhatrí, چهتري छत्री

A small ornamented pavilion, generally built over a place of interment, or a cenotaph in honor of a Hindú chief. Literally, "an umbrella."

Chihel, چهيل चिहेल

Wet oozy land. From chihlá چہلا mud.

Chikhar, چكهر चिखर

The husk of Chaná, *q.v.*

Chikharwái, چكهروائي चिखरवाई

Wages for weeding.—E. Oudh; called generally Niraí and Naulaí elsewhere.

Chiknáwat, چکناوٹ चिकनावट

A clayey soil. From Chikná چکنا greasy; oily.

Chillá, چله चिल्ला

A holy place where fakírs abide: so called from the initiatory abstinence of forty days (in Persian چهله chahilá) which they undergo.

Chilwáí, چلوائي चिलवाई

See an explanation of its meaning under Chík.

Chimbur, چمبر चिंबुर

An inferior kind of grass which grows in the Bhattí territory. It is perhaps the same as the Chaprúda of Hariana.

Chin, چن चिन

A kind of sugar-cane.—Upper Doáb and Rohilkhand.—See Ikh.

Chirchirá, چرچره चिर्चिरा

Name of a medicinal plant (*Achyranthes aspera*). Its ashes also are used in washing linen. It is also called Chíchara, Chitirra, and Satjíra. In Sanskrit it is known by the name of Apámárg अपामार्ग. There is a white and a red kind. The former, if it is carried about the person, is firmly believed to render one invulnerable, particularly against scorpions, and the application of it to the part affected is as immediate and certain a remedy as was the application of basil according to the classical writers.

Chirchitta, چرچته चिरचिट्टा

The name of a grass which somewhat resembles young Bajra. It produces an ear like that of the Kangní کنگني (*Panicum Italicum*), and its grain is about the size of a barley corn. This plant also is said in native herbals to have secret virtue. If any one will eat a chatták of its grain he will not feel the pressure of hunger for twenty-one days. As the experiment is easily made, and it is not a common practice to eat Chirchiṭṭa, we may presume it is somewhat nauseous.

Chiṭṭhá, چِٹّھا चिट्ठा

A rough note; servants' pay; a memorandum.

Chiwáná, چِوانا चिवाना

A place for cremation; called also Chihaí and Chihaní. These three are derived from Ksháí, ashes. Marghaṭ, Bhoídagdha and Smasan, or Samsan (in Benares) are also employed to signify the same.

Choyá, چویا चोइया

A hole dug in the dry bed of a river to get water. Also a name commonly applied to rivulets.

Chohá, چوها चोहा

A small well. Both these words are derived from Chúná چونا to leak, to be filtered.

Choká, چوکا चोका

Rice.—Saugor.

Chonḍá, چونڈا चोंडा

Kachha wells where the water is near the surface.—E. Oudh.

Chúá, چوا चूआ

Chúá, Battú, or Marsa forms one of the chief Kharíf products of the hills. The flowers are of a fine red color. It is supposed to be the *Amaranthus oleraceus.*

Chúá is also the siliqua, seed vessel, or pod of a pulse.

Chugáí, چگائي चुगाई

Pasturage. From Chugná چگنا to peck; to graze.

Chonchí, چونچي चोंची

A tiny creeper which grows round the Piyází plant and ripens its seeds at the same time with it. The Piyází seeds are eaten by the poorer classes, and during the famine at Ambala in 1861 cases occurred of persons being poisoned by eating Piyází bread in which Chonchí had become mixed. I was not able to learn the botanical name of either plant. Piyází grows spontaneously in fallow lands in April and May.—B.

Chullí, چلي चुल्ली

The supports which are placed below stacks of straw or stores of grain; called by English farmers staddles. In some places the ground is merely cleaned and elevated, and no supports are raised; it is then called Gháí.

Chullú, چلو चुल्लू

The palm of the hand contracted for the purpose of holding water. Sometimes incorrectly pronouned Challú.—See Ajaulí and Chungal.

Chún, چون चून

Chúní, چوني चूनी

Flour; pulse coarsely ground.

Chungal, چنگل चुंगल

A handful of any thing dry; as Chullú is of any thing liquid. Khonch is used in the same sense. In Rohilkhand, Lap, or Laf, is as much as two hands joined can hold; but in Benares, Dehli, and the Doab, it means only one handful.—See Ajaulí, Chullú.

Chúntrú, چونترو चूंत्रू

Head man of a district in Dehra Dún.

Chopná, چوپنا चोपना

To throw water from a Daurí, *q.v.*—Úlchab dena is the equivalent term in Bundelkhand.

Chot, چوٹ चोट

An ingenious way adopted by shepherds and husbandmen of folding a blanket or sheet into a covering for the head and shoulders, making it nearly impervious to the rain. It is somewhat similar to the mode by which a Scotchman converts a plaid into a sleeved great coat. It also signifies the tying the end of a blanket in a knot, and so placing it over the head, which in some places is called Ghúnghí; but that word is generally otherwise applied.—See Ghúnghí.

Chau, چو चौ

A ploughshare.—See Hal and Halas.

Chaukhá, چوکھا चौखा

A station where four boundaries meet.—See Chaugadda.

Chaukaṛá, چوکڑا चौकडा

Division of a crop, in which the cultivator gives only one-fourth; called also by the name of Chaukúṛ.

Chaulá, چولا चौला

A kind of pulse commonly cultivated in Hindústan (*Dolichos sinensis*). It is also called Rawás and Ramás; but it is best known throughout the country under its Persian name of لوبیا *lobiyá*.

Chauláí, چولائي चौलाई

The name of a weed which shoots up during the rainy season, particularly in old buildings (*Amaranthus polygamus*). It is also sometimes sown and eaten as a pot-herb. There are two kinds of Chauláí, red and green. The one is called Gandar, and the other Marsaí.

Chaunṛá, چونڑا चौंडा

A subterranean apartment for grain.

Chauntálí, چونتالي चौंताली

Cotton pods, in which the fibre is equal to one-fourth of the whole produce. Tiháli, in which the fibre is one-third. Pachdúlí (*i.e.* two out of five) when it amounts to about 16 seers in the maund.

Chaupál, چوپال चौपाल

Chaupár, چوپار चौपार

A small shed in which the village community meet; generally built by the head man of the village, and used by him in former days as a kind of Kachahrí or office.

Chaur, چور चौर

A large open space in the forest.—Rohilkhand.

A large tract of low land.—Eastern Oudh.

Achaur is one of those long low strips of semi-marshy land, formerly beds of small streams so common in Northern Bihár. They are generally appropriated for the purpose of growing rice and indigo.—B.

Chauráha, چوراهه चौराहा

The junction of four villages, or roads.—See Chaugadda.

Chaursí, چورسي चौरसी

A granary above ground.—Rohilkhand.

Chaus, چوس चौस

Land four times tilled.—Rohilkhand.

Chausinghá, چوسنگها चौसिंघा

A raised mound indicating where the boundaries of four villages meet.—See Chaugadda.

Chauthiyá, چَوتهيا चौथिया

A measure in general use for grain and about equal to a seer of wheat. Chaukarí is a quarter, and Adhelí is a half Chauthiyá. Five Chauthiyás are equal to a Kuro, or Paserí, and twenty Kuros to one Khanrí. These words are equally used in superficial measures. Thus an area which would require five Paserí of seed to sow it, is about equal to a Bígha (which in Hoshangabad is a little more than a statute acre, being 4,900 square yards), and was rated at about a Rupee of Revenue. A Khanrí would be about equal to four Rupees, and a Mání to twice that amount.—Saugor.—See Bísí and Jaríb.

Chautrá چوترا चौतरा

A Court; corrupted perhaps from Chabútra.

Chah, چه चह

A platform; a pier-head.

Chahlí, چهلي चहली

The wheel on which the rope revolves at the top of a well. —See Chák.

Chahorná, چهورنا चहोरना

To transplant.—Rohilkhand. Elsewhere it signifies to stick

up, to fix. The word Rompna is also frequently used to signify transplanting. In Dehli and the Upper Doáb, Chahorná, though rarely used, is preserved in the word Chahora, which signifies rice dibbled in a field, after being sown in a nursery.

Chahal, چهل चहल

A strong soil, ranking between Rauslí and Dákara, or Dánkra.—Dehli.

Chakká چکا चक्का

The weight (generally of clay) used to press down the small arm of the Dhenkla. The usual meaning is a wheel or circle, and the word may be therefore applied thus, as the Chakká is almost always of a circular form.

Chakkat, چکت चक्कत

The loss of a whole plot of ground by diluvion; the contrary of Ritkat.

Chakwand, چکونڈ चकवनड

A common weed, of which there are generally reckoned to be four kinds, though they bear but little resemblance to one another.—Chakwanḍ, Chakaundí or Kasaundí, Gulálí, Batoka. The Chakwanḍ, which grows from about eight inches to two feet high, and bears a long legume, is very common in Mango groves, and in fields grown with Kharíf crops. It is used by the poor people as a potherb.

Chaltí, چلتی चलती

Cultivated lands.—Dehli.

Chambal, چمبل चमबल

A log of wood with grooves, fixed on banks of canals. It is used in drawing water for the purposes of irrigation.

Chaná, چنا चना

Gram. *Cicer arietinum.* The origin of this word has been much disputed, but is, I believe, a corruption of the Portuguese *grama,* meaning *grain* in general.

There are generally reckoned to be three kinds of this widely-used legume:—1. Pílá (also called Rakswá, Chaptáí, and Kasárí in the Eastern part of these provinces); 2. Pachmil, which is a mixture of Pílá and Kassá; 3. Kassá, the superior kind.

There is also a small kind of Chaná, called Chaní and Batúrí, and Chaná itself is frequently to the Eastward called Rehla and Lona. But in general Lona is the name of the oxalic and acetic acid which forms on the leaf of the Chaná. It is used in this country in alchemical processes, and in the preparation of nitric and muriatic acid. Cloths are spread over the plants of the Chaná, and being well moistened by the deposition of dew, they readily absorb the acidulous salt, which the plants secrete abundantly on the surface of their leaves and shoots (Royle, "Antiquity of Hindu Med." p. 42). The presence of this acid is found to injure the feet occasionally when people walk in Chaná fields, and a local tradition has hence arisen that Sítá, when she was going to bathe in the Manwa river, is said to have cursed the plant, and directed that it should not be grown between that stream and the Gogra, and consequently no Chaná is now cultivated between those two rivers.

In the Western part of this Presidency there is a Kabulí Chaná sometimes grown. It differs from the Desí, or country Chaná in having a white flower and smaller leaf. It is also grown in the extreme East, and in Bengal, to the North of the Ganges. It is there considered a fit offering for the gods, probably on account of its rarity.

This useful grain is highly valued in India, and its praises have been sung by the poets. The following doggrel lines, which are attributed to the celebrated minister Bírbal, are greatly esteemed by the natives:—

सब देवों में महादेव बड़े सब अन्न में चकरवत चना
जाकी लमबी सी डार गुलाबसा फूल खूंटत खांटत होत घना
कहैं बीरबल सुनो साह अकबर नून औ मिर्च से अजब बना

Which may be thus literally translated,

"Among all gods, Mahadev is greatest; among all cereals, channá is king:
Whose stalk is longish, its flowers rose-coloured, the more it is picked the thicker it grows.
Quoth Bírbal, listen, Sháh Akbar, with salt and pepper it is wonderfully good."

The favorite way, however, of cooking grain is to parch it. It is then called Chabená, and is generally carried in the corner of the scarf to eat on a journey. By far the most common use of grain is as food for horses, for which purpose it is unrivalled.—B.

Chanchar, چانچر चंनचर

Land left untilled for one, two, or three years.

Chandá, چندا चन्दा

Subscription; assessment.

Chandelí, چنديلي चंदेली

A very fine species of cotton fabric, which is of so costly a description as to be used only in native courts. It is made from Berar, or Umrávatí, cotton, and every care is taken in its manipulation. The weavers work in a dark subterranean room, of which the walls are kept purposely damp to prevent the dust from flying about. The chief care is bestowed on the preparation of the thread, which, when of very fine quality, sells for its weight in silver. It is strange that women are allowed to take no part in any of the processes. From a correspondence published in Vol. X. of the "Journ. As. Soc. of Bengal," it would appear that the Chandelís are made solely from Narma cotton; but this is a mistake, for Umrávatí cotton is alone used, and the Narma, or Narma-ban, instead of being confined to Malwa, is cultivated in small quantities all over Hindustan, and its produce is in great request for the manufacture of the best kind of Brahmanical thread. It is a bushy plant, grows to the height of about seven feet, and lasts about six years.

Chandelís derive their name from the town of Chanderí, on the left bank of the Betwa, in Sindhia's territory.—(See Chandel.)

Chandeyá, چنديا चंदेया

Deep places.—Eastern Oudh.

Chaní, چني चनी

A small species of Chaná; called Batúrí in Benares.

Chaneṭh, چنيٹھ चनेठ

Drugs for cattle.

Changel, چنگيل चंगेल

A herb which springs out of old Kheras, or ruined buildings. It has a round leaf, and its seed, which is used as a medicine, is known generally by the name of Khabají. Also a round basket of straw.

Chanwán, چنوان चनवान

Name of a small species of millet.—Eastern Oudh.

Chaprí, چپري चपरी

A puddle. Also the name of a small pulse somewhat resembling Chaná.

Charí, چري चरी

Unripe Jawár, cut as fodder for cattle. It is always sown

much thicker than the Jawár which is intended for the threshing floor.

Charí is also the name given in the Lower Doáb to small portions of land held rent-free by cultivators: derived either from its chiefly producing fodder, or by a corruption from Sír.—See Chhír.

Charkhí, چرخي चरखी

The pulley by which water is raised from a well by two water-pots tied to the ends of a rope and raised alternately. Literally, a spinning wheel. It is generally made of pieces of bamboo lashed together in the form of a cylinder.—See Chák.

Charní, چرني चरनी

A feeding trough.

Charas, چرس चरस

The exudation of hemp flowers. It is collected in Nepal, and elsewhere also it is said, by persons running through a field of Ganja with leathern aprons to which the exudation adheres. In these provinces the Charas of Bokhara is most admired, and fetches double the price of the country product. Bahadúrgarh in the Dehli Territory appears the grand depôt for the Charas of the Western and Northern States.

Also, the large leathern bucket, or bag, used for filling water from wells; derived from چرسا leather. In some parts of the country it is called Púr and Moṭh. All parts of the apparatus of a well are differently called at different places. Thus, the upright posts over the well's mouth are in one place, Fílpáya (elephant leg), in another Thuní. The beam which they support is in one place called Bharsahá, in another Patao and Bharet. The rope is in one place called Bart, in another Lao. The reservoir into which the water is poured is in some places called Pareha, in others Chabacha, and so on.—See Arhaṭ, Bahoro, Chák, Chaktí, Charkhí, and Gararí.

Charwáhí, چرواهي चरवाही

Wages of a charwáha, grazier or herdsman, in grain. From Charná چرنا to feed, to graze.

Chatṛí, چتّري चटरी

The name of a herb which springs up with the rabi' grains. It is used as fodder for cattle, and the poorer class of cultivators eat the seeds of it mixed up with barley.

Chail, چيل चैल

Land twice tilled.—Rohilkhand.

Chain, چين चैन

Cultivated land.

Chaití, چيتي चैती

The harvest of the month Chayt (March-April). In Bundelkhand it is applied generally to the Rabi', or spring harvest.

Dáb, ڐاب डाब

The name of a grass, better known by the name of Kús or Kúsha. *(Poa cynosurides,* Kœn:) It is generally applied only to the first shoots of the Kús grass, and is called Dabsa in Rohilkhand. The extreme acuteness of its points is proverbial amongst Hindus. The intellects of a clever man are said to be as sharp as the point of a Dáb, or Kús, leaf (Sir W. Jones' Works, Vol. V. p. 79). Dáb is not in much request as fodder for cattle, but, when soaked, it makes very good twine, and is occasionally used in thatching houses. These are, however, profane uses: for the grass is especially holy, and is in great demand in almost all the votive offerings and religious ceremonies of the Hindus. It is considered very desirable that a man should die upon a bed of Dáb; and it is consequently the duty of attendant relations to spread the grass on the floor, and after covering it with a cloth, to lay the dying man upon it, in order that he may emit his last breath in that hallowed position.

Dábí, دابي दाबी

See Dabiya.

Ḍábak, ڈابک डाबक

Fresh well water.—Dabká is used in the same sense.

Ḍábar, ڈابر डाबर

Low ground where water settles; a small tank; a vessel for washing in.

Ḍákará, ڈاکرا डाकरा

Is the name of the best, or second best, quality of soil in the Upper Doáb or Dehli. It is sometimes pronounced Dhákar and Dankra.

The soil called Rauslí in many places ranks above Dákará.

Dál, دال दाल

"A pulse, *Phaseolus radiatus*, Linn., *Phaseolus aureus*, Roxb., green gram, or rayed kidney bean."—Ḳánún-i Islam.

In the North Western Provinces it is applied only to the split pea of Múng, Arhar, Urd, and a few other pulses (from *dalná* دلنا to grind coarsely); and there appears reason to apprehend error in the passage quoted from the "Ḳánún-i Islam." The Printed Glossary also says of Dol that it is a sort of pea.—See Dalia.

Ḍál, ڈال डाल

A bough. In Dehli and the Upper Doáb it is applied to the basket used for the purpose of raising water by artificial means from a canal. From *ḍálná* ڈالنا to throw, to fling. It is made sometimes of leather, but generally of Múnj or of Jhao. Ḍál irrigation is used where the course of the canal is much below the general level of the country, and is, in consequence of the labour attending it, more expensive than irrigation by Tor, which consists in merely breaking down the field ridge, and allowing the water to pass through it.

Dal, دل दल

Wild rice.

Dámcha, دامچہ दामचा

The platform on which a person is posted to protect crops.—Dehli. Jaunda and Tand are also used in this sense in Dehli; and the latter in Rohilkhand also; in the Doáb, Mattúla (from *maṭṭi*, earth), and Menra and Maiṅra* (from its position on the border of the field); and in Saugor, Marwa, for the same reason. Machán and Mácha are in common use elsewhere, and even within the limits of the local words above-mentioned.

Ḍámar, ڈامر डामर

Resin—more especially, in commerce, the resin of the Sál tree (*Shorea robusta*): also called Dhumná and Dhúná.

Dand, ڈانڈ डांड

High ground, opposed to Ḍábar; sterile Bhúr land; elevated land of Domat soil; also a fine; a land-mark; a stick. The word is spelt with either an initial ड or द.

Dáng, دانگ दांग

A hill or precipice; the summit of a mountain, as Lál-dáng. In Dehli, and generally in Upper India, the word is used to signify the high bank of a river. It is provincially corrupted into Dháng and Dhayang.—E.

Dángrá दांगडा is common in Nepalese for a hill.—B.

* *Meṅr*, *Menḍ*, مینڈ signifies a limit.

Ḍángar, ڈانگر डांगर

Superannuated horned cattle. It is applied also as a term of abuse to a fool. But Ḍángar, in Dehli, is not confined to old cattle; for it is there applied generally to horned cattle, exclusive of buffaloes.

Dántí, دانتي दांती

A sickle. From *dant*, a tooth.

Ḍánṭh, ڈانٹھ डांठ

Refuse of harvest floors, especially applied to Kharíf products; and so is synonymous with Jhora, *q.v.* It is also called Daṭuá and Ḍanthlá.—See Ḍanthlá.

Dánwán, دانوان दांवान

Burning stubble, or a conflagration in a forest. This word is provincially corrupted into *damar* and *do*, and is derived from the Sanskrit दावानल, a conflagration in a forest.—"Yates' Nalodaya," p. 353.

Dánwarí, دانوري दांवरी

See Daurí.

Dáo, داو दाव

A hatchet with a hooked point; a sickle. Among the Singphos and other savages of the north-eastern frontier it is the name of a heavy knife about two feet in length like the Nepalese kukarí.—B.

Dárú, دارو दारू

Spirituous liquor.

Dás, داس दास

This name, which literally means slave, is borne chiefly by men of the Baniá caste, by Bairágí Fakírs, and by Kayaths and

Brahmins. It is usually coupled with the name of some deity, as Shib Dás, Náráyan Dás, etc., etc., to imply subjection to some special tutelary God. It is a mistake to suppose that it is the name of a particular family, as was asserted by a celebrated statesman, who when inveighing against the treatment of some Dás of Lucknow, stated him to be a member of "the Doss family, one of the most distinguished in India."

In the time of Akbar we find it was not uncommon for Rajputs also to bear the name of Dás. Thus we read of Raja Bhagwan Dás, the Kachhwáha, who was the father-in-law of Jahángír, and grandfather of Sultán Khusrú, and who is stigmatized as the first who sullied Rajput blood by a connexion with the Imperial family of Dehli. The name is now seldom given to Rajputs, except to illegitimate children.—E.

By Europeans in India this word is often written and pronounced "Doss," and in that shape it appeared in the earlier editions of this work. The last (or perhaps I should say the last but one) generation of Anglo-Indians always pronounced the long *á* (आ or ا) like *aw* or *o*, this error was originated by that able but eccentric scholar, Dr. Gilchrist, who taught that the sound of *á* was the same as that of the English *a* in *ball*, *wall*, *water*, etc. Hence his pupils persisted in speaking and writing حاضري breakfast, as *hauzree*, پاني water, as *pawnee*, *nabáb* (the Hindi corruption of نواب *nawwáb*) as *nabob* and the like. The fact however is that the long *á* in all Indian languages is sounded like the English *a* in *far*, *father*, *past*, etc. In Persian the long *á* is sounded as in *water*, *war*, etc., and the Persians are said to dislike to hear Indians talk their language because of their pronunciation of the *á*, which they consider effeminate. Thus, a Persian would say نام شما چه باشد *nawmi shumaw chih bawshad*, while an Indian would say *náh*mi shum*áh* chih b*áh*-shad. The name Dás is in Behar indicative of the possessor's holding the office of village patwárí. It is one of the recognized appellations of the Káyaths, who are all called so-and-so Lál, Parshád, or Dás; also, though less frequently, Singh.—B.

Dásá, داسا दासा

A reaping hook. Also dáṅsá दांसा.

Dháḍá, دھاڈا धादा

Water falling from above; a waterfall.—Rohilkhand. The word is perhaps a corruption of Dhárá, a flowing stream.

In Saugor, Bhadbhada is used in this sense; but its general application is somewhat different.—See Bhadbhadána.

Díyáṛá, دیاڑا दियाड़ा

Díára, or Dáwara, or Díará, signifies an island formed in the bed of a river.—Eastern Oudh and Benares.—E.

It is a Hindi diminutive of Sanskrit द्वीप an island, and means a large sandbank formed by a river, which, after being in existence for a couple of seasons, frequently becomes sufficiently consolidated to be cultivable, but is always liable to be carried away again by a change in the course of the river. Some of these diárás or díaras, as they are also called, are very large and old. The Rámpúr díará in the Ganges near Maldah for instance is forty miles long and two or three broad, and is as firm as the high land on the banks of the river.—B.

Ḍíh, ڈیھہ डीह

Used in the Benares Province and the Lower Doáb to signify the site of a deserted village. The Persian Deh being used for an inhabited one.

Ḍíhá, ڈیہا डीहा

A small mound; same as the above.

Dihúla, دھولہ दिहला

See Dhan.

Dahnímí, دہنیمی दहनीमी

Five per cent.—Dehli. The literal meaning is half of ten.

Ḍehrí, ڈیہری डेहरी

A marshy soil.—See Dahr.

Dihindah, دہندہ दिहन्दह

A Persian word signifying one that is willing to pay or give; a good payer.

Dahyek, دہیک दिहयक

An allowance of 10 per cent., which used to be given to the Amil as his profit, and for the charges of Mofassil management. See Sec. 6, Reg. II. A.D. 1795. In the Printed Glossary it is called Dahyck.

Ḍel, ڈیل डेल

Land ploughed and ready for Rabi' crops.—Bundelkhand. Land prepared for cotton after having been cropped with Gram. —Saugor.

Ḍeulá, ڈیولا डेवला

Mounds; high ground.—Eastern Oudh.

Dháman, دہامن धामन

A grass, of a good quality, which is found in the Bhaṭṭí territory.

Dhán, دہان धान

The rice plant. Very many kinds are grown in these provinces. The best known in the North-West and Rohilkhand are Basmattí, Hansraj, Raímunia (called also Bandlí and Tilokchandan), Kamaura, Motíchúr, Píla, Súnkhar, Jabdí, Súngkharcha, Sohágmattí. These are all of superior quality. The inferior are Anjana, Chakua, Badámí, Dalganjna, Anandí, Kaldhanna, Seodhí, Sáthí, and Seodha.

In Saugor the most common kinds are Maltí, Síamjírú, Nunga, Láyachí, Dilbagsa, Antarbed, Tilsein, Batrú, Seinkhir, Deodhan, Khurában, and Jhanásar.

In the central part of these provinces we find the names chiefly of Deokala, Dúdhí, Sáthí, Bákí, Raímunia, Batásí, Naurangí, Dúnkharcha, Lumbha, Motíchúr, Kála, Hansraj, and Basmattí.

Those cultivated to the Eastward and in Benares are, for the most part, Bagarí, Dehúla, Dúdha, Mutmurí, Selha, Nanhya, Raníkajar, Ríngan, Naindosh, Basmattí, Jiria, Kalíjír, Nainsukh, Khattar, Birinjphúl, Bangalia, Bangkí, Súmbha, Selhí, Motísirrí, Rát, Raibhog, Motíjhúl, Naurangí, Kharrar, Samundar-phen, Hansraj. Of these the best kinds are Naindosh, Basmattí, Hansraj, Nainsukh, and Birinjphúl. Basmattí and Hansraj appear to be the only kinds which are known generally by the same name. The varieties are still greater in Behar and Bengal.

It appears from Abu'l Fazl that the most noted varieties of his time were the Sukhdás of Bharaich, the Dojírah of Gwalior, and Khanjan of Rájaurí.—E.

In Bengal and Behar, where rice is the staple crop, the people say there are two hundred distinct kinds, but, as usual with these exaggerated sub-divisions, they are seldom able to name them all. Many of the names are as purely fanciful as those given by English gardeners to their apples and pears. The better sorts are classed under one head as Arwá, and are the only sorts eaten by Europeans and the upper class of natives. The inferior second sorts are Joshándar avyal, Joshándar doyam, and Lál.—B.

Dhána, دهانه धाना

The Gond portion of a village, which is always separate from the rest. Also applied generally to Marza, Nagla, and Púrwa in the North-West.—Saugor.

Dháp, دهاپ धाप

One-fourth of a koss.—See Ḍhapiá. Also applied to a Ghat, or passage; a large expanse of low ground.

Ḍhár, ڈهار ढार

A heap of corn.—Benares. It is called more correctly Dher in the North-West.

Dhár, دهار धार

A hollow tree inserted in the mouth of wells in the Tarái, to keep them from falling in.—Rohilkhand.

Dhár or Dhára is also used in the sense given under Dhala and Dharbachh: it is frequently pronounced Dharua.—These words may either be derived from Dhala, as above-mentioned, or from *dharná* دهرنا, to place down, to impose. The word is entered in the Printed Glossary under Dara.

Dhárdharná, دهاردهرنا धारधरना

See Dhariyana.

Ḍhí, ڈهي ढी

A high bank of a river.—Saugor.

Ḍhíhá, ڈهيها ढीहा

Rising ground; mounds. Díha is similarly used.

Ḍhínkhar, ڈهينكهر ढींखर

Is the name applied to the bundle of thorns tied together and drawn by bullocks over corn for the purpose of beating out the grain. It is also used as a harrow for eradicating grass and weeds from ploughed land.—Dehli and Upper Doáb.

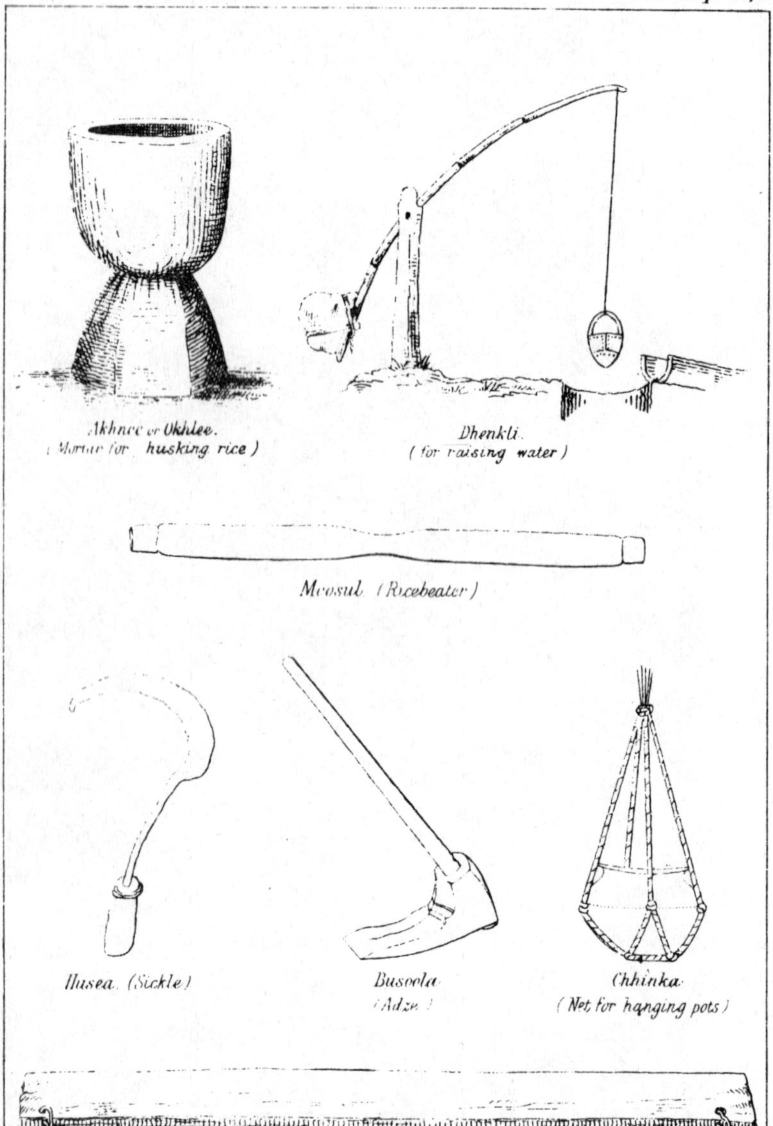

Vincent Brooks Day & Son Lith London WC.

INDIAN IMPLEMENTS.

Ḍhelá, ڈھیلا ढेला

A clod of earth.

Dhen, دھین धेन

A milch cow.

Ḍhenka, ڈھینکہ ढेंका

Dhenkí, ڈھینکي ढेंकी

An instrument for pounding rice, tobacco, etc. It is worked like the Dhenklí, and is similarly derived; corrupted by Europeans into "donkey."

Ḍhenklí, ڈھینکلي ढेंकली

A machine for raising water, consisting of a horizontal lever with a weight at one end and a bucket at the other. The name is provincially corrupted into Dhúklí, Dhiklí, and in Gorakhpúr into Dheokal. The word appears to be derived from ḍhalkáná ڈھلکانا to roll, to overturn. The posts which act as the fulcra are called Thúnia; the rope, Bart; and the bucket Karwala.

Dhenṛí, ڈھینڑي ढेंड़ी

Has the same meaning as Dhondh.—See Dhondh.

Ḍherí, ڈھیري ढेरी

A heap.

In the Upper Doáb it is used to signify a sharer, principally in landed property.

Dhingá, دھنگا धिंगा

See Jelí.

Dhoka, دھوکہ धोका

See Daria.

Ḍhoka, ڈھوکہ ढोका

Small stones of an inferior quality, extracted from the Chanár quarries. In Regulation XXII. 1795, the names of several other stones are mentioned, such as Chauká, Húrsá, Solí, Jántá, for grinding; and for building, Dápá, Chapetá, Ábhot, Bujautí, Patera, Pattea, Khúnth, Khamha.

Dhonḍá, دهونڈا धोंडा

Dhonḍí, دهونڈي धोंडी

A grass which grows in rice fields, and sometimes chokes the plant. It produces an ear, and the seed is frequently used by cultivators for making bread. In some places, as in the Bareilly district, it is called Bat; and in Eastern Oudh, Dhauní. It appears to derive its name from Dhán, rice; if we may be allowed to judge from the following familiar couplet, in which both words occur—

बोए थे धान होगया धोंडा।
क्या खाएगा लौंडी लौंडा॥

"We sowed rice, it has come up dhonḍá;
What will the family (*lit.* the male and female slaves) eat?"

Ḍhonḍh, ڈهونڈه ढोंढ

A capsule, or seed vessel; especially of the poppy, cotton, or gram.—See also Ḍhúnḍí.

Dhúí, دهوي धूई

Soaked pulse.

Ḍhúnḍí, ڈهونڈي ढूंडी

The pod of gram *(Cicer arietinum)*.—Benares. The correct word is Dhendí, or Dhenrí, *q.v.* It is also in Benares and many other places called Thonthí. It is known by the local name of Ghittrí in Rohilkhand, Tát in Dehli, Dhaurí in Bundelkhand, and Ḍhúnḍh, and Ghentí in some places. When it is somewhat unripe, it is called Patpar, Chatká, Ghegará, and

Satpar, in different parts of these Provinces. – See Ḍhonḍh and Ghegara.

Dhus, دھُس धुस

A sloping elevation of ground; and hence applied to the glacis of a fort; sterile sandy eminences. It is also the name of a soil in some parts of the Lower Doáb and Benares.—See Dhúh.

Ḍhorá, ڈھورہ ढोरा

Ḍhorá, or Ḍhola, is the name of an insect very destructive to stored gram.

It is also applied to the mound of earth raised by the side of a ditch.

Dhaul, دھول धौल

Dhaur, دھور धौर

A kind of sugar cane.—Rohilkhand, Upper Doáb, and Dehli.

Ḍhaḍḍá, دھڈّا ढडा

Ḍhaḍḍí, دھڈّي ढडी

A term applied to low ground.—Rohilkhand.

Ḍhanḍhoí, ڈھنڈھوي ढंढोई

The scum of the sugar cane juice, of which half goes to the Jhokia, and half to the Jhímar.—Dehli. It is called also Mallí. The corresponding word in Rohilkhand, Benares, and Bundelkhand is Mailia; in the Doáb, Patoí, and Lado.

Dhaniá, دھنیا धनिया

Coriander seed (*Coriandrum sativum*, Linn.).

Dhankar, دھنکر धंकर

A stiff soil producing rice (Dhan), which can only be ploughed and sown in the event of sufficient rain falling.

Also a field which has been cropped with rice during the previous season.

Dhanthiyá, دهنتهيا धंथिया

This also signifies a field on which rice has been cut.—Rohilkhand.

Dhapiá, دهپيا धपिया

A short koss. From Sanskrit धाव going or running; from which also is derived Dháp, a fourth of a koss, or that distance which a man is supposed to be able to run without stopping to take breath.

Dharáwaṭ, دهراوٹ धरावट

Land ascertained and apportioned by estimate; not measured. —Benares.—See Regulation LI. 1795.

Dhariyáná, دهريانا धरियाना

To separate the good from bad grain; to winnow. The word is used throughout the North-Western Provinces, but the process is usually called Dhárdharna in Dehli, Suretna in Rohilkhand, and Usána in Bundelkhand; but this latter, as well as Barsana, is also general in the North-Western Provinces.

Dharingá, دهرنگا धरिंगा

A kind of rice.—Rohilkhand.

Dharohar, دهروهر धरोहर

Deposit. From Dharná, to place.

Dhartí, دهرتي धरती

Land; the earth.

Dhaṛakhá, دهڑکها धड़खा

Dhaṛallá, دهڑلا धड़ला

A scarecrow.—See Bijhgah, Dhokha, and Dhúha.

Dhasán, دهسان धसान
Dhasan, دهسن धसन
Dhasáo, دهساو धसाव
Dhasam, دهسم धसम

A swamp; a quagmire. From Dhasná, to sink into, to enter.

Dig, دگ दिग

Dig, or Dik, is one of the regions of the earth, of which there are reckoned to be ten. They are frequently called by the names of their supposed regents; as Isan for North-East, Nairit for South-West, Agni for South-East, Báyu for North-West, etc. These regions are more usually considered to be eight, but there are in reality ten, by adding Ananta and Brahma, the regents of the nadir and zenith. "Decem mundi partes pro omnes mundi partes, quarum octo quæ sunt hyperbolice decem dicuntur."—Lassen, "Anthologia Sanskritica," p. 234. See also Johnson's Selections from the "Mahabharat," p. 91; Lassen's "Gita Govinda," p. 84, and Bopp's "Nalus," p. 198.

Dighí, دگهي दिघी

A large oblong tank. Corrupted by the English into Diggy.

Dil, دل दिल

A small eminence; the site of an old village.—Benares. Called in other parts of the North-West, Dhíha, Pútha, Tíla, Theh, and Thera.

Docha, دوچه दोचा

Docha or Dohcha is the second reservoir to which water is raised by the Berí and Daurí for the purposes of irrigation. The third is called Tehcha, and the fourth Chauncha. These words are used chiefly to the Westward. To the East other terms prevail.—See Daurí.

Dofaslí, دوفصلي दोफसली

Lands producing two crops a year. It is also known as Dohar, Dosaí, Dosahí, and Juthelí.

Dabehrí, دبيهري दबेहरी

Is the name given to a light kind of plough in the Western parts of Oudh and Rohilkhand. In Eastern Oudh it assumes a masculine form, Dabehra, and is there applied to a large ploughshare.

Ḍabrá, ڈبره डबरा

A marsh; a puddle; a small pond.

A small field, applied synonymously with Tapra.—E. Or rather a plot of land, whether consisting of one or more fields.—B.—Upper Doáb.

Ḍabrí, ڈبري डबरी

Division of profit amongst the village community according to their respective shares.—Upper Doáb.

Dach, دچ दच

Homestead.—Eastern Oudh.

Dadrí, دَدْري ददरी

Unripe corn, chiefly barley, which is cut from time to time, and brought home to be eaten, instead of being taken to the threshing ground. The word is in general use, but Alo, Arwan, Awásí, Kawal, and Kawarí, are also terms in local use.

Daftarí, دفتري दफतरी

A man employed in the vernacular offices of the Civil officials in India in preparing and taking care of articles of stationery, and in ruling or binding sheets of paper for official purposes.

Ḍagar, ڈگر डगर

A path. Also डहर ḍahar. The word is derived from Dag, a pace, a step; now rarely used, but we find it in the familiar couplet describing the fertility of Malwa, which is given in the article Gambhír.

Dahenḍí, دهينڈي दहेंडी

A vessel for holding dahi, or curds, *i.e.* the solid part of the milk separated from the liquid. Dohní is the name of the vessel which holds dúdh, or fresh milk.

Dahiyá, دهيا दहिया

A field; land near a village.—Benares and Saugor. The name perhaps is more generally spelt with a cerebral or lingual *ḍ* or ड.

Dahmardá, دهمردا दहमर्दा

A cart smaller than a Gárí and Chhakrá, and larger than a Rehlú.—Rohilkhand. The name is derived from its capacity to carry ten men. It is also called a Dobardá or Dobaldá, the origin of which is different, being derived from a word signifying two bullocks.

Dahr, دهر दहर

Dahrí, دهري दहरी

Stiff clay soil (in low ground). It is usually applied to a marsh or any inundated land in Dehli.

Dahal, دهل दहल

Sometimes used as the equivalent of Daldal, for a quicksand or quagmire. From Dahalná دهلنا to tremble, to shake. In an extract from a History written in Jahángír's time, and ascribed to Ferishta,—(the author seems wrongly quoted)—it is stated that the name of the Imperial city of Dehli (correctly Dillí,

Díhlí, or Dhillí) is derived from this word—the ground on which it was built being so loose and infirm (dahal) that tent-pins could not be fixed in it.

و دهلي از شهرهاي قديم و جديد است و در شهور من سبع و ثلثمائه اوديت راجپوت از طايفه تؤران در هندوستان قلعه اندرپت بنا كرده چون جاك او بسيار نرم بود ميخ بدشواري درانجا استوار ميگرديد آن شهررا دهلي موسوم كرد

"And Dihli is one of the cities which are both ancient and modern, and in one of the months of the year 307 (Hijri = A.D. 919) Udit the Rajput of the Tuar clan built the fort of Indarpat in Hindústán, and as the earth there was very soft so that they could with difficulty fix a tent-peg in it he called the city Dihli."

The same origin is ascribed to the word in the Nuzhatu'l Ḳulúb.

Histories usually ascribe a different orign to the name, saying that the city was founded by Raja Delú. Common tradition differs from these accounts. It is universally believed that the name is derived (ढीला or ढिला loose) from the sacrilegious attempt of the Tomar (Tuar) to see whether the iron pillar had really, as was supposed, penetrated the head of Sahesnag.

किल्ली तो ढिल्ली भई तूमर भयो मत हीन
पहिले ढिल्ली तूमर पीछे चौहानु
और पीछे मोगल पठानु

"The pillar became loose (dhillí), the Túmar was foolish :
First in Dehli was the Túmar, then the Chauhán,
And afterwards Mughal and Pathán."

Colonel Tod says the name of Dehli was not given to the Imperial city before the eighth century.—Trans. R. A. S. Vol. III. p. 150. See also Quart. Or. Mag. No. XVI. p. 133.*—E.

* See also J. A. S. B. 1866, vol. XXXV. Part I. p. 199, for a long and carefully elaborated topographical description of the city of Dehli by C. J. Campbell.—B.

General Cunningham fixes conjecturally the original foundation of Dilli in 57 B.C., but says that after a few years it was deserted for 792 years by the kings, though probably not by the people. In 736 it was rebuilt by Anang Pal or Biláu Deo (see Tomar in Part I.). As to the origin of the name the safest course is to acquiesce in the opinion that it has been lost in the lapse of ages. In 57 B.C. the Hindi word ḍhillí certainly was not in existence as far as we know, and the corrupted modern spelling Dihli or Dehli seems to point to a different source. The General's article is too long to quote here; it may be found in J. A. S. B. Vol. XXXIII. for 1864, Appendix.—B.

Ḍahaṛ, ڈهر डहर

Applied in Benares, Oudh, Lower Doáb, and Bundelkhand to a road; elsewhere, Dagar or Dagra is used.—See Dagar.

Daldal, دلدل दलदल

A quagmire.

Daliyá, دليا दलिया

Any sort of split pulse, ground finer than dal—in which the seed is understood to be split only into two pieces.

Dalganjaná, دلگنجنا दलगनजना

A kind of rice.—See Dhán.

Dalhárá, دلهارا दलहारा

A grain seller. From dal, split pulse.

Damká, دمکا दमका

A hillock.—Eastern Oudh.

Damrí, دمري दमड़ी

In the Dehli territory, the term is applied to the sub-divisions of a village. Thus in Gopálpúr of Rohtak, there are 150

Damrís, each Damrí being equivalent to twenty-five kachcha bíghas. But Damrí is commonly known as a nominal coin, equal to 3⅛ or 3¼ Dáms; or between two and three Gandas—so that a Damrí varies from 8 to 12 Cowrís, according to the good will and pleasure of unscrupulous Banyas.

It may be useful to subjoin from the "Díwán Pasand" a table showing the value of Damrís and Dáms:

1	Damrí	3¼	Dáms.	
2	„	6¼	„	1 Chhadám.
3	„	9¼	„	
4	„	12½	„	1 Adhela.
5	„	15	„	
6	„	18¾	„	¾ Paisa.
7	„	22	„	
8	„	25	„	1 „
9	„	28	„	
10	„	31¼	„	1¼ „
11	„	34¼	„	
12	„	37¼	„	1½ „
13	„	40	„	
14	„	44	„	1¾ „
15	„	47	„	
16	„	50	„	1 Taka.

The table is given with some slight variations in the "Zubdatu'l Ḳawánín," but in neither are the smaller fractional amounts given with correctness.—See Chhadám, Ganda.

Damaí, دمئي दमई

Amount of assessment. The word is derived from the Dám of account, which was formerly used in revenue accounts.—Central Doáb.

Dandá, ڈنڈا डंडा

A collector of market dues, in which sense Ḍanḍia also is

used; the beam of a pair of scales; the step of a ladder; a staff.

Ḍanḍí, ڈنڈي डंडी

A handle; a weighman; the beam of a pair of scales.

Ḍanḍwára, ڈنڈواره डंडवारा

A south wind. Khán Arzú says it is sometimes, but improperly, considered to come from the opposite quarter—and that the real name of the North wind is Barban.

Darántí, درانتي दरांती

A sickle.—See Dantí.

Ḍangwára, ڈنگواره डंगवारा

Reciprocal assistance in tillage.—Dehli and Northern Doáb. —See Angwára, Harí, and Jíta.

Dantáolí, دنتاولي दन्तावली

A harrow, or rake. From Dant, a tooth.

Ḍanthlá, ڈنتهلا डंथला

The bare stalks of Bajra, Jowar, and Indian corn; apparently from Dant, a tooth; but it must be confessed the word is usually spelt with the hard or cerebral *d*, and Ḍanthal is so spelt on the high authority of Professor Shakespear, which, if correct, would militate against this etymology. They are also called Khúnthí, Khúntla, Dúnd, Danthal, Thúnt, Khutel, and Khobari. These names are in use in different places. In some, they represent the crop with the heads of corn cut off the stalks; in others they represent the roots which remain in the ground after the crop has been cut.—See Datoí and Danth.

Ḍanthal, ڈنتھل डंथल

This word bears the same meaning; and is also applied to the roots of Chana, remaining in the ground after the crop is cut.

Dares, دریس दरेस

A road-margin; any line very straight. It is derived from the drill-word "Dress," which has been introduced by our retired Sepoys into their native villages.

Darkhál, درکھال दरखाल

A cattle enclosure.—Benares.

Daṛar, دڑر दड़र

A water-fall, or impetuous flood; corrupted apparently from daṛeṛá دڑیڑا hard rain.

Dasotara, دسوترہ दसोत्रा

Ten per cent. From das دس ten.

Dastí, دستي दस्ती

A present given to native officials at the Dasehra. From the Persian دست a hand.—E.

Also the small portable kalamdán or inkstand which the native amlá use.—B.

Datoí, دتوئي दतोई

Land which has been lately cropped with Makha (Indian corn or maize), Bajra or Jawar.—Dehli or Upper Doáb.

There is much the same difficulty about spelling this word, as in spelling Danthal. Professor Shakespear, whose authority is not to be slighted, gives डठा as a stalk, which would make Datoí to be more accurately represented by डठोई or डटोई. Gilchrist also spells it डठा.

Datara, دتره दतरा

A large rake used for gathering high grass together into a cocklet. Kilwaí is a smaller implement of the same kind.—Rohilkhand.

Ḍorí, ڈوري डोरी

A chain, or line, with which lands are measured.—See Ḍaurí.

Doras, دورس दोरस

Literally, two flavours; used in the Eastern districts; as Domat in the North-West, to signify a mixture of two soils, Mattíár and Baluá, clay and sand; and, like Domat, is in some places, as in Azimgaṛh, considered the best quality; in others, as in Gorakhpúr, the second quality of soil, except in Tilpúr and the forest Parganahs, in which the Mattíár is considered too adhesive.

Dosáhí, دوساهي दोसाही

Dosáhí, or Dosáí, signifies lands yielding two crops a year.—See Dofaslí.

Dosarí, دوسري दोसरी

The ploughing of land twice; the land itself when ploughed twice. When ploughed three times it is called Tesarí; when four, Chaurasí.—Dehli.—See Dor and Jael.

Ḍaulá, ڈولا डौला

A boundary.

Daungṛá, دونگڑا दौंगड़ा

A heavy shower. The author of the "Araish-i Mahfil," in his preliminary chapter on the praises of Hindústan, speaks of the Asáṛh kí Daungṛí دونگڑي, Sawan kí Jharíán جھڑیاں, and Bhádon kí Daṛeṛí دڑیڑي.

Daur, دور दौर

The slings attached to a basket for irrigation. The more usual terms are Jutá and Jotí.

Dauṛáhá, دوڑاها दौड़ाहा

A village messenger.—See Daláhar.

Daurí, دوري दौरी

The rope which binds the bullocks together when threshing. This is the general name, but there are many others in local use, as Gandáwar, Dámrí, Garáwar, Dánwarí, Pakhar, and Jor. The stake to which the bullocks are tied is called Mend (limit); and hence Mendhya, the inner bullock. The outer or off bullock is called Pat in Benares, Pagharia in Rohilkhand, and Pankararí in Dehli. Daurí, which is spelt both with the Hindí and Persian Dal, appears to be derived from Dor, a string, a rope; whence Dorea, lace. In the gipsy language, Dorí, which means a riband, is perhaps the same word.*

Daurí is also used to the Eastward in the same sense as Puroha, Berí, Chhápa, Boka, Dúgla, or Leharí, to signify a sling basket used in irrigation, and is generally made of split bamboo. It means also the act of throwing the basket, as Daurí lagá, "irrigation by Daurí has commenced."

The lowest reservoir from which the water is raised is variously styled Nyaní, Gonra, Nandhú or Nadhao. It is raised from that to the Pachú, and from that again to the Thauka. The raised bank between the Nandhú and Pachú is called Odí; and the place where the throwers stand on each side of the Nandhú is called Paidha.

* Doriyá, a dog-keeper, is also similarly derived, because he is presumed to lead dogs with a string. Dorí dalna also is to prolong the stitch of a quilt, or dress; and hence is applied, metaphorically, to the lengthened note of the bird called Chittí, the female of the Amaduvade, or Avaduvat (*Fringilla Amandava*), *i.e.* the Fringilla of of Ahmedabad in the Dekkan, for so the word has been corrupted by the Naturalists.

Dabbiyá, دبيا दब्बिया

A box; also written Ḍibbiyá. A term applied to about ten handfuls (Muttha) of Kharíf produce. Lehna is the word used in the same sense with respect to Rabí produce. About four Muttha make a Lehna; about four Lehna, a Dabbiyá; about five Dabbiyá, a Bojh; and about a hundred Bojh make a Pahí. Five Dabbiyá of Kharíf produce amount to a Dhoka, and about ten Dhoka make a Bojh, or load, and an aggregation of several Bojh make a Kundar. The application of all these words varies very much in different districts, and even in different Parganahs. The text represents the words used chiefly in the Eastern portion of these Provinces.

Doháo, دوهاو दोहाव

The Zamíndár's perquisite of milk from Ryot's cows.

Dohur, دوهر दोहुर

A sandy sub-soil.—Central Doáb.

Dohra, دوهره दोहरा

See Koluh.

Dohar, دوهر दोहर

The old bed of a river.—Eastern Oudh. Johar is elsewhere used in the same sense.

Dohar is likewise applied to land which bears two crops in a year.—Central Doáb.

Dojíra, دوجيره दोजीरा

A kind of rice.—See Dhan.

Dokhí, دوكهي दोखी

A raised mound indicating the junction of two boundaries.—Dehli.

Ḍol, ڈول डोल

Applied locally to signify the richest black soil.—Baitúl.

Ḍol is generally used to denote a bucket for drawing water. From the Persian دلو.

Doláwa, دولاوہ दोलावा

A well having two Laos, or well-buckets and ropes. Dopaira is also used in this sense.

Dolchí, ڈولچی डोलची

A small bucket.—See above under Ḍol.

Domaṭ, دومٹ दोमट

A mixture of two Mattís or soils, clay and sand, Mattíár and Bhúr. Like Doras, in some places, it is considered the first quality, in others, the second quality of soil. In Agra, Farrukhabad, and parts of Bareily, it is considered the best, but it is more usual, as in Badáon, to rate it as second quality.

Ḍongí, ڈونگی डोंगी

A small boat. From which our dingy is derived, according to some, but there exists also a form डेंगी which is more likely of the two to have originated the word.

Dúb, دوب दूब

Name of a grass (*Agrostis linearis*, Kœn. *Cynodon Dactylon*, Royle). "Its flowers in the perfect state are among the loveliest objects in the vegetable world, and appear through a lens like minute rubies and emeralds in constant motion from the least breath of air. It is the sweetest and most nutritious pasture for cattle, and its usefulness added to its beauty, induced the Hindús in the earliest ages to believe it was the mansion of a benevolent nymph."—(Sir W. Jones' Works, Vol. V. p. 78).

There are generally considered to be three kinds of Dúb. The best, which throws out the creeper-like stem,* is called Paundá. This is essentially the same as the fiorin grass of English farmers. The second, which is smaller, grows on hard ground, and is called Khútya. The third is called the white Dúb from its peculiar colour, and is used by native practitioners as a medicine in fevers. This is called by Wilson ("Sanskrit Dict." p. 279) Gandálí. In Dehli it is frequently called Dhaurí. In Saugor the Khútya is known under the name of Chhattú. Where the division into three kinds is not known, the recognized varieties are Ghur-dúb and Ban-dúbia; the first being derived from Ghora, a horse, as it is excellent pasture grass; the second from Ban, a forest, or jungle, as it is a coarser kind.

The nutritive qualities of Dúb have caused it to be a great favorite with the natives of India, and frequent allusions are made to it by the poets. Its tenacity whenever it once fixes its roots has caused it to be used in a common simile when the attachment of Zamíndárs to their native soil is spoken of.

Nának Shah also, in exhorting himself to humility, uses the following simile respecting the modest charms of this herb, alluding to the fact that it remains green even in the hot weather.

नानक नन्हा हो रहो जैसा नन्ही दूब
और घास जल जाएंगे दूब ख़ूब की ख़ूब

"Nának, be humble like the humble dúb,
Other grasses are burnt up, dúb remains fresh and fresh."

Dúbáí, ڈوبائي दुबाई

A term sometimes applied to a bribe, given whether the donor gain or lose his cause; in distinction to Taraí, in which the

* From this peculiarity of creeping along the ground this grass derives its name, from डूबना to be pressed down. It would be more correct, perhaps, to write it डूब, but Hindi spelling is very capricious.—B.

bribe is returned if the suit is lost. The words are used in the Doáb and Rohilkhand, and their existence indicates a degree of refinement in the art of bribery, which perhaps no other language can parallel. The origin of the terms is in the one case, dúbná ڈوبنا to sink, to be immerged; and, in the other, tarná ترنا to pass over safely, to be ferried.

Dubsí, ڈبسي डुबसी

Inundated land, or land liable to be flooded. From ḍúbná ڈوبنا to sink, to be immerged.

Dúdhá, دودھا दूधा

A species of rice.—See Dhan.

Dudká, ڈڈکا डुडका

Is the name of one of the many diseases to which the rice plant is subject. There are various others, as Bagulí, Katrí, Purwaí, Kansí, etc.

Dúgla, دوگله दूगला

A sling-basket of large size, round and deep, used for the purposes of irrigation.—See Berí, Boka, Daurí.

Durkhí, دُرکهي दुर्खी

An insect whose ravages are very destructive to indigo, when the plant is young.

Dor, دور दोर

Land ploughed twice. When ploughed three times, it is called Tíar; when four, Chawar, the *ar* in these words being from हर a plough; thus dor = do-har; tíar = tin-har; chawar = chau (for chár) har, etc.—Central and Lower Doáb.—See Dosarí and Jael.

Dúmá, دوما डूमा

Is the name of the leather case in which tea is imported from Tibet into Gaṛhwál and Kamáon. It contains about three seers, and bears a price of six or seven rupees. About one hundred Dúmás are imported annually into Kamáon, which is consumed chiefly by the Bhotiyás of the passes, and seventy Dúmás into Gaṛhwál, of which a portion finds its way to Hardwár and Najíbabad.

Dún, دون डून

A valley. The word does not appear in Shakespear's Dictionary, but is locally applied in the Sewalik Hills under the Himalaya, in this signification: as Patlí Dún, Dehra Dún. The word may perhaps be formed by elision from the Sanskrit द्रोणी "the union of two mountains, the valley or chasm between them" (Sanskrit Dict., p. 431); and hence Dronakas, "the people of vallies (Vishnu Purana, p. 196).

Ḍúnḍá, ڈونڈا डूंडा

A bullock with only one horn. The word is in general use; but in parts of Dehli it is applied to a bullock with two horns, and Túnda to a bullock which has only one. This word also means the broken stump of a tree.

Dundká, دندکا दुन्दका

See Kolhú.

Ḍúngá, ڈونگا डूंगा

Deep; an excavation, such as that of a trough; a canoe.

Fález, فاليز फालेज़

A field of melons.

Farás, فراس फरास

(Tamaris farás.) The Farás occur in the drier parts of the Doáb, and in the neighbourhood of Dehli; where it is called Asal or Atal, because in Arabia the galls which are formed on the tree are called Samrat-u'l Asal. Chhotí Maí is the Hindústání name of these galls. Very little use is made of the tree, except occasionally in building, when nothing better can be procured.—See Jhao.

In the Doáb it does not appear to grow to the East of the Arind river.

Farrásh, فراش फरास

From the Arabic فرش a carpet; a person who spreads carpets; a sweeper. The term is correctly explained in the Glossary under Ferash, Firashe, and Farash. In ancient times his duty appears to have been that of a Khalásí, or tent-pitcher, and the latter term was applied chiefly to sailors.

تنڈیل بزرگ خلاصیان ملاح را بزبان دریا ورزان خلاصي و حاوره گویند

(Áín-i-Akbarí.)

"Ṭinḍel (our modern word tindal = the boatswain of a native crew) the head of the Khalamis (vulgo clashies) in the language of the sea-going folk; also called Háwarah."

Firárí, فراري फिरारी

Absconding; a person who has absconded. From the Persian فرار firár, flight. The word is more usually pronounced Farárí in India.

Fota, فوطه फोता

A bag; collections made from the tenantry in general; treasure; revenue.

Gáchhí, گاچھي गाछी

A pad put over the back of a beast of burden; called also Gaddí, Gathí, Bakhrá, Palán, Líwá, Padád, Chhaí, and by several other names, which are merely local, and even then not applicable to every beast. For instance, where the pad of the ass is Líwá, that of the bullock is Chhaí-Bakhrá; and so on.

Gád, گاد गाद

The sediment of dirty water.

Gádar, گادر गादर

Gádar, or, more correctly, Gaddar and Gadra, signifies half-ripe fruit or corn.—See Bhadahar.

Gáḍar, گاڈر गाडर

Sheep.—See Gaḍariyá in Part I.

Gáhná, گاهنا गाहना

To tread out corn.—See Daen.

Gáhan, گاهن गाहन

A harrow with teeth for eradicating grass from ploughed land. The Maira, which it resembles in form has no teeth. The implement is little known to the East of Farrukhabad.

Gájá, گاجا गाजा

The first rice sowing in the districts at the foot of the hills. The sowing is in Baisakh (April-May), the cutting in Bhadon (August-September). The word is, perhaps, derived from Gajána, to ferment, to rot, which aptly expresses the condition of this early crop. The second sowing is called Bhijoa; it occurs in Jeth, the cutting takes place in Kuár. The third is called Rassauta, or Rutiya, seasonable, because it takes place in the most natural *rut* (vulg. for *rit*, season). The sowing is in Asaṛh (June-July), or Sáwan (July-August), and the harvest in Kátik (October-November), or Aghan (November-December).

Gájar, گاجر गाजर

A carrot.

Gál, گال गाल

A sort of tobacco.

Gála, گالہ गाला

A pod of cotton, or, more usually, a ball of carded cotton, which is known also by the name of Goḍhá گوڈھا.

Gám, گام गाम

A village: more usually Gáṅw.

Gáṇḍá, گانڈا गानडा

Sugar-cane—See Agaund, Ikh, and Ganna.

Gáṇḍal, گانڈل गांडल

Gáṇḍar, گانڈر गांडर

(Andropogon muricatum). Thatching grass. Gáṇḍal grows in land subject to inundation; and its root yields the Khaskhas, or scented grass, so much used for ṭaṭṭis or screens against doorways in the hot weather in India. The produce of this grass has of late years much diminished, owing to the great extension of cultivation in those parts where it used formerly to grow spontaneously. Gáṇḍal is the common name of the grass, but it is known by the name of Pánhí in Dehli.

Gánja, گانجہ गांजा

Gánja, or Gánjha, is a plant from which an intoxicating drug of the same name is procured, which is used as a liquor in the Upper Provinces, and smoked like tobacco in Bengal. That which is procured from Balúgarrah in Bengal is of high repute. It is divided into Chapta and Golí,* of which the first is chiefly in demand in Hindustan.

Gánja is largely cultivated in the hills of Sirmúr and Gaṛhwál and the plant grows wild under the hills from Sehâranpúr to Tirhut, and on the banks of the Ganges; but it appears to be not the same as the smoking Gánja of Bengal, as it is declared to have none of the gum-resin qualities peculiar to the latter. O'Shaughnessy describes Gánja to be the dried hemp plant which has flowered, and from which the resin has not been removed. This resin in certain seasons exudes, and concretes on the leaves, stems, and flowers, and is called Charas, and separately taxed and sold.

Buchanan, in his statistical account of Dinajpúr, says that the hemp when young is called Gánja; and Siddhi when the flowers have fully expanded. Authorities, however, seem little agreed respecting the exact difference between Gánja, Siddhi, and Bhang; nor are they more agreed respecting the difference between the Gánja of the Upper and Lower Provinces, and the identity of the *Cannabis Sativa* and *Indica*.

It was only this year that some Gánja procured at Seharanpúr was sent for examination to the superintendent at Rajshahí, who thus comments upon it.

"The specimens sent bear more the character of the hemp plant grown for Sanni, than of the Gánja plant. The *Cannabis Indica*, or Gánja plant, is diœcious, annual, about six or seven feet high; the stem is erect, six or eight inches in circum-

* The three kinds of Gánja, or rather three qualities or methods of preparation, now known in Bengal are *gol*, or "round," which is the natural plant dried in its natural shape; *chiptá*, or "flat," which is the plant pressed flat for convenience of packing; and *ṛoṛá*, or "dust," which is the broken flowers and stalks and refuse generally, and is less valuable than the other kinds.—B.

ference, and branched; leaves alternate or opposite, on long weak petioles, digitate, scabrous, with linear lanceolate, sharply serrated leaflets, tapering into a long smooth entire point. Males lax and drooping; branches leafless at base. Females erect, simple, and leafy at the base. Small jattís, the size of a walnut, form on the branches, of an absorbing nature, containing resinous narcotic juice, which is the part of the plant used. Each plant will yield from 20 to 26 branches, weighing, when dry, from two to two-and-a-half seers.

"The natives prepare the drug in a very rude manner, the branches are cut off when the resinous jattís are ripe, and left to dry for a few days; they are then spread on mats, and the jattís are compressed with the toes. By this means a great portion of the narcotic resin is lost on the mats, and by adhesion to the toes. The sticks being retained is also very objectionable when the drug has to be sent to a great distance; for out of 1000 maunds prepared in the customary way, not more than thirty maunds of the drug can be obtained, the remainder being useless sticks."

It is evident, therefore, that in his opinion the Gánja of Bengal is of superior quality to that of the Upper Provinces, from which intoxicating Bhang only can be extracted, and that the *Cannabis Sativa* is not the same as the *Cannabis Indica*; yet Roxburgh, Wildenow, O'Shaughnessy, and several other authorities declare that Gánja is the *Cannabis Sativa*; and the former, on comparing plants raised from European hemp-seed with the Gánja plant, could not discover the slightest difference between them.—Asiatic Researches, Vol. XI. p. 161.—See Bhang and Charas.

Gánjar, گانجر गांजर

A kind of grass. It is known also by the name Ganjerua, and is considered very difficult to eradicate when it has once taken root.

Gánkar, گانکر गांकर

An inferior kind of bread made of Arhar and other hard grains. It is also, more generally, applied to any bread not baked on an iron plate (the primitive "gribble" of Ireland)—made, in short, in a hurry, and covered with embers till it is considered baked enough to eat. It is also known by the name of Gákar, Girdí, Angákar, Bhaura and Battí.—See Bhatula.

Gánṭá, گانٹا गांटा

Gánṭh, گانٹھ गांठ

Gánṭh is literally a knot, and is applied by agriculturists to the refuse of straw, consisting of the knotted parts of the stalk and ear-ends, which are known to English farmers under the name of "colder." This is formed into a heap, and put aside on the threshing ground. As an illustration of the difference which prevails in the agricultural terms of different parts of these Provinces, it may be interesting to give the names of the various heaps which are at different times raised on the threshing ground, during the process of winnowing the corn. The names which are given as synonymous with Gánṭh, do not all represent the same thing. The words beginning with S signify generally the "colder" after it has been re-winnowed; and some of the other names applied only to Kharíf, or only to Rabbí produce, specially; the same word being rarely used for both.—See Bhurarí.—E.*

* Káli Rai says, "The small heaps put aside for bhúmí ganesh (or the offerings to gods and penates) are called *ujarí* and *syáwaṛh* स्यावढ़; grain left on the threshing floor after removing the bulk of the crop is called *meṛ* मेढ़, and *thápá* थापा, and the grain which falls to the ground with the chaff in winnowing is called *ghúnḍar* घूंडर and is the perquisite of the Chamárs. It is also called *gaṭharwá* गठर्वा. Gleanings of fields which any one may carry off are called सिला *silá*.—E. *add.*

TABLE OF DIALECTIC VARIETIES.

Dehli.	Rohilkhand.	Upper Doáb.	Central Doáb.	Lower Doáb.	E. Oudh, or Gorakhpúr.	Benares.	Bundelkhand.	Saugor.	How composed.
Sillí ...... Dhar	Gurhao Sillí ...	Sillí ... Neora .. Dhar ...	Dehí ...	Kalha .. Guráṅw	Kunáo ... Aokán ...	Guraṅw ... Ukaṅw ...	Thúa	Udeyí...	Grain and straw, or winnowed corn unheaped.
Rás, or Tár..	Rás	Rás	Rás	Rás	Rás	Rás	Rás	Rás	Heaped grain.
Bhús	Osa	Osa ...... Bhus ...	Sillí ...	Sillí ... Bhusaur	Sillí ...... Bhusaur ...	Sillí	Bhusaul	Bhusaura ..	Heaped straw.
Dondlí ... Gantha ... Bhularí ...	Gánth .. Gántá .. Sánta ...	Gántha Gánteh	Gathurí Sathurí	Gánta .. Guthrí.. Jangra .	Khúntí ... Gethara ...	Ganth ... Ganteh ...	Gúthrí ... Súthrí ...	Gathua . Sathua .	Refuse straw, or colder.

Gowárí, گواري गोवारी

A dwelling house; a family; a cow-house.—Dehli.

Gabrauṭá, گبروٹا गबरौटा

A large beetle found in old cowdung and dung-hills. It is called also Gabrauṛa and Gobaraunda *(Scarabæus stercorarius*, Linn.). From गोबर cowdung.

Gaḍ, گڈ गड़

A boundary mark.—Dehli.

Gaddí, گدي गद्दी

A throne, or cushion.—See Gachí.

A sheaf of corn. Perhaps this would be spelt more correctly with a Hindí ड *ḍ*.

Gaddhrí, گدهري गद्धरी

The unripe pod of the Gram plant, or *Cicer arietinum*.—Dehli.—See Dhúndhí and Gaddar.

Gaddar, گدّر गद्दर

Gadrá, گدرا गद्रा

Unripe corn, or fruit.

Gadíchaṭ, گديچٹ गदीचट

A grass generally found growing with Dúb, which it resembles, except in being about three times larger. It is much used as fodder.

Gadgol, گدگول गदगोल

Muddy water.

Gaháí, گهائي गहाई

The custom of treading sheaveṣ of corn by bullocks, with the view of separating the corn from the ears and stalks. From the verb Gáhná, *q.v.*—See also Dáín.

Gahná, گهنا गहना

Anything in pledge; the original meaning is jewels, ornaments.

Gajjar, گجر गज्जर

Swampy ground.

Galiyá, گليا गलिया

Galiyá (sometimes, but incorrectly, pronounced Gariyár) is the name given to a bullock which lies down in the midst of its work; generally from its neck (गला) being galled—hence the derivation.

Galtáṛ, گلتاڙ गलताड

The name given to the inner pegs of a yoke. The word appears to be derived from गला Galá, a neck, and आड़ Aṛ, a protection.* Gáta, Shamal, and Pachaí are used in the same sense.—See Hal.

Galtans, گلتنس गलतन्स

Dying without issue. From انس right, lot, inheritance, and گلنا to melt, to be dissolved.

Gambhír, گنبهير गंभीर

A Sanskrit word signifying deep. It is generally applied to soil which is of a rich quality, and attains a more than usual

* I should prefer to write it with र, and derive it from galá, the neck, and तार a thread or string, as its use is to fasten the string which goes under the neck of the ox. The derivation in the text does not account for the त.—B.

depth before the subsoil is reached. This quality is ascribed to the fertile soil of Málwá.

देस मालवा गैहिर गंभीर
डग डग रोटी पग पग नीर

"The land of Málwá is deep and rich;
At every step bread, on every path water."

The two words Gaihar (for गहिरा) and Gambhír in the foregoing couplet are in fact the same; the former being the modified or Prakrit form of the latter. See Wilson's Introduction to "Specimens of the Hindu Theatre," and "Sanskrit Dictionary," p. 283.

Gandá, گنڈا गंडा

This word is given under Gandál, in the Printed Glossary. Like the Dám, the Gaṇḍa of account and the Gaṇḍa of practice do not coincide. Gaṇḍás of account are but little used in the North-Western Provinces, except in Benares and the Dehra Dún, and, in consequence of its former subjection to Oudh, the Nazarána accounts of Rohilkhand are frequently drawn out in Gaṇḍas. This Gaṇḍa is the twentieth part of an Anna. The Gaṇḍá known to the common people is not of stable amount, sometimes four, and sometimes five, and sometimes even six, go to a packa Damrí, or Chhadám, according to the pleasure of the money dealers, or the state of the market. Notwithstanding this variable amount, as a Gaṇḍa is equivalent to four Kaurís, "to count by Gaṇḍas" signifies to count by fours, or by the quaternary scale, to which the natives are very partial,—in the same way as to count by gáhís or panjas, is to count by fives, or by the quinary scale.

As four Kaurís make one Gaṇḍá, so do twenty Gaṇḍas make one Pan, and sixteen Pans make one Kaháwan. But there are grades of monetary value even below that of Kaurí; for the Hindús seem as fond of dealing with these infinitesimal quantities, as they are with the higher numbers, as exemplified in the article Kaṛoṛ. Thus 3 Krant, or 4 Kak, or 5 Bat, or 9 Dant, or 27 Jau, or 32 Dár, or 80 Til, or 800 Sano are each equivalent to one Kaurí. These are not in practical use in the N.W. Provinces, but are entered in several account books, and many of them appear to be employed in the bazaar transactions of Kattack and parts of Bengal.—See "Rushton's Gazetteer," 1841, Vol. I. p. 182.

The Kauṛi or cowry shell, the *Cypræa moneta,* has been subject to strange diminution of value, in consequence of the facilities of commerce, by which their worth has been depressed below that of the precious metals. In 1740, a Rupee exchanged for 2,400 Kauṛís; in 1756, for 2,560 Kauṛís; and at this time as many as 6,500 Kauris may be obtained for the Rupee.

Kauṛí in Persian is translated by Khar-mohra, literally, a jackass's or mule's shell; because mules are ornamented in that country with trappings of shells, as a Gosain's bullock is in this country. In Arabic it is known by *wada* ودع, which Ibn Batuta says is carried in large quantities from the Maldive Islands to Bengal, where it is used as coin; and therefore there can be no doubt that the *Cypræa moneta* is meant. The Kámús adds تعلق لدفع العين—that it is suspended from the neck to avert the evil eye, as it is in India to this day,* provided the shell is split or broken.—E.

These minute amounts are of great and constantly occurring use in calculating the shares of proprietors in the enormous Zamíndárís in Behar and Bengal under the perpetual settlement. Each estate, however large, being considered for purposes of partition as one rupee, a person whose share is only two or three kránts may have an interest in the estate equal to several thousand acres, and worth many lakhs of rupees.—B.

* Gaṇḍá is also the name applied to the knotted string which is suspended round a child's neck for the same purpose; but not, apparently, because it has any connection with the Kauṛí amulet.

Ganda-biroza, گنده‌بروزه गन्दाबिरोजा

Olibamum, male frankincense, the produce of the *Boswellia thurifera.* The same name is also given to the produce of the Chír *(Pinus longifolia)*.—(O'Shaughnessy's Dispensatory, pp. 283 and 612).

Gaṇḍásí, گنڈاسي गंडासी

Gaṛásí, گڑاسي गडासी

An instrument for cutting sugar-cane, Jawár stalks, or thorny bushes. Also, in Dehli, an assessment on the number of Gaṇḍásís, a tax which used to be levied in former days.—E.

The gaṇḍásá of Benares and Behar is a formidable weapon, like a battle-axe, capable of inflicting in the hands of a stalwart Rajput peasant severe wounds, as is demonstrated by the cases of wounding which so frequently come before the criminal courts. In Shahábád the village chokidars are often armed with it.—B.

Ganderí, گنڈيري गंडेरी

Gaṛerí, گڑيري गंडेरी

Pieces of sugar-cane.

Gandhel, گندهيل गंधेल

The sweet smelling grass known as Gandhel (from Gandh, perfume), is most probably the same as Gandbbel, which Royle ("Ant. Hind. Med." p. 143) says is the *Andropogon calamus aromaticus;* from the leaves, culms, and roots of which a fragrant essential oil is distilled.

Gaṇḍarwálá, گنڈروالا गंडरवाला

See Kolhú. Gareran, Gandrára, and Gandhra are also used in a similar sense.

Gandailá, گنديلا गंदैला

Gandailá, or Gandhiyá, is the name of a grub destructive to Chaná and Arhar.—Eastern Oudh. It is usually called Gíndar elsewhere, *q.v.*

Gangálá, گنگالا गंगाला

Lands subject to inundations of the Ganges.—Rohilkhand.

Gangbarámad, گنگ برآمد गंगबरामद

Gangbarár, گنگ برار गंगबरार

Alluvial land recovered from a river, especially the Ganges. —See Daryábarár.

Gang shikast, گنگ شکست गंगसीकस्त

Encroachment of the Ganges, or of any other river, by diluvion.—See Dariyáburd.

Ganj, گنج गंज

A granary; a market, and especially one of grain. It is used chiefly as an affix to proper names; as Islám-gange, Hardoa-gange, Captain-gange.

Ganjelí, گنجيلي गंजेली

The same as Bhangela, *q.v.*

Gankaṭá, گنکٹا गनकटा

Is the title of the man employed to cut the sugar-cane into lengths of about six inches for feeding the mill.

Ganná, گنا गन्ना

Sugar-cane. There are various kinds cultivated in these Provinces. The principal in Rohilkhand are Dhaul (white),

Neülí, Katára, Lakrí, Paunda, Chin, Manga; in Benares, Manga, Paunda, Baraukha, Reora, Khusyar, Sarautí, Katára, Rakra, and Khiwáhí.

The most noted of the Doáb are Saretha, Dhaul, Paunda, Chin, Kathorí, Dhúmar, Baraukha, Káláganda, Kinára, Karba, Matna; in Dehli, Súrtha, Kálásúrtha, Paunda, Bhúrasúrtha, Lálrí, Ghararí, Kinára, Dhaul, and Bejhar. Many of these names are identical; but the kind called Paunda seems to be the only one generally known. It is eaten raw, not manufactured.

The amount of acres under sugar-cane cultivation throughout the North-Western Provinces, in the year of survey, is shewn below:

Dehli Division....................	5,307	Acres.
Rohilkhand Division	168,277	„
Mírat Division......................	105,861	„
Agra Division	47,090	„
Allahábád Division.............	33,410	„
Benares Division................	317,535	„
Saugor Division	12,919	„
Total Acres	690,399	

Ganel, گنيل गनेल

A species of long grass, which is used for thatching, and grows on the banks of the Chambal. The word is a corruption of Gandal, *q.v.*

Ganí (gunny), گني गनी

The name given to the coarse bags made from the fibres of the Pát (*Corchorus capsularis*). It is derived from Ganiya, a name which Rumphius gave to the Pát from some native source.

Ganaurí, گنوري गनौरी

A bulrush.—Eastern Oudh.

Ganṭhá, گنٹھا गंठा

A fractional part of a Jaríb.—See Gaṭṭha.

Gaṛá, گڑا गड़ा

A large sheaf; except in the Dehli territory, where it is usually considered to be a small one. The word is in use chiefly to the westward.

Gaṛá baṭái, گڑابٹائي गड़ाबटाई

Division of produce without threshing, by stacking the sheaves in proportionate shares.—Rohilkhand.

Grám, گرام ग्राम

A village; more usually Gáṅw.

Gaṛáo, گڑاو गड़ाव

An instrument used for cutting Jawár stalks, etc., for fodder. —Central and Lower Doáb. It is called Gaḍásí in Rohilkhand, and Ganḍásá and Ganḍásí elsewhere.

Garárí, گراري गरारी

The block over which the well-rope traverses.—Benares, Bundelkhand, and Lower Doáb. Garílí, Garrí, and Girrá are also similarly used.—See Chák.

Garḍaunrá, گرڈوںڑا गरडौंरा

A small pit.—Baitúl.

Gaṛeran, گڑیرن गड़ेरन

See Kolchú and Gandarwála.

Gargawá, گرگوا गर्गवा

A grass which grows in low ground during the rainy season.

When it gets into rice-fields it checks the growth of the plant, and is very injurious. Buffaloes are fond of the grass, but other horned cattle do not like it.

Gáucharáí, گاوچرائي गौचराई

Grazing; a grazing tax. From Gau, a cow, and Charána, to graze. It is known also as Kahcharáí. From Kah, grass.

Gáolí, گاولي गावली

A cowherd.

Gáṛí, گاڙي गाडी

Gáṛí, or Gáḍí, is a cart, and the man who drives it is called a Gáṛíwán, given in the Printed Glossary as Gaḍíwan The following are the names of the different parts of the North-Western Gáṛí:—Harsa is the long wood extending on either side, from the front to the back; the transverse pieces are called Pattí; those extending beyond the wheels are called Takání. Bánk, or Painjaní is the wood that joins the two Takánís; and Chakol the pin by which the wheel is attached to the Bánk; Sújah, the pins which attach the Bánk to the Takánís; Bánkara and Gaz, two pieces of wood in the front of the Gáṛí, where it narrows to a point; Phannah and Untara are parts that project beyond the yoke; Kharruá, the upright posts that support the covering or awning; Dandelí, something like a drag; Nah, the nave; Putthí, the quadrant of a wheel. The native wheelwrights make their wheels in four parts, each with a double spoke, which are afterwards joined together. Each of these parts is a Putthí.

Gáṛah, گاڙه गाडह

Low lands on which water does not lie long.—Upper Doáb. It is, perhaps, a corruption of *gáṛha,* deep.

Gáṭá, گاٹا गाटा

The yoking of bullocks together for the purpose of treading out grain.—Dehli.

Gáṭá is also applied in Dehli to a Brahman, or Banya, that forms an illicit connexion with a woman.

Gáṭá is also used, generally, in the N.W. Provinces to signify a plot; a piece of land; a division of a village; a field.

Gehúṅ, گیہوں गेहूं

Wheat. There are several names of wheats in different parts of the country, but they all, according to native opinion, resolve themselves into the two families of red and white; the former is known by the names of Lál, Laliyá, Kathiyá, Bansiyá, Samariya, Rattiyá, Jaláliyá, Pisiyá, etc. The latter by the names of U'jur, Situa, Dhaula, Pílí, Dáúd Khání, etc. The beardless wheat (Múṅriyá, from मूंड़िया Múṅriyá, to shave), is also both red and white, and in seed, flavour, and price, does not differ from the bearded kind. In opposition to Múṅriyá, Tikúrárí, or Túndiyá, is used to represent the bearded kind. The beardless wheat appears to be much more common in the Eastern than the Western parts of these provinces.

The following table shews the number of acres under wheat cultivation in the N.W. Provinces, during the year of Survey:

Dehli Division	225,084	Acres.
Rohilkhand Division	883,009	„
Mírat Division	890,309	„
Agra Division	472,364	„
Allahábád Division	423,901	„
Benares Division	535,642	„
Saugor Division	953,687	„
Total Acres	4,383,996	

Ghána, گھانا घाना

Ghání, گھاني घानी

A sugar-cane press.

Ghár, گھار घार

Clay soil in low situations, where rain-water lies for a time. Land worn away by running water is said *ghár ho jána.*

A sub-division of Mattiyár. Also, a long strip of land* in Etawa, lying for the most part between the Jumna and the high road to Agra. In Sekandra of Kaunpúr it is called Khár.

All these words are probably mere corruptions of Gahra, a cavity. The former is spelt with a common, and the latter with a hard or cerebral *r*, and Ghár itself is also spelt indifferently with either letter. The word bears a close resemblance to, and is possibly a corruption of, the Arabic Ghár غار a cavity, a hollow.

Ghárí, گھاري घारी

Cattle sheds.—Eastern Oudh.

A valley, or ravine.—See Ghár.—Rohilkhand.

Ghenṭí, گھينٹي घेंटी

The unripe pod of gram, arhar, and other pulses.—See Dhúndí (correctly Dhendí, Ghegará, and Thonthí).

Ghonghí, گھونگھي घोंघी

Ghonghí, or Ghoghí, signifies the tying the end of a blanket in a knot, and so placing it on the head as a protection against

* On the opposite side of the river there are other strips of land called Ghár, as Kachhwáha-ghár, Tauhar-ghár, and one in Seháranpúr (see Gújar); but whether it is applied to the oblong shape of the land, or to the worn surface of the soil in the neighbourhood of rivers, on the banks of which those Ghárs occur, it is not easy to say.

rain. It also signifies the enveloping oneself entirely in a sheet or blanket, so that, when one sits down, no part of the body, except, perhaps, the head, is discernible. It is also applied as Chot, *q.v.* The application of these words varies in different provinces.—See Khúrhú.

Ghúí, گهوئي घूई

The name of a herb which grows during the rains on high ground.

Ghun, گهن घुन

A weevil, destructive to wood and grain; hence, Ghuna, weevil-eaten. The term appears generic as well as specific, for it is applied to the Bhábí, Dholá, Pápá, Páthá, Khaprá, Kírí, Pitárí, Sursarí, and various other insects destructive to stored grain. Indeed Ghun is in many places not known as a grain-weevil, but, that it is nevertheless properly so applied, the common proverb teaches us,

गेहूं के साथ घुन पिस गया

"The weevil has been ground with the wheat;" applied to any indiscriminate calamity which involves equally both high and low.—See Journal of Agricultural and Horticultural Society of Bengal, Vol. III. Part 2, p. 89.

Ghundí, گهنڈي घुंडी

The name of a herb which grows in rice fields after the crop is cut. Camels are very partial to this herb; and it is used as a specific in various diseases by the country quacks.

Ghungchí, گهنگچي घुंगची

A small red and black seed (*Abrus precatorius*). It is known also by the name of Rattí, Chhontilí, Chirmithí, and Surkha; and as it is the primary unit of Indian weights, it is important to establish its exact value. From a series of experiments detailed in the thirteenth number of the "Mírat Magazine," it appears that the average weight of 267 seeds amounted to 1·93487 grains. Prinsep, in his "Useful Tables," gives the weight of the Masha (8 Rattís) at 15½ grains, which, divided by 8, affords 1·9375 for the weight of the Rattí. As these results were obtained independently, we shall be quite safe if we assume the Ghungchí, or Rattí, as equivalent to 1·933 grains.

Ghúngí, گهونگي घूंगी

An insect destructive to crops of certain kinds of cereals.—See Gindar.

Ghúr, گهور घूर

The name given to the soil of the sandy ridge to the East of Muzaffarnagar. Also pronounced घुड or घुढ़.

Ghurat, گهرت घुरत

Cattle pens.—Eastern Oudh.

Ghusránd, گهسراند घुसरांद

A kind of creeping grass with a yellow flower. It bears a bitter fruit resembling the Kakorí. It is used as a condiment for horses, but it is considered poisonous to men.

Ghoṭí, گهوٹي घोटी

Land which has been under a rice crop.—Bundelkhand, Lower Doáb, and Benares. Dhankar is used in the North West. The word is probably derived from ghoṭná گهوٹنا to shave.

Ghalla, غله गल्ला

Grain. The word is Arabic, but in common use.

Ghangol, گهنگول घंगोल

The name of the water lily which produces the celebrated Nílúfar flower. It produces a greenish fruit about the size of an orange, and the seeds of it are eaten by the poorer classes.

Ghaná, گهنا घना

From ghaná گهنا dense, close; a sporting preserve; the same as ramná or shikárgáh.

Ghaṛá, گهڑا घडा

An earthen water pot.

Gharkí, غرقي गरकी

Overflowed; inundated. From the Arabic غرق ghark, drowning.

Gharaṛ, گهرڑ घरड

The dry Moth plant, cut and given as fodder to cattle.—Dehli.—It is in some parts pronounced Kurar.

Ghaṭṭí, گهتي गट्टी

Loss; decrease; deficiency.

Ghai, گهئي घै

A platform of earth, artificially raised and levelled and smoothed, on which stacks of corn are placed; when staddles or supports are used they are called Chullí, *q.v.*

Ginḍurí, گنڈري गिड्डुरी

A pad of grass to support an earthen pot.—See Jurá.

Gindar, گندر गिन्दर

An insect which is very destructive to growing Gram and Arhar. Júí, Jurái, and Ghúngí are similarly applied, but chiefly in Bundelkhand, Benares, and the Lower Doáb.

Gintí, گنتي गिनती

From *ginna*, to count, signifies number; reckoning; the first day of the month; a muster; of which word Gilchrist observes that "it is much used in India for a *sample*, but why I know not, except from *mister*, a rule." The truth is, that *muster* in its Anglo-Indian sense is derived from the Portuguese *amostra*, a sample, a word which, as well as our *muster* in its ordinary sense, is derived from the Latin *monstrare*, to show.

Giráni, گراني गिरानी

Dearness of provision; scarcity.

Girjí, گرجي गिर्जी

A sort of grass which grows about a yard high, and is found in certain parts of Hánsí, particularly in that part known as "Skinner's Bir." The names of other grasses found there are gaṇḍá, or "scented;" sarwálá, or "head-bearing;" kheoṅ, bur, ganthíl, or "knotty;" palwá, or "large-straw;" and roish.—E. *add.*

Giro, گرو गिरो

Giro, or more correctly girau, is a pledge, a pawn.

Girwí, گروي गिरवी

Anything pledged or pawned.

Girwí is also, in Persian, an insect mischievous to standing corn. This is the same, no doubt, as the Genrúí of the Hindús which is a disease of the *cerealia*, in which the plant dries up and assumes a reddish colour. The word is derived from Genrú, a kind of red earth or ochre, and is in common use, but Ratá is the term used in the Doáb, Benares, and Rohilkhand, and Ratwaí, Rorí, and Ratua in Dehli. From *rat*, or *rata*, which is the origin of, and bears the same meaning as, *red*.—See Halda.

It is a popular delusion entertained in some parts of the country that the neigbourhood of Alsí, or linseed, is necessary to generate this disease; but in most parts of the N. W. Provinces the opinion is now repudiated. Nevertheless, as the disease first attacks Alsí, and the ova floats in the air, the precaution is perhaps wise of eradicating it, as farmers do the barberry-bush at home, which in many parts is supposed to be a great generator of rust.

The real nature of the disease has hitherto, as in the case of similar diseases in Europe, eluded the search of enquirers, whether practical or scientific; but an interesting account of its ravages has been given by Colonel Sleeman.

"It is at first of a light beautiful orange colour, and found chiefly upon the Alsí (linseed), which it does not seem much to injure; but about the end of February the fungi ripen, and shed their seeds rapidly, and they are taken up by the wind and carried over the corn fields. I have sometimes seen the air tinted of an orange colour for many days by the quantity of these seeds which it has contained, and that without the wheat crops suffering at all when any but an easterly wind has prevailed: but when the air is so charged with this farina, let but an easterly wind blow for twenty-four hours, and all the wheat crops under its influence are destroyed. Nothing can save them! The stalks and leaves become first of an orange colour, from the light colour of the farina which adheres to them; but this changes to deep brown. All that part of the stalk that is exposed seems as if it had been pricked with needles and had exuded blood from every puncture, and the grain in the ear withers in proportion to the number of fungi that intercept and feed upon its sap; but the parts of the stalk that are covered by the leaves remain entirely uninjured, and when the leaves are drawn off from them, they form a beautiful contrast to the others, which have been exposed to the depredations of these parasitic plants.

"It is worthy of remark that hardly anything suffered from the attacks of these fungi but the wheat. The Alsí, upon which it always first made its appearance, suffered something, certainly, but not much, though the stems and leaves were covered with them. The gram (*Cicer arietinum*) suffered still less; indeed, the grain in this plant often remained uninjured, while the stems and leaves were covered with the fungi, in the midst of fields of wheat that were entirely destroyed by ravages of the same kind. None of the other pulses were injured, though situated in the same manner in the midst of the fields of wheat that were destroyed. I have seen rich fields of uninterrupted wheat cultivation for twenty miles by ten, in the valley of the Narbadda, so entirely destroyed by this disease, that the people would not go to the trouble of gathering one field in four.

"The great festival of the Holi, the saturnalia of India, terminates on the last day of Phagoon, or 16th of March. On that day the Holi is burned; and on that day the ravages of the monster (for monster they will have it to be) are supposed to cease. Any field that has remained untouched up to that time is considered to be quite secure from the moment the Holi has been committed to the flames. What gave rise to the notion I have never been able to discover; but such is the general belief. I suppose the silicious epidermis must then have become too hard, and the póres in the stem too much closed up to admit of the further depredation of the fungi."—Rambles and Recollections, Vol. I., pp. 250-262. See also Spry's Modern India, Vol. II., p. 282.

Girwínámah, گروي نامه गिरवीनामा

A deed of mortgage.

Goál, گوال गोश्राल

Unclaimed land.—Dehli.—See Gyal.

Gurhaur, گرهور गुरहौर

Stacks of cowdung.—Eastern Oudh.

Gurab, گرب गुरब

Deep weeding, in which the ground is broken and pulverized. It is the opposite of Nirái, which applies only to superficial weeding. The word is derived from a rustic word, Gurabná, to dig—a common verb, but not in Shakespear's Dictionary, in which we rarely have occasion to notice any omission.

It is also the name given to the process of ploughing through a field of Bájrá or Jawári when the plant is about a foot high. The operation requires some nicety to prevent the young plants sustaining injury. Gurab, as applied to this process, is in general use, especially in the Upper Doáb and Rohilkhand; but Bidáhná and Chhantá dená are more common in Dehli and the Central Doáb, and Dadahrná in the Lower Doáb.

Gurarí, گڑري गुडरी

See Júra.

Gophaná, گوپهنا गोफना

A sling used by persons stationed on a Dámcha, *q.v.*

From गौ a cow, and फना or फन्दा a sling, as it is used to keep the cattle from eating the crops.—B.

Gorá, گورا गोरा

Applied to men, it means fair-complexioned; but when applied to horned cattle, it signifies red.

Goṛait, گوڑيت गोडैत

A village watchman; an intelligencer. The meaning is correctly given under Gúṛáit and Goráyát in the Printed Glossary.

Goṛhá, گوڑھا गोढ़ा

The homestead; fields near the village.—See Goenḍ.

Gorú, گورو गोरू

A cow; cattle in general.

Gorasí, گورسي गोरसी

A milk-pail. From, *goras*, cow-juice, *i.e.* milk.—See Jhákarí.

Got, گوت गोत

In common parlance Got has the same meaning as the more classical Gotra of the Glossary. Properly, those only are Gots (v. Colebrooke, Trans. R.A.S. Vol. I. p. 237), which bear the name of some Rishi progenitor, as Sándilya, Bharadwáj, Bashisht (Vasishtha), Kasyapa; but it has become the custom to call all sub-divisions of tribes Gots, and, according to the Ṇirnaya Sindhu, there are no less than ten thousand. The early genealogies of the Rajputs frequently exhibit them as abandoning their martial habits, and establishing religious sects, or Gotras. Thus, Reh was the fourth son of Purúravas of the Lunar Race, "from him in the fifteenth generation was Hárita, who with his eight brothers took to the office of religion, and established the Kausika Gotra, a tribe of Brahmans."—See Colebrooke's Miscellaneous Essays, Vol. I. p. 115; Journ. R.A.S. Vol. III. pp. 354, 356; Sansk. Dic. p. 298; and Vishnu Purana, p. 405.

Gothán, گوتهان गोथान

Place of assembling the cattle of a village. From the Sansk. गोस्थानं.—Saugor.

Gauchaná, گوچنا गौचना

Gauchaná, or Gochaní, is a field of wheat and Chaná (gram) sown together. The practice of sowing culmiferous and leguminous plants together has been much ridiculed, and has been brought forward as a proof of the ignorance of Indian agriculturists. Mill emphatically declares it (Hist. of India, Vol. II. p. 26) to be "the most irrational practice that ever found existence in the agriculture of any nation." But, notwithstanding this denunciation, which is too much in accordance with the usual spirit of his comments on everything Indian, the real fact is that the practice is highly advantageous to the land, as well as to the crop. Dew readily forms on the leaves of the Chaná, or gram, which would not form on the wheat; and in seasons of drought the practice is very often the means of preserving both crops. It may be carried, perhaps, to too great an excess in Madras, but the same charge cannot be made against the agriculturists of these provinces. As for its being irrational, it is a practice encouraged by the first agriculturists of Europe. Nothing is more common than to sow clover with barley, flax, oats, and Lent-corn; and with the same object which has established Gauchaná in native agriculture as a highly rational and beneficial system (Von Thaër, "Principes Raisonnés d'Agric. Vol. IV. § 1304).—See Gojáí.

Gauhání, گوهاني गौहानी

Lands situated close round a village; the village itself; fields on which cattle graze. Gauhání is also a general term for the entire lands of a village.—E.

This word is probably substituted for गांवहनी *gáńwhani*, which is rather difficult to pronounce, and is derived from the Sanskrit ग्रामिनी (sc. भूमि), of or belonging to a village.—B.

Godhaṛ, گودهڑ गोढड

Is the name given to the weeds and grasses which are collected from a ploughed field by the Dhínkhar.—Dehli.

It is known to the eastward by the name of Khedhí كهيڈهي, Guṛhal گڈهل, Akan آكن, and Ghúı گهور.

Goḍarí, گوڈري गोडरी

See Júra.

Goín, گوين गोईं

A pair of plough oxen; sometimes called Dogáwa. Gorá is more used in Dehli.

Goend, گوينڈ गोएंड़

Goenḍ, or Gwenḍá, signifies a suburb; vicinage; fields near a village; homestead.

Goháí, گوهاي गोहाई

The treading out grain by bullocks. From Gahna, *q.v.*—Rohilkhand. More correctly spelt *gahái*.

Gohárí, گوهاري गोहारी

Rich, highly-cultivated land; derived, perhaps, from its capacity of growing Gohuṅ, the provincial pronunciation of गेहूं *genhun*, wheat.—Saugor.

Gojá, گوجا गोजा

In Behar an ox-goad; also a bamboo staff—B.

Gojhá گوجها गोझा

A species of thorny grass which springs up during the rains. It is used medicinally, and Chamars eat it as potherb.

Gojará, گوجره गोजरा

Barley and Chaná sown together. It is known also by the name of Bejhará and Jauchaní.—See Gojaí and Gauchaní.

Gojaí, گوجئي गोजई

Wheat and barley sown together in the same field. Adhgawán, Gojí, and Gojarí are used in the same sense. This mixed crop is scarcely known in Saugor, Dehli, Lower Doáb, and Benares, but it is very common in the Upper and Central Doáb, Rohilkhand, Gorakhpúr, and Bánda.

Gokhrú, گوکھرو गोखरू

The name of a herb which springs up on Bhúr land; called also Hathíchinghar, Kanthphil, and Bhankarí. It produces a small fruit, covered with several prickles. In famine, the poorer classes of Hariáná feed on the pounded seed of this plant. It somewhat resembles Chaná, or the chick pea, and is known by botanists under the name of *Tribulus lanuginosus* (Roxb.). There is a large kind called the Gokhrú dakhiní, of which the fruit is of a triangular shape, and has prickles at the angles; hence the name is given to the iron crowsfeet thrown on the ground to check an advance of cavalry.

Gol, گول गोल

A party from another village sojourning with their cattle for pasture.—Dehli.

Gond, گوند गोंद

The name of a rush which grows in marshy ground, and is much used in making mats and baskets.

Goṅrá, گونڑا गोंरा

This is the name given in the Central and Lower Doáb to the reservoir from which water is raised by the Leharí, or Berí, to the reservoir above it, which is called Parchha, Odh, and Ulaha.

Sometimes Goṅrá is applied only to the straw or reeds which are placed to protect the side of the upper reservoir.—See Doarí, Docha, and Ríkh.

Gudṛí, گدڑي गुदड़ी

A daily market.

Gúl, گول गूल

A channel cut to convey water to a field.

A road; a path.—Saugor.

An unripe bunch of Indian corn; when ripe it is called Kukrí.—Dehli.

Gulál, گلال गुलाल

A farinaceous powder which Hindús throw on each other's clothes during the Holi. It is generally the meal of barley, rice, or Singhara, dyed with Bakkam wood.

Gulkhár, گلخار गुलखार

See Bhatkataiya.

Gulphunaná, گل پهنا गुलफुनना

The name of a herb which grows in fields sown with Kharíf grains. It somewhat resembles the Gúma.

Gulú, گلو गुलू

The pod of the Mahwá tree (*Bassia latifolia*). It yields a very useful oil, and is sometimes eaten by the poorer classes; but it contains no intoxicating qualities, like the blossom of that valuable tree, from which a spirit is produced by distillation, which is much used in Benares and Bahár in spite of its sickly smell. The word appears to be a corruption of Gilaunda, which is said in Shakespear's Dictionary to be "the blossom after it has fallen off;" but this application of the word is not known in these Provinces. The blossom is called Mahwa, like the tree, and the pod only is called Gilaunda, or Gulenda.

Gúlar, گولر गूलर

Cotton pods which have not yet burst.—Rohilkhand.—See Dhúndá and Ghegara.

Gúma, گومه गूमा

A medicinal herb which grows on high ground during the rains, and in fields grown with Kharíf crops (*Pharnaceum mollugo*). It produces several small flowers, the beauty of which is much admired by natives.

फल पर फूल फूल पर पाती
तिस पर जुगनू सब रंग राती

"On fruit flower, on flower leaf,
On that a firefly all coloured red,"

Is a distich applied by some poet to the regular order in which the flowers of the Gúmá alternate with the leaves, as well as to the appearance of the flowers which are said to resemble fire flies.

There are two species of Gúmá, one grows to the height of about two feet, the other seldom exceeds a foot.

Gúnṭh, گونٹه गूंठ

Land assigned rent-free for religious purposes; the endowment of a temple.—Kamaon and Gaṛhwál. This word is sometimes, but incorrectly, pronounced Ghúnt.

Gur, گڑ गुड़

Molasses. The gipsy name for sugar is Gúrlo and Gadlo (Trans. R.A.S., Vol. II., p. 553). This is no doubt derived from our Gur.

Guráo, گراو गुराव

A stook, or collection of sheaves.—Rohilkhand. A similar

word, but with the addition of a penultimate nasal *n*, is used in the Lower Doáb and Benares, to signify a heap of mixed chaff and corn.—See Ganteh.

Gurbháí, گربهائي गुरभाई

Fellow disciple. From गुरु Guru, a spiritual teacher, and भाई brother. The priests and teachers of the Sikh religion generally take the title Bháí.—B.

Gurdá, گردا गुर्दा

See Kolhú.

Gaṛhí, گڑهي गढ़ी

A village fortification of mud, flanked with towers. Under the former government there was scarcely a village without its Gaṛhí. Under our strong administration it is scarcely known except by name.

Gaṛhai, گڑهئي गढ़ई

A small pond.

Garrí, گري गर्री

A hay-stack; a rick; a stack of thatching grass; more correctly, Kharhí.

A small mound raised between heaps of corn and bhúsa on the threshing floor.—Lower Doáb.

A large stack of wheat or barley, containing two or more senká, which generally comprises several thraves of corn, the produce of one field.—Dehli and Upper Doáb.

A large stack of Kharíf produce.—Rohilkhand.

Kundṛá کنڈڑا is in general use elsewhere in the same sense, and also within the limits in which Garrí obtains, but in the latter case is always larger than a Garrí.—See Chhaur, Dabiya, Garáhí, Jhúha, Pahí, and Sántrí.

Gashtí, گشتي गश्ती

Presents to a revenue officer on his tour. From the Persian گشت gasht, rounds.

Gathí, گٹهي गठी

See Gachí.

Gathaund, گٹهوند गठौन्द

A deposit, or trust bound up in a bag (gaṭhrí).

Gaṭhrí, گٹهري गठरी

Literally, a bag; and hence applied to money brought in payment of revenue in a bag.—Benares.

Gaṭhwánsí, گٹهوانسي गठवांसी

The twentieth part of a Gatha.

Gaṭhiyá, گٹهيا गठिया

A pannier; a sack; a bundle.

Gayárí, گياري गयारी

See above under Gyal.

Gairá, گيرا गैरा

A sheaf of corn.

Hálí, هالي हाली

A man employed for the duties of ploughing—from هل a plough. In the Glossary, Halís are said to be agrestic slaves; it would have been more proper to say, labourers.—See Harwaha.

Hápar, هاپر हापर

A nursery for sugar-cane.

Hár lená, هاڑ لينا हाड लेना

To examine the correctness of a pair of scales.—Dehli and Doáb. Tár lena is used in Rohilkhand. Sádh lena to the Eastward.

Háta, حاطه हाता

Premises; an enclosure; a compound in Anglo-Indian language. It is a corruption of the Arabic Ihata.

Háthíchak, هاتهي چک हाथीचक

Is the name of a grass which grows about a foot high, and is given as fodder to cattle. It is also, by an easy conversion, the name given by gardeners to the prickly, and to the Jerusalem (*girasole*) artichoke.

Híṭhá, هيٹها हीठा

A person appointed to take care of the standing crops.—See Ahíta.

Hengá, هينگا हेंगा

A harrow. This word, as well as Sohága, Mai, Maiṅra, and Siráwan, is in general use; but the implement is known locally by various other names, as Patoí, Pahtan, Patela, Patrí, and Dandela. The part to which the ropes, or thongs, are attached is called Marwah. The cylindrical harrow, or roller, is called Rarí in Rohílkhand; Bilna and Belan in the Lower Doáb and Benares; and Gherí, Girarí, and Kolhú in Dehli and the Upper Doáb. The harrow made of two parallel timbers joined together, is called Maiṅra Sohága in Dehli and the Doáb, and Sohal in Rohilkhand. Gáhan is the name of a forked harrow.—See Gáhan.

Hirankhurí, هرن کهري हिरनखुरी

The name of a creeping herb which grows in the rainy season.

Its leaves resemble an antelope's hoof, and hence it derives its name—Hiran, an antelope, and Khurí, a cloven hoof.

Hulhul, هلهل हलहल

Hurhura, هرهره हरहरा

A small herb which springs up in the rainy season, and is used as a culinary vegetable, The commonest kind has a white flower, and produces a long pod, like that of the Múng, and is used as a medicine in fevers (*Gyandropsis pentaphylla,* formerly *Cleome pentaphylla,* or *viscosa*). There are said to be four kinds —white, red, purple and yellow. The three latter are much sought after by alchymists.

Hunḍh, هنڈه हंड

See Jíta.

Haulí, هولي हौली

A liquor shop. The word is common, except in Saugor and Dehli.

Hadbast, حدبست हदबस्त

This word also signifies the demarcation of boundaries, preparatory to survey.

Hakárná, هکارنا हकारना

To drive oxen. A corruption of Hánkna, tc drive.

Hal, هل हल

Har, هر हर

A plough,—if an instrument may be dignified by that name which has neither coulter to cut the soil nor mould-board* to

* But when anything like a mould-board is required, the people have sufficient ingenuity to frame one. The only occasion which calls for such an expedient is when

turn it over. Nevertheless, simple as the Hal is, and wretched in construction, it is admirably adapted to our light Indian soil, and does its duty well under the able agriculturists of our provinces. Of the operations of this simple plough, Dr. Tennant, who has led the van in the abuse of everything Indian, observes ("Indian Recreations," Vol. II. p. 78), "Only a few scratches are perceptible here and there, more resembling the digging of a mole than the work of a plough;" yet this prejudiced and superficial observer remarks in another place that the average produce of the Province of Allahabad is fifty-six bushels* of wheat to the English acre: as if these "scratches and diggings of a mole" could by any possibility produce *double the average* of the scientific cultivators of England. He had forgotten also to remark that the drill, which has only within the last century been introduced into English field husbandry, and has even yet

sugar-cane is sown. Large and deep furrows are then required, and various means are resorted to, to make the plough accomplish the purpose. In Dehli and the Upper Doáb it is usual to bind canes on the part into which the sole is fixed. Generally not more than two ploughs are used when planting sugar, but in the Doáb as many as four sometimes follow one another, on two of which are fixed mould-boards of the name of Roh and Pákhí, the former being stronger and smaller than the latter. The Roh is made of one piece of wood, the Pákhí of two.

* The yield of wheat would certainly not be so great now, whatever it might have been in the Doctor's days. It may be as well to make this reservation, with reference to the very common remark, that land in Upper India does not yield now so much as it did in former days. Where this is really the result of observation, the causes are obvious—the greater infrequency of fallows—the little manure that is given being diffused over more fields than formerly—the decrease in the fall of the periodical rains, owing to the immense mass of forest and jungle which has been cleared away—and the fields being less cultivated than formerly, when ploughs and hands could only be employed upon a limited number of fields. These are all to be traced to the operation of a more remote cause—the entire security afforded by the British Government. The number of hands, ploughs, and bullocks has not increased in proportion to the increase of cultivation.

It should never be forgotten that the decrease in the fertility of the soil is an old and popular complaint, and arises chiefly from the universal tendency to depreciate the present and exalt the past.

in the northern counties to combat many native prejudices, has been in use in India from time immemorial. If he had only reflected on this single fact (leaving out of consideration the universal practice of rotation and complete expulsion of corn-weeds), he would have saved the poor Hindus from much of the reproach which has been so lavishly heaped upon them by Mill and his other blind followers.

The principal parts of an Indian plough are—हरस Haras, the beam; हथीली Hathílí, हथा Hathá, चिरिया Chiriyá, or मुथिया Muthiyá, the handle or stilt; पन्हारी Panhárí or परौथा Parauthá, the sole, which is generally at the end shod with an iron share, called फाला Phálá, चौ Chau, or कूसा Kúsá. The Hal, or नांगल Nángal, is the body of the plough, the main piece into which the Panhárí and Haras are joined; but these terms, besides being exclusively applied to a particular part of the plough, are used to signify the entire plough. The ओग Og is a peg, or wedge, which fixes the Haras firmly into the Hal; a second is sometimes added which is called गंधेली Gandhelí; the पचेला Pachelá, पछीला Pachhílá, or फन्ना Phanná, is a wedge which fixes the Panhárí to the Hal. The खूरा Khúrá, बर्नेल Barnel, or नर्हेल Narhel, is an indented, or notched, part at the end of the beam, corresponding to the copse, or cathead, to which the yoke is attached by a leathern thong, called a नदह Nadah. In some parts the beam is not notched, but drilled with holes, into which pieces of wood are inserted. The yoke consists of the जूआ Júá, or upper piece, and the तर्माची Tarmáchí, or lower piece. The सैल Sail is the outer pin, and Gata the inner pin which join the Tarmáchí and the Júá, and which are on each side of the bullock's neck when it is yoked. These are the names usually applied to the parts of a plough in the Doáb and North-West; but in Benares and the Eastward the names are somewhat different. There, the चन्दौली Chandaulí answers to the Chiriyá, पाथ or पाठ Path to the Og, नरेली Narelí to the Pachelá. Har is the part on which the share is fixed. There

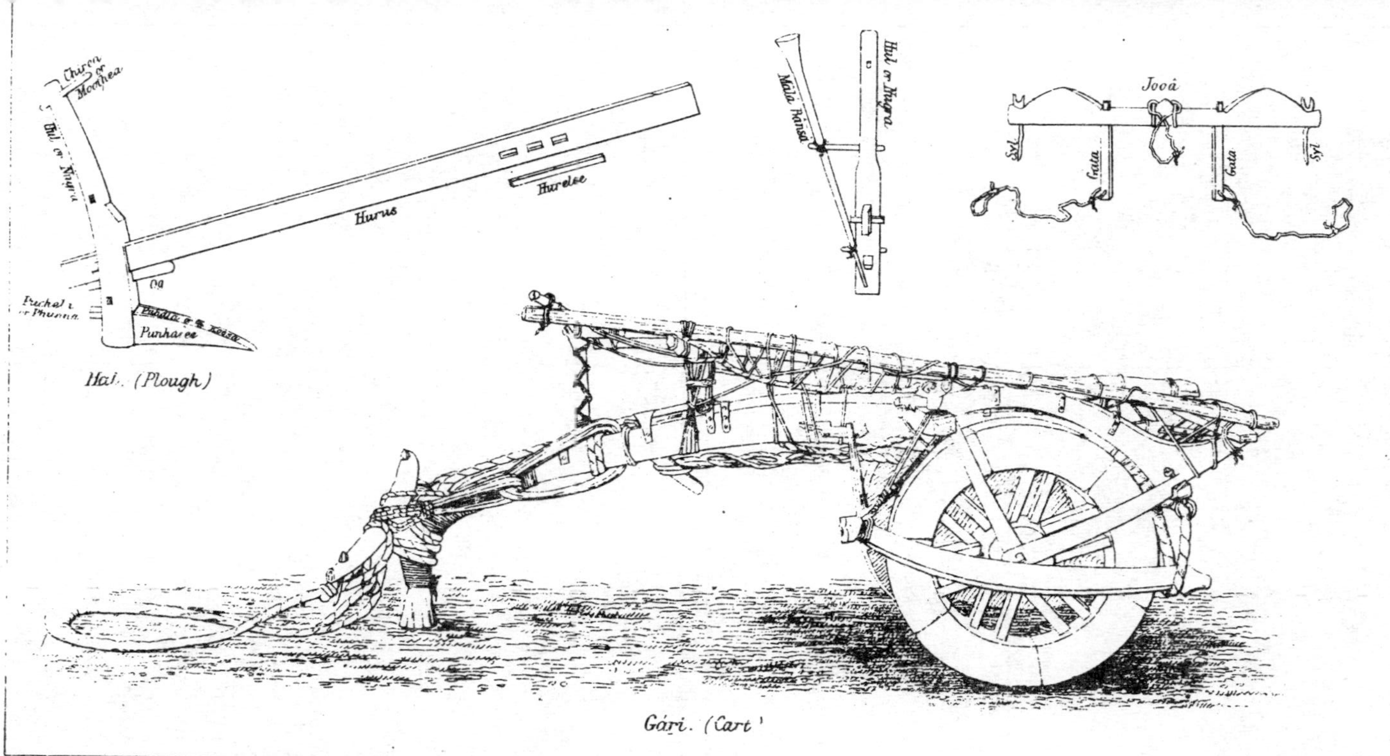

Vincent Brooks, Day & Son Lith. London W.C.

THE INDIAN PLOUGH AND CART.

are knots also, called Mahádewa, on the yoke of the Benares plough; and some other differences not worth mentioning.

Besides the common Hal of the country, there are others used in some places which vary but little in their structure from it. There is, for instance, the Nagar plough, which is used in Bundelkhand for planting sugar-cane. It is very heavy, requires six, seven, or eight bullocks to draw it, and enters very deep into the ground. The cane is put into a hole of the wooden part of the plough, through which it is passed and deposited in the earth, to as great a depth as the share can attain. The American cotton planters were much pleased with this plough, and preferred this manner of sowing sugar-cane to any they could adopt with the American plough. There is also the बाखर Bákhar, used to take off the crust when the soil is hide-bound, and by skimming the surface clears the soil from grass, weeds, and stubble.—See Bákhar. There are also the Kudhiya, the Kadh, the Kathú, the Kusiyar, the Pachranga, etc., which need no particular description.—See the illustration.

Haldá, هلدا हलदा

Hardá, هردا हरदा

A disease of the Cerealia, in which the plant withers, and assumes a yellow tinge. The word is derived from Haldí, turmeric. This kind of mildew differs but little from the Girwí, *q.v.*, except in attacking the plants in an earlier stage of their growth.

Haliyák, هلياک हलियाक

Wages of ploughmen.—Dehli and Upper Doáb.

Haltaḍḍí, هلتڈّي हलतड्डी

A drill plough.—See Bánsá.

Halas, هلس हलस

Hanas, هنس हनस

Haras, هرس हरस

The beam of a plough. Shakespear says wrongly Harís is the tail of a plough. Dr. Carey gives Is as the beam of the Dinagepúr plough.—Asiatic Researches, vol. x., p. 25.—E.

It is probably from हर and ईश ísh, 'lord or ruler,' as it is the principal part of the plough.—B.

Handá, هنڈا हंडा

A grass which is found on the banks of tanks and marshes. It produces a little red flower, but is not applied to any useful purpose.

Hansráj, هنسراج हंसराज

Literally, "goose-king," *i.e.* Brahma to whom it is sacred. A herb which springs up on brick walls during the rains. It is used medicinally.—Rohilkhand. It is known by the name of Pareshawáshan in the Doáb. It is also the name of a kind of rice.—See Dhán.

Haráí, هرائي हराई

The portion of land in a field which is included within one circuit of a plough. To commence another circuit is styled Haráí phándná, "to knot the plough-circle."

Harghasíṭ, هرگھسيٹ हरघसीट

All the cultivated land of a village is so called. From har, a plough, and ghasíṭna, to draw.—Lower Doáb.

Harhá, هرها हरहा

Unbroken and vicious cattle; plough bullocks.—Dehli and

Doáb. Besides these local meanings, it is generally applied to stray oxen.

Harjins, هرجنس हरजिनस

Grain of sorts. From har, every, and jins, species.

Harkára, هرکاره हरकारा

A messenger From har, every, and kár, business. The usual occupation of an Harkára at present is by no means in accordance with the derivation.

M. Garcin de Tassy, in a note to p. 219 of his "Kámrúp," observes on this word—" À la lettre factoton. Ce nom désigne un des trente-sept domestiques! que les Indiens, et les Europeans, ont a leur service." *

Harkaṭ, هرکٹ हरकट

Cutting rice while it is green and unripe.—Rohilkhand. From hara, green, and kaṭna, to cut.

Haraurí, هروري हरौरी

The occupation of ploughing, or place where ploughing is going on. Haraurí par jao signifies, " go and put your hand to the plough."

Also, an advance of about two rupees in money, and two maunds in corn, given to a ploughman when first engaged.—Benares.

Sondhár is the term applied in the North-West.

* In spite of the implied sneer in the text the learned French author is right both as to the literal meaning of the word, the original occupation of the officer, and the number of servants usually maintained by both Europeans and wealthy natives. In fact, to this day the indigo planters keep a servant called harkára whose business is precisely that of a factotum. He has to be constantly perambulating the land under indigo cultivation, and keep the ryots up to their work besides making himself useful in a vast variety of ways. The Hindu ryot of Behar and E. Oudh, however, corrupts the word into *halkára,* as though from *hal,* a plough, because one of the harkara's duties is to see that the lands are properly ploughed.—B.

Harsingár, هرسنگار हरसिंगार

The weeping Nyctanthes (*Nyctanthes arbor tristis*). It is a small forest tree growing to the height of about twelve feet. Harsingár yields a deliciously fragrant blossom, from which a yellow dye is prepared, which was borne on our tariff as an excisable article till the late revision of the Customs law. Harsingár is also much used in medicine by native practitioners, and is occasionally cultivated in gardens.

Harsot, هرسوت हरसोत

Harsot, or Harsotiya, signifies ploughing a furrow; the first ploughing of the season.—See Halaeta.

Affording assistance in ploughing.—See Angwara, Dangwara, and Jíta.

The term is also used to signify the bringing the plough home across the back of a bullock, or with the share inverted, after the conclusion of the day's work:

> Videre fessos *vomerem inversum* boves
> Collo trahentes languido.
> —*Hor. Epod. II.* 63.

These terms are used in Dehli; and, in the last meaning, in Brij also.

Harsajjá, هرسجا हरसज्जा

Literally, a sharer in a plough; reciprocal assistance afforded in ploughing fields.—Bundelkhand. From har, a plough, and sajja, partnership.—See Angwara, Dangwara, and Jíta.

Haraṭ, هرٹ हरट

A Persian wheel for drawing water from a well. The word is a corruption of Arhaṭ, *q.v.* Eight bullocks employed at a Haraṭ are capable of irrigating an acre of ground during the day.

Harwáhá, هرواها हरवाहा

A ploughman. The word is most commonly used in the East. Hálí is more usual in the West.

Hariyá, هريا हरिया

A ploughman; a worshipper; a devotee. The double meaning attached to this word is very elegantly conveyed in the following couplet.

हरिया हर से हेत कर ज्यों किसान की रीत
दाम घनेरा रिन घना तबहूं खेत से प्रीत

"Love Hara, o worshipper, after the fashion of the peasant,
The rent is heavy, his debts are many, still he loves his field."

The two first words signify "Ploughman and Plough," as well as "Worshipper and Hara (Siva);" which gives the poet the opportunity of conveying the moral, that no vicissitudes of fortune should affect a man's love for labor and devotion.

Hasiyá, هسيا हसिया

A reaping hook. Hansiya is also correct.

Hattá, هتا हत्ता

A large wooden shovel or spoon, about five feet long, used for throwing water into fields from aqueducts.—E. Oudh.

Íkh, ايكهه ईख

Sugar-cane; a field of sugar-cane.—Ganná.

Íkh is used in Western Hindustan, úkh in Eastern. In the Panjab the name is कुमाध kumádh.—B.

Ekfardí, يكفردي एकफर्दी

Land producing only one crop annually; opposed to Jútiyári and Dofarda. It is also known by the name of Ekfaslí, Fard, and Fardháí.

Ekfaslí, يكفصلي एकफसला

Land yielding but one crop annually.

Índhuá, اينڈھوا इंढुआ

A pad placed on the top of the head to support a water-jar.—See Júra.

Indurí, انڈري इंडुरी

A pad for supporting a round-bottomed jar.—See Júra.

Iráda, اراده इरादा

A term in arithmetic.—See under Bariz.

Isband, اسبند इसबन्द

The name of a herb which springs up on the banks of tanks during the rainy season. It produces a round thorny fruit, of which the seed is much used in exorcism and other superstitious practices.

Ismwár, اسموار इस्मवार

Literally, nominal. From ism, a name; entry in statements according to the order of individuals' names.

Istiklál, استقلال इस्तिकलाल

Confirmation; perpetuity; fixedness.

Istikrár, استقرار इस्तिकरार

Confirmation. These three last words are tenth infinitives of Arabic roots.

Itsiṭ, ائسٹ इटसिट

A root like osier-twigs, or like Chiretá, used in the Chaj Doáb, in the Panjab, together with other drugs, to procure abortion.—B.

Izáfa, اضافه इजाफा

Increase. These three words are also derived from the Arabic.

Jáb, جاب जाब

Jábí, جابي जाबी

An ox-muzzle. Jálí, Múnhchhínka, and Múncha are also used, as well as the words mentioned under Chhínka.

Jáíl, جايل जाईल

A term used in the Western parts of Rohilkhand to signify twice-ploughed land. When ploughed three times, it is called Tase; when four times, Chaus; when five times, Pachbásí; and so on. In the Northern Parganahs of Bareilly, the corresponding terms are Dobar, Tábar, Chonwar, Pacháwar; and the first ploughing is called Eksirí.—See Dor and Dosárí.

Jákhan, جاكهن जाखन

The wooden foundation of the brick-work of a well. It is generally made of the green wood of the Gullar tree (*Ficus glomerata*), because it is said to be less liable to rot than any other kind. The wood of the Pípal (*Ficus religiosa*) is also in request on the same account, but it is considered inferior to Gullar. This foundation is also known by the name of Newar and Nímchak. Sweetmeats are generally distributed, and sometimes a drum is beaten, on the occasion of its being adjusted and fixed. The word is perhaps derived from Jakarna, to tighten, to pinion; as great care and time are necessarily taken in binding the separate parts (gandwála) together, so that they may form a compact cylinder for the support of a heavy superstructure of masonry.—See Jamuwat.

Jálí, جالي जाली

An ox-muzzle; a net bag for weighing Bhus (chaff).—See Chhínka and Jab.

Jánt, جانت जांत

A wooden trough for raising water.

Jántá, جانتا जांता

A species of hand mill-stone; a stone mill for grinding.

Jáṭh, جاٹھ जाठ

The name of the post fixed in a tank to denote that its water has been dedicated to the deity, or has been married to a grove. Also the revolving beam or axis of a sugar-mill.—See Kolhú.

Játrá, جاترا जात्रा

A religious festival or fair.

Jíra, جيرا जीरा

Cumin seed.

Jítápatr, جيتاپتر जीतापत्र

A favorable decision.—Benares.

Jihát, جهات जिहात

Plural of Arabic جهت jihat, a cause, an object. Duties on manufactures. They were reduced by Akbar from 10 to 5 per cent., but were imposed during the decline of the monarchy at a much heavier rate by every petty ruler in his own principality.

Jel, جيل जेल

The chain of buckets on a Persian wheel.—See Arhaṭ.

Jelí, جيلي जेली

Jelí is a kind of pitchfork, or rake, for collecting and adjusting the ears of corn on the threshing-ground. It is also known to the Eastward by the names of Pancha and Panchángurá, from its having five (panch) prongs. Dhinka, or Dhínka, is a smaller kind of Jelí, which is used by a man in a sitting posture, and differs from a Jelí in having curved prongs.

جيلي در رساله چوبي دوشاخه كه خوشههاي كوفته كه در خرمن
باشد بدان برداشته برهوا اندازند تا غله از كاه جدا شود سكو بسين
مهمله مكسور و كاف مفتوح ليكن در جهانگيري سكو چوبي كه آنرا
سه شاخه و چهار شاخه سازند سه شاخه را سكو و چهار شاخه را
چهار شاخه خوانند و آنرا اشنه و نواشه و چك نيز كويند و بتازي
مدري و بهندي دنبالي گويند و صاحب جهانگيري سكو بفتح اول گفته
اما اول اقوي وهندي متعارف گواليار كه افصح السنه هنديست پنچانگرا
بيا و جيم هردو فارسي و نون غنه بعد الف و كاف فارسي و راي مهمله
بالف كشيده

(Gharáíbu'l Lughát.)

I translate only so much of the above as refers to the matter in hand: "Jelí is a piece of wood with two prongs, with which they toss into the air the ears of corn on the threshing floor after threshing them, to separate the chaff from the grain. Also called Sikau, but in the Jahangírí Sikau is restricted to a three-pronged fork; one with four prongs is called a 'Chahár-shákhah.' It is also called in Hindí dambálí, and at Gwalior Panchángurá."—B.

Jeonár, جيونار जेवनार

Is sometimes used in the sense of Jaunal, *q.v.*

Jenṭá, جينٹا जेंटा

A thick rope used for tying mould round the roots of trees when transplanting them.—E. *add.*

Jeoṛí, جیوڑي जेवडी

Bears the same meaning as Jaríb, *q.v.* A cord, a rope.

Jhábar, جھابر झाबर

Low land on which water lies, and which produces rice, or a grass called Tin. Sometimes, when the water dries up quickly, Rabbí crops are also sown in it.—See Jhab Bhomí in the Printed Glossary.

Jhad, جھاد झाद

Land on which Dhák, Híns, and other jungly bushes grow.—Upper Doáb.

Jháḍá, جھاڈا झाडा

Lands which remain under water during the rains. A swamp.—See Jhábar.

Jhákarí, جھاکڑي झाकडी

A milk-pail. From the Jhákarí, or Dohní, the milk is transferred into other vessels—the Kadhauní, the Jamauní, the Biloní, according to the particular process it has to undergo, till it reaches the ultimate stage of Ghí.

Jhám, جھام झाम

A large instrument in the shape of a hoe, or Phaurá, used for excavating earth in well-sinking. The use of it is peculiar to this country, and it is very ingeniously applied. The mode of its application has been fully detailed in the Asiatic Society's Journal.

Jhángí, جھانگي झांगी

Bramble and brushwood.—Eastern Oudh.

Jháú, جهاؤ झाऊ

(*Tcmarix dioica*). A common shrub in the Upper Provinces, growing in marshy or inundated ground. It is much used for thatching, hedging, and burning. Galls are produced on it, called Ṣamratu't turfa, or Baṛí-máí.—See Faras.

Jhárí, جهاري झारी

A pitcher with a long neck.—See Ghara.

Jháṛí, جهاڑي झाडी

Jungle; small bushes.

Jháwar, جهاور झावर

Flat or low land flooded by the rains.—See Jhábar.

Jhíl, جهيل झील

A shallow lake or morass, called in Bengal बील bíl.

Jhirí, جهري झिरी

Withered wheat; blight. The word is perhaps derived from Jhurna, to fade.

Jhojhurú, جهوجهرو झोझुरू

A grass to which camels are very partial, and which is occasionally given as fodder to horned cattle. It grows to the height of about two feet, and is known also by the name jangalí níl, or wild indigo.

Jhokand, جهوكند झोकन्द

Is the place at which the Jhonkayá stands.—See Kolhú and Jhonkayá.

Jhola, جهولا झोला

A cold wind which affects wheat by drying up the ears.—Upper Doáb and Dehli.

Jhonkayá, جهونكيا झोंकिया

The man who keeps up the fire when sugar is boiling. The word is sometimes pronounced Jhúkwa and Jhokya,—but incorrectly, for it is derived from Jhonkna, to supply fuel to an oven.

Jhúhá, جهوها झूहा

Jhúha is in Rohilkhand what Chaur is in Dehli. A large stack of Jawar or Bajra. A Jhúhá generally contains from ten to twenty Bojh, or loads.

Jhúlí, جهولي झूली

A cloth, or sheet, made into a fan for winnowing grain, when there is no wind.—Dehli. The word is derived from Jhúlna, to swing, or perhaps from Jhalna, to fan. The corresponding term in Bundelkhand is Sarwa. In Rohilkhand and Upper Doáb, Partwaí. In Benares, Páthí and Parauta; and in the Lower and Central Doáb, Parauta, Partowa, and Partí.

Jhúngá, جهونگا झूंगा

Bramble; brushwood. The word is sometimes pronounced Jhángí.

Jhúngá signifies also a bullock whose horns project forward. There are many similar words significant of peculiarities in the shape of horns.—मैना mainá is a bullock the tips of whose horns join in the centre. A superstition prevails against their use in draft or agriculture, and they are consequently always bestowed upon Brahmans.—Morá is a bullock whose horns grow backwards.—Múndrá, one whose horns are stunted and ill-developed. —Mundá, one whose horns are broken.—Phulsapel (literally one who shoves against a doorway), one whose horns project to the right and left.—Kainchá, one whose horns are one up and the other down. In some places, this is called Sarg-pátálí, *i.e.* heaven-and-hellwards.—See Dúnda.

Jhúnṭhar, جھونٹھر झूंठर

Fields yielding double crops. It is sometimes pronounced jhúṭhan and juṭhiyáíl. Júṭhiyan and júṭhelí are also used in a similar sense.—See Júṭiyan.

Jhúpá, جھوپا झूपा

A pile of mangoes or other fruit.—Lower Doáb.

Jhúṛná, جھوڑنا झूडना

To shake fruit from the tree. Jhuṛna, with a short vowel, is to fall as fruit from a tree.

Jhorá, جھورا झोरा

The haulm or stalks of leguminous plants, such as Múng and Moth, used as fodder.

Jhauwá, جھوا झौवा

A large open basket; so called because it is made from the twigs of the Jhaú, *q.v.*

Jhabrá, جھبرا झबरा

Jhabrá, or Jhabbúa, is an epithet applied to the ears of animals when they are covered with long hair. From jhabba, a tassel. One of the bucolic maxims respecting the choice of horned cattle says in approval of this point,

कार कछौटा झबरे कान
इन्हें छांडि न लीजिये आन

"Hairy ears
Buy these, do not let them go."

Jhajharká, جھجھرکا झझर्का

Early dawn before it is easy to distinguish objects.—Gharáibu'l

Lughát. The word is spelt jhajhalka in the Tuhfatu'l Lughát-i Hindí. Neither word is in Shakespear's Dictionary.

Jhakorá, جهکورا झकोरा

A shower.

Jhalár, جهلار झलार

A thicket; brushwood.

Jhamáka, جهماکه झमाका

A heavy shower.

Jhamjham, جهم جهم झमझम

Heavy continued rain. The term Jhamájham is similarly used.

Jhamarjhamar, جهمرجهمر झमरझमर

A light rain; raining drop by drop.

Jhaṇḍá, جهنڈا झंडा

Jhaṇḍí, جهنڈي झंडी

A flag staff; a flag used by surveyors as a mark by which to direct their observations.

Jhanjiá, جهنجیا झंजिया

A subdivision of the Mar soil.—Lower Doáb.

Jhankhaṛá, جهنکهڑا झंखडा

Jhankhaṛá, sometimes pronounced Jhankara, signifies a leafless tree,—the contrary of Jhaṇḍúlá جهنڈولا which is applied to a tree with thick foliage.

Jhaṛ, جهاڙ झड

Heavy rain; hence jhará-jhar, heavily, rapidly; and jharí, continued rain, wet weather.

Jhaṛberí, جهڙبيري झड़बेरी

From jhar, or jhár, a bramble, and ber the name of a tree, which appears to be the same as the sidar of Africa and Arabia, the *Zizyphus napeca* of modern botanists, and the *Rhamnus spina christi* of Linnæus, and probably identical with the tree which yielded the famous fruit of the Lotophagi (Herod. IV. p. 177).

The Jhaṛberí seldom exceeds two feet in height, but the Ber is a large tree which sometimes grows to the height of between twenty and thirty feet. The Jhaṛberí is often called the Pála shrub, and is used for many useful purposes. In appearance it is no better than a prickly bush, the fruit, however, which resembles a small plum, affords food to the destitute in famine, and is collected for that purpose by the women and children. It is either mixed with milk and water, or eaten in its natural state with bread, if procurable, and if not, by itself. The leaves are threshed and collected for fodder for the cattle; the briars and thorns form barriers for the fields, and cattle sheds, and, when no longer required, are used as fuel. During the year of famine (for it seems to grow equally luxuriant in a drought) the people to the West of the Jumna feḍ their cattle, and paid a large proportion of their revenue, from its sale. Indeed, in villages where the crop entirely failed, the only collections were from this source. In such cases the people retained one-half for consumption, and disposed of the remainder. Pála leaves, in an average year, sell from six to twelve maunds the rupee. The Jhaṛberí produces also very good gallnuts.

Jharuá, جهروا झरुआ

The name of a nutritious grass of which the grain is something like that of Shámákh (*Panicum frumentaceum*), of which it is reckoned to be a wild species. It springs up during the rains. The grain is eaten by Hindús on fast days, and Chamárs commonly make it into bread. The stalks are cut up and given to cattle, or applied to the purpose of improving the quality and quantity of milk. It is known also by the name of Sáwan and Sawaín, because it ripens in the month Sáwan.

Jharotá, جھڑوتا झडोता

The close of a season.—See Jhúrna.

Jins, جنس जिन्स

Grain; commodities; products.

Jinwár, جنوار जिनवार

See Janwar, which is the most usual pronunciation.

Jiriá, جریا जिरिया

The name of a rice cultivated in Benares.—See Dhan.

Jog, جوگ जोग

The name of the person upon whom a draft or bill of exchange is drawn.

Johar, جوهڑ जोहड

The name given to a large pond or lake.—Dehli.—See Ahar.

It is also applied in the Central Doáb to any inundated land, and is there pronounced Jhor.

In Shakespear's Dictionary, Júhar is said to signify "Pits filled with water at the bottom of mountains."

Jokhái, جوکھائي जोखाई

Weighment; the weighman's perquisite. From jokhná, to weigh.

Júá, جوا जुआ

The yoke of a cart or plough.

The word is preserved in many of the Indo-European languages.—See Garí, Hal, and Halas.

Júí, جوئي जूई

An insect destructive to certain crops.—See Gindar.

Jugálná, جگالنا जुगालना

To chew the cud.

Júná, جونا जूणा

Júṛá, جوڑا जूडा

A rope of twisted grass, or twine, made to support a round-bottomed jar. It is called also Indurí, Endhua, Chakwa, Gurarí, Ginduri and Godarí. The original meaning of Jura is the knot into which Hindús tie their hair at the back of the head.

Júṛemárí, جوڑيماري जूडेमारी

Literally, brought under the yoke. The term is generally used to signify land actually in possession, in distinction to that which a man is entitled to by virtue of descent from a common ancestor.

Jutá, جتا जुता

Is the name given to the rope connecting the leherí, or irrigating basket, with the killí, or handle. From jotna, to yoke.

Jútiyán, جوتيان जूतियां

Land which bears two harvests during the year,—opposed to

ekfarda, which bears only one.—Benares. The word is derived from jotna, to cultivate.

Júthálí, جوتهالي जुथाली

Júthálí bears the same meaning as Jútiyán above.

Jorí, جوڑي जोडी

A pond smaller than a Pokhur.—Dehli.—See Ahar.

Jot, جوت जोत

Cultivation; tillage; tenure of a cultivator. It is also sometimes used to signify the rent paid by a cultivator.

Jotá, جوتا जोता

Jotár, جوتار जोतार

Jotiyá, جوتيا जोतिया

Jotan, جوتن जोतन

A cultivator of land.—See above under Jot.

Jau, جو जौ

Barley,—but not exclusively such as is raised by artificial irrigation, as stated in the Printed Glossary.

The Jau, or barley-corn, is in India, as in many other countries, the primary unit of measures of length. The Asiatics, however, in that fondness for minute quantities which prevails with them, assume a certain number (6 or 8) of hairs of a horse's tail or mane, as equivalent to a Jau. Between Europe and Asia, there is also this difference in the use of the Jau as the basis of measures of length, that in the former it is more usual, though not universal, to take the length of the grain; in the latter, the breadth:—thus, in England, three barley-corns placed end to end make an inch, and in India, eight barley-corns' breadths make a finger. The former is more likely to be correct as an invariable standard than the latter.

The following table shews the quantity of barley in cultivation in the Upper Provinces during the year of survey.

Dehli Division	90,053	Acres.
Rohilkhand Division	182,476	„
Mírat Division	153,050	„
Agra Division	359,811	„
Allahabad Division	430,633	„
Benares Division	1,301,887	„
Saugor Division	854	„
Total Acres.........	2,518,754	

Jauchaní, جوچني जौचनी

A mixed crop of barley and chaná.—See Gojara.

Jaunál, جونال जौनाल

Land cultivated alternately by Rabí and Kharíf sowings. Land in continual cultivation.—Rohilkhand and Doab.

In Dehli and Oudh it is applied generally to land which has been cropped during the past season with wheat and barley, which in the Upper Doab is called Binar, and in some places, Narua. In Benares the same word, or rather Jaunar, means a field in which barley is sown without having borne a previous Kharíf crop. In Bundelkhand it means land on which any Rabí crops have grown.—See Jaunar in the Printed Glossary.

It is probable that the meanings ascribed to this word are derived from different sources. When it is applied to Rabí land alone, we may perhaps look for its root in Jau, barley. Where it means land under constant cultivation, we may perhaps look for its root in Jun, time. Thus, in many places land exhausted by over-cropping is styled Juní.—E.

The root of these words is probably to be found in the now little used Hindi word जेवना to eat.—B.

Jaunchí, جونچي जौंची

A kind of smut in barley and wheat, in which the ears produce no corn.

Juár, جوار जुवार

A species of millet.—See Jawar.

Jaunṛa, جونڙا जौंडा

Payment of village servants in kind. The word appears to be a corruption of Jiora, *q.v.*—Eastern Oudh.

Jabdí, جبدي जबदी

A species of rice cultivated in Rohilkhand.—See Dhan.

Jadhan, جڈهن जढन

Jarhan, جڑهن जढ़न

A large species of rice, cropped at the close of the rainy season.

Jagní, جگني जगनी

A small grain from which oil is extracted. It appears to be the same as the Ramtillí of the Gonds.—Saugor.

Jajmán,ججمان जजमान

A person from whom Brahmans, or menials, such as barbers, washermen and sweepers, have an hereditary right to claim certain perquisites, on occasion of any ceremonies or services which they are called upon to perform.

Jal, جل जल

A jungle shrub which grows in Bhaṭṭí territory.

Jala, جله जला

A lake. From jal, water.

Jaláliyá, جلاليا जलालिया

A fine species of wheat with reddish ears.—Saugor.

Jalása, جلاسه जलासा

A pool of water; a tank.

Jalkar, جلکر जलकर

The produce and piscary of rivers, jhíls, tanks, etc.; also, the revenue assessed thereon.—See Jelkora and Jalkar in the Printed Glossary.

Jalm, جلم जलम

Birth; birthright. Used to denote proprietary right, especially in the soil.—Saugor. The word is a corruption of Janam, birth.

Jalním, جلنيم जलनीम

A bitter herb which grows on the banks of tanks. It is used medicinally as a cure for the itch, and has a purgative quality. It has obtained its name from its springing up only in the vicinity of water.

Jal pípal, جل پيپل जल पीपल

A herb somewhat resembling the pepper plant. It is called also Aspabúta in the Taraí Parganahs. In the Talíf-i Sharíf it is called Jalpílbaka.

Jamúwaṭ, جموٿ जमूवट

The foundation of a well. From jamna, to join, to adhere. Hence the word is applied to the festive ceremony on the occasion of completing the foundation of a well.—Benares. In the Dehli territory this ceremony is called Naichak and Nímchak, which are names applied also to the foundation of the well. Newar (from नेव foundation) is the most usual word elsewhere.—See Jakhan.

Jamowá, جموا जमोवा

Indigo planted before the rains, and irrigated by artificial means.—Central Doáb.

Jamowá is also the name of a tree.

Jamaiya, جميا जमैया

The name of a grass in Dehli.

Jandrá, جندرا जंदरा

Shakespear says, Jandrá means a pitchfork; but in the Upper Provinces it is most usually applied to a kind of rake used during irrigation for dividing a field into small beds. It is used by two men—one holds the handle, and the other holds a string attached to the forks of the rake in a direction opposite to the handle. It is an inconvenient method of employing two men to do the work of one. The name Jandrá is used chiefly to the Westward. Elsewhere, the same implement is known by the name of Mánjho and Karha, and solid wood more sensibly supplies the place of the forks of the rake.

Janewá, جنيوا जनेवा

A kind of fragrant grass which grows in fields which have been cultivated with Kharíf crops. Its flower is like that of the Doáb, but its stem is erect, and grows to about the height of a foot and a half.

Jangrá, جنگرا जंगरा

The haulm of Kharíf produce.—Lower Doáb.

Jantrí, جنتري जन्तरी

An almanac, or register. It originally meant a perforated piece of metal through which wire is drawn, and may have subsequently been applied to an almanac on account of its having many open compartments, or ruled divisions.—E.

I should be inclined to think that the two meanings have no connection with each other; the wire-drawer's metal is merely a diminutive from the Sanskrit यन्त्र yantra, meaning a tool or instrument of any sort; and the almanac was so called because it contained the record of astronomical observations made with yantras or instruments, such as the wonderful stone and brass circles, etc., still to be seen in the Man mandil at Benares.—B.

Jaríbkash, جريب‌كش जरीबकश

Surveyor; measurer. Literally, a drawer of the measuring chain.

Jurímána, جريمانه जुरीमाना

From جُرم jurm, a crime; fine, penalty; given as Jerumana in the Printed Glossary.

Jaríṭá, جڑيٹه जडीटा

Brushwood; brambles. The word is used provincially, and is perhaps a corruption of the Hindí Jhúṛ झूड, which signifies the same.

Jarela, جريله जरेला

The name of a rice cultivated in Rohilkhand.

Jargá, جرگا जरगा

The name of a grass given as fodder to cattle, especially to horses. It grows generally on high ground.

Jaṛwí, جڙوي जड़वी

The name given to the small shoots of the rice plant, when it first springs from the ground.

Jaṛwaṭ, جڙوٹ जड़वट

The trunk of a tree.

Jatar, جتر जतर

Cultivated land.—Upper Doáb.

Jawálí, جوالي जवाली

Jawála, or Jawálí, signifies gram mixed with barley as food for cattle. Also, a small mixture of barley with wheat.

Jawár, جوار जवार

A species of millet which grows from a height of eight to twelve feet on a reedy stem *(Holchus sorghum)*. It is known also by the names of Jondhrí, and in some places, of Jaundí. There are generally reckoned to be four kinds of Jawár. The red kind, or Joginia Jawár, is large, bears a lower price than the other qualities, and its stalk is not good fodder for cattle. The Baunia (from Bauna, a dwarf) is small, very white, grows straighter than the other kinds, and its stalk is also considered an inferior fodder. The third and best is the Píria or Sáer. Its head bends more than the rest, its stalk is much approved as fodder, and, as the grain grows more compactly, it ripens later than the other kinds. The fourth and rarest is the Básmatí, which is a very fragrant kind, but scarcely repays the expense of cultivation.

These may be considered the kinds most ordinarily known in the Doáb; but there are several others known elsewhere, as the Alápúrí like the Joginia, Dúleria or Domunhí, Jaterya, Khowa, Charka, Bidara, Lukú, Gutwa, Málatí, Chúneha, Baksí, Magha, Gapuráí, Bhadelí or Kúárú, Dugdí, Kumaria, Latúghar and

Bánda; the specific differences of which it is needless to mention.

Jawára, جوارہ जवारा

As much land as can be ploughed by a pair of bullocks. If a man says he has two Jawáras, he may be considered to have cultivation sufficient for the employment of two ploughs. A Jawárí of the Central Doáb, in which province the word is chiefly used, could not at the most be considered as more than eight acres.

In Dehli, Jawára is used to signify the area ploughed in half a day, which is the same as the Chhakwár of the Doáb. A Sanjhlo (literally, till the evening) signifies that which is ploughed during the whole day, and comprises two Jawáras, equivalent to the Aratram, Arrura, Earing, and Avera of our law books.

The words Jawárí and Jawára are derived from Júa, a yoke, it being as much land as one yoke of bullocks can plough.

Another meaning of the word Jawára is a yoke, or pair of bullocks, especially when employed at a well.

Jawára is likewise the name of the barley which is forced in earthen pots by the Brahmans for presentation at the Dasehra, or by women, for presentation to their brothers or fathers on the same festival.—See Jaí.

Jawára also signifies, in some parts of these provinces, the small shoots of rice, which germinate when steeped in water. In Shakespear's Dictionary it is said to mean "large maize." I never heard of this application of the term.

Jawása, جواسہ जवासा

Jawása, under the name of Javassa, is described in the Printed Glossary to be "a slender thorny shrub, which assumes its most lively verdure in the heights of the warmest and driest weather, and languishes and fades under the influence of rain."

It is the prickly-stem Hedysarum (H. Alhagi), a thorny bush on which camels browse; hence, says Khan Arzú, in his Dictionary, it is also called Unt-katára. But Khan Arzú appears to be wrong in saying the Jawása is the same as Unt-katára. The peasantry look upon these as entirely different plants, and in appearance they do not in the least resemble each other. The real Unt-katára, or Katela, is something like a thistle (*Echinops echinatus*, Roxb.), and has a yellow flower. It is called in different parts of the country by different names, such as Ghamoí, and Bang-kateya, and Satyanásí. The Bhat-kateya and Gol-kateya are of the same family.—See Kateya. But, though the Jawása is not called Unt-katára, it certainly is a camel's thorn, and being therefore classed under the name of Ushtar-khar, Khan Arzú might easily have been misled. The name of Alhagi is derived from the root *haj*, which denotes in Arabic its connection with a place of pilgrimage. One of the species, the Alhagi Maurorum (which is said by some to be the Jawása itself) is celebrated for its production of the manna of the desert.

Jawása is áonsidered a good medicine in bilious disorders, but is chiefly known to Europeans as a substitute for Khas-khas in Tattís. In ancient times Jawása appears to have been eaten by bullocks as well as camels: for we find those animals represented in the Mrichchhakaṭi as chewing Jawása. If they were able to accomplish this, their palates must have altered considerably; unless, as perhaps was the case, the prickly herb was chopped up into little bits, and given as fodder in that state.

Jawáz, جواز जवाज

A Persian word signifying a wooden mortar; a sugar-mill; an oil-mill.

Jazar, جزر जजर

A term in arithmetic signifying *duplation*, or doubling a number, which, like *mediation* or halving, is considered in

Oriental works to be a separate operation from ordinary multiplication, or division, and is so entered in European books on arithmetic of the sixteenth century.

Jaichí, جيچي जैची

A weed which springs up with Rabí crops.—See Jaití.

Jaí, جئي जई

Oats. The name has been only lately introduced into the N.W.P., as the grain was not known before the acquisition of this country by the British. It may perhaps have been so called from its being considered a small kind of barley; thus, from jau, jauí, jaí; as from chana, chaní; and urd, urdí. The word, however, is not new, though the application of it is; for the small shoots of barley (especially cultivated by Brahmans for the purpose, in anticipation of the season) which are carried about in the turbans of Hindús during Dasehra, are in many places known by the name of Jai, or Jaí,* either because of the smallness of the barley, or in commemoration of the Jai, or triumph of Rama over Ravana, the demon-lord of Lanka.

It is worthy of remark that in Benares, Bundelkhand, and the Lower Doab, oats are called Ramjau, *i.e.* the barley of Rama. As the Hindus already had an Indarjau (*Echites antidysenterica*), Ramjau was not altogether an unnatural combination to represent a new grain which bore a resemblance to barley. Ramjau, therefore, being the name which the natives

* This is likewise the name given to the first sprouts of germinating rice (see Jawara) when the seeds are steeped in water previous to sowing. There is also a small species of barley well known in Rohilkhand as Jai, or Jaí, as is shown by the following couplet, in which its easy and rapid growth is remarked :—

कोठी चढ़े पुकारे जई
खिचरी खाकर क्यों ना बई

"The Jaí halloos out from the house tops, 'Why not sow me after eating Khecharí?'" (*i.e.* Makar Sakrant) which implies that its growth is very quick.

chose first to give this grain, it is not altogether improbable that we may derive our Jaí from the ceremony above alluded to, rather than from its being considered a small species of barley. The very name of Ramjau would instantly suggest Jai—both being words intimately connected with the festival of the Dasehra.

Jaití, جيتي जैती

Jaití, Jauchí, or Jaichí, is the name of an *Euphorbia* in the Western part of these Provinces, which springs up with the Rabí crops, and yields an excellent oil. The plant is about two feet high and three in circumference, and the seed yields about one-fifth of its weight in oil. In a paper presented in May, 1843, to the Horticultural Society of Calcutta, it is stated as an extraordinary thing that the seed will not come up on the ground on which it was last shed, if that land has in rotation been under a Kharíf crop. But there appears nothing wonderful in this (even if the statement is true to the fullest extent, which perhaps it is not), because land under a Kharíf crop is always most thoroughly weeded, and the Jaití seed would not be allowed to remain in it. If the land remain uncultivated during the Kharíf, a few Jaití plants would come up, but not of course so many as would appear had the land been ploughed and prepared for a Rabí crop. In these respects it obeys some of the conditions of Matauna.—(See Kodo.) The previous ploughing for the Rabí has such an effect upon Jaití, that it will spring up the third year after it is shed, even if the land has been under an intermediate Kharíf crop. It is not therefore necessary to suppose that it has any natural affinity with the Rabí grains; the mere ploughing, and exposure of the soil to the genial influence of the atmosphere, are sufficient to account for its germination.

Jaití does not appear likely to repay the trouble of cultivation, notwithstanding the expectation held out in the paper above-mentioned.

Kachhwara, کچھوارہ कछवारा

Any portion of ground cultivated by Kachhís. The Province of Katchh derives its name from the same source. (See Vishnu Purana, p. 190). In the Upper Provinces the term Kachhwara, or, more usually, Kachar, is applied to alluvial formations under the banks of a river, and the term has been said to be derived from Kach, a corner; on account of Kachars forming chiefly in the re-entrant angles of a river's bank: but this does not seem so probable as the derivation above given, as the land is well adapted for garden produce, and therefore cultivated, or fit to be cultivated, by Kachhís. Or the word may come from Kachha, new, fresh.

Kamla, کملا कमला

A caterpillar, so called from its woolly coat.—See below.

Kamal, کمل कमल

A blanket; a coarse woollen garment worn universally by the peasantry of the Upper Provinces.

The best Kamals in these Provinces are made in Alwar and in the neighbourhood of Mírápúr in Mírat. The Sánslá Kamal of the latter place sometimes sells as high as twenty-five rupees. It is made of the wool of lambkins, shorn about three days after their birth. The Sánsla is from six to eight yards long and about two broad. The ordinary Kamal sells for from twelve annas up to two rupees.

Karia, قریہ करिया

A village. From the Arabic قرا assembling together, concourse. The word is not frequently used now, but we have it preserved in Kariat Mittú, Kariat Síkhar, Kariat Dost, and Kariat Mendhú, the names of Parganahs in the Province of Benares.

Kás, کاس कास

Saccharum spontaneum. A grass which is found in every part of the Upper Provinces. Its existence is generally considered to be indicative of extreme poverty of soil, but this is not always the case. It particularly affects soils which have been allowed to remain long untilled, and as its roots strike deep, it is very difficult to eradicate.

In the Saugor territory it is said to grow in great abundance on lands which have been exhausted by over-cropping; it is also said that when the weed rots and disappears, it denotes that the soil has gained heart again, and is fit for cultivation; that it is stronger in proportion as the lands are richer; and that the strongest disappears in fourteen years.

Kás, however, is not altogether useless; it is sometimes applied as a thatch; is in much demand for twine; and elephants, horses and horned cattle do not object to it as fodder.

The grass grows from three to fifteen feet high, and it flowers in great profusion after the rains. The base of the flowers is surrounded with a bright silvery fleece, which whitens the neighbouring fields so much as frequently to resemble a fall of snow. It is hence frequently called in aid by the Hindú poets:

> "Like Siva's ashen whiteness, autumn bears
> The budding grass, and like the foul hide wears
> The dun clouds," etc.
>
> —*Mudrá Rákshasa*, p. 196.

The word is more generally pronounced Káṅs, with a nasal *n* as the penultimate letter; but it is correctly Kás, as in Kás-gange. The familiar couplet, in which the hunger and avarice of Brahmans are sportively alluded to, shows the correct pronunciation as well as the season of its flowering—

आया कनागत फूले कास
बामहन बैठे चूल्हे पास

"The Kanágat* has come; the Kás flowers,
Bámhans (low Brahmans) are sitting round the fireplace."†

* Festival of deceased ancestors; also called Shraddh, performed in Asin (Kuár).

† *i.e.* To get their doles of food, usual on such occasions.

Káshtkár, کاشتکار काश्तकार

A cultivator. This is a Persian word; the Hindí Kisán is in more general use.

Karíl, کریل करील

Capparis aphylla. The caper bush. It grows to the height of from ten to fifteen feet, and its evergreen branches, or twigs, which are leafless, produce a red flower, from which proceeds the well-known fruit called Ṭenṭ, which is eaten as a pickle by the poorer classes.

The Karíl grows chiefly in the North-West, and its being found in great quantities in the neighbourhood of Birj, has given rise to the following trite couplet, in which the taste of Raghonath is impugned for not giving the best article to the place of his own mortal abode.

कहा कहिं रघुनाथ की गई सतली मांह
काबुल में मेवा करी टेंट बिर्ज की मांह

"Folks say Raghunáth's capriciousness has not left him,
He has given fruit to Kábul, and (only) Ṭenṭ to Brij (his former house)."

When the fruit is large, it is called Tenta, when small, Tentí.

Kodo, کودو कोदो

A small grain, sown early during the rainy season (*Paspalum frumentaceum*, Kœn.). The season for sowing it is indicated in the following lines:—

पुख पुनर्बस बोइये धान
असलेखा कोदो परमान
मघा मसीना दीजिये पेल
फिर दीजिये परहल में ठेल

"In Pukh and Punarbas sow rice;
In Aslekha Kodo is directed."

The first word in each of the three first lines is the name of a lunar asterism, which points to the proper time of sowing various kinds of grain.

It is a very curious fact, but one which does not admit of doubt, that this grain is frequently found to have inebriating properties, when made into bread. Such Kodo is known by the name of Matauna (from Matt मत्त drunk, intoxicated); but in appearance it resembles Kodo in every respect. It is sown as ordinary Kodo, and comes up as Matauna, but only in those fields on which Kodo has been previously grown, and only, perhaps, in one instance out of ten even in such cases. If wheat or barley is grown, it will not come up, nor will it ever spring up on newly broken soil. It is therefore a necessary condition of the produce of Matauna, that Kodo was sown the preceding year. The effects of the mania are fortunately not very injurious, and death never supervenes. The intoxication which it causes is generally that of a cheerful kind, lasts for two or three days, produces no convulsion or ulcers, and inflicts no permanent injury on the constitution. In these respects it differs from Raphania, which is caused by eating rye affected by ergot.

These curious properties of Kodo have invested it with a degree of mystery in the eyes of the natives, and some classes even worship it as a god. Thus, the Kákan Rajputs of Gházípúr are said to pay worship to this divinity. They never cultivate or eat Kodo; and the reason assigned is that, while under the influence of Matauna, they were set upon by some of the neighbouring tribes, and thus lost the greater part of their once extensive possessions.

This intoxicating effect of Kodo is by no means imaginary, as many may be induced to suppose. Independent of its notoriety in these provinces, it has been witnessed in distant parts of the country by medical officers who have borne testimony to the fact. Dr. Irvine, in his statistical account of Gwalior, mentions it, and Dr. Francis Buchanan has seen its effects in Behar and and Bhagalpúr. He states that the natives, as they do in these provinces, attribute the narcotic quality of the grain in certain fields to its being infected by a large poisonous serpent, called Dhemna; and he is disposed to ascribe the lameness called Maghya lang to the common practice of sleeping on Kodo straw, which may, perhaps, emit narcotic exhalations.

Kisári *(athyrus sativus)* is another grain which is found to have injurious properties. A curious instance of a general paralysis caused by it is given in Colonel Sleeman's "Rambles and Recollections," Vol. I. p. 134.

Kolhú, کولهو कोलह

A sugar mill. To illustrate the difference of language in different Provinces of this Presidences, the names of the component parts of the mill are given below in the language of Benares and Rohilkhand. In Dehli and the Doáb other variations occur, but they are few. The Lower Doáb inclines more to the Benares dialect—Dehli and the Upper Doáb to that of Rohilkhand. Bundelkhand has a mixture of both. For instance, there Kattrí is the horizontal, and Jath the upright beam.

ROHILKHAND.	BENARES.	EXPLANATION.
Pát	Kattrí	The horizontal beam to which the bullocks are attached.
Láth and Játh	Pat	The upright beam which moves in the mill.
Malkham	Khúnta	The upright post which is parallel to the last.
Chirya	Dhenka	The wood by which the two preceding are joined to one another.
Orí	Orí	The basket on the horizontal beam, from which the mill is fed.
Nárí	Narí	The leather thong by which the horizontal beam is connected with the yoke.
Paith	Ghagra	The circle in which the bullocks move.
Saya	Saika	The cup in which the expressed juice is transferred into the boiler.
Jhokand	Jhokand	The place from which the fuel is supplied to the fire under the boiler.
Dhúndra	Dhúndka	The outlet for the smoke.
Dhor	Dohra	The spoon for taking the juice out of the boiler.
Chandwa	Gurda	The scrape to prevent the sugar resting at the bottom of the boiler.
Ota	Nesur	The raised blocks on which the cane is cut.
Gandarwala	Gareran	The receptacle for the sugar-cane before it is cut.

This simple mill has, like the native plough, been much ridiculed for the rudeness of its construction ; but it is, nevertheless, a very efficient instrument, gaining in power what it loses in rapidity of execution. Every particle of the cane is subjected to three crushings in the Kolhú. In the European triple-roller wheel it is subjected to only one. Native Zamíndárs repay us with their contempt for our process, by pointing to the juice in the refuse cane, which the European roller has been unable to express.—E.

These words are by no means the only set of words in use; in fact, every province and every district has its own long list for every small component part of every implement in use. It is not surprising, therefore, that no really complete dictionary of this exuberently copious language has ever yet been written.—B.

Korá, کورا कोरा

Is the mercantile name of plain silk cloth dyed. Bandanna is the same article dyed. The word is derived from کورا Korá, new, raw, fresh.

This article of Indian manufacture has lately been depreciated in the English market, in consequence of the dishonesty of the native workmen, who prepare goods of inferior quality and weight, and conceal the deficiency by a composition of rice-paste and sugar. It is said that a sound Korá ought to weigh from thirty to thirty-two Sikkas, faithfully woven throughout with 1700 threads. The deteriorated Korá has only 1400 threads, and weighs from twenty-six to twenty-nine Sikkas, brought up to the proper standard by the above-named composition, which may be easily detected by washing.

Kaulá, کولا कौला

Kauliyá, کولیا कौलिया

Derived from کولي Kaulí, an embrace or armful, and hence

applied to bundles of sheaves of corn given as perquisites to reapers and village servants. The word more generally used in Benares is Kakhíalí. From Kánkh کانکه an armpit.

Kerauny, كراني करानी

An English clerk in a public office, generally of mixed European and native descent. The origin of the name has been disputed, and is, it is believed, utterly unknown. It may probably be a corruption of some Portuguese* word, or it may be a mispronunciation of Karana, by which the Kayeth (Kayastha), or writing tribe, is designated in Bengal; and as most native writers in public offices are of the Karana caste, it is not unlikely that, by merely extending its signification, the same word might have been used to designate English† writers. The word from being utterly harmless in its application, has begun of late years to be considered decidedly dyslogistic (to use an expressive word coined by Bentham) and is consequently

* It is strange that Abúl Fazl, in detailing the officers of a ship's company, say the ship's steward was called Kerani.

كراني نپکچي خرچ كشتي و آب همه مردم رساند

This might imply a Portuguese origin, as many nautical terms are derived from that language.

† Should this really be the origin of the word, it is worthy of observation that Kayeths themselves at one time were called by a title, which was originally peculiar to foreign writers. In a treatise on Revenue Accounts by Raj Rúp, who calls himself a pupil of Raja Todar Mal, but who in reality wrote in, or after, Aurangzeb's reign, he says that, since those who in Iran followed the occupation of writing, were called Khwaja, it came to be considered an attributive word, and was in course of time appropriated to Hindú writers.

و ازانجا که در ایران نویسنده را خواجه خوانند همین سبب این لفظ
وصفي دانسته نویسندگان هنودرا نیز خواجه گویند

There is no reason to suppose that in India Kayeths are now ever called Khwaja, though that word is in common use for other classes. In other Muhammedan countries, however, the term is still applied to writers and teachers.

avoided by all officials of good feeling, for fear of giving offence.—E.

The derivation of this word still baffles enquirers. The simplest and most obvious derivation is from the Hindi काम करानेवाला Kám Karánewálá, which is equivalent to the English "overseer;" as this class of East Indians has generally been employed in the higher grades of the subordinate executive service, this name would be very appropriate and applicable to them, and is moreover very similar to the Bombay term Kárkan.—B.

Katían,

In the Printed Glossary, should be Khateoní, Khatauní, or Khátábandí, words signifying the posting of several items together, after abstracting them from the Khasra. From کهاتا Khátá, an account book. The meaning is correctly entered in the Glossary.

INDEX.

C.

H.

I.

K.

L.

R.

S.

STEPHEN AUSTIN, PRINTER, HERTFORD.